THE FUTU

Reform, Development, Progress or Progressive Decline

John W. Forje

Langaa Research & Publishing CIG
Mankon, Bamenda

Publisher:
Langaa RPCIG
Langaa Research & Publishing Common Initiative Group
P.O. Box 902 Mankon
Bamenda
North West Region
Cameroon
Langaagrp@gmail.com
www.langaa-rpcig.net

Distributed in and outside N. America by African Books Collective
orders@africanbookscollective.com
www.africanbookscollective.com

ISBN-10:9956-551-89-9

ISBN-13: 978-9956-551-89-7

Table of Contents

Acknowledgements

Even though views expressed in this publication are entirely mine, I am nevertheless deeply grateful and indebted to a number of people, friends, and colleagues who have, over the years been of particular help. I have and continue to benefit from books published by other colleagues; from institutions who have furnished me with numerous data and other materials. The list is long. It would be unfair to mention only some. To all, I extend my thanks and deep appreciation. I would like to extend my deep appreciation to my publisher for a wonderful job well done.

The preparation of this volume puts the entire CARAD Family into serious debts of appreciation to many people. To all, we extend our profound appreciation for the support and patience. Let us live in hope and not despair about the future of the continent and that we can get a little intoxicated on what we trust will be considered to be vintage results, for us all in the future. It is about transforming Africa's future or propelling Africa into a different future through exploring how the discipline of anticipation can have been shaped and applied in Africa and how it can be deliberately leveraged towards transforming the continent's future onto more positive trajectories.

We are very conscious that, in aiming at a moving target from moving a platform, my views on this vast complex subject and complicated continent with all its positive potentialities, diversities and conflicts, our views are not likely to coincide with those of the many helpers and the reading public. With more than the normal fervour, therefore, we absolve from responsibility all others the mistakes and shortcomings of the views herein expressed but deplore every reader to continue the discourse *(mijadala)* of moving Africa in the right direction and purpose.

Last, but by no means least, I am extremely grateful to all these who in different ways contributed to the publication of the book, It is my conviction that the fundamentals here discussed and analysed will govern power and politics and the process of socio-economic transformation in Africa and relations between the continent and the outside world regardless of which individual state governance or group of states may be in control of the governmental and administrative apparatus at any given time. Rephrased differently, no matter who takes over the reign of power in any African country at the dawn of tomorrow, and regardless of his/her ideological orientation, the reality here discussed will have to be contended and adequately addressed to save Africa from further decline and destruction. Actions not just words are needed to effectively make the changes that are required for our common good.

My family has been very supportive in many aspects. I wish to express my heartfelt gratitude for their support without which the publication would not have been possible. I remain responsible for the shortcomings of the publication. Let us jointly build the Africa We Want for Our Common Good and Posterity without Leaving Any One Behind.

John W. Forje
22nd April, 2019

Preface

This book is motivated by the events of 2011, "The Arab Spring" coming as a tsunami and, reshaping the political construct of the Africa continent north of the Sahara, as well as its eventual consequences on the rest of the continent, south of the Sahara. Events in Tunisia could be likened with the actions taken in the United States of America that faithful morning by Rosa Parks, the role of Martin Luther King Jr. and the eventual arrival of Barrack Obama in the White House in 2008. It is premised on the idea that Africa's future is up to Africans; and that the 21st century and beyond will be shaped by what happens not just in Berlin, Rome, London, Paris, Moscow, Washington, Mexico, Delhi but what happens across Africa, from Banjul to the Horn and from the Cape to Cairo. It is further strengthened by the quiet or silent revolutions that took place in Algeria and Sudan with the overwhelming force of 'people's silent power' overthrowing their long serving despotic authoritarian leaders. Will the rest of the continent follow these countries pattern of a progressive, non-violent silent political reaction in the change of long-seated heads of states that have for long clouded the political landscape of the continent? It is evidently clear that the recent events in Algeria and Sudan creates some new positive political dynamics for the continent's civil society to continue wearing the new garment of progressive Afrocentric game changing attitude without throwing a stone. Democratic empowerment of the African civil society is important as this touches every aspect of the political rights of the citizen. The emergence of new forms of democracy in Africa at the national, regional and continental level is important for the sustainable transformation the region. The democratic empowerment of the people is a healthy sign for development and quality welfare of the citizens.

One of the immediate effects of the Arab Spring was the disappearance of the strongest advocates of African Unity - Colonel Ghaddaffi of Libya - after Kwame Nkrumah. How this impacts the construct of a United States of Africa in 2017 has yet to be diagnosed. We are now biding fare voyage to 2017, the year Africa is expected to be united. Unfortunately, the continent is far away from the unity it started preaching as the bases for the self-determination struggle and building a new continent. What is clear – Africa is suffering from a serious leadership deficiency syndrome (SLDS) and passive civil society syndrome (PSCS). To a large extent, the ideal of a continental free trade zone is growing seeing the daylight to enhance the growth, integration and unity of the continent.

With the departure of Colonel Ghaddaffi another vacuum has occurred in the 'unity space' like the physical disappearance of Kwame Nkrumah from the African political scene? Another strong advocate of an Untied States of Africa, President Wade of Senegal was shown the exit door (like that of Obasanjo Olusegun and Thabo Mbeki), following his defeat at the presidential elections of March 2012. Another advocate of African Unity, Africa's longest serving Head of State, President Mugabe of Zimbabwe (37 years in power) on 21st November 2017 forced to quit the political scene. Is Africa an orphan or will Africa rise again? Will someone vindicate Ghaddaffi like President Julius Nyerere did in respect of Kwame Nkrumah? The answer is blowing in the wind. There is always something new in Africa as Zimbabwe exhibited a new form of military dictate in the governance structure of continent. It has been the end of road for Africa's dinosaurs – Robert Mugabe, Abdul-Aziz Bouteflika, and Omar al Bashir while others like Paul Biya, Idris Derby and many others are still hanging on to power and governing their countries with iron fist. The recent events in Algeria and Sudan show that new political dynamics are unfolding on the continent and that the continent needs collaborative environment in the spirit of a United Africa taking place under the Baobab tree – the true consensus of African cultural heritage. The continent since 2000 lost most of its visionaries, Nelson Mandela included (see Vandyck (2019).

Africa is currently undergoing a deadly game of chess but will triumph in the end – the result of people's power as the true custodian of authority in any society. In spite of the new scramble for Africa victory will be on the side of the people one day. But for this victory or potential to be unlocked the new rising force of the county/continent must have exploited in the right way. African youths and women hold the key to the future, but they must be empowered to have access to health and education – the essential engines of economic growth. Healthy and educated and empowered women and the youths will shape the future of not only Africa but the world. Therefore, the neglect of the youths and women in any development strategy is destroying the present and future of the continent. They hold the key to unlocking the doors of poverty and underdevelopment. It requires investing and empowering them. Even though the gender gap is shrinking, but progress remains uneven. African countries must seek for ways to chip away at the barriers preventing women from achieving her full economic potential.

Isa Shivji (2006:213) quoting Nyerere (1997) was emphatic on the disappearance of Kwame Nkrumah from the helm of African political limelight. "Kwame Nkrumah was the greatest crusader for African unity. We did not even discuss a mechanism for pursuing the objective of a politically United Africa. We had a Liberation Committee already. We should have at least had a Unity Committee or undertaken to establish one. We did not. And after Kwame Nkrumah was removed from the African political scene nobody took up the challenge again". Another advocate of African unity has just been thrown out of the African political landscape. Is the Renaissance Train receiving a setback or moving forward?

The publication begs these simple questions: what are the innovative foresight concepts, tools and planning methods that are necessary to transform Africa's future? How should we strengthen the anticipatory capabilities of African policy maker's practitioners and planners? In which ways can we allow the private, public and civil society to input debate and interrogate the thinking, application and potentials for partnerships as fundamental ingredients to shaping the continent's future? How can we encourage the conceptualisation – 'Thinking African Futures' as a discipline within the educational curriculum of the continent? There is increasing talk about the future of Africa; instead of focusing only on the present and the past. In addition, voices have been raised about an 'African Renaissance' and how Africans can take advantages of existing scientific and technological advancements and exert more control of their own future. African countries have shifted from the 'Five-Year National Development Plans to a longer-term planning vision of 2020, 2025, 2030, 2035, and African Union (AU) Vision 2063 as emerging new directions. Seen from these perspectives, the future has invited itself into the discourse of development. Therefore, it is time to interrogate how Africans are 'thinking African futures' as a basis for beginning to rethink the future of Africa. This publication is a part of evolving discourse on:

- Conceptualisations of African futures – comprehensive audit and history of African futures;
- How is the future of Africa being conceptualised?
- Why must the future of this great continent be conceptualised as a discipline?
- Who is conceptualising the future of Africa?
- Whose futures are being considered and why?
- Whose interests have been served?
- What must this generation do in ensuring a good future for Africa?

It takes an interdisciplinary approach identifying ranges of problems relating to the sustainable development and transformation threats the continent faces as it presents new means to addressing these challenges and changes in respective fields. As such, it provides to the reading public accessible information and policy-relevant analyses of vital and critical challenges to the leaders, policy-makers and peoples of the continent what is expected of them. The Future of Africa thus moves beyond current theoretical premise as it sets out critical debates on how the continent can pilot itself into the modern world.

Thinking about the future and in particular about the future of Africa raises eyebrows whether the continent with its vast natural resources yet sinking in endemic poverty has any future but remain as a raw-material resources exporting continent? The approaches and methodologies for thinking the future have grown exponentially, and many have been used to design the future of Africa. There is little knowledge about which ones have worked effectively, and why. Furthermore, the broader 'discipline of anticipation' which encompasses all these methodologies is itself fairly young and evolving. It is therefore useful to explore the underlying reasons and choices that justify the use of these methodologies for 'approaching the future' of Africa and think about the following questions:

- Hypothesis made about the future of Africa?
- Methodologies used to design the future Africa?
- Endogenous knowledge system used to deal with the future of Africa?
- Outputs and learning's from these methods?
- African foresight practitioners need for old, and/or adapted methods?
- The future does not mean Africa reinventing the wheel; it means Africa being a part of the evolution and contributing in that process.

The future of Africa focuses on the main policy strategic areas where African leaders and the people must in unionism correlate their activities, exhibit the political will and determination of taking comprehensive and decisive decisions on a number of significant issues plaguing the continent now and in the years ahead. The issues discussed include consolidating the democratic process, policies for greater depth strategic resolve on economic and monetary issues, the political union of African states, defence policies and citizenship rights, the economic and communication integration of the continent, appraising the achievements, failures or grounds so far covered and setting out new in-depth roadmap for the years ahead to better consolidate the sovereignty of the continent within the global environment of the 21st century and beyond.

Critically, the book examines the major issues facing Africa and makes proposals for the future from a position of strength and to be better placed in confronting emerging challenges. The principle reason for exploring the future is the purposing of claiming it. Decisions to change planning course lead to setting of goals about future plans. Much of the history of African foresight about the future of Africa articulating foresight into concrete decision planning exercises is a challenge in Africa. It is therefore paramount to examine and write on the historical past of the continent to determine local, national, regional and global case trends of successes and failure rates.

As a result, the publication reviews and analyses a number of inter-related issues that touches on a number of planning the future of Africa? Individual, local, national and regional key planning decisions cases, actions and programmes about the future of Africa. What lessons could be learned about various policy actions towards more effective planning decisions – political, economic, social and technological? Directions emerging about the continent towards positively transforming Africa's futures are given paramount space.

Above all, the book is not to forecast the future. Instead, it is an attempt to analyse the present situation and make proposals for the future. The cardinal objective of the publication is to promote 'future thinking' about the continent. We have to build the future by preparing today and by correcting mistakes made. Taking the bull by the horn the right way is what is urgently required now. The entire governance system has to be radically reformed. The media enterprise must throw its full weight behind curbing the power of the ruling elites as well as play the progressive role of defender of the rights of the voiceless and vulnerable in society. The collective public interest should stand tall under the canopy of the rule of law and justice. With open minds we can partner on behalf of the African continent and the rest of world to ensure prosperity for all.

However, one thing may likely occur, because of Africa's wonderful and irritating continental differences the likelihood is that Africa may not become politically united. A United States of Africa - one government, one economic market and monetary system may not take place. The possibility of "A loose African Confederation - a kind of African Switzerland" may eventually emerge. For now, except for common policy areas linked mainly with the achievements of Regional Economic Communities (RECs) may integrate more easily than in other areas. The end goal should the political and economic integration of the African continent.

Notwithstanding the odds, the wish is to see the consolidation of a Single African Common Market (ACM) (Forje, 1969) and Common Political Front (CPF) or a Union Government of Africa (UGA) piloting the affairs of the continent. These developments require a united front, common vision and resolved determination, political will and proactive actions for the common good. The admission that Africa is not a homogenous continent is clear. Nonetheless, there are many silver linings binding the continent than divide it. The hurdles and challenges are many but the possibilities for endurable solutions exist as well. It is a question of linking the two together from a rational, objective, constructive and scientific manner to obtain the best possible answers and constructive ways advancing the continent forward. But even with all these issues and concerns there is great hope and optimism for Africa in the near- and long-term future. The fundamental question is to make sure the current growth is continuous and sustainable. To achieve requires a new focus, change in mindset and the adopting of a progressive Afrocentric agenda placing the people as the focus and vision transformation. Theoretically, Africa has been liberated, practically, we are still colonised as we continue wallowing in owning and processing our natural resources. We need to emphasis the imperatives of African autonomy, ownership, control and sovereignty our natural resources. We are all challenged to vigorously move from transformation, decolonisation and decoloniality to building and sustaining the ideological nexus of sustenance, self-esteem and freedom without which we will remain slaves for eternity.

The reader will observe that there are no projections, scenarios or calculations situating what and where the continent should be, come another five or more decades. This is best left to experts to undertake the complex calculus for Africa. For now, the publication is concerned and committed to African Unity in all facets – from the hamlets to the urban centres, from the less fortunate to the educated class, from the poor to the rich – clearly a difficult blend of actors and demanding undertaking that calls for volumes and volumes to be written. What is written here is just a tip of the iceberg in a vast field of overwhelming challenges, yet engulfed with far-reaching opportunities to situate Africa within the context of a complex rapidly changing global environment. Above all, eradicating entrenched poverty and promoting the welfare of all citizens.

My vision as expounded in this publication may perhaps not be the most appropriate one: but may be and very likely many will come up with a vision that is doable better, and enhancing the current purpose of this work for pushing vigorously for that kind of vision; to see more serious discourses that should spur us to the next stage in African institutional development. What is important is the cross-fertilisation of ideas across the various disciplines to positively propel the continent forward. The goal is seeing Africa functioning within the precept of the virtues of democratic governance and quality services delivery. It is clear to us all from the perspective of our continent, that the time of the Nation States with all the usual trappings we were taught to love so much, has been overruled by a potent new reality. This call to globalisation needs to be properly understood. It offers both advantages and disadvantages; it has to be understood and in some cases to fight it, as if changes already in place could be undone. Not even the developed countries can stop the 'globalisation train', nor any nation can proceed according to its own free will in the global construct of the world today. Collaboration across borders is imperative to benefit from the virtues of globalisation. We should prevent globalisation being a vice to transformation especially of the African continent. Let us make it a 'win-win' factor for all the countries of the world. Africa needs an urgent new progressive diplomatic opening.

Nations are forced to consult, to seek alliances, to try to find a consensus and common grounds of some kinds, at least with other players. African countries should seek that common ground to construct the continent. The political processes during and after decolonisation, highlighted by a remorseless struggle for power; between local elites complicates the emergence of conciliatory intergroup relations on a multidimensional basis making it difficult to marshal a holistic new approach and structure. Africa has to evolve on the principles of political pluralism as the virtue of good governance. The absence of consensus on goals and values are regarded as a further threat to order, development and unity. What Africa most need is unity and prosperity; power and wealth to the people and in their pockets. People must be able to daily put bread on the table for the family; and quality livelihood constantly improved.

Inclusion, i.e. putting people first is what, the future of Africa depends on and what we want to make of it. What is important now is to improve on the lures of political kingdom with bread on the table for all so that the quality livelihood of the people is constantly improved upon and sustained? Results are what matter most. We must strive towards the best practices and excellent results. It is on this that the future of Africa should be constructed and on which it must depend to have its place on Planet Earth. So far it looks from developments since independence that the continent's development goals and objectives where not clearly and properly guided by the peoples values and perceptions of needs, resources, opportunities and possibilities prompting serious rethinking for clarification, of concepts and definitions, of understanding of processes and consequences, of mechanisms for monitoring outcomes and correcting processes and consequences and in charting a new way forward for the good of the people. We have to put in place the structures and elements for a genuinely African-oriented development strategy as well as ensure comprehensive policy implementation action plans.

The Eurocentric development strategy adopted by the continent has failed to produce the required results, There is an urgent need for an Afrocentric developmental strategy based on self-reliance, not dependence on hand-outs; self-sustaining development, democratisation of the development process, de-alienation, the creation of the right political and social environment, the recovery of self-confidence by the peoples of Africa in themselves, and the willingness to achieve effective, efficient and meaningful co-operation, coordination among African states. A new development strategy has to be envisioned and actualised. No one puts it better then former ECA Executive Secretary General, Prof. Adebayo Adedeji (1979); "the ultimate purpose of development must be the development of humankind – the realisation and unfolding of his/her creative potential through improvement not only in his/her creative potential through improvement not only in his/her material conditions of living which should enable him/her to fulfil his/her physiological needs but also through the satisfaction of his/her psychic needs. In short, development is a process by which the people's over-all personality is enhanced. And development for society means development of the collective personality of society. Thus, economic development cannot be treated as an independent variable divorced from its social and political bearings. Development of a society is social development, a process in which 'economic' and 'non-economic' elements interact organically with each other."

Let Africa sing a new song, the melody of constructive change, progressive development and sustainable quality livelihood. Let Africa incorporate critical enablers of structural transformation harnessing its vast local ad Diaspora resources for development. Building a New Africa of tomorrow requires laying new solid concrete foundation bricks today which should constitute the feelings of Africanness, sovereignty and cultural identity. An identity representing important cultural cornerstone for the fledging new but a different continent, coming out of abject poverty to affluence for all. For now, Africa is in serious trouble needing inputs and constructive engagement from all sectors of society. We should and must all be an inherent part of the process for change. Change we can and must for growing individual accumulation and material prosperity has not yet yielded concomitant human well-being; it is because humanity has lost its way in the pursuit of an insatiable, conspicuous consumption that has only created a rat race where individuals work ever more hours to purchase things that do not bring real or sustained happiness.

We should build an Africa of and for the future that rests on a number of 'basic needs', the possession of which constitutes sustainable quality well-being, namely; health, security, respect, harmony with nature, friendship, leisure, love, good governance, justice and personality, which can be defined as the ability to frame and execute a plan of life reflective of our tastes, temperament and conception of the good, call this sovereignty and autonomy. Let us bear in mind that the extremes of wealth and poverty undermine economic vitality, cripple participation, fans conflict, chaos and instability in society and in decision-making processes, obstruct the flow of knowledge, and distort the perception of human capacity.

What is most needed for the present and future of Africa is an effective process for exploring issues and making decisions that promotes genuine participation, facilitates collective action, and shared-prosperity as well as responsive to the complexity inherent in efforts to craft sustainable systems for the common good. The future of Africa must move 'towards a new 'we' – the collective good' of all Africans. "It is imperative that the Indigenous African Knowledge Systems (IAKS) and their underlying world-view should be unearthed, developed and harnessed for cultural, social and economic development. As well as Africa needs to return to a unifying spiritually and world-view that transcends race, colour and creed" (Motsheka 2005:44-45).

Finally, this publication is designed to continue fostering working towards the revival of political dialogue in Africa and to put before the people, an examination of leading issues in African politics from the perspective of sharply opposed points of view. An attempt has been made to select some of key burning issues as well as argue the points vigorously but in such a way as to enhance our understanding of which side of the shoes that hurts the people of Africa most. All is not lost. We need to rediscover, recycle and reconstruct and have self-confidence of ourselves – a most important asset lost during the colonial period. So great has been the down-thrusting impact of colonial governance on African values and cultural lifestyle and values that we have accepted this denigration as being part of our cultural upbringing. Although some grounds have been recovered much is still to be done resurrect and recover fully our self-confidence as human beings, the Africans we are, in building our lost capacities to initiate, organise and implement policies and instruments essential for engineering socio-economic transformation in building the Africa We Want and leaving no one behind Leaving no one behind means changing the **'tides of power'** and **'constructing an inclusive society.'**

It is hoped the reader who confronts lively and thoughtful statements on vital issues will be stimulated to ask some of the critical questions about African socioeconomic and political developments. Why is Africa underdeveloped in the midst of plenty? What are the highest priority areas which African governments should pay particular attention? What positions must these governments take on these issues? What should be the attitude of citizens towards their governments? How should civil society be organised as the watch dog and custodians of the rights of the citizens? Are we not forced to admit that Africa lives in what could be best described as 'absolute poverty' synonymous with pauperism and destitution? Can we escape from the reality that most of the 25 poorest countries on planet earth as well as which suffer from drought, the most appalling natural disasters and conflicts are in Africa? Is Africa prepared to make a dramatic turn from underdevelopment to a quality service delivery polity? What are these prioritised goals? What are the strategies to adopt? The list of critical cross-cutting goes on-and-on with no sight of ending any time soon.

The situation is all the more disturbing in that we cannot say when the predicaments will end and there seem to be no glimmer of hope in the immediate future given the growing number of sit-tight residents who change the constitutions of their respective countries with all impunity. The end of the crisis seems not to be in sight. Must we sit and fold our arms and transform ourselves through 'handouts'? Can we draw lessons from the words of Saint-Augustine, that great Africa: "Quis sum? Quae natura?" translated to mean, 'Who am I'? What is my nature and "Mihi question fui" (I become an enigma to myself)? How, in the words of the great poet Senghor, can we 'wrest the self from the self'? How can we usher happiness to the peoples of Africa reconciling them with themselves and restoring their lapsed heritage, while at the same time exposing them to the life-giving ocean air and the fertile flood tides from without? How can we break through the barrier of counter-development and avoid creating ugly, soulless societies while keeping as closely as possible in touch with the realities of the world around us through an intelligent acquisition of scientific and technical knowledge in order to ensure 'the harmonious development of the individual and of humankind? How can we change our internal structures and resist transnational corporations, or even harness them to our development (Kodjo, 1979)? These soul-searching questions by former Secretary-General of the Organisation of African Unity (OAU) some decades back remain extremely relevant today and need concrete answers from current leaders and the people of Africa.

These barrages of questions and many not asked clearly indicate to the continent the enormous problems and challenges Africa faces and must grapple with if it has to be an inherent part of the current global community of nations. It equally poses serious challenges to the international community of nations to constructively and in unionism with the people find endurable solutions to the problems plaguing the continent. The burden of the problem rest on the shoulders of the continent, whether they are psychological and ingrained in our mentality, whether they are natural, whether they are due to political or geographical factors, or the persistence of colonial structures, Africa is now in a position to seek lasting solutions and constructively and holistically reduce the plight of the continent. Africa stands at the cross-roads and quick actions are needed here and now. Africa does not need strong men, it needs strong institutions and visionary leaders. With better governance, the continent holds the promise of a broader base of prosperity and prospects of a better world construct. We all have a joint responsibility in constructing a better world for the common good.

Importantly, Africa is not the crude caricature of a continent perpetually at war with itself. But if we are honest, far too many Africans countries are in conflict as a part of life, and as constant as the sun. There are wars over land and wars over resources. And it is far too easy for those without conscience to manipulate whole communities into fighting among faiths and tribes (Obama, 2009). Must Africa continue in the negative form? Is it not time for the continent to build a new image that incorporates our cultural heritage with strong emphasises on the principle of human solidarity – the spirit of "Ubuntu and 'Harambee" leading to global participatory management of the resources enjoyed by one and the same species. It is the thesis that one of the criteria of justice in social policy is the maximisation of benefit to the least advantage, consistent with the safe-guarding of other practices. The publication acknowledges Africa's pitfalls, dating to the transatlantic slave trade, colonialism and the ongoing state of neo-colonialism (Fobanjong, 2018) the need to chat a new forward is imperative for this generation through consensus democracy (Matolino, 2018).

Borrowing from the vision of Kwame Nkrumah on the issue of a Continental Government for Africa should seek a number of objectives; (i) Over-all economic planning on a continental basis for Africa to avoid the continent remaining balkanised regionally or territorially and avoid remaining at the unholy mercy of colonialism, imperialism and neo-colonialism; a united states of Africa like the United States of America is there for us all to see; (ii) the establishment of a unified common military and defence strategy and command for self-defence, even though it could be ineffective in any major attack upon the separate states; yet we must realistically examine which African state can protect its sovereignty against an imperialist aggressor?; (iii) building on the two mentioned issues, the need for a common and unified foreign policy and diplomacy to give political, economic and technological direction to the continent's joint efforts for the protection and economic transformation and development of the continent – Africa should be able to speak with one voice on vital and imperative issues; and (iv) deepening the democratic and governance process throughout the continent. Africa of the future must speak with one voice and act from a common perspective that upholds the unity, sovereignty and progress of the continent.

Indeed, the survival of a future free Africa, the extending independence of the continent, and the development towards that better and brighter future on which out hopes and endeavours are pinned, depend upon our resolve for political and economic unity now; and it is from here that a new Africa could emerge, great and powerful, in which the territorial borders, the relics of colonialism become obsolete and superfluous. The AU should be tailored towards what Annan Kofi (2006) sees as; (a) African and global solidarity; (b) the rule of law; (c)mutual accountability; (d)multilateralism; and (d) collective responsibility. By all standards, this is the time for Africa to move-away from the entrenched dichotomy of inequality, corruption and poverty-stricken strategies that clouds fragile states that the continent has bestowed on itself and engaged in a new power structure of policy, profit and development for all.

We need that compass to plough and sow a better continent; for it to take its rightful place within the global community of nations. We can only do this if we are properly equipped with the tools and knowledge defining and knowing what is meant by politics, policies, governance and by development; define and recognise the different phases the policy and developmental cycles; and understand how social transformation impact the policy, democratic governance and development processes, Democracy offers vast possibilities to organise a collective-decision-making process which when properly executed offers quality livelihood to citizens. In the words of Bernard Crick (1992:33), 'politics should be considered as a way of ruling divided societies without undue violence – and most societies are divided, though some think that is the very trouble'. To put it bluntly, the book is entangled with the definition of politics as; who gets what, how and when (Lasswell, 1958)?

Apparently, the conviction is that a healthy, stable democracy with a progressive economic and stable economy requires a citizenry that considers these and many more pertinent questions and actively participates, however indirectly in reshaping society for the common good. In providing some answers to them. Stay aloof is the answer. The alternative is apathy, passivity and, sooner or later, the hegemonic rule of tyrants will triumph. Africa should avoid this form of government but ensure that the rule through democratic governance, rule of law prevails at all times. The forces uniting Africa are far greater than the difficulties that presently divide us. The goal must be the establishment of Africa's dignity, progress, prosperity and sustainable quality livelihood for all. That is the Africa we aspire to and want for this and coming generations.

All said and done, this publication like most CARAD books are out to promote the sharing of knowledge, building the framework for dialogue, academic discourse, creating meaningful understanding and cooperation for social and economic development that furthers the well-being of the peoples in society. We must in different ways encourage, support and facilitate the creation of a sense of national unity, integration and community within the national boundaries and across the continent and ensure that social justice at all levels of societal strata prevails.

As such we at CARAD have reached the stage of passing the baton to you the reader as primary actors and the people of Africa to shape the continent's future. We have from a realistic perspective backed by scientific objectivity and academic analytical framework present the case as it is, stating the dynamics as well as incorporating the factors and forces at play influencing the continent today. These factors and issues highlight key underlining elements that bring to your attention as citizens of the continent to know and how they might play out in the distant future. The scope of this publication is limited to the extent we do not aim to deliver recommendations that can immediately be put to test in prevent the free-fall of the continent given the state of poor governance and the corruption nexus that has and continues to bedevil the region. It should be rather considered as an attempt to explore the argumentative stances of institutional actors provide insights to underlying patterns of perceiving underlying issues of underdevelopment, poverty, injustice, bad governance, exploitation and corruption that have eaten deep into the marrow of the African society. Africa is poor as a result of these vices. It must be eradicated, the sooner, the better for the good of the continent. This in turn can deepen our knowledge of those cultural concepts and contexts in the broadest sense of the term which any progressive development strategy must necessarily take account of. The future of Africa rest on learning from the past; transforming the present, distributing lights to places of darkness, feeding those who have not to better prepare for tomorrow. Indeed, the future is about change - transformation of the present, implying transforming ourselves now by doing what is right for the common good. We should since 6th March 1957, show our maturity and sovereignty as a people, nation and continent. In no way does the publication claim to present a comprehensive record on the past and present to map the future, it just the beginning of a long journey necessary in moving towards a bright future. It is a journey that calls for the full participation, hearing and learning from those who have written about our past and present envisioning the new dawn. Seen within that context and spirit the publication seeks to make history available to present and future generations of this great continent. Africa is at the cross-road of development or destruction. It has to heal the past as well as prepare for the future. This is the hour for us in concert to challenge and contribute to contemporary discourses about the shared sovereignty, governance and wellbeing of our continent. No other person will do that for us. Only Africans can change Africa.

From our part, we want to focus the attention of you the reader, to what you would do, and what you need to do or not do in order to attain a certain desired future. It is time we escape from what Mhango (2017) sees as 'Africa's Dependency Syndrome. We should jointly workout our choices for the common good of every citizen as well as play our parts that constructively advance in building a common vision and welfare for Africa. This is a responsibility we all must carry and execute diligently, with a clear mind for the good of our people, continent and the world at large. As such, we are called to re-examine ourselves and honestly question whether what we are doing now can build the country and Africa of our dreams?

Finally, it is for Africans to choose what future for the continent. They have to tackle consequentially challenges and changes the continent now faces by confronting the state of underdevelopment and poor governance architecture head on with determinism, hope and optimism, even with new challenges now posed by Corona virus. The reality is that COV-19 puts Africa on trial. Critics say it is a poison pill with time-release formula and Africa will be the ultimate victims in the long-run. It should be a serious wake-up call to African leaders to critically rethink their development policies especially in the healthcare, infrastructure development and human capital development sectors. The writing on the wall is visible for us all to see. COV-19 is a serious time-bomb ticking silently and its principles are to set the continent's moral and social disintegration because the current governance structure in many countries is based on false premises of centralised authoritarian ethnical governance. We have to face a new continental ambition.

May be COVID-19 will usher signs of new life for a new brave Africa. The badness in us should be hunted out, acknowledge and, possibly, avoided in the future. To pore over the literary and developmental short-comings of the past fifty years, to attempt to patch a faulty work into perfection it missed at its first execution, to spend one's middle age in trying to mend the developmental sins committed and bequeathed by authoritarian self-cantered leaders – all this surely vain and futile. We have to silence the guns and fight the COV-19 by articulating policies that place the 'human-being' at the centre of all our developmental activities.

That is why we need a Brave New Africa totally different from the old. It is now a question of waiting to see how the new pandemic unfolds and the reaction of our leaders. Everyone wants to know there will be a positive end to the emerging darkness. We need to get out of current development apathy that makes the rich richer and the poor poorer. COV-19 spares no one. Our leaders should know and let it sink deep in their minds and actions. But the virus is also showing them that walls, large armies, and chauvinistic authoritarian governance construct does not provide the security their greed politicians and political administrators lie to them about. This is the time to connect and cross the 'it's and dots where necessary. We will never go back to "business as usual" but with a difference. The sooner we stop listening to greedy politicians and **Godfather Syndrome,** take responsibility for own future, and organise, the sooner we can overcome and create a better brave Africa. But in the face of such uncertainty, our leaders should do better to court hope and optimism.

The organisation of this volume reflects a concern for the processes by which character has been forced on the future of the continent as well as for specific countries, institutions, nodes of behaviour, and faiths have grown out of the African experience in it remains the unfinished journey towards a new brave continent.

Omissions have been as unavoidable as they are regrettable, and each reader will make his/her own list of lacunae. Whatever the case, it is hoped the publication will provide sufficient structure and starting points for the topics to be more meaningfully addressed. It is fervently hoped that the book like others can serve as a basic course text in the curricular setting; others will factor models suitable for particular audiences in various disciplines. The reader who chooses to go through the chapters sequentially should experience the dynamics of the skills evolving character and deepening nature of the challenges, changes and prospects of the continent. Others may decide to go through in a selective pattern, pursuing different interest, but still not missing the dynamics of the essence of the book.

In course of preparing this book, I have benefitted tremendously from the constructive criticism of a succession of observers that no amount of thanks is sufficient to appreciate their inputs which forever will be treasured

Chapter outlines

Together, the different sections depict the immense wealth and width of how people engage politically, culturally, socially and economically outside and inside the state, political parties and social groups to purse their different and common interests. Most importantly, the need to have a common front towards building a united and strong continent is imperative

The collective role of civil society organisations is vital. Partnership between state, civil society and the private sector and relationship with the rest of the world are all part of the shadows, illusions, challenges and prospects that fan and fuel the process of change. All of us, or most of use at any rate, are struggling continuously to discover the true reality behind what we know or suspect may be a mirage, an error, or at best a very tenuous proposition of transforming society that the masses of the population enjoy sustainable quality living standards. Continuously we should be searching for the right path to development. The challenge seems to be most severe where ascertainable reality is remote from us in space and time, or where it is obscured by think layers of self-articulate interests over the collective good. The 'Introduction' – Facing the Realities and Challenges of our Time – presents the problems of perception, the challenges and the prospects. It sets the tone of the publication with an attempt of mapping the way forward.

Chapter One, presents a historical perspective looking at issues according the gospel of the developed countries, what they think is good for Africa and not what Africa wants is good for her people. The long-road to African Unity is discussed scratching only the surface of the struggle. It addresses issues of why Africa is still underdeveloped. No doubt, poor leadership and institutional incapacity have not only fuelled the perpetuation of poverty and underdevelopment more than everything else, but have also created a system in which Africans citizens are entangled in an overlapping economic, political and legal systems that hinder market economic and growth Africa's local bourgeoisies mainly the political or corporate ruling elites have and continue to monopolise and personalise state resources to ensure the perpetuation of their economic privileges and supremacy in society.

We cannot deny the reality that Africa is trapped in a number of different nuances and ways: (i) the forces and legacies of slavery, imperialism, colonialism and neo-colonialism; (ii) the operational dynamics of capitalism fuelling the entrenched role and powers of multinational/ transnational corporations backed by the powerful Bretton Woods conglomerates (World Bank, International Monetary Fund, GATT and other agencies); (iii) the hegemonic forces of politicians and state inheritors of power who oversee, depend on the benefit from a reinter state; and (iv) the culture of self-inflicted poverty perpetuating and reproducing poverty and inequality globally.

Concentrated and generational poverty in Africa is therefore an absence of intellectual, political, social and cultural capital necessary and adequate to increase and expands the continent's resources base. A people caught in this circular process experiences economic decline, low income and infrastructural decline. That is Africa toady, which should be avoided in Africa of the tomorrow. The chapter addresses some of the consequences that seriously contributes to the marginalisation and exploitation of the continent; taking for example issues like poverty, education, healthcare and quality of livelihood.

Chapter Two, delves on the nexus of science, technology and indigenous know architecture emphasising the importance of human capital development as the ingredient or engine that can kick-start reversing the gospel according to western indoctrination. The need to improve the human resources of the continent is a vital aspect of transforming society by giving added value to the rich natural resources of the continent. Africa needs to demonstrate a new behaviour change. A given country is not forever prudent or profligate. Just as countries change – as a result of political, social, institutional, or economic developments – so does their degree of fiscal, technological, economic prudence or profligacy. This simple observation implies that African policymakers and the public at large should not take a long-established tradition of the Eurocentric for granted; conversely, African countries are no doomed to hang on this Euro-centric attitude and behaviour but pursue an Afrocentric when appropriate corrective measures underscore the approach.

Chapter Three, hammers on an important yet neglected aspect of what is contributing to the continued underdevelopment of the continent – the marginalisation of the female gender. The gap between the sexes is growing nor decreasing which is not good for the sustainable transformation of the continent from a backward to a service delivery society. Of course, reductions in gender disparity do not translate to equal opportunity. There are radical changes taking place, but not enough. Apparently, one of the most dramatic developments in the 20th century was the entry of women into the economic and political spheres previously occupied almost exclusively by men. The section stresses the benefits of further reducing gender inequality to allow women to realise their full potential in economic and political activities in civic and national life. Cameroon for example, has witnessed following the 30 September 2013 twin elections municipal and parliamentary) a substantial increase of elected women to parliament and councillors including many female mayors. Rwanda holds the highest number of females in the legislative assembly and in key decision-making position. Though women are making progress in closing gender gaps in the economic and political spheres, but they are still far from achieving equity. There is an urgent need to articulate constructive and comprehensive guidance for the design of policies to tap the full potential of women.

The focus of **Chapter Four** is on Regional Economic Communities (RECs). It is argued that the integration of Africa should evolve through regional economic communities. Some argue that a Union Government for Africa has strong roots in RECs. Whatever the stance taken, RECs are important for the economic growth and sustainable transformation of the continent. The diversity and disconnectedness of the continent makes it vulnerable for exploitation. Here lies one of the greatest weakness and deficits of the continent. As such Africa needs a stronger and united political, economic and an enabling environment in pursuit of its development agenda. There is a need for harmonisation and integration across markets that will allow for the free movements of people and goods to stimulate economic growth of the inter-Africa trade and scalable markets, more regional markets and trade blocks. One of the fundamental questions confronting the continent is the creation of regional trade blocks. Will these trade blocks ensure the creation of a common continental trade block? These and other related questions are better answered by political leaders, politicians and policy makers.

As far as the continent is concerned, there are many reasons why concentration on domestic factors of production, endogenous and self-sustaining development is to be achieved. To begin with, many African countries are too small in terms of geographical and economic life and variety, and size and income levels to assure a self-reliant, endogenous and self-sustaining development. Second, many countries are landlocked making development to be inevitably linked to the opportunities for economic cooperation with other countries. Third, and of course, we cannot rule out advances in science and technology which can dramatically turn around for the better the misfortune of some of the currently handicapped countries, Chad for example. And finally, even in these countries with reasonable geographical size and respectable income levels, economic co-operation arrangements can be very beneficial particularly when such arrangements are made with countries with different climatic and socio-economic conditions. The bottom-line solution of these difficulties point in the direction of creating *regional economic communities* as the lead to the establishment of regional collective self-reliance and as the important complement to national self-reliance for the sustainable and credible transformation of Africa.

Chapter Five, pays attention to the Diaspora. How can the *"brain drain'* phenomena be converted into a veritable *'brain gain'* input factor transforming the continent from what is known as a backward into a service delivery society with sustained quality livelihood standard. The new term is 'reverse migration,' or 'reverse brain drain'. From *'Brain Drain to Brain Gain'* happens when professionals return to their mother country to take advantage of the new growth and employment opportunities. Tapping into the knowledge and financial prowess of the Diaspora is an asset which for now is not appropriately utilised by African countries. Across Africa, from the Cape to Cairo, from Banjul to the Horn, the story is the same: Africans are coming home from abroad – for patriotic or family reasons, or simply because of the continent's increasing opportunities. The prodigal sons and daughters are coming home with a difference. Africa should take advantage of the new patriotism, as these young lions returning have been dubbed the 'repatriation generation' and are a fast-growing subculture of African émigrés. African Diasporas remittances can reduce poverty and spur development related activities. However, this is not a sustainable strategy in engineering the socio-economic transformation of the continent. What in case things take a different and dramatic turn against these people in their host countries?

While **Chapter Six**, addresses issues of African Renaissance and African Unity. The critical question is whether or not an African Renaissance and African Unity are truly possible, and why is Africa finding it so difficult to achieve political and economic unity, growth and stability are fully discussed. It is noted that 'the highest political expression of black power is Pan-Africanism and the highest expression of Pan-Africanism is Nkrumahism" (Hadjor 1988:104). The African continent is in turmoil. Imperialism, colonialism and neo-colonialism feeds on it like a vulture; and hungry elite worsen it as they thoughtlessly implement their master's military designs and economic schemes opines Shivji (2008: xv).

Chapter Seven, looks at the new invasion or re-colonisation of the continent. Re-colonisation is taking place at the age scientific advancement. This new invasion said to be headed by China present challenges and prospect for development if only carefully articulated to ensure a 'win-win' situation or else if could be moving Africa into a very dangerous trapping in the future. Re-colonisation is coming at the era of globalisation, the highest stage of scientific imperialism, and with Africa suffering serious deficit in the scientific and technological domain and the brain drain which puts the continent at variance on the struggle for development or continued exploitation and destruction.

Chapter Eight, is on the military dimension. African countries pay more attention on building their military capability than undertaking development related activities that improves the quality wellbeing of their citizens. Africa is not war with any continent. But Africa is at war with poverty and underdevelopment. Here is where the military arsenal must be deployed. Not paying attention to the development aspect leads to insecurity and conflicts. But military build-up partly comes as result of "sit-tight presidential" phenomena that have gripped the continent. A 'sit-tight' president working for the ultimate good of the people is not bad. What is bad is when a sit-tight president converts state property in a personal estate of dynasty; when an elected post becomes a self-acclaimed dynasty or monarchy that should go from father to wife or son.

Chapter Nine – The social dimension is one of disparity not equity. The gap between the rich and poor, urban and rural areas is widening not closing. Affluence at the expense of the suffering masses is the order of the day. Africa has to be re-calling and genuinely practice the *"Ubuntu Spirit"* of sharing and caring for each other. It is part of the cultural heritage of the people, unfortunately lost due to greed and articulate self-interests. There is need for a new social construct. There is the growing tendency of leaving most people behind; Citizens see no trickledown effect of the globalisation bandwagon in improving their livelihood. Rather globalisation leads to serious polarisation in society widening the gap between the rich and poor. Poor livelihood becomes a fixed agenda for the vast majority of the population. This is not building the kind of Africa the people want. The emigration of highly-trained and skilled Africans from the continent enlarges the requirements for technical assistance from the very countries which now take advantage of their talents and skills in improving the welfare of their citizens.

In **Chapter Ten** the focus is on the pandemic of corruption which has eaten deep into the social fabric of the African society impeding all genuine efforts towards quality livelihood to the people. Development projects are never realised due to corrupt practices. A new moral/ethical value for the society should be cultivated if the continent is to make any progress. Indeed, development in Africa is fast witnessing increased corruption and poverty, increased lawlessness, conflicts and insecurity as well as unemployment that challenge the apparatus of the state in unparalleled ways.

Chapter Eleven: The engine of development looks at the energy potentials of the continent to power its development drive to a service delivery society. What is the power base of the continent? Are these resources properly developed and utilised in its transformation process? There can be no industrialisation without constant power supply to keep the industrial wheels in constant rotation. Africa has failed woefully in utilising properly the vast abundant resources given her by Mother Nature in transforming itself into a quality services delivery polity. Across Africa, there is bountiful wind and solar power; geothermal energy and biofuels. The continent's boundless natural gifts can generate its own power, while exporting profitable, clean energy abroad.

Chapter Twelve: Conclusion – sums up the discourse under the title of "A Wake–Up Call for Africa" to regain its lost position within the community of nations. There is need for a new mindset, focused leadership, vibrant or proactive civil society, and an innovative, competitive and productive private sector in building the New Africa of our time and for the future. The human-being should be a focus of development. Thus 'individual plays a unique role in the development of society. Individuals are the birthplace of the rising aspirations, creative ideas, inventions, organisational innovations and dynamic initiatives that characterise a vibrant productive society. The individual is the most precious form of capital any society possesses and the source of its highest achievements. A truly human-cantered science of economics and politics dedicated to the fullest promotion of human welfare and well-being reaches maturity when it conceives and supports measures designed to promote the greatest well-being and blossoming of individuality in all (Jacobs, 2016:93) for the collective common good.

The strong points of the book are manifold. Most obviously, the publication takes theory seriously; and the author is meticulous in selecting quality building materials and ensuring they fit together brightly. In so doing, makes manifest who is doing what to whom, why, and what to do about it. The publication brings balance to the strategic discourse ***(Mijadala)*** on "Africa's Rise".

There is the strong and sincere conviction, which with a common deep-rooted wisdom and integrity, the innate respect for us, backed by the intense humanity that is our heritage and cultural values, and keeping aside over diversity which should be an asset (not a liability), a strong and brave continent will emerge. Now is the right hour to start the reconstruction of a New Africa; not allowing this golden opportunity to pass us by now; and may we all avoid breathing disaster for the hope of a free Africa survival of the future.

References

Adedeji Adebayo (1979). "Perspectives of Development and Economic Growth in Africa Up to the Year 2000", paper presented at The Monrovia Symposium on the Future Development Prospects of Africa Towards the Year 2000, Monrovia (Liberia), 12-16 February 1979. See also OAU (1979) What Kind of Africa by the Year 2000? OAU Secretariat, Addis Ababa, Ethiopia and The International Institute for Labour Statistics, Geneva, Switzerland

Annan Kofi (2006)". Kofi Annan's Farewell Speech as United Nations Secretary-General"; 11 December 2006 at the Truman Presidential Museum and Library, Missouri, USA

Crick Bernard (1992). In Defence of Politics. The University of Chicago Press, Chicago, IL. USA

Fobanjong John (2018). State of The Continent. A Mid-Century Assessment of Political Performance in Africa, Spears Media Press, Cameroon

Forje W. John (1969). "An African Common Market", New Africa – Africa Trade & Development, Vol. 11 No. 3/4, London, pp ii-vi (see Danish version. "Et Afrikansk Faellesmarked: EF or Afrika" in Daniel S. Odoom (1973) Afrikansk Synspunkt – "Essays", Jorgen Jensen Bogtrykkeri, Copenhagen – Denmark, pp115-136

Jacobs Garry (2018) "Foundations of Economic Theory. Money, Markets and Social Power", ASPJ – Africa and Francophonie, Vol.9, No.1, 1st Quarter 2018, pp71-94

Kodjo Edem (1979), "Building Today.... the Africa of the year 2000" paper presented at the Symposium on the future development prospects of Africa towards the year 2000, Monrovia (Liberia) 12-16 February 1979. (See also OAU 1979)

Lasswell, H. D. (1958). Politics: Who Gets What, When and How? Meridian Books, New York, USA

Mhango Nkuzi Nkwazi (2017). Africa's Dependency Syndrome. RPCIG Publishing, Bamenda, Cameroon.

Matolino Bernard (2018). Consensus Democracy in Africa. NISC (Pty) Ltd. South Africa

Mawere Munyaradzi, Ngonidzashe-Marongwe & Duri Thomas Peter Fedilis (eds.) (2018). The End of an Era? Robert Mugabe and a Conflicting Legacy, Langaa RPCIG, Publishing, Bamenda, Cameroon.

Motshekga Mathole (2005) "The Cultural Historical Unity of Africa", AU Magazine, Vol. 1. Issue 4, June-2005 – August 2005, Pretoria, South Africa, pp42-46

Nkrumah Kwame (1957) Speech to the Parliament of Ghana Accra.

Nhemachena Artwell and Warikandwa, Victor Tapiwa (eds.) (2019). From African Peer Review Mechanisms to Africa Queer Review Mechanisms? Robert Gabriel Mugabe, Empire and Decolonisation of African Orifices, Langaa RPCIG, Cameroon

Obama H. Barack (2009). "Speech by the President of the United States of America. Remarks to the Ghanaian Parliament, Accra International Conference Centre.

Organisation of African Unity (OAU) (1979) What Kind of Africa by the Year 2000? Final Report of the Monrovia Symposium on the Future Development Prospects of Africa Towards the Year 2000, Addis Ababa, Ethiopia., pp39-52; and The International Institute for Labour Studies, Geneva, Switzerland

Shivji G. Issa (2008). Pan-Africanism or Pragmatism. Lessons of Tanganyika – Zanzibar Union. Mkuki na Nyota Publishers, Dar es Salaam / Organisation for Social Science Research in Eastern and Southern Africa (OSSREA

Vandyck Ofosua Agnes (ed.) (2019). African Visionaries. Sub-Saharan Publishers Ghana.

Introduction

"Africa is a Lion with a Problematic Head. The leadership in Africa is depressing, but what are the rest of us doing, to be sensitive to problems and the needs of our people"?

(Ama Ata Aidoo, New African, No.515, March 2012, p94)

"The Map of Africa is a Question Mark. Only Africans have the Answers to their Problems; and yet Africa holds the key to the Future of the World but fail to realise its potentials in crafting a sustainable society for the good of its people"

(John W. Forje, 1st June 2012)

"It can no longer be denied that Africa is the victim of South-Americanization. That Africa is politically unstable is a fact. We can't even talk any more about 'balkanization' since the Balkan regimes are stable, whereas in Africa we have a change of regime almost every week or every month; at any rate, every year. And this instability is growing. In my opinion, what is been lacking are national leaderships which could set an example. Had this been the case, military overthrows would have been made much more difficult. At any rate, stability in Africa would have been much greater. Political selfishness is killing Africa; it is the basis of the problem once African interests become merely a pretext for individual selfishness, instability necessarily rears its head. When the only organised force in the country – the army – ceases to respect the civilians in power; it will seize power for itself"

(Cheikh Anta Diop, 1974, 1987)

Facing the Realities and Challenges of Our Time

The Africa of today finds itself at the most historical crossroads since 1884 and no less since 1945 which marked the constructive move towards the political independence of colonial territories into sovereign states. World War 11 – the war to end all wars did not end wars but created the pathway for the independence of colonised African States. Africa's transition from an oppressive, colonial-oriented and racially discriminatory system of government to people-oriented democratic governance took place over many years. The historical past of the continent is best known for the dramatic granting of independence – British Prime Minister Harold Macmillan's famous statement; *"wind of change blowing across Africa"* for the granting of independence to former colonies. There are many other aspects to the evolving development of the continent, and many factors that underlay the changes.

Attainment of independence in Africa marked a turning point in all spheres. However, not much after these profound breakthroughs, which many African states experienced sporadic interruptions occasioned by avaricious dispossessions of power and an attempt at expanding economic, political and geographical frontiers by certain groups or individuals. Most significantly, the large-scale rupture of the continent by the colonisers engendered strife, dislocation, separation and balkanisation which culminated in divisive delineations. The sense of disorientation caused by these invasions is reflected in the epochal 'transformation' that atavistic elements have witnessed, in political, social, cultural, and economic terms. Some of the effects experienced in the former colonised territories are captured by Appolo Amoko (2006:133) who enthuses that *"the political economies of many formally independent nations also continue to be characterised by fundamental contradictions, inequalities and dependencies brought about by colonial rule"*.

Commenting on the mapping of landscapes and the concomitant political implications, J. B. Hartley, cited in Tony Bitch (1996:179), opines: "as much as guns and warships, maps have been the weapons of imperialism" Africa has sought new ways of transforming itself. This trend continues in formal colonies where boundaries were constructed to achieve the 'us' and 'them' order which in turn necessitated the hoarding of opportunities in achieving the task of outplaying others in the quest for relevance and respect in the committees of nations More specifically, this idea assumed a state of particularly as the appropriation of opportunities was individualised (Mekusi 2011).The new ruling elites are directly or indirectly replicating the oppressive and dominating role of the departed colonial masters in an African style.

The formation of monolithic political party structures immediately after independence greased the exploitative machinery of the ruling class. In addition, establishing the impression or concept that black colonialism is worse than white colonialism; and that the blame theory of underdevelopment being attributed to colonial rule, should be given a different scientific research and inquiry fifty years after independence. Slavery, imperialism and colonialism (SIC) the tools of dehumanising and destruction, subjection and insecurity should be shown the red card or else development can never come the way of the African people. A heavy burden lies on the shoulders of every African, for we are responsible for nothing less than the destiny of the continent; and as such obliged to chart a new course of coherent action, ensure an integrated form of development for the welfare of all citizens. We have to move away from endemic and absolute poverty, synonymous with pauperism and destitution to equitable affluence for all.

Africa has decayed through human neglect and poor leadership: it is now the least habitable continent because of disease, lack of communication and political instability. Though Africans have not yet in the late 20th century and in the start of the 21st century experienced a holocaust as that experienced in the colonial raid for slaves and colonies or the kind of indigenous genocide (apart from the Rwanda debacle in the 1990s) at the hands of white people, have been the most humiliated people in history through the slave trade, colonialism and racial discrimination. In Africa, immense mineral wealth and agricultural potential coexist with extremely low living standards. Africa, the second largest continent, is the most fragmented, split into more than fifty nations, many of them tiny. Finally, Africa, a large continent centrally and strategically located in the world, plays only a marginal role in world affairs (Bauer 1981:191-2). The causes of the predicament of humiliation, poverty and political impotence, and the possible solutions are main concern of this book. The prime responsibilities for these predicaments rest with all the stakeholders – Africans and foreign powers. The remedy equally rests with them, though the Afrocentric strategic approach must receive top priority. The book is not only an attack on Africans, but the West and call on Africans to reconstitute their mindset and be responsible for the transformation of the continent.

Today, Africa stands before ***The Court of Highest Decision*** for the choice of integration or disintegration, underdevelopment or development; entrenched abject poverty for the masses and affluence for a few; growth or decline of varying degrees The need for making the right choice in the ultimate interest of the people is imperative. In particular, the 54 states are confronted with the choice of a Union Government or each nation going its own way. The consequences are clear – united they stand, divided they fall. The Arab Spring injected new dynamics into the body politics of the continent, especially issues concerning the creation of a Union Government by 2017, the split of Sudan into two states, and the assassination of Ghaddifi, the remaining frontline leader for African Unity - A United States of Africa (Forje, 2011). President A. Wade of Senegal has bowed out putting into jeopardy the proposed Union Government of Africa. African Union Government is in a fix. Will it ever be realised as the *'Talk Shop Dream'* remains unfulfilled. African unity is sliding deeper and deeper into an 'unrealised venture' like the many white elephant projects on the continent. Which leader is championing the Unity Crusade? We must therefore turn away from the existentialism which characterises Africa and the world of today and embrace an essentialism which combines form with substance to achieve essence.

For now, the continent is caught between optimism and pessimism. No doubt, Africa has made tremendous progress since the end of World War 11 towards the consolidation of democratic governance, though much remains to be accomplished. For example, colonial territories became independent states with seemingly no authority to govern. How independent and sovereign these countries are, constitutes the million-dollar question requiring in-depth research. The optimism is that Africa has a future: the future of the world is Africa. Do African realise they have a future? The pessimistic view pivots on deficient leadership and poor governance structures that fail to deliver fundamental needs. The region is still an unexplored research desert. Only the tip of the iceberg has been scratched so far. There is a second re-colonisation tsunami rush on the continent. The coming of China, Brazil, India, and of course, the second coming of Europe in a grand destructive style are indications of the importance of Africa to the rest of the world. Are there countervailing forces to these invading tsunamis? How can the continent mobilise and deplore the forces of resistance? What are the strengths, weakness, opportunities and threats for building the defence line or fortresses walls for Africa?

A contextualisation and localisation of these developments shows a potential emerging defence line in the making provided by Nigeria and South Africa with a number of foot soldier-nations, for example, Ghana, Mozambique, Ethiopia, Angola Kenya and others gearing up for the battle. However, Africa must first fortify itself with the necessary ammunition to better address the seven or more blunders Mahatma Gandhi outlined before his assignation on 30th January 1948. In short, the future of Africa rests on how it is able to confront existing blunders that continue contributing to the existing state of underdevelopment, exploitation, exclusion and marginalisation in global politics backed with poor services delivery nationally. Unfortunately, African leaders have and continue to give their citizens a bad check. The new generation must begin to define their new journey, work for and attain it. Remember the words of Martin Luther King Jr. *"I have a Dream that One Day..."* The new generation must have a dream and to be free from the scourges of authoritarian tyrannical governance structures that overshadows the transformation of the continent.

It is this future beautifully but categorically described by Nelson Mandela as *"A Long Walk to Freedom"*; eloquently elucidated by Odinga Oginga as *"Not Yet Uhuru";* Tom Mboya's *"Freedom and After";* Chinua

Achebe's *"Things Fall Apart"* contextualising the problems and challenges confronting the continent as Kwame Nkrumah's greatest wish *"Africa Must Unite"* constitutes the *prima facie* for constructing a united and strong continent in the wake of the globalisation onslaught. The globalisation bandwagon cannot be halted. It will accelerate its impact world-wide as it engulfs Africa. Rather the continent must prepare, learn how to accommodate and be part of the fast-moving express globalisation train. The globalisation train is a fast supersonic speed. It requires all hands on deck to make the best out of the fast-moving train; and drawing valuable lessons from other countries that have made it to the mountain top. The cases of Malaysia and South Korea present telling examples. Remember, Malaysia was at par economically with Nigeria in the mid-1950s. Where Nigeria is today compared with Malaysia? What magic wane did the Malaysians use that African countries cannot apply and even perfect on it?

To being with, the Malaysians adopted at least three significant strategies that drastically paid off in creating a new society. Today, oil-power is given the country a kind of economic miracles that drastically has changed their status. A five-year development plan was put in place. The Malaysians at the time of independence immediately embarked on a rigorous and diversification economic strategy. Instead of depending on what was their major export items (rubber and tin), they started growing other crops such as palm oil which today is the main crop; and cocoa added to their new crops for cultivation and production. The agricultural sector was broadening. Second, they intensified the industrial sector. With a focus of being an industrialised country, they opened up for foreign and domestic investors with attractive tax systems, for example, these investors were given a ten-year tax-free period, backed with low salaries. Many jobs were created. Third, a selective development policy was enacted. Investors were guided on what the country needed which contributed to a resource-based industries scheme and these investors were to fit into the industrial map carefully mapped out for the country. In addition, a strong tax regime was established. External factors like the Vietnam War boosted their industrial take-off.

In contrast, for example, a country like Cameroon, abandon its five-year development plans under the regime of Paul Biya (since 1982-to date). There is no industrialisation policy. The idea of Cameroon becoming an Emerging Economy in 2035 falters in many respects. Since independence in 1960 and reunification in 1961, Cameroon can hardly boost of a dual-carriage motor way of fifty kilometres; electric power supply is erratic; so also, pipe-born water supply; corruption is institutionalised, with poor governance taking pride of place in the structural-functional scheme of the country. Presently, the one greatest obstacle is the continued practice of centralised hegemonic ethnic authoritarian regime structures and the exclusion of the people from the development process as well as growing inequity in benefit-sharing of the wealth of the nation. The great divide between the rich and poor continues to widen. Poverty and corruption have been institutionalised and legalised. For now, reasoning has not yet crossed the minds of the power-brokers on this sinful episode of their activities towards fellow citizens. Africa cannot grow with such a mindset directed towards self-aggrandizement of the nation's wealth for a select few.

In some countries, you have absentee landlords as Head of State. They only visit their country making Europe their permanent abode at the expense of their taxi-payers. Can one describe such leaders as exhibiting a high sense of 'responsive, accountable, relevant and ethical behaviour? They have been overtaken by articulate self-interests. Are they better than their departed colonial masters who only went on annual leave but never abandon their posts? Who in this case is exploiting the country more - the former colonial masters or the indigenous leader? Fanon describes these leaders as *"Black skins in White Masks"*. The Fire Next Time is to sweep clean the continent of such absentee landlords.

There is need for a new generation of visionary servant leadership to dominate the continent's political landscape and change the state of pathetic development has gripped the region for decades, making the people into monstrosities. The African governance system with such leaders operates on over-exploitation which continues to ruin the region. Let us waste no time in sterile litanies and nauseating mimicry. These leaders have and continue to stifle almost the whole of their society in the name of a so-called *'advanced democracy'* their own way and with band played by sycophants and greedy individuals. Progress can hardly come the way of a country with absentee presidents who spend the greater part of the year in foreign country only visiting the country he is supposed to be Head of State and Commander of the Arm Forces.

The one determination we must all cultivate is to construct a democratic functional governance structure making the system and its institutions operational for the common good. The challenges are numerous but must be confronted holistically and with the involvement of the different stakeholders. Development has to be a holistic encounter for the total benefit of the community, not for an individual. Incidentally, the post-colonial era produced Chinua Achebe's *"Things Fall Apart";* as colonialism had severed the ties that bound the Africans together to the extent that the centre could no longer hold. The educated few became too euro-centric, losing their Africanness according to Ngugi Wa Thiongo (1986). This type of education produced an educated African who was, in fact, a hybrid as colonial education*: "…. annihilates a people's belief in their names, in their languages, in their environment, in their heritage of struggle, in their unity, in their capacities and ultimately in themselves. It makes them see their past as one wasteland of non-achievement and it makes them want to distance themselves from that wasteland. It makes them want to identify with that which is furthest removed from them".*

Since independence, the ruling elites have constructed what could be termed the blunders of destruction contributing to the underdevelopment of the continent, Fig.1:1 perpetuating the ideological orientation of slavery, imperialism, colonialism and neo-colonialism. Even though it may not be a good example of the New Headquarters of the AU in Addis Ababa, (see section on the New Invasion of the continent). It should be noted that the "ancient and modern history of the donation of buildings and structures from one nation to another is filled with intrigues and subterfuges, consequences, diplomatic scheming, espionage and counter-espionage, economic manipulations, political statements and domination" (Ezeanya, 2012:68). Whatever the plus side of the gift, (which at best be interpreted as a poison) in the end leads to the 'rape of paradise' leading to the death of the continent.

Failure to begin addressing the urgent problems of the continent contributes and exacerbates as well as, unnecessarily prolongs the plight and sufferings of the people. Can a new page be turned by Africans? Demonstrable political will, on the part of African governments, to implement good policies and change the current ways of doing things is a vital component in the process of change, progress, development and sustainability. The Future Africa chooses must build on different but solid tenors of ideological orientations and strategies and strong commitments of a comprehensive renewal, reconstruction and rebuilding of a strong united continent through the constructive and comprehensive involvement of all citizens. Africans can structurally do this by reverting into their cultural heritage, improving on it and benefiting from best examples around the world. In short, it is imperative for African countries to exploit positively the vast opportunities provided by the 'late-comer advantage' to accelerate the development of the continent. Science and technology offers that vast opportunity. But Africa should not allow its emerging scientific power through the late-comer advantage to be overrun its spiritual power and cultural heritage. In the words of Martin Luther King Jr, *'we have guided missiles and unguided men.'* The emerging era of the continent's science, technology, innovation and entrepreneurship, should be used for developmental purposes and not for destructive goals that benefits a few well-placed individuals.

Colonial rule may be dead, but the reality still exists as we hang on the Eurocentric developmental agenda – "the triumphant manifesto of the post-Cold War and post-colonial era, which granted capital its freedom of movement – arrived with more trouble than its architects anticipated. Capital is free but everywhere men and women are rediscovering their chains; and chafing against them" (Kantai, 2016:12). These developments challenge Africans to *consensually, constructively and comprehensively* take the 'reality theory' seriously as the compass for placing the region within the global context. A good example here is the new vision reached at the African Union Summit in Kigali July 2016 for launching of an African Union Passport as the first bold step in freeing Africa of its colonial borders and in creating the Africa We Want. The Kigali Passport Decision must be truly, rigorously and religiously implemented so that no African is a foreigner in Africa. The Kigali Passport accord has been followed by the Kigali Continental Free Trade Area (CFTA) intended to make Africa the world's biggest trading blocs and effectively become one country.

The rest of the world has the right to laugh at us that the continent wallows in gross despair but in the midst of abundant precious mineral resources, and corrupt African leaders engineering Africa's sufferings of epic proportions. Through poor leadership, Africans have been brainwashed to believe that a falsehood constantly repeated several times becomes accepted as the truth. The continent's political leadership and establishment is under serious trouble to restore trust, hope and confidence in the people and demonise all orientation of the continent as being weaklings, and light weights, failed and collapsed states. We need a new Africa that does not erode political legitimacy, but build strong faith, trust and hope in the political leadership and establishment offering sustainable quality livelihood to all citizens.

African leadership have entered a sustained stage of eccentric self-aggrandising personalities with the sole goal of personal accumulation, promoting and propagating the xenophobic ideology to win votes and by telling them what they want to hear without the interruption of reality. But holding on to reality is the gateway to solving the problems of the continent. If we are to build the Africa We Want, holding on to the truth and reality is the only weapon to restore faith, trust and confidence in leadership and government establishment of the region.

Apparently, the less people trust their government, the more likely they are to put their trust in fake demagogues and leaders. There is growing degree of impatience with the continent's poor leadership if Africa's future has to be bright. The current leaders should begin embarking on the historical mission of building an equitable, non-ethnic, non-racial, non-sexist and socially-democratic society as articulated in the Africans' Claims, the Freedom Charter and the Strategy and Tactics strongly expressed in AU Agenda 2063. Our past and present blunders must be adequately addressed as depicted in Fig 1 which presents just a tip of the iceberg of blunders inherent in our society today. Change we can, and change for the better we must undertake now.

Fig. 1.1: Addressing Blunders Leading to Underdevelopment

	Wealth without Work;
	Pleasure without Conscience;
	Politics without open space
	Stability without justice
	Religion without morality
	Knowledge without Character;
======================= →	*Technology without Direction*
Addressing Blunders leading to the	*Commerce without Morality*
Exploitation and underdevelopment of	*Science without Humanity*
Africa	*Worship without Sacrifice;*
======================= →	*Politics without Principles;*
	Work without wealth;
	Poverty in the midst of plenty;
	Rights without Responsibilities;
	Connection with Community
	Teach without Joy;
	Learning without Hope
	Deepening democracy without practice;
	Etc; etc; etc. (Source: Forje, 2012)

Source: The Author -Forje 2019

These and other blunders could be seen as passive destructive violence. If the continent can prevent these acts of passive destructive violence, Africa would be well equipped to wage the war against exploitation, poverty, underdevelopment, exclusion, inertia, corruption and marginalisation. Some of these blunders are interrelated, and some more pronounced in country A than country B. Together, they subject and compromise the future of the continent. No wonder Rene Dumont coined the granting of independence as *"False Start in Africa"* (1962): and Chinua Achebe (1958) half-a-century ago aptly discussed the evolving event through the periscope of *"Things Fall Apart".* Chinua Achebe was encouraging Africans to stand up to the realities of the existing situation, the evolving and changing circumstances as well as preparing adequately for the challenges and opportunities of the future. In short, the *'beautiful ones are yet to be born'* to guarantee the future well-being of the continent.

Democracy can be frightening. It can force partisans and ideologues to confront the difficult truth that public taste often fails to conform to their own tidy theories. Rather than deform democracy to hide from this, the honest ruler seeks to learn from the uncomfortable lessons democratic outcomes often teach. The most realistic alternative to democracy, in other words, is not a tyrannical government, but a deeply deluded one. African leaders should rethink their roles and responsibilities to their population. The people should see democracy as an expression of common sense at its best for the good of all. Thus, democracy in its most broadly understood definition, is a system where the rule themselves based on the idea that a free people must consent to their government.

The flaw of this is philosophy is that 'the people' are not angelic. They can easily misrule themselves, assent to forms of tyranny that erode their freedoms, or even destroy their system of self-rule. This paradox is not exclusive to democracy, of course – all forms of government possess the seeds of their own destruction, as Plato exerted much effort to explain. As subsequent philosophers came to conclude, democracy survives because it's proven to the system that does the best for the greatest number of people and can most easily rationalise restraining its dangerous potentials without undermining its larger principles (McCullough, 2017)

Africans must '*have a dream*' that one day Africa will be on top of Mount Everest, having climbed to the top of Mount Kilimanjaro and Mount Cameroon. The dream must be reflected in Kwame Nkrumah's speech on the eve of Ghana's independence. *"Ghana is Free for ever"*. Africa should be free for ever. This is the time to work towards that goal realising the reality of the Dream of African Unity and the progress of the continent. Undoubtedly, building the human capacity of the people is what will yield substantial benefits to individuals, families and to society towards achieving a united and integrated continent.

Interpreting Dumont's thesis, Professor Paul Nkwi (2009) wrote:

> ...scholars and experts chided him of ethnocentrism; he was unjustly equating Europe and its culture to that of Africa. Due to their Afro-optimism or emotions, his critics mostly Africans accused him of egocentrically judging Africa through the periscope of an imperialist. To

> them the book was a mere reminiscence of the odious system of colonial egoistic manoeuvres aim at reducing Africa to an ignorant schoolboy in a state of dilemma. However, Rene Dumont's crime was his foresighted and bold depiction of certain negative trends on Africa's route to underdevelopment. He blamed Africans for being the architect of their own demise, even if it meant accepting others to teleguide their pace of 'underdevelopment.

The Future of Africa is to be constructed today requiring the unflinching constructive engagement of all the stakeholders for the good of present and future generations. The right institutions must be crafted and made to function within the parameters of the *'rule of law, justice, equity in benefit-sharing';* and in the overall interests of the people and not against the wellbeing of the people.

Yet, when fears of lost democracy manifest, they usually take the form of some gothic dystopia in which constitutional checks and balances are methodically dismantled and replace with difference to a Hitlerian leader. Yet a considerably less theatrical, but no less substantial, erosion of democracy takes place when broad social agreement about its philosophical importance no longer exists, and citizens and elite alike instead cite wildly diverse, context-dependent, self-interested arguments to rationalise either ceding government to the majority's opinion or egging on those with the power to overrule said opinion. The end result is a new system in which the reigning philosophy is neither populism nor meritocratic aristocracy, but a mad scramble of partisan opportunism. That doesn't set the stage for dictatorship, but it does provide a ready-made excuse for both sides' attempts to rig the existing system as much to their benefit as possible, imposing a hodgepodge mixture of democratic and anti-democratic institutions and traditions that don't collectively make any philosophical sense (McCullough, 2017, op cit.)

The destruction of the people by those in power is what takes priority place in the governance of African states. African cannot and will never develop without mainstreaming the essentialities of developing the human intellect of its population. Promoting inclusive growth should the watchword. Africans must work under the umbrella of a renewed commitment to national unity, continental cooperation and integration. The well-being of the African economy and the family of nations depends on an enduring willingness to work together as one unit to solve the challenges facing the continent; reducing national and continental imbalances, and providing the solid foundation for economic growth and good governance that benefits all. It is time to give democracy and governance in Africa a new dimension. We have bathed ourselves with the unholy waters of a system that has gradually grounded the steady weakening of critical institutions, such as the press, judiciary, legislative leading to the erosion of long-standing of political norms that has given birth to authoritarianism. The good news is that at least some form of sovereignty descended on the continent in March 1957. The bad news is that by threading on the path of authoritarianism and Eurocentrism Africa remains enslaved and underdeveloped. The continent needs a comprehensive forward-looking strategic approach in transforming the continent.

Though plagued with diversity, the national, cultural, economic, and social differences make Africa richer. Unfortunately, Africa's riches have become a curse not a blessing. Consequently, the main concern, especially after the Arab Spring, the vast unsustainable exploitation of the natural resources of Africa over the centuries; after the numerous civil wars, political divide, the goal should be focused on reconstructing a Renaissance Africa within the contextualised development of a global-based knowledge economy and localised with the imperatives of the respect of fundamental human rights, delivery of peoples' basic needs and respect for the sovereignty of nations. This is an issue area we shall constantly return to throughout the book. We must constantly communion and avoid any form of disconnect between government, civil society and the private sector in constructing a capable developmental continent. A new mind set as the *'game changer'* is imperative to transform the continent from a backward into a quality service delivery society. It is important to ensure that everyone has the opportunity to benefit from national, continental and global economic integration and technological progress.

No one should be left behind in this age of scientific and technological advancements. Unfortunately, the wealthy are getting wealthier and the poor poorer for each passing day. In reality, growth does not help all. Some African economies have been growing and poverty has been on the decline, but inequality remains stubbornly high in many African countries. Male – female inequality in Africa is not on the decline thereby impeding the progress of the continent. Gender equality is more than a moral issue; it is vital economic issue. For the African economy to reach its potential, we need to create conditions in which all men can reach their potential. Gender equality would increase economic growth; and African countries of all income levels would see significant increases as well as benefit immensely by empowering the female gender in the process of development. This is the time for the people of Africa to restart the growth engine as well as creating a rebalancing action plan and address long-standing weaknesses in the development trajectories that has and continues plaguing the continent.

Whether harbouring an optimist or pessimist perspective, the challenging issue is the future of the continent. Where is the continent coming from? Where is the continent now? And where is it headed? These loaded one million-dollar questions are challenges to the consciousness of Africans and the rest of the world. Africa the cradle of civilisation is now the dumping ground for industrial waste of the West. But it can rise again. It calls upon the Diaspora to bring in new architectural engineering strategic plans for moving the region forward. The ball is in the court of Africans to gannet support from the global community in supporting African grown solutions to Africa's problems and in the overall benefit of humanity. Gaining external support entails keeping the house in order by sowing the good seeds of democratic governance, rule of law, justice, equity, social justice, equality between the sexes, partnership among others.

A divided house can neither constructively face external forces, nor build the strong solid foundation for erecting the structure. In other words, the obligation and responsibility for the socioeconomic-transformation of Africa rests solely in the hands of Africans. Africa should not deceive itself that Europe will develop the continent. Or that the newfound marriage with China will last for ever. When the natural resources are consumed the marriage will come to an end. In reality, Europe only helps in under-developing the continent for its own interests. It is the interests of Europe that matters to Europe. It is the interest of the Chinese that matters to China, not African interests. Africa should equally adopt such a strategy. Exploiting other continents provides the satisfaction needs. Therefore, the interest of Africa must come first in the priority policies ranking in articulating strategies for the techno-socio-economic transformation of the continent. Africa can only rely on its people and resources for its development. It has not got the capacity to invade other continents for its development like the West did in colonising Africa and continue doing so through the exploitation of its vast natural resources.

Existing regional fragmentation deprives the continent of new sources of economic growth, new jobs, and sharply falling poverty, (which intensifies corruption, inertia), factors which accompanied significant trade integration in East Asia and other regions. The cross-border production networks that have spurred economic dynamism in other regions, especially East Asia, have yet to materialise in Africa. These forms of change should trigger new thinking within the continent. African leaders should now be calling for a continental free trade area by 2017, to boost trade within the continent. The recent World Bank Report (Bretton, 2012) show that African countries are losing out on billions of dollars in potential trade earnings every year because of high trade barriers with neighbouring countries, and that it is easier for Africa to trade with the rest of the world than with itself. What kind of education is being implanted into the minds of the people to critically think through the problems and solutions confronting the continent? People are poorly educated to understand the reality of their plights. The very reason why human capital development must be accorded top priority in the development nexus of the continent?

Though Africa has made some significant progress over the past decades, conflict and growing diversities still exists. In some countries, economic growth rates have been robust, with significant improvements in macroeconomic indicators. In some countries, we see how progressive fretting by some leaders contributes to the anti-democratic evils of gerrymandering and voters rigging, depriving the people from making their choice of leadership. We see conservative intellectuals demanding a return to the 'smoke-filled room' system of imposing candidates on the voters. No doubts democracy is on the rise, even though military coup d'état and flawed elections remains a black spot on the political landscape and consciences of some African countries. Democratic bankruptcy has gripped the continent. Much remains to fix the democracy landscape of the continent. This is the one serious area bleeding African dry. Fixing the democratic environment is crucial for the economic recovery of the continent. Equally important is also fixing the economic environment to accelerate the democratic process. Though the economy of the continent has been moving forward relentlessly in the past few years, this economic development does not give us a reason to be complacent about participation and the human rights of people. The forces and virtues of democracy and democratic governance penetrating the continent of Africa can no longer be held back. But this does not entailed imposition of western perception of what kind of democracy is good for Africa. Or Africa should violate the fundamental rights of the people to please their ego or their pay masters. The pay masters are prepared to increase the pay cheques as long as the goods keep coming. The suppliers do their utmost best to ensure that they are on the right-side of the paymasters.

Is Tunisia - *"The Arab Spring"* - the litmus-test bed for Africa's new political dispensation or what? To what extent will the events in Tunisia penetrate into the annals of the political structure south of the Sahara? Will this popular revolt for system change be strong enough and accountable to answer to the desires of political popularisation and fulfilling the virtues of democratic governance and consolidation in Africa? Will it be a wild-wind leaving no substantial reconstruction traces for system change? After all, Africa South of the Sahara has had its share of conflicts, since independence (Laremont, 2013). The Central African Republic (CAR) is in flames. The positive outcome of the power struggle debacle has been in the sense of propelling Africa's Third Female Head of State on the continent with hope of bringing sanity to the people and region, the most turbulent in Africa. The Arab Spring in Tunisia seem to produce a positive changing element seen from the 2014 elections which sets the space for positive and constructive changes to take place.

The African summer brought about the ousting of Burkina Faso long serving President Compaore. It is yet to be seen whether the trend will continue further south to the Limpopo. People's power and uprising has triggered the passing of a law banning free demonstration with the death penalty in the Cameroon Legislative Assembly, November 2014 sitting. Cameroon is yet to have its true war of independence given the onslaught and domination of the majority Francophone over the Anglophone community. There is a fear that peoples' uprising could trigger a seminar effect in Cameroon like in Burkina Faso. It is interesting to see how leaders have started fearing their own shadow. Some leaders remain adamant to the plight of their citizens, but remain determined to hold on power forever. The fire this time is no longer external colonialism but *'internal colonialism'* by selfish leaders. Black smoke and dark clouds continue to hang over the continent. The question of a *'white smoke'* billowing from the continent remains a distant dream. Nonetheless, a new president has to be elected or appointed in countries like Cameroon, Congo Brazzaville, Equatorial Guinea and Zimbabwe.

Africa's conflicts show no signs of abating. Regional unity and solidarity remains a distance compass in the build-up towards a capable developmental continent. The efforts of the various regional economic communities, the role of the African Union and that of NEPAD are yet to be felt by the poor. The failure of Regional Economic Communities (RECs), the New Partnership for Africa's Development (NEPAD), African Union (AU) and national governments impacting on the lives of the poor throws the continent into confusion. This is a dilemma besieging the progress of the continent. It could also be a blessing in disguise. Freedom from hunger and want, peace and stability, unity and progress, growth and development seem further away from the shores of the continent more than ever before. The need for deepening the process for comprehensive change is here and now.

A typical example is the Democratic Republic of Congo which has known no peace and stable governance system the morning after Patrice Lumumba became the Prime Minister of the vast and natural resources rich country (see Delbert 2013; Maund 2013). Lumumba's fault like that of Nkrumah, Mugabe and others of the radical school was the resolve of speaking truth to the colonial masters. The West dictates to Africa but cannot stand any African leader criticising or standing up against western inhumane policies towards the continent. Puppet leaders condone to the dictates of the West. The apartheid governance system is now an issue of the past. Unfortunately, we are trying to replace dictatorial and centralised authoritarian regime structures with an extreme xenophobic or ethnic governance system.

In so doing, Africa plays into the long-term strategic policy articulation of the West for the destruction of the continent. Central African Republic, Somalia and Sudan contrive being a source of headache to the continent. For how long remains the question. Yet the continent continues and remains a region divided into compartments. The dividing line, the frontiers are shown by affluence and abject poverty and the frontiers between the rich and poor are protected by barracks and police stations with the agents of government speaking the language of force. The language of reconciliation and consensus is a distant commodity. Africa forgets its cultural heritage value concepts - *batho pele, ubuntu, harambee*, etc. - in building a strong and united continent as the pride of the people. Yet the continent cannot progress without an intellectual justification outside the b*oundaries of consensus and reconciliation and justice as the anvi*l on which to build a new ***soc****iety within the framework on the overarching principles of law, justice and equitable sharing of the nation's wealth.*

Bad as Africa's economy plight may be, the appalling situation that can be found in many countries has less to do with a lack of material resources than with breakdown of the machinery for distributing. The food is there in Africa, what is lacking is the ability to put it into hungry mouths. As is the case in poorest or backward countries, Africa's social system is based on patronage, with handouts awarded to the poor in exchange for their loyalty and votes. It is no longer how *Europe under-develop Africa* but how *African intellectuals and poor leadership under-develop their own people* to state the least. How can African solutions to African problems be effectuated with this kind of attitude? The ***"Arab Spring"*** is just the beginning of greater revolts on the way coming if drastic measures are not put in place to address existing pathetic situations across the length and breadth of the African continent.

What the West and its cohorts in Africa best understand is the power of force, exploitation and destruction often aided by zealous citizens who think only of their self-interests. Yet the power and force of argument, consensus and dialogue provides the best way for reconciling differences. Unfortunately, the power and force of the barrel of the gun is bought by the ruling class against the desires, needs and aspiration of their people. White colonialism is replaced by authoritarian black imperialism. The immediate post-colonial and post-Cold War era became the darkest, bloodiest and bleakest period for Africa. Dersso (2012:18) asserts: "outside the colonial era, at no other time has violence been more horrific and tragic than this period. It was as though Africa had gone 'from the frying pan into the fire', the military coups in Togo, Congo, Ghana, Nigeria, Ethiopia, Uganda and others signalled a bleak future for the continent; the post-Cold War saw the fall of Said Barre in 1990 resulting in the collapse of the Somalia state accompanied by internecine violence between rival armed factions destroying the infrastructure and livelihood of most parts of the country with hundreds of thousands pushed to starvation and death.

The period under Mobutu's authoritarian rule plunged the then Zaire into one of Africa's brutal civil war which is still ongoing. The civil war that ensued in Liberia, Sierra Leone, Uganda, Sudan and the genocide in Burundi and Rwanda among others was besieged with every act of brutality committed against citizens. Have we forgotten what happened during the civil war in Nigeria? Why are we blind to the genocide in Rwanda, Liberia and other parts of continent? We have equally remained silent with the ongoing genocide in the two English-speaking regions of Cameroon. While the 'blame theory' should not cloud our analytical approach to building a new future for the continent, these conflicts are the aftermath of the forces of slavery, imperialism, colonialism and neo-colonialism currently advanced by the forces of Eurocentrism, which Mentan (2015) sees as structures of knowledge imposed through the production of knowledge worldwide. The Eurocentrism of social science has justifiably come under increasingly vigorous scrutiny, especially in the period since 1945 with the formal decolonisation of Africa, Asia and much of the Caribbean.

In addition, African countries have managed to prevent anything remotely resembling a professional civil service from taking shape. Having stuffed the public payroll with their own dependents and people who would otherwise be unemployed, the political bosses and their propagandists can point out that any reforms designed to upgrade the state machinery throws millions of deserving citizens out of work. This point of view is raucously supported by the captured or sycophantic trade unions and by the *'intelligentsia'* whose main purpose in life is to discredit all genuine alternatives to the status quo by labelling them 'neoliberal'. What Africa needs is not 'neoliberals' but *"Pan-Africanism"* and how to balance Renaissance Africa with the ongoing global evolution. Renaissance Africa and African Unity should find its place within the context of the rapidly changing hostile global context. In short, Afro-centrism should constitute the cardinal point in Africa foreign policy. African interests should shape, as are those of Western states. Africa should define its interests and seek to use institutions to attain its objectives. The individual member state of the AU must equally work in that direction. Consistency in strategy as an ideological orientation should be encouraged and effectuated.

That Africa could rightly be classified as a continent of failed, collapsed or fragile states is no surprise (Mutua 1995:505; Lewis 2008:71-78; Asonganyi, 2015). Adebayo (2003:3) asserts thus: "where Africa had once feared intervention during the cold war, marginalisation had now become a greater concern in the post-apartheid era. Attention, aid, and investment shifted to the emerging democracies of Eastern Europe, and resources were later diverted from African conflicts to reconstruction efforts in Afghanistan and Iraq by 2003." This view is supported by the statement that "Across Africa, undemocratic and oppressive regimes were supported and sustained by the competing super-Powers in the name of their broader goals but, when the cold war ended, Africa was suddenly left to fend for itself" (Annan 1998: para.11).With increasing Western state imposition, the multipolar international system that has replaced the cold war bipolar system has assumed responsibility for ending deadly internal conflicts and reconstituting failed and collapsed state.

Seven of the thirty-three countries are in a critical state of failing were in Africa according to the 1995 Failed States Index compiled by the Fund for Peace, as were 12 of the 42 countries with strong signs of failure. The more detailed 2006 index has four clusters: critical conditions strong signs of failure, basically unstable, and stable countries. All the African countries fell into the first two categories; fifteen of the twenty-eight critically failing states were in Africa. No African state was considered to be stable (see index at www.fundforpeace.org/web) Are these states being reconstituted in the interest of the people or converted in what could best be termed *"state reconstruction industry"* (Ottaway 2003) or Roland Paris calls the *'contemporary liberal peace thesis'* benefiting the military industrial complex of the West. Doe (2009:1) notes: "Africa is hosted the largest number of multilateral peacekeeping and state-building missions in the world, and given the growing social, economic, and political debility on the continent, this trend is likely to continue for some time.

The scale of the multilateral state reconstruction project and its primacy in international policy agendas and trade, is what Chandler (2005) rightly observes is a marked contrast to the political norm that had governed the post-independence and *cold war periods* – present a conundrum with a steep learning curve. Africa in the 21st century finds itself caught in a serious state of tramps requiring the attention of the best medical experts the continent can mobilise to diagnose and treat. The issue or diagnoses circumvents on three key questions. Who leads in reconstructing collapsed states and what is the moral, legal, and strategic basis for their role? How are states being reconstructed? How viable are the outcomes? African Universities, Research Institutes and independent 'Think Tanks' and Individuals are charged and challenged with the responsibilities of seeking plausible arguments and solutions to be made in the process of indigenisation guarantees for the most viable outcomes in State reconstruction. Who is actually benefiting from state reconstituting or reconstruction? Not the people, of course. Where is Africa? Africa is where it is because it has opted to be where it should not be. The continent has embraced Eurocentric and not Afrocentric orientation as its policy options. Hence the continent is often treated with all contempt and ills by the developed world.

Jacobs (2018:78) notes; ...economic theory clings to a concept of static equilibrium by externalising the power forces compelling the rapid evolution of the entire global political, economic and social system. It is understandable that the wealthy, the corporate sector, politician's dependent on them and central bankers obeying narrow constitutional mandates should cling to the resent dogma and endeavour to holds it above scrutiny or approach". But this does explain why the vast majority of African leaders engage themselves in unhealthy policy actions and rather than in-depth question of the underlying premises and efforts to conceptualise a better alternative that advances the progress and development of the region.

Whatever the case there is need for a paradigm shift for the people to derive the best of the governance system of *'government of the people, by the people and for the people; and not against the people.'* In other words, the Arab Spring should intensify and consolidate the governance process of "Here The People Rule" (Forje 2009) or the slogan "Power to the People". Indeed 'Power to the People' (Moksnes and Melin 2010); but are the people using properly the power that belongs to them? The people must be proactive and judiciously deploy power for the common good. To mention the "elusive, confuse, incomplete elastic character of the concept of civil society is not surprising as it remains a revolving problem requiring solutions. Based on one school of thought as correct and the other as false, but the extent to which different frameworks can generate insights that lead to more effective action" (Edwards 2004:7).

However, what is important in the debate, and how many of these attributes result from the debate, is the fact that, civil society has become such a powerful and instrumental political tool, and has been incorporated into a number of different political projects and discourses, receiving, in the process, a variety of different meanings without distorting the reality that power belongs to the people. What is the role of the people in the politics of the continent? How do they intend to shape the socio-economic transformation of the region? Are they prepared to do so? Can the people be demarcated from the state? Just as civil society movements are not homogenous entity, one faction of the state may mobilise society against other factions of the state. Some political parties extend into social movements which are pitted against a military style regime. Adherence to law per se cannot be the hallmark of whether any group is legitimately part of civil society or not or even tell us anything about whether such a group or movement stands for democratic change. However, a vibrant and progressive civil society as the custodian of power is imperative.

Civil society is commonly imbued with a series of normative assumptions linking the notion both to protection of human rights and democratisation. People's participation in civil society is regarded as the exercise of their civil and political rights to freely form associations, freely express their opinions, to pursue their interests among other values. What matters is that those who aspire to be in government must see government office as a platform for public service and not for personal gain. Putting into practice the principles of services to the nation, transparency, integrity, justice, accountability, rule of law, honesty, competence and responsibility should be the watchword of political parties, leaders and all citizens. Above all, seeing the public office as a privilege to serve, and that simply to serve is itself a blessing remains an attitude to be cultivated, nurtured and consolidated by every citizen. The role of civil society as promoter of democratic change "from below" is not always as evident as some would argue. The legacy of anti-colonial struggles has meant that many states have been a progressive modernising force, compared to conservative populations. Examples here can be drawn from Cameroon, where the pre-independence political parties were not as conservative and the post-independence parties. People's movements or social movements are not always agents of progress or democracy, and some in fact may be both civil and uncivil (see debate between Alexander 2008 and Turner 2008).

For now, the continent is gripped by a tsunami with its deadly tide of disease and hunger which sails, steals silently and secretly across the continent. Africa is left in a devastating state and exposed to exploitation, ridicule and disgrace impacting negatively to its present construct and future sustainability. The issue of unity is at stake, even though 'unity' can never be just a simple, straightforward ideal given the many centuries of colonial policy of divide and rule. To unite now is a challenge, and this is complicated by the realities of diversity and disunity. But African unity has been the main ideal not only of the AU over one decade but also a conception of the OAU, over five decades ago. It is high time to go beyond the 'good, the bad and the ugly' to find out the different and conflicting perspectives as well as look at the opportunities, prospects and challenges that can further Africa's constructive engagement in world politics. However, the unequal access to power and resources between different social organisations make local organisation engaged in struggles in dire need for outside support.

That is why individual African states must build bridges to attain a Union Government for Africa and to collectively challenge Western dominance and hegemonic dominance over Africa. The world today is faced with institutions and power structures functioning within the dynamics of shifting powers in a shifting world. Africa has to find its place in these emerging trajectories of the new form of balancing shifting power structures but within the context of ensuring sustainable quality livelihood for the people. As always in Africa, both the present and the future remain contested, and civil society is simultaneously in conflict with and in partnership with the state to bring about democratic change, and to take on other actors in civil society who have other visions of the nation. The important lesson that African civil society must learn is that it has and can only be successful when it forges creative partnership with the peoples' struggles and its progressive leadership. The struggles for change or democratisation are not always neat, linear and devoid of contradictions (Okello, 2010:104).

The continent since the end of World War 11 catapulted itself from colony to nationhood. The difficulty has been finding its rightful place as equals within the international community of nations. It has not been able to adequately address the numerous blunders earlier listed. The colonial powers have not fully come to grips with the idea of a slave becoming a master and dinning on the same table. The idea of once a slave always a slave is stuck in the mindset of the centres of western major powers. There should be no alteration in the status quo. African countries to an extent continue to behave within the laid down principles of remaining a colony for ever. The reality is that the world of the 14th century is not the world of 21st century. Africa of the 1950s is not Africa of 2013, and will not and never be Africa of 2080s and beyond. This means that the continent must crawl from the colonial design to African reality designed by Africans to serve African interests. The formation of the OAU as the first continental organisation of African states and governments was geared towards the eradication of colonialism as well as facilitating economic and social development; as an instrument for the maintenance of peace and security and to solidify the unity of the continent.

Though the OAU failed in addressing the issues of security and peace, it has to its credit by the time of its transition to the AU, no part of the territory was still under colonial duress so to state. Such a milestone accomplishment has to be maintained and improve upon by the new continental institution. But African solution to African problems failed in Libya exposing the lack of unity of purpose among African states (Nathan 2011). This makes imperative for Africa to have a coordinated and common approach and for the AU to be afforded the right and opportunity in playing a leading role (Ebrahim 2011) in finding solutions to African problems in future debacles confronting the continent. Are there any movements in that direction? Or must Africa continue to rely on foreign assistance like in Mali, Central African Republic, DRC and others solving its conflicts?

The Libyan problem highlighted the issue of status quo maintenance on sovereignty focusing on states' rights without duties. For now, most or all member states are still not enthusiastic about developing sovereignty to the continental organisation as a supranational body. This lack of unity and a common approach has been responsible for the perceived failure by the AU to attain a single and united position on critical issues. Therefore, diverging views among African leaders regarding Gaddafi's regime quickly translated into a lack of coherence within the African countries (Cole & McQuinn, 2015; Wright 2012). It also highlights the absence of strategic coordination between the AU and African semi-member permanent states serving within the United Nations Security Council insofar as protecting the AU's position/interest is concern. The AU 'common position' on Libya encapsulated in its roadmap to peace, had already been crafted by the time United Nations Security Council voting took place (Koko & Bakwesegha-Osula 2012). Lack of unity of purpose and patterns of enmity among African countries also became evident as the Libyan crisis unfolded This happened notwithstanding the AU's declaratory commitment to a culture which precludes disunity and in particular behaviour that privileges armed conflict (Vrey 2008). Stark poverty in the midst of abundance has always been common in Africa but political bosses have been more interested in exploiting it than in taking such measures as might allow the continent to bring it down to irreducible minimum. Effective governance is not inevitable but an imperative in transforming the continent. This is what Africa should be gunning for and should be enshrined in all developmental activities.

Change is bound to come. The emancipated slave has come of age at least, or on the way to maturity. Based on the superiority or inferiority complexes or conspiracy theory the West holds on the strategic approach that builds on*: (i) domination and sabotage: (ii)plan economics and self-interests: and (iii) the West wants to prove the point that Africans are not up to the task of governing themselves.* Africa seems to have condescended to the "inferiority complex theory" as a way of life. For the West, and apart of the fear of communist penetration into Africa, the continent was of no strategic benefit to America in the Cold War, though the Democratic Republic of Congo was the main supplier of the resources needed for the 'space-race' between the USA and the Soviet Union. Since the continent did not future on the strategic radar and benefit to America in the Cold War, it was of no significant importance; therefore, it was and is kept as a raw material exporting source. It is possible if it had become a battle ground in the East-West conflict, development would have taken place at the expense of many lost lives.

The destructions of Japan, the Korean and the Vietnam Wars helped in boosting the economic transformation in the region. The Congo War has not triggered economic transformation of seminar magnitude in the neighbouring countries like the Wars in Korea and Vietnam. Why? One cannot rule out a hidden or unhidden agenda to keep Africa underdeveloped. Keeping Africa underdeveloped is good business for the industrial West. There can be no future without justice. It does not mean Africa should be a battle ground for it to develop. Taking equity seriously after fifty years of policies that have further widened the gap between rich and poor and exacerbated inequities and inequalities, not least regarding access to resources must be properly addressed. Unbridled market forces and inhumane policies have favoured the strong, thereby widening the economic divide. This requires the state to redress the imbalance, eliminate discrimination, and ensure sustainable livelihoods, decent work and social inclusion.

Historically, the creation of the Organisation of African Unity can be traced to a compromise between the 'cores' of the true believers in the movement's end goal and the 'periphery', the majority of conservative states that sought more limited objectives. In this idea propounded by the American political scientist, Immanuel Wallenstein, "the radical minority (Ghana, Guinea, Mali Egypt and Morocco) reluctantly accepted that they had to move at the pace of the slowest, and that unity was more important than momentum. The OAU Charter of 1963 did not even mention Pan-Africanism or political union. Its summits were little more than 'talk shops' with no implementation mechanisms. The Accra summit of 1965 effectively buried Kwame Nkrumah's dream of African continental government and an African Military High Command for two generations in favour of a more gradualist approach through regional integration (Whiteman & Nagar 2008:20) Importantly was the meeting of Three Heads of States. Sekou Toure (Guinea), Kwame Nkrumah (Ghana) and William Tubman (Liberia) in Sanniquellie, Liberia, July 15-19, 1959 that laid the foundations for African Unity. The three leaders were trying to strike a compromise between the philosophy of Kwame Nkrumah – who was advocating immediate unity for the continent – and the gradualist approach to African unity preferred by the Liberia President William Tubman (Paye-Layleh, 2011:74). The three presidents met to discuss the possibility of African Unity and the eventual formation of a Pan-African body. Liberia went to host a conference of independent African states in Monrovia in1961. Ethiopia hosted the meeting that led to the creation of the Organisation of African Unity (OAU) in May 1963; which transformed into the African Union as the organ in preparing the continent to facing the growing challenges of the 21st century and beyond.

The challenge for African Union (AU) is to live up to the expectations of the people and deliver the goods without leaving any citizens behind. The essential critical action of the AU is to ensure the unity of the continent, that the critical mass of the youth from across the length and breadth of the continent are called upon to articulate a vision of the kind of continent as well as the global world of which they part; ensure that justice and peace reigns and that poverty and corruption becomes history. Equally important is for the AU to develop a strategic inclusive and prosperous society. Therefore, it needs new ideas that will lead to new ideologies and new models to meet the challenges of the continent and ensure its place within the contemporary world. This the hour for a new social contract – existing models for good governance between governments and their citizens, existing social contracts are challenged by today's global conditions.

The Laying of African Future in Sanniquellie – Liberia in 1959

Source: Saye-Guannu Joseph (2011)." All Together Now;" Jonathan Paye-Layleh speaks to Joseph Say-Guannu (prominent Liberia Historian), BBC, Focus on Africa, January-March, 2011, p74 (Sanniquellie is sometimes referred to as the birthplace of the Organisation of African Unity (OAU) – now known as the African Union (AU) *(see:wwafricaunion.org/root/AU/DConferences/2007/December/euu/docs/Eas2007_lisbon_declaration_en.pdf)*

The six or more decades of Africa's rise to nationhood offers the region with contrasting realities: from the apprenticeship or struggle from the yoke of domination and colonial rule to the attainment of nationhood to the tyranny of the one-party state: from political murders to the heroism of the liberation wars; from the repetitive coups d'état to the re-establishment of democratic rule; from the identity crises (civil wars, authoritarian rule, etc.)to the revival of the African unification spirit: from unjust external interference to the construction of an authentic African destiny. These positive developments should spur the people towards achieving greater heights and consolidate the continent's position within global politics. From its establishment in 1963 and transformation in 2002, the AU seems to have more clout to intervene when conflict threatens and happens. In the Constitutive Act the principle of 'non-interference' in internal affairs is applied to member states among themselves, but the immediately following principle is *"The right of the Union to intervene in a Member State...in respect of grave circumstances, namely war crimes, genocide and crimes against humanity"* (AU 2000; art. 4 (g) and (h). In addition to this is "The right of Member States to request intervention from the Union in order to restore peace and security" (AU 2000, art, 4(j); a principle endorsed in the Protocol for the establishment of the Peace and Security Council of the AU (AU 2002; art 4 (f), (j) and (k).

With the new, reinvigorated Pan-African organisation in existence, it was inevitable that new proposals would be made to accelerate the pace of political and economic integration. Libya's mercurial leader, Muammar Kaddafi, pursued his 1999 proposal for a United States of Africa' at the July 2007 AU summit in Accra, Ghana. It had qualified support from Senegal's President Abdoulaye Wade, but the debate was a historical, quixotic, and impractical. The majority of Africa states favoured moving towards a "Union Government" by 2015 rather than an immediate "United States of Africa". Federalist schemes were rejected as lacking in priority, sequence, or reality. Domestic houses still needed to be put in order with strong economies and stable democracies. Qaddafi became Chair of the AU in February 2009, and continued his efforts at federating the continent (Whiteman & Nagar, op cit.)

African countries have even failed to attain the Millennium Development Goals (MDGs) of halving poverty by 2015; establishing a continent of a robust peace and security architecture; strengthening of investment, growth and prosperity through regional integration and closer economic ties; promoting and consolidating 'good governance' and ensuring 'human rights and freedoms; and the creation of opportunities for shaping global governance in an open and multilateral framework We should have done better with the MDGs than any other region. We did not. Our leaders failed in exhibiting the sense of prudent management and democratic governance. We all jumped on the bandwagon of corruption and bleeding the state to death.

For Africa to develop and prosper it needs to have a more prudent management of its economic and practice at best, the basic tenets of democratic governance. Africa should scrutinise any policies borrowed from elsewhere which are negative to its economic growth and not wholly beneficial to its peoples. Therefore, the continent must learn to be shrewd when dealing with either the East or the West and have a tough bargaining position with the interests of the vast majority of the people in Africa the sole priority and objective of development. We must the architect to the solutions to our economic problems. Being architects means forging together competing interests and diversities and weaving them into a dynamic whole of a governance structure that rewards merit but leaving no one behind as well as rejecting nepotism and cronyism, with the flag of the rule of law and justice flying high and all citizens contributing their quota and ripping benefits as well.

Following the independence of African countries, and based on the fact that no society is static, Western countries will have to learn to live with the dynamics of the emerging nations and how they affect the global balance of power rather than resort to smear campaigns against positive changes taking place which impedes the articulate self-interests of the West. They would have to adjust accordingly to the strategies put in place as confronted by the blunders mentioned. Of course, the West, however, is and would continue to be infuriated in the wake of African countries coming to maturity as they systematically attend to the blunders that have slowed their development path. They need to develop a new and positive mindset about the continent and its place within the global community. The best option is to evolve on the path-wave of acceptance - that Africans are human-beings with blood running in their veins like white people. They must come out of their age-old xenophobic attitude towards black people.

The colonial mentality harboured by Africans should give way to positive thinking, pride and love for their continent. Positive thinking should be backed by commitments, obligations and responsibility. Are Africans up to the task for change and reconstituting the continent or merely paying lip services and accepting the existing status quo? The people must in unionism help to halt the invading new form of c*olonialism with all the enthusiasm that social mobilisation harbours, a dose of caution is in place.* A new development and state construct nexus is imperative, and this better phrased by Burawoy (2010:312); *"alarmism but a careful and detailed analysis of the way capitalism combines the commoditisation of nature, money and labour, and thereby destroys the very ground which a 'counter-movement' could be built."*

Given the structural wideness of Africa's current development deficit, any future upgrades of its development construct must be construed on the platform of returning power to the people; and the people taking charge of the obligations and responsibilities given. Peoples' power must be enhanced and consolidated by exhibiting a high sense of obligations and responsibilities for the common good. This is a task that best can be accomplished only through an interface of all working together and in partnership. The obligations and responsibilities can best be scrutinised within the context of four scenarios as depicted in Fig 1:2, Scenarios for moving Africa Forward.

There is no other way for Africa's future without unity and being Afrocentric; in short, ***'do not agonise; organise'*** for Africa to remain a veritable player in world politics and in meeting its social contract with the people in terms of quality services delivery. The future of the continent depend on the currently articulated development policies which puts the interest of the people first and not articulate individual interests at the centre of transformation. The continent faces the dilemma of the good, the bad and the ugly. The choice should be the *'good'* for the common interest of all.

The signpost for the common good is *good governance* and inclusive *participation* by the different stakeholders. The neglect in addressing difficult challenges in good governance and anticorruption reflects the silent crisis plaguing the developmental progress of the continent. An evil spectre is haunting Africa – the continued forces and destructive nature of colonial rule and capitalism Colonialism is not dead, but transformed into neo-colonialism. As the triumphant manifesto of the post-colonial era granting the Eurocentric strategic approach more leverage of destruction than its architects anticipated. A new uprising with a different package of rising expectation, hope and trust in the governance establishment is needed in piloting the continent's passage into a new world construct.

With growing uncertainty among African governments, a new form of colonialism looms over the continent. Today, the African continent is facing a new colonial invasion no less devastating in structure and impact than what it faced during the nineteenth century. We have lost steam and sense of direction due to poor leadership and a passive civil society. We have failed to exploit the advantages of the 'late-comer advantage' in reshaping the continent for the good of all. It is time we wake-up from slumber and face the realities of the challenges of *'self-determination'* and sustainable development as the anvil for quality wellbeing of all citizens.

Moving to the post-colonial era of Africa, it is perhaps unfair to expect a single African voice to emerge from African governments and the African Union given the multiplicity of African views expressed by its 54 member states, and given the context of Europe, which, despite the EU's successful integration efforts, continues to lack a single voice in many areas (Centre for Conflict Resolution: 2016:7). Because Europe fails in uniting itself is no prelude for the failure of Africa adopting an Afro-centric approach and attitude towards its development agenda?

At the same time, the continent is poised to develop and implement for scenarios as depicted in Fig.1:2 Success in executing these scenarios requires unity, consensus, reconciliation, hard work, and new ethical values to turn their difficult historical past into a growing portfolio for a better Africa – the Africa the people want.

Fig. 1.2: Four Scenarios for Moving Africa Forward

The Lions are trapped. Economic growth is very slow or non-existent, and minimal integration into the global economic system has occurred. The continent remains primarily an exporter of raw materials, despite declining profitability, and provision of public services remains inadequate. However, crisis and collapse are averted.

The lions are hungry: External shocks, such as decreased raw material prices and lower aid flows, destabilise a number of countries. Regional institutions are unable to deal with this instability and violence spreads

The Lions come out of their dens: The provision of public services, building human capital of the people through quality education in all sectors. Developing a comprehensive long-term attitude of regime change that identifies the strongest pillars of the state for attack towards creating a capable developmental state; Together with infrastructure improvements and a favourable international environment, this supports sustained economic growth;

The Lions mark their territory: Economic growth occurs along a uniquely African grown path. African solutions to African problems for the ultimate good of the people should be the ideological path of action. Taking control of its development agenda is what all states must gun for. Developing a clever and pragmatic mixture of market incentives and state direction should be guiding lines of actions. Indigenisation, empowerment and establishing a socio-economic and political system which serves to improve the standard of living of the broad masses of the country should be prioritised high on the development agenda. Many examples worldwide exist to draw valuable lessons from countries that have it. The newly oil rich countries in Africa can learn from the Norwegian experience as compared to Nigeria where oil wealth has become a curse rather than a blessing.

Source: South African Scenarios The UNDP African Futures Institute (2003) Africa 2025: what Possible Futures for Sub-Saharan Africa? South Africa. See also Nick Segal (2007) Breaking The Mould. The Role of Scenarios in Shaping South Africa Future, SUN Press, Stellenbosch, South Africa, p91, and my inclusion.

The reality of these scenarios can have serious impact only when significant restructuring takes place in the decolonisation of our current mindset. And it means building on a progressive Afrocentric ideological orientation and action process. The people must begin now with a critical and dynamic interpretation of power relations of domination, struggle, emancipation and self-reliant participatory development process.

There is the issue of the unexpected and unforeseen injected by the Corona Virus (COVID -19).The long-term devastating impact is blowing in the wind. Africans must begin earnestly searching for the truth in a complex human relation as a never ending-quest within the complex global setting of our contemporary world construct. A progressive Afrocentric construct starts with the process of our human capital development which should begin with the deconstructing of the current dominant Eurocentric educational curriculum. The new educational curriculum should focus on breaking free from the chains of colonialism and its oppressive legacies.

No budding African child should be allowed to leave any institution of learning without this new ideological orientation inherently and strongly implanted in his/her skull. The continent's future is interwoven with histories, politics, and cultural considerations of its historical past; and drawing valuable lessons, with critical examination from there, and mindful reflections woven together to make a meaningful and strategic onslaught in building a better future for the continent. This is a significant aspect of the book urging us to articulating policies making the presently worse of in society better-of tomorrow. The continent's distinctiveness remains distinct, but there are more important things where our future intersects, and which gives us the identity of the Africans we are. And African we are and shall remain.

Reality and Blame Theories

The awakening Lion must of course be prepared and well equipped in all facets of (human capital development, policy articulation, governance, etc.) to launch the much-needed counterattack, as well as stand its ground for constructive change. That preparedness requires changes in openness. Increasing openness should be seen as involving some or all of the changes across the following areas: Greater transparency in procedures for information-gathering, standard-setting; and behaviour-modification;

- Wider public participation, inclusion and shared-prosperity, and
- Heightened accountability, transparency across the various components or segments of society in terms of increased obligations and responsibilities on the part of those responsible for state governance;
- A proactive vibrant civil society acting truly as the custodian of power and instrument for change, progress, development and quality livelihood for the people.

Can African countries make a long-term gain and success from the Tunisian/Arab Spring uprising? Are there other ways for system change? Political polarisation and economic stagnation, social injustice and unshared-prosperity underscore the plight of the vast majority of the people. The state of inequality and bad governance gives ample ground for crisis and revolts, calling for system change. Society cannot remain stagnant. Change is imperative. But a change that is holistic, comprehensive backed by constructive engagement and bringing the best to the people. Without change there can be no progress; without progress there is development, and without development, there is no sustainable quality livelihood for the citizens. This is the kind of ideological orientation that should be implanted in the population, ensuring that the people work in that direction. There is need for a kind of 'state dominated society' with a difference. A good example is drawing valuable lessons from the paradox of the Swedish political culture – the relationship between state and society.

Indeed, the Swedish political tradition is marked by a seemingly mysterious paradox, writes Lars Tragardh (2010); "....Sweden is also often celebrated as an open, democratic society in which citizens enjoy easy access to political culture and the political process...and where representatives of the state – elected officials as well as civil servants – have increasingly sought to govern in cooperation with civil society actors, ranging from traditional unions, new social movements, foundations, and voluntary organisations to national business organisations, multinational companies, and transnational non-governmental organisations, NGOs. The notion that Swedish political culture is particularly statist has shown itself to be an enduring one, not least among critics of Sweden. Viewing Sweden as the incarnation of Huxley's Brave New World (Huntford 1971) castigate the Swedes, who he deemed to be *"not quite of the West"*, for their "worships of the State" (p14). To be sure, they possessed the trappings of constitutional democracy, *"but they do not have democracy in their hearts*", rather they have a preference for governments by bureaucrats rather than by politicians under the rule by central administration, they love their servitude" (p.9, 348). Leading political scientists from Gunnar Heckscher (1946) in the 1950s to Bo Rothstein (1992) in the 1990s, describe Sweden as a *'corporatist'* state, even though they would carefully distinguish Swedish 'democratic' corporatism.

This brings to the fore two vital components; a democratic governance system working in partnership with civil society, and the state focused on service delivery with civil society responding positively towards government policies which are people-oriented. The Swedes demonstrate what could be rightly termed the holy marriage between *"democratic governance and an obeying society"* which makes the society to function according to the needs of the people. Today, Sweden like the other Nordic countries is the *"chosen land of democracy and freedom"* to state the least and this makes the place an envy of the world good governance system. It is not perfect, but the Nordic countries have established themselves as the place to be in terms of governance and service delivery. While one does not advocate a direct transposition of the Swedish model to Africa without some critical adjustments, some lessons of a *'democracy of popular movements'*, or *'associative democracy'* that can propel the continent from backward into a service delivery society can be copied and modified to meet the exigencies of the continent. There are obligations and responsibility responses and sharing by state and civil society. Civil society input into government is balanced with government output in terms of quality services delivery; making the Nordic countries the anvil for the ***"place to be".*** Trust, confidence, justice, rule of law, accountability, transparency, equity and legitimacy are assured. These aspects are missing in the African structure-functional governance system.

Some have identified a false start in the conceptualisation of democracy, development, the granting of independence, wrong policies and politics as the main problem to the attainment of democratic governance in Africa; fifty years after the attainment of independence, some will rightly argue that the faulty line is inherent in the African being, i.e. his/her perpetual inability to learn the essentials of governance through the governance system of the People Rule; government of the people, by the people and for the people. The operation of this virtue of governance system operates in the principle of *"government against the people."* While others harbour the ideas that the false start has roots in historical context – the dislocation of the continent through colonial rule, slavery, neo-colonialism and the name the rest cannot be dismissed lightly. Therefore, the continent should seek its own perspective and deal with pressing and concrete problems as well as offer conjectures or approaches to better understand where Africa is and how the continent can proceed from here to progressively forge ahead towards a better continent.

Between the two lie the theoretical truths of post-colonialist and realities. The main argument is that Africa must confront its situation from the strategic position of "reality" and in so doing be allowed to make mistakes and learn from them. African must construct its own learning process but drawing from the experiences of other countries that have threaded on the road of development. In short, benefit from the *"Late-Comer Advantage"* in correcting past mistakes, crafting the present and constructing the future. In a way, *"the blame theory"* should be put into the wastepaper basket or constructively reconverted into a progressive forward-looking developmental approach. This is the only way for building a new Africa of hope, vision, passion, and justice, equitable sharing, unity, and cooperation and building bridges across the state of social divide. There is a clash of culture and bridges must be constructed to connect harmoniously the various parts together. Without that connection, African cannot properly move forward. There is continued western dominance and western bias in reporting Africa. The problem is not about Europeans and Africans not interacting enough, the problem is that in their quest for continued global dominance, the Pan-European or Eurocentric world are relentlessly engaged in a war of disinformation about parts of the world and cultures (Africa in particular) dissimilar to them. It is, therefore, the place of Africans to look after their interests critically and objectively in the ultimate interest of good of Africa.

The book is emphatic that the *"blame and reality theories"* complement each other, but that emphasis should be focused on the *reality theory* for reuniting and the reconstruction of Africa as the way of laying the solid foundation for the future of the continent. It is time high-time for Africa to stop blaming everyone for its problems and get to work. It is now or never for the continent to work towards assembling its resources (human and natural) to galvanise, support, build ideas and aspirations towards constructing the Africa we want in the new globalised world construct. Building on the **"Reality Theory"** provides the structural anvil for confronting existing structural constraints and weaknesses to democratisation and sustainable development in Africa.

The reality approach should be seen as the foundation of a New African Order (NAO). And on that Order must the new continent be constructed. It is a clarion call f*or Africa*n countries to develop a new mindset towards addressing the plethora of problems and challenges plaguing the region. Africa has suffered a lot, slavery, colonialism, financial ups and downs, corruption, poverty, patronage, clienteles, dictatorships, institutional dysfunctions in democratic times, etc. It occurs, and rightly so, that outsiders believe that the situation has become inherent in the societies of the region, that these dysfunctions are almost synonym of Africa. The reality and truth is, however, that this kind of dysfunctions is very much present in some parts of the world but with a difference - a collective search and willingness to craft and apply agreed solutions. If Africa wants to become a reference in the international political system, it has to assume its parts of responsibility for a better world, for democracy, good governance, economic growth and social justice. The time for positive action and change is now, to forge ahead new lines of actions and build a new brave continent.

Without this New African Order (NAO), it will be difficult in understanding the evolving trends on the continent and of its place within the global context. The **"Blame Theory"** is a destructive strategic approach that engraves Africa within the destructive realm of a New World Order (NWO). Has the developed world genuinely included Africa in the New World Order Construct? Continuous building on the *'blame theory"* only peripherals and perpetuates the marginalisation of Africans. Seen within this perspective, Africa must ponder much deeper into the ideologies of two renowned scholars, Francis Fukuyama and Samuel Huntington which critically places Africa as a non-existent continent or one populated by objectives that are merely acted upon by history. This falls in line with Hegel's inaugurated thesis construed on ignorance or arrogance. Africa must develop the attitude and ability of learning; but winning requires ability, stamina, and building the capacity and will to win is what must be cultivated and implanted in the mindset, behaviour, attitude in every African from Cairo to the Cape; from Banjul to the Horn.

A new educational curriculum is much needed to reconstruct the continent. The educational establishment is put to task, articulating an educational system that adequately respond to the changes, challenges and needs of the people. Teaching African history from African perspectives with the literally scholarly works of historians like Yosef Ben-Jacaneen, Chancellor Williams, Ivan Van Sertima, Cheikh Anta Diop and a long list of others to dispel the wrong image often presented to the outside world by foreign writers. For a long-time past, Africans are fed a history of themselves based on materials written, controlled and approved by white academics. A liberal attitude is envisaged; since liberals believe in detachment, disinterestedness, impartiality, open-mindedness, objectivity and political independence and neutrality. Africa has to evolve on the principles of objectivity, reality and independence. The new educational curriculum must be vigorously inculcated in the mindset of Africans – seeking African solutions to African problems within the context of scientific realism from an African perspective and objectivity for the good of the people. Africa of the future should build on objectivity, impartiality and open-mindedness as well as bearing in mind that Africa operates within a rapidly changing hostile global environment. The adherence to the *'reality theory'* should be seen within this frame.

First, the continent should be aware that any development policy implies both selection of issues and a selection within subject matter –

a selection of theoretical method as well as a selection of relevant facts. The continent must prioritise its priorities according to its means and in relation to the needs and aspirations of the people. Second, selection will naturally be a function both of the interests and values of society or culture of which s (he) is a member. What is taken as expressive of the value-system of society in which such a choice be made. Third, in order to eliminate any possibility of misunderstanding of hidden persuasiveness, the continent should start by making and explicit and unreserved declaration of the regions values and interests in its development path, goals and realisation. Four, there is more than one sense in which choice and interpretation of the facts may be expressed or represent certain values. African should be able to stand its grounds on its development path. It must seek ways and means to establish its own values even in circumstances that are less than ideal.

The continent should be equally bound to admit the impossibility in principle of finding criteria which could, if satisfied, provide a guarantee that action of a given problem has reached a standard of perfect objectivity and impartiality. To admit that perfect objectivity and impartiality cannot in any practical terms known to exist. Open-minded is after all to be unremittingly sensitive to the possibility that one may not yet have succeeded in being as impartial and as objective as one may have intended and hoped; that there may still be new facts to be discovered, old facts whose relevance has yet to be reassessed, new interpretations to be considered of the total situation or of certain aspects of it. Objectivity and impartiality exist as ideals of reason; or that while to aim at objectivity is necessarily to aim at truth, in actual practice the most objectively presented account may always in as yet unknown fact turn out to be known to exist in the facts of things actually said and done is not at all the same thing as to say that they exist in no meaningful way whatsoever. The crucial point here is for the continent to know what it wants and how to go about obtaining just that as well as consolidating on the gains made so far.

Africa should show high degrees of disinterestedness in western manufactured policies for its socio-economic transformation. To be disinterested implies having no interest the articulated and imposed development path imposed by the developed polities. Africa should interest itself in what is at stake and to determine policy actions accordingly. Therefore, a progressive Afro-centric prioritised strategic approach is imperative for the continent to take charge and own its development trajectory. What is at stake for Africa is its state of underdevelopment despite its wealth of natural resources? What is at stake is to improve the quality livelihood of the people. What is at stake is to secure its independence and to deploy it in transforming the continent from backwardness to a service delivery modern society. This takes the continent to the concept of the political. Making right political decisions and choices for the overall good of the people is required of the leaders and policy-makers. Here is where the academia must make its impact felt in being objective, scientific, impartial and suggesting the right possible path for actions. The continent requires a broad framework marring the political and academic as these two have direct practical bearing on each other within a general framework or social structure; but a structure recognising at the same time one in which the possibility of their essential distinction is taken seriously. Before we start contemplating about the future, we should study and understand the past and present. That is why a scientific, objective and realist approach is highly recommended. We have to study ourselves as well. Who are we? What do we want? How do we obtain what we want? In other words, not only is there disagreement on how the subject should be approached, but one approach commits one to making this disagreement clear.

Whichever approach creates its own problems. First when should this clarifying occur? There is the danger in doing it too early that the complexity involved will put the continent off. In the case of the continent urgency is the issue. The magnitude of the problem is so enormous that issues must be tackled at all fronts. Second, which ever approach implies the application of different theories in the sense of logical proofs there is an absence of an established body of theory. The conflict is between leaving the continent to sort it itself which may again end up confused, or on the other hand inculcating Africa with a set of models which make it more difficult to think about new situations as they arise. Institutions and rigour can unfortunately be competitive as well as complementary. Third, and most difficult of all, is the stress which approach lays on the context of transformation issues. Here we are faced with a number of challenges; (a) the approach can be accused of a bias in favour of the status quo – the allowable knowledge is what is imposed on the continent by the West; (b) there are no agreed criteria of relevance – the approach assuming there is little theory which is agreed to be generally applicable, one does not know how to decide what is relevant and what is not; (c) this lack of settled criteria of relevance implies that there are no ground rule by which to judge accusations of bias. Obviously, these problems overlap. Africa should not exclude the intelligent anticipation of facts before they occur. Here criticism of bias is replaced by criticism of lack of objectivity. Africa must set its own criteria, guidelines, scholarship and objectives as well as means for realisation. African solutions to African problems must be given the ideological orientation and inculcated in body politic of society. The African society has to be proactive to realise its objectives of being a veritable player and equal partner in the rapidly changing global settings.

Holding on to the **"blame theory"** constitutes a defeatist approach which constraints the continent in the deeper depth status of underdevelopment. The marginality is the result of Africa holding too long on the blame theory which does more harm than good to the socioeconomic transformation of the region and as a significant player in world politics. The *"blame theory"* puts Africa on the line of being Afro-pessimists. Afro-pessimism is a line of t be approached, blinking that has given up on Africa; nothing positive ongoing; and nothing positive could occur. It is a lost continent. The future of Africa construed from the *"reality theory orperspective"* is constructing a New Africa of Hope and Positive Changes to kick-start Africa's political, social and economy transformation. The 'blame theory" is like the Whiteman who says shoot them before they grow up; and the *"reality theory"* is like the Whiteman who says give them education, build up their skills to face challenges, adopted by the colonial powers in governing the continent.

Africa is still paramount uncharted territory economically, and the withdrawal of the colonial rulers from political control is interpreted as a signal for the descent of the international monopolies upon the continent's natural resources (Nkrumah, 1965:109). African problems have to be dealt with in African terms of objectives, interests and cooperation. Solving African problems and meeting the challenges are tasks to be carried out both locally, regionally, and in cooperation with the world community. Africa cannot go alone as an isolated Island. This requires the availability of common resources and coordinated use of them. Without it the problems remain unsolved, or scanty resources directed to targets of secondary importance, or otherwise used ineffectively if not embezzled. Even though the continent is currently rent apart by various strife, ethnic conflicts, civil wars, piracy, religious insurgencies, corruption and poverty, the unity of the continent is still possible and achievable. European Renaissance flowered at the exact period when violence and war was most wide-spread; This does mean that Africans should go to war to enshrine their Renaissance construct. Africa should copy what is right and accelerates their transformation process.

We should not dismiss the reality of existing weaknesses of our institutions, communities and social forces. These weaknesses do not entail writing Africa off. Rather, "by avoiding undue romanticisation of dislocation, and generate the necessary political will, alliances and consciousness required for Africa's genuine liberation" (Ihonvbere 2000: xi), but providing the structural reformation basis for reconstructing a New African Order (NAO). The reconstruction of a New African Order necessitates both obligations and responsibilities. In this regards we can construct a chain of thought. The chain runs from choosing the targets and recognising the challenges, to defining the means and the actors. It involves 'inclusive, accountable and responsible governance construct. The need for strengthening democratic governance and overcoming fragmentation is imperative.

To overcome the fragmentation of governance for sustainable development and ensure policy coherence, it is essential to re-arrange and re-configure the institutional arrangements that cover all aspects of the policy cycle: agenda-setting, policy analysis and formulation, decision-making, implementation and evaluation. We can frame this as a model for ethical structure based on rational grounds though it could be constrained and framed by the reality existing in each African country.

African countries must take into consideration two complementary prerequisites for bearing national and full global responsibility for human's development: (a)the acceptance of mutual dependency and interdependency: and (b) taking care of one's own self-development and contributing in mutual exchange. Rationally, the stronger are morally obliged to support the weaker in their development, and in their contributions to the common good for sustainable development and a dignified life for all. In the contemporary, the challenges are global, long-term and holistic in nature. The environment, the economy, politics, culture and security are firmly interdependent, and affect each other. But because of articulate self-interests globality is downplayed by the nations that are technological and scientifically advanced subjecting the technologically and scientifically backward state to their dictates. At the same time failing to understand that the world has only one "nature" for all people – "an interwoven whole" or living in "global village". We can no longer escape the reality of global and real-time communication connect events, currency flows and human awareness in a way removes the buffers based on the geographical disparities of day and night, as well as on seasonal differences (FICOR, and FSFS, 1997).

It is important to be conscious and not associated with the ideal of rolling back the state and the obsessive labelling of the African state as a lame leviathan. The future of Africa should gun for increasing and sustaining the welfare of the people and not increasing the wealth of the nation without equitable distribution which makes no sense to the wellbeing of the people. The call is for participatory democracy, asserting that flawed democracy of the ballot box constitutes only a truncated and deformed form of citizen power. A new post-independence politics should be such in which the gap between governors and governed should be close by virtue of to overcome the fragmentation of governance for sustainable development and ensure policy coherence, it is essential to re-arrange and re-configure the institutional arrangements that cover all aspects of the policy cycle: agenda-setting, policy analysis and formulation, decision-making, implementation and evaluation. We can frame this as a model for ethical structure based on rational grounds though it could be constrained and framed by the reality existing in each African country, as depicted in Fig. 1:3 Chain of Intellectual Process of Searching for National Responsibility a political form that inducts everybody into the realms of political and administrative decision-making (Adler and Steinberg 2000:8; Forje 2009). Fundamental changes at three levels are needed in redirecting policies towards present and future administrative structures, namely:

- Changes in the mindset, the guiding concepts and indicators of development, progress leading to sustained quality livelihood;
- Changes in fiscal and regulatory policies at national, regional, continental and international levels in order to effectively overcome social inequalities and the degradation of nature and to strengthen sustainable economies;
- Changes in institutions and governance mechanism at continental levels

Therefore, the Future of Africa should be embedded with a programme for socio-economic and political renewal and the total democratisation of the African political landscape. The phenomenon of 'sit-tight' presidents or 'absentee landlord' should be discarded from the political dictionary of African leaders. This equally puts pressure on the African ruling elites to cloth themselves with a new mindset focused on addressing basic needs like food, shelter, clean water, health care and security critical to the welfare of the people, not to continuously be stuck at the esoteric level of articulate self-interests. The new elite's wish of simply replacing the old dictators and departed colonial masters with *"democratic oppressors"* is not what is expected of them. The present and future of Africa should be people-focused on the platform for democracy, accountability, social justice, popular participation, rule of law, transparency, gender equality, and empowerment of all constituencies and communities needs to be strengthened so that shared-responsibility and shared-prosperity is incarnated for the sake of canalising state energy into limiting exploiting the already poverty-stricken citizens.

If the various countries do not get the issue of state construct right, then you will not get a United States of Africa right. Getting state construct right is returning power to the people. Returning power to the people tells us the health and wealth of the nation and the continent. Building the human capacity of the people, backed by the rule of law and suppression of articulate self-interests for the collective-interests (the common good of the nation), should receive priority. It is on these ideals that the future of Africa can be x-rayed and constructed. A mindset change is needed to re-frame goals and objectives within limits and reclaim and redefine the role of the state, with principles and rights occupying the governance apex for public policies and budget allocation. Presently, a precarious partnership or relationship exists among African countries. As a result of these precarious partnerships, African states are not able to synchronised policy actions. Just as there has to be accountability and transparency in governance at the national levels, this should equally extend to the continental level to reinforce coherent approaches to attaining objectives. Democratic governance and full respect for human rights are pre-requisites for empowering people to make sustainable choices. Africa must constitute itself into a solid body that a future worth choosing for the people can be crafted.

We should all rejoice that we are able to make a humble contribution to the discourse which has begun about the continent's future and to share some perspectives, drawn from our experiences of the past and present within the rapidly evolving global context, as the prerequisites for walking the path towards constructing a future in prosperity. We cannot deny the fact that the rapid changes occurring; the outcome demonstrates the collective desire for Africa to exercise greater control or ownership over its independence, sovereignty and destiny. Our collective historical past and present should teach us one thing – that there is no shortage of articulated self-interested forces in the world that would not prevent us from determining our own future or, alternatively, should invite us to voluntarily abdicate this responsibility. The continent needs to guide against destructive forces obstructing and delaying the transformation of the region into a veritable force within the community of nations.

Many interrelated factors, colonialism, religious orthodoxy, ethnicity, authoritarian rule, and outright tyranny have all played their part in the past, and continue to do so in derailing the present and future of the continent. But this should not deter us from forging ahead with a comprehensive priority strategic approach towards building a better future free from past and present mistakes and calamities. However, we must equally recognise the existence of various forces in obstructing a smooth transition to the new Africa. Hence, today, 'gentler' force of consumerism and the gross erosion of ethical and moral values which it fosters are equally capable of holding us back, under the pretence of making us freer. It means overcoming governance gaps at all levels, local, national, regional, continental and global. It entails strengthening institutions to promote coherence for sustainability at all levels. Continental unity will not function to the best interest of people without commitments and coherence at the national levels. Therefore, creating more effective and coherent continental governance will be a futile exercise if it is not reflected in, and 'owned' by effective national counterparts and placed under influential democratic governance and leadership position vis-à-vis other bodies and interest groups.

In short, the embracement and consolidation of *"good governance, rule of law, electoral reform, the fight against poverty and corruption, provision of essential basic infrastructure and shared-prosperity"* must take pride of place as the foundation on which to build a sustainable future for the African population. Existing deficiencies must be corrected through a holistic, consensual and implementing roadmap strategic approach involving the entire various stake holders: state, civil society and the private sector, female gender empowerment and the incorporation of the youths under the banner of obligations, hard work and responsibility. Equity, fair play, inclusion and justice must underscore the development agenda from a raw material-based economy to a knowledge-based quality service delivery economy. African states must reconstitute their minds in the direction of moving, slowly and perhaps inexorably, towards a new federation, the Union Government for Africa, where Nation States will act as local intermediate entities, for they inevitably suffer, in this process, 'losses in sovereignty, functions and powers'. The 'weakening of states', and the perception that there are 'failed states', remain facts that cannot really be denied. The first, inward shifting of power away from the Nation State is clear not only in Europe (European Union) but also in the United States (Noonan, 2002). Africa will only be a part of that phenomenon, with emphasis on a premature loss of power of the nation state towards a continental body and a supranational organ. By contrast, the tendency towards inwards regionalisation (Regional Economic Communities, RECs) though emphasised by the AU is also weak in Africa, where the tradition is that of continuous 'state centralisation, under authoritarian hegemonic leadership' bleeding society to death.

Following the McKinsey Global Institute (2010) "…sometimes in the late 1990s the African continent began to stir. Gross Domestic Product (GDP) growth picked up and then bounded ahead, rising faster and faster through 2008. Similarly, The African Competitiveness Report 2011 notes that "Africa's recovery from the global economic crisis has been faster than it has in many other parts of the world. Indeed, Africa has seen what can be termed an "economic resurgence" over the past decade: between 2001 and 2010, gross domestic product growth on the continent averaged 5.2 percent annually – a rate expected in 2011, and higher than the global average of 4.2 percent *(ADB/World Bank and Economic Forum Report, African Competitiveness Report 2011*). Africa is one of the fastest growing economies, but this does not reflect on the quality livelihood of the vast majority of citizens. The degree of the divide between the rich and poor is rising with no signs of abating. Well-being is related to a context and so is the notion of poverty. People are said to be living in poverty if their income and resources are so inadequate as to preclude them from having a standard of living considered acceptable in the society in which they live. An absolute majority of Africans live in poverty making it impossible for MDGs to be achieved by 2015. Not only democratic governance is needed but economic growth and shared-prosperity is imperative for the sustainability of a Union Government for the continent. Africa needs rapid growth and to build economies that ensures the sustainability of well-being.

The improved economic performance notwithstanding poverty remains a major problem. Additionally, the robust economic growth has not been successfully translated into human development. Of the 182 nations ranked in the UNDP Report, Africa hosts 19 of the lowest scoring. Most Africa economies are locked into a natural resource trap and many are specialised in only one or two commodities. Only a few countries have successfully transformed their economies on the continent. In fact, only four of the 52 Africa economies can be considered diversified (NEPAD 2011). The result is a continent with only about 2.5 percent share of world exports on average between 2000 and 2007. The decline in Africa's share of world trade represents a loss equivalent to $70 billion annually since the late 1960s. The events occurring throughout the continent should be seen as a response to forces that are, in fact, drawing the entire African population towards greater interdependence and maturity and unity. The momentum towards greater maturity and unity began by Africans in the Diaspora by some thirteen students' in 1944 leading to the formation of the Pan-

African Congress that met in Manchester in 1945, with clear demands for independence and whose rallying cry was: Africa for Africans" should continue building the structures of Renaissance Africa for future generations.

Apparently, this should put African countries on the offensive. African countries must structurally transform their economies to effectively compete in the global marketplace. Transformation however can only occur if the states are able to successfully build innovation-driven economies. Innovation in all aspects of society is what Africa needs. It is necessary for African countries to be able to fundamentally alter the nature of their economies and to support economic transformation. The good news is that Africa's new generation is cognisant of the need for innovation. In many aspects, innovation is taking place on the continent from Nigeria's multi-billion Naira movie industry, *"Nollywood" to "M-Pesa"* which began in Kenya and is spreading in East and Southern Africa and gradually capturing the world. This is new export commodity rising out of African culture and knowledge acquisition. Knowledge transformation with a focus on indigenous knowledge system, seeks to liberate the African voice and the African genius and to marry this within the mainstream of the general corpus of scientific knowledge, helping to dispel racist and intellectual arrogance. For example, Hegel once declared that Africans have not been and are not capable of contributing to human development. His most infamous quotes read:

> At this point we leave Africa, not to mention it again. For it has no historical past in the world, it has no movement or development to exhibit. Historical movements in it, that is, in its northern part – belong to the Asiatic or European World. Carthage displayed here an important transition phase of civilisation, but, as a Phoenician Colony, it belongs to Asia. Egypt will be considered in reference to the passage of the human mind from its Western phase, but it does not belong to the African spirit. What we probably understand by Africa is the unhistorical underdeveloped spirit, still involved in the conditions of mere nature, and which had to be presented here only as the threshold of the World's history" (Teffo, 2011:25-6; Hountondji 1995; Hegel, 2007)

Dispelling this view is the fact venerable institutions of higher learning were established in Africa long before such institutions saw daylight in Europe, for example, the University of Timbuktu in Mali, University of al-Karsouine, Morocco founded in 859, University of al-Azhar, Egypt founded between 970-972 as compared to the University of Oxford, England were teaching stated in 1096, University of

Bologna, Italy, founded in 1088. Africa's contribution to knowledge cannot be challenged from these perspectives. Education and scientific excellence and contribution to knowledge slowed in Africa due to horrendous acts of slavery and colonial rule. Nonetheless, it is challenge to the African Academic Community (AAC) to revamp the continent's lost academic and scientific contribution to humanity. African Indigenous Knowledge must come to play and be properly taped. It was through the help of African indigenous knowledge holders and slaves, that botanists and anthropologists acquired local knowledge without acknowledging the sources and valuable contribution these persons made in developing a codified corpus of knowledge (Augusto 2007:159).

Throughout the continent, technology start-ups are emerging, and we now also have many examples of social innovations, applying technology to monitor elections, corruption or counterfeit pharmaceuticals. The malaise facing Africa is far-reaching even though the continent is on the move. The vulnerability to egocentric betrayal is self-evident. The need for audacious developmental strategies should be the concern of us all and the prerogative of a select few. The positive momentum for Renaissance Africa must be accelerated. This entails Africans re-thinking over their present strategies of governance. There is need crafting a democratic governance system reflecting the will and participation of the people in the entire process of governance. The continent continues to suffer from negative perceptions and imposed foreign values. What is important to note is that Africa is on the road to "Uhuru". Though it is still a long walk to freedom, Africa's place in the global development jigsaw, the continued imposition of Western culture on Africans, helps in derailing the walk to freedom and quality livelihood. On the other hand, by equating the West with modernisation, and local African traditions as backward, a fundamental problem arises that immediately prohibit progress of any kind. This is the very reason why the continent must put on a new thinking hat that shelters it from further destruction. The continent is challenged to appropriately utilise most of its cultural heritage values - *batho pele, ubuntu, harambee* - in building a strong, unified and developed polity.

What are the choices before the continent? Of course, many choices are on offer. The scenarios vary from a collective living championed by various interested parties. Are we to move towards an individualistic, fragmented society, wherein all feel liberated to pursue their own articulate interests, even at the expense of the common good? Will we be tempted by the lures of materialism and its be-holden agent, consumerism? Will Africa opt for a system that feeds on religious fanaticism like what is happening in Nigeria and other parts of the continent? Is Africa prepared to allow elites emerge that will be oblivious to her collective aspirations, and may even seek to manipulate our desire for change? Or will the process of change be allowed to lose momentum, dissolve into factional squabbling, and crumble under the weight of institutional inertia. The choice is Africa's. Especially when "the seeds of disunity that Europe had planted in Africa through the balkanisation and acculturisation of the whole continent, followed by artificial boundaries they imposed to divide brother and sister from sister and brother, will finally be destroyed by the process of the decolonisation of the African mind. Then Africa will once more experience its "Golden Age" of development and restore its leadership in the forum of nations as the creator and preserver of those values that once benefited humankind" (Koka 1985:3).

This generation should not make the wrong choice that will plunge future generations into destruction. Our choice must not result into disappointment but happiness and joy for future generations. The catalyst for change must be enshrined in love, trust and confidence and the strong ability to foster unity among disparate peoples and interests as the essential elements for the feature that ensures its success, but rather because the realisation quickly dawns that is far easier to find common grounds against the status quo than it is to agree upon what should replace it. It is vital that Africans endeavour to obtain broad consensus on the operating principles that should shape a new model for the Africa of tomorrow. Such broad consensus should be enveloped within the *"Ubuntu and Harambee Spirit"* and tied to the virtues of democratic principles and quality services delivery. Africa now and beyond 2017 should necessarily be a better continent, just better systems and societies controlling and influencing and exercising some measures of power at home and abroad.

A mature Africa of tomorrow should be the goal. A mature society demonstrates one feature above all others: recognition of the Africanness, the oneness of humanity in us. How fortunate, then, that African of tomorrow will be when it puts aside its cultural, religious, ethnic and political party divisions in favour of a common cause though in diversity with the sole objective of a strong and united continent. Our instinctive ability, as a people, to recognise the truth that we all belong to the African family serves us well as the starting point in developing common institutions and social structures that promote and faces our development challenges and prosperity. All must be involved in the discourse, from intellectuals, generals, foot soldiers and the layperson. It is through such a discourse that we can debate and agree and disagree to agree on many crucial issues in Building a New Democratic Africa through "linking our intellectual life together indissolubly" (Nyerere 1968:217) is what we must gun for and to progressively develop a brighter and better focus for the continent and generations yet to come

Nevertheless, significant challenges remain, which must be adequately addressed to construct a better future. For example, innovation on the continent continue facing major obstacles: the policy environment and bureaucracy which are not conducive to innovation; the state of inadequate financing and support to take innovative ideas to the market; and an educational system facing tremendous challenges; limited links between industry and academia, and the state of limited public support for research whether in academia or in the private sector and the fact that in many cases too many African countries are simply too small and lack the resources (whether human or financial)to build a robust ecosystem for innovation. African countries need an articulate indigenisation policy to give credence to their socio-economic transformation. It is imperative that indigenous people have control over the economy otherwise their sovereignty will be compromised and their ability to plan for future development serious curtailed.

Africans must bear in mind that no foreign nation will go out of its way to develop another nation. Actions by nations will always be executed on the golden principles of enlightened self-interest, implying the pursuit of permanent expedient interests rather than permanent friendship. Seen within this context, it is important that people and its institutions develop the capacity to understand and appreciate the country's national interests as well as enable it to develop the capacity to articulate, protect, defend, and expand its sphere of national interest. This idea should equally be inculcated into the mindset and actions of the arm forces to fully understand this orientation. Any arm force that fails to understand the national interest would be incapable in defending indigenous values, assets, and related indigenous human aspirations. The continent's security and defence forces as an organisation must evolving on a learning process capable of defending the continent while simultaneously appreciating and understanding the environmental forces, economic and political strategies and influences, and ICT-based asymmetric interventions that impact the national development and defence paradigm (Magosvongwe 2013:68). Africa has to develop a broad-based DNA for its population that makes it do things go against the foreign hidden agenda of destruction and exploitation. At the same time, regional cooperation on innovation continues to face the usual problems. The overriding purpose of this transformation must be embedded within the following key principles:

- Equal political rights and opportunities – which encompassed both the 'sovereign equality' of every citizen to participate in the political process and 'respect of human rights and fundamental freedoms as inscribed with the UNO charter and national constitutions
- Equal Economic Opportunities; enabling every citizen to a sustainable higher standards of living, full employment, and conditions of economic and social progress and development;
- The Rule of Law – implying governance based on equality before the law with a judicial procedure through which law and justice applies to all;
- Science and technology used for peaceful purposes and in the progress of humanity not science and technology for human destruction. In short, the prohibition of the use of armed forces for destructive purposes, 'save in the common interest'.

These principles together with others provide the bases on which to craft the future of the continent. African ruling elites and the developed countries remain reluctant to seeing the full implementation of the second principles – the promotion of *'equal economic opportunities'*. And the governments of some other countries are equally loath to see it actively promote *'respect for, and observance of, human rights and fundamental principles for all'*. The overriding purpose of constructing such a community is to save succeeding generations from the scourges of war, want, oppression, exclusion and destruction. It is important that the next generations be adequately equipped to face future eventualities. For now,

> "there is something inherently wrong with the educational and institutional systems across Africa. There must be a serious change in direction and orientation. How else can we explain why Africa is not producing entrepreneurs, inventors, scientists, famous public speakers etc.? Yet within the Diasporas there are Africans and people of African descent excelling in all manner of fields. For example, people such as Dr Mark Dean, an African-American inventor and computer expert who played a key role in the development of the PC and David Adjaye, the award-winning, world-renowned architect. It must therefore be because there is something seriously wrong with education across Africa" (Djanie 2011:46).

Without a solid educational background or human capital development, Africa cannot be competitive in the fast growing global-based knowledge economy; nor can added-value be given to its abundant natural resources. It is imperative now to build, support and encourage a growing network of talented generations to give new dynamism to the transformation of the continent. The relics of colonial educational system must be replaced with something akin to the realities of the continent and in line with global developmental changes. There has to be a change and not to blindly foreign ideologies without really thinking through whether they suite our own circumstances and in line with global changes. Africa must start thinking about home-grown solutions to her problems. We can learn and borrow ideas from different places, but we need to adapt hem so that they suit our prevailing local conditions.

Most of the continent's academic curriculum is archaic needing a new Pan-African structured-curriculum. Much of the learning is rote memorisation which will not solve the pressing problems and challenges Africa is facing today. We urgently need improved quality education construed on the basis of Science, Technology, Engineering and Mathematics (STEM) approach as the cardinal axis of the continent's change. There is need for critical thinkers who know how to solve problems, not simply memorising facts. Education system needs to create problem-solvers. We need therefore, to "radically rewrite the rule-books as much as possible as the educational system is based on the remnants of the colonial era. There is need to focus on problem solving and making it relevant to Africa and the world we live in. It is not just learning about British, French Spanish or Portuguese history. How can we solve our own problems if we do not know African history or understand our own economies and evolutionary past? The education syllabus must be relevant to the problems of the continent and in tone with the evolving global situation.

This generation should not create situations compromising the future of generations yet to come. The Africa of tomorrow has to be positively constructed and consolidated now and the right and bright touch-light handed to future generations. Now is the time to plant the right and healthy seeds about the moral rightness of the struggle for the total emancipation of the continent and restore human dignity to the people. Possibilities of triumph or victory are clearer and more realisable today than ever before. Such a widespread state of mind among the people is the very reason why most research on the continent should no longer happen outside of the continent itself. This new awakening is all part of the African Renaissance, Pan-Africanism, and Africa Must Unite Agenda for a better future of the continent. It will not be attained on a golden platter but through hard work, commitments and from very segment of society. Participation and inclusion should underscore the process. The cacophony of exclusion is what contributes to the kind of dismal development the continent is witnessing. There must be something fundamentally wrong in a society where people cannot think beyond raining fire and brimstone on each other. It is time Africans took serious consideration of how to take good care of their interests. Doing so equally requires sharing knowledge and actions among themselves as a long-term commitment and the right way to cut a devastating swathe that left the permanent wound, on Africa by western countries that occupied the continent named and claimed under imperialism and colonial rule.

Africa is what it is due to the forces of imperialism and colonialism to which neo-colonialism can be added. Smith (2012:22-24) asserts: imperialism and colonialism are two interconnected terms as colonialism is but one expression of imperialism, and imperialism, is used in at least four different ways in describing the form of European imperialism which started in the fifteenth century: (i) imperialism as economic expansion; (ii) imperialism as the subjugation of 'others'; (iii) imperialism as an idea or spirit with many forms of realisation; and (iv) imperialism as discursive field of knowledge. Colonialism became imperialism's outpost, the fort and the port of imperial outreach. Colonial outposts were also cultural sites which preserved an image or represented an image of what the West or 'civilisation' stood for. Colonies were not exact replicas of the imperial centre, culturally, economically or politically.

Colonialism was, in part, an image of imperialism, a particular realisation of the imperial imagination. It was also, in part, an image of the future nation it would become. In this image lie images of the other, stark contrasts and subtle nuances, of the ways in which the indigenous communities were perceived and dealt with, which make the stories of colonialism part of a grander narrative and yet part also of a very local, very specific experience. We need a new mindset to overcome the effects of our disastrous past and to build a new image for the future of the continent. Seen within this context, we should place justice and good governance on the agenda of our transformation, without which we would never ever make it to the promised-land. Justice, equity, the rule of law, and democratic governance should be on the personal agenda of every African as the cardinal anvil for building a new continent. 'The Brandt Commission Report and the World Development Movement have highlighted the fact that the world's trade and banking systems are fundamentally unjust to the poor in the Third World. Given aid is no longer seen as enough. We must actively campaign for just structures. There is no doubt that injustice spoils the states of Christmas with the distressing pictures of famine in Ethiopia, Somalia, Sudan, Chad, Central African Republic or the Ebola outbreak in Sierra Leone, Gambia, Liberia and name the rest. Are we not tired of seeing these horrific pictures?

We need a new African Development Agenda (ADA) which should build on the concern for justice, rule of law and the practice of democratic governance as the basis for leaving no one behind as we struggle in building a capable developed state. All hands must be on deck as all mouths must receive something from the fruits and wealth of the nation. The wealth of the nation is not only the exclusive use by the rich.

Africa's underdevelopment is intertwined on a number of interrelated and interbinary factors which could be summarised under the blame and reality theories. The 'blame theory' has long dominated Africa's approach to eradicating its economic backwardness and political immaturity. Simply put, the 'blame theory' goes thus Africa is underdeveloped because of slavery, colonialism and external domination. Of course, we cannot run away from the truism that Africa suffered the worse casualties in human history the inhumane actions of slavery, colonialism, occupation and exploitation. Importantly we can scrutinise this as 'a double edge sword'. Undoubtedly the impact of slavery, colonialism and exploitation left an uncompromising destruction on the psychic of the African continent.

At the same time, it challenges the African people to get out of this destructive and dehumanising nexus. Africans are challenged to sort out the wheat from the under (developed) chaff. Yes, Africa underwent a period of slavery, colonialism and is still confronted with the axils of the evils of our past construct. The question and most challenging issue is must the continent continue folding its arm because of the mistakes? We must rethink the past evils and move forward to solidify the struggle started by the Nkrumah's Nyerere's, Nasser's, Azikiwe's, Steve Biko's, and hundreds of the founding fathers and citizens who sacrificed their lives for a free, united and progressive Africa failed in their mission. No, they did not fail; we have failed because of our hanging on the blame theory. We have failed to show that slavery, colonialism, imperialism and exploitation was wrong, is wrong and should be eradicated on the surface of the earth. We can only do this by adopting a new mindset, attitude and cultivate a stronger political will that our forefathers laboured to save the continent from the destructive attitude of the West. Yes, we can, and we must to advance further, by leaving no one behind.

The blame theory shows that Africa is held hostage, kept behind the unscrupulous dictate of the tyranny of the minority. The tyranny of the minority has developed an attitude of being the representatives of the departed colonial masters; as such, they have succeeded in using the political influence, military might and ill-gotten financial muscles to continuously silence and keep in perpetual check the silent majority. A critical analysis of the 'blame theory' points in the direction and challenges Africans putting on a new thinking hat – that of a 'fast, progressive forward march to a New African Continent of the 21st century and far beyond. Choruma (23018) notes: 'we blame slavery, imperialism, colonialism neo-colonialism, sanctions, climate change and so on for our inabilities, weakness and failures. African leaders never accept their own failures. They are ready to blame someone else – the British, French, Americans, Chinese and even the opposition for their failures. In all we attribute our failures and shortcoming to external forces and have develop a vicious cycle of denial and blame. Thus, the blame and denial game has become and entrenched part of the DNA for African leaders'. The result is genuine Africa cultural heritage and values like ubuntu, harambee, batho pele not playing the role it should in developing the society. Africa remains an orphan so long as these cultural heritage values are not contextualised in the transformation strategy of the continent.

It is therefore imperative for Africa to develop a new line-of-thinking by embracing the 'reality theory'. First, Africa was colonised, and it is still under the old nexus. Second what has she done, or is doing to show that slavery, colonialism was wrong? Third, what must we do, how, where and when to forge a true realistic image of who we are, what we want and how to get around in achieving the right image of the continent in a rapidly, hostile and changing global context? Facing the realities of our predicament and in building the Africa we want is what should rigorously occupy us to wipe out once and for all, the roots of backwardness, underdevelopment and poor living standings

The reality is that Africa is underdeveloped with poor quality livelihood for the vast majority of citizens. What strategic policy approaches must be articulated and implemented to get the region out of this entrenched mess? We have to blame ourselves for failing to dig deep and exploit the truth of the realities of our predicaments. We can only make progress when we face the realities of our underdevelopment and exploit from a scientific and comprehensive perspectives to move forward; but above all to put to rest the 'blame' nexus. The new line of thinking should be couched in new progressive ideological perspectives of being a continent entrenched with vast opportunities (natural and human resources) and to realistically and constructively exploit these vast opportunities in improving the quality wellbeing of all Africans. Africa needs to rebuild a new relationship with its cultural past and to adequately exploit existing opportunities to advance the wellbeing of its citizens.

Speaking truth to power and facing the realities of our backwardness in all spheres means taking the bull by the horn we will make progress by pointing out existing ironies and mistakes, as these signal a real wrong; but the wrong is not the end of the world or of Africa. It is the right injection to progress. It is the challenge and medication towards constructing a new and progressive Africa for Africans and humanity to benefit from. If the West has not realised its destructive approach, it is not too late to repent and build a new world order (NWO). Such a NWO is the structural basis for a; win-win' sustainable world for all – East-West-South-North.

The problem is easier to define than the solution. The solution lies in facing the realities of our predicaments, attacking poverty, poor governance, injustice, inequality, exclusion, domination and the forces that fuel it. Since the independence of Ghana in March 1957, through the destruction of the apartheid system in 1994, the reorientation of the Organisation of the African Union (OAU) towards a progress continental body (the African Union- AU- in 2002) to the recent Kigali Agreement –formation of the African Continental Free Trade Area (AFCFTA) - 2018) the continent can never and will never be the same. Let us build on that new wave of Pan-Africanism, unity, integration all geared towards improving the wellbeing of citizens. We should ensure that Ghana's independence and the destruction of the apartheid governance system set in motion a new scene for Africa within the global context.

No one needs to remind us of an Afrocentric progressive looking continent. Africa remains the future of the world and the world depends on the progress of the African continent. This reality is constantly and progressively down-played by the industrial military polities. The reality is that the world is hungry for constructive change, change that cans only come from the constructive changes unfolding in Africa. To maintain its hegemony, the developed countries continue to pursuing economic policies that deepens the crisis and divide between the rich and poor nations and within the poor countries. The fact remains that world economies, led by the industrial countries continue to conspire to squeeze dry the economies of the developing countries in Africa in particular.

We must begin accepting the realities that the current levels of the continent's state of abject poverty, hunger and underdevelopment is intolerable; to realise that actions taken by our government remain woefully wrong and inadequate in the face of such suffering masses that have been left behind since March 1957. Every second another child dies the number of poor increases. There is a 'silent emerging' force that has started ringing the true bell of confronting the 'blame' theory and constructively embracing the progressive 'reality' theory in the best way forward towards building a new African within the current world context. Africa has to get its priorities right. Africa can only overtake its current poverty by a multitude of prioritised development projects that people-oriented and focused to substantially improve on the quality wellbeing of its citizens. Africa must be controlled and governed by a new social and economic contract and reforms that makes the presently disadvantage better off tomorrow. The decolonisation process started in 1957 and the new democratisation that is blowing across the continent provides a good foundation of the continent's wealth for all Africans in the 21st century. Africa must overcome its long series of antiquated governance structures and political disputes castigate ethnic divide and embrace national unity that enables the poor, marginalised and excluded to get a large share of the national cake.

Involving the Marginalised, Downtrodden and Disadvantaged

The reality towards the continent's sustainable development is involving all the stakeholders. The poor, female gender, and excluded must be made an inherent part of the evolving process of change, Continuous marginalisation of the poor, youths and the female gender exaggerates existing imbalances within the communities, nations and continent. Given these huge problems, how can governments most effectively, efficiently and productively meet the needs of the currently excluded in society?

Confronting the blame problem and embracing the reality nexus means (i) involving the poor; (ii) empowering the female gender; and (iii) equity in benefit sharing of the wealth of the nation; this implies involving the public, private sector and civil society. Popular and inclusive participation remains the most favourable ideological orientation of reality theory. The poor and women must be brought to the plus side of the (under)development continuum. Harping on the blame theory makes the continent the greatest looser in the global development nexus. A constructive approach to accepting the 'reality theory' is selling and building a comprehensive African future. This is the only way Africa can confront her existing problems. The 'blame theory' only protects the rich countries rules and hegemony. It fans and strengthens undemocratic governance structure, authoritarian and dictatorial systems that have taken grip of the continent.

African governments continue to thread on an approach that is streamlined within the paralysis of crying from the heart than to negotiate a new deal in development. They continue on the blame theory and fail to recognise their own very weakness and bargaining strategy and power, but continue to fine tone the 'blame theory as their underdevelopment fault. Africa has failed to cultivate and develop the 'reality theory' to better put their house in order, and fortify their bargaining position from the nexus of strength in terms of their 'natural resources and expanding market that the 55 or more Africa countries provide to the world. Without developing the 'new spirit of realism' African leaders cannot advance and bring quality living standards to their people. The progressive political process that the continent has witnessed within the past couple of decades and economic growth should be intensified as the new building block for a new Africa on the move. The developed countries should welcome ongoing positive political and economic changes.

Aware of the sea that surrounds the structure-functionality of African state, all must put hands on deck in searching for new ways of thinking and working, it is counterproductive for Africa to stay silent, impotent in the rapidly hostile changing nexus of today's world construct. The progressive democratically polities in Africa must not crate islands of survival but to export best practices to other lacking nations so as to pull our country/continent (harambee) on the struggle and challenges of constructing a healthy continent for the common good.

Facing the Changes and Challenges

The achievement of Africa in obtaining independence could be hailed as Harold Macmillan's "wind of change blowing across the continent which started on 6th March 1957 in Ghana. In reality, Africa has made tremendous strides towards the construction of a nation out of its colonial construct of many centuries past. While Africans deserves some pat on their backs for their achievements of fifty years, which indeed is a short period in a nations existence, it is often and perhaps imperative been fully for Africans to themselves if indeed their potentials have been fully exploited? Whether they could not have done better? The answers to these and other pertinent questions will invariably reveal to Africans the fact that the task ahead is awesome and that the continent still very much need to redouble her efforts to achieve real independence. This can be only done if Africans can realistically and objectively determine the obstacles to its progress, towards the realisation of a strong and real continent before its set about the task of tearing down those obstacles. We need a new benchmark to progress from the current stalemate that has gripped the continent.

Africa could have done better within this short span of 50 years of its independence taking into account Gerschenkron's *'later-comer advantage'*. Advances in science and technology and drawing from the failures and successes of today's developed countries in the West, but above all, what has transpired in South East Asian countries. China provides another good example judging its long march in the immediate post World War 11 era. It is too often mentioned that the first quarter century of Africa's post-colonial era was marked by deliberate policies of divide and rule, which gave access to the *'blame theory'* to linger too long in the minds of Africans. An opportunity for change was lost because of the embracement of the 'blame theory' instead of realistically looking what should be done given the new uniform the continent was wearing. Having found such a good but stupid escape goat and whipping horse, Africans with much complacency sit back and congratulate themselves for real imaginary successes. The road to real freedom is still miles away, needing courage and determination to overcome eventualities. Are the architects of state craft looking in this direction?

A critical and objective examination of the record shows that African elites – educational, political, business or in short, the ruling class, have been the greatest stumbling block to African unity. As result of their close contact with Western culture, the members of this group have and continue to suffer from a colonial hang-over that has developed various complexes in them. The silent majority (elites) suffer from a minority complex while the loud minority suffer from majority complex. These complexes have above all developed in the knee jerk reactions and phobias that make them behave more like protectors of the colonial heritages than as complexes constructors of a better, stronger and united Africa. The majority complexes develop the strong believe in might and infallibility as well as, a strong conservatism that encourages opposition to everything new and strange. The ruling elites do not want any change that will alter the status quo; they feel it is their inherent right after requiring western education and culture to replace the departed colonial masters. It is this attitude that explains their opposition to power to the people and better quality livelihood for all including the current disadvantage in society.

While the majority/minority complex has developed an all righteous syndrome in the African ruling elites, the minority/majority complex has developed a systematic alienation syndrome across the society particularly in the mindset of the excluded building a kind of hard core of rising destructive frustration and fear, mistrust and lack of confidence and trust in the governance system. The State under such situation lacks legitimacy and right of authority to govern. Chaos and instability results leading to failed and collapsed states; instability as well contributes to the non-construction of a union government for the continent. This is what happened prior to the creation of the Organisation of African Unity in the sixties. The African Union and the move towards a Union Government for Africa should not suffer the faith of the 1960s. Commitment to continental unity is still on the draft board and its realisation is still years ahead.

All these achievements no matter how token it is failed to satisfy the expectations of an increasingly demanding population. However, one cannot with good conscience fail to acknowledge the fact that the OAU/AU has in different ways play noble roles in pushing towards continental unity. Even national developments will not be achieved without the total commitment and participation of the masses in nation-building. Above all, there has to be harkened movement towards the cry of unity by the founding fathers for the independence struggle to put the interest of the continent first before the individual interest. The ideological orientation should be "the common good" not the 'individual good'. The "Ubuntu Spirit" should reign supreme. The growing challenge is that Africans more than ever before must let reason and rationality triumph over sentiment, blame and periodical attitudes, perhaps now more than yesterday.

It can no longer be denied that Africa is the victim of its own making. That the continent is 'politically unstable' is a fact. Africa cannot, given the prevailing situation talk anymore about 'balkanization' since the Balkan regimes are stable, whereas in Africa we have a change of regime almost every week or every month; at any rate, every year. The state of instability is growing not decreasing. This underscores a calamity of the gross absence of national leadership to set the right examples of leadership and good governance. Good leadership will drastically reduce the growing rate of instability and military takeovers. Political selfishness is killing the continent. Here lies the underlying problem of Africa. Once African interests become merely a pretext for individual selfishness, instability necessarily rears its head. When the only organised force in the continent – the armed forces – ceases to respect civilian administration, it seizes power for its articulate interest. Yet each time the armed forces undertakes a coup d'état and controls power, it perpetuates the same evils if pretended to address. A vicious circle is created; one military takeover replaces another. On the other hand, the armed forces are aware of the reality that the institution is merely an instrument of civilians wielding power; and that the survival of civilian rule depends on army-backing. The contradiction is solved by a seizure of power. When the army overthrows civilian rule, without having had any political education, and when this very army is itself devoid of any profound ideals, the result of army rule cannot be any better than civilian rule it overthrew (Diop 1987).

Africans need to start asking themselves what they have personally done to promote and hasten the advent of a strong, united and prosperous as well as a more harmonious and sustainable continent. The task is daunting. Yet there seem no viable alternative than for Africans to remain proactive, relentless and resilience in their efforts towards a united Africa. The price of success, i.e. the Unity of Africa, is perseverance and above all vigilance, resilience, courage, hard work, duty consciousness, and commitments. It is time Africa must start decoding its weakness and errors committed in the past and to fix all in the right perspective, constructively and comprehensively with the view of sustainable quality livelihood for all citizens. The politics of inclusiveness mutt constitute the corner stone of the transformation agenda. It should be noted that the "politics of exclusion" is destroying the unity of the continent and quality living standards for the down trotted citizens. No matter how well the economic reforms are constructed or critical but once the fail to be broad-based, transparent and inclusive will fail because they will take place in isolation, and without parallel political reforms will not impact meaningfully and evenly in society.

This is not intended to be an apology for any body's failure. Neither is it intended to discourage criticism. Rather, it is meant to encourage and promote a new line of critical, scientific and objective thinking and criticism of wrongs of the past and the rights about the future of the continent. It is intended to spur broad based approach to a New Africa under the canopy of a whole of which we are all part. Until we give precedence to that bigger whole, Africa may never get the opportunity to fully develop and fulfil those little parts that are found in a whole Africa will never make it to service delivery society. Only by opening up with the 54 or more African states in transition achieve the broad-based growth these state so desperately need to accelerate the process of integration, free movements of people and goods. More integration, the free movements of people and goods would not only create growth and jobs, it would provide discipline and incentives to help get the reform strategy right.

What should be the way forward for Africa? The publication adopts an eclectic epistemological approach with the conclusion of a simple message, namely constructive Afrocentric relations with the global community of a kind of cordiality enhancing autonomy and empowerment of the people. The promotion of self-esteem, human dignity and entrenched with values of integrity and respect of progressive cultural values and integrity as well as respect for cultural diversities not as liabilities but asset for promoting the progress and well-being of citizens. Our diversities should be a harmonious intercourse between civilisations geared towards fostering national cohesion and continental unity and making us the Africans we are; proud of our cultural heritage and values and dignity as human beings with blood running through our veins like any set of human-beings on planet Earth.

This volume offers suggestions and advances proposals along the way and offering specific views voiced by President Thabo Mbeki underlying sources of Africa's predicament, the actions required to restore her dignity and as a veritable player on the global scene, as well as the painful options to grapple with the leaders to reclaim Africa's humanity. Africa should not forget that the present World Order Construct (WOC) is part of the problem and not the solution to the continent's unending barrage of woes and nightmares. The solutions must come from Africans. Serious soul searching is what Africans must undergo to reclaim what is theirs by building the confidence and trust for out of every conflict lie the possibility of a more equitable and self-reliant development strategies that benefit the greater majority of the people (Langdon and Mytelka 1979:21). Will Africa rise from the ashes and ruins injected by slavery, imperialism, colonialism and neo-colonialism?

Fifty or more years of political instability and economic chaos and the silent acceptance of ethnic hegemonic authoritarian or western direct support of non-democratic practices that suits their interests and political consciousness, Africa finds itself in a fix. The most suitable out is the promise of inclusion through the virtues of *'democratisation* 'symbolising *'shared-prosperity'*; than the entrenched principles of '*winner-takes-all*' that cements and ferments chaos, exclusion and underdevelopment. It is time civil society takes its responsibilities through popular struggles and the involvement of organised social, political, cultural and economic groupings. Taking into consideration Africa's recent history and nature of pragmatic commitments of social scientists, there is little doubt that the continent is poised for a revolutionary reconstruction and transformation in the management of political and economic related matters. The long walk needs a bit of further pushing and in the right direction to avoid things completely falling apart.

Consciousness and commitment are refined and real when the people have the dream, hope and confidence to rise up to the reality and statue of what the continent is and what it must be for future generations. Vision without action is a nightmare. But vision plus action leads to development and progress. It is time to cut off the heat of oppression, exploitation and exclusion. We just have to realise that dream through the various resources at our disposal. The mountain of despair must be conquered knowing that Africa will be united, strong so that freedom, justice, quality livelihood and dignity can ring from the Cairo to the Cape and from Banjul to the Horn; and those worse off from the hill-tops to the plains and valleys; from the forest zones to the savannah regions become better-off tomorrow. Africa must recover from a string of serious socio-eco-political set-backs and open up for essential agents as drivers of change and sustained development. Sustained development calls for hard work and prudent management of resources. We should bear in mind that development is basically a human affair and should be treated like the concept of democracy – a basic model for development should be viewed as development for the people, development by the people, but also development of the people. Building the human capacity of the people is essential in transforming the quality of livelihood, without which, the African people will forever is condemned into the horrors of perpetual underdevelopment and exploitation by foreign bodies.

Conclusion

Toward A New Common Sense and Nationalism

This section has sketched out the basic approach and method for describing and comparing variety. It has brought some of the variety in the ways that crises are handled and controlled by the state within a society. It has been argued that the basic approach lends itself to successive category disaggregating to draw over finer distinctions and the degree of discrimination that is appropriate depends on the material to be compared and purpose of comparison. The important message here is build a solid foundation of patriotism, unity and sense of purpose. Of course, clashing views on controversial socio-political issues cannot be avoided as it is part of building the requisite knowledge for the sustainable transformation of the continent. We are Africans, must remain Africans and show the worth of the Africanness in us. Africans we are and must remain so. That is our dignity and sovereignty. Nature was not stupid to create us 'black'. We have to take pride in our 'blackness' and show case what it means to be black and Afrocentric. The dynamism of the business of black influence must remain paramount. Africans must face-head-on the reality of political power and economic conditions to restructure their governance system for the ultimate good of the people. It is only through this that the political and social climate can be transformed, and Africans treated with respect and dignity the world over.

In mapping a way for tomorrow's Africa, a proper understanding of the past is imperative to better understand the present in order to be properly armed in constructing tomorrow. We have been made to understand that Africa had no history until the Whiteman's arrival and celebrated in Rudyard Kipling's ***"The White Man's Burden"*** that ensured the Eurocentric's ideology. As such, African history is only the history of white people on the continent. This implanted a sense of permanent *"inferiority complexes"* and other derogating behaviour that continues destroying the continent. The new slogan should evolve within the ideological prescient of **"The Blackman's Pride and Duty'** ensuring an "Afrocentric" approach to constructive engagement for sustainable quality livelihood. eurocentrism affected all social scientists that grew up in an environment where European supremacy or the centrality and universality of the European experience were taken as supreme. These contribute to the development of a world view in which the superiority of Western culture, institutions and knowledge over the institutions, culture and knowledge of other societies was unquestioned (Mlambo, 2006). The present generation must detest from passing over this kind of physical and intellectual subjugation to the coming generations that reinforces both Western and Black elite imperialism and domination. Educating the population is extremely important. Unfortunately, the current African schooling system has failed the continent and continues to fail in critically engaging learners to the reality of their continent in a way that powers them to be agent of transformational change. To begin with, citizens lack critical knowledge about essential facts (social, economic and political) relating to the continent, but whatever they know has no relevance or impacting in creating a vision and an imagination for an empowered Africa. It should be noted that the lack of critical knowledge of the African continent among the population – should be considered a state of moral and strategic emergency in our current education system. An Africa focus must be introduced in the education curriculum of the continent. With little engagement and knowledge of Africa countries, it further leads to the development of a very insular and closed mindset among the younger generations which is a deterrent to African Unity and development.

Even within the educated class we have been brought up in the uncomfortable intersection of power and experience – and with West having total monopoly of power to define Africa and Africans. The educated African is caught within the trappings of accepting the West description, definition and perception of Africa or the African may make efforts to critically resist whatever frame of cliché labelled on him or her. As a result of colonial rule most Africans in this cohort, fail to engage effectively with the very complex theories that the West projected and promoted in the education curriculum of African states (Adams 2011, Mbembe 2001, Asante 1998, Wa Thiong'o 1986, Woodson 1933). This kind of miss education or brain washing that contributed to even the Vice Chancellor of the University of Ghana to order that Nkrumah's books be removed from the university's library after the coup d'état of 24 February 1966 that toppled Kwame Nkrumah from power. Some sections of the Ghanaian and African elite did not understand the essence of Nkrumah's politics then. Go to our law courts, see how the lawyer are all dressed in wigs, 50 years after independence from the Western colonial rule. "Real education for the colonial people would have inevitably meant unrest and resistance against the colonial order and as such colonial education was designed to inculcate obedience, servility and inferiority complex in the African" (Adams 2011).

The success of powerful nations is often based on their ability to prey on the economic, cultural and political weakness of poor countries. It their own prosperity or wellbeing that they are mostly concerned with rather than that of African countries. To ensure their own progress, for instance, the West mobilises its capital to construct a union or a cartel to fight and prohibit the emergence of a strong and united African continent. This underscores the hostility of the West towards a Union Government for Africa. Hence the reasons why the developed polities were and are prepared to deploy all the means including military arsenal at their disposal to stop or even eliminate Kwame Nkrumah's Africa Must Unite project, and based on the fact he not only understood the real nature of Western imperialism but, more importantly determined to confront it in Africa. No wonder people of the same school of thought, Lumumba, Sankara, Biko and many others were and are seen as stumbling block to the expansionist agenda of the West. Western orientation was clear, if Nkrumah succeeded to opt out of the orbit of global imperialist system and succeeded at some form of independent development approach, there was nothing to prevent other African countries following suit.

The ramifications of this fundamental truth are so profound that many other vital principles, essential for the future transformation of the continent, can be derived from it. A principle example is the equality of men and women. Is there anything retarding the progress of Africa more efficiently and effectively than the persistent exclusion of women from full participation in the affairs of nation-building and development? Redressing this imbalance will by itself engineer great improvement in every aspect of the African life" - cultural, social, economic, political and religious. Apparently, like the bird that cannot fly if one wing is weaker than the other, so humanity's ability to scale the heights of real attainment are severely impeded so long as women are denied the opportunities afforded to men. Nowhere could the equality of the sexes more helpfully be established than in human capital development (education) which exists to enable men and women of every background to fulfil their innate potential to contribute to the progress of society (One Country, 2011).

Given the opportunity to participate in constructing a New African Order (NAO), we will be confirmed in our newly awakened consciousness that we have ownership of our present and future and come to realise the collective power we already possess in transforming ourselves and continent for the better. This is the time we must make the right choices for the good of present and future generations. The mass of the people can never become the agents or partners of neo-colonialism. The function of neo-colonialism is to exploit, not to share with, the people. In like manner globalisation, the highest stage of scientific imperialism and benefits those with a strong and scientific background. Developing the scientific and tec*hnological capacity of the c*ontinent will enhance the region to properly reap the virtues of globalisation. Presently, the continent is suffering under the yoke of the vices of globalisation. In order to govern with a clientele-oriented style, as most African countries have constituted themselves into, you need to have accomplices at all levels of government.

Whistleblowers make that difficult to happen. Foreign representatives might act as whistleblowers, if nothing else. The greater perils of corruption do not only lie in the execution of the budget, they mainly lie in the decision-making process: when you contract something that is not needed, on terms that are unfair to society, for a price that is not market-savvy, there you have made the first and most important step of corruption; when bribery occurs, the biggest bribes are paid at that time (up to a hundred million dollars), the rest will be pocket money in comparison (up to a million dollars). From there on, everything falls in place. So, you have to try to stop the flow of corruption at the decision-making stage, not merely at the execution stage. The first one is of paramount importance; the second one is really secondary. In fact, there are various reasonable systems for internal control in small affairs. The continent's educational system and research institutions including the administrative set up must operate in a manner of inculcating a new mindset and vision in this domain of ethical behaviour.

Science and technology brings yet another controversial aspect to mutual dependency among humankind. Current wellbeing is based on technology which is very much the same all over the world. New innovations help everyday living for those who have purchasing power. People in different parts of the world become more and more unified and dependent on the same centralised technology and innovations, and humankind is losing its cultural and social differences. For now, the technological base of Africa is weak and deficient. It has to be strengthened and appropriately used in uplifting the living standards of the people. How can Africa use science and technology in accelerating its developmental process? How can indigenous knowledge contribute to the scientific and technological reawakening of Africa in the modern age? Answers to these and other pertinent questions will contribute to the enlightened understanding of African countries that, in the end, it is also in their own interest that they should try to send good people with serious intentions. Reclaiming lost educational and scientific prowess implies appointing the right people in the right places. Presently, we can be scared or furious with what is happening in the administrative and educational construct of African countries. Yet these are institutions that should become centres of excellence for democratic governance and a treasury of memory and the beacon of sustainable development. Our universities should be the sine qua none for building responsive and efficient state institutions in a new constitutional construct and order with new rules of the game, a new polity, new sets of relationships between the state and its citizens, and a new social contract, between Africa and the global community.

Indigenous knowledge should be developed and married with modern science and technology. The basis for such structural change is created through education. Indigenous knowledge forms the basis for innovation. It equally entails Africa moving from reactivity to proactively and from passivity to creativity and innovation. It is only through serious technological changes that the continent can transform – the changes have made the world more and more a single unit of growing interdependence between nations. For now, the grand and demanding goals *per se* – the abolition of poverty, increased security, the abandonment of weapons of mass destruction, stopping the destruction of Nature, and consideration for the privileges and rights of future generations – have been talked about, but they have not been used as the main guidelines in directing actual operations.

This is a strong deficit in the annals of the colonisation and transformation of the African continent. Globalisation does not share and develop: it grabs and exploits people who are scientifically and technologically weak. It is the people, therefore, and only the people, who can save Africa from the forces of neo-colonialism, imperialism and uncontrolled globalisation. Development and progress do not come by themselves, neither desire nor time can alone ensure sustainable transformation and. Africans have to work, strive and toll, tame the elements, combat the environment making safe, recast institutions, subdue circumstances, and at all times be ideologically alert and awake. Understanding the causes of European and American prosperity requires studying the policies of those who created it, not the advice of their forgetful successors.

The German economist, Johann Heirich Gottlob von Justin warned the countries forced to produce only raw materials would soon understand that they were being kept 'artificially' poor. Africa has been kept poor through colonial policies forcing then to producing and exporting only raw materials. Just like Adam Smith under the notion of blind patriotism requested Britain's American colonies and the rest of Europe not to follow England's example of industrialisation. Adam Smith argued that any attempt by the Americans to 'stop the importation of European manufactures would obstruct instead of promoting the progress of their country towards real wealth greatness.'

The Americans did not listen like the continent of Africa but went on to establish their own industries. An underlying element of the America war of independence in 1776 was that, as colonial masters have always done, England had prohibited manufacturing industry in the American colonies. America under British rule was given colonial treatment. It was denied the use of tariffs to protect its new industries. It was prohibited from exporting products that competed with British products. It was given subsidies to produce raw materials. Moreover, outright restrictions were imposed on what Americans could manufacture. The spirit behind the policy as noted by William Pitt (the Elder in 1770) was clear: 'hearing of the emergence of new industries in the American colonies, the New England should not be permitted to manufacture so much as a horseshoe nail' (see Boateng, 2011; Reinert 2007; Chang 2007) Africa should not be permitted to process its coffee, tea, cocoa or palms.

Reading Reinert (2007), Chang (2007), Nkrumah (1963) and others of the same school of thinking - must constitute a fundamental ground text books for all universities in Africa - puts people to understanding how to build strategies to address poverty and underdevelopment - to better construct an innovative, entrepreneurial and industrial society that leaves no one behind and in meeting the needs and aspirations of the people. Africa has to get out of its current ignorance. "We live in an age of ignorance today, when established qualitative arguments exploring the process of economic development have been abandoned…the banality of today's explanations about poverty being a result of climate and corruption amply testifies to this ignorance, fortified by the absence of historical knowledge and interest in proven principles that have brought nation after nation from poverty to wealth over five centuries.

We have collectively forgotten how to create wealthy nations – an art that was successfully employed as recently as 50 years ago – and so our responses to the challenges of poverty today, however well-intentioned, amount to an attack on the symptoms of poverty rather than in deep causes. After the Second World War, the world understood that economic development was the result of synergies and increasing returns. Combined with the political threat of communism, this understanding made it possible to overrule the free trade ideologies in Washington, and *reindustrialise* Europe and parts of Asia. In order to restart growth, it is necessary to reinvent this type of theory. When it was important to build a defence line to protect Asia and Europe from communist threat, the United States understood that the way to create wealth was to *industrialise* the nations bordering communism – from Norway and Germany to South Korea, Japan and Taiwan – and to support the project wholeheartedly economically, politically and militarily. Once the communist threat had dissolved, the developed countries rapidly started applying a policy that resembled old British colonial policy at its worst" (Boateng 2011, pp10-11). We have failed to practice neither socialism nor capitalism with a human face. Rather, we have become the worst colonial masters inflicting serious pains on the people. With such acts, the people have lost self-esteem and sense of belonging to Africa.

Europe's Double Talk and Strategic Approach

Here lies Europe's double talk and strategy towards the development of Africa. The West fails in bringing industries to Africa. Africa fails in creating an enabling environment that attracts foreign and domestic investors to kick-start the continent's industrialisation. Lessons should be drawn from Asian countries, Malaysia for example. The future of Africa must build on increasing the wealth of a people by improving and increasing their quality of living standard, building their human capital and ensuring that they get valuable returns for their exported raw wealth and natural resources (which should be converted and into transformed into finished products).

Why was a Marshall Plan not put in place on the eve of the independence of African countries as it did for the reconstruction of Europe after World War Two? Apparently, nothing so much contributes to promoting the public well-being as the exportation of manufactured goods and the importation of foreign raw materials. The ideologically thinking explains why the colonial powers stuck to the orientation of African countries producing and exporting only raw materials and never to be involved in the industrialisation nexus which would compete with Europe's manufacturing and exporting sectors. Industrialisation was the preserved domain of Europe.

Producing and exporting raw materials and human capital was the entrenched obligations of African countries. Africa has to crack that secrete code without which there could be no breakthrough for the continent's take-off to a services delivery society. More than fifty years after the granting of independence to the continent, the people live without industries but are encouraged, wooed, and even cajoled with the destructive policy strategy of free export of agricultural products and other raw materials all geared towards enticing Africa to forget the ideal and desire to industrialise. Yet no country has ever become rich by exporting either foodstuffs or raw materials without having an industrial sector.

Either the continent concentrates its forces for a decisive assault to achieve the objectives of transcending from a raw materials producing or exporting continent to one of exporting processed raw materials quality services provision to all in society. "In order to repair effectively and quickly the serious damage done to Africa - the result of imperialism and colonialism, emergent African states need strong unitary government capable of exercising a central authority for the mobilisation of the national effort and the co-ordination of reconstruction and progress" (Nkrumah 1962). The ball for the socio-economic transformation of Africa lies in the hands of African countries. The books by Reinert, Chang, Rodney and a long list of others bring to the forefront the cracking of the underdevelopment and exploitation code. Africa now has the choice – either use the new code to unlock the secrets to growth, wealth and development or wallow forever in abject poverty and exploitation.

Few Africans like Nkrumah understood the orientation that political independence without economic power was meaningless, that the industrialisation of the continent was crucial for sustaining political independence. Seek ye the industrialisation and economic independence of the continent and all others would be added. Economic independence strengthens the political independence and unity of the continent strengthens the political construct of Africa. Only technological and industrialisation changes can create an effective agricultural sector to propel the continent into a different world construct in the 21st century and beyond.

Without a shadow of doubt, this brings into sharp focus what Nkrumah attempted to do for Ghana, emulating the toolbox that developed Europe and America in his pursuit of economic independence for Africa, for as he noted; without abundant electricity to power industrialisation to propel economic independence, political independence would be valueless. Under colonial rule, a country had very restricted economic links with other countries. Its natural resources were developed only insofar as they served the interests of the colonial powers. In planning national development, the constant, fundamental guide is the need for economic independence. Leaders with a clear vision for the continent are not tolerated by Western powers. This explains explain the reason why Nkrumah, Lumumba, Sankara and other progressive leaders were overthrown by the industrial military complex of the West. The situation in Ghana is most telling. Nkrumah's efforts to make Ghana an industrial entity was thwarted by the military coup consecrated by the Khaki boys in 1966 and the country returned to the colonial era as western experts flooded the country to advise the military government to abandon the development plans designed to usher Ghana into a new development orbit. Sad enough, the Encyclopaedia Africana in progress was destroyed by the western intelligent units. What a shame for the continent, as its historical past could no longer be documented. Intellectually, the continent became an orphan; creating room for further exploitation and domination.

In a booklet written between 1942 and 1945, Nkrumah was equivocal on African unity as he wrote:

> There is, however, one matter on which my views have been expanded, and that is regarding African unity. Since I have had the opportunity of putting my ideas to work, and personally experiencing the better and arduous test of wit, patience and endurance that was necessary before our own victory over colonialism was won, I lay even greater stress on the vital importance to Africa's survival of a political union of the African continent. Twenty years ago, my ideas on African unity, important as I considered them even at that time, were limited to West African unity. Today, as I sit at my desk in Accra and glance at the several maps of Africa surrounding me, I see the wider horizon of the immense possibilities open to Africans – the only guarantee, in fact, for our survival – in a total continental political union of Africa."

He came out most strongly with Africa Must Unite in 1963 on the eve of the creation of the Organisation African Unity (OAU) in Ethiopia. In his autobiography 1957, he wrote:

> It is right and proper that we should know about our past; for just as the future moves from the present so the present has emerged from the past. Nor need we be ashamed of our past. There was much in it of glory. What our ancestors achieved in the context of their contemporary society gives us confidence that we can creates, out of that past, a glorious future, not in terms of war and military pomp, but in terms of social progress and of peace. Our battles shall be against the old ideas that keep men trammelled in their own greed; against the crass stupidities that breed hatred, fear and inhumanity. The heroes of our future will be those who can lead our people out of the stifling fog of disintegration through serfdom, into the valley of light where purpose, endeavour and determination will create that brotherhood which Christ proclaimed two thousand years ago, and about which so much is said, but little done.

In advancing that course, Nyerere spoke passionately against neo-colonialism: "Neo-colonialism correctly describes that phase in Africa when authentic leaders were destroyed, and a bunch of African puppets were installed for the purposes of presiding over the looting of our Continent. That phase is still alive in Africa. It has produced African millionaires, even billionaires. Their loot is rarely invested in Africa, it is invested or hidden abroad for the African looters have no more confidence in the future of our continent than their foreign friends and masters" (Nyerere 1997). New strategic thinking and approach is required for crafting the future of Africa far beyond 2063. The first move is political and ideological orientation and mobilisation towards a common purpose. Since independence African leaders have been making efforts in that direction. The continent has only one thing to gain, and that is by pulling itself out the crunching dilemma of underdevelopment and poverty through a constructive process of threading on the path of innovation, creativity and entrepreneurship by converting its resources into finished consumer products

This has not materialised to a large extent. Why? Cheikh Anta Diop (1987) opines:

> Simply out of selfishness, out of personal and egoistic power interests. However, the defence of power interests is in direct opposition to the avowed wish for regional economic cooperation and unity. Selfish African Heads of State want to reduce continental and regional exigencies to their own personal and national egoisms. In other words, they latch onto power, have no intention of abandoning it and they talk about creating regional economic interests. However, the defence of power interests is in direct opposition to the avowed wish for regional economic cooperation and unity. It is not just true that Africa is uppermost in the minds of these heads of state. It is in the interests of Africa to latch onto power and monopolise it to the extent of refusing to relinquish even a portion of it to a supra-national executive body so as to be able to arrive at an economic union. No one wants to relinquish an iota of national power. That is why previous regional associations have failed.

Globalisation the new sing-song has gripped the continent. Africa cannot escape from this invasion but strive to part of the fast-moving train. On the other hand, globalisation must also mean justice on a global scale. For now, it spreads injustice and Africa is unjustifiably marginalised due to a number of inter-related factors: (i) poor leadership; (ii) poor scientific and technological base; (iii) bad governance and wrong mentality of citizens towards the socio-economic and political emancipation of the continent. These and other impediments prohibit the continent from connecting to the world economy as successfully as Asia. Globalisation has and continues to work for China and the Asian countries. For example, the Gulf of Emirate of Dubai has enjoyed a boom by reinventing itself as a major and trading hub for international companies. It is not working the same way for Africa.

> "The seeds of disunity that Europe had planted in Africa through the balkanisation and acculturisation of the whole continent, followed by artificial territorial boundaries they imposed to divide brother from brother, will finally be destroyed by the process of the decolonisation of

the African mind. The African will once more experience its 'Golden Age' of development and restore its leadership in the forum of nations as the creator and the preserver of those values that once benefited humankind" (Koka 1985).

Why the poor now seems to be missing out on the spoils of globalisation is a matter of debate among scholars. Part of the reason could be the greater use of technology in manufacturing. With factors even in low-wage countries like China and India shifting to higher--positions out of the reach of unskilled labourers calls for a rethinking of current development strategies. Moreover, as more nations try to advance, ever hungrier mouths are chasing foreign investment and export sales. There is not enough to go around. Countries, like African states, coming late to the globalisation party now may never get a foot in the door. Indeed, once the giant, poor population of China entered the fray, it crowded out many other developing countries, especially those with slightly higher costs, such as some Latin American nations.

For now, with its low technological development, Africa is doomed as a raw material exporting nation. Much more needs to be done as competition for export markets and foreign investment intensifies, African governments need to develop better education programmes that can churn out qualified workers, build efficient ports and airports to smooth trade and introduce business-friendly tax and regulatory policies. Trade among African countries is low and should be increased. Economic growth and self-sufficiency and undisputed legality and political legitimacy and credibility are crucial inputs enhancing the sovereignty of the continent in the global space.

The legacy of all this is that in spite of its rich natural resources, Africa had a very weak starting point in the race for socioeconomic transformation. Apart from the fact that modern African states lack any natural geographic, ethnic, political or economic coherence. By contrast to the Indian sub-continent, where an effective administrative system was established, Africa was poorly served. Africa emerged from the colonial era with far weaker governance structures and infrastructure than other ex-colonies. Political borders have become economic barriers (Commission for Africa 2005:18; Achebe 1958; Dumont 1962).

The political and economic outlook has to change drastically to make the continent an interesting destination for investors. The continents policy strategy must evolve on a new ideological orientation, moving away from being puppets of Euro-centric to an Afrocentric revolutionary agenda that accelerates the promotion of the transformation of the continent in the best interest of the people. One can only agree with Patrick Chinamasa (Zimbabwe's Minister of Justice and Legal Affairs); *"we want to maintain a Pan-Africa vision for our country and the continent, and we want to align ourselves internationally with countries that respect the sovereign rights of others".* The continent needs to regain her lost soul by being proactive and giving added value to its human and natural resources. The rights of the people must be asserted, its sovereignty a certain and recognised. Indeed, the ideological orientation of Afrocentrism must be implanted in the mindsets of the people for them to better understand as asserted by Koka (1998:3):

- The injection of African values, concepts, beliefs and ethics into all sectors of human activity – including a workplace, economic and political activities, educational and health institutions, industrial relations and labour practices, social interactions and moral codes, etc.;
- A deliberate, yet essential activist movement which is necessary for the transformation of the African Continent into a 'paradise' that is worthy of human habitation.

In short, serious s*oul searching* is needed to put in correct perspectives what the continent wants and where it is heading and how to get there. A gist to that could be seen at the turn of the century with the 1990 OAU declaration on the political and socio-economic situation in Africa and the fundamental changes taking place in the world, the Heads of the State and Government of OAU member states noted;

> We reaffirm our commitment to revise the ideals of Pan-Africanism and commit ourselves, individually and collectively, on behave of our governments and peoples to maintain and strengthen our unity and solidarity and to pool our resources and wisdom in order to face the challenges of the decade of the 1990s and beyond, change the bleak socio-economic prospects of our continent and guarantee a better life for all peoples and future generations yet unborn. These objectives are well within our capabilities. We, therefore, pledge to apply ourselves fully to the achievement of these objectives" (OAU 1990: para.12).

True to their words, backed with efforts of leaders like Mandela, Obasanjo, Mbeki and others, heed unequivocally the clarion call for Africa to stand together *for itself reflecting seriously on Kwame Nkrumah's urgency* for African unity: "Divided we are weak; United, Africa could become one of the greatest forces for the good in the world" (Nkrumah 1961 xii). With this stand, the stage was set for African solutions to African problems, rightly bestowing Africa with the inherently right and role to ownership in the endeavour to prevent, manage and resolve conflicts in the continent. The continent stands at the cross-roads of development or destruction.

Only Africans can make the choice. The protracted nature of Africa's continuing malaise, of growing impoverishment and deepening deterioration, cannot be explained in terms of the rhythmic vagaries of cyclical fluctuations that characteristically plague 'free' market economies. Africa is not occupying the trough part of a business cycle because the logic of market events dictates so. Rephrased differently, Africa's long-lasting downswing is not bred by the dynamics of an erstwhile upswing; the plunge in her fortunes was not a natural consequence of internally-generated and system-engendered economic forces linked to a preceding prosperous phase.

True, African economies have, over the years, been subject to the ebbs and flows of international business fluctuations. For many decades now, Africa has been wallowing in stagnation and low-level equilibrium. Sadly, enough, most Africa regimes have, by and large, become pear-shaped because of the sheer recklessness of and economic miss-governance by, the political leaderships. Whatever the causes of the prolonged ebb in economic activity in Africa, the need to re-activate the pear-shaped economies has received considerable attention over the past many decades. The question that arises is whether the recovery blueprints have embodied strategic measures capable of initiating a process of sustainable economic recovery and renewal of the continent and in the best interests of its citizens (Timamy 2007:11)African unity and Renaissance

A new Africa has to emerge out of the excruciating hardships the region has endured in the face of disruptive spoliator incursions which the continent must be ready to face the new challenges with optimism and determinism and through a progressive Afro-centric agenda embedded with optimism. The good news is that Africa can aggressively pursue a new course of socio-economic transformation. It is for these reasons that human capital development training should incorporate books like those by Reinert, Chang, Nkrumah, Rodney, Achebe and others should form the cornerstone of the education curriculum of the continent's institutions of higher learning.

These books are the roadmap and compass for building the Africa we want. Wealth begins from wisdom and knowledge and what Africa need is to change our way of thinking so that the people can engage the global community with a chance to make an impact on it. We have to learn, for example in the North, *'time is money'* while *'there is no hurry in Africa'* which has contributed to the continent's state of underdevelopment and exploitation. Honestly, how do we hope to engage the West on the same level economically and technologically when we have lost our compass and sense of direction? The bottom line is for Africa to be proactive and pro-Africa in a way in which Africans should be politically, economically and socio-culturally upright and at least correct in actions.

Vital Dimensions and Optimism

Two vital dimensions are significant here. First, the control that Africans exercise over the analysis, understanding and definition of the peace and security challenges facing the continent. Africa had for too long had very little inputs over the definition of its challenges. Rather such inputs were externally engineered. This being knowledge generated based on epistemology and deploying methodologies developed elsewhere and often irrelevant to the indigenous framework and approaches. The orientation of African solutions to African problems was geared towards reversing this and giving indigenous framework and approaches. The orientation of African solutions to African problems was geared towards reversing this and anchoring the analysis and understanding of the peace and security of the peace and security challenges in Africa on the needs and particular circumstances of those directly affected (Dersso 2012:22).

Second, a call on African leadership to play significant roles in the articulation and implementation of solutions properly tailored to respond positively to the specific conditions and needs of those affected. Instead of treating them as objects of clarity and people incapable of redeeming themselves, this acknowledges and reinforces the agency of African actors. Thus viewed, *'African solutions to African problems'*, is a Pan-African ideal that seeks to accord Africa both ownership of and a high stake over the process for resolving the problems confronting the region. Essentially, this encases the ideals of 'Afro-centrism' epitomised by conflicts and weak institutions. It was espousing the ideological orientation of "Black Consciousness" strongly advocated by Marcus Garvey, W.E.B. du Bois, and Steve Biko among many others, inspired by the achievements of their forebears, and intellectually challenged by the arrogance of their white oppressors, and/or colonisers. Egyptian and Nubian pyramids were achieved without foreign inputs and participation. Many scientific and technological fates were attained without the West. Today the tide has turned against Africa. Tomorrow, Africa will again rise to its past glories but that requires taking the right measures and making the most appropriate choices now. Africa's future development depends on African solidarity and degree of Afrocentrism in us.

As the cradle of civilisation, lost due to centuries of slavery, colonisation and neo-colonialism, Africans need to work harder to regain the legacy of its past civilisation. Regaining lost heritage begins by curbing widespread state fragility by ensuring genuine state authority and legitimacy. Legitimacy is fundamental to stable political authority. State failure should be avoided. Insecurity and exclusion, breeds conflicts, instability, chaos eventually leading to failed or collapsed state system as witnessed in many parts of the continent. The situation in Sudan, Somali, Central African Republic and other countries contributes to what could be termed the *"misbehaviour"* of Africa states and societies. Overcoming the evils that have befallen the continent requires a new articulated way forward under the canopy of Afrocentrism which lead to the "emancipating from the deadly clutches of neo-colonialism", through democratic elections which should result in governments that are people-oriented and accepted by the people as being genuinely representative of the will of the citizens (Mbeki, 1998). This is the only way to avoid 'state contraction' as these can lead to complete collapse of state structures as has happened in the Democratic Republic of Congo (DRC), Somalia and the Central African Republic (CAR).

For now, the continent is suffering from two dangerous trends; *"state contraction"* and *"over-centralisation through ethnic hegemonic centralised authoritarian power."* This has to be replaced with democratic governance, rule of law, inclusion, responsibility and equity in benefit-sharing. Indeed, this is the finest hour for awareness creation as well as we must persistently challenge ourselves, our communities, our states and social institutions to reassess and refine established patterns of thought and interaction in order to better shape the course of African development and place within the world community. The voices and lived experiences of the people especially the poor must be heard loud and clear and taken in policy-making and execution. Present current decision-making and implementation processes excludes the masses, perpetuate conflict and encourages divide in society, place too much emphasis on the concerns of a power few, are often subservient to struggles for political ascendancy, which have proved inadequate for the task of building a better continent in which all are able to prosper

To state that Africa is on 'free fall' path is no exaggeration. The dismal performance of the state in Africa is attributed to the lack of democracy as understood by western imposed process and as understood by western scholars. But democratic elections through the barrel of multi-party system, does not necessarily lead to drastic change in the situation when those in power are puppets of the West. The transition to democracy rests with the people, the individual mindset to change and see through a functional system for the collective good. What is the individual contribution to ensure good governance? It is the sum total of the positive collectively of individual inputs that ensures, guide and drives the democratic process of good governance. Explanations of the deplorable state of democracy and good governance in the continent and of the role of the state in creating this situation abound. Characterised by two phenomena *'dependency and underdevelopment.'* (Leys 1996; Berman 1990; Chabel 1986; Bayart 1993), the main thrust of Africa's future should evolve out of economically weak and still dependent on former colonial powers dictate. Given that African states have created a civil society of their own woven in the dictates of violence and anger r destructive frustration as a response to abnormality of the state order (Monga 1996; Liebenberg 2000)

A critical dimension of the design and implementation of a new economic, political and institutional framework is an African encompassing trusteeship – the idea that each state is part of the whole of the African continent and bears a measure of responsibility for the welfare of all. It is this principle of trusteeship that calls into question the efficacy of present-day expressions of sovereignty. Unity should strengthen and expand cooperation among nation states; it has not removed the struggles for power that dominate relations among them. The mere collaboration of self-interested actors in a multilateral enterprise does not ensure favourable outcomes for the community of nations as a whole. As long as one group of nations perceives its interest in opposition to another, progress will be limited and short-lived.

Africa therefore needs a *new positive order* of constructive Afro-centrism; a new constructive mindset and the determined will to brave through the odds of the period in preparation to facing the emerging challenges of the future. A new mindset is necessary to internalised and empower the people to determine their destiny and own their development path. Africans should be owners not caretakers of their continent. The African continent must be consolidated by the people seeking comprehensive solutions to their problems and being masters of their development agenda. It is on this optimistic value belief structure that the 'Future of Africa' must be construed without which Africa has no future. A robust Africa tomorrow will significantly contribute vital changing balance of power on the world stage and this could have a precarious challenge to existing power centres of the world.

Of course, the West would not sit and fold her arms to see progress in Africa that threatens her security and well-being. For the past fifty years or more, the policy of the West has been in love with dominance and suppression of African approach which has and continues to play under the umbrella of science, technology and the forces of globalisation. Strong in-roads must be made by African countries in areas that have become the weapons of oppression and the tools for change, progress and development. Apparently, neither the visions of the future nor the lessons of the past, but the tyranny of today's commitments imposes constraints on our thinking. The challenge now is to accelerate the process of building the human capital of the people; redouble efforts in the ongoing good governance and democratisation restructuring process in Africa. The Africa of tomorrow needs new face uplift. Changes we cannot afford to forego. The process of change should involve all in society. Only through constructive change in mindset, behaviour, attitude, ethics and moral can Africa make the requisite transformation so needed. It is a question of the continent sharpening its ploughshares for the common good of the people. The continent must adopt a 'people-centric' transformation focus instead of the 'personal state-centred' concept approach that has characterised the Africa since the attainment of independence. Each African country in unionism with a Union Government must 'elevate' change, progress and development as a core pillar of African power, and as part of a strategy of exercising its natural resources potential advantage power internationally.

Africa is fuelled with the tragedy of humiliation. The tragedy of humiliation results from the continents failure of tackling democracy, modernisation and cultural imperatives. In the form of aculturalisation impacting on factors and trends leading to state failure, collapsed or fragile state construct in Africa. The absence of democracy leads to authoritarian rule. Though the continent is host to long-serving presidents in the world, significant progress has been made within the last couple of decades in the direction of returning traditional democratic states construct; making Africa one of the region most resistant to democratic ideals, indeed it has yet to experience a wave of democratisation. On the other hand, one can attribute the absence of democracy in Africa to a complex mix of factors, the most notable being the salient nature of civil society, though as custodian of power is passive and condescending as in Cameroon (Tiffiany 2010). The passiveness is assumed due to the fact that the type of state construct makes 'public grievances' not being addressed and are therefore allowed to fester to the point that citizens turn to extremist actors for relief. The dictatorial nature of regime construct in Africa further retards the public virtues of political moderation and compromise which are necessary ingredients of non-violent political expression.

The code of power in Africa needs a new baptism of inclusion, good governance and shared-prosperity. The legal separation of 'power' among several branches of government is unrealistic when the material sources of power are not also separated. Although one can appreciate the problems facing civilian regimes in Africa, efforts should be made to incorporate in the constitutions of African countries with firm guaranties against recurrence of person rule were quixotic. The sure way to avoid the abuse of power by government agencies is to divide the political power and vest it in the hands of diverse persons /institutions so that there is effective check on power by power. Consequently, efforts to cope with conflict of interest involving members of society, public establishments and beyond that with the control of power are reminiscent of the council of mice considering ways of belling the cat.

Civil society has to be proactive as in the hey-days for the struggle for self-determination, sovereignty and independence of the country. The introduction of monolithic party system destroyed the structural bases of a vibrant civil society. The return to political pluralism has not brought back the vibrancy of civil society as the custodian of the rights and power of the people. The situation in Cameroon is worse. The ruling party has cast a spell on civil society. With the *'politics of the belly'* taking centre stage in the structure-functionalism of the governance, the birth and existence of a passive civil society entails, seeing black and labelling it green or blue or white. This has given birth to the *'sycophant syndrome and the motion of support syndrome'* contributing to a state of failed democracy in the country and in other parts of the continent.

A vibrant civil society working in synergy with a people focused government quickly takes advantage of the *'latecomer advantage'* to greatly enhance the quality livelihood of citizens. The state and civil society are empowered as one unit in beating the drum for quality services delivery and in building a strong and united country and continent. What the continent needs is constructing a strategic framework and action plans in building an integrated and holistic society where everyone is the caretaker of the other. There is need for a patriotic civil society and government in articulating, consolidating and satisfying the needs and aspirations of the people, country and continent

It is only by pulling our resources together that the continent can in unionism facing the new invasion of the region. The role of human resources, particularly performance management, rewards and incentive systems, is crucial in embedding or sanctioning certain behaviours and attitudes. It is therefore necessary to bid fare voyage to archaic attitudes that derails the progress of the society and embrace a progressive new mindset, attitude and behaviour towards the construction of a better society for the common good of all. By changing the way, we think and work to a more human-focused and more service-centric attitude, we ensure that everyone in society receives the best quality of service s (he) deserves and serving everyone with an attitude of care and human dignity. Our rich cultural heritage, beliefs and value systems, ***('ubuntu, harambee, batho pele')*** provides us with the best development arsenal we can think of, but fail to utilise in transforming our development nexus

Given the current context of the world construct, African countries in unionism should cast away the blame developmental approach as it only intensifies the cause of poverty and underdevelopment. We must admit that there are many inhibiting factors which only the government and people have the ultimate power to decide how to reconstruct the region, ensure that wealth is shared justifiably among the citizens. The powers or forces that are should stop annexing benefits of economic growth for themselves and showing scant interests in the wellbeing of their citizens. There is an urgent need to develop a progressive and caring strategy in the interests of their population. Articulate self-interest must be shone. Developing collective interest should be encouraged. We cannot run-away from the reality that we as inhabitants of planet earth, our lives, the rich and poor are intertwined.

Departing from the premises of an intertwined world construct entails that political and not military solutions is what is required to ensure a sustainable global world. A sustainable Africa or world entails building and properly utilising the human capital of the people not exaggerating military spending. Military spending for useful purposes is not bad or unnecessary. It is not enough merely to remove the weapons of war and human destruction. It is essential to address and resolve the causes of poverty, marginalisation and underdevelopment by converting these weapons of destruction into the armoury of human development. It is not enough merely to remove the weapon of war and human destruction. It is most essential to address and resolve the causes of poverty, manipulation and underdevelopment. It is time for African countries to articulate and implement an agenda for development and peace, cultivating the habit of completely ending underdevelopment and conflicts, but building an enabling environment for participation, inclusion and quality livelihood. We need a collective approach to addressing the problems that confront the continent.

These problems underscore the roots of Africa's economic backwardness as it highlights the necessity for constructive change.

The way forward should be construed on the fundamental orientation of 'optimism and hope'. Optimism and hope geared towards a common African Future. This generation has an unfinished agenda. The non-realisation of the LPA, MDGs paved the way for constructing a new Africa, the AU, NEPAD and Agenda 2063. Today we possess greater collective capacity. More than fifty years down the lane, since the independence of Ghana, the continent has developed greater collective capacity and human power (though not sufficient) that should add value to natural resources as prelude to quality wellbeing.

Africa is better equipped to facing the economic and social realities than before 1957; these challenges remain daunting and must be addressed by accepting the realities of the situation. The challenges cannot be addressed by hanging on the 'blame predicament'. It is time to take truly continental and global perspectives of the present world context. The independence of Ghana and the shattering of the apartheid system in South Africa imply a new strategy of the 'unfinished agenda'.

Now the struggle for a race to the finished agenda begins. It begins with a fundamental change in our mindset, a radical revolution in our thinking and behaviour to start moving beyond the present square, where we have been stuck for the past sixty or more years. Moving beyond square one implies taking people living in absolute poverty to a new better livelihood. Since the decolonisation process, we have a better understanding of why we must move towards sustainable development and quality livelihood, if Africa is to get beyond square one.

Now is the hour for African leaders to recall the words of Prime Minister Indra Gandhi at the Stockholm Conference in 1972: poverty should be seen as the greatest pollutant; and the views of the Brundtland Commission; 'those who are poor and hungry will often destroy their immediate environment in order to survive. They will cut down forests; their livestock will overgraze grasslands; they will oversee marginal land; and in growing numbers they will crowd into congested cities. The cumulative effect if these changes in so far-reaching as to make poverty itself a major global scourge.'

The growing exodus of many young people t out of Africa in search of greener pastures in the developing countries should strongly prick the consciousness of African leaders to 'innovate, concrete realistic policy approaches with which to confront the critical issues underpinning Africa's underdevelopment and backwardness. Africa has to change. In the words of President Barrack Obama, "change will not come if we wait for some other person or some other time, we are the ones we're been waiting for. We are the change that we seek." We have to connect with African realities and in light of the global changing environment. For example, in line with AU Agenda 2063, African leaders have pledged to accelerate growth, development, and prosperity on the continent going forward 2063.

Without justice and equity in the distribution of wealth, growing inequality and backwardness will never subside. The continent is growing sick of injustice and inequality. It is high time it rides itself out of colonial mentality. This is what makes us the hopeless continent according the Economist cover in 2000. Importantly, African leaders should stop trying to reinvent the wheel. Grey Mills (2017) is categorical on this point that African leaders should go about changing the face of their countries; and thus, extricate themselves from socioeconomic poverty. The continent needs dedicated government with a comprehensive economic, political and security infrastructure agenda to turn-around as situation that has remained hopeless. The severity of the situation requires focussed leadership taking the bull by the horn and showing greater responsibility for both the problem and solution.

The entire people are confronted with one vital question – 'restructure or perish'. It is also a challenge to civil society facing the realities of the country and taking appropriately measures ensuring that their leaders deliver to their societies what is expected of them. Delivering what is expected of the leaders is a clarion call for mapping a new African Order (NAO) to analysing and addressing the important issues for the good of the people. In short improving the wellbeing of everyone in society should be the goal. We have to turn to Bache et al (2016; Schneider et al 2016; Popov, 2017) to better understand the signification of a New African Order (NAO).

To remember that a New African Order should be visualised as an *order for the people, order by the people, but also and order for the development of the people.* That is the most legitimate way for Africa to transform itself for the common good of the people. Africa has to focus its analysis on the contradictions in national development processes, criticising in particular the wasteful appropriation of development resources in excessive and imitative consumption by the privileged classes in African countries and the lack of distributive justice in national policies. It requires that Africa has to adopt a dynamic and progressive realist approach to the reconstruction of the region encompassing comprehensive long-term, medium and short-term structural and cyclical fluctuations trends and bearing in mind that we cohabit in an 'interdependent' world construct. The notion of catch-up with the developed world should be erased from our minds. We have to transform ourselves following the daunting challenges we encounter, with the resources we have, including the strategic approach of building and adding, drawing from what is available in our global world of today without subjecting ourselves to a beggar. We have to develop the strategic status-quo of a 'win-win' not a losing approach in our dealings with the rest of the world; as well as emerge out the current economic and political problems with the series of night-mare scenarios predicated by the Economic Commission for Africa (ECA) early in the 1980s, threatening African countries as the 21st Century approached. Africa is suffering from *'brain drain'* as well as *'drained brains'*. Globalisation has enabled talented Africans with marketable skills and experiences to immigrate to the developed countries, thereby creating 'brain drain' in their own countries where they are most needed. They are overworked in their own jobs; and because they have to supplement their domestic budgets to make ends they have to take extra jobs. They are thus compelled suffer from *'drained brains'* (Mohiddin, 1998)! Whether due to lack of jobs or personal insecurity at home or expectations of better life in the developed countries many Africans flee their countries. This creates a sad and somewhat pathetic situation where Africans feel proud and safe to be citizens of a non-African country. And they are ever willing to defend it with his/her life. This testifies serious failure in the structure-functioning of our governance system. Politics and governance are meant to find solutions to the problems afflicting society and to establish the best possible mutually acceptable means by which quality livelihood and improved standards of living for all citizens. Government is one of the means by which human beings can deploy properly for their collective objectives. Africa seems to have failed in this domain. The challenge now is to promote good politics, governance and the reinvention of government appropriate to the emerging Africa.

The starting point for the future of Africa should be the people. That is why producing home grown solutions provides the best way forward. The conditions created by partition and divisions hamper the development of the people. We have to ensure that truth and justice reigns to have peace; and we need peace enforcement and peace imposition at least to ensure the security of the individual, the nation and the international level. There is no loftier or more responsible mission than that of safeguarding and strengthening peace and curbing the forces of aggression and militarism for the sake of the life of present and future generations.

Africa's capability and will to fight the scourges of poverty, corruption, injustice, underdevelopment and the rest of the ills that undermine the sustainable transformation of the continent rest on us. And that is why we have to put in place a governance system that ensures and guarantee the fundamental human-rights and freedoms of every individual to freely choose the form of representation that should take care of the affairs of the country, without fear and favour. It is time we create the structural basis for equal opportunities for all.

Avoid building walls, fences and barriers that separate rather than unite citizens. Walls and fences create inequalities. Inequalities are so prevalent on the continent that no sustainable progress in the quality well-being of the people can be made. For example, "One single Norwegian has the same economic value as 491 Congolese; one Swiss person the same as 426 Ethiopian. These differences are common enough between Europe and Africa, but they also appear on other continents. One person from the United States has the economic weight of 239 Burmese" (More, 2011:11).

Africa is today confronted with the politics of poverty and underdevelopment leading to these countries having weaker but authoritarian governments that are susceptible to corruption, authoritarian rule and guarantees its citizens only a nominal observance of civil and fundamental human rights and freedoms. All these come about through a perverse interaction of many factors that impoverish the people. It is a multidirectional misunderstanding, where causes and consequences are mutual and interchangeable in a process that makes the step steeper instead of levelling it. The process started long ago with territorial claim, and the resulting antagonism may have been rekindled later by various factors including poor governance that have contributed to the state of the continent's underdeveloped status-quo. We have to reverse that status-quo, promote the unity and integration of the continent and ensure quality welfare for all citizens.

References

Achebe Chinua (1958) Things Fall Apart. Heinemann. London

'Adams Nyaradzo Rachel (2011). "Africa Unknown: Address the effects of an Alienating Education among Learners in South Africa. International Journal of African Renaissance Studies, Vol.6, No.1, June 11, UNISA Pretoria, South Africa, pp149-162

Adam Masser Gamel (2013). "Independent Africa. Why Kwame Nkrumah Was Overthrown," The African Courier, April/May 2011, pp 2011, pp38-41

Adebayo Adekeye (2010). The Curse of Berlin: Africa After the Cold War. University of KwaZulu-Natal Press, Durban, South Africa.

Adler Glenn and Steinberg Jonny (eds.) (2000) From Comrades to Citizens: The South African Civics Movement and the Transition to Democracy. Macmillan Publishers, Basingstoke, UK

African Development Bank, (2011). World Bank and World Economic Forum. The Africa Competitiveness Report 2011

African Union (2000) Constitutive Act of the Africa Union, Lomé, Togo.

African Union (2000), Protocol Relating to the Establishment of the Peace and Security Council of the African Union. Durban, South Africa.

Ake Claude (1996) Democracy and Development in Africa. The Brookings Institution, Washington DC

Alexander, C. Jeffrey (2008)." Civil Sphere, State, and Citizenship: Replying to Turner and the fear of Enclavement", Citizenship Studies, vol.12, no.2, pp185-194

Amoko Apollo '2006) "Race and Postcoloniality". The Routledge Companion to Critical theory. In Simon Malpas & Paul Wake (eds.) (2006) Routledge Publishers, London, pp127-139

Annan Kofi (1998) The Causes of Conflict and the Promotion of Durable Peace and Sustainable Development in Africa. Report of the Secretary-General to the Security Council April 1998.

Anta Diop Cheika (1974). Black Africa. The Economic and Cultural Basis for a Federated State. Lawrence Hill Books, Chicago, USA (1978)

Asante, M.K. (1998). The Afrocentric Idea. Temple University Press, Philadelphia, United States of America

Asonganyi Tazoaacha (2015). Cameroon: Difficult Choices in A Failed Democracy(Memoir), NGT Publishing, Madison, USA

Augusto, G. (2007). Knowledge Free and 'Unfree': Epistemic Tensions in Plan Knowledge at the Cape in the 17th and 18th Centuries". International Journal of African Renaissance Studies, 2(2):136-181

Bache Ian & Reardon Louise (2016) The Politics and Policy of Wellbeing, Edward Elgar Publishing, London, UK

Bauer p. T. (1981) Equality, The Third World and Economic Delusion, Methuen & Co. Ltd, UK.

Bayart, J.-F (1993). The State in Africa: The Politics of the Belly. Longman, London and New York

Berman, B. (1998). "Ethnicity, Patronage and the African State: The Politics of Uncivil Nationalism", African Affairs, No.97, 1998

Berma B and J. Lonsdale (1990) Unhappy Valley: Conflict in Kenya and Africa. James Currey, London

Birch, Tony (1996) "A Land So Inviting and Still Without Inhabitants: Erasing Koori Culture from (post-colonial Landscapes". Kate Darian-Smith, Liz Gunner and Sarah

Boateng Osier (2011) "Cracking The Code: Unlocking Africa's Secret to Wealth", New African, No.505, April 2011, AN IC Publication, London, pp8-17

Brenton, Paul (2012) Presentation of the World Bank Report – "De-fragmenting Africa Trade" – Deepening Regional Trade Integration in Goods and Services", 22nd March, 2012, ECIPE$, Science 14 Atrium, 124b Rue de la Science, 1040 Brussels, Belgium

Burawo Michael (2010). From Polanyi to Pollyanna: The False Optimism of Global Labour Studies. Global Labour Journal, Vol. 1. No. 2. Pp 301-313

Centre for Conflict Resolution (2016) Africa and External Actors, Policy Research Seminar Report, Cape Town, South Africa

Chabel P. (ed.) (1986) Political Domination in Africa: Reflections on the Limits of Power. Cambridge University Press

Chandler, David (2005). "Introduction: Peace Without Politics", International Peacekeeping 12.3 (2005)

Chang Ha-Jong (2007) Bad Samaritans. The Guilty Secrets of Rich Nations and the Threat to Global Prosperity; Random House

Chorum A. (2018) "End The Blame Game" in New Africa, No.581, March 2018, London p.6

Commission for Africa (2005) Our Common Interest: The Commission for Africa – An Argument. Penguin Books Ltd, London

Cole Peter & McQuinn Brian (2015) The Libyan Revolution and Its Aftermath; Hurst Africa Publishers, United Kingdom

Deibert Michael (2013). The Democratic Republic of Congo: Between Hope and Despair (African Arguments) Zed Books Publication, London

Dersso A. Solomon (2012) "The Quest for Pax Africana: The Case of the African Union's Peace and Security Regime", in African Journal on Conflict Resolution, Special Issue on the African Union, Vol.12, No. 2, 2012, ACCORD, South Africa, pp11-47

Doe Gbaydee Samuel (2009). "Indigenizing Postconflict State Reconstruction in Africa. A Conceptual Framework", Africa Peace and Conflict Journal, University for Peace, Vol.2, No.1, June 2009, Addis Ababa, Ethiopia, pp1-16

Djanie Akua (2011). "Education in Africa is Failing its People", New African, December 2011, London, pp46-47

Dumont Rene (1962) False Start in Africa

Ebrahim, I. Ebrahim (2011). Speech on the occasion of a public lecture on Libya. The United Nations, The African Union and South Africa: Wrong Moves? Wrong Motives? Presented at the University of Pretoria, 15 September 2011, Pretoria, South Africa

Edwards, M. (2004). Civil Society. Polity Press, London

Ezeanya Chika (2012) "Why I Hate the New AU Headquarters". New African, 46th Year, No.515, March 2012, London, pp68-59

FICOR (Finish Association for the Club of Rome (1997) Finish Society for Future Studies (FSFS) On the Way to Sustainable Development. Helsinki, Finland

Forje W. John (ed.) (2011). Century of Change: Symposium On African Unity. Nova Science Publishers Inc, New York, USA.

Forje W. John (2009) The Challenges of Administrative and Political Renewal in Africa, Nova Science Publishers Inc. New York

Forje W. John (2009) Here The People Rule: Political Transition and Challenges for Democratic Consolidation in Africa. Nova Science Publishers Inc, New York, USA

Fukuyama Francis (1992). The End of History and The Last Man. The Free Press, New York, US

Hadjor, K. B. (1988). Nkrumah and Ghana. Kegan Paul International, London

Heckscher, Gunnar (1946). States och Organisationerna, KFs Bokforlag, Stockholm, Sweden

Hegel, G. (2007). The Philosophy of History. Dover Publications, New York

Hountondji. P. (1995). Producing Knowledge in Africa Today. The Second Bashorum M.K.O. Abiola Dis*tinguished Lecture; Africa Studies Review 38(3)1*

Huntford, Roland (1971). The New Totalitarian, Stein and Day, New York

Huntington Samuel P. (1997). The Clash of Civilisations and the Remaking of World Order. Simon & Schuster, London

Huntington, P. Samuel (2004). Who Are? America's Great Debate, The Free Press. New York

Huxley Aldous (1977), Brave New World. ATRIAD Panther Books Granada Publishing Limited United Kingdom

Ihonvbere O. Julius (2000) Africa and The New World Order. Peter Land Publishers, New York.

Jacobs Garry (2018) "Foundations of Economic Theory. Money. Markets and Social Power' in ASPJ Africa and Francophonie, Vol.9. N1, 1st Quarter 2018, pp71-94

Johansson, Hilding (1952) Folkrorelerna och det demokratik statskicket i Sverige. Glerups, Karlstad, Sweden

Kantai Parselelo (2016) "The Signature Tune of a Generation", New Africa, No.564, August/September 2016, IC Publication, London, pp12

Koka, K. M. (1985) "The Concept of Black Star and Pan-African Unity, Unpublished paper delivered on the 40th Anniversary of the Pan-African Conference, Manchester, England.

Koka, K. M. (1998). "Africanisation of the Workplace. Unpublished paper of the African Study Programme, Midrand, South Africa.

Koko, Sadiki & Martha Bakwesegha-Osula (2012). Assessing the African Union's Response to the Libyan Crisis. Conflict Trends, 2012 (1), Durban, ACCORD, pp.3-10.

Langdon S. & L. K. Mytelka (1979) "Africa in the Changing World economy", in C. Legum, et al. (eds.). Africa in the 1980s: A Continent in Crisis. McGraw Hill, New York

Leys C. (1996). The Rise and Fall of the Development Theory. James Curry, London

Laremont Richardo (2013). Revolt and Reform in North Africa: The Arab Spring and Beyond. (Routledge Studies in Middle Eastern Democratisation and Government) Routledge Publishers, UK

Lewis, Joan (2008) Understanding Somalia and Somaliland, Hurst and Co. London, United Kingdom

Liebenberg I. & H. Solomon (eds.) (2000). Consolidation of Democracy in Africa. A View from the South. Ashgate, Aldershot. UK

Mandela Nelson ( ) A Long Walk to Freedom

Magosvongwe George (2013) "Armies Have a Role in Indigenisation," New African Special Report, July 2013. London. Pp68-70

Maund Margaret (2013). Congo Calling: The Memoir of a Welch Nurse in 1960s Africa. Y. Lolfa, Talybont, UK

Mbeki Thabo (1998). Statement at a Conference on the African Renaissance, 28 September, Johannesburg, South Africa.

Mbembe, A. (2001). On the Post-Colony University of California Press, California, USA

Mboya Tom (1963). Freedom and After, London

McCullough, J. J. (2017) 'Democracy Versus Opportunism: National Review, Politics and Policy, 11 December 2017, 9.00am

McKinsey Global Institute (2010) Lions on the Move. The Progress and Potential of African Economies, June 2010.

Mekusi Busuyi (2011) Corruption, Disruptions, And Socio-Political Disconnects in Africa. Department of African Literature, University of the Witwatersrand, Johannesburg, South Africa.

Mentan Tatah (2015) Unmasking Social Science Imperialism: Globalisation Theory as A Phase of Academic Colonialism, Langaa RPCIG, Bamenda, Cameroon

Mills Grey, Jeffrey Herbst, Olusegun Obasanjo & Dichie Davis (2017) Making Africa Work. Hurst Publishers, UK

Mlambo S. Alois (2006) "Western Social Sciences and Africa: The Domination and Marginalisation of a Continent", African Sociological Review, 10, 1. 2006161-179.

Moksnes Heidi & Mia Melin (eds.) (2010) Power to the People? (Con) Tested Civil Society in Search of Democracy. CSD Uppsala, Sweden

Monga C. (1996). The Anthropology of Anger: Civil Society and Democracy in Africa, Lynne Rienner

More Inigo (2011). The Borders of Inequality – Where Wealth and Poverty Collide. The University of Arizona Press, Tucson, United States of America.

Moore Carlos (1987) Interview with Cheikh Anta Diop in Cheikh Anta Diop – (1978) Black Africa – The Economic and Cultural Basis for a Federated State, Africa World Press Edition, USA

Mutua, M. W. (1995) Putting Humpty Dumpty Back Together: The Dilemmas of the Post-Colonial African State, Brooklyn Journal of International Law, 21.

Nathan, Laurie (2011). Remarks at University of Pretoria Centre for Mediation Seminar Presented at University of Pretoria on 15 September 2011, Pretoria, South Africa.

New Partnership for Africa's Development (NEPAD) (2011) Africa Innovation Outlook, June, 2011

Ngugi wa Thiong'o (1986) Decolonising the mind: The Politics of Language in African Literature, Heinemann Nairobi-Kenya, James Curry, London, Portsmouth N.H. Heinemann

Nkrumah Kwame (1963) Africa Must Unite, Panaf Books London

Nkrumah Kwame (1962) Telegram to Cyrille Adoula, Congolese Prime Minister, 17 August 1962

Nkrumah Kwame (1965) Neo-Colonialism. Panaf Books London.

Nkrumah Kwame (1962) Towards Colonial Freedom. Heinemann, London

Nkwi N. Paul (2009) "Foreword" in Forje W. John (2009) State Building and Democracy in Africa: A Comparative and Developmental Approach. Nova Science Publishers Inc. New York

Noonan, Jr. T. John (2002). Narrowing the Nation's Power. The Supreme Course Court Sides with the States, University of California Press, USA.

Nyerere K. Julius (1997) "Africa Must Unite", Edited excerpts from a public lecture delivered in Accra to mark Ghana's fortieth Independence Day anniversary celebrations, United New Africa Global Network Website: http://www.unitednewafrica.com/africa%20unite.hitm

Nyerere K. Julius (1968). Freedom and Socialism, Oxford University Press, London, pp173-188 Website: http://www.unitednewafrica.com/africa%20unite.hitm

Nyerere K. Julius (1968). Freedom and Socialism, Oxford University Press, London, pp173-188

Nuttall (eds.) Theory and Space" Land, Literature and History in South Africa and Australia, Routledge Publishers,

Oginga Odinga (1963) Not Yet Uhuru. Heinemann Publishers, London, Ibadan & Nairobi

Okello Duncan (2010). "Tensions in civil society participation in governance and politics in Africa", in Heidi Moksnes & Mia Melin (eds.). Power to the People? (Con-) Tested Civil Society in Search of Democracy. CSP Uppsala – Sweden, pp97-104

One Country (2011)"Reflections On Recent Events in Egypt", Vol.21, Issue 4. April2011 – August 2011

Organisation of African Unity (1963) Charter, Addis Ababa

Organisation of African Unity (1993). Resolving Conflicts in Africa: Implementation Options. OAU Information Services Publications – Series (11) 1993, Addis Ababa, Ethiopia.

Ottaway Marina (2003) "Rebuilding State Institutions in Collapsed States", in J. Milliken (ed.) State Failure, Collapse, and Reconstruction. Blackwell Publishing, Oxford

Popov Vladimir and Dutkiewicz Piotr (2017). Mapping A New World Order. Edward Elgar Publishing, London, UK

Reinert S. Erik (2004, 2007). How Rich Countries Get Rich and Why Poor Countries

Stay Poor. Norway and United Kingdom,

Robinson Rothstein, Bo (1992). Den Korporative Staten. Norstedts, Stockholm

Schneider Michael, Pottenger Mike and King, J.E. (2016). The Distribution of Wealth Growing Inequalities? Edward Elgar Publishing, London, UK

Shivji G. Isa (2006) "Pan-Africanism or Imperialism? Unity and Struggle Towards a New Democratic Africa", African Sociological Review, 10. 1. 2006, pp208-220

Smith Tuhiwai Linda (2012) Decolonising Methodologies, Second Edition, Zed Books London/New York and Otago University Press, Dunedin

Teffo Lesiba (2011) "Epistemic Pluralism for Knowledge Transformation", International Journal of African Renaissance Studies, Vol.6. No.1. June 2011, Routledge & Taylor Francis Group/UNISA, University of South Africa Press, Preto1ria – South Africa, pp24-34

Tiffiany O. Howard (2010). The Tragedy of Failure, Praeger Book Publishers.

Tragardh, Lars (2010). "Contested Notions of Civil Society" in Moksnes Heide & Mia Melin (eds.) (2010) Power to the People? (Con-)Tested Contested Civil Society in Search of Democracy, CDS Uppsala, Sweden, pp11-22

Turner, S. Bryan (2008). "Civility, Civil Sphere and Citizenship: Solidarity versus the Enclave Society", Citizenship Studies, Vol.12 No.2, pp177-184

Very François (2008). "The African Union from a Security Culture to an Emergent Strategic Culture. Paper presented at the 11th Conference of Africanists – Africa's Development Possibilities and Constraints, 22-24 May 2008, African Institute, Moscow.

Wa Thiong'o P. (1998) Decolonising the Mind: The Policy of Language in African Literature. Heinemann New Hampshire

Whiteman Kaye & Nagar Dawn (2008). From Eurafrique to Afro-Europe. Africa and Europe in A New Century. Centre for Conflict resolution, Cape Town, South Africa.

Woodson, L.G (1933). The Miseducation of the Negro. Associated Publishers, Trenton, NJ. USA.

Wight John (2012) A History of Libya. Hurst Africa Publishers, United Kingdom.

Chapter One

A Historical Perspective: The Gospel According to the West— From Colonialism to Independence and from the OAU to the AU

"Hide nothing from the masses of our people
Tell no lies. Expose lies; Whenever they are told
Mask no difficulties, mistakes, failures.
Claim no easy victories.

[Amilcar Cabral]

"When the missionaries arrived,
the Africans had the land and the missionaries had the bible.
They taught us how to pray with our eyes closed.
When we opened them, they had the land
And we had the Bible"

(Mzee Jomo Kenyatta, Founding President of Kenya)

"African nationalism is meaningless, dangerous, and anachronistic if it is not at the same time Pan-Africanism"

(Julius Nyerere –Founding President of Tanzania)

"The independence of the Gold Coast is meaningless unless it is linked up to the total liberation of Africa."

(Osagefor Kwame Nkrumah, Founding President of Ghana).

Understanding the Great Dialectics of SICN

This chapter is inspired by the critical woks of many scholars, in the revolutionary struggles for the sovereign rights of oppressed people and independence of the African continent. From the era of the slave trade through the colonial period to the collapse of the apartheid system, the continent has gone through a wake of turbulences, a time of frustrations, unfulfilled dreams and disillusions. Contemporary Africa though still clouded with the failures and disappointments of the past and present does signify some degree of hope for a brighter tomorrow. Some of the problem arises from Africa's historical past which cannot be detached from understanding the reality of continent's present. Capitalism, imperialism, colonialism backed by the forces of neo-colonialism continues subjecting the continent to the bottom pit of world economic and social system. The impact of this cannot be assessed in simple language in terms of monetary calculations. How many people were shipped abroad as slaves? The legacy of slavery has left a big hole in the transformation of the continent. One can begin to look at the continent's evolution from the lenses of the slave trade, colonialism and exploitation to understand the continents history and evolution.

On the whole, Africa was the last continent to be colonised by European powers under modern imperialism, which for the first time brought almost all the countries of the world under European control. Following Packenham (1991) "the scramble for the African continent bewildered everyone, from the humblest African peasant to the master statesmen of the age, Lord Salisbury and Prince Bismarck". What did this state of bewilderment? Apparently, Europe on the hand knew nothing about the interior of the African continent, just as the African peasant knew extremely little about Europe and the rest of the outside world (Nabudere, 20019). The saga on the colonisation of the continent continued and Africa remained a mystery even till today as:

> ever since the Roman times, Europe had been nibbling at the mysterious continent to the south. By the mid-1870s much was still mysterious. It was known that Africa straddled the equator with uncanny precision. It was known that Africa straddled the equator with uncanny precision. But no explorer had penetrated far along the dangerous latitude of zero towards the interior. No one knew what Africa was' greatest river or where it led. Europeans pictured most of the continent as 'vacant': legally **res nullius,** a no-man's land. If their states and rulers, they were Africans. If there were treasure, they were buried in African soil. But beyond the trading posts on the coastal fringe, and strategically important colonies in Algeria and South Africa, Europe saw no reason to intervene Africa was sliced up like a cake, the pieces swallowed by five rival nations – Germany, Italy, Portugal Britain and France, with Spain taking some scraps – and France and Britain were at each other's throats. At the centre, exploiting the rivalry, stood one enigmatic individual and self-styled philanthropist, controlling the heart of Africa: Leopold 11, King of the Belgians" (Packenham 1991).

The scramble for Africa could be seen as the scramble for the *"civilisation mission"* Or put differently, *"civilisation mission"* or *"scramble mission"* to achieve what? Has Africa been civilised? No; otherwise, we would not have been having wars and conflicts on the scale that exist on the continent today. Has the scramble stopped? No. Otherwise, China would not be invading the continent to the scale it does now? Answers to these and other questions provide in roads to the plethora of issues and kinds of crisis that confronts the continent: the crisis of legitimacy, governance and service delivery in post-colonial states, the response of the Africans and Europe's continued ignorance of the people and continent. The reality is the rebirth of the 1884-5 Berlin Conference which could be seen as intensifying the underdevelopment of Africa. Berlin has been replaced by Brussels and the scramble will be signed by free African people, supposedly democratic governments, and in contexts where African people again have neither voice nor choice (Soludo, 2012:12).

Europeans persuaded and coerced Africa into becoming a subordinate part of the modern world. The continent had become a magnet for the high-minded, the philanthropic, the unscrupulous and the insane. Visionary pro-consuls rubbed shoulders with missionaries, explorer, soldiers, adventures, engineers, big-game hunters, entrepreneurs and physicians. Between 1830 and 1945, Britain, France, Belgium, Germany, Portugal, Italy and the US exported their languages, laws, and culture, religious, scientific and technical knowledge and economic systems to Africa without a second thought. The colonial powers imposed administration designed to bring stability and peace to the continent, which seemed to lack both. The justification for occupation was emancipation from slavery – and the common assumption that the late 19th century Europe was the summit of civilisation. By 1945 a transformed continent was preparing to take charge of its own affairs. Through inertia and a desire for a quiet time, Africa's new masters left much undisturbed, and so this history also pauses to ask, what did not happen and why (Lawrence, 2016)? The future of the continent beacons for orderly change and transformation. Africans must search seriously for answers to stamp out foreign wills imposed on the continent.

These questions equally should provide answers as to why African Unity has never been fully realised despite some important achievements in that direction. Therefore, it is not fair to look back on the last fifty years with the conclusion that it has been wasted, it has not. Some resources-rich countries have made impressive strides in improving the lives of their people. But overall progress has been uneven – and in some areas it has fallen short of expectations. Rising expectation converge into rising destructive frustration. The benefits of economic growth have been skewed and disproportionately shared. A tiny group of less than three percent captures a large chunk of the income and wealth in Africa's changing tide of capitalist progress. In this landscape, a nouveau riche has arisen, a transnational capitalist elite class who are the primary beneficiaries of Africa's economic growth.

The continent seems to have lost its cultural heritage value system of the *'Ubuntu philosophy'* – of community solidarity, care and responsibility that seeks expression in the phrase. *'I am, because we are; and since we are, therefore I am'.*

No doubt, Africa has grown in many ways that are positive and progressive during that period. It can only be noted that much more could have been achieved if 'unity and integration' had been the underlying agenda and the focus of the people underscored the policy actions of the leaders. The leaders seem not to have a compass. And so, the problem is not so much that development has failed as that it was never really on the agenda in the first place. At least three factors could have induced this situational development. First, the character of the state in Africa was such that the struggle for political power was so absorbing for the political leaders that everything else, including development, was marginalised. Second, there has been no consensus on the development agenda with externally determined and driven development policies holding sway in an inconsistent manner. Third the Eurocentric agenda was allowed to take prominence over the Afrocentric agenda expressing the true and genuine desires and aspirations of the people.

Hence Ake's conclusion that 'the development of Africa will not start in earnest until the struggle over development agenda is determined: (1996:41).In other words, meaningful development must be domesticated with some spoonful of democratic salt, incorporating popular participation, wishes, desires and aspirations of the people, as well as the cultural practices and values of the people for which it is designed. It has to be Afrocentric. Democracy and development should under no circumstances be amalgamated and forcibly pushed down the throats of the people. There are countries that have developed without democracy, for instance, Singapore, Japan, Germany, Taiwan, and South Korea. But democracy and development constitute a source of human happiness in society. The Eurocentric agenda was part and continuation of the colonial agenda.

In the "Heart of Darkness" (Conrad, 1998) whose real name was Konrad Korzeniowski describes the Congo colonial state under the service of King Leopold as an "inferno" in which "a lot of people mostly black and naked, move about like ants" building the railway. The 1884-1885 Berlin Conference was a bit of *a "diplomatic mess"* brought about in the most *"undignified rush for slices of the African cake"* and with Britain's attempt to hand over the Congo to Portugal. The Berlin conference was simply for 'land acquisition' – the urge to occupy all 'vacant' lands in the name of their empires and exploit them for their needs. With very little knowledge of the people or their cultures, the Europeans nevertheless found it necessary to occupy these lands for their own profit. Following existing international law at the time, *'all land occupied by 'uncivilised' natives was vacant and civilised nations had a moral and legal right to occupy and exploit them in the interests of 'human progress'. If the natives proved a hindrance to this basic objective, they had to be eliminated.'*

The "Gospel' according to West through its civilisation model continues unabated today, the reason why the exploitation of the natural wealth of the people continues to reign through torture by electric shocks and by grazing the people with bullets in shirt, spreading the reign of terror to continue the so called 'civilising mission' and exploitation of the resources of the people. Apart from exploiting the resources of these countries there are numerous stories of human slaughter and murder of Africans once they resisted. In short, punitive measures and expeditions against 'a group of Africans who had rebelled against the colonial regime' (Hochschild 1997) were common. The 'civilising mission' and its extension under centralised authoritarian regime structures on the continent claimed more than ten million Congolese lives in the course of the brutal rule to exploit the Congo and open up the country for commerce. But when the European countries scrambled out of the continent, they ensured that they left behind a duplicate regime structure that would continue serving their interests. We do not need further analysis why radical African nationalist leaders found themselves on what could be seen as the wrong side of the emerging political dispensation of the continent. Patrice Lumumba, Kwame Nkrumah, Sekou Touré and others were victims of the left-over of puppet regimes by the departed colonial lords.

According to the Economist which had describe Africa as the "*hopeless continent*" (May 20-26, 2000), that African ethnicity, nationalism and war did not forge the post-colonial states. Rather, they were simply bequeathed by departing imperial powers that left behind centralised authoritarian states to a tiny group of western-educated Africans who rushed in to fill the gaps left by the retreating colonial masters. The Economist further notes in providing part of the answer as to why these African dictators 'simply continued the practice' of colonialism and its most damaging impact of European imperial rule was not so much economic and political by 'psychological'. Hence, *"in most places, effective European rule lasted a couple of generations or less: just enough to undermine African societies, institutions and values, but not long enough to replace them with new ways of life or establish new systems of government. Colonialism, in short, undermined African self-confidence. A full 40 years after independence it still looks to Europe and America for aid, goods, services and guidance"* (The Economist. 20-26 May 2000). The reality is that psychological impact of colonial rule contributed that African leaders' gross lack of self-confidence which has and continues to serve Western interests in every facet of development / under-development. The lack of self-confidence constitutes the very basis on which economic and strategic policies are implemented. Apparently, the few African masses who have some degree of self-confidence left are undermined by the activities of Western-educated rulers who, together with their 'donor' supporters and beneficiaries, 'simply continue the practice' of colonialism.

It is this lack of self-confidence that explains why Africa's post-colonial state can never serve the needs of the people of Africa (Nabudere op cit.). The acculturation did not stop here. It went further in denying the people their aspirations but inducing them promoting the aspirations desired by the colonialists. Western educational system was imposed on the people as it undermined the self-confidence of the Western-educated elite because Europe imposed its culture through its western educational system. The result today is that Africans are neither practising European culture nor African cultural values. Having lost our cultural values and heritage we are easy prey to destruction and exploitation and can be tossed around anyhow.

The three contributing factors or contributors to the continent's independence – the peasantry, workers and the middle class (see Melber, 2016) - with the latter as the driving force or the wielders of local political power on behalf of 'the people' Melber points out that across the continent, a burgeoning middle class has become the poster child for the 'Africa rising' narrative. Ambitious, inspirational and increasingly affluent, this group is said to embody the values and hopes of the new Africa, with international bodies ranging from the United Nations Development Programme to the World Bank regarding them as important agents of both economic development and democratic change.

With their privileged position as western-educated class or acquiring western cultural values gave them access to European culture and ideologies of nationalism, but never turn them into true nationalist, except of a select few, Nkrumah, Kenyatta, Nyerere and others. Basil Davidson (1992) opines in his publication, "Black Man's Burden", the African post-colonial nation-state became a "curse" to its people almost immediately after independence.

The immediate post-colonial African states failed to emerge from the word go as a 'nation' designed to serve African interests, but foreign interests. The nation-building project which the African independence leaders' espoused was thus flawed from the very start. Anderson (1991) and Gellner (1983:1-7) argue that nationalism is not the awakening of nations to self-consciousness; on the contrary, nationalist "invent nations to self-consciousness; and nationalists *'invent nations where they do not exist'*. The anti-colonial movement in the views of Oginga (1962) describes how the colonial powers put in place a leadership structure which would continue to serve their interests rather than those of the African people.

The former Governor of Uganda, Sir Andrew Cohen argues that what 'caused' nationalism was the frustration and discontent which arose out of the atmosphere of economic grievances, but that the new policy of the British colonialist was crafted to *'skilfully anticipate'* those concerns and instead of confrontation, *"guide the energies of nationalists into constructive channels to secure their co-operation in a programme of steady, but not headlong political advance"* (Wilson 1994). Services delivery was and is a major fundamental issue. It is services delivery that contributes to the quality of livelihood which the vast majority of the population are being deprived from receiving. The authors note that the majority of states emerged without help the help of the nation. The African colonial state is good examples of the 'nation' being superimposed on a pre-existing state.

What the African nationalists did was to harmonise and mobilise 'popular participation' in the project of 'nation-building', which falls within the concept of an 'imagined community': the mobilisation for independence was one of the processes of imagining the evidence of a community 'which had to be inserted into the territorial bastion'. The post-colonial state that emerged with African political independence inherited all the attributes, institutions and structures of the colonial state, including the colonial administrative principle and its ideology, values of greed and exploitative culture.

The cultural values and heritage principled on the *"Ubuntu Spirit of sharing and caring for one another"* was destroyed with greed, excessive accumulation and self-articulate interests cropped in. The idea of shared-prosperity was lost replaced by grabbing and stealing from the people's livelihood. The viruses of colonialism linger on making it impossible for the continent to conquer the fundamental enemies of 'ignorance, poverty and disease. Poor governance and bad leadership have contributed to create imbalances between the rural-urban development and between the affluence few and the vast and poor majority, which keeps increasing as the years go by. So continues the 'gospel' and saga according to the West to keep Africa poor and a supplying continent.

To a large extent, this explains Lord Palmerstone's assertion that: *"There are no permanent allies, no permanent friends, only permanent interests."* Reading George Orwell's classic 1984, the Libyan situation expose the reality of 'kissing somebody today and raining bombs on him tomorrow. The gospel according to the west blindfolds the leaders from seeing and reasoning the realities of their relationship with the developed west. It can be noted that when independence dawned on Africa, it was doomed from the start. It has continued unabated fifty years after. The challenge against 'the gospel according to the West' is by making 2017 as an illustrious date that will keep indelibly engraved in the hearts of present and future Africans as the glorious history of Africa's fight for liberty – free at last.

The independence of Congo exposed the 'Gospel according to the West'. Above all, declassified United States cables show that Lumumba scared the heck out of the Eisenhower administration. The best answer for the administration was to eliminate all those who dire speak ***'truth to power'*** in defence of the national interests of their citizens. The truth is yet to come out. See Williams (2016) and (Melber et al (2017) asserting that the Congo being important element of Washington's geopolitical strategy in the context of the Cold War, could not passively standby and let the people determine their destiny.

Many western countries had and continue to have a geostrategic and economic interest in remaining in control over the Congo generally and the then Katanga region (Lumubashi) specifically. This collided with the opposing interests of the Soviet Union, which was keen to secure a stake in the rich territory – or at least to prevent the West from establishing another satellite regime while ignoring the aspirations of African leaders for self-determination asserts (Melber 2017:20-23).

Nkrumah's attempt to reverse the situation was faulted by the fact that the Chief of Defence Staff of the Ghana Army, General H.T. Alexander a white lacked the imagination or confidence to reconstitute the Ghana units that went to Congo to be officered by Ghanaians. Was it part of the western plot to see white officers commanding Ghanaian soldiers when the Congolese where fighting the rebellion imposed by Belgium on the government of Patrice Lumumba. Apparently seeing that Congo had only six university graduates at independence and Ghanaians were capable of piloting planes could hardly believe their eyes. The mere fact that the Ghanaian troop incorporated white officers sent a wrong signal to Belgian soldiers. Lumumba's appeal to Nkrumah for assistance to stop Belgian sponsored coup d'état against his regime resulted with the latter dispatching within a week 1,193 troops to Congo, equipped with 156 military trucks and 160 tonnes of store. This gesture was not welcome by the West judging from the letter by The Head of the American Central Intelligence body (CIA) under the leadership of Allen Dulles who had dispatched the following message to the Head of CIA station stationed in Congo –Leopoldville.

> In high quarters here, it is the clear-cut conclusion that if [Lumumba] continues to hold high office, the inevitable result will be disastrous consequences...for the interests of the free world generally. Consequently, we conclude that his removal must be an urgent and prime objective (Duodu 2011).

Operation Barracuda" was the code name given to eliminate Patrice Lumumba, with Belgian Minister for African Affairs, Count D'Aspremont Lyden in charge of the plan and supported by the CIA. In the book by Ludo De Witte, detailed account of the happenings in Congo is well documented, noting that "Belgian military chief made nightly visits to Mobutu and President Kassavubu to plot Lumumba's down fall with the Belgian military officer, Colonel Louis Matlere carrying millions of francs for the purpose." The Time Magazine of 16 September 1960 gives a hilarious count of the unfolding events in the country noting: "it was the height of the Cold War when Sidney Gottlieb arrived in Congo in September 1960. The CIA man was toting a vial of poison. His target: the toot-brush of Patrice Lumumba, Congo's charismatic First Prime Minister, who was also feared to be a rabid communist.

As it happened, Lumumba was toppled in a military coup just days before Gottlieb turned up with his poison. The plot was abandon, the lethal potion dumped in the Congo River; the Americans were informed of the transfer because they actively discussed this thing for weeks" (Duodu 2011:83). Ludo de Witte (2001) shows how Belgium state archives document the conspiracy to assassinate Lumumba. From Lumumba through Nkrumah to Ghaddafi the ***"gospel"*** according to the West, has not been abated. Who is next in line? That remains a million-dollar question. But the gap between Western Europe and Africa continues to widen. The divide between the affluent and poor is not decreasing. It is on the increase. Society is torn into a perpetual state breeding conflicts, chaos and instability which destabilises the continent.

The gap continues to widen between the rich and poor. The granting of independence seems to have instead quenched the desire in narrowing the gap between the haves and have-nots. For many and rightly so, independence gave the leverage for the battle of inequality to be waged on many different levels and intensified the gap between the well-to-do in society and those left at the bottom of the livelihood ladder. While there are many educated Africans today than at the end of World War 11, the subjective conditions essential for the mobilisation of the down-trodden no longer seem to be present. The bottom many keeps increasing as the middle class increases and some are joining the ranks of the few top privileged rich. It is not surprising the initial euphoria of rising expectation at the dawn of independence has given way to rising frustration; optimism is now tempered by despair which shortcuts in the process of state-building, but, amplifying 'state destruction'. The internal frailties and vulnerabilities of some African states have attained a magnitude of no return to democratic governance without external assistance forcing such democratic changes.

While other countries are making significant strides towards the consolidation of democratic rule, Africa continues trailing behind with failed and collapse states. On the other hand, signs of democratic optimism can be spotted here and there on the African political landscape. This gives concerns for optimism and hope that the unity project would be attained sooner or later. The optimism view builds also the conception of Africanism *(Pan-Africanism, Renaissance Africa)* with the struggle for cultural survival and human dignity – a struggle against enslavement, racism and colonialism. Pan-Africanism is an embodiment of all black people of the continent and the Diaspora. According to Shepperson (1960), the birth of the Pan-Africanism in the Diaspora is 'a gift of the New World of America to the Old World of Africa.

In most campuses in African universities, the students are more interested in fraternity and sorority parties and getting their names on government registration pay roll slip than in analysing the contemporary political, economic and cultural situation of their respective countries and Africa in general. For these reasons, they are more interested to bribe at any length to obtain a certificate. Critical studies are shelved aside. The struggle is for belly politics and no longer the collective good. After all, political independence has been attained. It is the survival of the fittest that matters. The pivotal aspects of revolutionary transformation are the development of an educated elite corps, a new vanguard unprepared to offer much for a worthy and common cause. The social transformation of any peoples' societies is a gradual culmination of material and ideological conditions building towards a new form of social reality. The Africa of tomorrow should not permit the social divide reality to escalate and bequeathed to future generations. This generation has the moral and ethical obligations to bring to order this pathetic situation and to handover a viable and sustainable society to next generations.

African elites seem to have turned their backs towards constructing or completing the social revolution started many decades ago for the total emancipation of the black race. To say the least, the ruling elites failed to reinforce their basic strategy of gradual reforms within the state. In some cases, the process has been intensified widening the gap between the poor and rich. Neither, cultural integration within the existing system nor the advocacy of an immediate, violent confrontation between a handful of revolutionaries and the forces of law will create the conditions essential for the liberation of neglected Africans.

We need a new common sense and vision so that we can begin to make the right choices for the common good. The dream of Africa many years ago was that the intelligentsia would be indispensable as a vanguard of the great army of civilisation, of a new vision for present and future generations. Unfortunately, it is precisely this role that the African elites are refusing to play, to redeem the continent of the bondage of poverty, bad governance, corruption and marginalisation. They instead reinforced the pandemic disease of corruption, bad governance and maldevelopment. Chinua Achebe [1979] writes: *"we have stood too long on the side lines. Too many of us have adopted the cynical action constitute a serious betrayal of our education, of our historic mission and of succeeding generations who will have no future unless we save it now for them"*

African intellectuals like Azikiwe, Nkrumah, Nyerere, Kenyatta, Fanon, Cabral and many others that went through the machinery of racial relations in the United States, United Kingdom and other parts of the western world, equated the complex problem of uprooting racism in the West with the struggle to overcome colonialism and neo-colonialism in Africa. Making the right choices become imperative. Such choices usually appear to be determined by the individual, one decision at a time, on rational or irrational grounds. But these choices, when considered within the framework of all human creativity and productivity, are usually made within a common consciousness or sensibility shared by other people within one's immediate class or social group.

This consciousness, which is conditioned by a people's material needs and general pattern of human-productive activity, is the basis for any groups understanding of its own history. Common sense is that popular philosophy or folk consensus for what is right or wrong in the world, moral or immoral, aesthetically pleasing or ugly, possible or impossible. It expresses the final product of specific, collective historical decisions and the forces of material production and their impact upon humanity within a given period of time (Marable 1980:13).

Complicating the African struggle is the central factor of under-development, western domination and exploitation. Why? History provides ample evidence that the developed countries are unable or unwilling to struggle against their deep-seated attitude of superiority. Unfortunately, African elites defend the illusion of racial or ethnic integration without directly combating existing ethnic divide within their own society, rather using it as the saddle for political power or wealth accumulation. The state is bloated from its own fiscal wastes and unplanned economic development, and black bourgeois culture is the accumulation of state property as private property by those who control and walk through the corridors of power. The new ruling elites acted as replacement of the departed colonial rulers which further complicated and compromised Africa's journey to genuine self-rule and claiming ownership of its development path.

This generation must find practical alternatives to these immense social and economic contradictions that add to the continent's state of underdevelopment and global exploitation. If we fail, we must inevitably face the possibility of the complete disintegration of the black people as a group, along with the destruction of the total fabric of the African society. The political and economic transformation of Africa calls for a holistic development of new ideas within civil society which in turn promotes the ethos of a new generation of Africans able to stand their grounds in the fast-growing globalised knowledge-based economy. This transformation could not have occurred before 1945, because colonialism was still the mainstay of the exploitative policies of the West. It was and still is the West's common sense and notion of superiority and reality. A defence of superiority among the old democracies in the West is like a defence for the roundness of the earth. It is like the British Empire where the sun never set.

The bible came first, and land was seized from the people establishing a hegemonic control over the citizens. There is a new form of land grab ongoing in the 21st century dispossessing the people of their form of livelihood. President Mugabe of Zimbabwe has shown his visionary leadership in pursuing land reforms. The strategic vision has been the return of the land. Mugabe like Kwame Nkrumah, Patrice Lumumba, and many others are not liked by the West. Speaking truth to the master is not welcome. The servant must remain subservient to the master with no right to freedom and independence. Colonies must remain voiceless and retained in abject poverty and should know nothing other than poverty. For too long Africans have lived in poverty and lost all hope. They still fought hard to escape the pains and indignities, but they have equally learned how to accommodate them. No one puts it better than Harry Belafonte (2011) in his Memoir of Art, Race and Defiance. Harry Belafonte was a silent but very active member in the struggle for race equality and the recognition of the black race in the United States of America and the world over.

Defiance should culminate in African Unity or else the continent has failed to read into the words of Lumumba's letter to the wife: "I prefer to die with my head unbowed, my faith unshakable, and with profound trust in the destiny of my country." Doudo (op.cit: p.83) rightly opines; "no African with a brain in his/her head will ever forget that it was because Lumumba only tried to preserve the interests of his people and his continent that he was murdered. We have been forewarned that this can happen to all Africa leaders. And to be forewarned is to be forearmed." Akomolafe Femi (2011:33) reintegrate the issue by noting that; "African leaders often fail to learn is the issue of taking care of their security and welfare. It remains sad that apart from South Africa, no African nation has a military capability that counts for anything in the global balance of power. It is time African leaders also questioned their role at the United Nations. African leaders continue to think that by purchasing Western military surplus equipment (that is good only for 'independence' parades or to intimidate opponents), they are defending their countries. Ghaddafi reportedly spent $25bn in the last 10 years on military expenditure. That is good money that could have been spent on building viable indigenous defence industries and systems. If it had been, the result would not be the humiliation Africa is forced to witness today." The greatest and best defence of a country is building their human capital, educating them to love their country and continent first before extending whatever largesse to others.

The ideological orientation of these nationalists challenged the gospel according to the West most determined than ever before to make and retain Africa their Guantanamo. The orientation of the nationalist was a comprehensive policy of 'indigenisation', tacking back the economic and political initiatives in the overall interests of the people. They preached the gospel of empowerment to ratchet up the livelihoods of millions of Africans, only an indigenisation and people's empowerment policy reform programme could meet the aspirations and goals of the people. There was and still no other alternative but unapologetically intensify the implementation of the African Must Unite strategy as an imperative for the people to have control over the economy otherwise the sovereignty of the continent will be compromised and the ability of the people to own their development curtailed. Most Africans fail to realise that no foreign nation or nationals ventures out of their way to develop another people. Actions by nations are always undertaken on the basis of enlightened self-interest, implying executing the pursuit of permanent expedient interests rather than permanent friendship.

The return of the land is a foundation to liberation in countries that suffered settler colonialism. There are few great black statesmen alive today in Africa. Greatness here must be evaluated on the criteria of whether the person who claims the position of leadership of his or her people against colonialism, apartheid, and white rule has been able to guide the nation to greater liberation, dignity, and independence. There is a total silence on the underlying causes concerning the land issue taken by white settlers in Africa.

To what extent did the United Kingdom and United States honour the **"Lancaster House Agreement"** in respect of the return of land to the people of Zimbab**we?** The agreement was a taken obligation and responsibility of the two countries to provide funding for land redistribution. Both countries reneged on the agreement. Western media kept silent. The West will praise you only if you are doing things that please them. Most African leaders have gone too far to displeasing their citizens in praise and support of the West. Such acts do not help in fighting colonialism and exploitation, but perpetuates neo-colonialism at the expense of the socio-economic trans-formation of the continent. To be considered a saint in Western eyes is a curse African leaders should avoid like the plague.

The success of the land return makes Zimbabwe to regain her soul, turning the state into an instrument of transformation through a brave and economic transformation through the *'indigenisation programme'*. The gospel according to the West must be resisted. Or what Thabo Mbeki notes as having a new generation of Africans who; "must resist all tyranny, oppose all attempts to deny liberty, to resort to demagogy... and reassert the fundamental concept that we our own liberators from oppression" (Hadland and Rantao 1999.173).

But this western common sense has and continues to be precondition by two historical realities: (a) the factor of western hegemony (so to say) as it concerns the exploitation of the colonial territories, and: (b) the factor of economic exploitation. Seen within the parameters of *cheap labour*, Africa is the most exploited sector of the west or capitalist economy. Within civil society, western hegemony afflicts the entire set of social relations between the rich and poor. Therefore, the choices which African make concerning its socio-economic transformation and social behaviour is constantly condition by these omnipresent factors. To a large extent, it will not be wrong to state that Africa's transformation is conditioned by the willingness of the West.

The gospel of the West is not to see or permit the development of Africa. The mind of Africa and the inner logic of its ruling class is condition by this established ideological orientation established by the West. Africa is deeply ingrained in colonial legacies requiring a surgical mental decolonisation. Constructive engagement or integration with one another is essential through which all subsequent co-operation between African states – geared towards elimination all forms of colonialism and ethnics from the continent and developing trade and economic relations with one another. There is an urgent imperative and to take-off the 'white mask" and regain our true and genuine colour of 'blackness' or the 'Africans' we are.

Africa needs to establish new parameters for its transformation and productive activities, mindset of Africans call it 'consciousnesses'. (i) the desire for integration within the dominant western culture and am part of them and as a tool of acceptance: and (ii) contradictory impetus towards an autonomous sovereign African culture as the basis of its identification. The African culture under no circumstances must be made inferior or compromised with any other culture. Otherwise, we are no longer the "Africans we are." Our cultural heritage cements our identity and enhances our sovereignty. Our sovereignty has no meaning without our cultural imprint.

Civil society is the embodiment of our cultural setting under the prescient of '*diversity in unity and unity in diversity*' with a common vision and goal; promoting democratic governance by manifesting civic engagement, with egalitarian and transparent structures, promoting democratic ideals and by standing free from state influence. Here is our African identity by which we must stand, protect and treasure to pass on to generations yet to come.

The Dialectics of Slavery, Imperialism, Colonialism and Neo-colonialism (SICN)

Colonial rule did everything possible to destroy the cultural identity of the people by creating and confusing two publics – civil society and cultural society and placing the two entities at loggerhead with one another. The African civil society in terms of structure and function is unique. The public realm in Africa is a product of Africa's historical intercourse with the West through colonisation. The psychological and social implications of colonisation were revealed in the emergence of the two publics: the 'primordial' and the 'civic'. While the 'primordial public' consisted of traditional groupings and communities, the 'civic public' consists of African western-educated bourgeoisie, developed during colonisation and historically associated with the colonial administration.

The social divide between the two publics created tensions that have persisted into post-colonial times (Ekeh 1975; Osaghae 2006; Comaroff & Comaroff 1999). It is the African western-educated that injects confusion and tentacles of destruction of the African cultural heritage as a veritable input factor for sustaining the value of "am an African". The primordial public is regarded as being amoral, privately and publicly, while the civic public is regarded as being amoral and lacking the generalised moral imperatives that work in the private realm and the primordial public.

The contours of Africa's transformation are etched permanently by this divided and conflicting behavioural attitude – a strong identification with the values of Western Cultural Attitude versus, an equally strong rejection and revulsion of the Double Deal Western Political Institutions, Economic System and Culture, Behaviour and Attitude of western leaders. Ontologically, Africa as a result of slavery and colonial rule were pushed to being a part of western culture but not accepted as human-beings: inherently and simultaneously outside of it; being a member of the household but never allowed to be a member of the family. The best expression of this duality is noted by Dubois in *"Of our Spiritual Strivings"*, and Fanon's *"Black Skin, White Mask"* [1967]. Dubois wrote; *"the history of the America Negro is the history of this strife – this longing to attain self-conscious manhood, to merge his double self into a better and truer self:"* *critically observing*, *"one ever feels his twines – an American, a Negro; two souls, two thoughts, two unreconciled strivings; two warring ideals in one dark body whose dogged strength alone keeps it from being torn asunder."* In a way Senghor's 'Negritude' is not short of 'Black Skin White Mask' and the imposition of the Eurocentric agenda on the African people.

It is time for Africa to begin building concerted political, economic, cultural and technological agendas within the contextualised and comprehensive understanding of the continent's historical and ideological experiences, both nationalist and integrationist. Politics is mainly about the authoritative allocation of values and resources. It is about who gets what, when and how. The African liberation struggle was a reaction to the marginalisation of the black people in their own land as well as their programmed exclusion from owning their land and resources as well as using these for their development. The only hope was a struggle through concerted efforts, *"seeking the political kingdom"* for other things to follow. Hence the policy strategy of indigenisation and economic empowerment seeks therefore to correct the injustice created by the years of slavery, subjugation, deprivation and colonialism.

It is about creating a new society controlled and by Africans. The colonial policy was engraved within the contours of 'milking the cow without feeding it'. Since independence, Africa's bountiful natural resources has not ceased to be 'owned' by foreign companies which are in the continent to exploit them and give Africa peanuts in return. When there is a shift in this perception and attitude, African's rabbit will have the honour of being king among its peers chasing the fox in the world. The future of Africa is entangled with African Unity, Pan-Africanism and African Renaissance Agenda.

As globalisation entangles the continent in its web, there is a resurgence of African nationalism, as a form of both resistances to and reconciliation with imperialism. The creation of the Organisation of African Unity and its subsequent reconstitution into the African Union has evolved with the framework of imperialism, colonialism and neo-colonialism. Apparently, chauvinist nationalisms based on race, ethnicity or territory is on the rise within and between African countries leading to wars and civil strife. The continent is in turmoil. Imperialism feeds on it like a vulture; power hungry elite worsen it as they thoughtlessly implement their masters' military designs and economic schemes. The first-generation African nationalists feared that left on their own African states would become pawns on the imperialist chessboard. They pleaded for African Unity with little success witnessing their fears materialising in their lifetime. Some, like Nkrumah, became early victims of imperialist machinations; others like Nyerere, survived by practising pragmatism while preaching Pan-Africanism. Nonetheless, they were great visionaries, and like all visionaries, their legacy lies in their vision more than in their practice. Others like Gaddafi's African Union concept is opposed because he is perceived to represent 'Arab colonisers' who invaded Africa centuries before Christ (Shivji 2008); and so, the saga goes on contributing and confusing the real issues at stake – Africa's exploitation and domination by external powers with the complacency of puppet African leaders.

Debates about the slave trade in Africa will linger for many decades to come. But how many people know that the Transatlantic Slave Trade (TST) in Africa was started by Islam" (Azumah 2001; Ronald 2002)? The Arab Slave Trade (AST) that typically dealt in the sale of castrated male slaves. Black boys between the ages of 8 and 12 had their scrotums and penis completely amputated to prevent them from reproducing. About six of every 10 boys bled to death during the procedure according to some sources but the high price brought by eunuchs on the market made the trade profitable. Some men were castrated to be eunuchs in domestic service and the practice of neutering male slaves was not linked to only Black males. The Calipha in Baghdad at the 'beginning of the 10th century had 7,000 black eunuchs and 4,000 white eunuchs in his palace" (Segal 2002). Some historians estimate that between AD 650 and 1900, 10-20 million people were enslaved by Arab Slave Traders. Others hold that over 20 million enslaved Africans alone had been delivered through the trans-Saharan route to the Islamic world (Little 2011, Moor, 2nd June, 2014).

The continent has and is suffering from the 'wounds inflicted upon it by the vultures of imperialism and colonialism. The OAU and subsequently the AU remains a Pan-African and African Renaissance construct expounded under the umbrella Africa Must Unite which laid the foundation for the continent's commitments to fighting a common enemy – imperialism and colonialism. The creation of the OAU no doubt constitutes a grand political vision for the continent. Of course, unity will not make the continent automatically rich, powerful and independent, but harness its potentials making it difficult for Africa and the African peoples to be disregarded and humiliated. We only need to give value to what exists. Africa has to be seen as the "elephant as a whole" containing and connecting between diversities and divisions in unity. The politicisation of diversities contributed to the construction of a weak organisation for the continent, but the vision was not lost. But the politicisation of diversities coherently applied also constitutes the anvil on which to construct a strong and united continent.

And as noted by Wendell Berry; *"The past is our definition. We may strive to escape it or escape what is bad in it, but we will escape it only by adding something to it."* That something Africa adds to its diversity has to be positive. The positivism of the continents diversity is its strength which should be used positively and in the collective good of the people. The cultural diversity and heritage values of the African people are envy to those who have lost these human values and heritage. Incidentally, Africans failure to value and appreciate this wonderful gift of nature to the people contributes to their underdevelopment and undermining in global politics. However, Africa seems caught within the trappings of modelling the continent in Europe's image and creating something different. What turned out was neither of the two but a state of chaos and anarchy that evolved. So, the first years of rising expectations, optimism, and of boom were followed by a long period of destructive frustration, crises and stagnation. Africa is yet to truly recover from the failures of the immediate years of independence.

Given the changing dynamics of politics and global evolution, the AU had completed its assignment. It was time to move forward with new vigour, vision and a comprehensive agenda compass to chart a new course for the continent. Hate or love the OAU. Something new and robust was required and urgently to properly make use of what the OAU had put in place. In short, if no use is made of the labours and efforts of the OAU, the continent would always remain in the infancy of knowledge and transformation. Both at the national and continental levels drastic measures for constructive change must be articulated and implemented with the focus of prudent management and democratic governance all geared towards the ultimate objective and interests of placing the people first in all developmental activities. No one should be left behind in the new Africa we want. Africa's identity and diversity must be harmonised as a veritable asset for the sustainable transformation of the continent for the good of the people and humanity.

African states individually and collectively should play the leading role in the shaping the future of the continent. Unfortunately, the African state construct has earned itself many formulations, from the 'collapsed state' and 'weak states' to the 'criminalisation of the state' and 'aborted states'. Many African states are indeed very weak; some have even collapsed. A state is considered 'weak' or 'collapsed' if it fails to execute its functions as a sovereign authority, a decision-making institution and a security guarantor. The democratisation waves since the 1990s not-withstanding, African leaders must still deepen democracy in their own countries and support those that are still struggling in this regard. Furthermore, every part of our continent is faced with some form of conflicts, and this affects the extent to which the state can play a positive role in the realisation of shaping the continent we want. Worse still, the African political elite itself is fragmented and lacks cohesion both politically and as social force, due to the struggle over resources (Maloka, 2001).

Resources have become the dagger sword destroying the continent instead of being the anvil on which the region should reconstruct itself after many decades of colonial rule. The resources of the continent have become a curse not blessings to the people in improving their quality livelihood. For how long will this continue? The people need to put in place a forum for critical examining, informing, and debating national and continental issues that transform the quality livelihood of all citizens.

From the OAU to the AU

"Africa Must Unite. Together, we the African peoples will be incomparably stronger internationally than we are now"

(Julius Nyerere)

"We are already experiencing the instability that existed under colonial rule. We are fast learning that political independence is not enough to rid us of the consequences of colonial rule"

(Kwame Nkrumah)

"Contrary to what some have written that ours is a 'hopeless continent', the decisions taken at Sirte cannot but give hope to the millions of Africans from the confluence of the Indian and Atlantic oceans in the south, to the Mediterranean in the north, that the enhancement of African unity will enable all of us to overcome the problems that have confronted us for centuries

(Thabo Mbeki, ANC Today, Vol.1. No.7, 9-15 March, 2001)

The Humble Beginning

Pan-Africanism and Renaissance Africa unlike Africa Must Unite agenda evolved consensual visionary approach while the later was compounded with the controversy of crafting ***'immediate continental unity'*** as advocated by Nkrumah and ***'territorial nationalism'*** as propounded by Nyerere. A clash of ideological orientation and conflict existed between NKU's (national radicalism) and NYE's national (pragmatism). There was no reconciliation as the two divergent opinions overshadowed the creation of the first continental political union of states. Pan-Africanism and African Renaissance was about uniting people, and Africa Must Unite was about the construction of a Union Government uniting states. What emerged on 25 May 1963, in Addis Ababa, Ethiopia was eventually a celebration of the "Ubuntu and Harambee spirits" of keeping alive the vision of unity in diversity. By 1962 a total of 32 nations were independent states. The decades leading up to the formation of the OAU were simmering with agitation and expectation across the African continent as increasing number of nations became free from European colonialism.

The roots of the OAU dates back to the 1945 Pan-African Congress in Manchester, England which brought together activists from the African Diaspora in the United States, Europe and the Caribbean with leaders of the various nationalist movements on the African continent. The Congress with Kwame Nkrumah (Secretary) and W. E. B. Du Bois (Chairman) was an unambiguous call for Africa to be completely freed of colonial rule. Twelve years later, Ghana became the first British colony to gain independence, and in 1958 Nkrumah hosted an assembly of the eight independent African countries including South Africa in Accra. This was followed by the All African Peoples Conference (AAPC). In the aftermath of the Accra conference, colonialism began to rapidly recede across the continent. Harold Macmillan's (British Prime Minister) wind of change blowing across the continent could no longer be halted. More than a dozen former French colonies joined the independence bandwagon. A new continent had come on the stage of international relations. A continent clothed in diversity forging unity to ensure the Africanness in us without which as noted by Nkrumah, *"we will be mocking the hopes of our people if we show hesitation or delay in tackling realistically the question of African unity."*

In the excitement of the dawning post-colonial era, several different views developed within the Pan-African diplomatic circles about how these new sovereignties should relate to one another and the rest of the international community and at what pace unity should be manifested. Two divergent views and blocs emerged with alliances of different African governments – the Casablanca (radical) group and the Monrovia (moderate) group. The ideological orientation on achieving African Unity was divisive between the two blocs. Ethiopia played a pivotal role in bringing the different parties together which culminated in the Addis Ababa Summit of independent African nations in May 1963. In his opening speech to the Summit, Emperor Haile Selassie sounded the clarion call in these words: *'We cannot leave here without having created a single African organisation possessed of the attributes we have described. If we fail in this, we will have shirked our responsibilities to Africa and to the peoples we lead. If we succeed, then, and only then, will we have justified our presence here"?*

History in The Making: OAU First Summit, 25 May 1963, Ethiopia

On May 25, 1963, delegation from 32 independent African nations gathered in Addis Ababa for the historical launch of the Organisation of African Unity (OAU). The assembly of independent African states agreed to quickly establish a unifying Pan-African institution. After extensive deliberations, the conference of Independent African Heads of State and Government in Addis Ababa ended successfully with the signing of an official charter establishing the Organisation of African Unity. After the signing of the charter, the meeting hall was filled with the 'euphoria of Pan-Africanism. The OAU charter was just the beginning. After the signing of the charter, Kifle Wodajo (then a young Ethiopian diplomat) was appointed Acting Secretary General. At subsequent meetings, it was decided that the OAU would be headquartered in Addis Ababa, with Diallo Telli (then Guinea's ambassador to the U.N.) would become the OAU's First Secretary General in 1964. The decades leading up to the formation of the OAU were simmering with agitation and expectation across the African continent.

Source: Credit: Selamta - Ethiopian in Flight Magazine, (2013). 50 Years Uniting Africa – Celebrating the African Union, May/June 2013, Addis Ababa, Ethiopia, p23

On his part, Nkrumah famously declared; *"We must unite now or perish."* The assembly of independent African states ended up establishing a unifying Pan-African institution and signing of an official charter establishing the Organisation of African Unity. The euphoria of Pan-Africanism filled the hall with Kifle Wodajo of Ethiopia becoming interim Secretary-General of the organisation before handing over to Diallo Telli of Guinea as OUA's First Secretary General in 1964. On the hole, OAU achieved its objectives of decolonisation. Some significant initiatives included the African Charter of Human and Peoples' Rights and African Priority Programmes for Economic Recovery as well as addressing the severe challenges faced by many African countries. This gives room for drawing from the best practices of other countries, for example, countries from the Asian regions.

The OAU did have some achievements in its first decade as well setbacks. Rank erring among states on the construct of the organisation and the reluctance to empower the Secretary-General and with very few countries showing and desire to surrender real authority to the organisation either, these and other draws helped in weakening the authority of the body. None payment of membership dues helped slowed down the output functions of the organisation. Some of the challenges could be seen within the context of the infighting between the two main camps – the Casablanca group which was the most radical proponents of 'African unity' calling for a political union based on common defence, foreign affairs and diplomacy, a single nationality, and African currency, an African monetary zone among other items; and the Monrovia bloc consisting of sceptics and gradualist in contrast calling for economic unity as 'the best approach possible towards political unity, with regional groupings forming a useful step'.

Both parties on the divide saw themselves as continental groupings with Charters signed in Casablanca and Lagos respectively. Africa's ideology was systematically divided before the meeting of Heads of State and Governments 1963 Addis Ababa conference. The diversity of policies articulated and implemented by Africa states is a logical consequence of the division of the continent since the independence period and reinforced by the OAU Charter. The various Summits replicate this division though it often gave the impression of continent and a community of spirit reflecting the Pan-African ideal and the eventual Unity of the continent.

Given the polarised situation, the Prime Minister of Nigeria, (Tafawa Balawa Abubakar) opined that under these conditions, "any rigid institutional form at present seems premature. Thus, for now, we do not call for a federation or confederation, but progressive and close co-operation, slow but efficient on the economic and technical levels, and regular meetings of all Africa Heads of State on the political level." From the onset, strong emphases were not directed towards the economic transformation of the continent.

In short, the basic needs of the people received little attention. The majority were and are still neglected today in the political dispensation of the continent. As a result, many economic reform programmes benefit only a small elite rather than the general population. The consolidation of benefits in favour of a small group further hamstrung the economic impact of the reform effort. In the absence of strong parliaments able to exercise proper oversight, the privatisation of many state industries often take place without complete transparency leading to a perception, often justified, of corruption. The governance system instead of fighting corruption only intensified the act. Some governments consciously or not seem to have legalised corruption by not adhering to the constitutional provisions which call s for appointed officials to declare their assets before and after leaving office. Giving a blind eye to such acts implants the lack of trust and confidence in the government.

The Development

Coming in the heat of the Cold War era, the OAU went through periods of trials and triumphs. It was plagued by member states not meeting their financial obligations. Nevertheless, the OAU limped on, promoting Pan-African cooperation and working to end colonial rule as well as minority rule in South Africa, Rhodesia, including creating a forum for mediation and the resolution of intra-state conflicts. A range of important Pan-African conventions, treaties and charters were adopted covering issues ranging from civil aviation and environmental conservation to culture and technical cooperation. Mention can also be made of significant ones like the 1981 African Charter on Human Peoples' Rights and Africa's Priority Programme for Economy Recovery; The Abuja Treaty creating a unified African Economic Community as well as laying the foundation for the transition to the African Union.

Of course, the OAU had many setbacks as well as achievements. By far the most important was that of simple survival. That the OAU could fall apart was evident from the divisive nature between the radicals, moderates and conservative's perception of the Union's structural-functional construct. Not only had the OAU survived its first decade; it had also grown in strength, hence its transformation into the AU. The failings of the OAU merely demonstrated that the dream of African Unity has at least as far to go as any other dream. Its areas of agreement – opposition to white minority rule in the South for example – were too often marred by the factionalism that divided the very people that the Organisation supported.

Member states were divided on the Nigerian Civil War in the 60s. For example, Tanzania and Zambia including some West African states supported and recognised the break-away Eastern Nigeria State of Biafra. The Chairmanship of Idi Amin, the conflict between Tanzania and Uganda, the over- throw of General Gowon (Nigeria) were some of the issues that threatened the c*ollapse of the union.* The same split could be registered within the AU on the invasion of Libya by the European Union 2012. The turbulent period in the Cold War era threatened the structural-functioning of the year. It can be noted that the collapse of the Berlin Wall in the late 1989 injected in spirit and dynamism in an organisation that was limping back to existence, bringing the ideals of Pan-Africanism to bear fruit and fostering unity and solidarity among the different states.

Generally, and from analytical perspective, the OAU reached its climax with the last vestiges of colonial territory attaining impendence and with the collapse of the apartheid regime structure in South Africa.

Thus, by the turn of the century, the continent needed a new body to advance the course of African unity in the sense that:

- The OAU Charter created a purely intergovernmental organ, whose resolutions were not legally binding on its member states;
- The Secretariat (i.e. the Secretary General) had only a purely administrative character lacking executive powers. It could be compared with the role of the UN Secretary General especially during the Cold War era which also characterised the failure of the UN to take decisive action during the outbreak of the Congo Crises of the 1960s;
- The triumph of the principle of the sovereignty of states instituted by the Charter condemned the notion of a continental government as well as any attempts at leadership by a person or a country;
- The official objectives assigned to the Organisation by the founding fathers indicate they did not intend to create a supranational power:
- African state continues to play a role within international organisations out of all proportions to their effective possibilities of action in the relations between states

It should be noted that the fifth Pan-African Congress held in Manchester in 1945 was attended by a large delegation from continental Africa, and charted the course for post-war liberation struggles in Africa. Participants such as Ghana's Kwame Nkrumah and Kenya's Jomo Kenyatta would latter lead their countries to independence and champion the Pan-African case. This period equally witnessed the emergence of divergent interpretations of Pan-Africanism and alternative strategies to achieve it, as evidenced in the enduring tensions between the advocates for an immediate continental political union (the Casablanca group) and the (Monrovia and Brazzaville blocs) which favoured a gradual approach to unity. The creation of the OAU in Addis Ababa, Ethiopia in May 1963 brought an end to these rival blocs, which reflected a gradualist approach to continental unity over its radical counterpart.

There were high expectations of independence ushering a new era of democratic governance and socioeconomic development throughout Africa. However, despite its success in achieving the decolonisation of the continent and ending the horrendous governance apartheid system in South Africa, the OAU proved to be ineffective in moving forward the Pan-African ideals of regional and continental integration and development, amid the proxy wars waged by the United

States of America and the Soviet Union (USSR) across Africa, and the over 40 French military interventions in the continent to prop up or replace assorted autocrats. Poor governance and military rule also proliferated throughout the continent (Adebajo 2016).

Some African leaders in countries like Uganda and Equatorial Guinea hid behind the shield of sovereignty and committed gross human rights abuses against their people. Following the independence of African countries after 1960, over six million Africans died in a bid to defend colonial boundaries in Nigeria, the Democratic Republic of the Congo (DRC), Sudan, Ethiopia, and Eritrea. The OAU was further criticised for its lack of engagement with their African Diaspora, thereby undermining the global unity of Africans in their struggle. A new wave of optimism about Africa's future swept through the continent, resulting in the creation of the African Union in July 2002 in South Africa's port city of Durban under the stewardship of host president Thabo Mbeki.

African Heads of State and government at the opening of the African Union summit in Accra, Ghana (July 2007).

The birth of the AU was expected to mark a new era in the quest for Pan-African unity. Although the African Union has contributed to efforts to transform Africa's security and governance landscape, and has brought renewed attention to the ideal of Pan-Africa unity, Pan–Africanism as a political movement appears to have lost its appeal. The existence of the AU over the past decade and a half has been animated by the same debates over the meaning, timing, phasing, and sequencing of the Pa-African project of regional integration and socio-economic development. It is now evident that the creation of the AU was not underpinned by a shared understanding among African leaders of the organisation's place in the global order, nor is there consensus on the degree of sovereignty that member states are expected to cede to the AU in order for the organisation to achieve its integrationist goals and make it relevant to the aspirations of Africa's one billion citizens in order for the organisation to achieve its integrationist goals and make it relevant to the aspirations of Africa's one billion citizens (Adebajo, 2016). Both the defunct OAU and the current AU have failed to silence the guns, usher peace and security most needed by the people. Africa institutions have failed to put up a strong deterrence in the destructive acts of poverty and corruption and in fighting the resurgences of dictatorial regime structures that glitters the continent's socio-eco-political landscape.

The Renewal – The African Union (AU)

Significant changes have occurred over the years that empowered the OAU to address the challenges facing the continent. The Togo Summit of 2000 saw the transformation act that led to creation of the African Union (AU). The African Union held its first official Assembly in Durban, South Africa in 2002. The transition from the OAU to the AU represents much more than a simple change of name. The new constituted organ has established more complex structural organs with a broader sphere of activities geared towards a peaceful and prosperous continent. Some significant organs created include (a) New Partnership for Africa's Development (NEPAD) with a focus and strategic drive for African states in pursuing sustainable socio-economic development, African integration and increased trade in the context of democratic governance.

The African Peer Review Mechanism (APRM) of NEPAD is a major stride to entrenched good governance, curbing endemic corruption and promoting best practices. NEPAD has since become the main instrument for advocating Africa's position and interest on the global stage, including the G-8 and G-20 Summits. Just like Emperor Haile Selassie 1, Prime Minister Meles Zenawi equally played a significant role in the creation of the AU. At the adoption of the AU Charter in 2002, Prime Minster Zenawi noted:

> if we are considering a Union as a panacea, as a magic wand which removes all our economic problems, clearly we will be disappointed. When we in Ethiopia support this union, we support it not because we believe it will be a magic wand, but because we believe that a bigger

> economic space is in the interest of all of us. I agree with the African union because I assume it will be an instrument of fundamental transformation of our economies from that of rent collection to that of value creation.

But the road to the creation of the AU was long and winding with challenges and opportunities to brave the odds of failure and embrace success for the new Africa. Prior to the Extraordinary Summit of the OAU in March 2001 in Sirte, Libya seen as the historic move forward in Africa's quest for unity, the Lagos Plan of Action (LPA) could not be effectuated as the continent's economic crises were in full swing, the impact of the 1981-82 recession, the burden of external debt, and natural misfortunes such as famine, floods, desertification and drought had entangled the region. The adoption of "African Priority Programme for Economic Recovery" by the 1985 Summit aimed at revitalising the LPA also resulted in a United Nations Special Session adopted a similar action plan for the continent – ***"Programme of Action for African Economic Recovery and Development, 1986-1990".*** Seeing that the well-articulated LPA could not be achieved as a result of the serious economic and political crisis that had befallen the continent, the OAU Summit of 1991 adopted the Abuja Treaty as an attempt to revive the LPA and move forward in concrete terms, the question of regional integration and the creation of an African Economic Community (AEC) by 2025 (see OAU 1991, UNECA 1995, 1994; Muskias & Thompson 1995). The Treaty envisaged a 34-year, six stage, linear process through trade integration approach beginning with trade liberation and advancing on to a Common Market and eventual Economic Community.

The African Union was established on 26 May 2001 in Addis Ababa and *launched on 9 July 2002 in Durban, South Africa.* Of the 54 African states, *Morocco is the* only African state not a member of the AU. The most important decisions of the AU are made by the Assembly of the African Union, a biannual meeting of the Heads of State and Government of its members. The future goals of the AU include the creation of a *free trade area, a customs union, a central bank and a c*ommon c*urrency*, thereby establishing economic and monetary union. The AU's new principle include the right of the Union to intervene in a member state; respect of democratic principles, human rights and good governance; the promotion of social justice and the promotion of gender equality. The conversion of the OAU to AU should be seen as moving the continental body from an emphasis on decolonisation and self-governance to prioritising the issues of the day, namely; a general improvement in people's lives, safeguarding its sovereignty, the security of the individuals and properties, the rule of law (with strong emphasis on democracy) and economic emancipation through investment in infrastructure, agricultural reforms, free trade, customs unions, and improvements in the health, education and employment sectors, amongst others.

Of course, the Treaty has its shortcomings which can largely be attributed to the economic and developmental approach adopted. In addition, the relevance of the OAU came under scrutiny, given that the mission of the organisation was conceived with the framework of the struggle against colonialism and narrow concerns with national sovereignty. According to the Consultative Act establishing the Union adopted at the OAU Summit in Togo in July 2000, including the draft Pan-African Parliament (PAP) protocol by African Parliamentarians in Pretoria two months earlier, the March 2001 Extraordinary Summit in Sirte, Libya was convened mainly for the purpose of advancing the ACT and PAP protocol. Apparently, the Act adopted in Togo was based on a 'moderate, gradualist approach, *a la* Nyerere; which evoked a reminiscent of the old debate between Kwame Nkrumah and Nyerere in the 1960s; while the PAP adopted in Pretoria envisaged a body with, for now advisory and consultative powers only.

Parallel to these moves towards the Union, another plan was uncovered "The Millennium Africa Recovery Plan (MAP) unveiled by President Mbeki at the 2000 Davos World Economic Forum anchored on five areas that must be targeted for the realisation of Africa's recovery, namely:

- Peace, security and governance;
- Investing in Africa's people;
- Harnessing Africa's strategic advantages;
- Investing in infrastructure and information technology; and
- Developing financing mechanisms.

Governance system based on either the *"tyranny of majority or minority"* must be discouraged. Policies and administrative procedures must not be determined by 'patronage, tribal considerations or regional balance/allegiance, rather than issues of policy or strategic leadership. The AU is tasked to work in uplifting the burdens of poor or marginalised silent majority, poor governance and cyclical poverty from the shoulders of the people, the continent can expect to see limitless expansion of creativity, innovation and entrepreneurships, progress, development and sustainability. The AU should feed member states with good policies to feed the continent with development and sustainable quality livelihood for the people. Member states should positively respond to constructive policy strategies of the AU in making the continent what it should be in years ahead. The words of Kwame Nkrumah like that of Thabo Mbeki and others being significant in this context. *"I am not African because I was born in Africa but because Africa was born in me."*

Its first decade of creation has seen many achievements across the continent, for example, the election of the first female head of state in person of Ellen Johnson Sirleaf of Liberia, followed by Joyce Banda of Malawi. For the first time (2012) a female in person of Nkosazana Dlamini Zuma (South Africa) was elected Chair of the AU Commission. On 28 January 2012 AU's new Headquarters funded and built by the Chinese was inaugurated in Addis Ababa. Efforts in promoting democratic governance and quality management are on course to change the face of the continent. Seen within this light, the AU's achievements so far can be linked to the statement by Barrack Obama; *"if you are walking down the right path and you are willing to keep walking, eventually you will make progress."* The AU is breaking grounds, making Africa proud and propelling it into a future of great hope. The organisation so far is on the move, putting into correct perspectives the progress and potential of the continent. There are many obstacles to overcome. China constructing the new AU Headquarters should not imply that the continent must become a permanent supply line of raw materials to China or any other country. The AU should not be subservient to the dictates of any other continent or country. Drawing from the views of Steve Biko, 'the most potent weapon in the hands of the oppressor is the mind of the oppressed'. It is time to nourish the mind of Africans, if we stand together. And standing together provides the most strategic and constructive way forward for Africa.

Challenges and obstacles that can be overcome through the determined and committed resolve of the various stakeholders, reducing excessive bureaucracy, ethnic diversity, corruption, poverty, exclusion; but building and promoting partnership, inclusion and quality services delivery. A new crop of leaders and citizenship mentality must emerge proud to say, *'I am and Africa.'* The decisive steps towards a better Africa has been taken. The challenge for the AU is whether the date of 2017 will be honoured with the creation of a Union Government of Africa. The growth of the AU is assured, its development inevitable. Member states must equally play their parts constructively and comprehensively. They need to move from rhetoric to concrete actions. The challenge now is for all stakeholders in unionism should go boldly forward, into a greater future made in

Africa, by Africans. Africa remains one continent, one people and one nation.

Chairpersons of the AU since Creation in 2002

Name	Country	Period
Thabo Mbeki	South Africa	9 July 2002
Joaquim Chissano	Mozambique	10 July2003
Olusegun Obasanjo	Nigeria	6 July 2004
Denis Sassou-Nguesso	Rep. of the Congo	24 Jan.2006
John Kufuor	Ghana	30 Jan.2007
Jakaya Kikwete	Tanzania	28 Jan.2008
Muammar al-Ghaddiffi	Libya	2 Feb 2009
Bingu wa Mutharika	Malawi	31 Jan.2010
Theodore Obiang Nguema Mbasogo	Equatorial Guinea	31 Jan.2011
Yayi Boni	Benin	29 Jan.2012
Hailemariam Desalegn	Ethiopia	27 Jan.2013
Iddris Deby	Chad	30 Jan. 2014
Paul Kagame	Rwanda	17 July 2016
Abdel Fattah al-Sisi	Egypt	30 Jan 2019
Cyril Ramaphosa	South Africa	10 Feb.2020

Unfortunately, this sense of solidarity was lacking during the Libyan crisis. The dictates of the payment master prevailed over some governments for fear of losing thirty pieces of silver in form of aid assistance. African countries one after the other started extending recognition to the invading forces in Libya. These divisions across the continent shock the AU's new and fragile foundations designed to promote democracy and the prevention of conflict (Sturman 2012; Kasasira 2011, Massoni 2011; Khawaja 2011). The Malian situation exposes the weakness of African unity and solidarity. The AU is engulfed by the crisis in Mali and the intervention of the French. Fifty years after individual countries and the OAU (through the liberation committee) fought to win independence-neither the Malian army, the regional economic community (ECOWAS) nor the AU's own peace and security mechanism could defend this independence without outside help.

One can seriously question African Independence. What does this independence really mean if a determined enemy can still walk into any African country? Where is the investment in our collective armed forces for this most fundamental and existential of things? If the Malian political class or military cannot guarantee their independence, why are they and their people so reluctant to take Kwame Nkrumah's advice and truly pool their sovereignty and merge their country into a bigger African structure that can guarantee that independence? The questions throw into relief some of the continuing challenges around unity – between full integration and something looser. Even then there are huge issues around the current loose status. Why is it easier for Westerners to move around our continent than ordinary Africans? Why is intra/African trade so tiny? Why can't Africans own property/ land in their own right in Addis Ababa, Africa's capital city? The OAU/AU has spent 50 years and perhaps a billion dollars setting up structures and establishing norms of behaviour. This is an important process, but Africa now needs an accelerated movement towards implementation and the reality of unity (Wambu, 2013:98).

The Central African Republic, Congo. Mali, Somalia, South Sudan and Libyan situations including others should teach Africans to work together, negotiate and communicate as one unit to have a common position in enforcing policy decisions and deepening African unity. Even though change does take time, the various complex political, social and economic challenges faced by African countries calls for urgent political consensus and the subsequent appalling rise of political violence, a major problem that Africans are urgently invited to manage, makes it imperative in searching for urgent solutions to prevent the total collapse of the continent. Fifty years after the cutting of the biblical colonial governance cord, a large portion of the Africans express increasing worries about the intense ideological polarisation that threatens national, regional and continental peace unity and the poor progress in improving the living standards of the people. The lack of a consensual spirit and the absence of real channels for fruitful and open dialogue between political opponents deepen tensions and discords, pushing each country in particular and the continent in general to an endless series of violence, which will inevitably have disastrous results. Africans are fed up with sterile political debates and unfulfilled promises.

Now is time for concrete, effective and efficient actions. Actions requiring that political *'freedom and bread'* go together. Economic reforms must go hand in hand with political transitions and must benefit all segments of society and have buy-in from everyone. What the people want is 'seeking the bread kingdom' before any other thing else. If the OUA operated on the slogan of *'political freedom first'; the AU should operate on 'seeking and placing bread on the table for all'* first approach. Fifty years after, it is not wise to continue harping only on political reform with serious structural economic changes. In other words, it is even dangerous to continue on political reforms before supplying citizens' basic needs. Only when those needs are met could people make responsible political decisions. Necessary economic reforms must be accompanied by development of a political system of checks and balances, otherwise abuses by key economic actors would go unchecked, permitting impunity as the rule.

It is time for leaders and politicians to advance beyond their ideological affiliations, ethnic, religious and partisan loyalties and to exhibit a greater sense of patriotism. It is sad that fifty years after the wind of change blowing across the continent, Africa is still struggling with poverty, underdevelopment, free and fair elections, ethnic conflicts, abject poverty and wars and name the rest. Seeking the political kingdom has converted into seeking wealth and good life for a select few. The promise of and expectation of quality livelihood remains nothing but illusions. Yet to the amazement of all, some of the leaders are still preaching to the top of their voices the promise of sweet words, heaven on earth as if Africans are still in an era of dark ages where they do not see that they are being deceived and lied to.

Collective bargaining, inclusion and shared-prosperity are not a popular motto in Africa. Yet no nation progresses without adhering to the virtues of these concepts. Adhering to the vices of poor governance highlights the reality that there are no solutions to give hope to the **people.** Africa now and beyond 2017 should address burning political, economic and social issues, setting out clear strategies for an equitable and sustainable development. But most importantly to ensure a healthy democratic atmosphere for coming generations to continue a better state construct. Fifty years after independence Africa is acting and allowing itself to be re-colonised. To a large extent, this explains the penetrating impact of colonial administration in the psychic of African intelligentsia. And why the African post-colonial state came to be recognised as a member of the international community but with a difference - not as equal partners but as a subordinate member. Africa's weaknesses are glaring and, contradictions inherent in the colonial state project gained more momentum than the African unity construct.

These developments leave room for the exploitation of region by both external and internal forces. The question and the most challenging obstacle is how to reinforce Africa's capacity to stand up to the challenges of the new millennium? How can the African people attain their destiny and conquer war, poverty, corruption, hunger and diseases before 2017? How can African countries ensure that they do not miss the right turning point? Who are the main actors in the transformation processes? To what extent are the grass-roots actively engaged in the process of constructing a United and Integrated Continent (UIC)? To what extent has the Millennium Development Goals been realised? Are there potentials for the continent to recover from the devastating economic development of the 1980s? As things stand, the prospects are good, and with good governance optimism and extra positive input efforts things can only be better as Africa remains the fastest economic growing continent.

The challenge is creating a new brand of leadership, education system and civil society well-articulated and equipped with, national, continental and global issues. Education is the key to understanding and solving the problems and challenges facing the continent. The founding fathers did their very best given the situation at the time. Swaniker (2011:4) opine: "there was a problem as a lot of the leaders we had at independence found themselves in a very difficult situation in terms of the efforts of colonialism. When Ghana got its independence in 1957 and other nations soon after, across Africa there were 19,000 university graduates if you exclude South Africa, and those, 15,000 came from two countries, Ghana and Nigeria. In the Democratic Republic of Congo, for example, there were only 19 university graduates. Think of a nation and you need to form a cabinet. You must select a minister of finance, education, health etc., yet they themselves had not been properly educated. Also the leaders we have had were the remnants of the liberation movement and the skills you require to liberate a country are not necessarily the same as the ones you need to govern a country; And unfortunately in many cases they were more concerned with holding on to power and acquiring resources for themselves and that is where Africa stumbled in the post-independence era."

The Triple Helix – Gospel According to the West

The gospel according to West (Eurocentric) is tied within the framework of three dynamics call it the triple helix seen as "process, drivers and parameters" (PDP) as depicted in the Box 1.

The gospel according to the West can only be counteracted through a progressive yet aggressive Afro-centric ideological approach and taking into consideration the reality of the forces and impact of globalisation. Three factors are the determinant of the gospel according to the West, namely: (i) Globalisation: (ii) Regulation of modernity; and (iii) Dynamics of humiliation. Thus globalisation, modernity and humiliation (GMH) places Africa at the cross-roads of development or decay. It is not a lost battle but requires vigilance, determination and resolute political will to overcome existing deficiencies. It requires visionary leadership, responsive civil society with a strong focus on putting the welfare of people topmost on the development agenda; to significantly address the postcolonial era pattern of development that bypassed popular participation but revolved around (a) the dictatorship and centralisation of development which was prevalent between 1960 and 1980; (b) The criminalisation of popular participation in development which occurred under the structural adjustment programmes, 1980s-2000s; and (c) the reengagement and struggle for popular participation in development , 2000-to-date.

Box 1. Processes, Drivers and Parameters

Process	Drivers	Parameters
Globalisation	**The Pursuit of** - Power - Prestige - Profit	**Frames of Globalisation** **Imperial impulse** **Logic of the market** **Cosmopolitan Condition**
The Regulation Of Codes of modernity **Regulation of Modernity**	- Social Competition - Treatment of the vulnerable - Access to social benefits	**Honour Code** Human rights code Mix of codes
====➔ **Dynamics of - Humiliation**	The imposition of - Conquest - Escape - Fear cycles - Relegation - Exclusion	Modes of response to humiliation: Acceptance ==➔ Victimisation cycles Rejection ===➔ Revenge cycles

Source: Dennis Smith (2006). Globalisation: The Hidden Agenda, Polity Press, p.10

The Sustainable Development Goals ISDGs) provides the platform for the global community to take over and continue the results of the Millennium Development Goals (MDGs) so that we have a sustainable world environment. We need to learn from the shortcomings of the MDGS and move forward. CPOVID 19 pandemic challenges us to seek a new more cooperative approach to facing the huge problems the pandemic poses to the entire world. We have to face the realities and strategically organise ourselves to finding a common agreeable solution. Given the fragility of African countries, the only out is a forge a harmonious agenda to ensure we develop the much-needed political will for democratic governance as the uniting common platform that for facing the challenges confronting the continent.

The gospel according to the West is the highest stage of scientific imperialism expressed under neo-colonialism and globalisation as the hidden agendas. It is within the hegemonic right of the West for Africa to remain a dependent entity under the stewardship of the developed economies. The so called granting of independence to these former dependencies has not changed the situation. Globalisation only adds to the woes of the continent because of their technological under-development. But globalisation makes victims as well as victors. Africa is the victim of imperial, colonial and capitalist impulses.

As such, and perpetuating the Euro-centric approach makes the continent to lord their assets and sense of direction and capacity to uphold the virtues of the struggle for self-determination. The gospel accord to the West backed by globalisation as a hidden agenda gives added advantage to the dynamics of globalisation as the pursuit of power, prestige and profit in order to enhance and harness all available inputs that ensure the survival factors. The reality is that globalisation makes victims as well as victors. People or nations get wounded. These include victims of the imperial impulse.

The Triple Helix

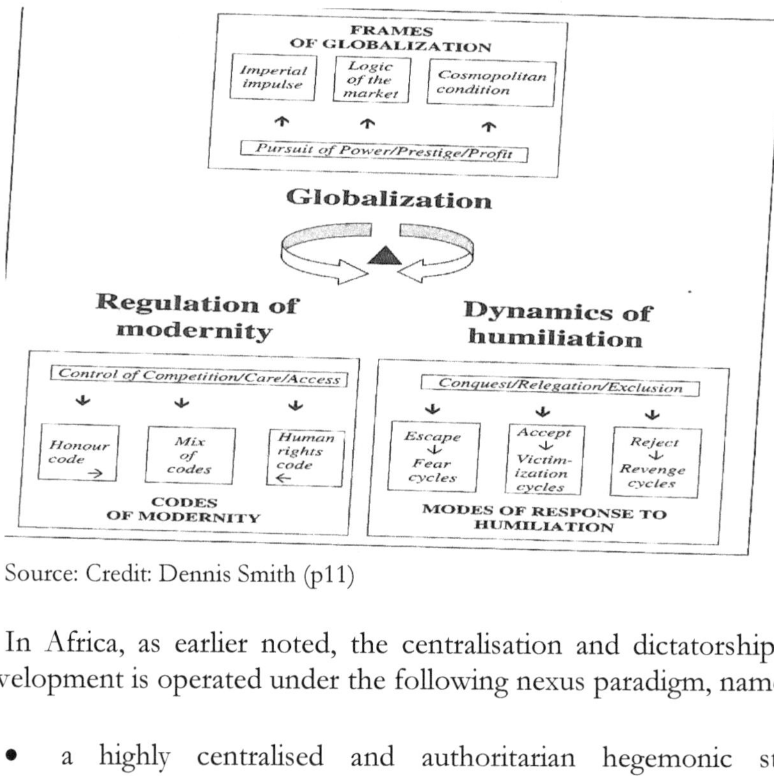

Source: Credit: Dennis Smith (p11)

In Africa, as earlier noted, the centralisation and dictatorship of development is operated under the following nexus paradigm, namely:

- a highly centralised and authoritarian hegemonic state construct;
- the emergence of monolithic party politics - competitive party politics was replaced a single no party system;
- strong reliance on a centralised or unified bureaucratic /administrative structures exclusively accountable to the head of state or centralised administration, in defining, organising and executing the

production of public goods and services along specific determined lines and patterns;

- no legitimate, significant role allowed for local authorities despite the mammoth local governments created in the postcolonial era throughout the continent particularly in English-speaking colonies;
- executive authority extremely maximised at the expense of other branches of government and society – legislative, judiciary, civil society organisations, and the media etc;
- political parties and organisation totally silenced or criminalised;
- national budget or wealth of society used as a personal budget of the head of state (thereby creating what at best could be envisioned as the dictatorship of development without a human face as a Eurocentric conspiratorial and ideologically programmed agenda by the political leadership to remain in power or implement the Eurocentric vision);
- some factors engendering the centralised dictatorial governance system included the fall-out of the cold war politics, and as such, accountability was shelved to the background and politics focused on serving as political proxies to the two ideological power blocs;
- thus, the fragility of African states impeded or made the task of national unity and integration an overriding political objective for political leadership;
- interesting enough, the dominant political and intellectual discourse has tended to support centralised hegemonic authoritarian governance system Cameroon for example; but the coming into being of the Africa Union opened a new perspective for participation and progress development – strengthening the Afrocentric agenda. seen within the context of new continental initiatives like – the New Partnership for Africa's Development (NEPAD). African Charter on Democracy, Elections and Governance; The African Charter on the Values and the Principles of the Public Service and Administration; The African Peer Review Mechanism (APRM); the African Charter on Human and Peoples Rights among others convention engineered a new developmental atmosphere for the continent.

Africa has been destroyed and its future ruined, through the logic of the market forces and the hegemony of political domination. The quest for modernity and the destruction of its indigenous cultural heritage and value belief systems makes Africa a vulnerable target for destruction. Ethnic clientelism, political boot licking by sycophants shapes outcomes as various voting, public goods investment and welfare distribution. Clientelism is an institution, however, for the ruling elites it makes sense as politicians remain in power by using it; clients receive benefits by acceding to it even if those benefits may be societal suboptimal which gives added advantage for pursuance and flourishing of the Eurocentric agenda and so goes the cycle of humiliation. With humiliation follows siege and destruction. A new resurrection is needed best put by Amara Essy (former interim chair of the AU Commission, 2002) in these words: "never again wills another mind than the African mind defines Africa. Never again will Africa's children accept slavery, racism or any form of oppression. Never again will non-Africans define Africa".

Defining the new Africa implies economic growth and development and increased employment with improved welfare for citizens; reduction in poverty and inequality; diversification of productive activities, enhancement of international competitiveness and increased exports; greater trade, integration among African countries to facilitate the free movement of goods, services, capital and peoples across national borders. Only by understanding the dynamics of great power politics can the cycle of humiliation be addressed.

The Afrocentric agenda provides such a framework. Three types of humiliation can be distinguished here, namely: (a) conquest humiliation; (b) regulation humiliation; and (c) exclusion humiliation with three possible responses; escape, acceptance and rejection. With the Afrocentric agenda, Africa can totally reject and escape from the Eurocentric agenda. Building the structural framework and good governance architecture for African unity becomes imperative.

The political framework of African unity should be now receiving a common consensus. Nkrumah (1963) averred this issue eloquently with these words: 'We in Africa who are pressing now for unity are deeply conscious of the volatility of our purpose. We need the strength of our combined numbers and resources to protect ourselves from the very positive dangers of return colonialism in disguised forms. We need it to combat the entrenched forces dividing our continent and still holding back millions of our brothers. We need it to secure total African liberation. Kwesi Kwaa Prah (2004:15) states:

> At the beginning of the 21st Century, the literate culture of Africa remains arrested in a colonial time-trap, in which production and reproduction of knowledge, the media and technological culture which goes with these features are held captive by creative sources located outside Africa; this is a recipe for cultural atrophy and death. For those of us whose literacy is imprisoned in a single European language, our source material is limited to that specific literature either as original texts translations from other languages. Our familiarity with ideas tends to

follow what is written in the language we know. Most of this is not written with Africans as audience.

We need it to carry forward the construction of a socio-economic system that will support the great mass of our steadily rising population at all levels of life which compares with those in most developed countries. *The AU Agenda 2063 – Building the Africa We Want* – echoes the same message. Here Smith defines what globalisation is and its humiliation impact on the continent. Africa is being humiliated because she is not an inherent part of the globalisation bandwagon. In another context, globalisation is the highest stage of scientific imperialism, especially as African countries are scientifically and technologically still underdeveloped and cannot harvest properly from the process like the technologically developed polities. Africa should be charting a new path forward especially in the domain of human capital development and infrastructural development. Africa should build its capability and capacity in this domain, particularly as Africa continues to struggle with economic, political, and social upheavals related to its status as an the most underdeveloped region of the world.

Africa's vast natural resources mean nothing if added values are not given to them. It is high time we question past approaches, target solutions, and promote new thinking on the continent's transformation which must be sustainable as well as ensue that it brings maximum benefits to its people. It means African scholars and colleagues the world over must disrupts old knowledge pathways and builds new ones to a better Africa and the world. Only Africans can take the bull by the horn and dislodge the entrenched notion of 'centre-periphery' relationship. Research has to be intensified. Situating research within and between African countries must be seen in a wider African context of collaboration with research institutions. Another important pillar should emphasis a proactive outreach strategy to the media and constituencies. Enhancing the visibility of research institutes and their outputs to wider public demands that it develops a very proactive media and outreach strategy. Research results must be package in a manner that it attracts the private productive sectors.

There has to be cluster or framework to integrate perspectives of different disciplines and to take a broad view on globalisation processes and questions related to national, regional and international trade integration and poverty eradication. Trade integration should evolve on the basis of win-win for the stakeholders and not the current structure of a 'win' for the powerful, technologically developed polities.

More financial resource allocated, and cross-cutting research activities stimulated within and between the various centres of learning especially on issues that have tremendous impact on the everyday realities in the continent – abject poverty, injustice and inequality. The governments must open windows to fascinating, facilitating and innovating research without which the region cannot benefit from globalisation. Africa must get into the scientific and technological age and be entrepreneurial. It has to get into the age of a private sector been assertive and a free press playing a central role in articulating an independent and authentic African developmental agenda.

The continent was misled in the 1970s and 1980s giving birth to an aborted well comprehensive, articulate development plan the first of its kind – *The Lagos Plan of Action* (LPA) of the 1980s. It should not allow the AU 2063 Agenda to fall victim in the same manner as the LPA. The invasion of the continent with a new giant like China should be well scrutinised. It could be a new form of colonialism that could lead to Africa being defined and exploited in terms of negativity – the absence of rights, The aim of development policy should be the expansion and entrenchment of people's involvement in a monetary economy and to increase economic growth, formalisation is probably a necessary and justified step. Policies that structurally reduces the qualitative and quantitative state of poverty, inequality and injustice must be strongly promoted to secure a better and sustainable quality of livelihood of the overwhelmingly population. Poor infrastructure and inadequate human training hampers access to larger markets. Therefore, the state, private sector and civil society must marshal a common concerted strategic approach for the sustainable transformation of the continent in this aged of a globally based-knowledge economy.

Given the rapid technological changes of the past couple of decades, Africa is now the global agenda attract the attention of traditional western powers as well as the leadership of emerging powers such as Brazil, China, Malaysia and South Korea. The pervasive "Afro-pessimism" of the 1980s and 1990s with the Economist magazine aptly charactering the region "*Hopeless Africa*" has given way to and image of Africa that is socially and economically vibrant and politically more open, with and assertive civil society, and entrepreneurial indigenous private sector and an articulating and independent and authentic development agenda, for example AU Agenda 2063. To take advantage of globalisation we need to intensify and improve on issues advanced by the Sustainable Development Goals (SDGs), The AU Agenda 2063, and the progressive National Development Plans (NDPs) of African countries.

Box 2: What are Globalisation and Humiliation?

Globalisation	Humiliation Impact
Globalisation is the large-scale, long-term when; making links between groups outrageous displacement or exclusion become increasingly dense This displacement and / or extensive, complex and dynamic; gain advantage and exclusion. Impose order within those relationships	Humiliation occurs when people process of: and are subjected to the Expansion of societies undergoing an an outrageous displacement or exclusion links that tend to become increasingly dense, exclusion from struggling. to gain advantage, avoid costs. Impose order within those relationships; and from a position they feel is rightfully 'their own within a group, network or hierarchy which they feel they rightfully 'belong' and; coming to terms with the fact that influence and initiative this process is perceived by those who suffer it as a painful and within social networks and hierarchies has tended, over and destructive attack on their identity and interests which they cannot prevent or ignore. The long term, is to shift upwards towards the global-regional and global levels.

Source: Forje, 2018 and compiled from Smith (2006:21)

Secondly, improve on the democratic governance nexus, While the continent can be said to have achieved some successes in the rule-based political system, much is still to be done to ensure economic governance, and decentralising authority to local structures, by putting an end to the existing centralized authoritarian hegemonic governance system. The good governance democratic train must be accelerated. For now, even though with an impressive progress, the democratization agenda remains unfinished in a handful of African countries. Pockets of centralised authoritarian hegemonic regimes are still waxing strong across the continent. Therefore, the continent is challenged to either unite or perish under the weight of globalisation. Mammo Muchie et al (2015) assert:

> "Understanding how Africa will manage to navigate the tumultuous waters of globalization as Africa has just recently emerged out of the horrors of slavery, colonialism, apartheid, neo-colonialism and genocide, and is still wrestling with unceasing conflicts, popular unrest, neo-imperialism, coloniality and mushrooming insurgency."

Thirdly, African countries have to strengthen and foster the New Partnership for African Development (NEPAD) Agenda and ensure that these governments improve on their governance structure, intensify inter-African trade and regional cooperation; diversify its economy (see Cheru, 2007:5). While Africa's tragic pitfalls dates to the transatlantic slave trade and colonialism, the people have to move away from the 'blame theory game' associated with dependency school to fashion out a new development path. It is a question of focusing on 'the reality theory' anchored within the framework of a new political kingdom which must be married with a new orientation on economic development. Improving the "State of the Continent" (Fobanjong 2018) is imperative. It is necessary to construct and usher a solid form of "*Inclusive Development in Africa*" (Gumede 2018).

To ensure effective transformation in Africa the changing imperatives of international development, the reform of international finance institutions and the growth-development nexus should be take off as well as varied implications for Africa emanating from global economic crises are critical is Africa is to make any serious headway in the global arena. One can only but agrees with Moyo (2014) that "*African states should invest time, energy and resources to develop and implement policies which takes into consideration African realities.*" In solving the 'globalisation' saga, Africa must combine with an imagination with down-to-earth political economy and to put in correct perspectives the continents attempts at growth and development since the independence era, attempts at recovery from a string of serious socio-political set-backs; while also advocating and ensuring the role of universities as essential ingredients in the drive to sustained development (Mkandawire 2015). There should be an inter-locking interface between the State, Private Sector, Civil society and the University / Research Institutes in accelerating the transformation process of the continent. The interface will enhance value being given to the natural resources abundance which presently, is not properly used to improve the quality livelihood of the people. To benefit from the fallouts of 'globalisation' the continent must get rid of its dependency syndrome (Mhango 2017).

Apparently, the humiliation is backed by a revenge act. After humiliating Africans from constructing a strong and powerful OAU as the first towards a Union Government for Africa, the West went ahead on the revenge spree with NATO military arsenal destroying Tripoli and assassinating Col. Ghaddafi perhaps the last strong advocate for a union government. The United Nations Security Council resolution 1973 was a deliberate attack, humiliation and revenge politics of West against Africa. It took Africa fifty years to get where it is; but a couple of minutes to reverse all the good things it had achieved so far. The West makes itself the one and only legitimate engine for humbling others in the world, imposing punishment on those they do not like or who broke their gospel or of displeasing the West.

Violating the gospel of the West entails (i) the capacity to humiliate others by inflicting damage on them, either disabling or destroying them; (ii) the capacity to humiliate others by making them bow down in subservience; and (iii) the capacity to defend them against being humiliated by others. Looking at the first scenario, the West humiliated Africa when they did everything possible to prevent the establishment of a strong African organisation by dividing the Casablanca, Monrovia and Brazzaville groups; fanning Nyerere against Nkrumah. Turning to the second point, we see how the west pressurised Malawi not to host the AU Summit because of the President of Sudan or in cases of threatening to withdraw financial assistance from countries not supporting homosexuality, Uganda and other countries were targets. If the West accepts homosexuality as their pattern of lifestyle it does not mean African countries should be the same. Because of the dependency factor, African countries accept Western dictates which is humiliating.

The West deplores three forms of humiliation, namely: (a) *conquest where the conquered party* (Africa) is forced into subordination. A hierarchy is formed with the conqueror on top of the mountain; (b) *relegation where an individual*, group, institution or society is forced into a lower position within an existing hierarchy against their will and in a way that conflict with their own perception of their social identity and interests. A good example here is the English Cameroon within the Republic of Cameroon dominated by French speaking Cameroonians (Forje 1981; Sobseh 2011; Ntumazah 2001; Ndiva 1980; Tumi 2006; Awasom 2011; Ngunjoh 2013; Wakai 2009). Ngunjoh asserts: "... *with these acts of mistrust, there was no doubt that the assimilation, demolition and marginalisation of Cameroonians West of the Mungo had been concluded. The constitution of Cameroon is tailored to ridicule the Anglophones who have been made captives in their own country.*" Relegation should be perceived as 'unacceptable' although in some cases the 'victims' may eventually find themselves accepting, or at least, acquiescing, in it. Anglophone Cameroonians have acquiesced to their fate in the Republic of Cameroon. African has accepted the relegation syndrome; and (c) *the exclusion phenomena*, as a continent at the receiving end are forcefully excluded or ejected from membership within the specific groups, hierarchies or networks which they believed they have a right to belong (Smith, 2006:40-42). The African Union was not listened to by West when NATO undertook the destruction of Libya and the assassination of Colonel Ghaddafi.

But African leaders due to articulate self-interests misplaced their role of defending the interest of the continent and gun instead for state sovereignty. The Centre for Conflict Resolution (2013:24-25) Cape Town South Africa, on the Libyan saga states and lengthily reproduced here:

> "In a manner reminiscent of its previous term, South Africa's apparently shifting positions on the crises in Cote d'Ivoire and Libya in the first of its second term – 2011 – sparked controversy, and were

> perceived by critics to be undermining Tshwane's historical role since 1994 as a leading defender of human rights. In Cote d'Ivoire, South Africa initially held out against recognising the electoral victory of the challenger, Alassane Ouattara, over the incumbent president, Laurent Gbagbo, before eventually recognising Ouattara as president in March 2011, when the Security Council mandated the UN mission to use 'all necessary means' to protect civilians. In March 2011, Tshwane also voted in favour of Security Council Resolution 1973, which established a no-fly zone over Libya and effectively authorised a military intervention by NATO in the country. Though fellow African Council members, Nigeria and Gabon, also voted for the resolution, South Africa faced criticism for having provided diplomatic support to Western powers for the action, which has not supported by the AU as a whole, particularly when NATO also interpreted the Council's mandate expansively to pursue a policy of 'regime change' in Libya. Tshwane responded to this criticism by insisting that it had supported resolution 1973 in good faith and in keeping with its commitment to the protection of human rights, and noted that the AU's failure to articulate a clear position, and to communicate this position in a timely manner to African permanent missions at the UN, had left the African members of the Council with a difficult decision. Furthermore, according to this view, when NATO countries went beyond the mandate of the resolution to carry out a policy of 'regime change', South Africa strongly criticised the shift and supported the AU position in favour of a peaceful and negotiated solution to the crisis. More generally, South African diplomats have sought to highlight the often-complex nature of the cases that come before the Security Council, and to emphasise the need for a balance between human rights ideals and pragmatic concerns pointing to the decisive influence that national interests continue to play in international fora like the UN."

Therefore, a common Africa positions on conflicts afflicting the continent are essential to avoid this kind of humiliation and undermining and to achieve a strong and influential African voice on the Council, or in any international fora, not least because its absence enables the P-5 to exploit the opportunity to advance competing interests. For example, the AU did not have a clear position on Libya in 2011, but the Arab League did, and the US, France, and Britain were able to rely on the latter as evidence of regional support to push their 'regime change' agenda forward in the country. In this context, the AU must also more clearly articulate and communicate its position to both the African delegations in New York, as well as the mass media. Furthermore, South Africa's experience on the Security Council between 2011 and 2012 demonstrates that African countries have to leverage a range of often fluctuating partners and groups at the UN on different issues in order to strengthen their influence within the Council. Fr example, while South Africa and France were on opposite sides of the debates on Libya and Syria, the two countries have worked together on addressing the situations in Mali and the broader Sahel, where their interest have coincided. Even in configuration such as the IBSA and BRICS groupings, homogeneity is sometimes lacking. For example, South Africa voted for Security Council Resolution 1973 in 2011, while its IBSA partners abstained. This tells of something – strong and visionary leadership is required if the AU has to make its presence felt.

It goes without saying that notions of a common voice and shared interest are key test of the degree of integration in any political union. The foundation of the OAU in 1963 represented a compromise between a Pan-African ideology that sought the rapid political unification of the continent as the best means to liberate Africans (a view most eloquently expressed by Ghana's Kwame Nkrumah), and a more pragmatic approach adopted by the majority of African governments that aimed to integrate the continent through the strengthening of sub-regional bodies responsible for creating common policies and shared institutions for the OAU's member states (Centre for Conflict Resolution 2012:28). Strong leadership is forged by effective responses to important contemporary issues. NEPAD's drive to promote Africa's socio-economic development and to eradicate poverty, and the continent's continued marginalisation, represent major causes around which continental leaders can campaign and frame global debates. However, the preponderance of the voices of the more powerful African states at different multilateral fora on these and related issues can sometimes fragment African voices than provide continental leadership. The Libya case is a good example of poor leadership, poor means of communication and enhancing state sovereignty impact negatively on the future of the continent.

The only way out or potential responses to the challenges of humiliation are; (i) escape; (ii) rejection: and (iii) acceptance. The first potential response is to escape from the humiliating situation. An Afro-centric approach provides such escape route. However, the 'escape route' is bounded with the 'fear cycle'. Another avenue is that of 'rejection' which may take either a 'passive' of active resistance approach. African leaders did not reject the secretly imposed union on them in 1963. The last possible means is that of 'acceptance'. To a large extent, Africans have embraced the 'acceptance' code. Without a radical change in perception and action, the next fifty years will be guided by the humiliation code with the acceptance factor playing a bigger role.

The gospel according to the West show more spectacular but developmentally inconsequential factional squabbles, personality conflict, or other effervescent phenomena of the passing political parade.

Based on long - rather than short-term phenomena, reflective of historically more consequential events and relationships, the future if Africa will be rendered socially more meaningful, diagnostically more rewarding, and intellectually more satisfying to all concerned especially the people of the continent if they embark on people-focused Afro-centric approach as the guiding star in addressing their problems and in exerting the continent within the realm of the community of nations. Then and only then, will Africa be crowned with sustainable future and its resources used to improve the living standards of its population. There is no other way. To tether it to the already calcifying invading forces and tenets of the new colonisers – the Chinese thought and hidden strategy or to be mummified remnants of the declining Western hegemonic doctrine would be no improvement at all. The future of Africa is hoped, though limited in scope will enhance our efforts and its reliability but broad enough to be representative of the ideals most Africans long for, and that together will other works will serve Africans and friends of Africa in articulating and supporting a progressive and more encompassing quest for a better understanding and constructive development of the continent as it really is and should be. An Afro-centric alternative is the only way forward for a strong and united continent that can stand the test of time even in this age of 'globalisation' as the highest stage of scientific imperialism.

An Afro-centric Code as a countervailing strategic force should entrench and solidify the sovereignty and independence of the continent reinstating the fundamental human rights of the people; the right to be empowered as human-beings not as second class citizens – the right of African to be enabled to develop as a fully rounded human-beings participating creatively in as many aspects of a civilised society as they can or wish to the right of self-determination. The innate search for democratic governance should occupy. The point has been made that the legal-constitutional structure under which African countries were granted independence was obsolete before the ink dried on the relevant documents. This chapter shows why political thought and development on and about Africa went astray and will continue to do so unless and until radical changes occur in the mindset of African leaders and the people embrace progressive Afro-centric approach to addressing the throes of legal, administrative, political party structures and systems that bedevilled the continent and were already doomed at birth back in the 1960s.

Africa has been subjected to the following historical phases which has influenced or uprooted by the processes of socio-political transformation, left the continent stranded between the old and the emerging new. Seen within this context, Africa feels humiliated and liberated at the same time; humiliated by the loss of its cultural heritage and loss of sovereignty and sense of identity and purpose; liberated by the weakening of constraints on their behaviour and creating a new sense of awakening – Renaissance Africa. The policy strategic articulation should be seen in light of the following phases and valuable lessons drawn to craft a new brave continent.

- **European Imperialism:** A period that entrenched the continent into slavery, colonial rule and exploitation of the rich cultural, human and natural resources of the continent up to the end of the Second World War;
- **Global Imperialism:** Events during the post-European imperialism or after the Second World War that gave birth to the Cold War Confrontation between East and West or between the 'Capitalist Bloc' and 'the communist Bloc; and the American-led 'free World' against each other with Africa paying the price. By the 1990s only the American Empire remained standing although beset by deep internal conflict, especially between Europe and the United States;
- **Global Multi-polarity or Post-Communist Collapse Era**: The uni-polar world dominated by the United States but such power hegemony reaching its peck and starting the descent. The start of 21st century saw the beginning of a new structure – the rise and increasing independence of the European Union, the rise of China, the revival of Japan, the gradual resurgence of Russia, the emergence of India, Brazil and other sending a new signal to American weariness with distaste, for, its present role as a 'global monarch.
- **An Emerging Post-Independent Africa:** The collapse of the Communist bloc injected a new dynamism in Africa as the continent gradually graduated from its weak organisation the African Unity (OAU) which was Euro-centric conceived into the birth of the Africa Union (AU) or an Afro-centric inclination. A period giving birth to a new feeling – moving away from the 'slave morality or believe attitude' into a '*Renaissance Spirit*' or sense of belonging – The *Africanness of Africans*. The Afro-centric cradle seriously strengthening the 'strength and sovereignty of African states.

Africa is at the crossroads of change as it gradually drifts towards 2017 envisaged as the period of establishing a union Government of Africa (UGA). As Africa's grip on the world events strengthens, as it takes seriously the reconstruction of the declining status of the continent in global politics, the resurgent of the continent requires new structures of power distribution or at least the surrender of some degree of sovereignty to a union government, it sends new messages of a rising continent to the rest of the world. Africa has only possible best option – moving away from the politics of exclusion, the frustrated high-school graduate, the frightened poor, the overzealous affluent few elites to a new era of 'power to the people with equally opportunities to all, benefit-sharing and quality livelihood of the people. The ruling elites should reserve their greedy attitude, contribute to a new look with the dynamic interaction between honour and human rights, the two codes of modernity. Valuable lessons should be drawn from the words of Albert Einstein:

> A human being is a part of the whole, called by us 'universe', a part limited in time and Space. He experiences himself, his thoughts and feelings as something separated from the rest – a kind of optical delusion of his consciousness. The delusion is a kind of prison for us, restricting us to our personal desires and to affection for a few persons nearest to us. Our task must be to free ourselves from this prison by widening our circle of compassion to embrace all living creatures and the whole of nature in its beauty.

The challenge is for Africans, now more than ever before, should let reason and rationality triumph over sentiments, the 'blame theory' and parochial attitudes. Perhaps now more than yesterday should see the emergence of a new mind construct behaviour and attitude. Africans need to begin to ask themselves what they have personally done to promote and hasten the advent of a more prosperous, a more harmonious and united continent. The task may appear daunting yet there seems no viable alternative for Africans but to embrace the Afro-centric orientation and remain relentless in their efforts of creating a new brave continent. The price of success is perseverance and above all vigilance and unity. Can African countries monster these values to better direct their development struggles so that the citizens harvest the best of the globalisation saga?

Apparently, the process of globalisation specialisation has greatly radicalised the already existing process of structural differentiation, witnessed since the beginning of the industrial revolution in the 18th century. The entire process has processed through the following stages:

(i) increasing degree of interdependence; (ii) degree of specialisation which has become institutionalised; (iii) complexities arising from interdependencies; (iv) as a result of this interdependency, exchange relationships exist; and (v) flows come together in specific nodes. How does Africa fit into these changes? How does Africa intend to use the process-change to ensure that her interests are sustained? Has Africa been able to define its interests? Is Africa prepared to find out its interest and to work towards creating a new future in light of the rapidly changing global context? These and many other questions need answers that drive the continent forward.

We cannot deny the fact that Africa is the worst hit by the deepening crisis of survival under the orgy of globalisation and underdevelopment. Underdevelopment, exclusion, and globalisation is splintering many societies and doing little to eradicate poverty and to create a level playing field for all societies. The African Union and institutions like NEPAD should emerge as major policy breakthroughs in search for Africa's development. The gross absence of an independent African Think Tank places the continent in a bad shape of independently articulating policies that should drive forward the transformation of the continent. This makes African governments to be heavily reliant on the Bretton Woods Financial Conglomerates for policy formulation. As a result, the continent faces the most daunting challenges of development among all parts of the world. It continues to witness a scourge of violent conflicts leading to the death of countless civilians, not only as direct result of conflict itself but also from the consequence of conflict.

But Africa has to move forward by reclaiming lost grounds, preventing conflicts, taking the responsibility to care for and protect Africa, and importantly ensuring that peace and unity reigns throughout the region. Understanding and tackling the root causes of conflict is a long-term process requiring the commitment of leadership as well as citizens at the national, regional and global levels. The various actors should from their different perspectives work in unionism for the well-being of all citizens. It requires pulling together all available resources – human and natural; building the human intellect of the people to give added value to their natural resources and creating a level playing ground for the people.

We have waited too long and things have gone out of hand. It is time to take the initiative and be the masters of our own development for the good of the people. The time for creative thinking and concrete action is now. Everyone should be on board, participate and be listen too. It is the people's project and a process that should not be hijack by anyone. This is the only way of creating a *"sense of belonging"* and of strengthening patriotism to and allegiance to mother country and continent. We have to become Afrocentric without succumbing to flimsy myth-creation and distortion of facts. It is time the people take back their development nexus and ensure it travels on the right path and vision.

References

Achebe Chinua (1979). A Man of the People. Heinemann Books, London

Adebanwi Wale (2005). Techno-Politics and The Production of Knowledge: Democratic Activism and The Nigeria Exile, Occasional Paper Series, Vol. 10. No.1, African Association of Political Science (AAPS), Pretoria, South Africa,

Adebajo Adekeye (2016)" Prophets of Pan-Africanism" in Daniel H. Levine and Dawn Nager (eds.) (2016) Region-Building in Africa: Political and Economic Challenges, Palgrave Macmillan, New York, pp144-146

Adebajo Adekeye (2016)." Pan-Africanism and The African Diaspora" in The African Union: Regional and Global Challenges, Policy Research Seminar Report, Centre for Conflict Resolution, August 2016, Cape Town, South Africa, pp8-11.

Ake Claude (1996). Democracy and Development in Africa, Brookings Institute, Washington DC, United States of America.

Akomolafe Femi (2011). "Kissing Him Today, Raining Bombs on Him Tomorrow," New Africa, May 2011, London, pp30-34

Anderson B. (1983). Imagined Communities. Verso Publishers, London

Awasom Fru Nicodemus (2011). "Towards Understanding the Anglophone-Francophone Conundrum in Post-colonial Cameroon and the Belasis (Nigeria) Addendum." In Abdalla Bujra (ed.) (2011). Political Culture, Governance and The State in Africa. DPMF, Nairobi – Kenya

Azumah Alembellah John (2001). The Legacy of Arab-Islam

Belafonte Harry (2011). My Song: A Memoir of Art, Race and Defiance. Canongate Publishers, Edinburgh & London

Cheru Fanta (2007) "Africa on the Agenda", Nordisk Afrikainstitutet – The Nordic African Institute, Annual Report 2007, Uppsala – Sweden

Comaroff, J. And Comaroff, J. (1999) Civil Society and the Political Imagination in Africa: Critical Perspectives. University of Chicago Press. Chicago and London,

Centre for Conflict Resolution (2013). Africa, South Africa, And The United Nations' Security Architecture. Cape Town, South Africa

Centre for Conflict Resolution (2012). The African Union at Ten: Problems, Progress, and Prospects. Cape Town, South Africa.

Chinweizu (1987). The West and The Rest of Us. PeroPress, Lagos, Nigeria

Conrad Joseph (1998). Heart of Darkness, Wordsworth, London

Davidson B. (1992). The Blackman's Burden: Africa and the Curse of the Nation State. James Curry, London

De Witte Ludo (2001). The Assassination of Patrice Lumumba

Dubois W.E.B. [ ] Of Our Spiritual Strivings, USA

Duodu Cameron (2011) "Patrice Lumumba from a Mere Man to a Lasting Symbol (2)," New African, May 2011, London pp78-83/

Ekeh P. (1975) Colonialism and the Two Publics in Africa: A Theoretical Statement" Comparative Studies in Society in Society and History, Vol.17, no.1, pp 91-112

Fanon Franz [1967] Black Skin, White Masks. New York

Fanon Frantz [1960] The Wretch of the Earth, New York

Fobanjong John (2018) State of the Continent. A Mid-Century Assessment of Political Performance in Africa. Spears Media Press, Cameroon

Forje W. John (1981). The One and Invisible Cameroon. Lund Political Studies No.35. Department of Political Science, University of Lund, Sweden

Gellner, E. (1983). Nations and Nationalism, Blackwell, UK.

Gumede Vusi (2018 Inclusive Development in Africa. Africa Institute of South Africa, Pretoria, South Africa

Hadland, A. and J. Rantao (1999). The Life and Times of Thabo Mbeki. Zebra Press, Rivonia,

Hochschild A. (1997). New Yorker 14 April 1997

Khawaja, Noor ul-Ain (2011). The Libyan Crisis and UNSC Resolution 1975: Authority, Legitimacy and. Prospects Pakistan Horizon. Pakistan Institute of International Affairs, pp7392

Kasasira, Risdel (2011). Uganda: Museveni, Zuma Dump Gaddafi. Allafrica.com. 16 September 2011

Kwesi Kwaa Prah (2004). Local Cultures, Local Memories and Local Meanings in the Era of Globalisation: African Studies Under the Searchlight. Keynote Address, Pan-African Anthropological

Association 12th Annual Conference, Accra, 2nd-6th August 2004, Ghana

Lagos Plan of Action (LPA). (! 980) Lagos Plan of Action for the Economic Development of Africa: 1980-2000. Addis Ababa – Ethiopia OAU 1981.

Lawrence James (2016). Empires in the Sun: The Struggle for The Mastery of Africa. Orion Books

Little Tom (2011) Beyond Mercenaries: Racism in North Africa (see also: Think africanpress, com [http://atlantablackstar.com/2014/06/02/10-facts-about-the-arabs-enslavement_of-black-people-not-taught-in-schools]

Maloka Eddy (ed.) (2001) A United States of Africa. Africa Institute of South Africa, Pretoria, South Africa.

Manga C. Fombad (2004)." The Dynamics of Record-Breaking Endemic Corruption and Political Opportunism in Cameroon" in Mbaku, J. M. And Takougang Joseph (eds.). The Leadership challenge in Africa – Cameroon Under Paul Biya, Africa World Press Inc. Trenton, NJ

Marable Manning [1980] From the Grassroots: Social and Political Essays Towards Afro-American Liberation, South End Press, Boston, MA

Massoni, Marco (2011). African Crisis: Libya, Morocco and Tunisia. Quarterly Africa 9 (1) Spring

Melber Henning (2016) The Rise of Africa's Middle Class. Zed Books, United Kingdom

Melber Henning (2017). "Lumumba, Hammarskjöld and The Cold War in the Congo", New African, No 568, January 2017, IC Publication, London, pp20-23

Melber Henning, David Wardrop & Susan Williams (2017). "Rewriting History, Rescuing The Truth", New African, No.568, January 2017, IC Publication, London, pp26-27

Mhango Nkuzi Nkazi (2017) Africa's Dependency Syndrome. Langaa RPCIG, Bamenda – Cameroon

Mkandawire Thandika (2015) Africa: Beyond Recovery. Sub-Saharan Publishers, Ghana

Moyo Theresa (ed.) (2014) Trade and Industrial Development in Africa. Rethinking Strategy and Policy, ODESRIA, Dakar, Senegal.

Muchie Mammo, Vusi Gumede, Phindile Lukhele-Olorunju and Hailemichael Teshome Demissie (eds.) (2015) Unite or Perish – Africa Fifty Years after the Founding of the OAU. Africa Institute of South Africa, Pretoria – South Africa.

Mukisa R.S. & B. Thompson (1995). "Prerequisites for Economic Integration in Africa: An Analysis of the Abuja Treaty", Africa Today, 4th Quarter, 1995.
Nabudere Wadada Dani (2001)" African Political Unity in Historical Perspective", in Eddy Maloka (ed.) A United States of Africa? Africa Institute of South Africa, Pretoria, pp29-40
Ndiva, Kofele-Kale (ed.) (1980) An African Experiment in Nation Building. The Bilingual Cameroon Republic Since Reunification. Westview Press, Colorado, USA
Ngunjoh Pa Tafoh (2013). "Cameroon Constitution is Tailored to Ridicule Anglophones" The Median Newspaper, No.094, Tuesday 22 October 2013, Yaoundé, p 1 &.5
Njogu Kimani and Adem Seifudein (eds.) (2017) Critical Perspectives on Culture and Globalisation. Twaweza Communications Kenya
Nkrumah Kwame (1963) Africa Must Unite: Heinemann Educational Books, London
Ntumazah, Ndi (2001). A Conversational Autobiography. Patron Publishing House, Bamenda – Cameroon
Odinga Oginga (1962) Not Yet Uhuru. Heinemann Educational Books London
Organisation of African Unity (OAU) (1991) Treaty Establishing the African Economic Community, Addis Ababa,
Organisation of Africa Unity (OAU) (1991). Treaty Establishing the African Economic Community, Addis Ababa.
Oliver R. (1991). The African Experience. Weidenfeld & Nicholson, London
Osaghe, E. (2006) Colonialism and Civil Society in Africa: The Perspective of Ekeh's Two Republics," Voluntas: International Journal of Voluntary and Non-profit Organisations, Vol.17, No.3, pp253-245
Pekenham, T. (1991). The Scramble for Africa. Abacus, London.
Robson P. (1985). "Regional Integration and the Crisis in the Sub-Saharan Africa", Journal of Modern African Studies, Vol.23, No.4 1985.
Segal Ronal (2002). Islam's Black Slaves: The Other Diaspora
Shepperson, George (1960). Independent Africa. Edinburgh University Press, Edinburgh
Smith Dennis (2006). Globalisation: The Hidden Agenda, Polity Press.
Sobseh Y. Emmanuel (2011) Rethinking Citizenship, Politics and Governance in Cameroon: Towards A Better Future, Bamenda – Cameroon

Soludo Charles Chukwuma (2012). "From Berlin to Brussels: Will Europe underdeveloped Africa Again?" New African, No.516, April 2012 AN IC Publication, London, pp10-17 pp

Sturman, Kathryn (2012). The African Union and The Arab Spring's: An Exception to New Principles or Return to Old Rule? Instituto per gli Studi di Politica Internazionale (ISPI), 108 (May).

The Economist, 20-26 May 2000, London

Thompson V. B. (1999). Africans of the Diaspora. Africa World Press, New York

Tumi, Christian Cardinal (2006). The Political regimes of Ahmadou Ahidjo and Paul Biya, and Christian Tumi, Priest. MACACOS, S.A. Printers, Douala, Cameroon

United Nations Economic Commission for Africa (UNECA) (1994, Policy Convergence for Regional Economic Cooperation and Integration: Implementation of the Treaty Establishing the African Economic Community", Addis Ababa, Uneca 1994)

United Nations Economic Commission for Africa (UNECA) 1995 "Implementation of the Abuja Treaty Establishing the African Economic Community: Progress Made and Prospects. Addis Ababa, Ethiopia.

Wakai Nyo (2009). Under The Broken Scale of Justice: The Law and My Times. Langaa Research & Publishing CIG, Mankon, Bamenda, Cameroon

Wambu Onyekachi (2013). "Deepening African Unity", New African, No.526 March 2013, London, p.98

Williams Susan (2016) Spies in the Congo, London

Williams Susan (2013). Who Killed Hammarskjöld? The UN, the Cold War and White Supremacy in Africa. The Hurst (Publishers, London

Wilson, H. S. (1994). African Decolonisation. Edward Arnold, London

Wilson, H. S. (1977). The Imperial Experience in Sub-Saharan Africa. University of Minnesota Press, Minnesota, USA.

Chapter Two

The Nexus of Science, Technology and Indigenous Knowledge Architecture

Introduction: The Perils of Neglect and Re-cooperating indigenous Knowledge

This chapter looks at the often-forgotten rich potentials of indigenous knowledge architecture and the role it can play in uplifting the continent. In addition, that role should be played in partnership with modern scientific and technological achievements for example, information and communication technologies (ICTs) have changed and revolutionaries the process of development the world over. In Africa, illiteracy backed by the forces of colonial rule helped deprived the people from documenting their indigenous knowledge for posterity. Africa's underdevelopment as a result of illiteracy and the perpetuation of oral knowledge not the written word makes knowledge to be distorted and undervalued as the year's role on.

Today Africa is chasing only its shadow of its indigenous knowledge; and even undermines the practices and pursuit of it in the transformation process. The social production of knowledge remains negative not impacting properly on the well-being of the people. The far-reaching consequences of these can be seen in the context of the level of prevailing knowledge not properly applied in the development of the continent. A concrete move towards the awakening of indigenous knowledge should be a drawing board of African leaders, first by intensifying the process of human capital development and second encouraging the idea of documentation of our cultural heritage and values.

Technology has emerged as a fundamental part of contemporary social formation. The circulation of knowledge through new technologies of information and communication – which are developing at exponential; proportion – and the mediation of relations of power by these technologies are consequently crucial in the total organisation of social relations. As these technologies spark off significant expansion, redefinition and reformation of old concepts and the mode and terrain of producing, mediating and contesting power and knowledge, it becomes increasingly possible to follow the logic on the inherent revolutionary potential of these new technologies and to seize and re-function them in the service of democratising polity (Adebanwi, 2005:5). The possibility of empowering people, promoting democracy and producing new and counter-knowledge towards achieving social change through technologies are clear, they, however, contain within them what could be described as a 'new dialectic of empowerment and powerlessness in social relations (Levi-Faur & Waarden. 2018: Slein, 2000:4). This ambivalent nature of the new technologies is, perhaps, responsible for a paradox: in spite of the fact that the literature of social theory, and specifically the literature of communications, is yet to focus comprehensively on how the Internet meshes with cultural transformation in the modern world, the realisation that communications technology is fundamental to contemporary social, economic and political life rather than incidental, continues to grow (Adebanwi, op cit.). Essentially, human agency or human activity has been altered in significant ways by the new technologies (Caldwell, 2000:4). Despite worldwide disparities in access to information technologies, everyone everywhere is being ratcheted into a participatory Internet-based culture (Choucri, 2000:253).

Development and survival increasingly depends on the art of self-effacement and self-censorship. African universities must become the bastion and centres of excellence of knowledge and protection of indigenous knowledge. Africa's indigenous knowledge is indicative of power in Africa's past; knowledge is power as exhibited by institutions of higher learning on the continent long before the penetrating impact of slavery, imperialism and colonial rule. Times have changed and today Africa is at the bottom ladder of the human capital development. Globalisation and the continent's unflinching love for everything western subjects the region into a perpetual state of dependency and exploitation. Globalisation undermines the articulation of indigenous knowledge and the dehumanisation of the African people. Awareness of the complexities of the African past should not derailed the continent from advancing new inroads of analysis, interpretation and the marriage of indigenous knowledge and modern science and technology. For too long, the continent has neglected its most useful sources of indigenous knowledge in accelerating its development construct. Now is the time to marry that piece of asset with modern science and technology for the viable transformation of the continent and to restore its place among the community of nations, as equal partners not servants in advancing the course of humanity.

Modern technological developments have had significant effects on power relations of states, on the concerns of governments in their domestic policies and their relations with each other, and on the means that are available for furthering – as well as damaging – the common interests of the people. The technological development that was most revolutionary and far reaching in its effect was the production and practical application of the atomic bomb which demonstrated the effectiveness of a new weapon of mass destruction and suggested possibilities not only of further developments for war purposes but also of a new and relatively unlimited source of energy for peaceful uses.

The success of the Soviet' Union in putting a human-being in orbit following the launching of the Sputnik in October 1957 led to the rapid development of technology for the exploration and use of the 'outer space' with the result that national governments found it desirable to seek agreement on such matters as the permissible uses of outer space, the acquiring sovereignty over celebrated bodies the possibility for damages resulting from outer space activities and the possibility of joint enterprises.

An aspect of outer-space technology that has been of special concern to governments has been the possibility it offers through the use of satellites greatly to expand the content speed of communications, and more particularly to extend that speed of communications, and more particularly to extend broadcasts across national lines, thus fracturing the tight control which many governments seek to maintain over what their people see or hear.

Only with relatively recent times have we come to recognise that as the result of our success in harnessing the forces of nature and applying modern technology to the production of goods to meet the ever-increasing demands of higher consumption standards, we are actually endangering our environmental and risking the very survival of the human race. Humankind's mastery of science and technology gives him/her unprecedented power, but his/her living world is threatened as at no time since his/her planetary home first gave him/her warmth and shelter.

Advances in science and technology are at the centre of the triangle of communication, development and globalisation (CDG). The success of modern technology in penetrating the secrets of the outer space, and sea and in making available for exploitation and use the resources above, on and below the seabed for increasing distances from the shore and even-greater depths, has made it a matter of pressing urgency to determine the extent of national control and the nature of the regime under which resources beyond national control are to be exploited.

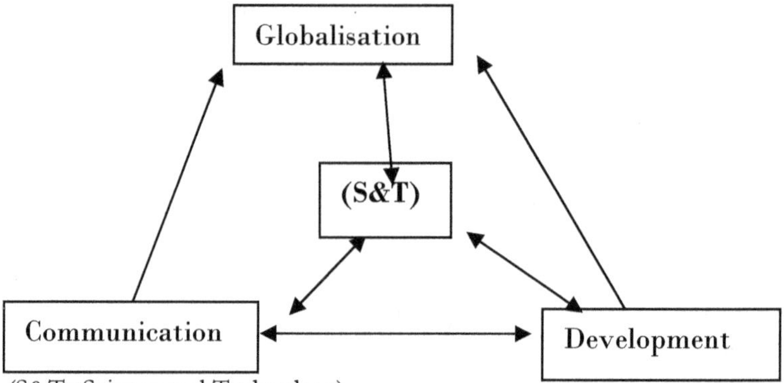

(S&T=Science and Technology)

We have to recognise that as the result of our success in harnessing the forces of nature and applying modern science and technology to the production of goods and services to meet the ever-increasing demands of higher consumption standards we are actually endangering our environment and risking the very survival of the human race. The development of our human knowledge capacity and capability through science and technology gives us greater power to manipulate the resources of the earth positively or negatively.

However, the widening gap between the developed *(centre)* and developing *(periphery)* countries has become a central issue of our time. An important aspect of this widening gap has been the limited development of science and technology in low-income (periphery) countries. It is now a challenge for developing countries to explore the application of science and technology for their transformation. It is a question of making the best use of the "late-comer advantage" to explore the possibilities of accelerating development through a better utilisation of human, raw material, and energy resources; the development and use of advanced industrial technologies, the organisation of scientific research and improvements in public health.

Outer Space

//

Science and Technology==➔Atomic Bomb==➔ **Planet Earth** =➔ Promoting Economic and Social well-being

//

Bottom of the Sea

The battle for development, security and peace must be fought on two fronts. The first is security from where victory spells freedom from fear. The second is in the economic and social front where victory means freedom from want ensuring peace. Only victory on both fronts can assure the world of an endurable peace, sustainable development and quality livelihood without leaving any one behind. Science and technology is not the panacea but provides a viable way forward if properly harnessed and utilised to meeting the social well-being of all citizens. So far Africa to a large extent has failed to untapped the potential of the people's knowledge and skills.

If African countries are to achieve the Sustainable Development Goals, African Union Agenda 2063 and National Development Plans, the 54 countries must ensure the proper development and deployment of science and technology in preparation for its second revolution, without which it will remain at the bottom ladder of the transformation continuum. The deployment of science and technology should not be geared towards the destruction of human lives but improving the quality of services delivery to the people. African countries should stop articulating policies and actions deliberately designed to thwart the rise of a New Africa from the fall-outs of the advances in human knowledge and skills in science and technology.

No society develops without building a strong scientific, technological and entrepreneurial base. The search for solutions to Africa's crippling problems and dismal economic performance must be a matter of serious concern for its leadership and academic community. It also challenges the private sector and individuals to wake up, be creative, innovative, productive and entrepreneurial. While admitting that post-colonial Africa inherited weak-states and dysfunctional economies that were further aggravated by poor leadership, corruption and bad governance in many countries. These two factors, together with the division caused by the Cold War, hampered the spread of responsible and accountable governments across the continent. Fifty years after, unfortunately, the lessons are not learnt by African states to craft policies that make them masters and owners of their resources and development agenda. It is not Africa that owns its resources.

The situation in the Niger Delta Region depicts the plight of the continent in policy articulation and implementation. According to a UNEP Report; *"Oil contamination in Ogoniland is widespread and severely impacting many components of the environment. Even though the oil industry is no longer active in Ogoniland, oil spills continue to occur with alarming regularity. The Ogoni people live with this pollution every day"* (UNEP Report; http://www.unep.org/nigeria). Osodi George (2011) notes that; "...the images that confronts in their awful beauty are of a hellish nightmare. I noticed there was so much injustice being perpetuated in the region. So much had been heard about the situation in the Delta region but very little had been seen in images, presumably due to the hostile topography of the region"

That oil has been described as ***"the devil's excrement"*** and resources in general as a 'curse' comes as no surprise since the continent continues to witness the devastation that it has wrought the people's lives and what was once a pristine environment is being rendered uninhabitable for a long time to come. Travel across the continent, is the same story and picture you find as the poor struggle to produce crops on their lands for existence; and, importantly, the heavily armed groups that are waging war against governments, oil companies and other external exploiters acting in collusion with their governments to deny the people their birth right. The process of land grab occurring throughout the region tells it all to the despoiling of an entire continent by an industry's rapacious lust for crude oil and other resources taking place in a continent rich in natural and human resources, History, and beauty second to none on planet earth – but where many of the people have been left with absolutely nothing but misery and poverty. How much benefits have the people of the Democratic Republic of Congo derived from their vast natural resources?

The situation is not different from the existing situation in countries like Cameroon, Angola, and many others. But why is governance failing Africa so badly? African states have reneged on the democratic values they committed themselves to uphold, and governments have become less accountable to the people. Universal norms and standards are being ignored or sidestepped by new rules that favour markets. It is not out of place to presume that both people, with the needed political clout will be particularly keen to open a refreshing new page in government's relationship. Resources have been destructive to Africa's economy to state the least. The case of Ogoniland is just a tip of the iceberg. The oil companies or any of the companies exploiting the continent's resources do not obey national or international standards, or even their own in-house standards. In many cases, they are simply getting away with murder and other criminal acts.

To a large extent, government has betrayed the people. The people have lost confidence and trust in the administration. With trust and confidence lost in state institutions, conflicts are bound to persist. As long as the root causes remain, possibilities of conflicts remain. The root causes of discontent are several - environmental degradation, un-employment, poverty, corruption, poor infrastructure, social dislocation, general neglect, exclusion and the absence of good governance. Decades of wrong-headed policies and the impact of multiple policy failure have inevitably highlighted the role of the state and how important it is. The required stronger role of the state must be based on democratic legitimacy and accountability - and balanced by the effective participation of civil society in an autonomously creative role – and not on 'technocratic knowledge' that has led to a takeover by a financial-political complex in many countries around the world.

The whole of Africa trembles under the impact of colonial, neo-colonial and capitalist brutalities maintained through the systematic use of violence, exploitation and racism. The call now is to 'lift up the torch of a United Africa' as a call to all African peoples to reject an international community conspiracy dominated by the legacies of colonial and imperial powers. The African peoples' have no future in a community that see their struggles for self-determination and quality well- being as everything from 'naive' to 'illegitimate'. Is Africa facing a battle with the stream of consciousness or what? Confronting ourselves and the reality of the challenges is a task that must be done. It simply means *'mental decolonisation', building self-esteem and confidence* as well as *wearing a new dress* that rights the wrongs of the past. Without such inbuilt strong attitude, the continent cannot break the existing building blocks placed by the developed countries.

The failure to carry out this noble task can be seen in Mazrui's (1980:79) statement: "a belief in the efficacy of market forces, faith in the profit motive and private enterprises, distrust of state initiatives in the economy, and optimism about the developmental value of foreign interests" constitutes some tendencies, in conjunction with other salient anomalies, have conspired to condemn Africa to a state of disenfranchising retardation. This retardative distortions have been responsible for institutionalising Africa's dependency on the outside world, in particular the West, and that her prospects to realise prosperous liberation hinges on her capacity to decolonise modernity. This includes, among other things, practical efforts to enhance indigenisation at human, resource, and institutional levels, promote diversification financially, culturally, and ideologically; facilitate genuine interaction and cooperation between Africa and other Third World countries.

Economic recovery requires building a strong scientific, technological, entrepreneurial, and innovative background. Indigenous knowledge is an asset not a liability as some make it. The development of such inherent knowledge backed with modern scientific and technological knowledge is an added vantage to quick start the continent on its upward climb to quality services development. No development can be expected to be deep and dynamically sustainable without the entrenchment of technological preconditions. Rostow (1959) heightened the significance of technological change in stimulating growth-oriented dynamics in an economy. Gerschenkron (1962) emphasises this with the *"late-comer advantage"* to advance and accelerate their take-off.

Of course, Schumpeter (1943) sees technology as the quintessential factor and fundamental driving force of all economic systems. Gee (1981) asserts that industrial revolution in the United States dating back to the Industrial Revolution and have witness major role that American technology played in the economic resurgence of West Germany and Japan since World Two. The developing countries in particular realise that, in order to reap the full benefits of an increasingly technological world, they must align their governmental infrastructure for effective utilisation of technology imported mainly from the industrial countries. The three-sword approach under the canopy of *'The Three T'* approach, technology, technical assistance and training should enable African countries to address economic issues. Addressing these issues means investing in human capital, building the knowledge base of every African and ensuring the proper use of the vast resources embedded in every country. Africa should start by building on what it has – 'indigenous knowledge' and strengthen that with advances in modern science and technology. It is wrong to discard what we already have as the foundation of our historical past and as basis for advancing our transformation. We need to add to what we already have, not to destroy it.

Timamy (2007: vii-viii) sounds a note of warning here, calling for a new approach to the sustainable transformation of the *c*ontinent, as he notes: "Has Africa ever paused to reflect why she stormed out of the meeting in Seattle? Was it not becoming apparent to African leaders that the West's legendary inaction on the subsidies front was a manifestation of the latter's desire to have her cake and eat it too? Was it not becoming obvious to Africa that the West was using all manner of gimmickry to preserve the global status quo inimical to her? Had it not occurred to African leaders that their economies were, to a large measure, the only ones embracing the neo-liberal conditionality's with virtually no reciprocal movement b*eing observ*ed on the other side? Pius Okigbo (2002:118) proclaims technology as the grammar of the future; we need to modify it by proclaiming technology as the language of the future with science as the grammar of the language. And the future of the world is in Africa. Therefore, building its scientific and technological base now is imperative.

The technological imperatives in Africa's quest for economic renewal are issues that should haunt all policy-makers and stakeholders genuinely keen to see Africa play in the global setting. For now, Africa has shot itself in both feet running the risk of immobilising its entire body almost completely, and conceptualising technological change in very narrow terms. The heterodox view of science-technology-research relationship has to be recognised and create new windows of opportunities to push the science and technology package in the development process of the continent. Africa has been reaping a whirlwind for centuries under successive regimes of organised spoliation. The seeds of this degenerative decay have been sown at different times during her evolution. What Africa needs most is a National Code of Science, Technology and Research (CSTR). The NEPAD initiative on Science and Technology should be given greater credence, more than the ill-fated Lagos Plan of Action (LPA that never took off but remains Africa's well best and well-crafted policy plan for the continent's technological take-off).

The marriage of Science, Technology, Research, Creativity Innovation, Production and Entrepreneurship (STRCIPE) is an imperative for Africa to claim ownership over its development agenda. Africa's present condition of (deepening poverty in the midst of plenty) and precarious destiny awaiting it need to be b*lamed ultimately on the leaders, even though powerful exogenous forces share the guilt of responsibility of Africa's malaise real and potential.* Without developing the science, technology, research, innovation and entrepreneurial base of the continent, African leaders would be condemning several generations of Africans to a life of the *"walking dead"* grinding poverty and other incalculable risks. Scholars are implored to show commitment to the problems of the continent, to study its institutions and values; in short, to provide solutions to the national / continental problems of economic development and political integration. A major drawback on the continent is the gross absence of textbooks that adequately reflect the state in Africa which constitute a threat to the cultivation of consciousness among students. Existing history textbooks in particular tend to portray the history of the pre-colonial era as static. The treatment of the period since independence also leaves a lot to be desired. The factors behind the failure of scholarly research in African history to raise the levels of historical consciousness among the general public are quite complex but not forthcoming. They are determined by general economic and political developments in each country and the specific processes and practices involved in the production of social knowledge. This has equally had a spill-over in other subject areas.

Africa's scientific and technological spirit grossly subverted and criminally crushed by forces of organised spoliation over the centuries, but so quintessential for her dynamics revival can only be rekindled with an Afro-centric agenda and the unity of the continent to be the ignited through a neo-liberal approach being propagated by the West and happily accepted by the paid servants of the continent. Timamy (2007) asserts; African leaders should "not waste time with models that have a potential to undermine domestic technologisation, participatory empowerment and self-reliant autonomy." Simply stated, if a proposed development paradigm embodies measures and programmes likely to deepen Africa's dependence on others then that model is not for Africa. Such a project should be rejected out rightly as it only enslaves rather than empower; such schemes only fossilised the predicament of African states to continue being hewers of wood and drawers of water in the world economy. The right-tide for transformation must be ignited from visionary historical past in tune with modern science and technological development. Fortunately, Africa has an indigenous cultural knowledge heritage value to build on. Since most of the historical knowledge past oral, serious research and documentation is required to piece-together the forgotten rich past as the road-map for a better Africa of tomorrow able to stand its ground.

It is time for African leaders to do their serious mathematical homework to distinguish between *dependence – increasing and autonomy-enhancing development* initiatives. Revitalising Africa in the field of science and technology is a call for rebellion in the eyes of the West like the African Renaissance or Afrocentric approach which gives the continent its identity as it helps in maintaining its sovereignty. Africa has no choice but to embark on the path of developing competence in the domain of science and technology. It will never please the West, just like the West never liked "*the cultural revolution or long-march*" of China. But where is China today? At no point in history will the West condoned any policy articulated by Africans to enhance the wellbeing of their citizens. Such policies must emanate and be executed by the West under their control. Lessons should be drawn from what happened to the Africa Must Unite agenda crafted by the radical school of leaders under Kwame Nkrumah and other leaders like Lumumba, Ghaddafi, Sekou Touré and many others. Any developmental strategic approach that will enhance the quality livelihood of the people is often thwarted by the developed countries.

These leaders were labelled as rebellious and dictators. But the real dictators oppressing their citizens and responding to their paymasters are hailed as the liberators of the African continent. They are the sit-tight leaders who have introduced centralised authoritarian governance nexus on the continent. The genuine and patriotic rebellious leaders who no longer can bear the degree of widespread discount and oppression of the people are moved to act to restore ad bring dignity to the people. Hugely influenced by the socio-political ideological context of the time, and inspired by including the ideals of a socialist revolution and a scare courage showing a love of their country these leaders were bound to react and restore order and dignity to the people to better improve their livelihood.

Such leaders are not welcome by the West. In the words of Russell Botman former Vice-Chancellor, University of Stellenbosch, South Africa, *"Africa needs a generation of responsible leaders who will be willing to place the public good before self-articulate interests"*. We should look at scientific and technological development trends that are focused at shaping Africa's future and strongly invest in those areas. All key growth sectors, from technology to energy, manufacturing to agriculture, education to health care, tourism to design, improving on indigenous knowledge and other areas driving change and ensuring quality services delivery and sustainable well-being must receive the top priority of policy-makers, civil society and the private sector. Presently, the vast majority of African youths are either unemployed or underutilised. Implying that policies must be articulated and implemented to first educate and absorb the currently underemployed/unemployed youths as well as make constructive provisions for the expected youth bulge the continent will face in the next couple of decades. Africa's current population is put at 1.2 billion, with over 20 million coming onto the job market yearly. It is estimated that by 2100, the continent will need to find jobs for 100 million youths coming into the labour market annually. The greatest challenges will be how to educate these numbers, equip them with the requisite knowledge and skills as well as provide employment or self-employment. How does Africa perfectly respond to turning challenges into opportunities along the development nexus?

African Rebellion

Agitation for African unity and improved quality wellbeing of the people is a calculated rebellion towards the West. Revitalising Africa's endogenous knowledge empowers the people towards improving the livelihood of the poor. This endogenous knowledge need to be developed through application, research, investigation, modification and innovation. Most indigenous knowledge has disappeared because too often and too long Africa has relied or 'oral' and not 'written' channels of information. These oral ways of knowledge depreciate rapidly and often distorted depending on who is transmitting the information or knowledge. As a result, indigenous knowledge systems, however, are under serious threats from contemporary forces, in particular the current wave of globalisation (Brahy & Tobin, 2005).

An incursion of foreign religion as well as western styles of conflict resolution and peace-building, among other forces, has contributed to the displacement of aspects of traditional methods for the production and transfer of knowledge in Africa. Other key factors associated with this trend are a decline in the use of endogenous African languages and shifts in culture and in identity. These changes have inspired global concern and movement towards the protection and promotion of indigenous peoples' rights and their knowledge systems. Undermining the saliency of local cultures and traditional authority structures endangers social cohesion and local Conflict resolution mechanisms. The challenge is for Africa to protect and promote its endogenous knowledge systems. The relevance of endogenous knowledge is linked to its ability to enhance the capacity of communities to solve their own problems. (Kwaja 2009:71-72). The problem-solving approach found in a number of African communities is that "whereas the Westerner is geared towards using a *"problem-solving"* approach following very trenchant analysis, our approach is that of *"situation-experience"* (Stubbs (ed.) (1978). In the same vein Nelson Mandela (1994) opines: *"in African culture, the sons and daughters of one's aunts or uncles are considered brothers and sisters, not cousins. We have no half-brothers or half-sisters; my mother's sister is my mother; my uncle's son is my brother my brother's child is my son, my daughter. Anyone who claims descent from a common ancestor is deemed part of the same family".* We need to build that sense of belonging across the continent and the spirit of living and eating together as one big family.

Whether a *'problem-solving'* approach or a *'situation-experience'* approach, the anvil in capacity-building and the capability stance to strategically harness and embed capacity building as an integral part of the continents development framework is important. Many African states lack the capabilities to achieve development results. These include:

- The capacity to design, implement, monitor, and evaluate economic and social policies;
- The capacity to determine the investment priorities and make sure that the investments actually get delivered
- Being able to manage conflict within national boundaries and outside;

- Managing uncertainty and have the leadership that manages to put in place mechanisms to manage those uncertainties;
- Bringing together sectoral, geographical and generational boundaries for decision-making that will influence future development; and
- The capability to deliver basic services

Even with these capabilities, the bottom line, of course, is to have the capability also to produce cheaply textbooks affordable to the people or else, the risk is high that the books will remain on the shelves as a monument to irrelevance. The ultimate responsibility for the promotion of accurate and relevant historical knowledge rests on the shoulders of African scholars (Zeleza 1997:163). Our textbooks should be Afro-centric as well as incorporating the global scientific and technological evolution. An African Scientific Think Tank" operating several working groups, task forces, and cooperative research programmes pertaining to various aspects of development, monitoring, and control. We need to see more philanthropic groups awarding prizes for excellence in research, creativity, innovation, entrepreneurship among others. We need to see more bilateral as well as multilateral programmes. We need to see institutions promoting regional integration, promoting free movements of people and goods and fertilising knowledge as well as learning from best practices.

Putting Africa on the science and technology podium is simply asking for a rebellious approach to Africans dictating its development path and owning it. Under no circumstances is the West prepared to condone such a developmental approach. The future of Africa rests on how far it can exert its weight in the domain of science and technology. Yet scientific and technological inventiveness is t Africa needs. Africa is not out to develop the wheel but to become a proper user of the wheel and to add more value to it. Africa has to be science and technology-based. For now, the idea of building technological capabilities from existing world technology and indigenous knowledge does not feature in the policy frames of states. The continent has neither evolved with the context cultivating the culture and tradition of technology acquisition, nor cultivated the habit of institutionalising indigenous knowledge and value systems as a springboard for the continent's take-off to an industrial and services delivery society: Therefore, the prevalence of weak economic and development foundation of African state.

Africa is in a crisis situation. Independence has been achieved. Some progresses have been accomplished but the continent is not yet there when it actually concerns genuine independence – economic and political. The ruling elites have abridged the rights of the vast majority of the population from quality livelihood and equity in sharing the wealth of the continent. The region finds itself in a climate and situation that is threatening what was achieved some fifty years back. It should now be firmly fixed within the sector of science, technology, innovation and entrepreneurial kingdom. This is not the case. Now is the appropriate moment to educate the youths in particular and society in general to embark on the journey of reawakening of indigenous knowledge and know-how within the premises of STRCIPE (science, technology, research, creativity, innovation, productivity, and entrepreneurship) in the socio-economic transformation of the continent.

It is unacceptable that a continent like Africa with much wealth and resource and so much ingenuity is ranked as the least developed region on planet earth. Yet under the shining light of underdevelopment pessimism grows; yet there is a silver lining beaconing with positive energy and vibration emanating from the continent which is too great and irresistible provided by the rapidly growing youthful population. To attain Africa's ambition which is the development of the continent, the people should of course be confident, optimistic, realistic and hard working. Whatever billions earmarked for infrastructure development should not undermine the place of education, since thousands of Africans as of now cannot read or write which inhibits their progress and development. Africa is the continent with countless opportunities and where everything is possible. The youths in this age of science and technology advancement should not go the way of our forefathers – but made to embrace, and properly utilise the magic powers of science and technology. The youths beacon for one thing – empowerment – with education as the foundation for sustainable development.

The recently concocted marriage between China and Africa (see George, 2014; Manji & Marks, 2007; Simelane & Managa, 2018) is a love affair woven with blessings and curses. It is a love affair because the old husband – the west failed in meeting his side of the marriage vow; as a new boyfriend, China wants to out beat the failures of the West with new conditionalities that look more attractive. But these conditionalities may turn out to be the curse in the long-run not the short-term blessings as is the case. The curse is that Africa is not prepared for the union. And this is because the managers of the economy have not actually keyed and taken into consideration two-fold tasks:

- ➢ to integrate the technologies of the most advanced and the most primitive sectors through a wider diffusion of technologies; they must ensure the strict observance of the rules and regulations governing the use of raw materials and intermediate inputs and promote the emergence of a wider network of transaction between sectors;
- ➢ have the responsibility to strengthen the machinery for deepening of the technology in each sector through active and deliberate promotion of skills formation and the domestication of science and technology.

China policy is not geared towards the transfer of skills to the African people. Their policy is not different from that of the West in this respect. Zeleza (2014:161) asserts. 'poor worker safety standards and low wages, failure to comply with domestic labour and environmental laws, excessive use of Chinese labour and failure to train African workers.' Again, we revert to the importance of human capital development as a predominant input factor in the development, promotion and utilisation of science and technology for sustainable transformation of the continent. Seen within this premises, we can without hesitation and proof advance some pertinent proposition:

- investment in human capital development constitute a fundamental link in the kick-off transformation of Africa into a new world orbit of development;
- the efficiency of investment is determined by the rate of growth of aggregate technology in the economy which, at the simply rate of abstraction, can be represented by the sum of the rate of growth of technology in the sections into which we have divided the economy;
- the rate of growth of technology is an increasingly function of the investment in skills formation;
- the maturation of investment in skills takes longer than maturation of investment in physical capital;
- the quantity and quality of achievable results in science-based development are inherently determined by the competence and vision of the science and engineering manpower available
- the quality and quantity of achievable results in science-based development are manpower available;
- the environment including the architecture of laws and regulations as well as the political will to apply them effectively for the purpose of development and growth must be in place for the propositions advanced here.;

- technologies adopted in Africa must be tailored to suit the needs of the people they are intended to save and must imply lifestyles which do not conflict with the natural and cultural environment;

On the other hand, the Chinese have within a reasonable short period produced tangible results (roads, infrastructures, hospitals, water supply etc,) that significantly contribute to improving the welfare of citizens. However, Africa should not be blindfolded with these gestures but critically and strategically also probe into the long-term negative sides of the give attitude. Africa should by all means avoid the Chinanisation of the continent through the confucianisation of the region, as we are now undermining the teaching of indigenous African languages in place of Chinese (see French, 2014; Duan and Gao, 2014). This calls for strong institutions and constructive strategic approach towards the China-Africa relationship. Specifically, 'African countries should develop robust laws and strengthen their monitoring and enforcement mechanisms and institutional capabilities for labour, safety and environmental protection applicable to all investors, domestic and foreign, including the Chinese.

Most critically, African countries must articulate more clearly, coherently, and collectively what their fundamental interests are in this crucial relationship' (Zeleza, 2014:166). As such, the fundamental standing but yet critical issue for the continent is to cultivate a clear and strategic policy plans in the pursuit of its short-term, medium-term and long-term interests in its relationship with China as with any major power. African countries embedded with such coherent visionary policies and democratic accountability would benefit more from relationship with China. Bear in mind and be aware of strangers bearing gifts. China like any other country is no different and no country is a philanthropist. Countries are businesses for themselves. For African countries, the only safeguard is to endeavour as much as possible to negotiate advantageously for it.

Investing in human capital development, infrastructure and institution-building and deploying the use of ICTs remain imperative in reconstituting and restoring the lost cultural heritage and indigenous knowledge of the people necessary in constructing a capable developmental state most needed for the continent at this stage of its transformation versus simply memorising facts and figures, as is the case in the past. Technology as Swaniker (2017:51) points out has provided the opportunity to remove learning from the old domain of the lecture hall and to make it a far more interactive, holistic, social and continuous experience. The entire world evolves at the speed of technology. We have a unique opportunity to leverage it in rethinking our education models as well. Technology also has tremendous potential for students to personalise their learning – choosing courses from various universities with the best content, and not being constrained to the limited (and often badly taught) content at their particular university. Technology enables students to take ownership of their own education. The idea is to build of scholarly independence, to enable students to learn how to learn, to be creative, innovative and entrepreneurial.

One of the many weaknesses of the Structural Adjustment Programme (SAPs) was their inability to relate the core problem of designing efficient 'democratic institutions' in Africa to the structural problem of underdevelopment and making science and technology a key component in transforming the region. More0ver, the absence of science and technology and a clear structural framework for equitable global trade has exacerbated Africa's weak economies. The Lagos Plan of Action (that never was implemented) showed the shortcomings of the continent. It is therefore imperative that African governments strengthen the collective capacity of their continental and regional institutions to address contemporary challenges of democracy, science and technology, development and globalisation as envisioned in the AU's Agenda 2063.

UN Sustainable Development Goals and AU Agenda 2063 should be geared towards ensuring that the African people no longer remain the poorest in the world, both in real income and in access to quality services delivery; importantly to bear in mind that the large number of people in poverty implies an inefficient use of resources and increases the risks of social upheaval. They should remember that the poor have much potential energies and capabilities to contribute to economic development, which implies that an enabling environment be created so that their potentials that often go wasted, underdeveloped and underutilised are effectively put into good use. The existence of a poor and unconducive environment leads to a situation where the people are often effectively disenfranchised and politically frustrated. Lastly, bearing in mind that disenfrancisation and politically frustrated accelerates the risks of social upheaval is further increased by high and growing inequality within nations and across the continent. The importance of creating a dynamic science and technology infrastructural base and integrating the sector to the wider system of development is imperative. Africa should perceive technology as an object and tool to be constructively deployed for the benefit of the humanity. We cannot ignore the potentials of technology to generate wider socio-economic benefits, just as we should not fail to recognise the limitations of science and technology in solving social problems, as these will not be solved by technology alone.

Creating an enabling environment for a sustainable socio-economic and technological take-off for Africa means creating at a conducive atmosphere to socio-eco-techno change as a process of learning for a country and continent in three ways; '*invention, innovation and production processes and learning how to learn*' (Stiglitz and Greenwald, 2004). Human capital development or learning that allows the people to increase their knowledge and to push the frontier of knowledge to improving their well-being is imperative. Providing an enabling environment entails governments putting in place constructive developmental and industrial policies that spur domestic firms to innovate, learn and retain that learning at home.

Globalisation and technological advances have lifted billions out of poverty but also contributed to the rise in income inequalities. But this does not mean that we cannot work towards constructing a future where tensions and risk arise in different dimensions, develop more suddenly, and build on each other, challenging our ability to deliver continued stability and shared prosperity. For example, interconnectedness and diffusion of power could point to a future that is both increasingly integrated and politically and socially fragmented, with profound implications for policy cooperation at different levels. Thus, the complexity and uncertainty of the future present opportunities and challenges to the leaders and peoples of the African continent to provide a fresh perspective in stimulating growth and well-being for all. In short, the future belongs to those who actively, constructively and holistically prepare for it now.

References

Adebanwi Wale (2005). Techno-Politics and the Production of Knowledge: Democratic Activism and The Nigerian Exile, Occasional Paper Series, Vol.10. No. 1, African Association of Political Science (AAPS), Pretoria, South Africa.

Braby N. & B. Tobin (2005). "Protecting and Strengthening Traditional Knowledge, Innovation Systems", Work 17-2 (2005). (www, unu.edu/hq/ginfo/wip/wip17-2-summer 2005 pdf)

Caldwell, John Thornton (2000). Electronic Media and Technoculture. Rutgers University Press, New Brunswick, New Jersey, USA

Choucri, Nazli (2000). "Introduction: Cyber-Politics in International Relations", International Political Science Review, Vol. 21. No. 3, July 2000:243-263

Duan, Changrui & Gao Jiayong (2014). "Confucianism and China Business Doctrine." Paper presented at the Academy of International Business – US North East Chapter 2014 International Conference Beijing Technology and Business University & Tianjin Foreign Studies University, China, May 21-24, 2014

Forje John & Funeka Yazini April (2014) "Rethinking Africa's Development through Science and Technology: A Partnership Opportunity for South Africa and China" in Funeka Yazini April & Garth Shelton (eds.) (2014). Perspectives on South Africa- China Relations, Africa Institute of South Africa, Pretoria – South Africa, pp83-104

French Howard (2014), China's Second Continent: How a Million Migrants Are Building a New Empire in Africa, Alfred A. Knopf. New York

Gee, S. (1981) Technology Transfer, Innovation and International Competitiveness. John Wiley and Sons Inc. New York.

George, Francis Stevens (2014). China and Africa Love Affairs. CreateSpace Independent Publishing Platform.

Gerschenkron, A. (1962) Economic Backwardness in Historical Perspectives. The Belknap Press, Harvard University Press, Cambridge, MA

Kwaja M.A. Chris (2009). "Globalisation and Africa's Endogenous Knowledge Systems", Africa Peace and Conflict Journal. University of Peace, Vol. 2. No 1, June 2009, Addis Ababa – Ethiopia, pp71-74

Levi-Faur David & Waarden van Frans (2018). Democratic Empowerment in The European Union, Edward Elgar Publishing, UK.

Manji, Firoze & Stephen Marks (eds.) (2007) African Perspectives on China in Africa. Oxford, Fahamu Mazrui A. Ali (1980). The African Condition. The Reith Lectures, Heinemann, London

Nelson Mandela (1994). Long Walk to Freedom. Macdonald Purnell Publishers, Randburg, South Africa

Okigbo Pius (2002) "The Grammar of the Future", in Animalu O. Alexander (ed.) (2002) Science Today in Africa, 2002. The Nigerian Academy of Science, Lagos, Abuja. SNAP Press Ltd, Enugu, Nigeria, pp110-151

Osodi George (2011). Delta Nigeria – The Rape of Paradise, Trolley Books, London

Rostow, W. (1959). The Stages of Economic Growth. Economic History Review, August.

Schumpeter, Joseph (1943) Capitalism, Socialism and Democracy. Unwin Publishers, London

Simelane Thokozani and Managa Lavhelesani (eds.) (2018) Belt and Road Initiative: Alternative Development Path for Africa. Africa Institute of South Africa, Pretoria, South Africa,

Slevin James (2000). The Internet and Society. Polity Press, Cambridge, United Kingdom

Stiglitz E. Joseph and Greenwald C. Bruce (2014). Creating a Learning Society: A New Approach to Growth, Development and Social Progress, Columbia University Press, New York, USA

Swaniker Fred (2017) "Time to Modernise", New African, No.578, December 2017, AN IC Publication, London, pp50-51

Timamy M.H. Khalil (2007). The Political Economy of Technological Underdevelopment in Africa. CBAAC Lagos, Nigeria and DPMF Addis Ababa, Ethiopia

Zeleza Tiyambe Paul (1997). Manufacturing African Studies and Crises. Codesria Book Series, Dakar – Senegal

Zeleza Tiyambe Paul (2014). "The Africa-China Relationship: Challenges and Opportunities", Canadian Journal of African Studies, Vol.48. No.1, April 2014, pp145-169 [http://dx.doi.org/10.1080/0083968.2014.964298]

Chapter Three

Gender Power – Neglected, but Rising and Important

"The genuine emancipation of women is that which entrusts responsibilities to them and involves them in productive activities and in the different struggles the people face. May my eyes never see, and my feet never see, and my feet never take me to a society where half the people are held in silence. I hear the roar of women's silence. I sense the rumble of their storm and feel the furry of their revolt. I await and Hope for the fertile eruption of the revolution through which they will transmit The power and the rigorous justice issued from their oppressed wombs"

(Captain Thomas Sankara: Former President, Burkina Faso, 8 March, 1987)

"African women have always been aware of the gender disparities in their societies. There is a Ghanaian saying which goes 'even if a hen does not crow she sure knows when it's daybreak".

(Liz Ticharewa, Bethelwet, Zimbabwe)

"More than 50 per cent of the population does not benefit as much as their male counterparts from the fruits of their labour and independence. There is need to arrange the world differently to enable women to access equal benefits of the wealth they have participated in creating, control of the fruits of their labour and become part and parcel of the decision-making process in their world".

(Jenifer Riria, Kenya Women's Finance Trust)

"Women and men are equal. Women are even in government these days. The church teaches us not to be violent so men should never be violent to women and children".

(Male client in Sustainable Livelihoods Programme, Angola)

Introduction

Africa remains underdeveloped and exploited because the gross absence of proper utilisation of both its human and natural resources potentials. Part of this failure can be attributed to a gross misunderstanding or misinterpretation of cultural values and belief systems. The victims in this category are women. Male chauvinism has misguided our priorities towards a building a humane and sustainable society. The failure to bring women on board is Africa's greatest dilemma and source of underdevelopment and exploitation. The world has evolved. Women cannot remain stagnant. Changes are bound to take place. Africa has to wake up to the realities of the twenty-first century. Women have and continue to proof their worth as veritable partners in the process of socioeconomic transformation. They are not competitors but complimentary partners and deserve to be treated as such. For too long they have and continue to pay the prices of the inadequacies of male chauvinisms and outdated cultural factors and other constructs that discriminate against women. Change of attitude and behaviour towards women must occur in the mindset of African men. This is what will show the 'manness' of the African man. I am inclined to believe that African men are changing for the better and for the common good of the people. Steady Chioma Filomina (2012) using the concept of *'mothering the nation,'* argues that female leadership can humanize the state and provide a powerful alternative to the male-dominated status quo.

Gender inequality is a multifaceted concept that is hard to measure and the United Nations Development indexes (UNDP); constructed by combining several indicators are clearly tentative. A more robust, but partial, measure of gender inequality is differences in schooling. The direct effect of inequality in education is illustrative. First it reduces the average amount of human capital in the country, since qualified girls are not given the opportunity to study. Second, it is also an efficient allocation of resources since the marginal return on educating boys and girls most likely are different; Third, there are many externalities deriving from female education; for instance, child mortality decreases with the mother's level of education, while the nutritional status and school performance increases, Fourth, higher female education reduces fertility, which indirectly affects Gross Domestic Products (GDP) per capita growth in the long run (Bigsten & Durevall, 2008:44-45).

This measure can be used to illustrate the development of one important aspect of gender inequality. A major problem is that the state of statistical update is poor and often not available in most African countries. The reason for choosing education is that studies show that female education is more important for labour productivity than male education (Kowles et al, 2002; Klasen 2002). On the other hand, Blackden et al (2007) conclude that 'gender inequality acts as a significant constraint to growth in sub-Saharan Africa, and that removing gender-based barriers to growth will make a substantial contribution to realising Africa's economic potential Investment in female education has a high pay-off in terms of economic growth, as well as in reducing gender inequality. This pay-off both is high in Sub-Saharan Africa due to existing large imbalances (see Stotsky 2006).

As the world pays lip services to the Rural Woman on 8 March and 15 October every year by commemorating what has been pompously called Women's Day and Rural Women's Day respectively, it behoves Africa to speak to the inter woven tapestry that binds the African woman to her bondaged society. Ngwane (2007:4) questions: *"African women, who are you? Are you a product of your own traditional evolution or an imitation of Eurocentric images? What values do you uphold? Those that maintain our strong African solidarity: or those that pursue the blind alley of separate individual advancement? African women are you still the one that Leopold Senghor eloquently asset as 'clad in your black beauty strikes me to the heart as lightning strikes the eagle? Are you still the one who majestically ploughs the farms; replenishes the energy when we flag and ruin the entire humanity? Are you still the nightingale who sings the lullaby when the world is still snoring? Yes, my African woman you remain to us the cradle of African civilisation and the fertility of your womb shall be as perennial as the River Nile. Tell the African man to turn his gun into a spade and his military truck into a tractor so together we can build a confidence-prone and conflict-proof Africa."*

African women are challenged to 'stand up and be counted not just as one who attended Beijing but one who speaks truth to power and in the face of human greedy as one who fights against the unequal distribution of our resources; as one who stands by the flag of the Africa Union – the flag of the United States of Africa.' The African women have become the paradise of rape. From Mexico, through Copenhagen, Nairobi to Beijing, it is still the long but unfinished march. Yet some progress has been made, with some achievements and still some setbacks which should only encouraged you to move faster on the long-road to equality, partnership, ownership and shared-prosperity. The disease is still there at the state, regional, continental and world level; it should not be signs of *'despair'* but *'hope';* the male chauvinist world have risen to a certain extent in renouncing female gender discrimination and embracing equality. Levinson (2016) gives a detailed but challenging account of the struggle for the rise of Africa's first woman president – Ellen Johnson Sirleaf of Liberia. Getting to the top is not a journey on a platter of gold but of hard work, endurance and conviction.

A number of African women have made it to the top, Joyce Banda of Malawi, Specioza Naigaga Wandira Kazibwe (former Vice President, Uganda and UN Special envoy for HIV/AIDS; Dlamini-Zuma (AU Chair), Polonomi Venson-Moitoi (current Foreign Minister of Botswana, and her bid to become AU Commission Chair; Winnie Byanyima (Uganda) Head, Oxfam International; Fatma Samoura (Senegal, FIFA Secretary General; Maria Ramos (South Africa) CEO,

Barclays Bank Africa; Fadumo Dayib (Somalia) Presidential Candidate; Ameenah Gurib-Fakim (Mauritius) First female President sworn in June 2015; Luisa Diogo (First Female Prime Minister of Mozambique; Immaculee Nahayo Nyandwi (Burundi) First female Speaker, National Assembly of Burundi; Speaker of the African Parliamentary Union (APU); Mary Catherine Nkosi (Malawi) first Female Deputy Governor of Malawi's Central Bank; Simbi Veke Mubako (Zimbabwe) Judge, High Court of Zimbabwe and Ambassador to the United States; Madam Sheila Sisulu (South Africa) Executive Director of UN World Food Programme; Amina J. Mohammed (Nigeria) UN Deputy Secretary-General; Vera Songwe (Cameroon) First Female to lead UNECA; Olga Johnson (Benin) Secretary General of the Energy for Africa Foundation; Haben Girma (Eritea/Ethiopia/US) World first deaf blind person to graduate from Harvard Law School; Vanessa Mounger (Chad) Director of Gender Women and Civil Society, The Africa Development Bank (AfDB); Prof. Ruth Oniang'o (Kenya) Winner of 2017 Africa Food Prize; Yvonne Mburu (Kenya) Member of French President Emmanuel Macron's |Presidential Council for Africa; Prof. Yaye Kene-Gassama Dia (Senegal) Member Expert Panel of 10 of African Union (AU)(Commission on Existing and Emerging Technologies to foster Economic Development; Nunu Ntshingila (South Africa) Head of the African Division of the World's biggest Social Media site - Face book; Isabel dos Santos (Angola) Chairperson of Sonangol, state-owned oil and gas company, and Africa's richest woman; Dr Matshidiso Moeti (first Woman WHO regional director for Africa); The list goes on, impressive but not sufficient in bringing the female gender in parity with male gender. Much has yet to be done to change the male-female dynamics of equality and respecting fundamental human rights.

You have the ammunition - the vote - use it wisely and properly to drive sense and greater awakening in the African man's world of domination and suppression. The use of 'bottom power' is strongly advocated by women to get their men register for upcoming elections. Mishi Mboko (Member of Parliament for the coastal city of Mombasa) strongly advocates women to withhold sex from their husband until they register as voters for the August 2017 elections. Deny them sex until they show you their voter's card" (The Times Journal, 2017). Bottom-power has emerged as powerful weapon in the political chess game. Calls for sex boycotts are common in Kenya. In 2009, women activists held a week-long sex strike to get then President Mwai Kibaki and Prime Minister Raila Odinga and their allies to reconcile after falling out. Continue with your strategy of "Non-violent Social

Change". During the era of political turmoil in Cameroon, the Takemben Women (old Mothers) in Bamenda became the body-guard of Ni John Fru Ndi (Leader of the Social Democratic Front (SDF) held captive by the security forces of the state for more than three months after the presidential elections.

Women have always exhibited their resilience in championing the right cause for the common good. Often, some of their actions are misunderstood or under-rated. In the majority of conflicts, it is women and children who the greatest price of these conflicts. There is need for society to pay serious attention to the plight of the female gender and ensure they become veritable partners in the development process. The hatreds that fuel the divide between male and female concept of development is causing the continent serious problems of Africa being left behind in the global development saga.

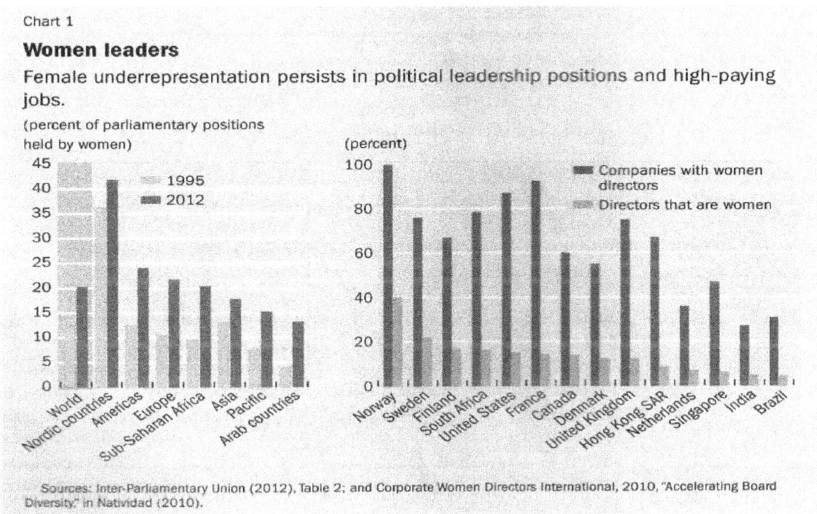

See also Finance and Development 2013, p13 Chart 1.

It will soon be three decades since the Nairobi Conference which transformed the African women from staying in the shadows, out of the limelight of Mexico and Copenhagen. Western women were in forefront occupying centre stage. It is a different chess-game today. The new ball game is for African women to go for what was denied them decades back by placing knowledge at the forefront of development and their emancipation. Building the human capacity of women will hasten the long unfinished march to human equality. The best weapon to empowerment is human capital development and putting in places the necessary enabling environment. Empower the African women and see the changes that will occur throughout the continent.

Drawing from the United Nations Fourth Conference on Women in 1995, Aung San Suu Kyi asserted: *"There is an outmoded Burmese proverb still recited by men who wish to deny that women too can play a part in bringing necessary change and progress to their society; 'The dawn rises only when the rooster crows.' But Burmese people today are well aware of the scientific reasons behind the rising of dawn and the falling of dusk. And the intelligent rooster surely realises that it is because dawn comes that it crows and not the other way round."* The fallout of the Beijing jamboree being 'The Beijing Platform for Action', which compelled governments to enact legislation to include women at all levels of power and decision making, including parliaments. Since 1995, the world will never be that of the chauvinist male dominated, but a world of equal partnership and cooperation between male and female for the common good. African governments are doing tremendous jobs in advancing the course of women as veritable players in the transformation nexus of the continent. Like Oliver Twist, they need to do more and go beyond the 30% quota in increasing the political representation of women at the local government level to the highest policy marking organs of the state, as well as encourage the private corporate sector to do same.

Presently, and looking at the World Economic Forum's 2012 Global Gender Gap Report, there is a marked increase in equality between the sexes in human capital investments and economic opportunities, female under-representation persists in political leadership positions and in the highest paid positions. Policies are powerful tools but not enough in expanding women's political voice; construction actions are vital in ensuring that these policies are implemented. South Africa is making tremendous strides in this direction on the continent as demonstrated by Chart 1 – Women Leaders. Only Norway, France and the United States have passed the 80 percent mark in respect of companies with women as directors; while South Africa is slightly near the 80% mark above Sweden according to Chart 1. Again, South Africa is above the United States, France, Canada, Denmark, and United Kingdom in respect of Directors that are women.

Changing Perceptions

These changes are taking place in more forceful and right pattern. Thus the recent election of a woman to head the African Union coming after the hills of the election of Africa's first women President, Ellen Johnson-Sirleaf, Africa's first woman Noble Peace Laureate, Late Prof Wangari Maathai, the rise to the Presidency in Malawi, Joyce Hilda

Banda, the appointment of Fatou Bensouda of Gambia to the helm of the International Criminal Court, the first Speaker of the Southern African Parliament following the rise of Black majority rule was a woman as Speaker of the South African Parliament; followed by Baleka Mbete (2004-2008) later to be Deputy President of South Africa (2009-2009); Dr Ramphele Mamphela (Former Vice Chancellor, University of Cape Town), Dr Ngozi Okonjo Inweala as World Bank President for Africa; Assistant Secretary General of the United Nations; Africa's First Anglican Female Bishop Ellinah Wamukoya (Swaziland): Prof Dorothy Njeuma (Cameroon's First Woman Vice-Chancellor (University of Buea) and the longest ever in that post and founding Member of the African Peer Review Mechanism): Catherine Samba Panza (Central African Republic) as the African Woman Head of State; Asha-Rose Migiro (Tanzania) as the UN Secretary-General's special envoy for HIV/AIDS in Africa. Phumzile Mlambo-Ngcuka (first Southern African woman to hold the position of Deputy Vice President of South Africa; later to be appointed as UN Secretary-General as Executive Director of UN Women; Ms Baleka Mbete, Speaker, South African Parliament and current Executive Director of the UN Women); Women Vice Presidents in Gambia and Zimbabwe; and in 2010 Rabioatou Serah Diallo was appointed Deputy Prime Minister in Guinea; Speciosa Wandira-Kazibwe was Vice President of Uganda from 1993 to 2004; and as UN Special envoy for HIV/AIDS in Africa; Hiroute Guebre Sellassie (Ethiopia) as UN Secretary-General as his Special envoy for the Sahel; Pramila Patten (Mauritius) as UN Special representative on Sexual Violence in Conflict; Sahle-Work Zewde (Ethiopia) as UN Secretary-General as Director General of the UN Office in Nairobi; Margaret Vogt as UN special representative as Head of the UN Integrated Peacebuilding Office in the Central African Republic; Najat Rochdi (Morocco) as UN Special representative for the UN Multidimensional Integrated Stabilisation Mission to the Central Africa Republic; Vera Songwe (Cameroon) as the first Woman to the post of Executive Secretary of the United Nations Economic Commission for Africa (ECA);the first female WHO Regional Director for Africa; Aichatou Mindaoudou Souleymane (Niger) as special representative of the UN Operation in Cote d'Ivoire are just a few of the cases of the changing landscape of women in leadership position on the continent and the world at large. Women have to bring into centre as equal participants in the transformation of the continent otherwise sustainable and balanced development cannot occur.

But as the number of women in executive positions continues to grow in Africa, they must find ways to translate their presence in politics into action and influence. Enlisting the support of men across government bodies is one way to effect reforms. Stated in another way, political gender quotas in Africa are not enough to simplify the voices of women. Given the increasing number of female legislators, and women's defining role in the economy, one might think that women in Africa would have more influence on policies that directly concern them. However, cultural practices and deep-seated traditions have been hard to budge. The urgent need for men changing perception about gender equality and participation as partners in the sustainable transformation of the continent is imperative and a must for the region to be a veritable play in the global chess game of development and quality livelihood for its citizens.

The question arises: Can a public policy that forcibly changes the gender balance in leadership really influence voters' belief systems? Can it lead to an acceptance of women as leaders? And can it improve girl's confidence and increase their aspirations to study, have a career, and become a leader (Pande and Topalova 2013:13)? Turning to Chart 1, African women have made tremendous strides in political representation Sub-Saharan Africa which was at 10 percent in Beijing 1995 had by 2012 attained 20% ranking fourth after the Nordic Countries, Americas, and Europe. Today Rwanda tops the World list on female representation in parliament. In no small way the first Southern Cameroon Parliament established on 26 October 1954 took the bold lead in appointing a female representative representing Women's Interest in the person of Mrs Idowu to be followed by Mrs J. Mua and Mrs Diffo; Mrs Mua who was the deciding factor to whether Southern Cameroon joined the Federation of Nigeria or integrated with La Republic du Cameroun. Mrs. Mua was carried from the maternity ward to cast her vote in the Assembly.

African women are on the move towards constructing a capable developmental state. Emphasis certainly needs to be devoted to fostering equitably the partnership now emerging between the sexes. The priority agenda should be deepening male-female interrelationship and partnership for the constructive and sustainable socioeconomic transformation and advancement of the continent. The process requires empowering the female agenda by building their human capital capacity as well as enforcing at least the 30% quota in all spheres of public and private sector appointments and especially representation in the legislative assembly and other institutional decision-making bodies. Despite the proliferation of the literature on women, including women's history, women remain largely invisible or misrepresented in mainstream, or rather 'malestream' African development Zeleza

(1997:167) notes: "they are either not present at all, or they are depicted as naturally inferior and subordinate, as eternal victims of male oppression. Alternatively, the romantic myth is advanced that the roles of women and men were equal and complimentary in good old, harmonious, pre-colonial Africa, or the lives of notable, exceptional, heroic women are celebrated". In short, most institutions of higher learning in Africa women's history are still marginal and lack recognition and academic respectability (Awe 1991:211: Iman 1998).

Building the Africa of tomorrow needs more than ever before the potential investors of women's skill and knowledge to develop business opportunities and share ideas on how to propel the continent in the right path of socioeconomic transformation. Men's failure in the transformation could be seen as the failure of structural adjustment. Male chauvinism advocated the solution for women to be treated as second class citizens and to continuously adopt austerity measures, second fiddle role by the women. It is no longer, let's cry for African women but let is praise and up-lift the African woman. Top priority should be given to the role of African women in development which falls in line with African Solutions to African Problems and respect for fundamental human rights. Yet you cannot solve African problems when more than 52% percent of the population is marginalised and excluded instead of being active participants in the process of reconstruction and development.

Excluding women implies delaying the constructive development process of the continent. Seen within this context, it is worth emphasising steps necessary to institutionalise the ideal and the necessity to incorporate women as partners in the development agenda. Challenges that need to be overcome in the continent's renewal effort in order to better achieve sustainable and endurable development for Africa. Presently, and for long time past, African women have been left on their own to deal with their marginalisation and the distortions of the chauvinist attitude of the male gender towards the female gender. This is the period of putting women at the forefront of Africa state construct and development policy agenda. The 30% female representation in decision-making bodies is not enough. There has to be equal participation of women in leadership position not only at the AU but also within national governments and institutions including the private sector.

If Africa is to be prosperous, it will require a gender revolution. Women in agriculture, enabling women to grow their enterprises, this is what will create jobs. Women must be empowered in all spheres of activities. Women were at the forefront of the independence struggle.

The election of Dr Dlamini Zuma to Head the AU Commission and Dr Vera Songwe the United Nations Economic Commission for Africa (ECA) is a significant milestone in a journey of more than a thousand miles. But women still lack behind, and most unfortunately, they are their own greatest enemies. They need to be more proactive and cooperative among themselves to better face male domination and the propagation of discrimination and inequality waged against them. There are still many social, cultural and religious impediments constraining women's participation in society as equal partners in development. In many countries, laws often favour men, or are unfavourable to women. Women still do not have land-tenure rights. Land and housing are critical to women in numerous ways. Land and housing remain a key resource for women; it is an asset important to their economic condition and central to their physical and social well-being. It is the site of child rearing and inc*ome generation and a nexus for so*cial networks of support and c*ommunity-based relianc*e. Land and housing is a s*ignificant economic asset to women that contributes to their independence, economic security and bargaining power with men in their households and so*ciety at large. Land rights for women are also highly resistant to reform. A glaring example is that women farmers in Africa have no leverage over agricultural policies in their countries and little access to credit, fertilisers and seeds, although they produce most of the food.

Most importantly, it helps women determine their own futures and make the decisions that affect their lives. Moreover, land and housing is crucial to the people's identity, dignity and sense of belonging, especially if their rights are upheld by law, and in constituting a pathway out of poverty (Moser 2006; 2009; Mitlin & Satterthwaite 2012; Forje 2013;) can also be a route to prosperity. Despite the fact that gender equality in rights to land and housing has been established in numerous international treaties and conventions (Chant 2011; Minujin and Nandy 2012), gender continues to be a major axis of shelter discrimination, with COHRE (2008;2) asserting that: "When addressing housing as a human right, it is impossible to adopt a gender-neutral approach. Women, either by law or by action, are excluded from or discriminated against in virtually every aspect of housing." Yet women's role and leadership is central in driving economic growth, promoting peace, development and social justice for the sustainable transformation of the continent. The opportunities for increasing the participatory role of women in the development of Africa are increasing but not as rapid as it should.

However, Rwanda has taken the lead as 56% of parliament consist of women, the largest ratio in the world, with Senegal not far behind with 43% are indicative of African women on the rise to prominence. South Africa ranks third-highest with 44 percent representation. The Kenyan 2013 March elections saw one-fifth of parliamentary seats went to women, doubling their representation. There is a steady increase in female representation in the Cameroon parliament and in local councils. After more than three decades of long campaign to implement a protocol for women's right in Africa resulted in October 2010 in the declaration of 2010-2020 as the African Women's Decade (AWD). The scheme puts women in the centre of every initiative that will be undertaken by African Union member states during the next decade in all aspects of development related activities. It should be understood that women are not competing with men. Rather women should be seen as complimentary partners in the development process. Therefore, both sexes must have to cope with the effects of infrastructural disorder and corrupt institutions though women are affected by these predicaments differently. As components of a common course, cooperation rather than division should underscore their joint efforts in crafting a sustainable developmental state.

Human capital development is not an option for the girls as it is for the boys. The girl child is marginalised and deprived of fundamental human rights compared to the male child. The female gender is subjected to sex trafficking, gender-based violence and maternal health care and other inhumane activities. Take for example Female Gentile Mutilation (FGM) and its disastrous effects and consequences on girls. These and other factors requires structured democratic principles necessary to both maintain and accelerate the ongoing developments demanding the imminent participation of women in top decision-making positions, access to victim and vital services, maternal health and legislature regarding women's rights. By and large, it can be noted that stability and progress is determined less by factors such as democracy and wealth than by how well a society safeguards the interests of women.

A society that protects the interests of women and incorporates their roles in the development process is sure to ripe greater and sustainable bounty for an endurable length of time. Presently, women are being systemically marginalised within the African society. This attitude should change to ensure parity between the sexes. At the same time, there is a need to afford greater recognition to women's special capacities to contribute. Women must be empowered as effective change agents in the field of disaster risk reduction, recovery and reconstruction, in line with similar recognition of their potential roles in conflict prevention, resolution and peace building. We must therefore take cognisance of the reality, that:

- Until African women occupy spaces where leadership equates with decision-making power, things will not progress as steadily and rapidly as they need to in African society as a whole.
- Women themselves must take primary responsibility for ushering more women into positions of power and most do so determinedly. It would not wrong to state women are their own greatest enemies;
- African women have failed to articulate comprehensive policy strategies as well as take measures to secure seats in leadership positions which contributes in their inadequate representation as a result;
- Nor have they constructively challenged patriarchal structures and social attitudes that exclude them from leadership, participatory and constructive engagement positions;
- Shared leadership and engagement encourages as it promotes unity and cooperation, bringing more women in the powerhouse humanises situations that we collectively encounter, seeking joint solutions to the predicaments of the continent is vital;
- Women's leadership and participatory role is central in driving structural changes, economic growth, promoting peace, development and social justice in Africa.

With such credible caveats, why should women be hold in the garage of underdevelopment, marginalisation and exclusion? They should occupy the centre stage as veritable partners with the male gender in accelerating the transformation process to sustainable development in Africa. Holding on to male chauvinism is perpetuating the centre-periphery syndrome. For too long we have been prolonging the period of slack and frustration in developing thinking. This could be seen as the result of the turbulence in the global economic process of imperialism, slavery, and colonialism. Africa should be doing better in post-colonial development and not falling back to the acts of yester years.

The frustration and the depressed mood of relegating the female gender to the background have lasted for quite some time already. As a rather natural course of events in human historical evolution, it should now give way to a change. That change is gradually coming around the corner, and there developing many positive signs of the search for a new orientation in development thinking and efforts towards bringing women as equal partners in the development process. The entire African society stands to harvest the best of properly utilising the inherent potentials of women which we have foolishly or stupidly neglected for too long in our development thinking. New development thinking with greater emphasis on the significant contributions of the female gender should eventually be put on the library shelf of an emerging Africa.

Therefore, it is important for the continent to protect her women folks as creators of emerging paradigms, sources of inspiration and of reference. With such male orientation, the continent stands a better chance of advancing the process of quality services delivery to the people. We should perceive women as the sustainable emerging mechanisms for transforming Africa in the new globalised world of era.

Until and unless poverty reduction, equality and empowerment goals are explicitly integrated in our development related activities, Africa will never make progress. This raises the important question of walking the talk and not just talking the talk of gender empowerment and incorporating women as equal partners in the process of change, development and quality welfare for all citizens. Quality livelihood is not just for men. Africa is challenged to effectively implement SDGs, AU Agenda 2063 and each country's national development plan.

References

Awe, B. (1991). "Writing Women into History: The Nigerian Experience", in Offen, et al (eds.) Writing Women's History: International Perspectives. Indiana University Press, Bloomington, USA

Blackden, Mark, Sudarshan Canagarajah, David Lawson (2007), "Gender and Growth in Sub-Saharan Africa: Evidence and Issues", in Mavrotas, G. and A, Shorrocks (eds.), Advancing Development, Palgrave, London, pp349-370

Bigsten Arne & Durevall Dick (2008). The African Economy and Its Role in The World Economy. Current African Issues, No. 40. The Nordic Africa Institute, Uppsala, Sweden,

Centre on Housing Rights and Evictions (COHER) (2008), Women, Slums and Urbanisation: Examining the Use, Causes and Consequences, COHER, Geneva.

Chant, Sylvia (2011)," Gender and the Prosperity of Cities", Final draft of lead Chapter prepared for the UN-Habitat State of Women in Cities 2012/13, UN Habitat, Nairobi, Kenya

Forje W. John (2016) Gender Empowerment, Equality and Economic Development as African Solutions to African Problems. Lambert Academic Publishing, Germany.

Forje W. John (2010). Cameroon Without Poverty. Civil Society Empowerment: Growth and Poverty Eradications? Mapping New Strategies for the Future. Lambert Academic Publishing, Germany

Imam, A. (1988)." The Presentation of African Women in Historical Writing", in Kleinberg, S. J. (ed.). Retrieving Women's History, Berg/UNESCO. New York.

Knowles, S., Lorgelly, P. K., Dorian Owen (2002), "|Are Educational Gender Gaps a Brake on Economic Development? Some Cross-country Empirical Evidence", Oxford Economic Papers, 54(1):118-49

Levinson Riva (2016) Choosing The Hero: My Improbable Journey and The Rise of Africa's First Woman President. Serpents Tail Publishers.

Minujin Alberto & Shailen Nandy (2012) Global Child Poverty Concepts, Policy and Action. Polity Press, Bristol, UK.

Mitlin Diana & David Satterthwaite (2012), Urban Poverty in the Global South: Scale and Nature, Routledge, London

Moser, Caroline (2006). "Asset-based Approaches to Poverty-reduction in a Globalised Context", Global Economy and Development Working Paper, The Brookings Institution, Washington DC, USA

Moser, Caroline (2009). Ordinary Families, Extraordinary Lives; Assets and Poverty Reduction in Guayaquil, 1978-2004, Brookings Institution Press, Washington DC, USA.

Ngwane George Mwalimu (2007) "The African Woman", The Post, No. 0899, Monday, 15 October 2007, Buea – Cameroon, p4

Pande Rohini & Topalova Petia (2013). "Women in Change", Finance and Development, A Quarterly Publication of the International Monetary Fund, Vol. 50. No. 2, June 2013, Washington, pp12-15

Steady Chioma Filomina (2012). Women and Leadership in West Africa: Mothering The Nation and Humanizing the State, Palgrave McMillan, New York, NY. USA.

Stotsky, JU. G. (2006)," Gender and Its Relevance to Macroeconomic Policy: A Study", International Monetary Fund (IMF) Working Paper WP/06/233

The Times Journal (2017). "Kenya Women Urge to Withhold Sex in Vote Drive", The Times Journal, Vol. 03, No.218, Tuesday, January 18, 2017, Yaoundé – Cameroon, pp10

Chapter Four

Regional Economic Communities

"Africa is rich. Our people walk on gold, diamonds, and oil. Yet our people are poor, and our mineral wealth has become a curse in itself."
(Jay Naidoo, Former Minister in Mandela's Cabinet; Secretary General, South African Trade Unions)

Introduction— Unlocking Africa's Economic Heart: Cross-Cutting Issues

Underlying Africa's failure to deliver the dreams of Kwame Nkrumah for *"one continent, one people and one nation"* is leadership failure and a passive civil society to be guided by the needs of the very people meant to benefit from the collective wealth and power. What are the successes or ugly failures of the continent given its abundant natural resources potentials? Is the continent evolving on uncertain policies for uncertain glory? What is actually happening? Are the leaders listening and very carefully to our citizens? Naidoo is explicit on these and other pertinent questions and issues plaguing the continent. *"Across Africa, from the slums of Kibeira and Khayalitsha to the villages of Turkana and Giyani, far from the ivory towers of our political discourse, I see and hear the rising tide of anger and discontent. Africa is rich. Our people walk on gold, diamonds, and oil platinum. Yet our people are, poor, and our mineral wealth has become a curse in itself. Our natural resources, now estimated at a third of the world's reserves, power the global economy. But we undervalue our assets. We undervalue ourselves."* We are not proactive but blame others for our failures. There is continued obsession for placing our shortcomings elsewhere.

Change we have before it becomes too late to reactive positively and constructively. We fail to plan and plan to fail. With the "Corona virus (COVID-2019)" pandemic having a serious toll on the lives of the people, we need to seriously rethink our current development strategies. We have to start providing life-changing appliances – which have for many years failed to reach the most vulnerable in society. This should be the growing priority. We need to formulate and respond positively to comprehensive policy actions that put the blame phenomenon to 'rest in peace' and encourage society still inclined to such destructive agenda to start thinking afresh and in a more positive direction. Rationality, objectivity, scientific thinking and reality have escaped our line of thinking and actions. It is time we moved from the fringes to the centre of a people-oriented development action plan. Africa remains a growing market with major untapped potentials and demands.

Anyone thinking Africa is a poor continent is making a serious mistake. Financial resources abound in the continent's institutional and private hands. The policies are good many. But the political will for implementation is in serious deficit. These resources need to be crowded in and channelled to bankable projects on the continent argues Mataboge (2017:48) who equally point out that "the rise of populism and populist economic rhetoric and policies, and the commodities slump have a negative impact on the fortunes of many African economies as the continent is heavily reliant on commodity exports.

It goes without saying that the increase in intra-Africa investment is manufacturing and infrastructure projects has become a prerequisite to increasing the new levels of intra-trade. There is a brighter future for the African continent; the only realistic hope for realising the "Africa Rising" narrative pivots in ensuring that Africans invest in each other's economies to demonstrate confidence for the transformation, participation and economic emancipation of the people in the rapidly growing and changing circumstances of global knowledge-based economy.

Without mincing words, it is a challenge to Africa's businesses and government to look into the issue of intra-continental resources mobilisation and strategic investments and projects that build much needed infrastructure accelerating the industrialisation of Africa. For a long time past, intra-African trade grew from 10% to 16% between 2000 and 2014 and remains far below that of other regions, and in arguably Africa's most underutilised growth opportunity.

Improved intra-African trade equally requires improved intra-African transport and communication network – road, rail, sea and airports etc. which the Chinese Silk Rod project – the One Belt, One Road (OBOR) could help facilitate its take-off. Thomas (207:54-55) states that "underpinning the ambitious bid to pull over 60 disparate nations into an integrated trading system in a plan to unlock vast flow of infrastructural capital. The ultimate goal is to create manufacturing-based industries which ca attempt to turn back the tide on decades of commodity-dependent growth. OBOR aims to build commodity improve and manufactured goods export supply chain infrastructure connecting China to markets in Asia, Middle East, Africa and Europe." See also Simelane and Managa (eds,) 2018).

The challenge is to seriously move Intra-African trade beyond political commitments to aggressive implementations Action Level (AIAL). There is a serious "mismatch between the high political ambitions African leaders hold and the harsh economic realities they face, they have set up no less than 14 trading blocs to pursue regional integration, Yet they have shown a distinct reluctance to empower these institutions, citing loss of sovereignty and policy space as hey concerns: Regional institutions remain weak, performing mainly administrative functions" (Tafirenyika, 2014:5).

Accelerating regional integration African leaders expand access to trade finance as well as reduce behind-the-border trade restrictions such as excessive regulations and weak legal systems. The African continent is saddled with weak economies, small domestic markets and 16 landlocked countries, governments believe they can achieve economic integration by starting at the regional level and working their way up, merging all regional trading blocs into an African Free Trade Area. But with 14 different trading blocs, and with overlapping members and many countries belonging to multiple blocs, the challenge becomes even more complicated.

However, trade flourishes when countries produce what other trading partners are to buy. This is not what prevails on the continent; to a large extent, African produces what it does not consume and consumes what it does not produce. It is a weakness that often frustrates policy makers; it complicates regional integration and is a primary reason for the low integration and primary reason for low intra-African trade, which is between 10% and 12%; Africa's total trade, as compared with 40% in North America and about 60% in Western Europe. Well over 80% of Africa's exports are shipped overseas mainly to the European Union (EU) China and the USA. Trfirenyika (op cit) notes further that African governments need policy space to address the development challenges they face but this does not appear consistent with the signing of many regional agreements. Lack of capacity to implement their obligations s also to blame; a view shared by the African Development Bank (AfDB) that regional integration and intra-trade in Africa imputed slow progress to a complex architecture of regional economic communities; while this arrangement has yielded positive steps towards common regional targets, progress has been disappointing." It is also because there is lack of progress in implementing agreements along with the absence of reliable transport, energy and information and technology infrastructure which impedes the journey towards regional integration long and arduous.

Building the corridor connection – Banjul to the Horn; Algiers to Lagos; and Cairo to the Cape will go a long way to ease Intra-African connectivity and boost to intra-regional trade. "African countries need to develop robust laws and strengthen their monitoring and enforcement mechanisms and institutions capabilities' (Zeleza 2014:166). Though many African countries have significantly made some economic progress, they need to embark on the path of diversification and aggressively enter the world trade market, especially in the Asian regions, which can boost exports. It is not enough export raw materials. These have to be processed to get more added values from them.

Nevertheless, African countries have to diversify and carry out serious domestic reforms to fully capture the economic benefits. So far, "Africa's exports to Asia have not yet significantly contributed to sustain widespread Africa's export diversification of either trading partners or products including with respect to greater value added though further processing. African countries need strategies to leverage the current export explosion to create opportunities for long-term economic benefit. Further reforms in at-the-border trade policies, such as reducing Asian's escalating tariffs or harmonising or consolidating Africa's overlapping regional trade agreements will surely help facilitate Africa's export to Asia and elsewhere. But dealing head-on with domestic constraints in Africa is likely to be every bit as, if not more critical. Indeed, if African countries are to enhance their global economic performance is Asia and key much it will have to take for more than simply liberalising trade policies to reach that objective" (Broadman, 2007:39).

No doubt, Africa will its vast natural resources has a comparative advantage in manufactured products to boost its exports to China and other Asian countries, India for example, and this positive shifts/complementarities can be reinforced by serious domestic reforms in Africa, namely; (i) the prospects for resources based value-added manufacturing exports which China and India are importing. Africa countries can increase their manufactured exports to China and India based on their existing exports of raw materials: (ii) the prospects for broader participation in global value chains between Africa and Chins and India are growing: and (iii) the diversity among African countries and political benefits from regional integration" (Broadman 2007).

Prof Zeleza (2014) remarks; "there is a need to deepen inter-cultural understanding through education, the media, cultural exchange and interactions. China is investing heavily in increasing its soft power in

Africa through peacekeeping missions, media, education and building cultural ties. It is clear that Africa's relations with China are situated in the exceedingly complex context of a rapidly changing global political economy. This makes it imperative and difficult for each party to manage effectively their relations with each other and with other major powers and economies," see also Brautigam, 2009; Bokilo, 2013; Chan, 2013).

In the final analysis, and most critically, Africa countries must articulate more clearly, coherently, and collectively what their fundamental interests are in this critical relationship. An interest that should be rooted in the historic and humanistic agendas of African nationalism for self-determination, sustainable development, democratisation, and regional integration (Zeleza, 2014:166). On their part, Hout and Salih (2019) bridge the gap in African literature on regional integration and asymmetric relation it is characterised by. They bring to the fulcrum issues concerned with regional integration and African development. The role of civil society is crucial in the process of integration; policy makers can benefit from using traditional institutions and indigenous knowledge systems. Is advancing the cause of functional, efficient and effective regional organisation.

Attempts at regional integration in Africa have a long history but a very uneven implementation record. The presence of too many different and overlapping regional arrangements, particularly in Eastern and Southern Africa, has created confusion and cumbersome administrative rules. The real change is to ensure that regional organisations are perceived as effective means of integrating Africa into the world economy, fostering mutual support among members in their reform efforts (Gondwe, 2001:33). Most importantly, these regional groupings should not be perceived as mechanisms for defending and promoting established interests. In order to truly become vehicles of the integration and development of member countries and the continent as a whole, they should equally be strategising for obtain the best out of the globalisation deal as well as also pushing for openness to the rest of the world. What is therefore needed for the continent to achieve these objectives is (i) the existence of entrenched political will to pursue regional/continental integration objectives and giving priority over domestic considerations; (ii) resolute effort made to rationalise existing arrangements; and (iii) efforts needed to coordinate macroeconomic policies by reinforcing peer-group surveillance of national economic policies, including adopting convergence criteria, as well as working intensively to harmonise standards and regulations.

The world is significantly whitewashed with materials on trade agreements and socio-economic growth. Looking just at a few cases, Hosny (2017:133-155) notes that regional integration is characterised by improved competing investment flows, economies of scale, technology transfer and improved productivity. Marinor et al (2014) arguments focus on the effects of regional economic integration as including increased investments, expenditure, the consolidation of production and increased specialisation, proper utilisation of resources, production efficiency and the enhancement of economic growth. Regional integration is an important step in integrating Africa into the global economy. But we must plan for it to get the best out of the global unfolding opportunities.

While Wandrei (2018) maintains that the trade agreements eventually lead to trade gains for participating countries. Participating countries stand to benefit from regional cooperation and trade agreements especially if they improve on their infrastructure, developing human capital, empowering women and the youths, attracting quality foreign direct investments, creating and enabling environment for the promotion of various productive activities including the practice of democratic governance. Chime (1977:32) defines integration as a "process of cohesion between two or more social units thereby these units come to constitute a political whole which can in some case be described as a community".

Galtung's definition of integration is "a process whereby two or more actors form a new actor when the process is complete, the actors are said to be integrated." Aker and Puchala (1968) hold that "the levels of economic interaction between nations can serve as a reliable indicator of their degree of political integration. "What is certain is that political integration will occur only as a result of positive political decision to bring it about, not as a result of economic pressure alone "asserts Krause (1967:24). Therefore, it should be stressed that the study of regional integration is unique and discrete from all studies of political unification because it limit itself to non-coercive effects (Chine 1977:388) and the dominating desire of regional integration is the identity toward the voluntary creation of large political and economic units between the participating unites and groups. As such regional integration is thus normative.

Chime (1977) advances four approaches to integration, namely; (i) the *pluralist thesis*; considers the nation-state as the basic units in the process of integration. The modern nation-state presides over enormous resources. Integration is defined as a process leading to an end-state envisaged as a 'community.' The nation-states exercise their sovereignty in choosing their own policies and are regulated in these choices by diplomatic and strategic accommodations, by a resolve to solve their conflicts within a peaceful framework without resort to war; and by a cohesive network of transactions and a feeling of affinity – the so-called 'we' feeling; (ii) the *functionalist thesis*; which argues hampers on the administration of things instead of the government of men/women. "Society' as maintain by Mitrany (1943), will develop by our living it, and not by policing it. In the face of technological revolution, the nation-state, according to the functionalists, stands out as increasingly inadequate as the supreme and exclusive unit for organising human needs. Implicit in this reasoning is a basic functionalists paradox: Technology is progressing by leaps and bounds while politic is running a mock; (iii) the *federalist thesis* is a method of dividing powers so that the general and regional government are such, within a sphere, co-ordinate and independent. Federalism upholds the outright securing of political union by a dramatic and immediate subscription to a blueprint allocating powers to the system and the units; and (iv) according to the neo-functionalist thesis, integration between states emerges from the pluralistic bargaining process among salient political forces consisting of interest groups, parties, governments and international organisation. As in the functionalist approach the bargaining is welfare-issue oriented and incremental (see Haas, 1958; Hazelwood, 1967; Ndegwa, 1968).

Regional integration is another major potential source of enhanced trade investment, economic efficiency, and growth generally. In sub-Saharan Africa, some regional trade arrangements have contributed significantly to structural reform by creating incentives for restrictive trade practices and licensing procedure. Furthermore, the importance of regionalism in stimulating efficiency and reforms should not be underestimated. Another problem with regional trade arrangements that is especially acute in eastern and southern Africa is the number of overlapping and internally inconsistent initiatives. The East African Region has for example regional groupings which include the Regional Integration Facilitation Forum, the Common Market for Eastern and Southern Africa (COMESA), the Southern African Custom Union (SACU), Region Integration Facilitation Forum (RIFF), East African Community (EAC) and Southern African Development Community (SADC) with overlapping memberships, conflict obligations, different strategies and objectives as well as conflicting rules and administrative procedures. See map on Regional trading Arrangements in Eastern and Southern Africa. This is in mark contrast with regional trade arrangements, such as Asia and Latin America, where regional trade arrangements consist of blocs of countries with little overlap between them (Sharer, 2001:16).

There are also those looking at the current precarious situation of the continent will argue that African countries are not mature enough for executing a free trade area partly because of its underdeveloped nature. The poor state of industrialisation prevents the continent of harvesting rightly from the process of a free trade; rather, it has made the continent a dumping ground for western manufactured goods. These arguments for and against a free trade area have their merits and demerits. What is important is for the continent to move forward by developing its human capital, infrastructure to proper utilise and benefit from its vast natural resources. It has to start from somewhere and the creation of AfCFTA could just be the beginning of that long journey to maturity. The continent at this juncture can draw valuable lessons from existing regional integration bodies like EAC, ECOWAS, SADC, COMESA, CEMAC, NEPAD, and the EU to sharpen their tools and ensure they make the best out of AfCFTA for the overall interest of the people.

There is no doubt that with NEPAD and under the canopy of the success stories of existing regional groupings and regional aspiration, Article 3 of AfCFTA (AU, 2019) identifies the regional objectives of the agreement is:

- The creation of a single market for goods and services facilitated by the free movement of people to deepen the economic integration of the continent with the Pan-African vision of 'integrated, prosperous and peaceful Africa as enshrined in Agenda 2063;
- The creation of a liberalised market for goods and services;
- Contribution to the movement of capital and people and to facilitate investments and regional economic communities;
- Laying the foundation for the establishment of a continent customs union in due course;
- Promoting industrial development through diversification and regional value chains in agriculture and food security;
- Resolving challenges of multiple and overlapping memberships as well as expedite regional and centralised integration processes.

It should equally be noted that AfCFTA's strong political backing from African Heads of State has garnered attraction from member of state level especially around the projection of intra-African trade gains. The enthusiasm is further strengthened that AfCFTA is coming at the heels of other continental initiative championed by the African Union, notably the launching of a single air transport market during the 30th Ordinary Session of the Assembly of Heads of State and Government at the AU on 28th January 2018 in Addis Ababa, Ethiopia, to boost connectivity and cut travel cost across the continent (AU 2018; Onwuka and Udegbunam, 2019).

With the introduction of an AU passport this will help eliminate travel restrictions and resolve glitches of intra-African mobility of people and goods. The realisation of a functional AfCFTA will be Africa's dream of unity come true. The challenges now include developing interconnectivity. Infrastructures, roads, seaports, air transport within and between the 54 countries to facilitate the movement of the people and goods from one point to another. African countries need to be connected not disconnected if it has to be part of the fast-growing globalised world of knowledge-based economy.

Beyond existing challenges of infrastructure deficit, poor access to finance to finance, political uncertainty, inter-regional restriction on free movement and growing demands for western goods by African consumers, AfCFTA could the game changer, opening new avenues for 'love of and produced goods' which should offer significant prospects in improving the quality livelihood of the people. We should develop a culture for the love of what we produce. Opening up the boarders and promoting connectivity would be of great importance to the emerging Africa of tomorrow.

For now, half of the continent's population today is under 20 and our 'youth bulge' will account for a third of the global youth population in less than three generations. What is the future we are nurturing for our youth when nearly half of them have few skills, no jobs and are unlikely to have the dignity of labour in their lifetime? It is time we change the education and social environment to create livelihoods. Technology holds the possibility to change the world we live in, how we work and how we organise our lives. That is the dial of hope we need to change; it is a matter of the greatest urgency. The current ferment demonstrates that the patience of the people is running out. Citizens alienated by corruption are demanding a voice. They want the dignity of work and social protection, safety and justice. Independent public institutions are a key pillar to prevent the incestuous web of interconnected, predatory political and economic elites who have a stranglehold on our growth potential. A third of our people lives in a conflict-ridden country and will never achieve any of the Millennium Development Goals (MDGs). A country that goes through a civil war will take at least 25 years to recover its pre-conflict GDP. In places like the Great Lakes, rape has become an instrument of war. It forces thousands of children into the brutal game of soldiers of war.

Regional economic integration – allowing the free movement of goods, services, people and capital between national markets – is fundamental to achieving robust and equitable growth in Africa. Only by giving Africa's producers access to regional markets and linking them up into more sophisticated value chains can Africa become competitive in an interconnected world. Regional Economic Communities is the key to boosting productivity and achieving lasting improvements in living standards. Therefore, RECs should help to unlock the continent's immense economic potential by better connecting its people and integrating its economies.

Creating bigger markets in Africa requires integrating their economies. Importantly, the right recipe for regional integration is that countries concentrate on commodities in which they have a competitive advantage. Presently, African markets are small and fragmented, which cancels out any competitive advantage smaller countries may have. Therefore, to create bigger markets, African countries should unite and integrate their economies and speak with one voice. As noted by the Carlos Lopes (Executive Secretary of the Economic Commission for Africa), "Togo with six million wants to survive on its toothpaste produced in Togo, and Benin with a population of nine million inhabitants also wants to produce its own.' The right recipe for regional integration is that countries concentrate on commodities in which they have a competitive advantage. For example, Benin and Egypt could concentrate on cotton. Togo on cocoa, Zambia on sugar – each country operating in bigger regional markets.

Challenges for Regional Integration

Presently, problems with regional integration, such as weak political commitment and a lack of policy harmonisation, are familiar but should be overcome for the overall good of the continent. One of the main challenges facing Africa's Regional Economic Communities (RECs) in implementing their integration programmes is overlapping membership. Consider the case of COMESA, EAC and SADC. EAC is already a common market, but it shares four member States with COMESA and one Member State with SADC. Five SADC member States are members of Southern African Customs Union (SACU). Ten countries in the region are already members of customs unions, but all of them are also in negotiations to establish alternative customs unions from the one they now belong to. COMESA and SADC have seven member States in common that are not part of a customs union, but all are preparing customs unions. So, of the 26 countries in COMESA, EAC and SADC, 17 are either in customs union and negotiating an alternative customs union to one they belong, or are negotiating two separate customs unions. Similar overlaps, though to a lesser scale exists among members of RECs in Western and Northern Africa (ECA 2012).

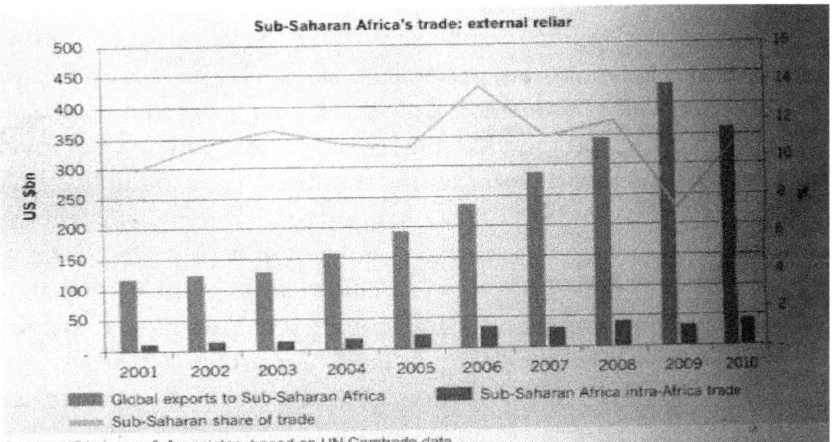

Source: Whitehouse & Associates, based on UN Comtrade data

There are attempts to merge three regional trade groupings (the Poor trade among African countries (see chart on Sub-Saharan Africa's Trade: External Reliance) imply that Africa cannot grow out of the poverty and underdevelopment syndromes. There has to be a magnificent shift in policy orientation and actions. Constructive engagement with civil society and the private sector is called for. Continental integration should no longer be driven by political agendas which due to policy articulation remain incremental and tedious. Other input measures should come to play. For example, the rationale for extension of roads, rail, telecommunications and power – and even the maintenance of existing infrastructure should be stepped up and given a new face lift (World Bank, 2009; Stiglitz, 2013; Bloom et al 2014)).

The East African Community, The Common Market for Eastern and Southern African; and The Southern African Development Community) into a "grand free trade area" incorporating 26 countries with a combined gross domestic product of US$1 trillion. Such a combined strength would give Africa a more assertive voice at the negotiating table. The establishment of a Continental Free Trade Association (CFTA) should be clear in articulating and aggregating matters relating to the responsibilities as well as the obligations of member states including accession and ratification of the protocol creating the organisation.

Problems with regional integration, such as weak political commitment and a lack of policy harmonisation, are familiar. The 2013 ECA/AU report is optimistic about the outcome of commodity-based industrialisation, which it insists 'must be grounded in the reality of each country. RECs have created a complicated web of competing commitments which, combined with different rules, result in high costs of trade between African countries, in effect undermining integration. Multiple and overlapping memberships occasion resource and effort wastage due to duplication/multiplication of effort. It complicates harmonization and coordination among member states and according to the ECA: tends to muddy the goals of integration leading to counterproductive competition among countries and institutions (ECA 2004). Ajayi (2001:7) asserts that "Africa's economic marginalisation, the result of its relatively isolationist policies and closed economies, explains why economic prosperity has eluded most of the continent."

Building up the continent's manufacturing is not that easy. Presently, the sector is not competitive for a host of reasons. To begin with existing policies have failed in promoting the technical capacities or specific knowledge needed to enhance efficiency, which is fundamental to successful industrialisation; second, the key to successful exporting lies in the technical efficiency of firms, which, in turn, is dependent on policies encouraging innovation and economies of scale.; and third, transaction costs in Africa is too high for a number of reasons including corruption, high tariff and nontariff barriers, high international transport costs, poor telephone/communication systems, unreliable infrastructure facilities for essentials like water, erratic power supply and many other difficulties.

Political and strategic reasons are cited as the overriding motivation for this multiplicity of memberships in RECs. Therefore, (i) there is need to rationalise the RECs since multiple memberships spread limited resources thin and complicate the integration process given diverse agendas: (ii) Need to expedite ratification and rationalise protocols to enhance convergence of sub-regional goals; (iii) Need for prioritisation to match goals with available resources, focus on achievable objectives and deepen fundraising: (iv) Strengthen private sector involvement in integration efforts: (v) Integration as part of Africa's overall development strategy: (vi) Integration ensuring equitable outcomes and guarding against deepening inequities:

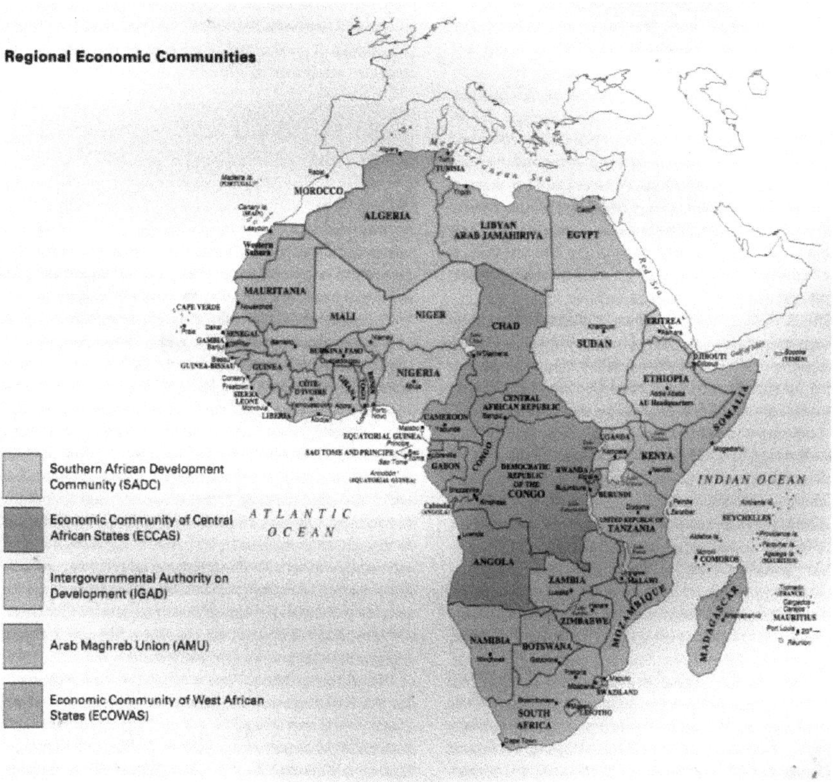

Source: Credit - Conflict Trends Issue 2, 2010, p 37

There is urgent need to intensify economic integration between African regions to help each African state to derive greater benefits from the fallouts of globalisation. There is not only divergence across disciplines, with economist, political scientist and sociologists focusing on different aspects and prioritising different dimensions, but also divergence within disciplines, with different theorists making different arguments. Given these disagreements, it is especially challenging to define globalisation. Although generic definitions do exist - for example, Rolandson (1992:8) defines globalisation as the compression of the world – they tend to reflect differing priorities often linked not only to changes in the social organisation of societies but also in the economic. We have to look at globalisation from three perspectives as (i) world system theory; with its emphasis on the division of the world; (ii) global culture theory; focusing on the forms of globalisation, such as the nation-state or individualism, or focusing on the 'contents' that globalisation represents a kind of cultural and scientific imperialism, the imposition of Western ideas and ideals onto the rest of the world; and

(iii) the global society approach; focusing on the structural dimensions of the world and examining the shifts associated with the turn to globalisation and outlining within each framework the role it allocates to economic development and democratic empowerment. The rise of global capitalism is something we should expect under these circumstances. The form taken by global capitalism is one that is, intimately linked to new media technologies.

So far poor and obsolete infrastructure hinders industrialisation efforts and the free movement of people, goods and services. To facilitate trade in goods and services, it is essential to reduce distribution costs. This is only possible through investments in roads, railways and energy infrastructure. Against the backdrop of the global economic and financial crisis and the stalemate in the World Trade Organisation (WTO) negotiations, intra-African trade could become a formidable tool for sustaining economic growth worldwide Yet, owing to a plethora of challenges comprehensively documented in ARIA 1V (UNECA, 2010), intra-African trade remains low. Its share of global trade is also limited – 3.2 per cent as against about 5 per cent in the mid-1960s. Table 4:1 Destination of Africa REC Exports, average 2000-2009, per cent of world total depicts the situation.

Table 4:1 Destination of Africa REC exports, Average 2000-2009, Per cent of World Total

	US	Japan	Brazil	China	EU	Africa	Rest of World
CEMAC	32.0	2.3	1.0	0.1	26.7	3.4	34.5
CEN-SAD	17.3	1.3	3.2	0.1	42.8	9.1	26.3
CEPGL	13.2	0.6	0.1	0.3	35.0	18.2	32.6
COMISA	5.3	1.6	0.8	0.1	50.2	9.1	32.8
EAC	3.8	2.1	0.0	0.9	30.2	33.6	29.4
ECCAS	29.0	1.0	0.6	0.2	22.2	3.9	43.0
ECOWAS	28.7	0.8	5.2	0.1	29.3	13.7	22.2
IGAD	2.4	7.1	0.0	0.4	17.6	19.4	53.1
IOC	14.0	1.3	0.0	0.6	64.7	8.5	10.9
MRU	7.6	0.2	0.0	0.1	54.2	9.0	28.9
SADC	13.7	3.9	0.5	1.0	26.3	13.5	41.1
UEMOA	6.2	0.4	0.7	0.1	49.6	31.4	20.6
UNA	11.9	0.7	3.0	0.1	64.6	2.5	17.2

Source: IMF Director of Trade, April 2011

In respect of exports, the European Union (EU) and the United States are among the leading export destinations for most African countries as depicted in Table 4:2, Sources of Africa REC imports, average 2000-2009, and percent of world total. The main trading partners of the African RECs are outside the continent. This is the main challenge for Africa to intensify trade among and within the continent's RECs. Intensifying such activities through the creation of an Africa Continental Free Trade Area (CFTA) will help construct African. To boost inter-African trade, African countries should equally invest in each other's economies. As the result of globalisation and changes in the global trading landscape have equally reduced flows of foreign direct investments from the rich to the developing countries Africa in particular even though the continent has the best potentials for rapid economic growth. Africa is not a poor continent; financial resources abound in African private and industrial hands. African countries need to be judiciously exploited and properly used. One way of incentivising such resource mobilisation is for African countries to build into projects being rolled out on the continent.

Table 4:2 Sources of Africa REC Imports, Average 2009-2009, per cent of World Total

	US	Japan	Brazil	India	China	EU	Africa	World
CEMAC	8.4	1.5	1.7	2.1	9.8	49.4	2.1	0.7
CEN-SAD	6.8	2.7	1.8	2.2	9.5	39.5	18.9	28.7
CEPGL	2.8	1.3	1.1	1.1	8.0	31.2	2.3	0.2
COMESA	7.1	3.1	1.3	4.1	8.8	30.0	17.7	18.6
EAC4.6	4.9	0.6	10.5	10.4	20.3	4.3	2.9	
ECCAS	8.1	1.3	4.8	2.5	11.4	45.7	5.2	1.6
ECOWAS	6.0	2.1	2.0	2.5	11.7	35.7	13.9	11.3
IGAD	4.2	3.4	0.9	7.7	13.9	18.8	3.9	5.3
IOC	3.4	2.5	1.0	9.6	10.6	24.4	1.2	1.3
MRU	2.8	1.0	0.9	1.1	8.0	33.7	1.3	4.9
SADC	7.4	4.4	2.2	3.5	12.2	31.8	18.3	13.1
UEMOA	3.6	1.6	1.6	1.9	12.2	32.6	7.3	2.2
UMA	5.2	2.0	1.7	1.2	8.4	53.8	3.5	9.3

Source: IMF, Direction of Trade Statistic, April 2011

Improved African markets and promoting intra-African trade (from the current low average of 10 per cent in the past decade will move economic activities forward. It will also help Africa to regain its lost share of global trade. As already noted, regional integration in the continent faces multiple challenges, which underline the need to strengthen coordination among the various RECs as individual countries cannot overcome them alone. Therefore, African leaders must accelerate integration reviewing current methods, by removing all obstacles that hinder integration, by making strong commitments to reach the goals by providing more resources to the AU and the RECs. various challenges stand out. Energy access and security constitute some of the greatest constraints on sustainable and inclusive growth. Despite the continent's vast energy resources, its energy access lags far behind than in the rest of the world. In addition, energy supply is hampered by inefficient utilities, and weak cross-border collaboration in energy trade. Hence some sub-regions need to spur themselves further, in order to harness the benefits of, for example, gas and power supply pools and regional energy markets.

The multiplicity of schemes holds back integration, by imposing a huge burden on countries' inadequate administrative and financial capacities and by leading to conflict obligations. A smooth integration process will also beef-up the lack of self-financing mechanisms for the RECs, limited progress on fostering production integration and regional complementarities, or for developing regional infrastructure (especially transport and communications) to drive market integration (ECA 2012). The general objective of establishing the CFTA is the creation of a single market with the free movement of goods, persons and services as a way of promoting social and economic development in Africa. In short CFTA should impact the continents socioeconomic and technological transformation by:

- movement of persons and labour and right of establishment
- movement of goods and service in Africa;
- movement of investment and capital in Africa, this should lead to;
- improving macroeconomic performance and harmonising policies;
- enhancing regional financial and capital market development and integration;
- improving the business environment;
- improving the stability and security of property rights;

- regulation and taxation;
- improving labour market

African countries mainly trade with countries and regions outside the continent, with only 10-18% of trade taking place between African nations. This compares unfavourably to Europe, where 69% of export were traded within the region, and Asia, where 52% exports were traded with other countries within the region. One of the reasons Africa's regional trade is so low is due to the fact that most trade with overseas countries is in the export of raw materials, such as copper and iron ore, which are rarely processed within the continent. Therefore, producing value-added goods which can be traded between African countries, as well as overseas countries, should be a priority for African governments and business. But this cannot happen until - and we keep - returning to this theme – we improve the continent's infrastructure especially in electricity power. Regional integration is a key to securing the future development of Africa. I do believe that the leaders are moving in the right direction and there is now better coordination between African countries (Elumelu, 2017:23).

On average, the trade regimes of African countries remain significantly more protectionist than those of other countries including Africa's major trading partners as indicate in the two charts, Sub-Saharan Africa's share of world exports of goods and Trade Regimes are more Restrictive in Africa than the rest of the world. It is evidently clear that without substantial improvement in its trade performance, Africa will be unable to reverse its weak growth performance of the past many decades and it is only by achieving sustainable high-quality growth that it will be able to meet its overarching goal of improving the quality livelihood of the vast majority of the citizens. Trade constitute a major engine of growth of which African countries should seriously bear in mind.

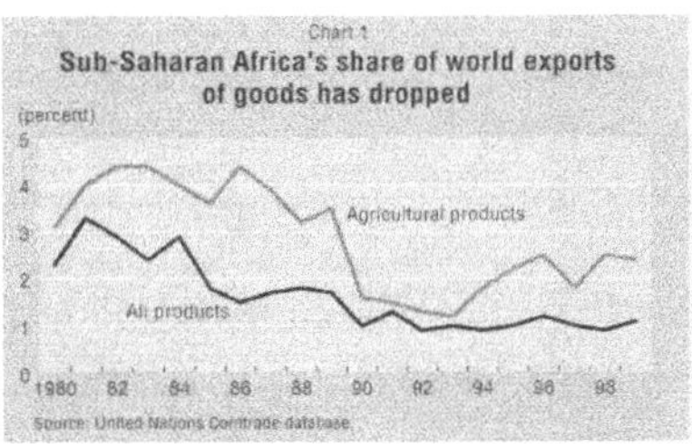

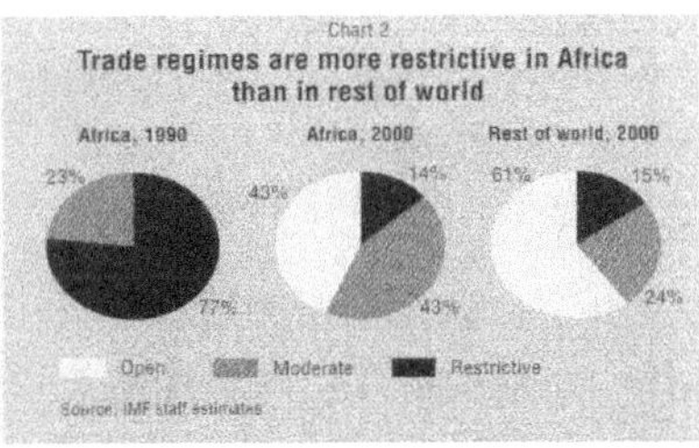

(See also Robert Sharer (2001)"An Agenda for Trade. Investment and Regional Integration" Finance and Development, December 2001, Vol.38 No.4.IMF Washington. Pp15

Given that Africa's share of world trade is marginal, at only 3.2 per cent in 2010, it is imperative that RECs should have new code of proactive colour of greater integration, coordination and political will to improve on the economic image of the continent within the global structure. RECs through CFTA should intensify trade among them and thus be a major contributor to the improved wellbeing of their citizens since neighbouring states have a tendency to trade among themselves. This requires removing trade barriers continent wide which should help facilitate the free movement of people, goods and financial transactions and other flows to enhance welfare (Krugman 1991). It equally entail opening up of a number of transport or infrastructure corridors and related projects that address road infrastructures, road transport facilities as well as rail infrastructure to connect countries. The Trans-African Road should be accelerated to link East and West, North and South and this should be backed by a continental wide railroad transport system. Africa should intensify its connectivity through air, land and sea as well as developing and using ICTs. Energy connectivity is important to keep the emerging industrial wheels of the continent rotating in order to meet global production and competitively.

Table 4:3 Features of Regional Integration

1	2	3	4	5	6
Preferential Trade	No	No	No	No	No
Free Trade Area	Yes	No	No	No	No
Customs Union	Yes	Yes	No	No	No
Common Market	Yes	Yes	Yes	No	No
Economic Union	Yes	Yes	Yes	Yes	No
Political Union	Yes	Yes	Yes	Yes	Yes

Source: UNECA (2006)

Note: (1) = Type of Arrangement; (2) => Free trade Among Members; (3) => Common Commercial Policy; (4) => Free Factor Mobility; (5) =>Common Monetary and Fiscal Policies: (6) => One Government

Intra-African trade in the first decade of the 21st century made very little progress. In 2009, it accounted for only 11 per cent of the continent's total trade compared with other continent's as depicted in Table 4:4 trade within continents 2009, a meagre 1 percentage point increase from 9/7 per cent in 2000 (Comtrade 2009/2010). This is far less than trade within other regions. For the sake of world peace and stability, developed and developing countries need to do something more drastic in improving the follow of trade within and between developing polities.

Intra-African investment is essential for realising the 'Africa rising' narrative. Africa has to industrialise and to stop exporting raw materials. It is imperative for Africa's business and government leaders to probe into an intra-continental resource mobilisation for strategic investments and projects to accelerate the continents industrialisation nexus. While some progress can be recorded – there are stays large lope holes to be addressed. For example, the African Development Bank asserts that while intra-African trade grew from 10% to 16% between 2000and 2014, this falls far below that of other regions, and is arguably Africa's most underutilised growth opportunity. No doubt, greater increase of intra-Africa investments in manufacturing and infrastructure projects remains a prerequisite to boosting the low levels of intra-Africa trade. Investments in each other's economies would demonstrate confidence and trust as well as increase the quest for African unity and renaissance. The continent need to wage a serious war on the economic marginalisation; as women's economic empowerment languishes in a black hole and underscores the continent's state of underdevelopment.

Table 4:4 Trades within Continents – 2009 (Per cent of Total Trade)

Intra-European Trade	72
Intra-Asian Trade	52
Intra-North America Trade	26
Intra-African Trade	11

Source: Comtrade (2009/2010)

According to Robson (1994), the larger the regional construct the more likely they are to be trade creating, because their members' production structures are most likely to have larger overlaps in their range of products and producers, thus creating a competitive environment. Most African countries' small size argues for the CFTA: For example, 12 African states have a population of less than 2 million, and 19 have a Gross Domestic Product (GDP) of less than US$5 billion in 2008 (World Bank, 2008). Thus, a continental approach would there provide a leverage and collective platform for Africa to increase the continent's influence in the global trade negotiations nexus. Africa must unite to exert its influence in the global community (Forje forthcoming).

Table 4:5 Average Export and Import Times (Days)

OECD High Income	10.5	10.7
Latin America & Caribbean	17.8	19.6
Middle East & North Africa	19.7	23.6
Eastern Europe & Central Asia	27.0	28.8
Sub-Saharan Africa	**31.5**	**32.1**

Source: World Bank, Doing Business, Doing Business in a More Transparent World. (2012)

(http://www.doingbusiness.org//media/fpdkm/doing%20business/documents/annualreports/English/db12-

Note: Times comprise inland transport, customs procedures and port handling

Table 4:5 illustrates the average export and import times (days). Trade within the regions is impeded by a number of factors including burdensome customs procedures, lengthy port handling and poor inland transportation Export and import times are far higher than for OECD countries as illustrated in Table 4:5. Following United Nations Conference on Trade and Development (UNCTAD), report on Economic Development in Africa 2009, it pointed out the difficulties confronted the continent added greater urgency to efforts to forge more links among African economies themselves. As of 2009, only 9 percent of African countries; external trade is with other African states and just 13 percent of inflows of foreign direct investment come from African the lowest shares of regional trade and investment in the world. But there is enormous potential to increase such intra-African relations. Unlike Africa's trade with Europe, Asia and other parts of the world, which is dominated by raw materials, trade within Africa is primarily in manufactured goods. Increasing intra-African trade can therefore help develop Africa's manufacturing and promoting greater diversification of its economies.

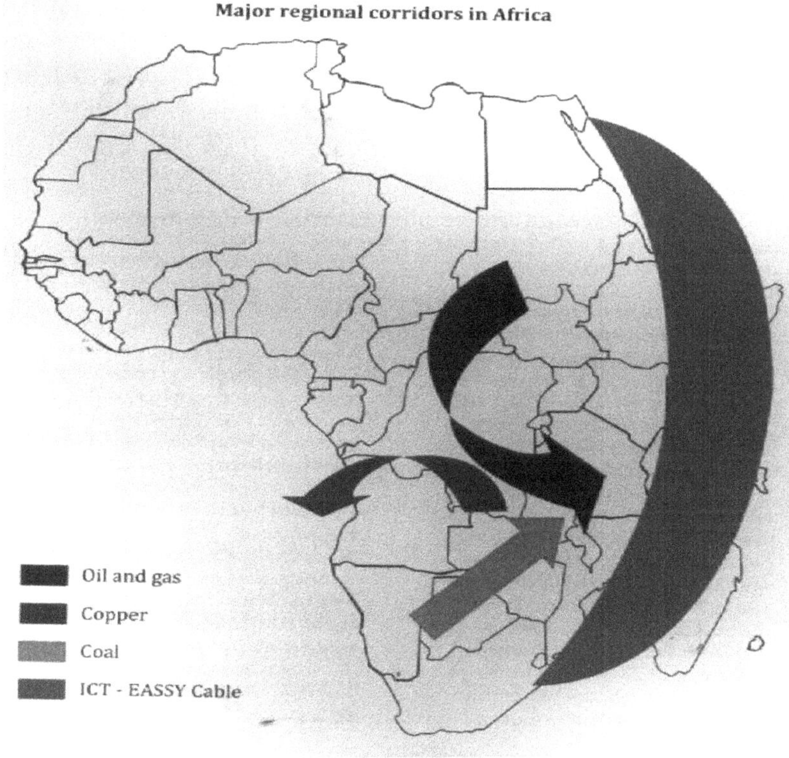

Source: Duncan Bonnet (2012) "Privately Motivated". In Africaninvestor, May-June 2012, pp74-77

Therefore, better trade and telecommunications and improved banking and insurance services across African borders can also strengthen investment among African countries. The report concluded that Africa needs to exploit opportunities within the continent which could help it achieve higher economic growth rates and development objectives (Africa Renewal, Vol. 23. No.2, July 2008, pp24, Washington USA). The Map on Major Regional Corridors in Africa depicts some of major key projects not only adding the gravitas needed to underpin the integration of the continent, but they are also providing the bedrock for the development of associated industries as well as the expansion of other industries – notably agriculture, but also construction materials, building and social infrastructure. For now, the continent is badly integrated; however, with large swathes of the continent have no direct access to logical trading points. This is changing quickly though as the desire to open up the potential of much of Africa's interior gathers space. The urgency for an integrated economic space in Africa remains imperative. Poor economic integration is serious inhibiting factor to the growth of trade. For example, a car exported to Abidjan from Japan would cost about USA $1.500 as compared to transporting the same car via land from Addis Ababa (Ethiopia) to the other side of the continent at a cost of USA$5.000, which shows Africa's starkest evidence that trading within the continent itself is hamstrung.

Apparently, African traded externally more comfortably than internally and investment patterns have followed this, but these seem to be changing. Poor trade integration among African countries can be related to many border posts, corruption linked to these, too little infrastructure, thus inhibiting too little trade, and thereby making the economies of scale too small. It thus becomes a self-perpetuating circle suggesting that new infrastructure cannot be justified because of the low levels of trade. Sub-Saharan African trade has averaged less than 11% a year for the past decade (see chart on Sub-Saharan Africa's Trade; External Reliance).

The Central African Region constitutes a vital corridor linking West and East, South and North of the continent but remains the least enclaves with poor communication infrastructure. Both the free movements of people and goods are hampered by poor means of communication. The earlier the Trans-African Highway linking East and West, South and North the quicker this is done the greater it would hasten regional and continental integration. These developments require private initiatives and the participatory role of various stakeholders. Government alone cannot undertake these massive infrastructural developments. No doubt the gross absence of an integrated economic space in Africa is a serious major obstacle to African trade and integration. For example, a car exported to Abidjan from Japan would cost USA$1,500 as compared to USA$5.000 for an identical car transported by land from Addis Ababa (Ethiopia) to West Africa, exhibiting the starkest evidence that Africa's ability to trade with itself is hamstrung. The reasons for such discrepancies are myriad; (a) too many trade regulations and too many border posts control; (b) corruption; (c) too little infrastructure backed by too little trade, which make the economies of scale too small. In the final analysis, it is evident that self-perpetuating circle suggest that new infrastructure cannot be justified due to the low levels of trade between African countries.

Presently, one can witness some form of increasing private investments that should give regional economic integration a boost. Private companies are becoming more and more important in the funding, building and operation of existing and new infrastructure in the region. Within the Central African Region, exciting mining developments, a form of regional cluster of large-scale iron ore projects with vast potential of positioning the region as the next global iron ore province is emerging. Bonnet (2012) notes that the deposits straddle an area in the northern Congo, northern Gabon and Southern Cameroon which have attracted investments from a number of private companies including; Sundance resources, Legend Mining, Core Mining, equatorial Resources and Xstrata. These deposits are in the remote regions and the development depends on the development of a route to sea. The key players have reached agreement on the development of a rail corridor through to a custom-built iron ore export terminal at the Port of Lolabe in Cameroon.

In East-central and East Africa, there are three major spines of resources development driving integration in southern-east-central and east Africa. The *first* is the 'new oil frontier' which roughly traces the Great Rift from South Sudan through Uganda, eastern DR-Congo, Rwanda, Tanzania, Mozambique and ultimately the northern reaches of Madagascar; the *second* area of development is the growing coal belt across southern Africa, stretching from Botswana through Zimbabwe and South Africa to Mozambique's massive Tete coal fields that are transforming central and northern Mozambique; the *third* major area of development is the great Copperbelt region of Zambia and the Congolese province of Katanga. See map on Regional Corridors in Africa depicting some of major areas of the newly found resources attracting foreign capital for infrastructure development. No doubt, private capital, private planners, private project developers and private operators are slowly but surely emerging and to have a far bigger role to play in the development of various infrastructure (roads, rails, ports, airports, industrial parks, telecom and pipelines) that are vital at both national, regional and continental levels.

Seen in broader terms, these major developments are slowly but gradually beginning to push forward and accelerate the process of integration so badly needed in Africa. In short, lack of integration in Africa is costing the continent billions of dollars in lost opportunity every year. With private companies becoming more and more interested in the funding, building and operation of existing and newfound infrastructure in the region, one can only hope and be optimistic of some form of movements towards higher levels of output and greater integration of the continent. Banks in Africa, Nigeria, Kenya and South Africa are getting more and more interested in infrastructural development in a number of African related development activities'. Together with these African Banks and in conjunction with other tradition financers from over the world including other emerging sources of private capital from Japan, Korea and the Middle East and Asia (Japan, Korea) China among others as funders, we can begin to see new shapes of things emerging.

Finally; a continental free trade area would be an efficient way to resolving the overlapping and multiple memberships of RECs. The conflicts and contradictions stemming from the complex "spaghetti bowl" of Africa Regional Arrangements undermining moves towards an African Economic Community by engendering poor coordination and costly duplication of programmes and activities (UNECA, 2006' AU, 2007). Administrative burdens on cross-border trade, and roadblocks along trading routes, bribery and corruption as well as robbery and piracy, all need to be tackled on a continental scale. Otherwise the benefits of continental economic cooperation and trade will be far below potential, working against the progress of the continent. Of course, nothing is certain. However, it is evident that with the resources boom underway in many African countries, it is likely that this will be accompanied by far more privately-led integration of the continent's infrastructure, trade and regulatory environments.

It is imperative that African states should pay greater attention to issues that divide them, address the dilemma of regional integration and development in Africa. The challenges posed by globalisation should not be underestimated. Indeed, the architects of the AU and continental integration should by now be strongly motivated by a desire to strengthen Africa's ability to engage with the rest of the world on its own terms. Globalisation has seriously contributed to the continent's vulnerability and exposure to global market forces and externally driven development paradigms. A more pronounced process of continental economic and political integration is therefore imperative for Africa to establish itself as an equally partner in the global economy nexus.

Therefore, the following crucial obstacles to political and economic integration must be looked into from an objective and critical mindset for the continent to own is development path. (i) there exist a 'cacophony' of regional groupings which fans an avenue of confusion, duplication and a dissipation of energies and resources; (ii) regional economic and political insecurity detracts attention from more positive and concrete measures of integration; as such, governments tend to devote time and resources to internal crises, thereby short-changing regionalist initiatives that would benefit their countries in the long-term: (iii) apparently, regionalism in Africa is driven largely by governments, and is often held hostage to the political will and dictates of the self-articulate interests of African leader; (iv) the prevalence of nascent and weak regional institutions, and rigorous and cumbersome regulatory procedures such as import controls and tariffs, have and continue to have adverse effects on regional integration; and (v) Africa must urgently tackle its infrastructural problems of poor and inefficient communication, road and transport systems as well as ensure the reign of good governance, rule of law and justice (Akokpari 2005; Forje 2009). It is shameful that the continent should be suffering from erratic power supply when we have sunshine the year round to power our energy needs.

Infrastructure Underdevelopment: The Impeding Factor

Infrastructure constitutes a vital link in promoting regional integration. Since he creation of the OAU to the present African Union, most of the summits of these two organisations have harped on the state of poor transport and communications infrastructure; deficient maintenance of road networks; and the inflexibility, unreliability and inefficiency of rail transport, power supply and water as key factors holding back inter REC and Intra-African Trade. It should be pointed out that regional cross-border infrastructure facilitates and boost intra-regional trade and investment, unlock national and regional comparative advantages, and address the special needs of land-locked countries in accessing the rest of the world.

The World Bank Development Research Group (2006) estimated that sub-Saharan Africa could gain in the range of US$20 billion annually ($203 billion over 10 years) from trade-related infrastructure upgrading projects. For Africa to attain the Millennium Development Goals on poverty reduction, the region requires an annual growth of 7 per cent, which requires a yearly investment of US$22 billion in infrastructure – 40 per cent in transport, 25 per cent in energy, 20 per cent in water and 15 per cent in telecommunications. For its part, the AU/NEPAD African Action Plan, launched in 2009, considers the following projects as priorities for 2010-2015, Table 4:6 – African Action Plan Priority Infrastructure Intervention, 2010-2015.

On the hole, it is envisaged that the realisation of these projects will build and consolidate African markets and promote-intra-African trade, reduce transaction costs and improve regional competitiveness. Unfortunately, these projects are slow to take-off and be realised. At least two input factors contribute to the delay; (i) absence of political will; and (ii) the financial resources. All these require comprehensive coordinated strategy for total and successful realisation without which

Africa cannot claim the 21st century and are part of the globalisation bandwagon. For the past two or more decades, shifting economic paradigms and conditions for investment and capital flows – globalisation – have underlined the importance of Africa countries' steps to broaden and deepen regional integration. Seen within this context, there is an urgent need to remove opens all impediments to capital flows, enabling investors to freely select among alternative destinations on the basis of comparative advantage destination countries. Secondly, African countries must embark on a vigorous internal mobilisation of resources and ensure stringent management of the economy. Good governance is the key to ensure and enhanced the country's attractiveness to foreign investment, and even domestic financial capabilities.

Table 4:6 Africa Action Plan Priority Infrastructure Interventions, 2010-2015

Sub-Sector	Project/Programme
Energy	Kariba – North and Itezhi-Teszhi Hydropower Expansion Projects Kenya-Ethiopia Interconnections Sambangalou-Kaleta Hydropower and OMVG Interconnect-ions. Zambia-Tanzania-Kenya Interconnection Project
Transport	Upgrading of Dobi-Galafi-Yakobi Road Section of the Djibouti to Addis Ababa (North) Highway Mombassa-Nairobi-Addis Ababa Corridor Development Project Missing Links of Djibouti-Libreville Transport Corridor Isaka-Kigali-Bujumbura Railway Maghreb Highway Project Missing Links of the Dakar-N'djamena-Djibouti Highway Corridor Gambia River Bridge Bean Port Development Kazungala Bridge Project Regional Infrastructure Development in Support of Trade Facilitation Programme Brazzaville-Kinshasa Rail/Road Bridge and Railway Extension Kinshasa to Ilebo Regional Transport Network Improvements Improvement of Maritime Ports for African Island Countries NEPAD ICT Broadband Infrastructure (UMOJA Terrestrial Network), including the following regional network projects East African Community Broadband Network Central Africa Broadband Infrastructure Programme (CA-BI) West Africa Wide Area Network Southern Africa Regional Backhaul Network North-Western Africa Backbone Project NEPAD ICT Broadband Infrastructure Network (UHURUNET Submarine Cable) Marine Communication for Safety on Lake Victoria
Trans-boundary Water	Senegal River Basin water and Environmental Management Project Water Resources Planning and Management in the Nile River Basin Niger River Basin Shared Vision Investment Programme

Source: AU/NEPAD (2011)

Weak financial infrastructure delays the economic transformation of the continent. Though African countries have liberalised and upgraded their domestic financial markets, the number of solid stock exchange markets has not increased as one would expect. During the period

2002-2009, stock exchanges increased from 8 to 20, and market capitalisation of the five leading stock ex-changes tripled over the period. The spread of cross-border banking investments and the emergence of Africa-wide lenders also suggest potential for increasing integration and in regional and international markets. Lukonga and Chung (2010) note that cross-border banking in sub-Saharan Africa has been boosted by various push and pull factors. "At present, the playing field in international trade is not level. The industrial countries should eliminate restrictions against imports of African products, while the African countries must develop a coordinate trade strategy, notes Ajayi (2001). The challenge for Africa is ensure faster economic growth and poverty reduction within the context of an increasingly interdependent global environment. Even though there is no simpler, universal blueprint for a successful development strategy, policymakers do know a lot about the elements of sustainable growth with equity and social justice. To be successful, Africa's reform programme will need to be coupled with increased and better-coordinated international technical and financial assistance.

The increase in minimum regulatory capital in Ghana, Nigeria and Zimbabwe pushed foreign banks' subsidiaries to attract additional equity from parent companies and to seek M&A. Intensified competition in Nigeria and South Africa also pushed these countries, in that their major banks had to seek greater opportunities outside the country, generating M&A. In fact, M&A – associated with privatisation, regulatory changes for minimum capital, and intensified domestic competition – has provided opportunities for banks, pulling them into host countries. Rapid roll-out of new products and services as well as new technologies has also stimulated cross-border activity.

Table 4:7 depicts Capital Market Structures in Sub-Saharan Africa. Instead of investing in effective deterrents, African countries should focus of creative conducive environments for effective economic growth and employment across the continent. Public-private sector harmonious participation is vital and should be encouraged. The dearth of trade between African countries is a missed opportunity to help boost growth as well as improve the quality of the livelihood of all citizens. There is need across the continent to improve the business environment and to push towards greater economic integration.

Table 4:7	Capital Market Structures in Sub-Saharan Africa		
No. Markets	**Treasury Bill Market Market**	**Treasury Bill & Treasury Bond Bond Markets & Corporate Bond Or Equity Markets**	**Treasury Bill All Four markets & Treasury**
Burundi			
DRC	Angola	Benin	Botswana
CAR	Ethiopia	Gambia	Burkina Faso, Ghana
Chad	Guinea	Senegal	Cameroon Kenya
Comoros	Guinea-Bissau	Seychelles Cape	Verde, Nigeria
Congo Repub.	Lesotho	Cote d'Ivoire,	Namibia
Eritrea	Madagascar	Gabon	South Africa
Equatorial Guinea	Malawi		Mauritius Swaziland
Liberia	Sierra Leone	Mozambique	
Tanzania			
Mali	Togo		Rwanda Uganda
Niger			Zimbabwe, Zambia
Sao Tome & Principe			

Source: ECA 2010

Presently, the national, regional and continental resources and markets are largely unexploited. These resources remain virgin, unexploited but with great potentials of expanding. Africa for a long time yet will remain an unexploited desert. It needs to be properly exploited to deepen, national, regional and continental integration. The hidden domestic financial prowess of the continent needs to be exploited to facilitate economic integration and cross-border movement of private capital investment. African countries are challenged to address the following questions and provide valid and functional solutions;

- What is Africa's experience in regional integration?
- How do regional and other investment arrangements affect intra-African (within Africa) and inter-regional (between Africa and other regions) investment and capital flows?
- What are the steps that could be taken at national, regional, continental levels to improve performance?
- What are the favourable conditions (or opportunities) and challenges (or constraints) for improved performance?
- Why is Africa descending from hope into destructive frustration?
- Why has Africa failed to industrialise?

These and other related question begs for good governance, proper management and the rule of law, removing bottlenecks to private investments among others. Creating an enabling environment should be prioritised. A number of documents come to play vital roles here: The AU Convention on Preventing and Combating Corruption entered into in force in 2006 and ratified by 31 countries; The African Charter on Democracy, Elections and Governance; The African Charter on the Values and Principles of the Public Service and Administration and others should be vigorously encouraged and implemented in regional arrangements to help harmonise rules and standards across the continent so as to better improve the living standards of citizens.

Mainstreaming RECs within the whole process of Africa's development is fundamentally important. Regional economic groupings could be viewed as 'add-ons' that provide certain levels of economic development and as input to an African Common market. Regional Economic Communities empowers Africa to achieve to achieve development goals as well as emancipate African countries from a position of pleading for small amounts of aid, thereby enhancing and maintaining external dependence and acting in accordance with externally formulated conditionality; or access to world markets based on unequal terms of trade, and unequal access to decision making markets; or minimal debt relief on the terms of creditors.

It is time that equitable global economic relationship is built on the basis of shared responsibility, accountability and participation while redress for past abuses and fair demands are addressed through international law and human rights system. Africa can longer afford to continue business as usual. The people must speak with one voice in convincing our leaders to fashion an African and world order in which all Africans/human beings would have decent life chances and the opportunity to grow and develop in peace, confidence, freedom, with equality of opportunity to the fullness of their potentials.

Brief Notes on RECs, SDGs, the AFCFTA and AU Agenda 2063

Regional integration is an imperative for Africa, in terms of enhanced competitiveness in global trading, prevention of conflicts and consolidation of economic and political reforms. Following the 1980 Lagos Plan of Action (LPA) *(that never was)*, envisaged the African Economic Community (AEC) which grouped the African continent into five regional areas, North Africa, West Africa, South Africa, East Africa and Central Africa. A six region was later added – the **Diaspora**. It should be noted that the configuration of RECs does not tally with the AEC regions. Importantly, a marriage between the ideals of the AEC and RECs should be and economic union with a common currency, full mobility of factor of production and free trade among all 54 African states; and the political union of the continent to ensure safeguard and consolidate its sovereignty.

The African Union Commission officially recognises 8 RECS in line with decision No.1 of the Banjul Summit in July 2006, downgrading all others to inter-governmental agencies. The eight recognised RECs are considered building blocks. Based on an agreed need for rationalisation and better coordination of RECs, a Protocol on the Relations between the African Economic Community (AEC) and RECs is in existence. A study by the African Capacity Building Foundation in 2008 hoped; "that the new protocol under development will lead to the emergence of a better working relationship anchored on the principles of subsidiary and partnership." By and large, African countries have large unmet investment need, in addition these countries are poorly equipped to keep up with the state of rapid urbanisation and changing demands on workers. Investment is also needed to smooth the transition away from growth driven by natural resources (in commodity exporters) or sectors that do not engage in foreign trade (in some commodity importers) toward more sustainable sources of growth. African Governments should focus on social development, particularly health and education and improving infrastructure. These are the keys to the sustainable transformation of the continent.

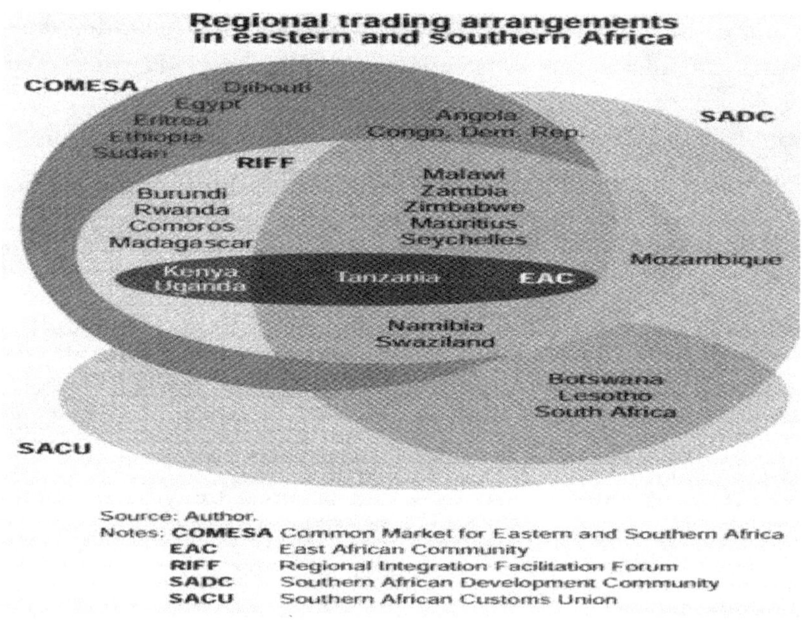

Source: (See also Finance and Development – Globalisation and Africa Vol.38, No.4, December 2001, Washington, p16)

This partnership should make the RECs the building blocks of the AEC, indeed with the AU playing its role as Africa's premier continental integration organisation. The eight recognised RECs in Africa according to the Banjul Summit in July 2006 appears on Table 4:8. Eight RECs and Six Integration Blocs. It is not just creating regional economic blocs but equally ensuring their structure-functionality to improving the livelihood of the people.

Table 4:8 Eight RECs and Six Integration Blocs

The Eight RECs Recognised by the AU	The Remaining Six Integration Blocs
Arab Maghreb Union (UMA)	1. Economic Community of Great Lakes Countries (CEPGL)
East African Community (EAC)	2. Southern African Customs Union (SACUS)
Economic Community of West Africa States (ECOWAS)	3. Mano River Union (MRU)
Southern Africa Development Community (SADC)	4. West African Economic and Monetary Union (UEMOA)
Community of Sahel-Saharan States (CENSAD)	5. Central African Economic Monetary Community (CEMAC)
Inter-Governmental Authority of Development (IGAD)	6. Indian Ocean Commission (IOC)
Common Market for Eastern & Southern Africa (COMESA)	
Economic Community of Central African States (ECCAS)	

The United Nations Sustainable Development Goals (SDGs) 2030

United Nations Sustainable Development Goals (SDGs) 2030 emerged in the wake of the failure of developing countries meeting the Millennium Development Goals (MDGs) of halving poverty by 2015. Few African countries attained the envisaged goals. The MDGs is now history and African countries have to move forward in a more structured way of realising the SDGs as well as meeting the AU Agenda 2063.

According to projections by Nicolai et al (2016), shows that Sub-Saharan African failing to reach most of the SDGs by 2030, which follows on from its relatively poor performance at the MDGs. Indeed, the MDGs emphasised the weak performance of Sub-Saharan Africa compared with other regions. This was notable in the mid-2000s when it was found to be the only region not 'on track' to meet any goals.

Sub-Saharan Africa's failure to hit uniform global goals in 2030 is an under stable in the context of its low starting position in 2015. Given absolute targets (getting to zero) in the SDGs, this is being set the most challenging targets compared with other regions. Nonetheless negative scores do not predict failure but as a warning sign that sets out the scale of the challenges and what should be done to ensure success. It should stretch African governments beyond current results trends as both SDGs and AU Agenda 2063 set out ambitious agenda and to inspire action good results (Takeuchi and Samman (2015). The challenge is for African countries to exhibit the good will of achieving these envisaged goals. The blame game theory should not repeat itself. African has to develop early warning systems for detecting factors that can impair the attainment of these goals.

Working towards the achievement of the SDGs, AU Agenda 2063 and integration of the continent we have to holistically take into consideration the need for the empowerment of the female gender and those currently left behind that undermine their dignity. Africa finds itself in a specific situation as the least developed continent needing urgent attention to address the situation. The continent needs open governance not the continuation of foreclose spaces for civic activism that breeds conflicts and underdevelopment. The need for bilateral and multilateral partnerships for economic growth has to be consistent with local civil society demands for basic freedoms of speech, assembly and movement or else integration cannot be achieved. African governments are challenged to ensure sustainable internal changes of governance, accountability and transparency that enhance the ideas of regional integration and the sustainable transformation of each country. The focus should be on improving the quality well-being of every citizen by fighting inequalities of all forms that perpetuate disempowerment of people and communities.

The African Continental Free Trade Area (AfCFTA)

The future of Africa means the eyes of the world are turning towards the continent. Speaking at the opening ceremony of the 12th Extraordinary Summit on the African Continental Free Trade Area (AFCFTA) on 7th July 2019, Egyptian president and Africa Union Chairman pointed out that "the success of the AfCFTA will be the real test to achieve the economic growth that will turn our people's dream of welfare and quality of life into a reality." The creation of a single market for goods and services, backed with the free movement of businesspeople and investments is closely being watched by financial markets and institutions around the world with keen eyes and great expectations. It equally constitutes a serious challenge for the continent.

Though the continent is currently plagued by internal conflicts for various reasons, it is envisaged and hoped that the market could contribute to lessening of some of the problems by improving on the quality livelihood of the people. It is envisaged that the economic benefits from the AfCFTA will be numerous and apparent and that the continental free trade area would also have other benefits beyond purely economic matters.

Source: Credit: Onwuka Nkechi Chinye & Udegbunam (Conflict Trends: Issue 3, 2019, p.3)

Presently, "the current state of competitiveness and conflicts within and between nations is a major obstacle. African leaders must begin by building confidence within and between their countries. This confidence can only be established by Africa developing a shared future, as envisaged in Agenda 2063. It cannot be achieved by another generation of selfish leaders motivated by personal benefit only. The AfCFTA should be a blueprint to develop the conditions at this time to benefit all Africans" (Gounden, 2019:2). Article 4 of AfCFTA (AU, 2019) highlights the following specific objectives as constituting the pillars of the economic group.

- Progressively eliminate tariffs and non-tariff barriers to trade in goods;
- Progressively liberalise trade in services;
- Cooperate on investment, intellectual property rights and competition policy;
- Cooperate on all trade-related areas;

- Cooperate on customs matters and the implementation of trade facilitation measures;
- Establish a mechanism for the settlement of dispute concerning their rights and obligations
- Establish and maintain an institutional framework for the implementation and administration of the AfCFTA.

Without an iota of doubt, a successful implementation and realisation of the AfCFTA objectives, prospects and challenges abound; in all this signals a renewal towards a more integrated Africa of tomorrow; as it will undoubtedly contribute to reinforcing African Unity as well as advance the notion of *"African Solutions to African Problems"*. According to Onwuka and Udegbunam (2019:3) many analysts argue that AfCFTA calls for caution celebrations and optimism. Currently intra-African trade only constitute 15% of overall African external trade. It is envisaged that with the elimination of tariffs, inter-regional trade could increase approximately 15-20% in the medium term; and the signing of the agreement by Africa's largest economies, indeed increases the prospects of the agreement becoming a reality that could improve industrialisation on the African continent and the welfare of the African people.

At the moment, intra-African trade accounts for only 16% of the total trade in goods and services within Africa. In comparison, intra-European trade currently stands at around 65% of goods and services traded within the European Union. The United Nations Economic Commission for Africa (UNECA) is of the opinion that the AfCFTA has the potential to boast intra-African trade by 52.3% by eliminating import duties and it can double this trade if non-tariff barriers are reduced. The AfCFTA is a giant step towards to the sovereignty of the continent. It is left to the people to make the best use of the various institutions in developing a sustainable climate for the quality livelihood for its fast-growing population so that the people can feel and maintain a sense of belong to the rising new continent.

Contextualise within this scenario there is a need for a strategic approach articulated on a number of building blocks, such as:

- Maintaining sound macroeconomic policies to contain inflation and avoid a recurrence of balance of payments difficulties;
- Liberalisation of domestic markets and increased openness – good governance being a key;

- Cooperation within and among African countries and other economic blocs of the world (EU, NAFTA, etc.) that offer the continent the opportunity and incentives to move forward with trade liberation and industrial restructuring;
- Regional measures that complement cooperation agreements with the rest of the world:

While regional cooperation is not a substitute for sound macroeconomic policies or needed structural reforms, it would eliminate the market fragmentation that currently makes the region unattractive to investors, thereby allowing Africa not to unleash its formidable economic potential. Presently, the economic potential of the region is unutilised or wasted. There is no magic wand for solving the numerous challenges associated with the continents developmental debacle. The continent need to be focused on what it wants, how it wants it and how to attain the goals set for itself. Although interregional cooperation is an important even indispensable tool in the development of individual countries, it cannot solve all the problems by itself. Internal incentives, the political will to preserve on the path of reform, and the understanding needed to make the right choices will also play a critical role in determining how much Africa is able to benefit for the opportunities offered by globalisation and African economic integration.

The world's poorest countries - most of which are in Africa – are likely to be hard hit by the economic fallout from events of the West like economic slowdown-, HIV/AIDS and especially now with Corona Virus (COVID-19) Pandemic – the focus on globalisation and its potential benefits and risks for Africa. Africa has yet to enjoy the benefits of globalisation, which could boost growth in the region through the expansion of markets for African exports, the stimulation of domestic investment, and an increase in foreign capital flows. There is need for both stronger domestic policies and international support to address causes of inadequate growth which requires promoting good governance and strategic development plans in all aspects; in defining and implementing its socio-eco-politico policies in all their myriad details and how it adheres to the rule of law.

The harmonious interface between the State, Private Sector and Civil Society as well as inputs from the international community remain fundamental in addressing the ailing economic down-turn of African states in advancing the sustainable transformation of the continent. Therefore, joint action will help to ensure success by shining the right light on the Africa.

References

African Capacity Building Foundation (2008). "A Survey of the Capacity Needs of Africa's Regional Economic Communities", Harare, Zimbabwe

African Union (AU) (2007). "Brief on Negotiations for Economic Partnership Agreements", African Union, 26 June - July 2007, Addis Ababa, Ethiopia

African Union (2010). Report of Meeting of 6th Ordinary Session of AU Ministers of Trade, Kigali – Rwanda, 29 October – 2nd November 2010

African Union (2018)"Assembly of the Union Thirtieth Ordinary Session: Decisions, Declarations and Resolution" (Available at: https://au.int/sites/default/files/decisions/33908-assembly_decisions_665_689_e.pdf)

African Union (AU) (2019) "AfCFTA Agreement Secures Minimum Threshold of 22 Ratification as Sierra Leone and the Saharawi Republic Deposit Instruments",(Available at: https://au.int/en/pressrelease/20190429/afcfta-agreement-secures-minimum-threshold-22-ratification-sierra-leone-and)

African Union/NEPAD (2011). Revision of the AU/NEPAD African Action Plan 2010-2015: Advancing Regional and Continental Integration together through shared values. Abridge Report 2010-2012. Johannesburg – South Africa

Ajayi S. Ibi (2001) "What Africa Needs to Do to Benefit from Globalisation" Finance and Development - Globalisation and Africa – December 2001, Vol. 38, Number 4, International Monetary Fund, Washington,pp6-8

Akokpari John (2005) "The Dilemma of Regional Integration and Development in Africa", paper presented at the Centre for conflict Resolution (CCR) Policy Seminar, Building an African Union (AU) for the 21st Century: Relations with Regional Economic Communities (RECs), the New Partnership for Africa's Development (NEPAD) and civil Society, Cape Town, South Africa, 20-22 August 2005

Alker H. And Puchaa D. (1968) "trends in Economic Partnership: The North Atlantic Arena 1928-1963 in Singer J. David (eds.) Quantitative International Politics (1968) Free Press, New York, USA

Amundsen Inge (2019) Political Corruption in Africa. Extraction and Power Preservation. Edward Elgar Publishing, UK.

Balassa, B. (1962) The Theory of Economic Integration, London

Bloom, J. Peter, Stephan F. Miescher and Takyiwaa Manuh (2014) Modernisation as Spectacle in Africa, Indiana University Press, Bloomington, USA

Bonnet Duncan (2012). "Privately Motivated", Africainvestor, May-June 2012, pp 74-77

Bokilo Julien (2013) China and Africa. Competition Between China, Traditional Trade Partners of Africa and BRIC Countries, L'Harmaltan, Paris France

Broadman, G. Harry (2007) "Connecting Africa and Asia" Finance and Development, June 2007, Vol. 44, No.2, International Monetary Fund, Washington DC, USA, pp36-37.

Broadman G. Harry (2007) Africa's Silk Road: China and India's New Economic Frontier. World Bank Publication, Washington DC, USA

Chan Stephen (2013) "The Middle Kingdom and The Dark Continent: An Essay on China. Africa and Many Fault Lines", In the Morality of China in Africa: The Middle Kingdom and The Dark Continent (editor) Stephan Chan. Zed Books, London and New York.

Chime Chimelu (1977) Integration and Politics Among African States. Limitations and Horizons of Mid-Term Theorising. The Scandinavian Institute of African Studies, Uppsala, Sweden

Comtrade (United Nations Commodity Trade Statistics Database) 2009/2010. (http://comtrade.un.org/db/default.aspx)

Deborah Brautigam (2009) The Dragons Gift. The Real Story of China in Africa. Oxford University Press, Oxford University Press, Oxford and New York

Dowden Richard (2010). Africa: Altered States, Ordinary Miracles. Public Affairs, New York, USA

Deutsch, K. Et al (1967) France, Germany and the Western Alliance: A Study of Elite Attitudes on European Integration and World Politics, new York

Economic Commission for Africa (ECA) (2012) Assessing Regional Integration in Africa (ARIA V): Towards an African Continental Free Trade Area. Addis Ababa, Ethiopia.

Economic Commission for Africa (ECA) (2004). "Assessing Regional Integration in Africa" Addis Ababa, Ethiopia

Elumelu Tony (2017) "Youth Unemployment is Africa's Greatest Challenge", African Business, No. 443, July 2017, London, pp20-23

Forje W. John (2017) Constructing or Withering African Unity? Fifty Years After Kwame Nkrumah, Lambert Academic Publishing, Germany

Forje W. John (2009) Here The People Rule. Political Transition and Challenges for Democratic Consolidation in Africa. Nova Science Publications, Inc, New York, USA

Galtung J.)1973) The European Community – A Superpower in the Making. Oslo – Norway.

Gondwe G.E. (2001) "Making Globalisation Work in Africa", Finance and Development, The International Monetary Fund, December 2001, Vol. 38, No.4, Washington, USA. Pp31-33

Gounden Vasu (2019) Editorial. Conflict Trends. Issue 3, 2019, South Africa, p.2

Haas, E.B. (1958) The Study of Regional Integration: Reflections on the Joy and Anguish of Pretheorising. International Organisation, Vol. XXIV; 1970.

Hazelwood, A. (1975) Economic Integration: The East African Experience, New York. USA

Hazelwood, A. (ed.) (1967).African Integration and Disintegration: Case Studies in Economic and Political Union, University press, Oxford, UK and New York.

Hosny, Amr (2013) Theories off Economic Integration: A Survey of the Economic and Political Literature. International Journal of Economy, Management and Social Sciences, 2 (5), pp.133-155

Hout Will and Salih M.A. Mohamed (2019) A Political Economy of African Regionalism: An Overview of Asymmetric development. Edward Elgar Publishing, UK

Krause, L. (1967) Economic Integration and the United State: The Brookings Institution, Washington, D.C. USA

Krugman, P. (1991). "Increasing Returns and Economic Geography," Journal of Political Economy, Volume 99, Issue 3

Lukonga, I., and K. Chung (2010). "The Cross-border Expansion of African Large Conglomerate Financial Institutions." Unpublished Research Paper. IMF, Washington, DC.

Mataboge D. Lerato (2017) "Africans Need to Invest in Each Other's Economies", Africa Business No.443, July 2017, London, pp48

Marinov, Eduard (2014) Economic Integration Theories and the Developing Countries, In Dautov, Rustem; Gkasis, Pavlos; Karamanos, Anastasios; Lagkas, Thomas; Prodomidou, Alexandra and Ypsilanti, Antonia (eds) Infusing Research and Knowledge in South-east Europe. South-East European Research Centre, Thessaloniki, pp.164-177

Mitrany S. (1943) A Working Peace System. An Argument for the Functional Development of International Organisation. London

Moremong, Tshepidi (2019) The AfCFTA is a Giant Step Forward. The African Report, July-August, p.8

Naidoo Jay (2013) "We Need to Listen to The People", New African, No.528, May 2013, London, pp36-37

Ndegwa, P. (1968). The Common Market and Development in East Africa, Nairobi, East African Publishing House, Nairobi - Kenya

Nicolai Susan, Chrisa Hoy, Tanyi Bhatkai and Thomas Aedy (2016). Projecting Progress. The SDGs in Sub-Saharan Africa. Overseas Development Institute, April 2016, London, United Kingdom

Onwuka Nkechi Onyinye and Udegbunam Chigozie Kingsley (2019) The African Continental Free Trade Area: Prospects And Challenges. Conflict Trends, Issue 3, 2019, South Africa, pp.3-10

Robson, F. (1994) The Economics of International Integration, 2nd edition, George Allen & Unwin, London

Rolandson, R. (1992). Globalisation: Social Theory and Global Culture, Sage Publications Limited, London

Saddem Abdellatif (2001) "How Tunisia Is Meeting the Challenges of Globalisation" Finance and Development - Globalisation and Africa-December 2001, Vol.38. No.4, International Monetary Fund, Washington, USA, pp28-30

Sharer Robert (2001) "An Agenda for Trade, Investment, and Regional Integration" Finance and Development, Issue on Globalisation and Africa, December 2001, Volume38, No. 4, International Monetary Fund, Washington, DC. Pp14-17

Stiglitz E. Joseph, Justin Lin Yifu, Ebrahim Patel and Joan Esteban (2013). The Industrial Policy Revolution 11: Africa in the Twenty-first Century. (International Economic Association), Palgrave Macmillan, UK

Tafirenyika Masimbe (2014) "Intra-Africa Trade. Going Beyond Political Commitments. Progress will when Agreements are Implemented. African Renewal, August 2014, Vol.28, No.2, United Nations New York, pp5-7

Takeuchi Rodriguez and Samman E. (2015). Patterns of Progress Towards the MDGs and Implications for Post-2030 Target Setting. Overseas Development Institute (ODI) London, United Kingdom

Thomas David (2017) "China's New Silk Road Gets off the Mark", African Business, No.443, July 2017, London, pp54-55.

United Nations Economic Commission for Africa (UNECA), (2006). Assessing Regional Integration in Africa 11. Rationalising Regional Economic Communities Addis Ababa, Ethiopia (http://www.uneca.org/aria2/full_version.pdf)

United Nations Economic Commission for Africa (UNECA) (2018) African Continental Free Trade Area: Towards the Finalisation of Modalities on Goods. Addis Ababa, Ethiopia, Economic Commission for Africa.

United Nations Economic Commission for Africa (UNECA) (2019) Experts Meet to Set the Stage for AfCFTA Phase 11 Negotiations. (Available at: https://.uneca.org/stories/experts-meet-set-stage-afcfta-phase-ii-negotiations)

United Nations Conference on Trade and Development (2017) Trade and Development Report 2017. (Available at <https://united.org/en/PublicationalLibrary/tdr2017_enpdf)

Wandrei Kevin (2018) Advantages And Disadvantages of Regional Integration. (Available at: https://classroom.synonym.com/advantagesdisadvantages-of-regional-integration-12083667,html)

World Bank (2008) World Development Indicators, 2008, Washington, DC.

World Bank (2011). Africa's Infrastructure: A Time for Transformation (African Development Forum) World Bank Publications, Washington, D.C.

Zeleza Tiyambe Paul (2014) "The Africa-China Relationship. Challenges and Opportunities", Canadian Journal of African Studies, Vol.48, No.1, April 2014, pp145-169

Chapter Five

The Sixth Region - The Diaspora

"I believe those with skills should be encouraged and rewarded to stay, work, and raise their families in Africa. When that happens, a large middle class will be created, thereby reducing the conditions that give rise to civil war and corruption. Then, a true revitalisation and renaissance will occur."

[Ngozi Okonjo Iweala, World Bank President for Africa, and Current Minister of Finance, Nigeria]

"Ten million Africans now constitute an invisible nation that resides outside Africa. Although invisible, it is a nation as populous as Angola, Malawi, Zambia or Zimbabwe. If it were to be a nation with distinct borders, it would have an income roughly equivalent to Africa's gross domestic product"

[Computer Wizard, Philip Emeagwali, (2010), Renaissance World]

"While these 70,000 skilled Africans are fleeing the continent in search of employment and decent wages, 100,000 skilled expatriates who are paid wages higher than the prevailing rate in Europe are hired to replace them".

(Computer Wizards, Philip Emeagwali, (2010) Renaissance World]

"African countries should now concentrate on transforming 'brain drain' into 'brain gain' by building and nurturing networks and developing strategies to harness the scientific and technical expertise of their Diaspora members."

(Kofi Anani, Washington, D.C. October 9, 2008)

"The continent's political leaders also appear to have arms open to receive the returning Africans. The New Partnership for Africa's Development (NEPAD), the African Union's economic development organ, even created an African Diaspora programme that it says is strategically important to Africa. In May of last year, NEPAD organised an Africa Diaspora Summit in Johannesburg, South Africa, to encourage Africans in the Diaspora to support economic integration and development on the continent. That was a thinly veiled invitation to skilled Africans abroad to return to help their countries."

(Aissata Haidara, 2013)

Introduction: Defining the Concept and the Turning Tide

The Diaspora constitutes Africa's Sixth Region. The concept "Diaspora" takes centre stage in the capable development states construct. The "Diaspora," according to the Merriam Webster dictionary, is 'the movement, migration, or scattering of people away from an established or ancestral homeland" or "people dispersed by whatever cause to more than one location" or "people settled far from their ancestral homelands." There are those who believe that the African Diaspora should be based on the ways and manner with which individuals left Africa, especially those who were forcibly abducted, enslaved and transported out of Africa. The acceptance of this argument would not only be contrary to the original meaning of the word" Diaspora," but would exclude millions of Africans who "voluntarily" left the continent, many through political persecution while others left for economic reasons and they still do today. However, on December 5, 2007, the African Union (AU) decided to put an end to the Diaspora discourse and argument when the organ agreed to define the African Diaspora as of "consisting of people of African origin living outside the continent, irrespective of their citizenship and nationality and who are willing to contribute to the development of the continent and the building of the African Union." The constitutive act declares that it shall "invite and encourage the full participation of the African Diaspora as an important part of our continent, in the building of the African Union."

Whatever definition accorded the African Diaspora, the cardinal point is that the African Diaspora has been accorded a legal entity. On the other hand, the African Diaspora, with all the love they have for the motherland, does not believe that the relationship should be a one-way street. The issue of "dual citizenship" comes into picture and that of land reform which recognises the rights of those who were forcibly removed from their ancestral lands, participation in the infrastructural development of Africa which takes into account the skills and experiences of the African Diaspora, as well as the fear and anger at Africa allowing itself to being exploited again, hearkening to a nightmarish vision of the 1884 so-called Berlin Conference which carved into fiefdoms of European hegemonic ambitions. Without diluting the importance of the African Diaspora as a whole, there is a need to understand the importance and enormous sacrifices that continental African Diaspora are making every year to the economic growth of Africa (Onyeani, 2012:9).

The concept frequently refers to the rallying of migrant citizens living in other countries as a result of interrelated factors, for example; first the most Herodotus crime ever committed against humanity – the slave trade and colonial rule; second, people leaving Africa for the quest of human knowledge given the poor and inadequate development of educational opportunities before and after the end of colonial; third, citizens chased out of their countries by authoritarian regimes because of the stances against such regime structures; and fourth, economic migrants triggered by the deplorable economic situation in the country specifically since the 1980s with Western financial conglomerates imposed structural adjustment programmes of the World Bank and International Monetary Fund and other western financial institutions and governments designed to cripple the continent. Migration is not a recent phenomenon. It has been with humankind since the creation of the world. The free movement of people and goods is encouraged to galvanise the globalisation idea. The dark side of migration is the entrenched xenophobic tendencies which have gripped the world.

Existing xenophobic attitude in many western countries against foreigners; the economic hardship and the struggle for self-determination in different ways fostered the unity of the Diaspora looking "back home". It should be remembered that the Diaspora was at the forefront of the independence struggle which gave birth to the Pan-African, African Renaissance and Africa Must Unite Agenda. People of African descent and Africans abroad rallied for the 'home coming' ideal to regain their lost Africanness flowing in the veins of this race is now a reality that cannot be stopped. It is not the intention here to delve into the pros and cons of the concept but emphasis its significance in the African states construct. However, let it be understood that the Diaspora is about the role and functions of a Diaspora, beyond its being a description of migrants in distance lands. The Diaspora could be seen as a social movement – motivated by a political struggle and a will to react to issues such as racism, discrimination and domination (Olsson 2012; Ogom 2009; Alina 2004; Gilroy 1993; Cohen 1997; Safran 1991; Sheffer 1995; Veney 2002).

According to Mwagiru (2012:74), the term, 'diasporas have sometimes run the risk of becoming meaningless. This was, and still is, because of the tendency to apply the term to a wide category of people who have been dispersed from their home-land. When used in this way, it is applied regardless of the reason for their dispersal. This is what Brubaker (2005) calls the universalisation of the term which thus implies that almost everyone is despotic. And if everyone is diasporic, then the term Diaspora is no longer able to delineate between categories. And if it is no longer able to do this, it will have a very short conceptual life. While not belabouring the definitional discourse, we can settle on three criteria for the constitution of a Diaspora. **First**, any form of Diaspora as long as territorial borders are crossed. Ethnic communities divided by territorial borders also constituting a Diaspora,

Second, homeland orientation requiring some loyalty to, or recognition of, a real or imagined homeland from which flow value, identity and loyalty. **Third,** boundary maintenance involves maintaining an identity distinct from host society, which can be done by resisting assimilation into the host society through self-segregation, or can be an unintended consequence of social exclusion (Brubaker 2005:6).

Seen within this perspective, an African Diaspora is a political term originally used to emphasis the experience of African people dispersed by the slave trade. It is also an analytical term permitting discourse about black communities across territorial borders (Patterson and Kelley 2004:14). Broadly stated, the Diaspora is not a nation as opined by Patterson and Kelley (ibid.15); "the Diaspora is not a sovereign territory with established boundaries though it is seen as 'inherently inherited' to people of Africa? Descent while there is no official language, there seems to be a consistent effort to locate a single culture with singular historical roots, no matter how mythical...many members of this Diaspora see themselves as an oppressed 'nation' without a homeland or they imagine Africa as their (future) home". In light of this interpretation the Diaspora are people who have been dispersed beyond the territorial borders of their country, but retaining some loyalties for the country where they come from, and who, in their new habitat retain also some social exclusiveness, which adds new dimensions within the diplomatic circles – the diplomacy of the Diaspora.

The diplomacy of the Diaspora while being at the fore front for the independence struggle injects new blood in state construct. The role and the social, economic and political welfare of the Diaspora as citizens take centre stage. Many African states today have departments catering for the interests of their citizens outside the country. This is done through the establishment of structures specifically meant to address Diaspora issues, such as Diaspora departments in ministries of foreign affairs (Kenya and Ghana). The Ghanaian government for example has, among other efforts passed citizenship legislation granting overseas-resident Ghanaians the right to vote. In addition, the government also has introduced a permanent Diaspora visa that allows descendants of the historical Diaspora to visit Ghana without visas after their first visit. The opening up of the diplomatic space for the Diaspora leads to the realisation of another political role for the Diaspora. The Diaspora takes part in elections for example, the Presidential elections in Cameroon 2011. The significant number of Diaspora voting can impact on elections results. The decision by the government of Kenya to have the Diaspora participate in the

Presidential vote was a first step in the right direction. But more needs to be done to ensure that Africans abroad are not disenfranchised.

African governments must listen to the concerns of their citizens abroad. However, there are arguments being raised against the Diaspora voting unless they first pay taxes (Kapur 2003, Mwagiru 2012, and 2011). What is important is the consensus for the Diasporas to be part of the electoral process thus giving them a voice in the construction of the continent. This recognition goes a long way to incorporating the Diaspora into the mainstream of the transformation process. It is a significant change from the past when African governments treated the continental African Diaspora with disrespect and nonchalance, often perceiving them as 'rebels', anti-nationalist and name the rest, yet failing to understand and appreciate the role of the Diaspora in the process of political restructuring and economic change. It cannot be denied that the various Diaspora organisations played key roles in the 1990s in pushing forward for political reforms and multi-party politics.

Nigeria has taken the right move of incorporating the Diasporas in the decision-making machinery by creating a Diaspora Committee of the Federal House of Representatives (the only such parliamentary committee of its kind in Africa) devoted only to Diaspora matters. The Committee is charged with the following objectives:

o promoting the exchange of ideas between home country and Nigerians in the Diaspora;

o collecting and maintaining data on Nigerians in Diaspora from consulates, Ministry of Foreign affairs, Education, Justice, the population registers, Censuses, employment agencies and statistics division of international organisations and International Census Bureau for domestic planning and use;

o initiating policies needed to recognise and harness the potentials of Nigerians in Diaspora networks and organisations and assist in their realisations and international changes to help public servants collaborate effectively with Diaspora representatives;

o participating in dialogue with Governments, regional and local on Diaspora matters in their homes and host countries.

In the context of the African Union which led to the creation of Africa's sixth region, the Diaspora, constitute, to paraphrasing Cross (2010:205); (i) dialogue among citizens that transcends national borders leading to stronger societal interdependence; and (ii) eventually some sense of common (African) identity. Citizens in the (Africa Union) can serve as cultural ambassadors. AU's definition of 'diasporas' is peoples of African origin, living outside the continent, irrespective of their citizenship and nationality, and who are willing to contribute to the development of the continent and the building of the African Union. Omeje (2007:95) holds the opinion that the definition should include not only those of African origin living outside the continent, but also those who may not even hold the nationality of an African country, but who consider themselves to have an African ancestry. This is an open call for Diaspora to connect and with 'Mother Africa' and re-tress their roots and fortifies it so as to consolidate their being in the world.

Take the case of India, and how its citizens dominating Silicon Valley have invigorated technological advancements in their motherland. Following the Asian Development Bank Indians living abroad started 19 of 20 software companies set up in the country. Technology transfer is absolutely important for economic development which Africa desperately need for its transformation. Another vital area is the domain of tourism and trade. Despite the grim picture presented by the exodus of skilled professionals, the African Diaspora remains the best ambassadors of the continent in promoting related developmental actives in these and other areas in boosting the economic development and growth of the continent.

The skills these Diasporas have horned in their newfound homes are vital inputs for any country's economic growth which must be properly harnessed and enhanced for scientific, technological, economic and innovative take-off for Africa to ensure sustainable quality livelihood for the people. African countries should concentrate on transforming 'brain drain' into 'brain gain' by building and nurturing networks and developing strategies to harness the scientific and technical expertise of their Diaspora members. Apparently a realistic agenda for the brain drain is to concentrate on utilising Information and Communication Technologies (ICTs), virtual networks and partnerships, short-term visitations and professional exchange programmes.

There is a growing improvement among African governments in recognising the potential contributions of the Diasporas to home country development. What is required by African countries is to undertake concrete actions and measures for harnessing the expertise and related resources of their Diaspora in a more coherent and comprehensive manner, The incorporation of the Diaspora is the start to the road of development and success for the new Africa that is rising Akesson and Baaz (2015) argue that in the wake of economic crises in much of the developed world, alongside rapid economic growth in its part of Africa, the impetus to 'return' is likely to increase in the coming years. Such returnees are often portrayed as agents of development who will bring with them economic capital, knowledge and skills as well as social connections and experience gained in the developed world.

The Diaspora – Who Are they and their Values?

The discourse, boils down to two types of 'diasporas' – First, 'historical Diaspora' consisting of the black people taken into slavery, ending up in the America's, Caribbean and other places (Black 2011; Veney 2002); Apparently, the historical Diaspora has the senses of connection to the continent or homeland, strong enough to resist forgetting, assimilating or distancing (Shuval 2000.43). The historical Diaspora neither born in Africa nor visited the continent. But they are pulled by ancestral bonds backed by the degree of exclusion and hostilities faced in country of residence. These two factors piloted their drive for the independence struggle of African countries. Tracing their 'roots' is fundamental for them. How committed and for how long this will last is a secondary issue. This category can be described as the third generation of Diaspora hood and largely retaining root-ties to the home country. Second, the 'contemporary African Diaspora' are Africans dispersed outside their home countries in the last sixty or so years. By and large, this group left voluntarily for education, and later in search of greener pastures. Importantly, they still maintain ties with the home country as well as supporting family members and community related activities in different ways through remittances.

It is estimated that this particular group is targeted by African governments and the AU for political and economic reasons. Economically this group remits home an estimated amount of USA$ billion annually. These acts seem to motivate AU's definition of the African Diaspora as being 'peoples of African origin living outside the continent and with the will to contribute to the development of the continent and in helping in the construction of the African Union'. Politically, individual governments use this to gain political credibility for caring for citizens outside, attracting some grown investments and gaining some degree of political credence before foreign governments. For the AU, it hopes in using this as platform for political cooperation diplomacy (AU 2011:4).

According to the World Bank and the United Nations, in 2010, African immigrants remitted the sum of USA$40 billion to the continent, dwarfing the so-called aids pledged to the continent by the 'developed' world. There is the spurious argument that these funds remitted are to individual's families, but without these huge remittances

Africa would not be growing at the accelerated rate of over 7% GDP. These remittances are used to lessen the burden of governments to provide essential services to its citizens. According to the Central Bank of Kenya documents show that remittances from North America increased by 18.2 percent from USA$44.02 million in January 2012 to USA$52.02 million in February 2012 and that over the same period, remittance inflows from Europe increased by 20 percent from US$24.39 million to US$29.27 million.

According to Carlos Lopes, former ECA Executive Secretary, current Fellow of Chatham House and Professor, Mandela School of Public Governance, University of Cape Town, South Africa; 'In 2018, remittances from the Diaspora attained 11.6 per4cent of Egypt's GDP, 12 percent and 14.7 percent of the GDP of Liberia and Lesotho respectively. Attempts to put cooperation on migration in one neatly isolated corner will not work. The continent hosts 26 percent of the world's refugee population. Many of these refugees come from regions such as the Horn. This sensitive region has been experiencing a palpable EU disengagement, as shown by the EU declining financial support to the African peace keeping operations in the region. From a pragmatic perspective migrants' remittances are guaranteeing a predictable resources flow to originating countries, largely surpassing development aid."

The Central Bank of Kenya has also established an infrastructure bond to tap into savings from the Diasporas which is a step in attracting Diaspora investment into the country. Recent estimates of the total remittances by African migrants into the region range from USA$10-40 billion (in fact there is no accurate figure). In 2007 for example, Bank of Ghana announced that Ghanaians living abroad contributed about USA$2 billion to the economy through remittances. These remittances have sustained families, stimulated new home construction and artisanal enterprise development, helped to extend and maintain public infrastructure such as schools and hospitals through efforts of hometown and student associations. It is projected that sub-Saharan African countries can potentially raise USA$1-3 billon by reducing the cost of international migrant remittances, USA$5-10 billion by issuing Diaspora bonds, and USA$17 billion by securitising future remittances and future receivables.

The Diaspora is ready to work with the African Union according to a declaration issued by the President of the "Black Mayors" of the United States Hon. Mayor Robert Bowser of East Orange, New Jersey] at their meeting with AU Deputy Chairperson, Ambassador Erastus Mwencha in New York on 19 April 2012. Mayor Robert Bowser asserted; 'it is time for us to unify all people of African descent, and I believe there is enough brain power in this room to make this happen, there is enough brain power here to change the world, and change the misguided opinions about the people of African descent.... about areas that are of great interest to Africa, areas that are vital to economic growth to the continent as well as providing jobs to teeming millions of unemployed Africans. We want to deal with tourism and technology and training for people and getting into the business world. As Majors, we can use our offices to be a vehicle to connect with what is needed in the whole Diaspora. So, use us, use us to accomplish some of these goals because we have the wherewithal to work together with the African Union and whoever wants to get onboard with us. So, the leadership of the African Union, we are here to work with you."

The Memorandum of Understanding [MOU] signed on September 2008 between the President of the African Union Commission [AUC] Jean Ping and Robert Zoellick [President of the World Bank] to cooperate in specifically areas of regional integration; governance; post-conflict countries relations with the Diaspora; and communicable diseases, including HIV/AIDS, malaria and tuberculosis. The Institutional Development Facility (IDF) grant from the World Bank to the AUC approved in July 2008 is focused at supporting, the following actions:

- strengthening knowledge sharing with Diasporas and development partners in the Americas;
- developing a reliable Database of African Diaspora networks and individuals;
- initiating resource mobilisation efforts from the African Diaspora and private sector in the Americas; and
- improving coordination with the African Diaspora in the Americas [North America, the Caribbean, and Latin America].

In connection with the foregoing, the African Region of the World Bank launched the African Diaspora Programme (ADP) in September 2007, with the strategic elements focusing policy development and implementations in finance, particularly the leveraging of remittances for (a) development, and human capital development for 'brain gain.' The strategy calls for among others, the following;

- working with the African Union (AU) in support of its global Diaspora policies, programmes and projects;

- working with partner countries to obtain improvements in the enabling policy and environments for engaging their Diaspora in economic and social development activities;
- working with the partner donors to understand better the flow of remittances, including issues related to the costs of, and approaches to the leveraging and securitisation of remittances for development;
- working with Diaspora Professional Networks to increase knowledge sharing and transfer (brain gain) between the Diaspora and their home country. [see www.worldbank.org/afr/diaspora]and [toafrdiaspora@worldbank.org] for submitting CVs or corporate profile]

Looking at the Diaspora in the African context, we discover the following silver lining running through their activities; (a) the struggle towards a united Africa – the struggle for self-determination and independence of Africa. The role played by the Diaspora by such great Afro-Americans and Afro-Carribbeans like Henry Sylvester Williams, George Padmore, W. E. Du Bois, C. L. R. James and many others through the Pan-Africanist Movement that saw the participation of Kwame Nkrumah, Jomo Kenyatta, Nnamdi Azikiwe, Julius Nyerere and many others especially at the Fifth Pan-African Congress in Manchester (UK) in 1945 standout very glaring; and (b) the struggle to have an identity. In many instances the Diasporas is neither here nor there; the question of recognition and a ***'home'*** is vital. A 'home' called their own means returning and belonging into society what they have achieved outside. Is the place called **'their home'** ready and willing to welcome them or we may ironically call the 'prodigal son' which in many cases is not their 'own fault or making' for leaving mother country.

The case of South Africa and other African countries during the independence struggle for example stands out glaring in this context. The struggle for independence under the apartheid regime drove many people out of the country. The eventual collapse of the Apartheid Governance System saw the massive influx or return of citizens back into the country. In some quarters these people were treated or looked upon with scorn; it was common to hear South Africans make statements like; they were out receiving education and leaving in peace, while we stayed home receiving the bullets and in constant fear and harassment; now they have returned and gotten all the good jobs, and we are languishing in misery.' While such reactions could be taken as normal human feelings, it should also be noted that these people in different ways equally contributed to the struggle while away from home in many fronts and aspects; somewhere targeted and assassinated abroad by the forces and instruments of the apartheid regime. Many returned home with acquired knowledge and other skills; linked-up with the forces that remained on the ground to construct a strong, healthier developed South Africa. South Africa is what it is today due to the joint efforts of all South Africans – Diaspora and the inherent ground forces. The developmental process in the country gives pride and honour to the continent. Africa should strongly encourage the leveraging of Diaspora skills for the sustainable development.

In connection with the foregoing, the African Region of the World Bank launched the African Diaspora Programme (ADP) in September 2007, with the strategic elements focusing policy development and implementations in finance, particularly the leveraging of remittances for (a) development, and human capital development for 'brain gain.' The strategy calls for among others, the following;

- working with the African Union (AU) in support of its global Diaspora policies, programmes and projects;
- working with partner countries to obtain improvements in the enabling policy and environments for engaging their Diaspora in economic and social development activities;
- working with the partner donors to understand better the flow of remittances, including issues related to the costs of, and approaches to the leveraging and securitisation of remittances for development;
- working with Diaspora Professional Networks to increase knowledge sharing and transfer (brain gain) between the Diaspora and their home country. [see www.worldbank.org/afr/diaspora] and [toafrdiaspora@worldbank.org] for submitting CVs or corporate profile].

There is a catch-twenty-two situation here; why must the World Bank collect and fund the African Database if one may ask. The same situation happened in Cameroon with the introduction of the electronic identity cards. Everything was undertaken by a French firm. Today France has the data information of every Cameroonian. The irony is that Silicon Valley is packed with African Diaspora expertise in this domain. Why not engaged them which will be of a lesser cost to the country concern as well as an honour for the Diaspora's contribution to the development of the continent? We repeat the same mistake like the construction of the AU Headquarters in Addis Ababa by the Chinese. The Chinese are building the legislative assembly of Cameroon. Whatever is discussed even in the inner circles of the AU and the Cameroon Parliament is already known in China giving China the leap-forward to articulating constructive counter strategies and other measures to enhance their economic interests.

How can the continent present collectively recognise and tapped the invaluable human resources perspectives of the African Diaspora leverage professional skills for overcoming the development challenges of Africa? The Diaspora want to a full participant in Africa's march into economic independence, and as such would want African governments to look to the African Diaspora to undertake projects which are being snapped up by other communities that ordinarily disdain the African experience. Is it wrong for the continent to collect and own its data base? Of course, the invaluable Diaspora human resources can and must be tapped to support the continent in overcoming its underdevelopment predicaments, but this should not be done at the future detriment of Africa. The African Diaspora should be constructively engaged and properly utilised for the growth and development of the continent's people.

With this spirit, at no moment the candle of hope, belonging, trust, reconciliation, reconstruction and forward march allowed to go dim. It must keep burning and glowing making South Africa in particular and the continent in general to prosper and become what it wants to be. In short, the spirit of "*harambee, Ubuntu*" etc. must remain the guiding star and forces making every African to refocus, reposition and readjust our thoughts, mines, behaviour and actions towards the common goal of sovereignty, human dignity justice, for the good of present and future generations is imperative. With our Diasporas spread over the globe, there is no reason why Africa should not be the citadel of knowledge and sustainable transformation and development. Africa ought to and should dominate the global intellectual and scientific scene. Unfortunately, what exists is an extremely low level of underdevelopment, innovative, entrepreneurial and industrial destruction in the midst of abundant human and natural resources. We witness daily bountiful resources continually being looted by the greed of global corporations. With this the continent is witnessing an economic re-colonisation that bounds its people to the perils of corporate handcuffs. Therefore, by tempering the ability of African countries to have a voice and use the Diaspora with respect to the wishes of the North and global corporations, the nations of Africa have itself kneeled to the economic colonisers and the Eurocentric developmental agenda.

Come to think of the *'Brian Drain Menace Syndrome'* (BDMS) that almost two decades ago, there were more Senegalese doctors in

Chicago (USA) than in the entire country of Senegal: and that the Kuwait General Hospital would close down if Nigerian doctors were to suddenly return home en masse. Of the 120-150 doctors Ghana trains yearly, the country loses an equal number to migration. The healthcare industry is particularly hard hit; 1227 health care professionals left Ghana in 2003 to work abroad. The sectors in Africa hardest hit by *'brain drain'* are the science and technology, education and health sectors. The list of such examples is long and need not be repeated here.

Looking at the manpower spread across the globe, the host countries are the [beneficiaries] or the Brian Drain Benefactors (BDB); though there is also the notion of the Brain Drain Gain Benefactors (BDGS) for Africa, other countries harvest more than Africa from the human potentials of the continent. For now, what most African countries benefit from the brain drain phenomenon is 'remittances'. For now, Africa fails to properly utilising its huge Diaspora professional skills, to build hope, opportunity and prosperity for the continent through sheer hard work and determination.

The Diasporas are determined to return home and contribute to the necessary changes taking place. Let Africa prepare the table for them to contribute to what could be termed; Diaspora Social Responsibility (DSR), in which equality, justice and ethics stands as the foundation of well-functioning societies. Africa must turn defeat into victory and use the experience of forceful separation in the era of the slave trade and humiliation in the era of colonialism and reconstruct the period of neo-colonialism and beyond as a framework for solidarity and rejuvenation of an emerging holistic Africa in the new world.

A visual snapshot of Africa's economic migration 2017 indicates that 244 million migrants living abroad. This is a 41% increase from 2000. The total number of international migrants living in 2015 was 21 million and increase of 6millon between 2000 and 2015. Migration across the Mediterranean shows that about 362,753 arrived by Sea to Europe in 2016; and 181,000 arrived by boat to Italy in 2016. The top sources country as of May 30th 2017 was Nigeria, accounting for 9,286 arrivals; and nine of the 10 source countries for arrivals by sea to Europe were Africans, coming mostly from Nigeria, Guinea, Cote d'Ivoire, Gambia, Senegal, Morocco, Mali, Eritrea and Sudan. The European Union hopes to stem migration from Africa through an External Investment Plan which it hopes could catalyse up to 88 billion Euros of investment. In 2017, Africa was home to around 30% of the world's displaced people.

Migrants rescued from the Mediterranean await transfer

(Source: Credit African Business, No.443, July 2017, pp14-15)

It is absorbed that the continent should allow its human capital to risk their lives in search of greener pastures abroad. The greener pastures are here in Africa. We only need to create the enabling environment for pour youths as future custodians of the continent to be active participants in the development process. Imagine that over 200000 migrants and refugees arrive on European shores in 2016 from the African continent. What a drain on the human resources potential of the continent.

Youth unemployment is Africa's greatest challenge. Unemployment among the young people aged 15-24 years old in sub-Saharan Africa has hovered between 12% and 14% since the global financial crisis of 2008. This is higher than 9-10% in South Asia over the same period. Therefore, African countries must boost private sector investment by creating the right environment in addition to ensuring articulating the right policy consistency, credible regulations, security and a sound power and energy base.

Of course, we cannot stop people wanting to migrant for one or the other reasons. It is their right to do so. Migration is not going to be stopped so we have to learn to make it work for all concerned and to govern it in a most sustainable way. What is essential is creating the enabling atmosphere at home for them to be an inherent partner in development. We need to create the space and feeling for a sense of belonging to the 'fatherland', not that of driving them away from the continent. If the people are leaving because of poverty, for example, we need to put instruments that fight against poverty, inequality and poor governance. Intra-African migrants face numerous challenges, including strict visa restrictions, while refugees in some countries are denied the right to earn a living. These are the barriers holding back the progressive transformation of the continent. African countries should stop building walls, fences and barriers for the progress of the well-being of the people.

Reorienting African governments towards a more responsive, comprehensive and coordinated approach to the goals and aspirations of the continent's technological advancement and social equity class for new strategic approach with a strong focus on human capital and infrastructural development. The expertise of the Diaspora must be brought to bear on the transformation of the continent. This calls for creating a more conducive and enabling environment that attracts them home. Creating an enabling environment for improving the welfare of citizens is a solid passport for attracting the Diasporas to return home. What kinds of changes do we need?

The first begins with radical, constructive and concerted policy changes in Africa, some of which has already been alluded to but constantly repeated to emphasise the importance of policy articulation, political will and greater investments in human capital development. A new mindset and hard work spirit is equally essential. Democratic governance is the key backed with total commitment to respecting the fundamental human rights of citizen. These policy changes require 'walking the talk' and not mere policies statements gathering dust on the shelves of government offices. The need for a strong and determined political and comprehensive implementation process is imperative. It requires a constructive plan to heal a body that has been lacerated. The two - *Diaspora and Mother Africa* - have to be reunited spiritually and physically and for them to do anything structurally and constructively for the good of the people.

Second, we should broaden the basis of technology assessment and to bring to the fore the role and impact of indigenous knowledge as a major contributor to development. There is much the continent can draw from its indigenous knowledge system. When married with modern science and technology will accelerate the transformation nexus of the region. It is something the people know and cherish; requiring only education to sustain the knowledge and avoid extension which has deprived the continent in advancing its transformation process. An expanded policy programme on human capital development and infrastructures for creating as health society is crucial as the vanguard of the efforts of building a rising, winning and progressive continent.

Third, in line with the preceding point is to develop a new mix of different types of technologies whether they are being referred to as Western/non-Western, or alpha/beta or whatever. As long as the condition is about the improvement of the livelihood of the people (not at any cost) but through striving to regulate the composition of a proper or balanced mix so that equity, equal relations improved and sustained human conditions are attained;

Fourth, the joint task of both the developing and developed polities developing together technologies that structurally contributes towards meeting the following criteria, namely;

Basic Needs ========➔	Contributing to the satisfaction of human basic needs - food, shelter, health, education infrastructure, communications, and transportation etc. providing goods and services accessible to the vast majority if not all the people
Factor Development: ===➔	The use of local factors optimally over time; Generating employment to produce growth; Building the short, medium and long-term high skills human power for R&D capabilities and for the purpose of furthering technological development; Avoid waste/save and generate capital/resources
Structural Development=➔	Reducing dependency and promoting self-reliance; Reducing inequalities between the rich and poor, urban and rural areas, male and female, etc. etc.
Human Enrichment===➔	Contributes to creative investment liberate human-beings from boring, degrading excessively activities, etc. etc.
Cultural Compatibility==➔	Makes use of, and builds on endogenous technical traditions; enhance the blend with valuable elements and patterns in the local, national, regional/continental culture
Ecological Balance ====➔	Minimising the depletion of resources and pollution of the environment; Proper usage of renewable resources/though built-in Waste minimisation, recycling, or re-use and blend with existing eco-cycles; Improve the material and human-made environment by providing a higher level of complexity or diversity of the eco-system, towards achieving balance **[Source. Galtung 1979 with my additions]**

What must be avoided most is development against the people: (i) The widening gap easily results as the accelerating perversion of science and technology into instruments of power, social control and destructive purposes: (ii) the widening gap between North and South in the capacity for technological advance across almost the full range of economic, social and military activities in which technological change plays a significant role resulting in increasing technological dependence of Africa on the developed countries: (iii) notwithstanding these widening gaps and growing dependence, growing strides are being made in some African countries, Nigeria and South Africa in a variety of sectors of productive activities in social services including high technological fields such as electronics, space and computers based on the rapid and discriminate import of capital intensive technology from the developed countries.

The *trickle-down* development analogy of the yester-years is gradually giving way to a more *trickle-upward* approach to development, i.e. endogenous technological approach thanks to the increasing and important human capital in these countries and conscious policies to tackle the issue their own way. Of course, there is a long-way yet to go to overcome this state of technological deficiency and dependency. Morehouse (1979) notes that this kind of skewed development effort based on imported technology, has not only exacerbated the equity crisis in the Third World, but has had two other adverse consequences. Instead of increasing the autonomous capacity for local problem-solving in respect of critical economic and social needs, it has stifled the development of this capability in African countries, because of the ready availability of apparently 'superior' outside (Eurocentric) solutions to local problems.

The acceptance of Eurocentric as against Afrocentric builds on Europe's strategic policy attitude of a systemic manipulations and de-industrialisation of Africa. The mechanisms or imperatives of the day-to-day de-industrialisation of Africa are:

(a) the quest obscene and gargantuan appetite of western industrial machine to the relentless search for more industrial raw materials wherever they can be found and to structurally displace the poor and despoliation of land which accompanies the extraction of these materials;

(b) mechanisms generated by the enormous consumption of non-essential goods by mass markets in the industrial north;

(c) mechanisms embedded in the North's capacity to control the direction of technological change for productive activities in Africa

Take for instance, the green revolution which is a western conception, implementation as well as its funding by Western agribusiness multinationals. Further extension of the green revolution jeopardises traditional agriculture on a magnitude beyond the imagination of industrial colonialism. The massive use of pesticide and fertilisers is not only destroying the soil but lead to serious food problems in the future. For now, the yields are high in some cases, but the long-term consequences may be greater than the short-term benefits. This may seem a doomsday prophecy; the number of landless people has increased since this expensive technology was introduced.

It has also triggered the scramble for land by the new colonial powers like China in Africa. Nevertheless, Africa must eek ways and means in ensuring food security for its rapidly growing population. The continent needs a more equitable food distribution and crop production more than it needs more output. There is a lot of waste in agricultural production due to many interrelated factors such as; (a) poor agricultural techniques; (b) poor road infrastructure that inhibit the transportation of products from the rural to urban areas; (c) poor preservation systems; (d) the growing quest for foreign products; and (e) gross absence in educating the people about their eating habit and the nutritious values of the different food species.

The Diaspora as the continent's sixth region should be given more and greater opportunities to invest both knowledge and capital like the new entrants exploiting the continent. Currently, the Diaspora through remittances overcomes foreign aid to African countries. They are more of a success story and blessings than the treats posed by the new and old colonial masters. The practice for investment-for-resources swaps and 'compensatory' trade that China developed in several African countries was copied from the Japanese model of resources-based confessional loans that it applied in India and China. Increasing Chinese aid serves as a spring-board for investment. The bundling of aid, investment, and trade became a powerful locomotive of China's economic entry into Africa' (Zeleza, 2014:152). The question of aid has failed the continent. Western aid efforts have done more harm than good serving only to strife the development and perpetuating corruption (Moyo 2009). African countries need to recognise that the sustainable transformation of the continent rest in their hands. Though handicap as they are, the diasporas can make a difference no matter how small this can be at the present moment, but it can blossom to something bigger tomorrow. The vast inequalities between the poor and the rich nations create one of the world's serious and urgent problems. Failure to reduce the international and national incomes, or even to prevent it from widening further, is a major source of national and international tension and a treat to peace. Admittedly, it is quite unlikely, with the best will in the world, that international inequalities can be reduced, or even prevented from increasing, for the rest of this century.

But looking at realities rather than appearances, this does not seem an insoluble problem. The immediately urgent objectives are to achieve a substantial absolute improvement in the levels of the developing countries (which is by no means identical with reducing inequality) and to bring about profound qualitative changes in all countries, Africa in particular, which are needed for their survival in a world of limited resources and delicately poised ecological equilibrium. Misdistribution of food is a technical and a political problem. Food security equals national security and world peace.

Generally, a 'global race for arable land that oftentimes lies at the centre of public policy among wealthy countries as an effort to secure future energy and food as productive investments in anticipation of massive profits, or as a hedge against the risk for potential food and fuel shortages in the future. In turn, developing countries pursue a development strategy premised on attracting foreign investment, the core feature of which is concessionary land deals to foreign investments involving huge tracts of land. In many instances, this approach results in a displacement of local populations, the further immiseration of the rural poor, and an overall socio-political framework in which basic rights to land, food, water, adequate housing – as well as the right to self-determination, freedom of assembly and right to fair exploitation of natural resources – are denied (Rosairo, 2016:56-9). Another position taken by Conteh-Morgan (2015:25) is that China's geopolitical objectives in Africa and globally is directly tied to the support of and maintenance of positive/cordial relations with all African states. China needs African states at the UN to counter condemnation of its human rights record by the West and to help advance its 'One Child' policy as well as other political objectives.

African countries must make proper use of its sixth region to lobby and establish a strong hold in the formulation of developmental policies, particularly in counteracting and seeking solutions to problems of: -

- Technology as the new instrument of global domination;
- The role of technology in accelerating the de-industrialisation process of Africa from the developed polities;
- Africa's strong search for technological autonomy, not capacity, as the goal for the continent's transformation;
- Selective technological delinking as a strategy for achieving Africa's greater autonomy;
- Technology for basic human needs and the imperialism of social priorities;
- The new development myth of technological change to alleviate poverty in the absence of a social transformation;
- Intensifying Diaspora role in building the knowledge capacity of African countries as they are better placed in identifying technological requirements in all economic and social sectors;
- Preparing periodically updated short, medium and long-term technology plans for the continent as an integral component of each

country's/continent wise plans for the technological revival and take-off in Africa;

- Expected positive responses from African governments towards the Diaspora in science, technology and development policy formulation especially giving priority to developing technology policies to fulfil the unmet needs of the poor.

From my perspectives, it is believed that the Diaspora when properly motivated and incorporated into the new transformation agenda do provide the knowledge chemistry for a New African Science, Technology and Development Order (NASTDO). Only by establishing a new science, technology order for the continent can the region own its development nexus. The Diaspora constitutes a vital link in this direction, breaking the unholy alliance that exists between the North and Africa (See Morehouse 1978; Link and Gottstein 1986). Africa's inadequate infrastructure limits the continent's economic progress, but funding roads, ports and power projects is difficult. While the Diaspora cannot carry out these projects on their own, they can lend their expertise in policy formulation, assisting in contributing knowledge to the execution of projects and so forth.

The continent is faced with what could be described as 'academic imperialism' which Streeten (1980) concludes that the backward countries potential to use their own forces to generate new ideas and execute research is undermined by the presence and activities of foreign specialists and that the West's research practices in developing countries are designed to justify the neo-colonial apparatus of exploitation. The Diaspora should promote the sustainable transformation of the continent, not acting in ways that destroys the region. Today there are mixed feelings in Cameroon on the role the Diaspora in the ongoing political crisis plaguing the country. While the original idea was to ensure the self-determination of the people of Southern Cameroons, poor management of the struggle has only contributed to the destruction of the country. No one appreciates the attitude of Yaoundé regime towards the people of Southern Cameroons; just as some of the restoration forces have contributed negatively to destroying their own people instead of defending them.

The transfer of technology, which is the fundamental form of spreading the scientific and technological revolution to developing countries, strengthens Western's corporations' position in these countries, much to their detriment, and increases the instability and uneven development of their economies. The scientific and technological revolution creates ample opportunities for the solution of the most troublesome socio-economic problems facing African countries today. As has been demonstrated throughout the publication, ways to these solutions are blocked by imperialist policies and the fact that the majority of African countries continue to depend on the forces of imperialism. Most of Western's monopolies have collected in their hands and laboratories the greatest part of the capitalist world\s scientific and technical potential, use it to achieve their own economic and political ends. Africa should use her Diasporas to achieve its own political and economic ends by improving the quality well-being of the citizens.

For the Diaspora to be active partners in the development process would require a number of interrelated coordinated activities; for example; (i) improvement in good governance and stringent management of the economy; long-term progress in building institutions of good governance and deepening democracy. Africa's surge for progress cannot persist without strong education health system; (ii) effective and efficient development of finances; and (iii) positive responses from the international community.

The International community has an important role to play. In addition, the richer nations should encourage further economic progress and economic diversification by reducing barriers to trade for products from African countries especially those whose economies are least developed. The export of technology to African countries has neither brought about any fundamental changes in the dynamics of their economic development, nor lead to these countries' achievement of economic independence. The only result of technology transfer has been or is the emergence of enclaves of contemporary industrial production within the African countries' multisectoral economies, enclaves weakly integrated into the national economies. The export of technology has given rise to a new kind of dependence, technological dependence, the essence of which is found in the exploitation and subjection of African countries within the modified system of capitalist division of labour.

To a large extent there is a correlation between the Diaspora and economic transformation in Africa. The Diaspora are part and parcel of the continent, they have more to gain by developing their ascentary home than destroying it; which the colonial powers or invaders are out to exploit. Here one sees the politics of *'assimilation'* as practiced by France in Africa and the politics of *'indirect rule'* practiced by the British colonial masters in play. The politics of assimilation and authoritarian centralisation, accounts for the greater share of the numerous political turmoil plaguing French-speaking Africa where democratic governance is slow in catching-up with the current wind of political changes blowing across the continent. This is no praise for the British colonial system, but compared to French colonial system as witnessed in Africa, there is praise on the British system of indirect rule which produced some degree of accountability, transparency and ensured the peoples' involvement in the governance process. Writing on her process of decentralisation, Joseph Owona (2012), assert: 'Great Britain has an advance system of regional autonomy...local and regional authorities are models of 'sui generis organisation' each having its peculiarities.

Economic development is impossible without reference to cultural aspects; not only because is a constitutive element of development but also because it is one of its cornerstones ever in the material field. The Diaspora has a cultural affinity with the continent. The Chinese for example have no such affinity with Africa's cultural heritage and values like the British and French out to exploit the resources and human power of the people. There is therefore no reason for shifting the viewpoint on the idealistic level. If one considers culture to embrace all that is not natural, then it becomes clear that culture cannot be something which we can regard as the ornaments added to life by aesthetes. Culture, and in particular the African grassroots culture found in the villages, can be compared with a factory manufacturing a broad range of products, both material and intellectual. Throughout the world, technicians and scientific discoveries are in the first instance the products of their intellect. Thus, if Africa were to be satisfied with merely adopting foreign technologies, any development based thereon would be unstable and one-sided. Development without cultural innovation would be not growth but merely a growth feeding on foreign development.

The expertise of the Diaspora adds to indigenous knowledge of the people to act as a link between modern and indigenous technological development. The Diaspora gives added value to indigenous knowledge for they are part of that cultural heritage. The invaders do not have that. The fact that Europe invented the word exploitation, invasion, colonialism, development etc. should not be judged positively. It would be more appropriate to enquire whether ***homo faber*** and ***homo sapiens*** and whether every promising civilisation did not leave merely a sense of emptiness in human hearts as these slowly but surely forewent wisdom for power and profit' (Mbaya 1986:95-96).

The Diaspora could in a way be seen as Africans chained in iron and transported to other lands where they laboured and put out their talents to promote the course of foreigners while dear Africa wept behind in barbarism, desolation and neglect. The Diasporas want to change that fate and bring the continent to the limelight of development for the good of the people. Therefore, the Diaspora must be part of the transformation of Africa - where he/she belongs – to believe that (s)he is really alive as it is part of his/her existence, Give the Diasporas a chance to transform Africa, no matter how small their contribution is at the present. It is a contribution that comes from the heart with no strings attached.

Using the Diasporas constitutes a dichotomy between indigenous knowledge and modern technology. This builds the way towards a more realistic and more pragmatic attitude towards integrated technology that is adjusted to social and cultural needs and potentials, helping to further a more effective usage of didactic role of science and technology for the sustainable development and transformation of the continent. Kaplinsky (2005:11) asserts that technological progress leads to the advance of global processes in the production of knowledge. This might be termed the benign side of technological globalisation. However, there is also a malign, more disruptive component to technologically induced globalisation which reflects a darker side. This is what economist call *'negative externalities'* and environmentalists refer to as the *'spoilage of the global commons'* creating fundamental conflicts in society. The ruling elites due to their foreign acquired values are part of the problem as well as they are an inherent part of the solution. The ruling bourgeoisie have contributed to what could be seen as technological imperialism.

A precondition for technological imperialism is existence in the continent of a social group which serves technological imperialism as a transmission belt and afford it, the necessary measure of legitimacy. The upper strata within the educated bourgeoisie normally discharge this function under the supervision of the ruling class. As part of the solution to the ongoing crisis on the continent they should emerge as the construction avenue of new enterprises as well as play large roles in the process of breaking the technological dependence on western imperialism and domination.

Again, AU's diplomacy of the Diaspora is the focus on economic partnership, creating incentives for innovation and entrepreneurship, research and development, encourages the mobilisation of capital. Financial remittances in this context entails payments by members of a Diaspora either directly to their families to for individual projects in the community. In addition, there also exit social remittances in the form of the transfer of ideas, values and norms (Levitt 1998). Remittance flows to Africa is what is keeping many families afloat. Western financial institutions are making high profit of these remittances sent as they charge up from 8% to 20% as transfer fees. The average cost of sending remittances to Africa is 12%. Globally, sending remittances cost an average of 9%. In Nigeria, where most migrants send money home from abroad, the fee is 10%. The G8/G20 plan aims to reduce the global average remittance price to 5% in five years, which could save migrants up to $16 billion a year.

The five costliest corridors are all intra-Africa and rates are as high as 25%. Ghana, South Africa and Tanzania are the most expensive countries in Africa to send money, with fees averaging 20%. The estimated annual remittances sent to African countries from the Diaspora in 2012 amounted to USA$61 billion. Somalia is not the only African country where migrant remittances have become an important source of external funding. Officially recorded remittance flows to Africa by the World Bank are estimated to have increased from US$9.1 billion in 1990 to nearly US$40 billion in 2010. These remittances equalled 2.6% of Sub-Saharan Africa's gross domestic product in 2009, or almost 60% of official aid flows to the region.

There is no doubt that African countries rely heavily on external funding for development. But foreign direct investments and official development aid have declined over the years, according to the African Development Bank (AfDB). It is believed that remittance flows can impact on reducing poverty and grow economies. However, a big chunk of the remittances goes to pay hefty bank charges. "High transaction fees are cutting into remittances, which are a lifeline for millions of Africans," according to Gaiv Tata, World Bank's Director for Finance and Private Sector for Africa. Remittances are an important share of foreign reserves for countries, but their impact on development and economic growth are minimal if they are only spent on consumption. Cash-strapped Africa governments are trying to get migrants to invest part of their wealth in their homeland in the form of Diaspora bonds. The capital raised could be earmarked for big development projects. The initiative is not new. The governments of India and Israel have raised about US$40 billion since the 1950s using these bonds.

In Africa, Ethiopia was the first country to issue Diaspora bonds to finance a hydroelectric power dam. The so-called Millennium Corporate Bonds, issued in 2009, failed to sell. Lack of trust in the government as a guarantor and the political risks are some of the reasons for the flop. In 2011, the government re-advertised the bonds as the Renaissance Dam Bonds, lowering the minimum denomination to an affordable US$50 and offering to pay yields or interest to buyers every six months. Waiving remittance fees associated with the purchase of the bonds was another new feature added. Rwanda found herself in a similar situation when the major donors suspended aid after the United Nations accused the government of backing rebels in the Democratic Republic of the Congo - a charge it denied.: Rwandans living abroad and those at home were called upon to donate to a 'Solidarity Fund' named Agaciro Development Fund (ADF) (meaning 'dignity' in local language. By August 2012, the fund had attracted pledges of about US$31 million, according to the UK Guardian Newspaper (Sambira 2013).

Table 5:1 Top 10 African Recipients of Remittances: (in billion US $)

Nigeria	**$20.6**	**Egypt**	**$20.5**	**Morocco**	**$6.9**
Tunisia	**$2.2**	**Algeria**	**$1.8**	**Senegal**	**$1.4**
Kenya	**$1.2**	**Sudan**	**$1.1**	**S. Africa**	**$.1.1**
Uganda	**$0.98**				

Source: Send Money Africa, World Bank. See also Africa Renewal, August 2013, p16 (Sambira 2013).

Egypt and Nigeria are among the top recipients of migrant remittances according to the African Development Bank's latest Report, the African Economic Outlook 2013. According to the report, the two countries received 64% of the total remittance to Africa in 2012: US$18 billion transferred to Egypt and US$21 billion to Nigeria. Table 5:1 depicts a bird eye perspective of recipient countries in Africa. These remittances help to keep afloat many families across Africa, from Mali to Tanzania from Senegal and Somali to South Africa, the story is the same. It calls for a holistic approach to improving the living conditions of people and for remittances to be deployed in creating small-scale as well as medium-type enterprises. These remittances sustain many families. Looking at the other side of the picture, given the state of economic instability in the West and growing signs of xenophobic attitude towards foreigners, the process cannot be sustainable in the longer-run, Remittances wrongly used increases dependency, destroys creativity and promotes inertia. Therefore, receivers of these remittances should embark on the road of judiciously usage of it as well as prepare themselves for an eventual rainy-day ahead.

Remittances, especially those from skilled migrants workers, and associated with the "brain drain nexus", remain a cause for serious concern to the continent. In many cases, one can associate the crisis in Africa's health sector to the emigration of skilled health care professionals, who increasingly find employment in the high demand countries of Europe, USA and Asia. Sanjeer Gupta, Catherine Pattillo and Smita Wagh (2007:41) pointed out that "about 80 percent of nurses from Liberia and equal number of doctors from Mozambique were working in industrial countries. High job vacancy or attrition is rates in the public health systems of countries like Ghana, Zambia and Zimbabwe are still attributed to migration. On average 20 percent of Africa's population over the age of 15 with a post-secondary education work in OECD countries compared with less than 10 percent in South Asia. Higher wages abroad is also an inducement in the increase of the regions supply of health-care professionals, even after accounting for emigration. At the same time, it was recorded following remittances sent home to the following beneficiary countries (see Chart 1 – Top African destinations relative to their size).

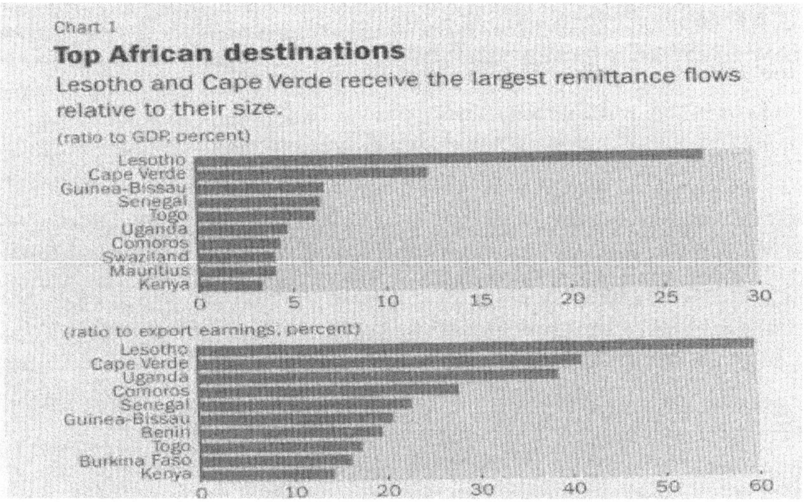

(See also Sanjeev Gupta et al (2007)"Making Remittances Work for Africa" Finance and Development. June 2007, Vol.44. No.2, International Monetary Fund, Washington, USA pp41).

An outstanding impediment to remittances is the prohibitive fees associated with transfers. The cost of formally transfer funds to Africa, especially small amounts is high. The figure on probative fees depicts the situation. (See Chart 3 Prohibitive Fees). Getting remittances is one thing, how it is properly used is another. Though most households typically spend a large proportion of their remittances, their propensity to save can be as high 40 percent; but the wish for policy makers, the challenge is how to channel these savings into productive uses (Gupta, op cit.p43). Banks and financial institutions in Africa should encourage emigrants (remittances) to use these moneys for more productive use and spur long-term related developmental activities.

It calls for restoring trust and confidence in financial and banking institutions given the corrupting rate and poor governance in most Africa countries (see Forje 2018) Cameroon Without Corruption; Christoph Sruckelberger (1999) Fighting Corruption and other related publications that pound on corruption as undermining of the common wellbeing through particular interests of individuals.

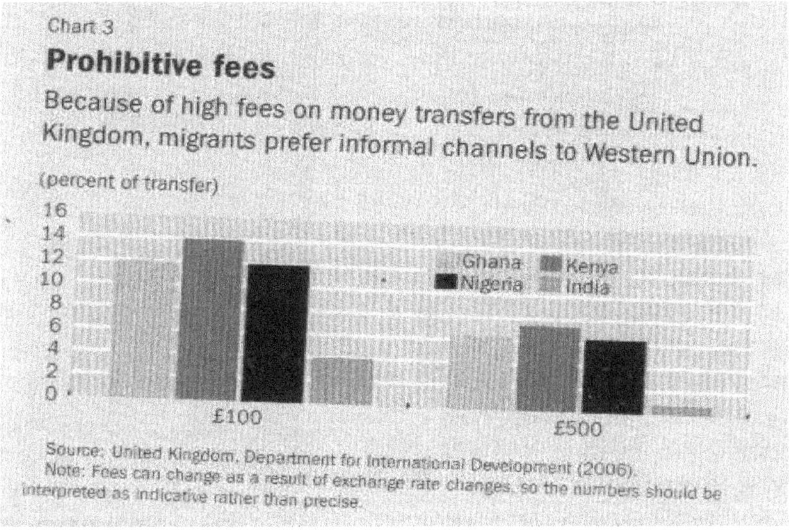

(See also Sanjeev Gupta 2007 op cit.)

The challenge is how African financial and banking institutions can promote investment from remittances by bundling financial services like saving products and entrepreneurial loans for household that receive remittances. As noted by Gupta et al (2007) remittances cannot be substituted for a sustained, domestically engineered development effort. Things can rapidly change where emigrants are resident and can no longer earn salaries to remit home. The Corona virus and fallout is a typical example, even if it is a very short period. The consequence of COVID 19 could be long-lasting. Let us reflect back to the "Dutch disease" effects on the real exchange rate. For now, migrants transfer, or remittances help to ease. The most fundamental question hangs on the uncertainty of remittances from the Diasporas in light of the corona virus.

The immediate household budget constraints of recipient households. Remittances to African countries far out-weight development assistance and have a more direct impact on poverty reduction for individual homes. African countries should not only rely on remittances in the development of the continent. Who knows what effect the Corona Virus is going to impact on the global economy. The answer is blowing in the wind. We just have to wait and see for the long-term consequences of the ongoing pandemic that has affected every country on Planet Earth. The entire world is in serious economic crisis following the corona virus pandemic. Fragile and collapsing states in Africa are in serious. COVID-19 as noted by the Centre for Analysis, Forecasting and Strategy (CAPS), entitle "The pangolin Effect: The Storm coming from Africa?" Obtained by the Ecolin Agency, the French Ministry of Foreign Affairs predicts a quasi- apocalyptic effect of COVID-19 on African states. According to the governments think tank, "seen from Africa, the Covid-19 comes in the form of a p chronogram which amplify the crisis factors of societies and states" (The Voice, (2020) Issue 216:5).

According to the report, the pandemic of the new corona virus will be "the crisis of too many which destabilises durably regimes which puts down fragile regimes (Sahel) or ultimately (Central Africa)". For Caps the rate of medication is almost zero and national health systems can be considered as saturated automatically". COVID-19 should therefore reveal the "inability" of African states to protect their populations. The health crisis that comes with the disease will, according to the note, lead to a political crisis that could be triggered by too many deaths or even the infection of an "elderly leader". In this scenario, the States most exposed to destabilisation would ne those of the Sahel and Central Africa, characterised by "falling public policies" unlike other countries with "more solid institutions" such as Rwanda or the Senegal (The Voice op cit.).

In West Africa, containment measures will undermine the fragile balance of the informal, an economy of daily survival essential to the maintenance of the social contract. In Central Africa, the shock could precipitate the final crisis in oil rent in Cameroon, Gabon and Congo-Brazzaville, there too, at the heart of social equilibrium" indicates the Quai d'orsay. In quasi-Hollywood scenario, the institution also indicates that the essential needs linked to the health crisis should reveal phenomena of urban panic in Africa cities. "The question of selection will not relate to the people to be saved medically (lack of reception capacities), but on the basic needs: which district to supply? Which credible local authorities can be the relay for organising distribution? What essential products to supply in an expected phase of shortage - indicates the CAPS. The situation should lead to increases in crime, making the authority of the state even more fragile. The opinion is consistent with several previous reports, which paint a complete bleak picture of African governance systems and public policies. However, if it is true that many African countries are considered fragile, are they also helpless in the face of the new crisis? One thing is certain, the so-called fragile and failing countries, according to the Quasi d'Orsay note, have already acquired a lot of experience in crisis management, whether political or health" (The Voice, Issue 216, 2020:5). Within these perspectives, Africa is in serious problems now and in post-COVID-19 era. It will take a very long time to overcome. There is a parallel her with what happened to the Lagos Plan of Action (LPA) in the 1980s which was toppled with the introduction of the Structural Adjustment programme to contributed to the Lost Decade of the continent.

Illicit Financial Flows

While the six regions [Diaspora] through remittances are boosting the economy of African countries, there is a growing outflow of financial capital from the continent. According to Tafirenyika (2013:14-15) "between USA$1.2 trillion and USA$1.4 trillion has left Africa in illicit financial flows between 1980-2009, roughly equal to Africa's current gross domestic product, and surpassing by far the money it received from outside over the same period. Illicit financial flows are money earned illegally and transferred for use elsewhere. The money is usually generated from criminal activities, corruption, tax evasion, bribes and transactions from cross-border smuggling."

According to the African Development Bank (AfDB) and the Global Financial Integrity (GFI) USA, the illicit haemorrhage of resources from Africa is about four times Africa's current external debts The Report, Illicit financial Flows and the Problem of Net Resource Transfers from Africa: 1980-2009, indicates there has been a cumulative illicit outflows from the continent over 30-year period which ranged from USA$1.2 trillion to USA$1.4 trillion. Following Raymond Baker, President of Global Financial Integrity, "the traditional thinking has always been that the West is pouring money into Africa through foreign aid and other private-sector flows, without receiving much in return." Mthuli Ncube, Chief Economist and Vice-President of the AfDB, agree: The African continent is resources-rich. With good resources husbandry, Africa could be in a position to finance much of its own development." The human capital and natural resources to Europe is not acknowledged. The ideological orientation and believe of the West is that nothing good comes out of Africa.

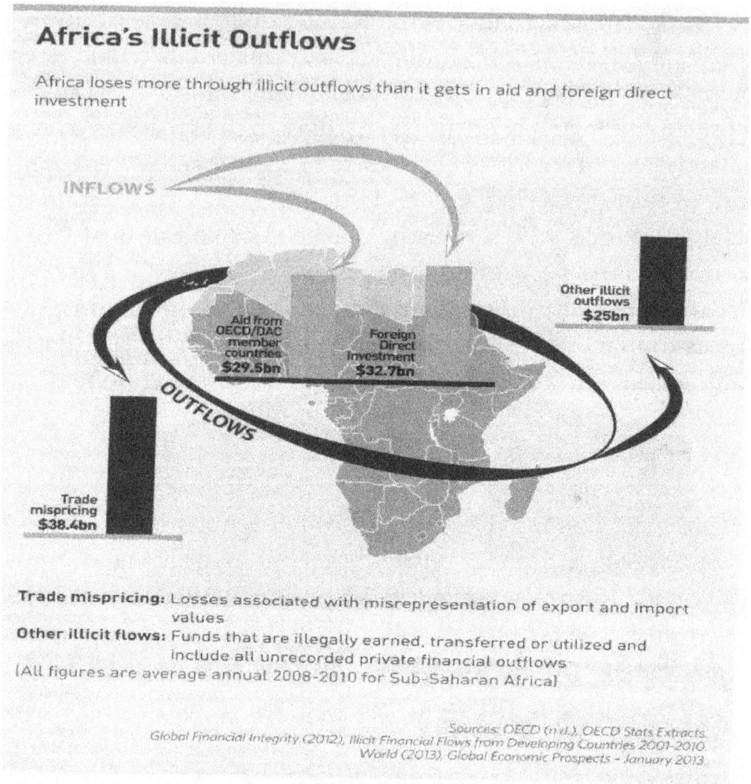

(See also Masimba Tafirenyika (2013) Illicit Financial Flows From Africa: Track It, Stop It, and Get It" Africa Renewal, December 2013. Vol.27. No.3, New York, pp14-15)

Following estimates by GFI, corrupt activities such as bribery and embezzlement constitute only about 3% of illicitly outflows; criminal activities such as drug trafficking and smuggling make up 30% to 35%; and commercial transactions by multinational companies make up a whopping 60% to 65%. It is argued that contrary to popular belief, money stolen by corrupt governments is insignificant compared to the other forms of illicit outflows; and the most common way illicit money is moved across borders is through international trade.

The United Nations Economic Commission for Africa Research Panel to probe into illicit financial outflows is headed by former South Africa President, Thabo Mbeki, with ECA Executive Secretary Carlos Lopes as vice-chair and, the following as members, Raymond Baker President of Global Financial Integrity and Ambassador Segun Apata of Nigeria, faces a daunting task. The ECA blames illicit outflows for reducing Africa's tax revenues, undermining trade and investment and worsening poverty. Apparently, developing countries lose three times more to tax havens than they receive in aid. The Organisation for Economic Cooperation and Development (OECD) holds that poor countries have weak bargaining power. Some have problems in enforcing their transfer pricing regimes due to gaps in the law, weak or no regulations and guidelines for companies and that poor countries have limited technical expertise to assess the risks of transfer pricing and to negotiate changes with multinationals (Tafirenyika 2013:15-16). Ambassador Segun Apata (Nigeria) points out that Africa loses USA$50 billion every year through illicit financial outflows. Moyo Dambisa (2009) makes the assertion that aid positively correlates with high levels of corruption and that reducing such aid will address this endemic problem. In reality, however, African governments become visibly more extractive toward their citizens when faced with diminished sources of income. Also, Africa has a fair number of the most highly taxed countries in the world, but much of the tax revenues do not reach the intended beneficiaries; instead they end up in the pockets of few rich and powerful.

Developing countries loose three times more to tax havens than they receive in aid. According to Nigerian Ambassador Segun Apata illicit financial outflows from Africa between 1970 and 2008 were over USA$800 billion. And Africa loses USA$50 billion every year which is quite a huge resource (Africa Renewal 2013:16). Africa Progress Report 2013 calls for multilateral solutions to global problems because 'tax evasion, illicit transfers of wealth and unfair pricing practices are sustained through global trading and financial systems. It urges African citizens to demand the highest standards of propriety and disclosure from their governments, and rich countries to demand the same standards from their companies.

Apparently, the public argument for a crackdown on tax dodging is gradually being won, but the political battle remains. This is an issue of good governance. African countries are challenged to ensure the practice of democratic governance and show the needed political will to curbing bad governance throughout the continent. It goes without say that countries embracing self-monitoring mechanism to shine light on domestic affairs stand a better chance of promoting sustainable development that improves the quality of the livelihood of their citizens. The African Peer Review Mechanism (APRM) a self-monitoring instrument created by African leaders in 2003 gives hope for fighting against bad governance. They need to beat the drums much harder in areas like democracy and good governance, socioeconomic development, corporate governance, corruption, human rights, particularly women's and children's rights, conflicts and judicial independence.

Mobilising civil society is crucial in the process of ensure democratic governance. Civil society organisations should work in partnership with the government for these civil society groups to become major actors in the fight against bad governance and corruption. The involvement of civil society actors is a necessary but not a sufficient condition to reduce corruption. Corruption frequently takes place in societies where there is considerable discretion for public officials, limited accountability and little transparency in governmental operations.

During the past couple of years, governance in Africa has improved considerably, aided in part by the African Peer Review Mechanism. There are fewer coups, more elections and better management of national economies, but also growing number of *'sit-tight'* presidents who manipulate constitutions to make it a dynasty. Presently, the Central African Sub-region holds the highest number of 'sit-tight' presidents on the continent. In the wake of all these short comings, there is still need for more accountability and transparency before Africa can claim credit for good governance, transparent, free, fair, credible and accountable elections.

Corruption is still rife and illicit financial flows are draining the continent's domestic resources. The developed polities need also to show good examples by calling to order the activities of their various companies operating abroad. It takes two to tango. Therefore, strong and independent institutions are required to ensure that the rule of law prevails. The judiciary must remain apolitical and totally independent in dispensing justice. In Africa, perhaps more than elsewhere, the success of a credible monetary policy depends crucially on a central bank that is wholly independent of political pressure. We all have the power to make a difference in the life and development of other people.

References

African Union (2011). Report of the Technical Experts Meeting on the African Diaspora (TCEM), Pretoria, South Africa, 21-22 February 2011, Addis Ababa-Ethiopia, African Union

Akesson Lisa & Maria Eriksson Baaz (2015). Africa's Return Migrants. The New Developers? Zed Books, UK.

Alina, M. (2004) Spaces of Diaspora: Kurdish Identities, Experiences of Otherness and Politics of Belonging. Department of Sociology.

Gothenburg University, Gothenburg Studies in Sociology No.22, Sweden

Apata Segun (2013)." Interview - Africa Loses $50 Billion Every Tear" Africa Renewal, Vol.27, N0.3, December 2013. New York, USA, pp16-17

Black, Jeremy (2011). Slavery: A New Global History. Constable and Robinson, London

Brubaker, Rogers (2005). The 'Diaspora' Diaspora. Ethnic and Racial Studies, 28, pp1-19

Cohen, R. (1997) Global Diaspora. An Introduction, UCL Press, London

Constantinou, Costa and James Der Derian (eds.) (2010) Sustainable Diplomacies, Palgrave – Macmillan, Basingstoke, UK

Conteh-Morgan Earl (2015). "China's World View and Representations of its Engagement with Africa", ASPJ – Africa and Franco phonier, 3rd Quarter, Vol. 6. No.3, 2015, USA pp16-34

Cross, M. Davis (2010) "Sustainable Diplomacy in the European Union. in Constantnou, Costa and James Der Derian (eds.) Sustainable Diplomacies. Palgrave – Macmillan, Basingstoke, UK, pp192-212

Emeagwali Philip, [2010] "How Do We Reverse the Brain Drain?" Renaissance World – Restoring Black and African Dignity, 1st April-31st May, 2010, pp11-12 &-74

Galtung Johan (1979). "Towards a New International Technological Order". In Ward Morehouse (ed.) (1979). Science, Technology and the Social Order. Transaction Books, New Brunswick, New Jersey, pp277-300

Gilroy, P. (1993) The Black Atlantic: Modernity and Double Consciousness, Verso Press, London.

Haidara Aissata (2013). "No Place Like Home. Africa's Skilled Labour Returns", Africa Renewal, August 2013, Washington D.C.

Kaplinsky Raphael (2005). Globalisation, Poverty and Inequality: Between A Rock and A Hard Place. Polity Press, Cambridge (UK) and Malden (USA)

Kapur, Devesh (2003) Indian Diaspora as a Strategic Asset. Economic and Political Weekly, 38

Lopes Carlos (2019) "Europe Needs to Make Min Up on Relations With Africa". 12th December 2019, Euro server.

Levitt, Peggy (1998) Social Remittances: Migration Driven Local Level Forms of Cultural Diffusion. International Migration Review, 32.

Link Gotz and Klaus Gottstein (eds.) (1986) Cultural Development, Science and Technology in Sub-Saharan Africa. Nomos Verlagsgesellschaft, Baden-Baden, Germany.

Mbaya Etienne-Richard (1986). "African Cultural Identity: The Conflict between Traditional Heritage and Modern Development', in Link and Gottstein (eds.) (1986), Cultural development, Science and Technology in Sub-Saharan Africa. Nomos Verlagsgesellschaft, Baden-Baden, pp87-108

Morehouse Ward (1978). "Technological Autonomy and Delinking in the Third World: Confronting the Unholy Alliance of Power, Privilege and Technology in Rich and Poor Countries", paper prepared for the International Workshop on Technological Dependence – A Major Hindrance for Autonomous Development", Bonn, FRG, 2-5 November, 1978.

Morehouse Ward (1979) "Science, Technology, Autonomy, And Dependence: A Framework for International Debate" in Ward Morehouse (1979). Science, Technology and the Social Order. Transaction Books, New Brunswick, New Jersey, USA, pp387-412

Moyo Danbisa (2009) Dead Aid: Why Aid is Not Working and How There is a Better Way for Africa. Straus and Giroux, London

Mutisi Martha (2009) "Book Review –Dead Aid" in Africa Peace and Conflict Journal, Vol. 2. Number 2. December 2009, University of Peace Africa Programme, Addis Ababa, Ethiopia, pp106-108

Mwagiru Makuni (2012) "The African Union's Diplomacy of the Diaspora: Context, Challenges and Prospects", in African Journal on Conflict Resolution, Vol.12, Number 2, 2012, Special Issue on the African Union, ACCORD, South Africa, pp73-85

Mwagiru Makuni (2011) Diplomacy of the Diaspora: Harness Diasporas in Kenya's Foreign Policy, Diaspora Studies, 4.

Ogom, Raphael (2009) The African Union, African Diaspora and the Quest for Development: In Search of the Missing Link. African Journal of Political science and International Relations, 3.

Omeje, Kenneth (2007) The Diaspora and Domestic Insurgence in Africa. African Sociological Review, 11

Onyeani Abba Chika (2012) "Genesis: Bridging the World Africa Diaspora" Global Diaspora Summit 2012, South Africa, May 2012, A Production of the African Sun Times, pp8-9

Olsson Erik (2012). Introduction: Diaspora Transnational Engagement and National Regimes" in Heidi Moksnes & Owona Joseph (2012). Decentralisation in Cameroon. L'Harmattan Publishers, Paris, Frances

Mia Melin (eds.) (2012). Global Civil Society – Shifting Powers in a Shifting World. Centre for Sustainable Development, University of Uppsala, Sweden, pp177-192

Patterson, Tiffany Ruby and Robin Kelley (2000). Unfinished Migration: Reflections on the African Diasporas and The Making of the Modern World, African Studies Review 43

Rosario Cruz-Del Teresita (2016). "South-South Land Grabs: The Case of Korean Investments in the Greater Mekong Subregion", ASPJ – Africa and Francophonie, 2nd Quarter, Vol.7. No. 2. USA, pp57-76

Safran, W. (1991) Diasporas in Modern Society: Myths of Homeland and Return, Diaspora Vol. 1. No. 1. Spring pp83-99

Sambira Joycelyne (2013) "Tapping Migration Wealth to Fund Development: African Diaspora Remittances Can Reduce Poverty", African Renewal, August 2013, Washington, USA, pp15-17

Schutter De Oliver (2011). "The Green Rush: The Golden Race for Farmland and the Rights of Landless: Harvard International Law Journal, 52. No.2, Summer 2011: 504-58

Sheffer, G. (2003) Diaspora Politics: At Home and Abroad, University of Cambridge Press, Cambridge

Shuval, Judith (2000). Diaspora Migration: Definitional Ambiguities and Theoretical Paradigms. International Migration 35

Streeten P. Paul (1980) Quoted in Scientific Cooperation for Development: Search for New Directions, New Delhi, Vikas Publishing House, PVT Ltd., p55

The Voice (2020)"COVI9-19: When a French Diplomatic Note Predicts The Fall of Certain African States" The Voice, Issue 216, Tuesday, March 07, 2020, Yaoundé – Cameroon, pp5.

Trafirenyika Masimba (2013). "Illicit Financial Flows from Africa: Track It, Stop It, And Get It". Africa Renewal, Vol. 27, No. 3, December 2013, Washington, pp14-15 and 32

Veney Cassandra (2002). The Ties That Bind: The Historic Africa Diaspora and Africa, African Issues,

Zeleza Tiyambe Paul (2014). "The Africa-China Relationship: Challenges and Opportunities", Canadian Journal of African Studies, Vol.48, No.1, April 2014, pp145-169

Chapter Six

Pan-Africanism and Renaissance Africa

"I have a dream that one day every valley shall be engulfed, every hill shall be exalted, and every mountain shall be made low, the rough places will be made plains and the crooked places will be made straight and the glory of the Lord shall be revealed, and all flesh shall see it together."

[Martin Luther King Jr.]

"According to Nelson Mandela, Africa has gone beyond bemoaning the past for its problems. The task of undoing that past is ours, with the support of those will to join us in a continental renewal. We the Africans must take responsibility for our own destiny if we must uplift ourselves by our own efforts in partnership with those non-Africans who wish us well"

[Ezeemoo Ndu, Editor –in-Chief, Renaissance World, 1st April – 31st May 2010]

"It is a historical reality that Africa has contributed and continue to contribute significantly to the wealth of the North, especially Europe and North America. This is in the form of mental and manual labour and natural resources. It is also a fact that the negative impact of transcontinental slave trade and colonial plunder is still being felt in Africa"

[Professor Shadrack B. O. Gutto, 2010]

"I reject the glorification of the nation-state which we have inherited from colonialism, and the artificial nations we are trying to forge from that inheritance. We are all Africans trying very hard to be Ghanaians or Tanzanians, Fortunately, for Africa we have not been completely successful. The outside world hardly recognises our Ghanaian-ness of Tanzanian-ness. What the outside world recognises about us is our African-ness."

(Julius Nyerere 1977)

Introduction: UNITY – The African Dream

Confronted with the crushing effects of a devastating situation of Africa, one can only have envisioned a time when the inequalities of life and the unfortunate twists and turns that throws the African continent off track would be erased and straightened out. Some African leaders like Martin Luther king Jr. embraced a united vision of a continent united and at peace with itself. Martin Luther King like Kwame Nkrumah; "African Must Unite" articulated on the eve of the creation of the Organisation of African unity for segregated or divided Africa, challenging the people and their moral consciences to reconstruct a united continent within a rapidly changing hostile world community. He equally challenged the moral complacency of African leaders and Africans the world over that had failed to live up to the essential creed and profession of faith; that all people are created equal and have the same rights to enjoy what God had created; that no nation had the right to place itself to subject others into slavery and domination.

The African dream lingers on. One day the Africanness in us will be realised to go by the views of Former South African President Thabo Mbeki speaking at the African Renaissance Conference; "I dream of the day when these: African mathematicians and computer specialists in Washington and New York, the African physicists, engineers, doctors, business managers and economists, will return from London and Manchester and Paris and Brussels to add to the African pool of brain power, to enquire into and find solutions to Africa's problems and challenges, to open the African door to the world of knowledge, to elevate Africa's place within the universe of research…education and information".

African Renaissance, Pan Africanism and Africa Must Unite agenda are one and the same because the concepts signal seeds of hope and progress. The concepts inspire the growth of people of genius to guide its socioeconomic and political rebirth and renewal. President Nnamdi Azikiwe (1936); Kwame Nkrumah (1953); Thabo Mbeki (1998) and many others remained passionate to the ideal and under the common umbrella of first ***"The Right Timing".*** Here the works of Nnamdi Azikiwe "Renascent Africa" coming at the peak of the "Great Depression" and at the start of the Second World War which inhibited people paying any attention to the concept; Before Africa Must Unite, Kwame Nkrumah spoke about ***"Black Renaissance"*** in the 1950s and 1960s, coming at the height of the 'Cold War' and the 'African Liberation Struggle Against Colonialism and Imperialism"; and "Post-Cold War", Mbeki emerged as the new inspirational advocate for the three concepts and agenda. Nkrumah's 'Black Renaissance' is part of the Pan-Africanism, African Renaissance and Unity project and within the context of sovereignty as part of the overall struggle for the construction of a Union Government for the continent to gain its rightful place as well as play a veritable role within the construct of the international system.

Therefore, the 1960 republican constitution of Ghana contained a clause showing Ghana's readiness to surrender its sovereignty in the overall interest of African Unity. Many saw this as a radical inspired Pan-African vision of a union government difficult to swallow. Yet the notion of Pan-Africanism remained a continental project and vision of uniting the continent irrespective of the butchering machinery put in place by the colonial invaders. It was paraphrasing the words of Nyerere (1997) a grand political vision, not a puny economistic design. Unity did not make Africa automatically rich but can make it difficult for Africa and the Africa peoples to be disregarded and humiliated. These are some of the fundamental issues which the future of Africa must continue to strive in protecting and showing that the forces of slavery, imperialism and colonialism remain the greatest crime ever committed against the humanity – the African people.

First, **African unity** is imperative and should structurally redress the wounds inflicted upon the continent by the vultures of the slave trade, imperialism, colonialism. The concepts of slavery, imperialism, colonialism are interconnected dating back to the fifteenth century or before and these concepts can be streamlined within the following context;

- imperialism as economic expansion;
- imperialism as a subjugation of 'others';
- imperialism as an idea or spirit with many forms of realisation; and
- imperialism as a discursive field of knowledge;

And

- Colonialism facilitated imperialist expansion to ensure European control of indigenous people;
- Colonialism became imperialism's outpost, the fort and the port of imperial outreach (Smith 2012:22)

Both Hobson in 1902 and Lenin in 1917 saw imperialism as being an integral part of Europe's economic expansion and as of the future nation it would become; (Giddens, 1998, Smith 2012). The struggle for sovereignty and independence of colonialised territories was to assert the claim to humanity and remains a consistent thread of anti-colonial discourses on colonialism and oppression. Contextualised within this frame, Smith (2012:27) notes; The focus on asserting humanity has to be seen within the anti-colonial analysis of imperialism and what were seen as imperialism's dehumanizing imperatives, which were structured into the language, economy, social relations and cultural life of colonial societies. From the nineteenth century onwards the processes of dehumanization were often hidden behind justifications for imperialism and colonialism, which were clothed within an ideology of humanism and liberalism and the assertion of moral claims that related to a concept of civilized 'man', The moral justifications did not necessarily stop the continued hunting of Aborigines in the early nineteenth century, nor the continued ill-treatment of different indigenous peoples even today."

So far Pan-Africanism, Renaissance Africa, and African Unity faces strong challenges from the advocates of Pan-Arabism' which provides a new domineering proclivities and machinations of creating a united continent which Gaddafi like Nkrumah and Nyerere and Nasser strongly believed in. The differences can be traced to the historically and culturally irresolvable antinomies of Pan-Africanism and Pan-Arabism dating back into the historical past of relationship between the two worlds. How can these differences be overcome? The fundamental and yet challenging issues that unite Pan-Africanism and Pan-Arabism are more significant than what divides them. It is in the ultimate interests of the two bodies to pull their resources together for the common good rather than deploying these resources in consolidating the divisive tendencies existing between the two.

The coming into being of the African Union provides a unique opportunity and desirability for creating an African Union Government, with exclusive and/or concurrent jurisdiction over certain strategic policy areas using the regional economic communities as 'building blocks' in the process of continental political integration (African Union, 2006) remains a remarkable and momentous landmark in the evolution of the Pan-Africa idea. It is 'momentous' because it provides a unique opportunity to adapt or modify Nkrumah's vision to the present historical conjunctures and to learn the correct lessons from either his mistakes or the inadequacies of his own formulations of the idea of Pan-Africa (Jinadu, 2009).

Second, ***"Strong Leadership"*** - here, advocates for a hope for the continent demonstrated strong and committed leadership as vital inputs in popularising the ideological orientation and accomplishment of a United Africa. At the launching of the Renaissance Institute in Pretoria on 11 October 1999 at the Presidential Guest House in Pretoria, South Africa President Thabo Mbeki saw it as shared vision of African Unity and solidarity, of African economic development and renewal and the need for returning to this vision to the people of African so as to initiate a popular movement for the African Renaissance. Just like Nkrumah emphatically believed in the unity of the continent, Mbeki remains vocal and passionate on African

Renaissance because of the various epochs of trauma each one of which has pushed her peoples deeper into poverty and backwardness. Simply put Mbeki notes:

- Slavery robbed the continent of its healthiest and most productive inhabitants;
- Imperialism and colonialism led to the rape of Africa's natural resources, and the destruction of traditional agriculture and domestic food security;
- Neo-colonialism leads to the perpetuation of a global economy in which Africa was subservient participant, the emergence of a new national elites who joined the dominant global force to exploit the continent, thriving on looting of national wealth and the entrenchment of corruption;
- The growth of an impossible international debt burden that is unlikely to be repaid in the foreseeable future

These developments challenges African countries to seek for alternative pathways to development as well as articulate concrete and comprehensive measures about the future of the continent taking into consideration certain objective s, such as: -

➢ Learning new initiatives and their future implications on the continent;

➢ Understanding the need and struggle for control on the technological resources and technological futures;

➢ Developing a critical awareness of the relationship between the future of technology and the future of the continent;

➢ Comprehend the difficulties and complexities of governing the new forces of the media, communication and information as veritable tools in the spread of the globalisation nexus;

➢ Building a strong pool of good leadership capability which is current major deficit on the continent as well as ensuring the practice of a democratic form of governance, management and organisation may prove to be the best, since it is based on the premise that all citizens and stakeholders are represented, and that this representation is based upon consent of those that are represented and governed.

➢ Developing the knowledge capacity of citizens to empower them as well as enhancing and harnessing such knowledge in the transformation of the society.

➢ Instil in the people a sense of belonging (patriotism) and love or country and continent.

Source: Credit. Renaissance World, 1st April-31st May 2010, Fela Anikulapo Road, Abuja, Nigeria. p4

Africa cries out for ethical leaders. Africa expects the best, but we are often left profoundly disappointed. While leadership programmes may feature ethics as part of the curriculum, the approach is often either simplistic or overly esoteric. The need for an African leadership that has the competence to comprehend the threats, challenges and opportunities of globalisation, the imperatives of democratisation and good of governance, the vision of a preferred future and the capacity and commitment to realise it, is clearly crucial. In light of the endemic problems facing Africa the first generation of African leaders have been subjected to severe criticism. It cannot however be maintained that they totally failed Africa and Africans. To do so would be both unscientific and unjust. Some of them responded to the problems confronting them in the best possible manner they could. There were successes and failures.

Strong leadership is essential and crucial to the realisation of these new development agenda for the continent's recovery and place in the global community of the 21st century and beyond. Africa is in dire need of strong and visionary leadership, strong institutions, and a vibrant and committed civil society to restore its lost glory and reclaim its rightful in the world community governed by the forces of a knowledge-based economy, scientific and technological prowess. So far, the continent has failed to use these God given resources for the benefit of the people. Africa remains poor in the midst of plenty. Governments have failed in developing better and more robust safety nets that target the needy. Given the current situation of poor governance, implementing a comprehensive economic reform agenda will be tough, and getting the political economy right will be critical. More than ever, policymakers' success will depend on listening to all stakeholders' views when formulating policy agendas – including those whose voices were not heard under previous regimes.

Third, ***"Resources"*** – no continent in the world can march the resources potential of Africa. Her resources have become a curse rather than a blessing. The resources of the continent can sustain the transformation of the region that it desperately need. Unfortunately, as mentioned several times, resources are curses not a blessing to the people. The continent has to pierce together these three factors; (i) timing; (ii) leadership and (iii) resources in solving instantly all of the Africa are endemic and deep-rooted problems. The new invasion or colonisation is the result of the continent's natural resources potential, its growing middle-class market and its youthful population. To unlock Africa's vast potential, many factors come into play, and the recipe for reform will naturally vary across countries but there are some common priorities, namely:

- Greater trade integration, both within each country, region, continent and in the world economy to boost growth and act as a catalyst for other important reforms;
- Business regulation and governance reforms are needed to ensure simple transparent, and even-handed treatment of economic activities to ensure simple, transparent, and even-handed treatment for

companies, and ultimately greater transparency and accountability of public institutions;

- Improving access to finance will help catalyse entrepreneurship and private investment;
- Public finance reform that can help free up resources for high-priority expenditures and reduce vulnerability, which will also spur growth;
- Education and labour market reforms will ensure adequate skill building and protection of workers.

Serious structural changes and challenges in transition is required having long suffered from a lack of dynamism, with high unemployment and poor reform efforts an inability to generate per capita growth on par with other emerging market and developing economies. African countries have to craft new ways forward and focus on the future. Africa as a continent in transition need a guiding vision for the future seen within this context, African Renaissance, Pan-Africanism and Africa Must Unite agenda should be given a chance to change countries in transition as well as consolidate their sovereignty and in owning their developmental process. The resources mean nothing unless added value are given them which can only come through the proper use of science and technology, innovation, human capital development, research, investments, entrepreneurship and an energy empowering manufacturing sector.

Currently a washed in a sea of troubles, Africa needs a gigantic leap forward to reconstitute and reconstruct its renewal agenda not by waving a magic wand but walking the talking of a comprehensive and endurable socioeconomic and political transformation able to stand the test far beyond the 21st century. This view is best captured by Mbeki (1998:11); *"Africa is readying itself for growth and development fuelled by her own efforts and the profitable and safe injection of international private capital. Let us do what we have to do together to achieve the sustained development of Africa."*The realisation of Africa Must Unite, Pan-Africanism, and African Renaissance project depends on a number of inter-related activities. If it is to be successful, Africans must not just engage on euphoric rhetoric, but put into concrete action pragmatic measures on short-term, medium-term and above all, long-term basis that will enable the continent to achieve practical, endurable and sustainable results.

The success of any agenda requires a strong and visionary ` leadership as well as important godfathers to push it, popularise within the national and international economic and political agenda of new revolution is imperative such as Kwame Nkrumah's variant of African socialism termed ***"philosophical consciencism"***; Julius Nyerere's vision of African socialism under the canopy of ***"Jamaal***; Kenneth Kaunda's "***humanist philosophy"*** which attracted a coherent world view through the strands of capitalist, populist and socialist views; Ahmadou Ahidjo's "***planned Liberalism***"; Mbeki's ***"I am an African"*** ; Modibo Kieta views as well as Paul Biya's concept of "***Communal Liberalism"*** seen as 'returning power back to the people'. All this brand of new development orientation indicates that at every turn of history of a people, a leader or group of leaders emerge who by the forces of their personality and providentially endowed vision, take it up them to guide the rest. They have gift of inspirational and courageous leadership (Okumu 2002). The Africa Must Unite, Renaissance project should create a new continent where the governed are free from, 'fear, the fear of oppression of one state by another or of national group by another, the fear of disempowerment of one social echelon by another; the fear of tyranny, and most importantly the fear of the use of state power to deny anyone their fundamental human rights. Therefore, a Union Government for Africa should exhibit a vivid picture of a New Africa where genuine and stable democracies would be established, and where systems of governance flourish because they derive their authority and legitimacy from the will of the people – here the people must govern (Forje 2009).

Existing interface between *"timing; leadership and resources"*, in cooperates a number of intertwined factors highlighting the role of civil society and culture. The cultural ties bind the Diaspora with homeland. Culture gives the Diaspora an identity and the call to come back to its roots. Renaissance Africa, Pan-Africanism, and Africa Must Unite hinges on the culture of the people. Cultural heritage and values underscores the identity and sovereignty of a people. This is the pull factor and on which the continent must build on. While Africa evolves on the inherent structure of *'unity in diversity'* and *'diversity in unity'*, the only left of the people after centuries of oppression, domination and exploitation, is 'the values of cultural heritage'. However, unity in diversity and diversity in unity took a different turn or given misconception by the invading forces of the West. Within the context of the African society, an African cultural civil society existed in promoting whatever form of governance that existed though the term democracy was not applied. The people could make and unmake their own rulers. Power was with the people in a way. The advent of foreign rule complicated, compounded and compromised the cultural structure-functional system of the people. Today, the people are thrown into total confusion. Unable to distinguish left from right or vice versa, external exploitation is reinforced as they continue to disconnect with their cultural past, an important instrument in establishing identity and sovereignty.

Generally, the idea civil/culture society is considered to promote democracy by manifesting civic engagement, having egalitarian and transparent structures, promoting democratic ideals, and by standing free from state influence. Renaissance Africa, Pan-Africanism and African Unity is envisaged to advance the democratic state structures by demanding transparency and accountability of governments, and by pressing for popular participation in political decision-making on different levels. A proper marriage between civic and culture, society is able to form a shared identity and bonds of solidarity, enabling them to resist state encroachments on their fundamental liberties." The nature of civil society in Africa in terms of structure and function is unique. The public realm in Africa is a product of Africa's historical intercourse with the West through colonisation. The psychological and social implication of colonisation was revealed in the emergence of the two publics: the *'primordial'* and the *'civic'*. The 'primordial public' consisting of traditional groupings and communities: while the 'civic public' consist of African western-educated bourgeoisie who helped in destroying their cultural heritage developed during colonisation and historically associated with the colonial administration. The social divide between the two publics created tensions that persisted into post-colonial times. The primordial public is regarded as being moral, privately and public. The civic public is regarded as being amoral and lacking the generalised moral imperatives that work in the private realm and the primordial public (Ekeh 1975, Comaroff & Comaroff 1999, Osaghae 2006, Suleiman 2010). What is and should be the role of African cultures in shaping the development of governance debate across the continent?

A culture is what makes a people and keeps them in a unique position in relationship to other people. Unfortunately, the African people have to a large extent lost their cultural value heritage. Many factors have contributed to this; first the legacy of imperialism; the slave trade; colonialism and neo-colonialism; and, second, the fact that due to illiteracy, our forefathers did not put pen on paper to ensure the continuity of our cultural values and belief systems. An analysis of the cultural flows between countries shows a serious imbalance. The power of the pen, backed by scientific developments in West gives an edge of western cultural values over the African culture. Africa is gradually descending into a cultureless society. The media in developing countries take a high percentage of their cultural and entertainment continent from developed countries. The flow in the other direction is a mere trickle by comparison. The West gets the selected of the culture (chiefly music and dance) from developing countries; the latter get a lot of what on any objective standard is the worst produced by the former. This unequal exchange is inevitably harmful to national culture in developing countries. The socio-cultural tastes of foreign values have been widely disseminated and are familiar to and often admired in developing countries, Africa in particular to the detriment of their rich cultural heritage and value systems.

Today Africa is suffering the viruses of cultural alienation; cultural imperialism, cultural decline and stagnation, cultural fragmentation, cultural illiteracy among others. The continent cannot progress with such deficiencies. Therefore deconstructing the African state requires faithful implementation and adherence to the numerous policy documents agreed by African countries under the auspicious of the African Union, (for example, The African Peer Review Mechanism, The African Charter on Human and People's Rights; The African Charter on Democracy, Elections and Governance; The African Charter on the Values and Principles of the Public Service and Administration) Regional Economic Communities, and international bodies, opening up access to the state in all-inclusive manner, which should facilitate people's participation in political and socioeconomic processes, so that no one is left behind (Forje, 2013). This is the way to deconstruct the current African state and strengthened it to face the challenges of contemporary globalisation and neoliberalism. Deconstructing or reconstructing the African state will enhance the development path of the continent. It requires a progressive Afrocentric attitude and mindset to establish the African we want for present and coming generations.

Pan-Africanism, Renaissance Africa and African Unity have entered a new and robust stage requiring new thinking to advance the idea of African unity. New players, new technologies are needed to pilot the rising demand for the Africa We Want. The battle for the soul of a United Africa has entered a new, intense phase requiring a new conscience, a new mind of Africa, a new strategic approach toward the African revolution; the articulation and elaboration of a new philosophy of African development based on an African epistemology and cosmology; reflecting and representing of Africa's fresh and reinvigorating contribution to the global knowledge industry are badly needed (see Jinadu, 2009; Nabudere, 2003; Fanon,!967, 1965; Mazrui 1967; Nkrumah, 1970; Shivji, 2005).

Kenyans being evacuated from South Africa

(Source: Raphael Obonyo (2014)."Peace in South Sudan Critical to Region Stability", Africa Renewal, August2014. Vol.28. No.2 New York, USA pp16-17

Unfortunately, powerful vested interest violently supports widening economic inequality and bad governance structure which is a legalised violence of the rich and powerful which has to be outlawed to enfranchise all. Historical precedent is no justification or rational basis for the future persistence of social injustice. It is time for African leaders and people to wear a new coat for economic and political renewal to fully acknowledge and impartially examine the underlying fabric of social forces and processes governing the operation of economic and political systems today. For too long African leaders, have exhibited optimal appetite for power accumulation, and holding tight to the realms of authority for perpetuity without thinking about the welfare of their citizens. Africa remains the only continent with too many long-serving Presidents, which could describe as 'self-articulate' leadership. But Africa is hungry for self-actualising individuals and leaders as persons able to think for oneself, chose for oneself, rely on one's own capacities, and act freely to realise one's highest aspirations, while respecting and supporting the equal rights of others and accepting the responsibility to contribute to the security, welfare, well-being and fullest development of the entire community (Jacobs, 2018:93). The problem with many African countries is the idea of adopting 'selective' development to please either ethnic groups, or fulfil political party interests. This form of 'discriminative' development is what is destroying African states. African countries should thread on the path of 'balanced' development.

The greatest input factor of democracy is its capacity to foster the development of individualism in its members, organise and coordinate such individualistic strength for the good of society. Africa's ethnic and cultural diversities are a great asset in fostering individuality for a common purpose – the wellbeing of the people. Thus, the need for democratic governance cannot be overemphasised as it offers the possibility of organising collective decision-making process in a manner considered by members of the political community as legitimate, without causing substantial disorder. Existing opaque governance system must be given the red card. The need for a structure-functional governance system and most needed in Africa, is one construed within the parameters of ruling divided societies, without undue violence, with justice and rule of law top of the agenda. By extension, priorities have to be formulated; in addition, priorities and values have to be balanced in order to establish an order of importance so that society can progress in serenity and harmony for the common good of all.

For African countries, the current state of underdevelopment should mark a turning point and be a decisive era for its subsequent development. New progressive strategies have to articulate and comprehensively implemented. The aggravation of the international context can never, however, be more than a factor opening up the way to a new dynamic course whose final evolution depends in the last analysis on the nature of internal responses. By now African countries should have derived valuable lessons from their status of underdevelopment and embark resolutely on the road to industrialisation and not to remain trapped in the old mould of primary-commodity exporters.

It has long been believed that democracy is a luxury beyond the means of poor countries. Centralised authoritarian hegemonic dictatorships have, however, brought wide disappointment with regard to their ability to spur growth and development. It is up to democracy now proving its superiority in the economic field as well. Indeed, this is the real essence of the challenge and changes for Africa. The continent of Africa is living in hard times. The continent's development requires transforming authoritarian regimes into democratic ones; transforming the military of destruction into a military of development and protection of the people.

Africa is strategically well placed and endowed with vast resources which places it in a position of strength that can seriously make former colonies of powers that divided the world among them plundered it for centuries today will constitute the underdeveloped countries, if only Africa plays its cards well. The current second scramble for Africa tells it all. The reality is that African countries have been and are being oppressed and terrorised by the developed countries. Naturally African countries are bitter and angry and have lost faith in justice and honour which should make it imperative for them to rethink and restructure their approaches to development and within the international community.

Africa has failed to use its independence and freedom to develop their respective countries and continent for the good of the people. Instead we have used independence to replace colonial rule with black imperialism, equality with greed and accumulation, which has made us to be busy overthrowing governments, setting up new governments, which in turn overthrows the other or remain as sit-tight-presidents for entirety. We have killed or continue killing our own people by the millions, take the case of Burundi, Rwanda, Sudan and the ongoing silent genocide in Southern Cameroons. And frequently, frustrated with anarchic democracy we resort to autocratic Governments, exposing ourselves to much vilification.

War solves nothing. War is primitive and destructive. We continue to inflict carnage to our citizens, and take pride as we press buttons of attacking innocent and unarmed civilians and see nothing of the mangled bodies, the heads and limbs and destroyed properties which are torn from disembowelled bodies, the blood and gore of the innocent people who, are instant before, were living people like them. We have embarked on the journey to carpet-bomb our citizens, using weapons we do not produce but import that keeps the industrial wheel of western factories in constant rotation.

Instead we have created and imposed an unsustainable and unbearable country and continent expanding the realm of poverty and injustice, with a continuous demand from the centre for the periphery to remain totally underdeveloped. The reduction in the gap between the centre and periphery, between the rich and poor is never strongly propagated but to the advantaged of the developed polities. It is therefore time for African countries to reorganise and act together as the only way to break the North's stranglehold on the continent.

In this age of increased globalisation, the global system, structures and institutions have everywhere assumed a critical role in all spheres of life and society, providing countries of the North with powerful leverage to pursue their interests. Thus, in various forms and to different degrees, African countries are experiencing a massive and multifaceted intrusion in virtually all domains of national policy, sovereignty and governance. The developed countries have arrogated to themselves the right to interfere at will, in complete disregard of the basic premises of the United Nations Charter. Some African countries work in the same way, by disregarding the African Union Charter on fundamental human rights. There is a great need for a new vision for African countries by placing 'people first' on their development related activities. Only a new paradigm shift, based on dialogue and on the people's participation, would likely to foster sustainable development, justice, peace, cooperation and democracy on the continent. This section strongly argues for a new human-and development-centred paradigm shift for the continent as the only way forward for Africa nations. The new paradigm would seek to resolve the myriad challenges on the national agenda and continental level through cooperation and participation, as well would more fully and equitably realise the immense and growing potential and opportunities that exist today, especially those offered by advances in science and technology and knowledge, and particularly with regards to the continent's grossly underutilised human resources. These are often misappropriated or wasted under the current regime, which has many of its roots in authoritarian nexus of the post-colonial era.

The cumulative consequences of the inability or unwillingness to respond to changes have incrementally tended to isolate Africa and Africans from major global events. For too long the continent has become progressively isolated, ceased to an active player in the global place. Instead it became victim or casualties of the global changes and challenges. It has in effect, emerged as a recipient of other peoples' ideas and ways of doing things, and of goods and services. The new Africa has to be involved and participate as free agents in the global marketplace. The survival of Africans as a distinct people with their own cultures and civilisation values to enjoy, nourish, promote and defend, will depend on their capabilities to respond to the global changes, challenges, possibilities and opportunities as the 21st Century unfolds.

No one can dispute the views of Prof. Mohiddin Ahmed (1998) that there exist persistent negative images of Africa, as a continent in deep troubles and of Africans portrayed as a people unable to solve their problems is unhealthy and damaging. If these images are not challenged they may not only continue to mislead the rest of the world, more seriously they may cause young Africans to doubt their own capabilities and self-esteem, and thus undermine their role as levers of change for an alternative better future for Africa. It is imperative that Africans begin to build now the requisite capabilities to respond to these changes otherwise the marginalisation of Africa from major world activities, like trade and politics, science and technology, would accelerate.

The challenge now is how the continent can mobilise its resources by facilitating the release of the energies, talents, creativity, innovative skills, enterprise and entrepreneurship of its citizens. Only competent, honest, visionary and committed leaders are likely to create the enabling environment within which such liberalising process can come to fruition.

References

African Union (2006). Study on an African Union Government: Towards the United States of Africa [Mimeo]. Addis Ababa, Ethiopia; African Union.

Azikiwe Nnamdi (1936) Renascent Africa, Frank Cass Books, London

Comaroff, J and Comaroff (1999) Civil Society and the Political Imagination in Africa: Critical Perspectives, University of Chicago Press, Chicago and London

Ekeh, P. (1975). Colonialism and the Two Publics in Africa: A Theoretical Statement, Comparative Studies in Society and History, Vol. 17, No.1, pp91-112

Fanon, F. (1967). Black Skin, White Masks, Grove Press, New York, USA

Fanon, F. (1965). The Wretched of the Earth. Grove Press, New York

Forje W. John (2009). Here the People Rule: Political Transition and Challenges for Democratic Consolidation in Africa, Nova Science Publishers Inc, New York, USA.

Forje W. John (2013) Emerging Perspectives on Capacity Building and Quality Public Services Delivery in Africa. Lambert Academic Publishing, Germany.

Giddens, A. (1989) Sociology. Polity Press, Cambridge

Gutto B.O. Shadrack [2010] Africa is Cradle of Humanity, Civilisation Says Varsity Don' Renaissance World, 1st April-31stMay, 2010, pp67-7

Jinadu L. Adele (2009)." Nkrumah, Pan-Africanism, And the Future of Africa|" in Adejumobi Said and Adebayo Olukoshi (eds.) (2009) The African Union and New Strategies for Development in Africa, CODESRIA (Dakar) and DPMF (Nairobi), Chapter 2, pp18-27

Mazrui, Ali (1967). Towards a Pax Africana: A study of Ideology and Ambition. University of Chicago Press, Chicago, USA

Mbeki Thabo et al (1998). The African Renaissance. Konrad Adenauer Stiffung, Occasional Papers Series, Johannesburg, South Africa

Mohiddin Ahmed (1998) African Leadership: The Succeeding Generation – Challenges and Opportunities.

Nkrumah, Kwame. (1970) Consciencism: Philosophy and the Ideology for Decolonization, Monthly Review Press, USA

Nyerere K. Julius (1997)" Africa Must Unite | ", edited excerpts from a Public Lecture delivered in Accra to mark Ghana's Fortieth Independence Day Anniversary Celebrations, United New Africa Global Network website: [www.unitednewafrica.com/Africa%20Unite.htm]

Okumu. A J. Washington (2002) The African Renaissance. History, Significance and Strategy, Africa World Press, Inc. Trenton

Osaghae, E. (2006) Colonialism and Civil Society in Africa: The Perspective of Ekeh's Two Publics. Voluntas: International Journal of Diversity. Princeton University Press, Princeton, USA

Shivji, Issa (2005). Pan-Africanism or Imperialism? Unity and Struggle towards a new Democratic Africa. Bill Dudley Memorial Lecture Series, 2. Nigerian Political Science Association, Lagos - Nigeria

Smith Tuhiwai Linda (2012). Decolonizing Methodologies – Research and Indigenous Peoples, Second Edition, Zed Books United Kingdom and Otago University Press, Dunedin

Suleiman Lina (2010) "Civil Society in the Making: Can NGOs contribute to Development and Democracy? In Heidi Moksnes and Mia Melin (eds.) Power to the People: (Con-) Tested Civil Society in Search of Democracy, Uppsala, Sweden, pp154-160.

Chapter Seven

Facing the Dynamics of the New Invasion

Africa is confronted with a new invasion or colonial trade with a difference, to put it in a subtle way. The new invasion is coming not from the old colonial masters, but from countries which earlier were characterised as developing polities. The penetrating force of China can be seen as new and total recolonisation of the continent judging from the constructed Africa Union Headquarters in Addis Ababa Ethiopia. Expressing his disgust on the construction, Chika Ezeanya [2012:68] expresses the opinion of many Africans as *"it is an insult to the AU and to every African that in 2012 a building as symbolic as the AU headquarters is designed, built and maintained by a foreign country.*" He goes further to indicate that "common sense dictates that in an era of increasing exploitation of Africa's natural resources by foreign powers, including China, the AU, rather than the apparent submissiveness signified by accepting the construction of its headquarter by China, should be an organisation advocating for fairness in the relationship that exists between the continent and the global powers".

It is a serious issue that fifty-five African countries are incapable of constructing their Headquarters but prefer deepening the "dependency syndrome". Where lays the sovereignty, pride and dignity of the continent? When will the idea of roaming the world with a begging cap come to an end? However, some see the relationship between China and Africa from a positive perspective for both sides. In this light, the exchange of essential natural resources for infrastructure to foster economic development is more likely to benefit than paternalistic and failed aid strategies. While some believe China's entry into Africa is simply another neo-colonial effort with a clear disregard for human rights and the legitimacy of governments, many believe China's pragmatic and business-like approach is more dynamic and well-rounded than classic Western aid efforts.

Not only are Chinese investments inherently different in their goals and strategies, but they are also significantly larger. There is no doubt that China will continue to need Africa for years, as its paradox of abundant human capital and scarce natural resources will make Africa a key partner in fuelling the double-digit growth rates needed to maintain political stability. Chinese investments is hoped would lead to the much need growth and development as input factors to maintaining peace and stability in African countries given that failed developments have converted rising expectations of the independence years into rising destructive frustration. There China and Africa have much to gain from the newfound partnership. Seen in this regard, china is providing African countries with tremendous opportunities for change which should make African countries relevant to global policymakers. Yet it is up to Africa to capitalise and drive a hard bargain so that it finally comes out on the winning side. For now, it can be concluded that Africa not only failed to develop and achieve economic take-off, but converged into what can be described as a *'lost continent'*, left out and marginalised by the globalisation process. Africa represents less than 10% of the world's population, yet only 1.2 percent of its gross domestic product (GDP).

Source: Credit – New Africa No. 557 January 2016. IC Publication. London, pp73

China needs Africa's resources and is actively seeking them. Africa needs Chinese capital and know-how and is making greater concession in providing these raw resources to China. As such, China's role in the continent is making what once seemed a 'lost continent more relevant' than ever before. Many feel China is the big investor Africa has been waiting for, while some feel its undemocratic nature will only aggravate Africa's true problems of governance and lacklustre political institutions. The world has seemingly advanced while Africa has stagnated since Ghana gained independence in 1957. In spite of the different fate that have befallen China and Africa, an intriguing strategic and beneficial relationship based on mutual needs and respect for one another can develop to the advantage of both parties. The Chinese are after wealth and improving their standard of livelihood, so also should Africa gun for without subjecting itself to colonisation and exploitation. It is imperative that in this section we penetrate into the issues on the drivers pushing the two continents together and factors pushing the growth behind the partnership between China and Africa, and salient factors or criticisms and why it might ring hollow; and the new opportunities and threats it presents Africa as it moves into the 21st century and beyond – indeed the pros and cons of Chinese involvement in Africa. The debate between Calestous Juma and George Ayittey (in The Economist is interesting in this respect. For more details, see http://www.economist.com/debate/days/view/465.

This gesture of receiving a quest is contrary to the views expressed by the founding fathers of the organisation. Emperor Haile Selassie in his historic opening address to the formation of the Organisation of African Unity [OAU) the forerunner of AU noted in 1963; "Africa has been reborn as a free continent and Africans have been reborn as free men. The blood that was shed and sufferings that were endured are today Africa's inspiration for freedom and unity". The Emperor was echoing the peoples' quest of bringing an end to colonialism and to embark on a struggle for a united Africa and economic independence, and development that would change the lives of Africans for the better. The quest for a rebirth of Africa – the Africa renaissance –began a long time ago, which Izaka Seme (1906) pointed out at New York's Columbia university, USA in these words; *"the brighter day is rising upon Africa. Yes, the regeneration of Africa belongs to this new and powerful period. The African people...possess a common fundamental sentiment which is everywhere manifest, crystallising itself into one common controlling idea. The regeneration of Africa means a new and unique civilisation is soon to be added to the world."*

The growing impact of ICTs especially with mobile is regenerating Africa's penetration in the new world communication order as the region is one of the World's fastest growing regions with a 38% growth rate which facilitates trade among nations. Africa's internet bandwidth has grown by an average of 51% since 2010, faster than any other region, reaching an expected 2.9nterabytes per second GDP. Mobile phones continue to dominate internet usage in Africa, accounting for

90% of connections; with Kenya as the global leader in mobile money while in 15 African countries, more people have more mobile money accounts than formal bank accounts (African Business November 2015). It is much easier to access mobile money accounts than going through the rigours entangle with the red-tap modalities associated with the formal bank account system. It is hoped that Africa's partners can help orient more direct foreign investment to the continent, using the appropriate incentives (guaranteed investments, lines of credit, and so on. Handicapped by the weakness of its infrastructure, lack of qualified human resources, and low level of industrial development, Africa is clearly not sufficiently integrated into the global economy. However, it is also clear that the region cannot afford to remain on the side-lines of globalisation for much longer. To facilitate its inclusion in the rapidly changing world economy based on knowledge, Africa most begin to make significant institutional and political reforms, especially by reducing the functions of the state toward the essential mission of delivering needed public services, promoting the development of a dynamic private sector and strengthening the role of civil society, which is critical for any social and economic change. Regional economic integration is also a necessary element for securing Africa's participation in globalisation (N'Diaye, 2001:21).

China-Africa Trade

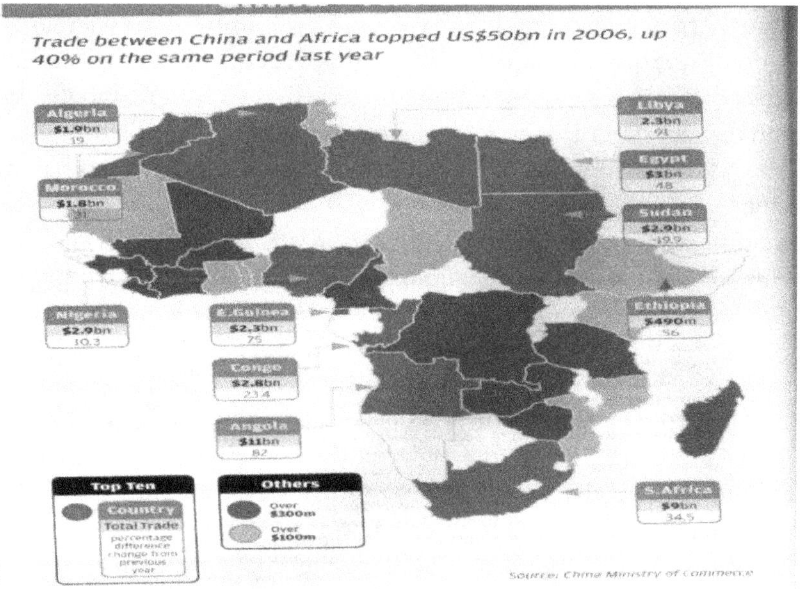

Source: Credit: New African [2008] No.471, March 2008, p36, London

What kinds of projects is China financing and where are the funds going? Apparently, Chinese funds are distained at projects for infrastructure for key suppliers of oil and minerals. A breakdown of Chinese funded projects in Africa shows the following: Public works 54%; extraction or production of natural resources 28.5%; humanitarian activities 2.5% and with the remaining 15% unspecified which spells out the intension of China in Africa. It is no hidden secret that their intentions are clear. With her intentions of spending up to US$23 billion to build oil refineries and other petroleum infrastructure in Nigeria in order to potentially strengthen its had in the country; and another amount of US$24 billion in aid between 2002 and 20076 in areas of infrastructure, mining, oil refining, hydropower, dam construction, national stadiums, telecommunications, electricity, medical training, universities and administrative buildings in countries like Angola, DRC, Sudan, Gabon, Mozambique and equatorial Guinea which exports oil, wood and ores to China.

China has substantially stepped up its aid, which it provides in the forms of technical assistance, with an emphasis on training in Chinese institutions; grants; interest free loans; preferential loans that have an interest subsidy; and debt relief. China's financial assistance to Africa is substantial as of 2006; existing loans and credit lines are total about $19 billion. The beneficiaries of the largest flows were Angola, Equatorial Guinea, Gabon, republic of Congo, and Nigeria-with Angola and editorial Guinea alone having credit lines totalling about $14 billion. The proportion of grants is small, but China also cancelled an estimated $260 million in debt for the Democratic Republic of the Congo, Ethiopia, Mali, Senegal, Togo, Rwanda, Guinea, and Uganda (Jacoby 2007:34).

The map depicts China-Africa trade that sends shock-waves into the spine of Western countries. The Chinese resurgence in Africa is not only transforming the continent's political, economic and social landscapes, but is sending nervous shivers into Western governments, hitherto the dominant forces in Africa. But the ball is now in Africa's court-to fully embrace the new-kid-on-the-block, or hang on to friendships and policies by maintaining the status quo. This time, Africa needs to play its card right. The West is confronted with an identity crisis, is in a pensions and employment trap, and remains ambivalent in its approach to Africa (New African 2008:12-18).

It is clear that China has strategic economic interest in Africa and is increasingly in need of certain strategic natural resources, mainly crude oil. In 2005, Nigeria, Angola, Equatorial Guinea, Gabon, Congo Brazzaville, Sudan and Chad supplied 28 percent of China's crude oil imports, compared to nine per cent from Nigeria, Angola and Gabon in 1995. This compares with the Middle East's 47 per cent and 45 per cent, respectively, in the same period. East Asia's seven percent and 42 percent and Russia are ten percent and 0 per cent. As a result of China's increased dependence on Africa for crude oil, trade between Beijing and Africa continues to rise (Centre for Conflict Resolution (CCR) 2007:14).

China emerges as Africa's main trading partner and a major source of investment for infrastructure. However, this partnership is crowded with much controversy concerning labour and corruption as well as sparking "Western bullying" following its move to lend USA$20 billion in credit over the next three years to African countries. From the Chinese perspective, Africa and China as developing countries should better coordinate their response to international affairs to counter the practices of "the big bullying the small, the strong domineering over the weak and the rich oppressing the poor". But is China's penetration into Africa a *"win-win"* strategy or a *"win-loose"* strategy for Africa? One cannot but question China's generous intention towards Africa; and Africa's failure to defend its interests and to own its development path. There is no doubt that China's penetration into Africa is for its own good and in support of African governments with dubious human rights records as a means to get access to resources. But we should not throw out the baby with the bath water. There are some positive sides with China's penetration into the continent. Exploit the positive side for the continent's benefit.

China's new marriage with Africa comes under strong criticism for using imported labour to build government – financed projects like roads and hospitals, while pumping out resources and leaving little for local economies. This new "cheque book" recolonisation of Africa by China should be strongly rejected or properly negotiated and scrutinised into a *"win-win"*, not a *"win-loose"* strategy between China and Africa. China is not losing but gaining in the marriage. Africa is losing. No wonder the European Union (EU) countries, most of them former colonial powers for fear of losing their strong hold on the continent are insisting for Africa/China countries to walk on the good governance path and transparent use of funds from trading partners. Whether Western Europe or China's invasion of the continent the idea of, *"good governance, and transparent government"*, must be ranked the highest priority by all African governments. This is an issue which should not be compromised by any African country. For now, it is Africa's greatest deficit, throwing the continent into serious dilemma and disadvantage within the global community. If the invasion of the continent by China is going accelerate the industrialisation of the region, Africa should seize that opportunity to industrialise.

Unfortunately, many African countries are de-industrialising while they are still poor, partly because technology is reducing the demand for low-skilled workers. In addition, weak infrastructure – lack of electricity, poor roads and congested ports – drives up the cost of moving raw materials and shipping out finished goods. But the continent's favourable demography, rising urbanisation and extensive agricultural resources base underscore the potential for the regions manufacturing industry. This calls for bold and creative policies imagination – creativity in crafting policies and for African policymakers to avoid being bound to any single theoretical policy. Therefore, African countries need to have the self-confidence to develop alternative policies and stick to them; they should not be hesitant to take alternative policies for fear of dictates and conditionalities of the West. The continent is faced with the good, bad and the smart approach or the so-called sophisticated or smart protectionism' of imposing temporary tariffs to shield budding industries from the negative effects of cheap imports as part of its strategy to industrialise.

Though China's friendship with Africa dates back in the 1950's when Beijing supported liberation movements in the continent fighting to throw off Western colonial rule. China's trade with Africa hit USA$166.3billion in 2011 according to Chinese statistics. In the past decade, Africa's export to China rose to USA$93.2 billion from USA$56,6billion. At the same time, China has found a dumping ground for poor quality products. It is not surprising that most of the goods imported have earned the name, "buy today use and throw away tomorrow". The quality of goods is questioned. But the problem here is the gross absence of a system of "quality control" mechanism in the country. Anything goes as long as the hands of the custom officers and police are greased at the expense of the lives of the people. Due to the state of poverty prevailing in many African countries, citizens opt for these poor-quality goods rather than stay without them.

Chang (2015) argues that rich countries have historically relied on protectionist approaches in their quest for economic dominance. There is nothing preventing African countries to do the same. Rich nations preach free market and free trade to the poor countries in order to capture larger shares of the latter's markets and to pre-empt the emergence of possible competitors. The World Trade Organisation (WTO) June 2016 Report notes that there is a rapid increase in trade restrictive or protectionist measures by the world's leading economies that make up the G20 group. Between mid-October 2015 and mid-May 2016, the report notes that G20 economies slapped 145 new trade-restrictive measures per month, a significant increase compared to the previous reporting period at 17 per month (Tafirenyika, 2016:28-29).

Total trade between China and Africa rose from roughly US$10 billion in 2000 to approximately US$107 billion in 2008, a tenfold increase. The key trade dynamic between China and Africa is that of natural resources in exchange for cheaper and more affordable Chinese products than those the West can offer, and Africans are currently able to produce. Mineral fuels such as oil were by far China's largest import from Africa, accounting for 71% of the total in 2008. Put together, mineral fuels, ores, precious stones and metals accounted for 87% of Chinese imports from Africa. As a result of this, the top five sources of African imports were Angola (40%), South Africa (15.5%), the Sudan (11%), the Congo (8.2%) and Libya (5.7%). With five important oil and mineral suppliers accounting for 80% of total imports, the trend for the remaining 20% remains the same. Other key suppliers to China on a smaller scale include Gabon (oil & minerals), Equatorial Guinea (oil) and Zambia (copper).

Africa is sitting on a goldmine, but lacks the kind of audacity to deal with its exploiters, making the continent most vulnerable within the community of nations. The giant continent has succumbed to the dictates of the 'cheque book' diplomacy. The *'cheque book'* diplomacy is not bringing the need social needs to improve the quality wellbeing of the population. The continent remains lacking in economic and social infrastructure but has embraced corruption and made poverty an entrenched sector of its being. The reasons can be attributed to poor leadership and passive or sycophantic civil society under the spell of a satanic religious cult. This is being exploited by the new invaders of the continent, through what is called partnership between African administrators and representatives of developed country donors to short-change an already poor people. This leaves no one with the painful conclusion that corruption, poor leadership and a passive civil society and political apathy are the main culprits in the slow progress at the provision of the infrastructure necessary for the development of African countries.

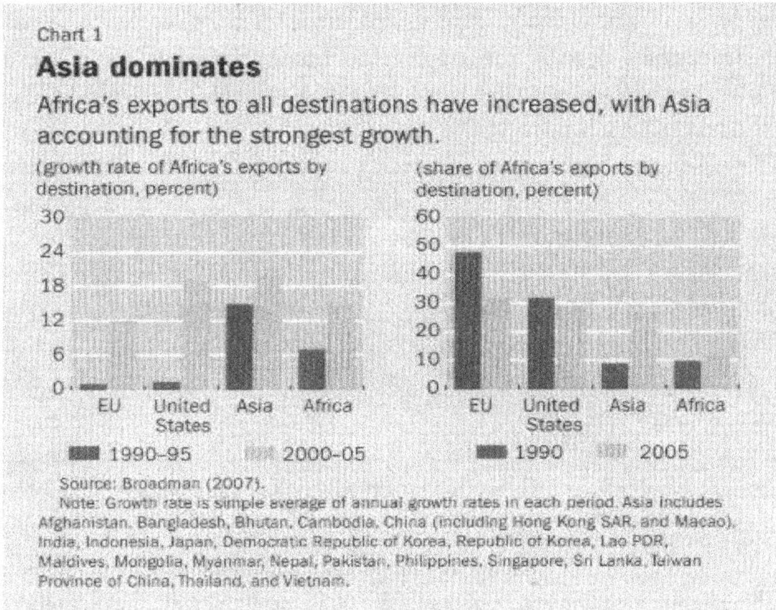

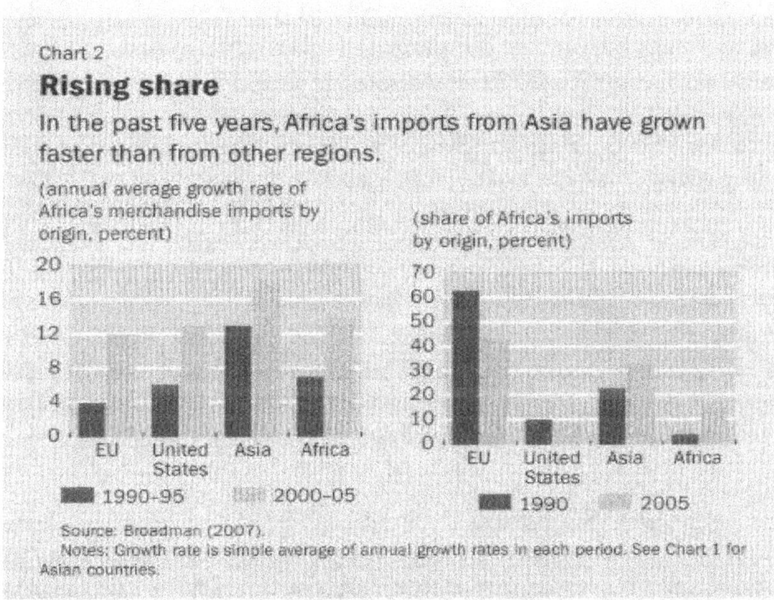

(See also Broadman (2007) "Connecting Africa and Asia": Finance and Development, June 2007, Vol.44. No.2, Washington, DC. USA, pp36-39)

It could be argued that the Chinese are trying to fill the missing gaps in the infrastructure shortage faced by African countries. But at what cost? Chika Ezeaanya [2012:68-9] is clear on this point as he notes: *"with the Chinese paying for the Head Quarters of the African Union, the move to reverse the derogatory perception of Africa and Africans by non-Africans has suffered a major setback."* But what attracts China into Africa? Clearly, the demand for commodities – raw resources – to meet the needs of its burgling population and to keep its new industrial wheel turning; and Africa provides all that China needs. The 2007 US Geological Survey's mineral yearbook shows how wealthy Africa is with regard to mineral resources of all kinds. In addition, Africa is a growing market with its population made of over fifty percent youths. Table 7:1 - Mineral Resources in Africa shows how prolific individual countries are which China is exploiting to its advantage. African countries are challenged to develop a *"Win-Win"* policy strategy and negotiating tactics in its dealings with China or any other country venturing in the exploitation of the continent's resources.

Packenham (1991) notes that Africa was sliced up like a cake, the pieces swallowed by five rival nations - Germany, Italy, Portugal, France and Britain (with Spain taking some scraps) – and Britain and France were at each other's throats. At the centre, exploiting the rivalry stood one enigmatic individual and self-styled philanthropist, controlling the heart of Africa: Leopold 11, King of the Belgians. Europe operated on the fundamental basis that it had the right to occupy all 'vacant' land in the name of their empires and exploit them for their needs. With very little knowledge of the people or their cultures, the Europeans nevertheless found it necessary to occupy these lands for their profit. So, the civilisation mission of the 'uncivilised' which meant free trade and exploitation of the continent and its vast resources was set-in-motion for European countries interested in these resources.

China doing its home-work exploits the dynamics of mutual needs (aid and investment in exchange for key resources). Time for Africa doing its homework and exploiting its resources advantage to benefit from China's rush into Africa. Balancing the act means a win-win situation for the two continents. The Chinese puts the interest of China first. Africa on the contrarily puts the interests of China first and not that of the African people. There has to a complete turn-around. Without any shadow of doubt, the division and lack of unity, in Africa as well as the Diaspora, is the ***sine qua non*** for African marginalisation, discrimination and exploitation. Under such condition, Africans remain enslaved people. The reasons for this reside in the fact that Africans have never assumed sovereignty. The African post-colonial state construct remains an inherent part of the European project. Attempts to create an African nation were doomed to failure by the fact that the inherited colonial state could not, by its nature countenance Pan-African unity.

Table 7:1. **Mineral Resource in Sub-Saharan Africa**

Commodity	Africa Relative To the World %	Notable Sub-Saharan Producers % of African Production
Platinum Metals	89	South Africa 89
Colbot	80	Congo 100
Diamonds	55	Botswana 35; Congo 34; South Africa 7; Angola 8
Chromite	50	South Africa 98
Cobalt	49	Congo 75; Zambia 22;
Manganese	33	South Africa 56; Gabon 32
Gold	20	South Africa 56; Ghana 13; Tanzania 10; Mali 8
Uranium	17	Namibia 46; Niger 44
Petroleum	12	Angola, Equatorial Guinea, Nigeria, Gabon, Congo-Brazzaville
Bauxite	9	Guinea 95; Ghana 5; Cameroon 5
Copper	5	Zambia 60; Congo 17; S. Africa 14
Aluminum Metal	4	South Africa 48; Mozambique 32
Iron	3	South Africa 73; Mauritania 20

Source: Richardson Gonzalez Patricio (2010) based on the US Geological Survey's Mineral Yearbook 2007

Chart 3 Dynamic Duo: Africa's Exports to China and India up, with these dynamos accounting for half of Africa's exports to Asia

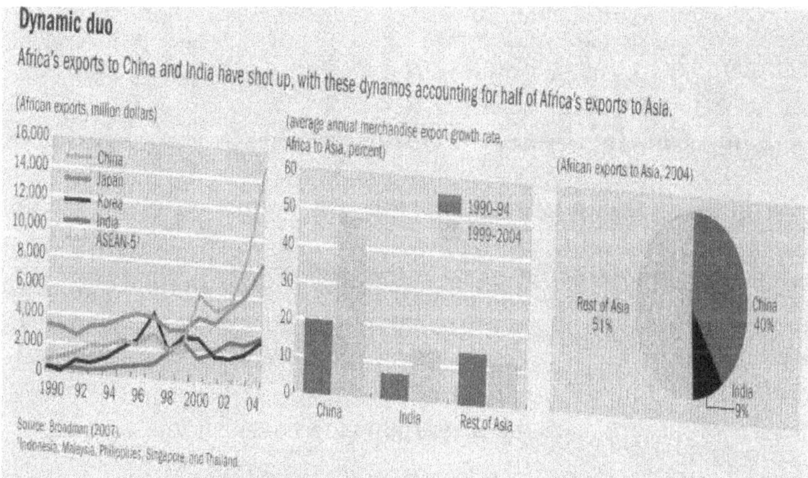

See also Broadman (2007) Connecting Africa And Asia. Finance and Development, June 2007 Vol.44, No.2, International Monetary Fund. Washington, USA. Pp38

It is interesting to note that China's fuel imports from Africa rose from US$10.1 billion in 2004 to US$38.5 billion in 2008, a 28% increase. Africa exports of non-fuel minerals rose from US$1.4 billion in 2004 to US$7.2 billion in 2008, up t0 402.7%. In the same period, exports of precious stones and metals (mainly platinum and diamonds) rose from US$742 million to US$1.77 billion in 2008, up 138.8% The intriguing thing about the Sino-Africa relationship, however, is how it has gone beyond simply a relationship based on trade to a boom in investment that is challenging the classic development paradigms established by Western IFIs such as the IMF and the World Bank. It is safe to say that barely a week goes by without Beijing signing a multimillion-dollar bilateral agreement with an African country. The results are everywhere, with Chinese workers building roads, ports, dams, railways, football stadiums, hotels and office blocks (Richardson 2010)

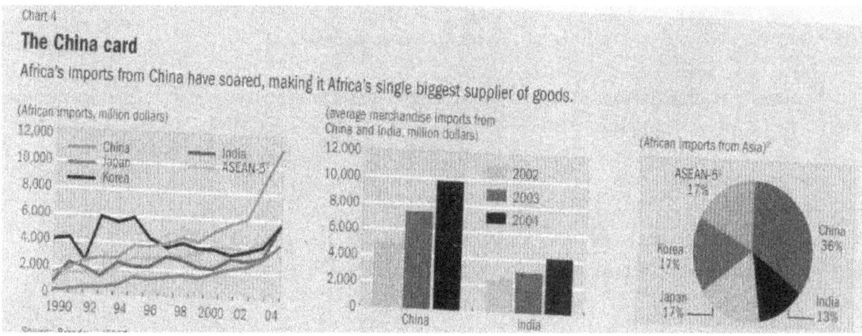

See also Broadman (2007) Connecting Africa And Asia. Finance and Development, June 2007 Vol.44, No.2, International Monetary Fund. Washington, USA. Pp39

Some Burning Issues and Opportunities

China – Africa relationship coming under serious scrutiny calls for constructive proactive strategic measures from Africa in their dealings with China. There are opportunities as well as concerns which have to be addressed for both sides to benefit equitably from the marriage. For now, the marriage is not balanced – the ideal of a *'win-win'* dichotomy is absent. It is a 'win' for china and a 'win-not' for Africa. Yet both sides need each other. Therefore, the following issues should be well looked into (see Richardson 2010):

- Competition over African resources, allowing Africans more leverage and say in the negotiation process and to haggle for terms. China's arrival as an alternative source of trade, aid and investment has created a competitive environment where African states are no longer exclusively dependent on western nations;
- China is driving up both demand and prices for global commodities, making the supply of natural resources more lucrative than ever before;

- China can offer its own experience of growth as an example and model for other developing countries to consider and learn from, something the United States, as the doyen of developed countries, cannot;
- Cheaper and more affordable Chinese goods for African consumers;
- US$2.5 trillion in currency reserves available for financing needs. The IMF possesses US$257 billion in usable resources, while China has US$2.5 trillion in currency reserves. That makes Chinese currency reserves roughly 10 times bigger than all the funds at the IMF's disposal;
- The creation of special economic zones across the continent as a means of boosting non-natural resources industries and trade. The building of special trade and economic cooperation zones focusing on boosting manufactured exports can help overcome the Dutch disease;
- Better terms and more flexibility regarding aid financing;
- Money for infrastructure, infrastructure and more infrastructures. Especially in countries that have been ravaged by conflict such as Angola and the Congo; this is absolutely the key to getting their economies back on track. Since infrastructure requires such huge investments, it typically needs to come from sources outside Africa;
- Shifting of some labour-and energy-intensive industries to Africa as Chinese firms move up the value chain. This could be a potential solution to reducing the dependency on extractive industries and revenues from natural-resource exports. China is visualised as interested in helping to create low-cost manufacturing bases in Africa;
- Finally, and unquestionably most important, Africa is relevant again on the global stage as everybody seems to be talking about it a lot more since China has been around.

Africa should make proper use of the opportunity provided by the 'late-comer advantage' to ensure that relationship between China and Africa is of positive and beneficial outcomes for both sides – a-win-win – signifying justice on the agenda for the two entities. There is a kind of trade by batter here: China has the finances and technical know-how which Africa has not got and badly needs. China needs Africa's resources which she does not have. Both sides have common grounds to interact and should do so from the position of collaboration and partnership not from the bases of a **'master-servant'** relationship. The premises of departure for a cordial outcome are simple. Africa should take full control of its development nexus. It should stop running around the world with a begging cap in hand. We have the resources and the people. All we need do is to build the human capacity of the continent so that they able to give added value to existing resources as well as develop new sources of resources. We need to democratically empower the people and ensure proper housekeeping of our resources. No nation or continent in the world will do that for Africa. What we need most now, is a new progressive mindset to take command of our transformation.

A new mindset should dictate how we view ourselves and the world around us. But it can also create self-imposed limitations within our belief system. We can learn from the Chinese who today dominate the world. We need both a fixed mindset of not destroying our cultural heritage values: just as we need a growth or progressive mindset of learning or acquiring the ability to progressively change in the direction of ensuring of improving the quality livelihood for all. We can call this as the psyche, attitude and ethos for a new outlook in life or a new mentality for progressive and sustainable development.

Source: Credit: Ross Hemingway 2016, UK's New Scramble for Africa; New African No 564 August 2016, IC Publication, London pp 18

With the current fixed mindset of being underdeveloped and looking on the developed world to resolve our underdevelopment nexus, we remain on the same spot. We have placed before us the platform of failures or setbacks as evidence that we are not good enough. This explains why we are stuck on the runway unable to take-off to quality livelihood. The right mindset means choosing growth and progress over negativity. We need to condition ourselves as people with brains and capable of achieving what we can. Africa had been a developed polity once; it fell on the wayside due to imperialism, slavery, colonialism and neo-colonialism. We need to recollect ourselves for a new change in a rapidly changing world construct. A new mindset should give us a new measure of our mental power or capacity and as people willing to consider new ideas, improve on it and move forward. This progressive growth mindset is what determines our place in the highly technologised global community of our time.

Source: Credit - New African No 564, August/September 2016, IC Publication London, p20

Both need each other. The exchange of essential needs such as natural resources and infrastructure to sustain or foster economic development is much more likely to achieve great things than paternalistic and failed aid strategies. China is not alone in the invasion wave. A Report by the War on Want shows that as many as 101 companies listed on the London Stock Exchange (LSE) have mining operations in Africa. Combined, these companies now control resources of oil, coal, gold, diamonds, gas etc. worth in excess of USA$1trillion.

Apparently the ongoing scramble for Africa shows how companies seek to control the continent's valuable resources and cash in at the expense of people and the planet. Take the case of Madagascar famous for its biodiversity. Yet the QIT Madagascar Minerals (QMM) project (80% owned by Rio Tinto, 20% by the Madagascan government) is wrecking the area's unique environment. The QMM mine is extracting limonite. Already, any have been affected by the mine, including being forced from their land. Farmers and fisher folks have seen their lives and livelihoods disrupted. Meanwhile, precious coastal forest habitat will soon be lost to dredging (Hemingway, op cit.). African countries should do everything possible in bridging the development, leadership and technology divide. The region has to take advantage of the emerging forms of technology – digital divide (Baskaran & Muchie, 2006) – which is creating global inequalities that emanates from different roles in the global division of labour.

Taking Essential and Beneficial Precautions

Seen within this context, China-Africa accord could be interpreted as a marriage made in heaven, of which perhaps the five most important underlying elements being:

- Chinese deals should not exclude African workers and firms from the bulk of the work in large projects by bringing their workforces from China. This idea also applies to African firms getting a share in development contracts:
- Cheap Chinese products should not flood African markets, putting local African products at a huge disadvantage, further hampering the diversification away from natural-resources sectors into textiles or manufacturing;
- There should not be a disparity in the size of the trading partners, potentially allowing China to dominate the relationship or impose terms;
- The Dutch Disease and over-dependence on natural-resource exports should be avoided;
- The failure to improve governance and political institutions will prevent the money going to the right places instead of enriching corrupt officials;

Source: See Richardson 2010

Washington versus Beijing Consensus

There is no reason why Africa should not emerge as winners given its centuries of ties with the West and little or no concrete ploughing back into the resources extracted from the continent for its transformation from a backward to an industrial continent. China's investment in Africa offers an opportunity for meaningful change as such "China's role could be seen to be wider, more sophisticated and more business-like than any other country's at any time in the post-war period" notes Zambian economist Dambisa Moyo (2009). Judging from China's super-cycle 10% annual growth puts pressure on the country to search for more resources from Africa. This should ring a bell to African policy-makers to articulate policy strategies that are beneficial to the people, to unify and re-invest prudently in its people and in developing its human capital as well as ensure and maintain political stability.

China's new engagement in Africa sends worrying messages to the West. At the same time western hypocrisy is facing serious challenges of classic development paradigms. The West criticises China's involvement in Africa yet depend of financial support from China. In all, it can be argued that ever-it-takes China to hunt for commodities is in Africa's interest. The most frequent critique is of China's foreign policy of dealing with undemocratic and highly oppressive regimes. It is said China is supporting dictators and undermining Western efforts to spread democracy and prosperity. How clean is the West from this? The west believes that a Chinese take-over in Africa would erode all possibilities of Western values and the concern for human rights from flourishing on the continent.

Must Africa remain the preserved hegemonic rights of the West? And so, goes the main argument against China in Africa that by aiding internationally-ostracised regimes, corruption, economic mismanagement and instability will proliferate. According to the West one can point to China's continued extraction of oil in the Sudan and its loans to a number of repressive dictatorships. Yet the west is doing business with corrupt and dictatorial regimes in Africa as well as financing conflicts which are clearly in their interests. This is part of why China's message and strategy resonates so strongly with many African nations and leaders, the appeal of their principle of non-interference in the affairs of sovereign states. The West believes a Chinese take-over in Africa would erode all possibilities of Western values and the concern for human rights from flourishing on the continent. After all, part of Africa's failure has been the lack of quality leadership and effective political institutions.

One can safely state that the behaviour of the West towards the African continent has been two-faced and hypocritical, as they have supported regimes just as corrupt if not more than those they accuse China of supporting. It is a fact that Western governments and multinationals have propped up dictators, financed conflicts, turned a blind eye to genocide and knowingly gone about business practices that used militias and child soldiers as a means to extract natural resources. There is believe if Chinese influence spreads too widely, the ***"Washington Consensus'*** of economic liberalism and democracy will find itself in competition with a ***"Beijing Consensus"*** of state-led development and disregard for human rights.

Africa is challenged to articulate and aggregate comprehensive policy strategies that safeguards Africa's interest in dealings with foreign powers – East or West. The views of Gin Din-Kariuki (Kenya) should be a guiding line of action and taken seriously: *'What had happened before is that we helped to prepare the meal, other people ate it…and we didn't even sit at the table. I think what we are doing now is that we are cooking it and we have brought our stool to the table…and we are taking our seat as global entrepreneurs (and) as a continent that needs to be watched."* In the same vein, the views of Tony Elumelu (Nigeria, one of the Founders of United Bank of Africa - UBA): opines; *"No one is going to develop Africa except us. The private and public sector must collaborate on long-term investment that will ultimately drive Africa's growth and development hours."* And to borrow the words of Carlos Lopes (Executive Secretary of Economic Commission for Africa, ECA); *"We must be the first to admit that there is still a lot more to be done… development challenges still abound… our narrative is still very much generated from outside"* Adding his views the President of the African Development Bank, Donald Kaberuk, notes: *"….but the colonial powers who were in Africa from 1884 to the 1960s left a legacy in many African countries of may be 5 doctors, a couple of university graduates, old infrastructure, no universities, few schools. Today, the things you see on the continent have been done by us, we Africans. There is now a new conversation about the bright economic prospects for Africa and this is true; so long as we have an understanding that although we've covered much ground, there are many more hills to climb"* New Africa 2013).

The continent has to contextualise its development from the perspectives of (a) Will Hutton (2006) – The Writing on the Wall; (b) Todd Moss (2007) African Development; (c) Gerschenkron (1962), The Late-comer Advantage; and (d) The Asian Tigers. It is evident that China's radical transformation from a moribund centrally planned country to the world's fourth largest economy is one of the fascinating stories of our time. Indeed, the transformation has been so profound as to prompt the question, will the 21st century be Chinese, just as the 20th century was American and the 19th century British? The writing on the Wall by Will Hutton (2006) addresses head-on, and with a narrative skill not always found in economic and political literature the question of underdevelopment and ways of transformation – a good lesson for Africa which supports the ongoing China-Africa newfound development relationship. China's rising star should be a serious learning process for Africa's political and economic transformation and what good and visionary leadership means to a society. African countries should seriously and thoroughly examine China's prospects for continuing rapid growth, given one-party rule. What did African countries do with their entrenched one-party rule from the 1960s to the late 1980s?

The current generation of leaders should learn from the economic travails of Chairman Mao years, including the early mass reorganisation of the means of production, the *"Great Leap Forward'* and the policy of radical egalitarianism. Of course, it had it failures of the time but created the consensus that a reorganisation of the economy was imperative, and such a reorganisation must now be spearheaded by new visionary leadership as the architect of modern Africa. Africa id obliged to start looking ahead 50 years or more by dismantling central planning and allowing for market-based activities with the total involvement of the people. With the new century, China began liberalising external trade with stunning success, and a flood of foreign investment helped turn the country overnight into the world's mass assembler of consumer goods. Africa can do the same by pushing ahead greater economic integration within Africa – free movement of people and goods across the continent. Africa has to pursue a pragmatic, gradualist, bottom-up and proactive approach to reform, 'crossing the river groping for steppingstones,' beefing up boom in small rural manufacturers or enterprises that should create jobs. We must cultivate the habit of consuming what we produce through giving added value to our natural resources and our products.

On the other hand, Africa's early post-independence years were hopeful – rising expectation – and an international development industry quickly emerged to help the new countries. But as we all know, the continent's experience has been deeply disappointing giving rise to destructive frustration and great disappointments. Hopes shattered, confidence lost and an uncertain future clouding the minds of citizens. To restore trust and confidence in the system and leaders remains an uphill task. The Future of Africa does not claim to provide the answer, but intends to give a simple, but hopefully not simplistic, introduction to the main themes, trends, and players in contemporary African development. What the publication does is providing a fast-moving account of development in the continent starting with an overview of the legacy of colonialism, the role of 'big men or leaders' and personal rule or self-articulate interest overriding the 'collective interests' of the people, conflict and civil war; and contemporary political change and democratisation in light of the challenges and opportunities offered by the unstoppable forces and process of globalisation.

The China- Africa accord as part of the "Future of Africa" addresses core questions, including the slow-growth puzzle, issues in economic reform, the role of international aid, leadership and others, all in the overall interest of improving the living standards of the African people and ensuring the sustainability of their sovereignty and the continent's place within the global economy. Fifty years after independence and fifty years on calls for serious rethinking and repositioning of priorities but bearing in mind the following realities as a compass of constructing a credible future for the continent:

- Africa has had an unlucky history and faces many structural factors that impede meaningful transformation; yet the challenge remains simple, which of harnessing the region's other advantages and work around these obstacles. It simply entails how the continent looks at existing issues of strength, weakness, opportunities and threats (SWOT) in advancing its transformation process;
- Transforming the African state to improve governance, accountability and the management of resources as key to attracting larger aid flows and improving the living standards of the people;
- Africa should not depend on 'aid', though there is no reason why 'aid' should not be increased, but also to be used more effectively and efficiently for the benefit of the people and ultimate satisfaction of those providing the assistance;
- The need to share responsibility and obligations between the various actors, citizens and state, local, provincial, national, regional, continental and the world to ensure that Africa is able to take advantage of global economic, scientific and technological opportunities.

Now is the time for African leaders and policy-makers to articulate 'magic bullet solutions' that adequately addresses issues dealing with the proper use of human and natural resources curse' the lack of good governance and accountability, weak institutions among others. It must be admitted that the imposed World Bank financial conglomerates imposed Structural Adjustment Programme (SAP) on Africa provide both challenges and opportunities for the continent to bring order in its governance and financial activities. On the one hand, it was a near or total failure imposing greater hardship on the people. On the other hand, structural adjustment had visibly improved macroeconomic management across Africa. It imposed social problems to the most vulnerable in society.

What is not clear is the role played by conditionality. Today, there is little debate across the continent among policy-makers that the first-generation reforms aimed, for instance, at achieving fiscal discipline and taming inflation helped created the conditions for the strong growth currently enjoyed by the continent. If the successes of the reform period are sharply and critically exposed to analysis, so are the challenges China and Africa now face: For China, with its ideological basis eroded by its embracement of the market growth, the Communist party is struggling for legitimacy and facing the social strains of rising income inequality, corruption, land theft, and environmental degradation. Africa's adoption of the centralised monolithic party structure and with the collapse of the communist system threw the continent into great confusion and development disarray. Both sides are now finding their feet on the ground and collaboration between the two become a matter of necessity. Both sides must develop a kind of 'balancing act' to succeed. For now, the ball is more in the courtyard of African countries to expand their vision, scale down economic waste and poor governance which leaves output growth increasingly reliant on unsustainably high levels of investment rather than driven by the prowess of the human and natural resources potential of the people. The African one-party nexus system was used for personal wealth accumulation and entrenching ethnic divide in society. It has not been positively used in forging unity and development for the common good of the well-being of the citizens. Africa is underdeveloped as a result of the centralised monolithic party construct.

Africa needs to strengthen its intra-regional trade, political and social integration and cohesion. Presently, potential benefits of intraregional trade and movement of people and goods is disappointing. This has to be boosted – with regional economic communities (RECs) playing a much greater role. May be, there are too many economic communities which imposes strained of multi-membership. The result is sometime conflicting and overlapping commitments which does more harm than good. Thus, complicated and restrictive rules of origin, together with other internal barriers, have kept intraregional trade relatively low compared with other developing regions. For now, it is sad to note that existing regional economic communities have not succeeded in boosting trade within their respective regions and the continent at large. The challenge for these RECs is to construct, deepen and consolidate the connectivity of African countries. Country, ethnic, political, cultural, religious and gender animosity or divide is dismantling progression towards the unity of the continent.

In addition, a close look at the new political landscape suggests that most of the political parties that emerged during the continent's transition to democracy follow ethnic lines. In many countries, ethnic political parties have flourished, and in those with a high degree of ethnic fractionalisation, no single party is capable of winning a majority of popular vote. To this should be added the incoherent bureaucratic institutions that results from a highly politicised administration leave the government incapable of resolving collective problems and transcending individual or group interests. Thus, rules and decisions are commodities, to be sold to the highest bidder. This produces an unpredictable environment of political rules and decisions. In these systems, state power reduces private productive capabilities, and distribution and growth both suffer. Thus, just enacting democracy is not a sufficient condition for good economic performance. There is need for a corrupt-free bureaucratic structure to handle the China - Africa newfound relationship. Effective and efficient organisation structure of government will facilitate the inter-link between the two continents, creates commitment and promote coherence in the best interest of the people.

A China-Africa relationship is one of overlapping, conflicting and complicated commitments towards one another. Politics is a game of interest. Complicated and restrictive rules of origin together with other internal barriers may impair the relationship. Who gains out of the deal depends on the strategic approach developed by the two continents and how their interest converges for the wellbeing of their citizens. Both continents can sustain their balancing acts and evoke the necessary changes to ensure a smooth outcome which in turn will determine how the world responds to the new Chinese-African century and the reaction of their citizens. Persistent poverty exists in both continents. The persistence of poverty is distressing both because we feel compassion for the poor and because poverty is associated with disruptive behaviours, such as crime (Karelis 2007) which their governments in respective continents must address. From a perspective of common grounds, China and Africa should work together and articulate policies to lift their citizens out of poverty as well as take into account the effects of poverty and underdevelopment on the motivations of poor people.

At the same time, a note of caution is necessary. Africa should draw lessons from "The Story of My People" (Nesi 2013) how Chinese competition devastated the Italian textile industry. Nesi lays out a clear diagnosis of Prato's predicament. The biggest problem was the dismantling of the international clothing regime, which allowed cheap Chinese textiles to flood into Europe. At the time, economists predicted that Italian firms would in return be able to sell their high-priced textiles to China. But this promise proved a chimera, except for a few firms with famous names. Moreover, to that the second factor was subtler, as the Italian government aiming to stamp out tax evasion levied a tax on firms' revenue. That meant that even as profits turned to losses, firms were stile liable for taxes. Instead, they just decided to shut down. The lesson African governments must learn from Prato's demise is to limit the process of *"creative destruction,"* or at least slow it down to make it more manageable. Poverty has to be eradicated in Africa. Chinese invasion into Africa could provide a 'golden era' but with a heavy price to pay in the long-run. Drawing lessons from the

Prato case, it should be noted that hundreds of textile factories collapsed across Nigeria because they could not compete with cheap Chinese garments; and the Tanzania government stopped Chinese from selling in that country's textile markets. Chinese are welcome as investors, but not as 'vendors or shoe shiners. Imported Chinese furniture which is not strong is crippling the furniture industry across the continent. Africa exports timber but imports sawdust furniture. What an irony?

Chinese products have flooded markets across the continent – from Cape to Cairo, from Banjul to the Horn, cities, towns and villages in Africa. These goods include clothing, jewellery, electronics, building materials and much more. Even little things like matches, tea bags, children's toys and bathing soaps are coming from China. To a large extent, African consumers go for Chinese products because they are affordable and with less quality control mechanism in place to check the quality of goods imported. As a result, Chinese goods are cheaper than those from Europe and North America – in business, price is very important to customers. The low level of the Yuan (the Chinese currency) compared to the other major world trading currencies such as the US dollar, the Euro, the Pound and Yen attracts African importers.

Already trade between Africa and China has grown tremendously at a breath-taking pace. It was US$10, 5 billion in 2000; $40 billion in 2005 and $166 billion in 2011. China is currently Africa's biggest trading partner, having surpassed the US in 2009. The Chinese government is eager to cement China's dominance by burnishing its image through initiatives such as $20 billion credit to African countries to develop infrastructure and the African Talent Programme, which is intended to train 30.000 Africans in various sectors. China's give-and-take relationship also plays out n other forms. Chinese construction firms are acquiring enormous construction contracts. The China Railway Construction Group (CRC) signed a $1.5 billion contract in September 2012 to modernise a railway system in Western Nigeria. That same month, China South Locomotive and Rolling Stock Corporation, the largest train manufacturer in China, signed a $400 million deal to supply locomotives to a South African firm, Transnet. In February 2012 the CRC announced projects in Nigeria, Djibouti and Ethiopia worth about $1.5 billion in total (Ighobor 2013).

The writing on the wall is clear for all to see. To that should be added Bhagwati and Panagariya (2013) perception, why growth matters and why African governments must embark on reform, dismantling step-by-step various myths about the continent's economic and social policy from independence to the present day; issue a call for additional reforms to bolster growth and further improve the lives of Africans. An Afro-centric approach clothed in a progressive reform agenda is imperative which advance a pro-growth reform on two tracks: (i) those that support growth immediately – for example, less regulation and more investment in infrastructure; and (ii) those aimed at more effective and inclusive growth – such as better education (the need for broader access to higher education and better roads is clear) and implementation of social programmes. China's land grab in Africa is a serious problem even though it is maintained that in the long-run China could well seek to import much food from Africa which, by World Bank estimates, has 60 per cent of the world's uncultivated land. Given Africa's potential, China is likely to turn towards it.

Cultural differences between Chinese and Africans, including the language barriers, often lead to social tensions, and poor infrastructure in Africa makes business operations difficult. Frequent power shortages in some countries raise production costs, while policies towards businesses are inconsistent. African governments do raise taxes at a whim. And most African economies are still fragile, subject to shocks from the global market. On the other hand, China is taking measures to bridge the information gap. In 2008 the China Africa News Service was launched to report 'China-Africa News Stories from Africa, Chinese and Western Sources". In early 2012 China Central Television (CCTV) opened a broadcast hub in Nairobi – Kenya – its first outside of its Beijing Headquarters. There is no doubt that China is actively introducing its culture and values through a push factor of what could be termed 'the rise of China's state-led media dynasty in Africa'. The overarching driver is the Chinese Government's strategic pursuit of resources and attempts to ensure energy needs within China. As the world's second-biggest economy, china currently buys more than one-third of Africa's oil; and its industries are getting raw materials such as coal from South Africa, iron ore from Gabon, timber from Equatorial Guinea and copper from Zambia (Shinn & Eisenman 2012).

Chinese industries require new markets for their products and Africa is a potentially outlet. In other words, China is repositioning itself continuously for the new Africa that is emerging. To boost up activities and relationship, Chinese President Hu Jintao at the Fifth Forum on China-Africa Cooperation held in Beijing in July 2012, listed yet more projects including the construction of 100 schools, 30 hospitals, 30 anti-malaria centres and 20 agriculture technology demonstration centres. The state-of-art complex Africa Union building with its 2,500 – seat conference hall in Addis Ababa (Ethiopia), a gift to the continent prompted the following statement from the late Prime Minister Meles Zenawi to Africa's current economic boom as a 'renaissance,' due partly to China's "amazing re-emergence and its commitments to a win-win partnership with Africa."

China's aggressive offensive in Africa sends shock waves and raises fear in the Western world. The West is nervous about China's activities in Africa. China's policy of non-interference in the internal affairs of African countries and its fast approach to aid delivery make it more attractive than Western donors, whose aid often comes with demands to improve human rights and democracy. Former US Secretary of State Hillary Clinton has warned against a *"new colonialism in Africa,' in which it is easy to come in, takes out natural resources, and pay off leaders and leave."* Apparently, China-Africa relationship will get stronger: so long as Africa's development requires huge foreign investments, so long will China continue to be relevant. Irrespective of the concerns being voiced in some circles in Africa, Chinese involvement is widely considered to be a positive-sum game. Importantly, Africa countries must develop a strategy for its dealings with emerging economic giants such as China, Brazil and India. It is important the African governments ensure that everyone benefits from the economic gains from the China-Africa relationship. There are no reasons to believe that China's newly articulated soft-intervention policy is a set of principles which are formed by shaping the national development policies as well as international affairs of other countries particularly regarding the African continent. With such a strategic approach, Beijing is preserving its traditional normative claim of non-interference, as well as protecting its various newly emerging national interests and consolidating its growing international powers. China's growing interest in African must be understood from a wide range of interconnected activities at home as well as abroad all geared towards consolidating a self-constrained rising power (Li Yin (2018; Chan Gerald, 2018). Chinese politics is not a "black-box" as commonly assumed but explainable and predictable (Luk Yuen, 2016).

Prasad (2017:23) points out that China now employs a multipronged approach to setting the global agenda; (i) gradually increasing its influence in international institutions and even establishing a toehold in those where it does not have direct and immediate interest. This allows China to change the rules of the game from the inside: (ii) it is setting up multilateral institutions where it gets to call the shorts, which allows it to control the rules of the game and also serves to subtly catalyse changes in the existing institutions; (iii) it is joining with other like-minded countries to establish institutions that are meant to build trust and stronger economic linkages with countries that it sees as partners as well as potential competitors; (iv) it is using other arms of the state, including state-owned banks and development agencies, to increase its global financial reach and power.

There are reasons to believe that high levels of Chinese aid have had a harmful effect on human rights and on economic development across Africa. It is argued, that aid from China is, in fact oriented toward poorer countries, although mostly resource-rich ones Chinese investors do seem more willing than Western countries to invest in countries that are politically unstable. Views are mixed. What is clear is that Chinese money has in some ways played a positive role in Africa's economic development, but with significant risks and costs to some sectors. What is clear is that the Chinese are quick learners, taking a pragmatic approach and adjusting strategy when circumstances demand it. Can African countries draw valuable lessons and tailor their developmental approach to respond to their needs, aspiration and activities in meeting the goals and visions envisaged in AU Agenda 2063?

Lessons to Learn

What can Africa learn from the economic miracle of China to transform itself? The continent must embrace itself in taking 'risk and complexity to make profit or derive gains in different forms. African and global integration and new technology entails rapid progress, but also embedded with higher risk. No one should be blamed but take advantage of the rapidly changing environment to do something good and progressive to improving on the well-being of the people. The challenging question or issue is how African countries can make good decisions when they cannot foresee the consequences? For example, institutions and regulations advance slowly, while technologies and their application in complex systems change much faster. The ongoing political crisis in Cameroon, shows how technology overtook the slow grinding machinery of the government (see Forje, forthcoming)

Kangai (2014:16-20) illuminates our minds on what can be described as the 10 commandments or lessons provided by China for Africa to properly tax on the runway for constructive and meaningful change as depicted here.

1. A nation that was once colonised can rise to become a superpower.

China like Africa was colonised. Colonisation is an instrument through which a country loses its pride, dignity, and self-respect. And Self-belief.

China has since the "Great Leap Forward" regained its dignity, self-respect, confidence and is today recognise a super-power.

Apparently, colonialism and slavery robed Africa and took away its pride, dignity and self-respect. Africa is yet to recover from its past legacy of colonial rule and the impact of the slave trade

2. A nation must create its own economic and political system guided by its national interest

Recovering from the status of a colonised status through the 'Long March', China embarked on the ideological orientation of "socialism with Chinese characteristics" The institutionalised one-party hegemonic structure directed and cushioned development in the best interests of the people. Today, one can describe the economy as a 'social market economy'. In addition, China to a large extent has not stuck on its socialist characteristic, but equally adopted other elements system to create a unique system that enhances its national interests. In short, it takes various parts of other systems and combine them to create a system that advances consolidates its national interests

African countries have tried the communist, socialist and capitalist systems without realising the impact of these approaches. They have failed in the just mentioned aspects. What is required now is some leverage of 'pragmatism' and adopt a system or combination of systems that necessarily serve further and protect African national interests.

Africa can begin to try its indigenous knowledge system – for example adopting and improving on the "Ubuntu, Batho Pele and Harambee" spirit that ensures that Africa interests (e.g., food security, education, health care, and access to opportunity for all is available.

3. A nation must always have clear programmes that are bold, innovative, creative and with vision.

The Chinese state construct has evolved or a number of programmes, starting with the "Long March"; the "Great Leap Forward" (1954-1964), "Cultural Revolution" (1966-76). "Open Door Policy" (1978-) and the "Go Abroad Policy" (2000) all with clear objectives and interests.

This is lacking on the continent. Even if they exist like vision 2020, 2025, 2030, 2035, there is a gross absence of the political will to ensure its realisation. There are mere political slogans for the leaders to remain in power. The "Africa Must Unite" agenda initiated by Kwame Nkrumah more or less died a still birth This could have being "Africa's Big Push" like Mao's "Big Push" (1949) land reform, construction of factories through the state, and reduction in consumption

4. A nation must train its youth skills that serve national interests (in short, human capacity building, job creation and employment). How do we tailor our education system to meet the pressing and essential needs of the continent? Is Africa's education system tailored to meet the needs of the job-market? How many engineers does a country need as compared to lawyers, political scientists? Should a kind of quota allocation be allocated for the different disciplines following the immediate needs of the country? "Africa has a young population; some estimates show that 60% of Africa's total population is between these of 15-25. Africa's population continues to get younger and the trend does not seem to be changing anytime soon. In fact, some estimates say that by 2015, 75% of Africa's population will consist of young people" (Kangai op cit)

5. A nation must be proud of its cultural heritage so it can have a strong national identity. (To what extent is the continent making use of its indigenous knowledge and cultural heritage values as a veritable input mechanism in accelerating its process of transformation?)

6. A nation's State-Owned Enterprises (SOEs) can be key drivers of the economy. (In China the key drivers of the economy are state-owned enterprises, where the state owns 50.01% of shares. The 2011 Global Fortune 500 list shows that three SOEs are in the top 10, namely; Sinopec, China National Petroleum, and State Grid, and top Chinese state-owned Banks – Industrial Commercial Bank of China (ICBC) and China Construction Bank (CCB) top the list of Banks following Global Fortune's 500 (Kangai ibid). In Africa, most of the State-Owned Enterprises milk the country to death. They have become the channel for corruption and used as

Lessons for Africa:

7. A nation must be quick and decisive in policy implementation: (Policy articulation, implementation and evaluation (PAIE). Government must be resolute in its policy strategies ensuring the constructive use of the 'stick and carrot' as well as recruiting the best brains into the public service sector; creating an enabling environment for workers within the administration.

8. A nation must be proud of and promote its own brands; (Taking pride and promoting the culture of the continent is vital. We seldom promote the rich cultural heritage and indigenous value system of the continent, but prone to embracing without questioning foreign values and cultures. In contrast, "the Chinese have pride in their good local brands and always make a conscious decision to support them whenever possible. The Chinese are very economically conscious. They understand the power of their currency, and they are extremely aware of the impact of their spending" (Kangai 2014).

9. A nation must have the courage to make decisions that are in the best interest of its people regardless of criticism. (The Chinese embark on a 'Go Abroad Policy' in 1999 with the intension of spreading and implanting its image abroad. ***(Chinese companies were encouraged to invest abroad and either acquire or partner with foreign companies. In short, the Chinese are in Africa to further their interest);*** they are not in Africa to further the interest of Africans. Africa should copy the Chinese policy of working in the overall interest of Africa.

10. A nation that exploits its competitive advantage can become globally competitive: (China has taken technology from Europe, and cheap raw materials from Africa combined them with its relatively cheap and efficient labour to manufacture and export finished goods to the world. From high quality goods typically found in the USA and Europe to the cheap goods typically found in Africa, China makes something for everyone, because it has capitalised on its strengths to be globally competitive (Kaangai 2014). Africa has failed to capitalise on its strength – rich natural resources potential, virgin and unexploited research desert. To bargain for greater development related activities from abroad. It has also failed in making good use of the 'late-comer advantage'. Equally, the continent has failed to improve and incorporate its indigenous knowledge to improve on the wellbeing of the people.

Source: Forje (2014) Complied from Kangai (2014) "Ten Lessons from China That Can Transform Africa', pp16-20)

Africa is caught within the trappings of structural dependency paradigm which has been with us for centuries. Africa needs to do something concrete about its dependency nexus. We need to articulate more rigorous tests of dependency or, more precisely, of theories and hypothesis that can get the continent out from the dependency construct. One such new framework is to penetrate into the late comer advantage; taking advantage in building the human capacity of the people as well as making proper use of nature's given resources. It is clear that without skilled human capital, added value cannot be given to the continent's vast natural resources potentials nor creates new resources for the sustainable transformation of the region.

In addition to this, we need to develop and mobilise domestic financial potentials in financing development related activities. Ensuring the existence of an enabling environment is equally crucial. The story being narrated here is not only real and true: it is made even more dramatic by the fact of technologies and robots shaping the way to future development prospects. Hence, building the human capital skills remains an imperative for the continent in transforming itself. Knowledge is power so goes the adage. We have to tap into the potentials of the African people to bring development back to the people and by and for the people.

References

Bask ran Angathevar and Muchie Mammo (eds.) (2006). Bridging the Digital Divide. Innovation Systems for ICT in Brazil, China, India, Thailand and Southern Africa, Adonis & Abby Publishers Ltd, London, UK

Bhagwati Jagdish & Arvind Panagariya (2013). Why Growth Matters. How Economic Growth in India Reduced Poverty and the Lessons for Other Developing Countries, Public Affairs, New York

Ezeanya Chika [2012] "Why I Hate the New AU Headquarters", New African, 46th Year, No.515, March 2012, London, pp68-69

Centre for Conflict Resolution (CCR) [2007] Crouching Tiger, Hidden dragon? China and Africa: Engaging The World's Next Superpower. Cape Town, South Africa

Chan Gerald (2018). Understanding China's New Diplomacy: Silk Roads and Bullet Trains, Edward Elgar Publishing, London, United Kingdom

Chang Ha-Joon (2015) Bad Samaritans: The Myth of Free Trade and the Secret History of Capitalism,

Forje W. John (Forthcoming – There Was Another Country – Southern Cameroons)

Gerschenkron A. (1962). Economic Backwardness in Historical Perspectives Cambridge, M.A. The Belknap Press, Harvard University Press

Hemingway Ross (2016). "UK's New Scramble for Africa", New African No.564, August/September 2016, IC Publication, London, pp18

Hutton Will (2006). The Writing on the Wall. Why We Must Embrace China as a Partner or Face It as an Enemy. Simon & Schuster Trade, New York

Ighobor Kingsley (2013) "China in the Heart of Africa: Opportunities and Pitfalls in a Rapidly Expanding Relations' Africa Renewal, January 2013, United Nations Department of Public Information, New York, pp6-8

Izaka Seme Ka Pixley (1906) Speech at the New York's Columbia University, USA

Jacoby Ulrich [2007] "Getting Together. The New Partnership between China and Africa for Aid and Trade" Finance and Development,

Vol.44, No.2, June 2007, the International Monetary Fund, Washington, USA, pp34-35

Kangai Manyika (2014). "Ten Lessons from China That Can Transform Africa" New African, No.543. October 2014, AN IC Publication, London, pp16-20

Karelis Charles (2007). The Persistent of Poverty: Why the Economics of the Well-Off Can't Help the People. Yale University press, New Haven and London

Li Yin Hak (2018). China's New World Order. Changes in the Non-Intervention Policy Edward Elgar Publishing, London, United Kingdom

Luk Yuen Ching Sarina & Peter W. Preston (2016). The Logic of Chinese Politics. Cores, Peripheries and Peaceful Rising. Edward Elgar Publishing, London, United Kingdom.

Moss J. Todd (2007). African Development: Making Sense of the Issues and Actors. Lynne Rienner Publishers, Inc, Boulder, Colorado, USA

Moyo Dambisa (2009). Dead Aid: Why Aid Is Not Working and How There Is a Better Way for Africa, Farrar, Straus & Giroux, New York. (See also her two thought-provoking books (a) Winner Take All: and (b) How the West Was Lost.

N'Diaye Seyni (2001)"The Role of Institutional Reforms" finance and Development" – Globalisation and Africa, December 2001. Vol. 38, No.4, pp18-21

Nesi Edoardo (2013). Story of My People. Random House, New York

New African (2013) "Most Influential Africans 2013, New African, No.534, December 2013, London.

New African [2008] "China-Africa: Why The West Is Worried", New African, Issue 471, March 2008. London. pp12-18

Packenham, T. (1991). The Scramble for Africa. Abacus, London, United Kingdom

Prasad Eswar (2017) 'Path to Influence. China Employs a Multipronged Approach to Enhance Its Role in Setting the Global Economic and Political Agenda', Finance and Development, September 2017, Vol.54, No.3, International Monetary Fund, Washington, USA, pp22-25

Richardson Gonzalez Patricio (2010) China and Africa: A Mutually Opportunistic Partnership"? (ARI) 99/2010, 17 June, 2010.

Shinn H. David and Joshua Eisenman (2012) University of Pennsylvania Press, Philadelphia, USA

Tafirenyika Masimba (2016) "Why Has Africa Failed to Industrialise?" African Renewal, Vol. 30. No.2, August-November 2016, United Nations, New York, pp28-29

Chapter Eight

The Security Dimension and Military Nexus Challenges: Problems and Solutions

The security of the continent is a major concern. No wonder an official could question: "what are we doing 50 years after independence calling our former colonial powers to resolve our security disputes?" France's recent intervention in Mali has prompted much soul search among Africa's military officials and diplomats. The plethora of challenges to be adequately addressed by African states is many and varied. Thus the securitisation and militarisation standards as a major problem of concern securitisation and militarisation of the continent has come under scrutiny, but militarisation continues to escalate in ups and bounds, security, militarisation and development have undergone a paradigm shift may be perceived as rapid they are usually part of processes of global change that, lead to a fundamental redefined imaginary, a sudden new reality, The new landscape of securitisation and militarisation of the African continent can be seen within the context of development of the region by the 54 or more states, and also for the developed economies to ensure the sustainability of the development wave as well. The industrial military complex comes to play. Strictly speaking, arms production is a burden on African countries. From the realities of Africa's underdeveloped status, the continent does not need the level of existing arms arsenal. We need an army for development and quality livelihood, not that of destruction. Apart from South Africa under the apartheid governance structure, there is little African countries gain from investments in arms production, or making fortunes on the arms race and the development of new deadly weapons.

Coming to play in the name of the so-called free world means that the sophistication of modern weaponry creates technical dependence on the supplier nation, just as its complexity creates continuing spare-parts dependence. Apart from South Africa and Egypt, Africa does not produce arms but totally dependent on imported arms from the Western and Eastern countries. Arms are also sold or given for base rights, or for staging or over flight privileges, thus creating two-way diplomatic power. Because of the state of growing political instability and ethnic fragmentation, the need for arm purchase continue to be on the increase. Africa's arms purchase since the 1960s has been on the steady increase so also have conflicts within and between nations increased. Expenditure on these weapons of human destruction is so huge that just a third directed to towards the social well-being of citizens would make a significant difference in their quality livelihood.

Unfortunately, the producers of these destructive weapons through their sales of arms and diplomacy attached to it have repeatedly tried to alter a landscape they do not understand. The export of weapons of human destruction to Africa reveals a continent beset by illogical boundaries, horribly mismanaged through poor political construct, financial aid and comically incompetent government structures. A better future for Africa requires powerful ideas and raw energy which, for reasons of politics and ignorance, have gone awry. For now, Africa remains a land of Eurocentric ineptitude superimposed on an inherent native harmony. Africa wants to construct its future not through building a fleet of destructive arms arsenal, but through positive construction of an army of well-educated and healthy citizens.

Securitisation and militarisation and development nexus remains a continuous growing big business in the world today. It is driven by the demand and rush for new markets. **First,** people wanting to invest in Africa looked for a high degree of security for their investment related activities. To maintain security requires some degree of militarisation; militarisation also requires resources and excessive use of military power. It is a vicious circle. Africa provides most of these resources in various forms, quantities and magnitude. All these linked together puts the continent at the centre of the development security and military nexus. Thus, the security and military nexus creates controversies for African states which has earned the continent with clichés such as 'failed, fragile, banana and collapsed' states emphasising the lack of state capacity to uphold order and implement policy: 'human security' and 'humanitarian intervention' both in indicating a shifting referent of security from 'state' to 'population' (Sorensen & Soderbaum, 2012).

Security – military-development nexus as noted earlier constitute the world's largest business which while purportedly aiming to dismantle itself, is continuously growing. In reality the security-military development nexus enhances the centre-periphery continuum. The centre calls the shot; the periphery due to its vulnerability dances to the musical tone of the big power brokers; and the waltz continues. Shall the cynical vicious circle be ever broken? That is the million-dollar questions Africa states must seek concrete and endurable solutions and make critical choices to move forward.

Second, the need for disarmament and quest for world peace is a course all nations should strive towards. For now, who are the peacemakers, and who are militarists? What is the role of civil society in promoting the course for peace or fanning the path for military and conflict actions? Which are the hidden hands behind African conflicts? Ankomah (2013;10-11) notes: "it may be currently unfashionable to assign Africa's troubles to colonialism and external powers, but in the case of the continent's second largest country, Democratic Republic of Congo, it would be difficult to come to any other conclusion. After 56 years of independence, Africa is now more mature and able to take responsibility for its own shortcomings without blaming external forces especially the West.

What about issues surrounding the assassination of the first elected Prime Minister (Patrice Lumumba) of Congo? And the sufferings still continue. There is a thread running through the serious harm done to the country by the killing of Lumumba on 27 January 1961 – 56 long years ago this January, 2017 – to the troubles in Congo today." United State Congresswoman Cynthia McKinney in December 2000 stumped Congress with this revealing by stating: "The whole world knows that Uganda and Rwanda are allies of the United States and that they have been given a ***carte blanche*** for whatever reason to wreak havoc in the Congo" (Ankomah, 2013:11). On 17 May 2001 Wayne Marsden acclaimed book, "Genocide and Covert Operations in Africa 1993-1999" testifying before Congressional Subcommittee on International Operations and Human Rights Committee on International Relations, "prepared testimony and statement for the record" was so revealing that the West's mainstream media refused to print it" But as Marsden pointed out; *"At the very least, the United States, as the world's leading democracy, owes Africa at least the example of a critical self-inspection"* (Ankomah op cit.).

Third, the concept of peace, democracy, security and development are intertwined. We have to understand what is meant by peace and its sustainability. Peace remains a vital condition that must exist for human development and progress; but this is not a sufficient condition since peace cannot just simply occur out of the blue; For example, peace can be achieved under a repressive regime construct where citizens are silenced as well as denied the basic political choices; for instance, a comparative analysis between Cameroon (Nigeria during the military era) or Ghana and Botswana. It should also be noted that weapons production diverts equity and skills from more productive enterprises; it also depletes a startling growing fraction of essential raw materials like bauxite (use to make aluminium) copper, lead, zinc and nickel. The Republic of Congo (DRC) has gone the way it has due to arms race between the superpowers. Given all these facts, is it cynical to consider whether the continual building of arms almost too devastating to use is a source of relative peace, an extension of the pax atomica which continues to reign between the superpowers to the detriment of Africa.

Durable peace is based on the existence of real social conditions and free-institutions, and justice than can sustain peace and ensure development and progress. Security entails peace and vice-versa, implying that when the conditions of human security, liberty and freedom are present, change, development and progress can be ensured. Lack of freedom, liberty and equality, entails absence of peace and this contributes to conflicts, wars, fear and human insecurity. Autocratic rule with no checks and balances, states devoid of democratic institutions are fertile grounds for conflict, wars and insecurity. Public policy can promote peace and development by establishing democratic institutions. Strong and democratic institutions are absent of the African political landscape which paves the mode for conflicts, wars, instability that underpins the state of underdevelopment and poor governance. Given the scores of entrenched conflicts in Africa calls for a new constructive and comprehensive approach that involves a triumvirate men and women in conjunction with civil society from the continent, regional peace keeping forces and the warring factions themselves working in concert to replace the power of firing rifle with the courageous tool of the "talking will" that everyone agrees should prevail.

When free and fair elections are not organised, and if the political impasse is not overcome or the political violence clashes, and other impediments as a result of injustice and other malpractices are not overcome, the issue of peace and progress cannot be assured, the Penelope for insecurity will swing to the highest level as been observed in many parts of the continent. The issue of peace is bleak on the continent due to the existence of poor policy articulation and implementation, weak state institutions and poor governance. These factors have a vicious impact on private domestic and foreign investments as investors are discouraged due to uncertainty, risk and insecurity for investments. Overcoming such negative results requires an enlightened population focused and responsible leadership including a democratic governance system within the rule of law.

The views of Mercieca (2012) on the role of governments in promoting peace are significant in this context. Governments of all kinds seem to share one thing in common, the conviction that all their actions are performed in the best interest of their respective population without no hind-sight, experience, demonstrates that this is not necessarily true in anyway whatsoever. One has only to critically and objectively x-ray their behaviour in terms of results since actions are stronger and more credible than words. Clear enough, and most unfortunately, there is not a single government in the world that can claim to be perfect. There is no perfect human-being. There can be no perfect government. But this is not an excuse or recipe for the existence of governments prone to destroying their people in the name of politics. Importantly, we must all strive towards constructing and operating a governance system that is as perfect as it can possible is. "We need government officials who genuinely and sincerely try to do their very best to alleviate problems and diminish needless suffering as much as possible. Every government has the potential to contribute all means toward the promotion of peace or war both within the nation and the world at large" (2012).

Quality services are expected of government officials and their performance actions should be positive, constructive, objective and embedded within the relics of justice and the rule of law and in fulfilment of people's dire needs without compromising the needs and aspirations of other and generations to come. Given human ingenuity, the world has evolved as a single unit – a global village with significant impact on our wellbeing or destroying it with whatever actions taken. For example, the pollution of air or water by one nation extends far beyond the borders of that country. That is all people of all nations tend to be physically strong or weak on a mutually beneficially or destructive basis. This implies that no government has the right to perform actions that are detrimental and harmful to citizen's ability to quality livelihood.

Like good parents, governments are obliged to look after the vital needs of all citizens without exception – this includes vital needs as sacrosanct human rights, healthcare, education among others. A nation may be viewed as strong or weak by the health status of the people. When people are healthy and strong, then we have a healthy and strong nation, when people are given the opportunity to develop one's talents to the maximum possible, then we will have a developed and affluent society with everyone sharing the cake equitably. Events over the past fifty years (i.e. the attainment of independence, show that we are very far-away from the goals of an equitable society. Politics and society have not attained a common ground of placing humankind at the centre of all development related activities. We continue operating an unjust and san unequal society. A just society is the source of hope for humankind, How and when to get there is the question. Are we doomed to operate an unjust and unequal society. We need a renewal of the current world construct. A just and equal world nexus means the poor and powerless getting their rights, That is why new political leadership is much needed in our world construct of today. Our world today is govern by the evils of injustice.

Crafting A New Approach

Weapons and wars have always served to create nightmares and to subject people into merciless sufferings. It was Pope Pius X11 on the eve of World War 11 who drew the attention of the British and Germans to the reality that in a war everyone is a loser, and no one is a winner. Germany lost the war and its economy collapsed and people were poor everywhere. England won the war so to say, its economy equally collapsed, and people were likewise poor everywhere. The old-aged dictum *"si-vis pacem para bellium,"* i.e. 'if you want peace prepare for war' should be critically reversed. Why? This explains why the USA gives priority in its expenditure on the manufacture and sales of weapons and the never-ending development of the military industrial complex. Apparently, the USA stands as the greatest debtor on planet earth with trillions of dollars in debt and the American people are suffering immensely as a result. Washington and the developed polities need armed forces to attain world domination and protection of the interest of their dollar and Euro corporations which fleece, like sheep, dozens of countries and peoples.

Through unequal exchanges and the exploitation of the cheap raw materials and manpower of newly liberated African countries, western imperialism earns hundreds of billions of dollar and Euros in profits. It is the developed polities that gain from the growing arsenal industries. Seen in this light, for the developed polities, it is indeed impossible, inadmissible and unscientific to separate foreign policy from home policy. That is why former USA Secretary of Defence, Caspar Weinberger in 1980 bluntly and arrogantly asserted that America needed military power in order to ensure itself access to crucially important raw material and energy resources in Africa, Latin America, and the Middle East, and to secure its 'vital interests' in Asia and Pacific, as well as in Western.

Africa countries have wrongly copied this dictum of preparing for peace by beefing up their military arsenal. Africa countries are at war with corruption, poverty, underdevelopment and poor-quality livelihood but they are not preparing for it. They are boosting their military expenditure to entrench sit-tight presidents not solving and meeting the needs of their citizens. Sit-tight Presidents addiction to power and wealth is so deep and so strong that African leaders continue to articulate and aggregate policies that promotes their being in office till death do them part. Jesus of Nazareth was not wrong when he noted: *Homo hominids cup us* – man is his own worst enemy. Most Africa leaders have emerged to become the country's worst enemy with their belligerent policies. Howe (1981: xxxiii) points out that arms predominantly exist to give political power, the tiger whose tail so many are seduced to hold. Arms-industry expansion, or increased defence budgets, does not imply that a war is on, or even near: We live in an age of sophisticated and expensive rattling sabers which determine the balance of power. The bloodless wars we fight are wars without much honour; in which friends and even protégés are fickle and sometimes vicious.

The vast majority of the African population want peace not war: development not destruction: progress not decline: sustainable and progressive quality livelihood not endemic squatter and poverty. Remember the famous statement by US President Dwight Eisenhower's farewell speech to the US Congress *"all people of all nations want peace, only their governments want war"*. A substantial number of African states continue to accumulate more weapons and never cease to resort to war each time they find an opportunity. These governments promote conflicts to make a lot of money. Poor governance and conflict are viewed as business venture and for money they seem to be ready to do anything conceivable, including the needless suffering and massacre of their citizens. Therefore, we should build and practice peace in our minds. In war everyone is a loser and no winner. We are all winners and benefit in an era of peace and stability.

We must bear in mind that that wars are negative sum games and irrational to every one of the parties. But unfortunately interests of all ruling establishments are not identical with the population and are based in favour of conflict. It is not surprising to observe time and again the opportunities for gains to agreement that are not realised and opportunities for sustained peaceful coexistence between communities are lost. In the light of this dismal development and hysterical record, the governing elite are perfecting the game of tactical agreement and strategies avoidance in order to buying more time in asserting its base of power by continuing exploiting the modalities of conflict.

Truth is treason in the empire of lies and dishonesty and bad governance. There is an alternative to poor governance, a bigger police state, billions of CFA Francs misused monies and a governance system that draws more on the energies of corruption and tribal hatred it has helped to cultivate in order to remain in power. For these reasons, insecurity, conflicts and wars are inadvertently reproduced by leaders or governments through a hidden agenda to stay put in power. But this is not what the country and continent needs. African countries need to work towards need to work towards institutionalising a culture of peace and a deterrent to war and insecurity. This requires a comprehensive policy focused on consensus, *reconstruction, reconciliation and rehabilitation* – the three "R" s and other factors needed to restore trust, hope and confidence in the people. It should be pointed out that insecurity, conflicts and wars arise due to a number of interrelated factors which include:

- Conflicts associated with political ethnic and religious allegiances;
- General climate of lawlessness creating tensions in communities and even between countries;
- Poor governance and justice system;
- Passive and condescending civil society;
- Foreign influence and interference

Conflicts over land use and national resources or competition over resources, land and mineral wealth by foreign investors impact in conflicts in the continent. We need an Africa that is at peace with itself. Without peace, there can be no meaningful development and progress. Peace indeed is a collective responsibility and the 'make peace happen' slogan should be enforced and made to guide the continent towards sustainable development. Therefore, this generation should not bequeath the issue of peace and development to the next generation. It is the ardent obligation and responsibility of this generation to carve out the structure for peace and endurable socioeconomic transformation and growth to coming generations. What will you do to make peace happen and ensure that conflicts and wars are eradicated on the continent?

The African Standby Force (ASF) must be oriented with an ideological Afrocentric agenda of; "in order to be free and at peace, we need to die for Africa." This ideological orientation must equally be implanted in the minds, behaviour, and attitude of Africans in building the continent as a veritable play in global politics and in ensuring the well-being of Africans. Turning now to the lessons of the past, we see that conflicts within and between the state in the continent takes an interesting shifting and periodical short-time patterns of rearrangement of broader alliances of interests between the conflict parties rather than integration of their strategic alliances of interest between the conflict parties, rather than integration of their strategic forces. The security challenges facing Africa are daunting and these security challenges as stated time and again concerns issues such as health-care, food security, shelter, human capital development, life and property.

In addition, poor governance gives the continent false dawns, and government's writ will run little further. The calamities of instability and insecurity have particularly stalled the African continent, mostly in terms of failure in meeting basic human needs and in the form of inter-ethnic wars. The continent has and continues to suffer by far the largest number of major conflicts during the 1990s, with more than 40% of the world's total (Novelli & Robertson, 2007:3) genocide in Rwanda; 'ethnic cleansing' in Sudan, diamond wars in Sierra Leone and Liberia, and ongoing rebel anarchy in Congo, Uganda, Somalia, Central Africa Republic to name a few incidents of grief magnitude and consequences. Apparently, the poster child of twentieth-century interstate conflict in the Republic of Somalia; what has been called "the planet's foremost failed state" (Bay 2008).

Much blood has been spelled in Africa's 54 current states since the creation of the Organisation of Africa Unity; and its transformation into the Africa Union has not abated the killing spree either. Will AU agenda of silencing the gun by 2020 be realised? What actually is wrong with the continent? Assuming the dynamics of Africa's 'failed state's requires a thorough x-ray of the notions of nationalism, decolonisation and nation-building concepts which must be adequately streamlined in light of the implication that violence affects social transformation as prefigured in the new humanism advanced by Fanon (1963:7). As much blood has been spilled in Africa's fifty or more years of independence, Cold war, underdevelopment and exploitation etc. much more irk has been spilled by academic and policy discourses to pathologies and dehumanise the African people. From the 'founding fathers' through the *'khaki-boys'* to the current sit-tight presidents, and without constructive and meaningful change, tomorrow for sure will be demonised in a way that Fanon rightly stated; the European seldom has a problem with figure of speech (1963:7). That statement stands tall today as it was in the 1960s, implying that Africa does not learn from history; but perpetuates the 'blame theory' which fails in providing the right approach to solving the predicament of the continent.

This no doubt, is what troubles one with reductionist narratives on the continent's people that is mired with cultural essentialism, social anomalies, and perplexity. The picture painted of Africa is a result of this narrative is not only fraught with assumptions that have constructed, conceptualise and even imbued with various clichés and different meanings through historical circumstances demarcating both the true construct of society and its cultural heritage. The African failed state construct is an extension of violence and the failure of the governance system in meeting basic needs – rising expectations – which have converged into "intensive destructive frustration" where the state has negated the fundamental needs of the people and equality with the in other parts of the world. Power to the people has only converged into money in my pockets for my use. The numerous inter and intra-conflicts make the continent very unsafe for citizens. The civilian dimension of security is very important as it concerns the security and safety of the ordinary citizens. Unfortunately, most states focus on the military dimensions not for the security of the civilians but to ensure the articulate self-interest of the various political leaders in power.

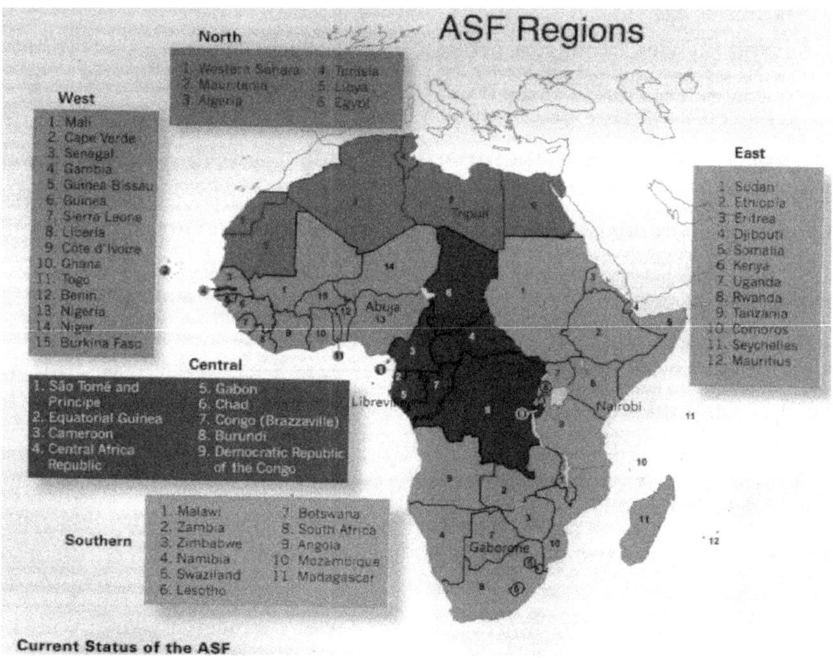

Source: Credit - Zinurine Alghali (2010) Conflict Trends, Issue 2. p.40

For these reasons huge amounts are invested in acquiring large quantities of weapons for human destruction. This is not what the continent needs at this point in time. Africa of the future should gun for friction-free region with happiness and quality welfare as the signpost. All these things are achievable with the right mindset, leadership and a proactive civil society backed by a competitive, progressive and productive private sector. Seen within these contexts, military solutions instead of political solutions are deployed for solving socio-economic problems. In most countries, the military nexus consumes the highest segment of the budget. While greater emphasis is centred on military security, little attention is directed towards meeting the needs of the people which is a source of growing insecurity within the continent.

Growing social and economic insecurity at home paves the increasing departure of Africa's human capital in search of greener pastures in the West. And so many young people continue to lose their lives as they attempt to cross the Sahara Desert and the Mediterranean Sea to fulfil their dreams of quality livelihood denied them back in their home country. Therefore, it is imperative to avert these situations to revitalise and entrench the belief set; 'we belong, we care, and we serve' (batho pele), which should form the core culture and re-orientation of the governance structure and functioning system. When the governance system puts people first and for real, the continent will make progressive development with enhanced quality livelihood.

Failure in addressing the security of the people in its totality, converges the place as "the future of the world" into a "crude empty barrel" – a land of hostilities, lawlessness, brutish, gangsters, war lords, militias and other imagery and sentiments befitting Western media's analysis. Insecurity of various kinds (food insecurity, health insecurity, road insecurity, water insecurity, and energy insecurity, insecurity to life and property and name the rest) is now a common phenomenon on the continent which breeds insecurity to human life and property. As part of the need to secure the safety of civilians in the wake of growing insecurity especially, arms conflict within the region, the creation of the African Standby force (ASF) could be seen as a welcome move to ameliorating the in secured status of civilians in the wake of armed conflicts. Violence, crime and insecurity in Africa appear to be motivated by poor governance, social phenomena and this is linked to the overall social struggle for survival. In short, violence, crime and insecurity are in many respects socio- eco-political phenomena and can only be addressed through a constructive and functional political and governance process.

In short, Africa strongly and urgently needs an African Social and Economic Standby Force (ASESF) to inject the idea and spirit of "*Ubuntu, Batho Pele and Harambee*" as the new ideological orientation for the sustainable transformation of the continent. There is no other way for the continent but taking proper sides on its development trajectory and owning it. Where does Africa stand at the moment on critical issues (a) democracy and the African political process (b) The institution of government; (c) social change and public policy including services delivery; and (d) Africa and the world? To be more precise, how has Africa realised the Millennium Development Goals (MDGs) as a barometer indicator for improving the wellbeing of the people. The cost of the economic or development policy Africa has embarked upon since independence is no more than what any society pays for eating its seed corn rather than planting it.

Such inconsistent and Euro-centric policy approach plunges the continent into conflicts, scorn and underdevelopment. The continent continues to operate in deficit and underdevelopment in ratio to its vast abundant resources that suffer from wrong exploitation, and waste leaving the people in wanton misery and abject poverty. With meagre investment in education, healthcare that continue to shrink compared to total investments in military hardware, the territory is well fertilised for insecurity, conflict and destruction. With so little investment in the basic structure of a strong economy, Africa's ability to produce the goods and services that people want has and continue to be disappointing even fifty or more years after independence. In short, Africans have been witnessing one disappoint after another, despite a marked improvement in the exploitation of natural resources. But this favourable exploitation has been swamped with corruption and waste leaving the vast majority of the population walloping in confusion and dismay.

Yet common sense teaches us that the idea of progress for the country as whole both reflect and demand continual economic betterment for the individual citizen. With such a development trend, Africans can hardly place or even imagine of an "African Dream" of quality living standards. It is not surprising that chaos, conflict, insecurity, and instability clouds the continent. It is not wrong to insinuate that the decision by African leaders to mortgage the continent's future emerges as a deliberate articulate interest of a select few in power positions to hold on to power no matter the cost infringe on the silent majority. It is time people, especially the silent and deprived majority should stand up as one and try to persuade one another of the truth, logic, and virtue of their own views and the falsity, irrationality, and downright evil of the others in order to secure the peace and security the society needs to make progress to maturity as a service delivery entity.

The Peace and Security Nexus

The peace and security nexus are intertwined factors for accelerating development. The June 1992 Agenda for Peace – report of the

Secretary General of the United Nations defines these concepts and examines them as integrally related and major elements of a holistic approach to maintaining national and international peace and security. To begin with Africa needs security in all aspects of life – food security, health security, water security, shelter security, energy security, security to life and property among others. The United Nations Development Programme (UNDP) in the 1994 Human Development Report links various humanitarian, economic and social issues to alleviate human sufferings and ensure security. The spectrum of peace and security activities are further codified in the 2008 UN Peacekeeping Operations: Principles and Guidelines (otherwise known as the Capstone Doctrine.

Security means more than the absence of conflict, and that sustainable peace will be achieved through a comprehensive approach to addressing issues relating to education, health, democracy, human rights, protection against environmental degradation, proliferation of deadly weapons, poverty alleviation and justice (see Annan 2001). As an integrally related and major element of the holistic approach, peace and security expands the prevention of conflict as well as post-conflict related actives that contribute to a comprehensive strategy for durable peace and security. It is for these reasons that socio-economic and political solutions are the sine qua non for resolving socio-economic and political problems and not through the barrel of the gun. The barrel of the ballot box provides the way forward to a better world construct. Supports early peace building, facilitates post-conflict peace building and security as well as prevents relapse of armed conflict and state of insecurity.

Source: Credit - Abiola and Otte (2014). Modern United Nations Peacekeeping: Towards A Holistic Approach to Addressing Conflict." Conflict Trends, Issue No. 2, 2014, pp5

The rise of private military or security establishments is growing significance of the failure of the regular security forces in maintaining law and order and ensuring the safety of citizens and the protection of property. The lost confidence and trust in government institutions is due to the pandemic of corruption that grips, and has eaten deep into the marrow of the body politics and governance structure of the country in question. As a result of this failure, people seem to have lost trust and confidence in the national security system and institutions of government. The security forces and institutions of government are now well established *'terrorist bodies'* acting with all impunity against citizens. This equally signifies state failure in ensuring the security of the state, lives and property. The private security forces are out for profit making like any other establishment. On the other hand, it equally undermines state apparatus. United Nation (2013) Security Council Resolutions 2086, of 21 January 2013, provides what could be seen as the minimum framework for sustainable peace and development. Figure on – Linkages and Overlaps in Peace and Security Activities depicts the interconnection between the various peace and security activities.

Once the education system, the judiciary and the security forces of a country are baptised with the spirit of corruption, insecurity and conflicts are bound to be a permanent feature of the politics and governance pattern of that country. This explains why many African countries have sunk so low in the governance, development, insecurity, chaos and conflict nexus of the country. A socio-political process is called for to restore normality and sustainable development. As noted by Hirschmann (2012); with the liberal peace paradigm dominating during the 1990s, peace was associated with democratisation and electoral participation was determined to be an integral human right hence, peacekeeping exit strategies were based on elections.

African countries need to improve on their governance architecture, human capital development, judicial system and other social areas that are mutually reinforcing, providing a holistic approach to addressing the underdevelopment pandemic characteristic of the continent. The policy and practice of participation must be reinforced, as well as the voices of the voiceless are made an inherent part of the policy articulation process. Development trajectory from below ensures some degree of trust in government, restores confidence and the feeling of belonging and partnership in state construct. It has to be partnerships that (i) reflect clear roles, (ii) comparative strengths and integrated approaches, (iii) exhibit some degree of local and national ownerships;

(iv) popular engagement and prioritisation availability of appropriate skills and equipment; (v) and rapid deployment capacity.

Status of Civilian Dimension Processes

Processes	AU Peace Support Operations Division (PSOD)	East African Standby Force (EASF)	Central African Multinational Force (FOMAC)*	ECOWAS* Standby Force (ESF)	SADC* Standby Force (SSF)	North Africa Regional Capabilities (NARC)
Framework documents	Have developed key documents and continue to generate the others required	Not yet approved	Not yet developed	Not yet developed	Not yet approved	Not yet developed
Civilian staff in Planning Element (PLANELM)	One position filled	All four positions filled	Two positions filled	Initiated the process to fill all four positions	One position filled	Planning to fill all four positions
Centres of excellence/training institutions	Utilises the regional centre of excellence and training institutions	Have one centre of excellence	None	Have tactical, operational and strategic centre of excellence	Have one centre of excellence	Have one centre of excellence
Civilian components	Utilises the civilian components of RSFs	Developing	Not yet developed	Not yet developed	Developing	Not yet developed
Civilian training for the ASF	Relies on APSTA* to coordinate training conducted by regional centres of excellence and training institutions for the ASF	Some conducted	Not yet initiated	Not yet initiated	Some conducted	Not yet initiated
Completion of Map Exercise (MAPEX)/ Command Post Exercise (CPX)	Completed a continental MAPEX and will be conducting a continental CPX in October 2010	Completed	Not yet conducted	Completed	Completed	Not yet conducted
Completion of Field Training Exercise (FTX)	To be conducted in the future	Completed	Not yet conducted	Completed	Completed	Not yet conducted
Standby roster	Have initiated the ASF Standby Roster process and will coordinate the RSF's hub roster	Developing database	Not yet initiated	Not yet initiated	Developing database	Not yet initiated

Source: Credit- ZINURINE ALGHALI, 2010, CONFLICT TRENDS ISSUE 2, 2010 P. 43S, South Africa

Nothing can be more valuable for the people of Africa than peace, unity, progress and stability. Indeed, there is no loftier or more responsible mission than that of safeguarding and strengthening peace and curbing the evil forces of aggression, inequality and militarism for the sake of the life of present and future generations. Africa without wars and without weapons or arms arsenal is the ideal Africa we all want. Africa has never striven for military superiority and never will. The goals of the people of Africa have been peace, development, equity since 6th March 1957. The continent has been steadily, slowly and progressively advancing towards this goal since the historic events that saw the creation of the Organisation of African Unity (OAU) in 1963. Though not as quickly as we would like. The transformation of the OAU into the African Union (AU) is just the first step towards the dream land of African sovereignty and development. It is now left to the AU to exert itself into the force of African peace, unity and development. African development is at a turn point and should shy any form of external and internal forces designed to derail the forward march to a united, strong and prosperous continent. Our thinking should be focused on eradicating endemic corruption, entrenched poverty; achieving these critical actions requires new approaches and new solutions. It requires readiness to abandon any selfish or narrow considerations and to take resolute steps to overcome the threats hanging over the African people.

Human Security and Sustainability

The security nexus embeds what economist Amartya Sen, terms 'the dangers of sudden deprivation.' Humanity must be protected from all forms of insecurity and deprivation. Society must work hard towards ensuring unanticipated threats to life which can take the form of natural disaster and conflict, which can also arise from economic crises and rapid environmental degradation brought about by climate change. African countries must prepare themselves to respond grievously to such threats which grievously undermine people's lives, livelihood and dignity. The dignity of life means ensuring security in all facets of life; food, health, education, shelter and water, which tighter ensures the right to the greatest happiness. When disaster strikes, society as whole must be prepared to offer short, medium and long-term support, sharing the responsibility to assist people in rebuilding their lives. The future of Africa must be constructed on the anvil of humanitarianism, human rights and sustainability. Three major challenges - natural and human created disasters, environmental degradation and poverty, and nuclear weapons – present future generations with threats and burdens that will only become greater the more we delay. Ikeda (2012:20) points out that humanitarianism, human rights and sustainability need to be the core elements of a future vision of:

- a world that, refusing to overlook human tragedy wherever it occurs, unites in solidarity to overcome threats;
- a world that, based on the empowerment of individuals, gives priority to securing the dignity and right of all people to live in peace;
- a world that, remembering the lessons of the pasty, does not allow unborn generations to inherit the negative legacies of human history and directs all its energies to transforming those legacies.

Due to increasing social disparity and growing inequality in society, most African governments deploy military rather than socio-politico-economic solutions to mounting tensions in society. Rising expectation has been replaced by rising destructive frustration. When two elephants fight it is the grass that suffers. The people though the custodian of power in society suffer most under the growing power of the military arsenal. What Africa of the future needs most is the arsenal and productive weapons for development not military arsenal for destruction? Africa has become the testing ground for western newly developed arsenal of destruction. Why the rise of terrorist and secessionist groups across the globe especially in Africa? The answer is simple: widening gaps in socio-economic livelihood of the people; the politics of exclusion and marginalisation, absence of the rule of law; social injustice; the rise of totalitarian or dictatorial regimes; majority domination over minority groups; the richer getting richer; and conversely, the poor and downtrodden getting poorer for each passing day and name the rest.

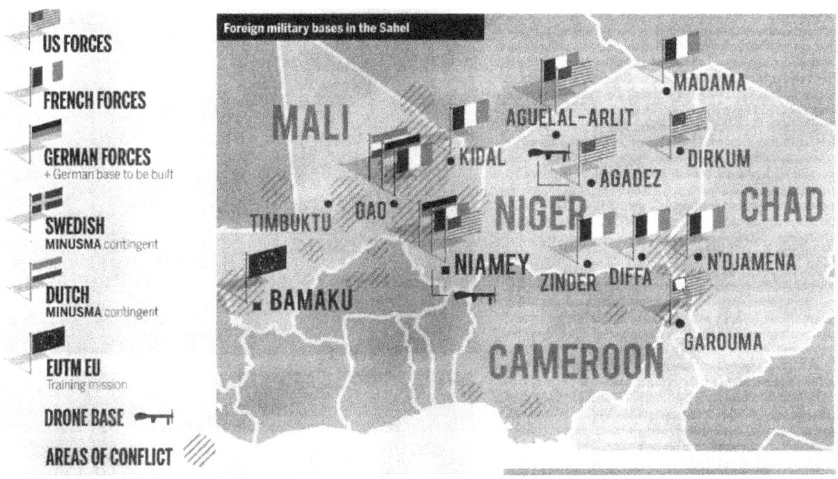

Source: Credit - Jeremy. Keenan 2017; War games in the Sahel; New African No 568 Jan. 2017 Pp 36- 41

The polarisation of inequality and affluence, marginalisation and exclusion fuels disgruntled, cheated and destructive groups ranging havoc towards innocent citizens. It was believed the end of the Cold War era would herald an era of peaceful co-existence daggering a new atmosphere for sustainable development. This has not been the case. Rather the end of the cold war has ushered an era of ostensible period of conflicts and terrorism worldwide. No one safe anywhere in the world today. Even countries like Sweden, the Netherlands, Canada and others that took a neutral position are today contributing troop to counter-terrorism. A combination of bad governance, poor leadership, and the politics of greed contribute to political instability; the spread of jihadism, Al Qaedaism, Arisal al-dinism, Boko Harmism and other destructive groups continuously contributing to a deteriorating security situation the world over.

Globalisation, the highest stage of scientific imperialism has injected new dynamic forces of destruction and conflicts within and between states. Some western countries have joined the bandwagon to pacifying the state of growing insecurity and conflicts. Today the Sahel region is the new testing ground where countries like Sweden, Holland and Canada are contributing troops particularly in Niger, Mali, and Burkina Faso. Keenan (2017:37) notes that Western concerns over the Sahel have been increasingly apparent since the late 2015, following the jihadist attacks on hotels in Bamako (Mali), Ouagadougou (Burkina Faso) and Grand Bassam (Cote D'Ivoire) in November 2015, January 2016 and March 2016 respectively, with contingents of several hundred Dutch (c.400), Swedish (c250) and German (c650) troops sent to the Sahel to support MINUSMA and the French forces.

Since mid-2016 there has been a worrying escalation of Western military intervene in the Sahel. The United States is financing the construction of a new three-kilometre runway and associated infrastructure for a drone base at Agadez (Niger). Apart from that the USA has drones, including MQ-9 Reaper drones stationed at Niamey supporting France's Operation Barkhane. Germany has equally joined the bandwagon with the establishment of a military base in Niger near the Mali border to house about 850 German troops in the Sahel. The French already have bases in Niamey and Madama close to Libya. France by 2014 had a 3000 troop across Mali, Niger and Chad. The United States has a contingent of 300 specialists from the air force and intelligence services deployed to its military base at Gaoura, Northern part of Cameroon. In conjunction with Israel, they are training Cameroon's Rapid Intervention Battalion (BIRs) in the fight against Boko Haram.

Of course, the Russians are not staying passively behind in this new race for the Sahel. Like the Gulf of Guinea with AFRICOM, already invaded by western military arsenal, the Sahel is now the surrogate region in the pursuit of European interest in Africa. During the Cold War era, the Democratic Republic of Congo was the centre of interest for the pursuit of precious minerals most needed in the space battle between the USA and USSR. The question that stands high on the agenda is whether Europe wants to *"Kill People and Break Things in Africa*" (Munson. 2009:35-44). According to the Russian authorities, they have heard the call of the majority of the Malian population for Moscow to be involved in resolving the crisis in Mali, and Russia is ready to help Mali fight against terrorism and to ensure its economic development. Is China staying behind? Of course not, as Africa has become the perfect springboard for Islamist, military and other destructive group extending their diabolic activities across the continent. Africa is also the solid testing ground for Western and Eastern new developed weapons of destruction.

The challenge for Africa is how to constructively reduce the state of ongoing conflicts contributing to the state of destructive development and creating a most conducive climate fostering sustainable, balanced and progressive development in the direction of improving the welfare of citizens. It is time the guns are silent once and for all on the continent with the military returning to the barracks where they belong. The continent's military arsenal for destruction should be converted into a military arsenal for constructive and sustainable development. Should not the engineering corps of the military be put into use for the development of society – building roads, bridges; farm-to-market roads and other activities that can improve on the income generating capacity of the citizens? African countries should not be at war with one another but at war with the state of increasing abject poverty, endemic underdevelopment, chronic corruption, injustice, marginalisation, discrimination and all that dehumanise the African as a human-being.

Apparently, the state of growing destructive military construct on the continent should be put on a journey of healing; cleansing it from the Eurocentric viruses that has invested the people for decades. The continent's governance system must be coaxed to solving critical fundamental questions; auditing itself in the direction of providing quality welfare to the people. Without Africans taking a deep look into its own soul, with a vision of the birth of desire to really change, the continent is set on a course of entrenched cultural and human destruction and underdevelopment. As noted earlier, military power is not and will never be the answer to the problems of the continent. The fight against poverty and underdevelopment; as well as against the various dissident groups calls for dialogue, consensus, reconciliation, the rule of law, equity in benefit-sharing; in short, a political process of give and take, participation, responsibility and obligations taking by all the stakeholders. It has to be a holistic and inclusive process. Too much money is spent throughout the continent on the weapons human of destruction rather than on the instruments needed for development and improving the quality of livelihood of the people. With such incoherent and yet wrong attitude and thinking, development can hardly come the way of the African people.

Some African countries are unrecognisable from the ramshackle structures of the yester years of colonial governance. With rapid increase in military expenditure, with a combination of weak economic performances, poor planning, a lack of experience and expertise and a dearth of investments in this sector has meant that the African continent has fallen behind the other developing nations even in the provision of basic needs such as clean portable water supply, reliable electric power supply, transportation networks, housing, ICTs, health and education infrastructure. Attention should be paid to the continent's infrastructure and building strong and functional institutions to accelerate the capable developmental process of the region; and not on the military arsenal gap that further puts the continent on the destructive and declining road into the world of poor-quality livelihood for most of the population.

Presently, the main problem for example, of the 34 African countries classified as least developed countries are most worrying. Can these countries ever catch-up with the industrialised North? I wonder given the numerous challenges African countries are confronting; the most outstanding being whether a United States of Africa will ever emerge or is this wishful thinking. We cannot run away from the reality of "the Iraqization of Africa" (Esterhuyse, 2009:21). But the Iraqization of the continent is perceived through western ideological orientation of providing military support to Africa in the form of (i) American interests and efforts coinciding with those of their traditional allies and partners in Africa; and (ii) the military effort must be integrated with the political and developmental efforts across the continent. Did the military effort of the USA and USSR in the Congo Republic ever coincide with the developmental interests of the people? It did not and will never be but contributes to the destruction and underdevelopment the country which is still ongoing; whereas in reality, the situation calls for a developmental process were Africa should take ownership of its own destiny as for too long the continent's future has been dictated by outsiders. This especially concerns the roles of Britain, Belgium, France and Portugal during the colonial era and the United States and the former Soviet Union during the Cold War. It further translates into an increasing uneasiness of the people of African with Western and other influences – sometimes interferences – in general and US influences – or interferences – in particular (Esterhuyse, op cit.).

Facing the new threat: Boko Haram and Ebola

The Preamble to the United Nations Organisation for Educational, Scientific and Cultural Organisation (UNESCO 2002) constitution states; "Since wars begin in the minds of men, it is in the minds of men that the defences of peace must be constructed." Joy (2015:41) opines that 'the Boko Haram insurgency is a war that begins in the minds;

therefore, to address this quandary, conflict transformation approaches and peace initiatives must target the thinking of people and communities." This new wave of extremism and form insurgency is causing serious havoc on the continent, different from the war of liberation so to state. What are the factors fuelling this kind of violence unleashed by a non-state actor across a number of African states? How can these group of actors justify what are legitimate desires? Why do others violate the freedom and liberty of others? What must be done to arrest these kinds of acts? These are challenging questions encircling the quandary of any insurgency group like Boko Haram. But what is Boko Haram?

Etymologically, Joy (2015:42) points out that Boko Haram comes from the Hausa and Arabic languages. In Hausa, 'Boko' literarily means, book, but figuratively is translated as learning or education. In Arabic, "Haram' is translated as forbidden, sin or unlawful.' Contextualised, this extremist group, Boko Haram stands for 'Western education is forbidden'. Emic studies reveal that this group prefers to be called '*Jama'atu Ahlis Sunna awaits wal-jihad*'. This means People Committed to the Propagation of the Prophet's Teachings and Jihad' or 'Association of Sunnas for the propagation of Islam and for the Holy War (see Sani 2011) This is a kind of religious crusade against western education, since etymologically, 'Boko' stands for learning or education. The group sees western education and culture as infiltrating through the forces of imperialism, colonialism, and globalisation into the Hausa / Islamic cultural values. The group Boko Haram is notorious in Nigeria, Cameroon, Chad and Niger. How to break down or transform such fundamentalist mindsets and radical behaviours that ignite extremism in many countries remains the challenging issue at hand?

A conflict situation arises between the Boko Haram ideology and western education and value systems. Such confrontation impedes development. This is not what the Africa of tomorrow should be gunning for. Ogoloma (2013) opines that conflict is a result of frustration when 'legitimate desires' of a person or group is denied them either directly or indirectly as a result of the way society is structured. The feeling of disappointment may lead such a man or group to express anger through violence that will be directed at those held responsible. This anger and violence can also be directed to people who are directly or indirectly related to those people that are said to be responsible. In the same vein, this could be seen consequences of rising expectation converging into rising destructive frustration. Here, Forje (2002:41) notes: The truth is the litany of Africa's woes is awful, painful and agonising. While the rest of the world is modernising, Africa remain a museum piece. The outcome of this coercive and alienative situation has seriously worsened prospects of development, leading to yet more alienation and coercion. The ultimate tragic consequences of this vicious circle since the granting of independence to former colonies are all to visible in contemporary Africa; with minor exceptions – physical infrastructures as well as social infrastructures have collapsed, economies are mires of chronic crisis, poverty has greatly intensified, and civil society is in revolt. The result is simply the outcome of denying and inhibiting the inalienable rights of the people.

It was the Greek historian Thucydides who in detailing the history of an infectious disease, called the 'plague of Athens,' and affliction that reduced its population by over one-third and contributed to that city-state's defeat in the Peloponnesian Wars. Turning to the Ebola Epidemic outbreak in a number of West African States in 2014 drawing from Thucydides; "The bodies of the dying were heaped one on top of the other and half-dead creatures could be seen staggering about in the streets or flocking around the fountains in their desire for water. For the catastrophe was so overwhelming that men, not knowing what would next happen to them, became indifferent to every rule of religion or law' (Price-Smith, 2009). Woldemariam and Giacomo, 2016:54) points out that epidemics have been critically important throughout history in determining the fates of communities, armies, states, and entire civilisations.

The 2014 Ebola epidemic threatened havoc in West Africa, undermining the recovery and well-being of the post-conflict states in Guinea, Sierra Leone, and Liberia while also bringing attention to how the affluent world is not immune to diseases in the global South in the context of a worldwide economy.' The disease was first discovered in 1976 in the Democratic Republic of Congo, with sporadic outbreaks in Uganda, Southern Sudan. Ebola is not the only diseases that has and continues to destroy the continent, but this was of a special character that it even threatened the West. And did highlight how poverty and inequality exacerbate the epidemic? How the legacies of violence and civil war complicate efforts against Ebola? What lessons can be drawn from crises and what does history teach the people of Africa?

Indeed, Africa is at the cross-road necessitating it to make the critical but right choice on which road to continue the journey. Of course, there the initial conditions that provide the options available at the juncture and provide incentives for the peoples' choices. Critical junctures are points in time at which a number of options are available to actors; often the choices are made necessary by the inadequacy of current institutions to deal with some problems at hand, hence the juncture. Africa failed with implementation of the Millennium Development Goals (MDGs). Today Africa is called upon to deliver on the Sustainable Development Goals (SDGs) and importantly to ensure a full implementation of the AU Agenda 2063. Such junctures are 'critical;' and provide the take-off direction for the continent to progressively move forward, increasing returns and not falling behind (Smith 2007:44-45). But take the case of my community, Bali Nyonga in the North West Region of Cameroon where not a drop of water has flowed in the pipe in the compound since 2nd March 2013. Why should people not suffer from all sorts of water borne diseases? What quality of livelihood are the Council and Government offering its citizens?

Ebola is not the only killer disease on the continent. But actions taken in bringing Ebola under control demonstrated that killer diseases like malaria could be easily tackle provided it started affecting people in the developed world. As long as Africans die of these diseases and Europe is safe so be it. The last Ebola outbreak in West Africa should teach African countries the need to deepen their healthcare system and to ensure the provision of basic health care facilities to all citizens. Must African leaders be parading the corridors of hospitals in Europe for their personal healthcare facilities? Why can a proper health system be put in place on the continent? The adequate provision of fundamental human basic care constitutes a crucial part of the security nexus of the continent. Richards Paul (2016) asserts that: "crucially, the humanitarian response to the disease was most effective in those parts where it supported these initiatives and actually hampered recovery when it ignored or disregarded local knowledge...the rest of the world ought to ponder their courage". Use must be made of local science knowledge in improving our security in all facets. What is happening is the application of wrong strategies as Gills (2016) asserts: *"when political meltdown and clan violence threatened a humanitarian catastrophe, almost the entire independent aid world called for military intervention...."*

Without security in all its facets we are not respected as human beings; and sovereignty remains nothing but shamble of a ghost town. Every state must defend itself against any attempt at interference in its affairs. It must defend itself against subversive and destructive elements and finally, against people spying for other countries. Respect for the sovereignty of a country means that the people continuously make efforts in keeping their homes clean and intact; there should be interference in its internal affairs and consequently no demands that it changes its laws and progressive pattern of development that is in line with the aspirations and needs of the people. If Africa embarks on the road that in effect is recommended by the Eurocentric ideological thinking, it will only be entangled in endless conflicts and constantly subjugated to the arena of permanent destructive development.

As such, SDGs and AU Agenda 2063 in partnership with the progressive national development plans of African states provides the basis for construct a developed and secured continent even with the turbulent global environment. Therefore, this book calls for strengthening, and searching for new forms of cooperation and partnership in the fields of education, medicine, culture, arts, technology, and security. The steady development of various ties among African countries and peoples on the one hand, and between the continent and the rest of the world on the other, remain an essential input condition for strengthening peaceful coexistence and relationships among all nations of the world. I strong hold the opinion like many other Africans that the continent is ready and will be doing everything necessary to achieve these ends

Promoting peaceful coexistence and progressive development that meets the needs of all citizens is the surest means of having a secured world free from hunger, wars and conflicts. Natural disasters may strike; but cooperation among and between nations provides the solid anvil for coming to the aid of the affected and needy. Can we provide that basic assurance to all citizens so that they can happily live well on planet earth with which African governments have failed woefully; we must respect our sovereignty for others to respect same? Therefore, cooperation in spreading the ideals of peace, stability, justice, rule of law, disarmament and international security; in providing more objective information and enabling nations to learn more about one another's lives; and in promoting a spirit of mutual understanding and concord among them is necessary

Facing the New Global Pandemic: COVID-19 Curse or Blessing for Africa

There is a new global health pandemic - Corona virus - that spears no one, king, queen, president, prime-minister, judge or the common citizens. We all are in for it. We are all naked. Is it a curse or blessing to humankind? So far, the causalities for the continent have not been heavy. When the COVID-19 tsunami strikes Africa, heaven or hell will open its gates given our super health facilities and living conditions which African leaders have neglected in building but prefer flying to Europe for their own treatment forgetting about the health of their citizens. Some leaders have been absentee landlords or own health facilities in Europe.

The general fear is that when COVID-19 hits Africa with the same tenacity and intensity with which it is terrifying Europe and America, the likelihood would be serious depopulation of the continent – call it the "New African Plague." The HIV-AIDS did render its destruction on the continent and still does; malaria and other killer diseases have been doing so for the past many decades. What hope is there for Africa when COVID-19 seriously strikes the continent?

Like in many areas, Africa has never been prepared to tackle serious crisis. We have been good at accumulating and siphoning the continent's wealth into personal accounts abroad. Could this pandemic provide the necessary wake-up call and opportunity for Africa to seriously rethink its developmental strategies; invest more in human capital development; put an end centralised authoritarian hegemonic governance and open the way to a more structure-functional democratic/administrative governance system. The entire world panics as a result of COVID-19. The world remained mote with malaria and other killer diseases in Africa and in the less developed world. The speed at which researchers the world-over are racing to fine a vaccine for COVID-19 shows how science and technology have greatly improved our way of livelihood. It tells us the importance of human capital development in the transformation and sustainability of society.

In some countries, Cameroon for example, that human capital development has been denied our children for five years because of greed, power and wealth accumulation by a select group that fell assimilation, annexation and centralised hegemonic power accumulation is the way distained form of governance. People wake up with gun-shoots as breakfast, lunch and dinner. The silent genocide goes on unabated. Genocide has killed more people in Cameroon. Coronavirus is yet to show its ugly head of death in this part of the continent. We pray it spares the people who have suffered so much for no crime committed since 2016, but because they ask for the full respect of their fundamental human rights.

There comes a moment of truth, which is to decide what form of governance a society should put in place to ensure the smooth functioning of that society. That moment has come for Africa to wake-up and fight the root causes of the numerous problems plaguing the African society. Strange enough, we know the answers, but the political will is lacking to do what is right, just, good, ignorance irresponsibility and true because of articulate self-interest. What gets into my pocket is what matters. The collective self-interest is thrown into the shadow of destruction.

What are African countries doing to face malaria and other killer diseases that are within the continent? What collective actions did we take or learn from the 'embola' out break. The realities are clear before our eyes now and puts into question the structures and functioning of our governments and institutions. The only way to save our continent from the flaws built into our governance system is to return power to the people and construct a continent that understands, appreciates and applies the basic tenets of democratic governance.

There those leaders who want to turn the democratic governance system into a personal or family dynasty; that the structure and change if governance leaves the husband to the wife or to the son. That is why the continent is pregnant with long serving heads of state, and constitutions have to be changed following how the incumbent sleeps at night. With such attitude, the continent will always remain at the receiving end or at the bottom of the ladder of development.

With COVID-19, whether or not it hits Africa with the same intensity and tenacity like Europe, we will have to face numerous challenges as well as drastically restructure how we govern ourselves. When the continent finds itself in a mess, its more excitable and forward-looking progressive leaders would warn us to pull our forces and resources together (like Kwame, Nyerere, Mboya, Biko, Mandela and others did); some like Mobutu and others conjured in trenches, others turn to still-darker horrors of selling the continent for thirty pieces of silver.

Following Hanson (2020) "Authoritarian and petty fascist, eager to issue endless edicts, moult their exoskeletons, as if under their chrysalis suits they were always caudillos, waiting to be reborn with sunglasses and epaulettes. But a free and empowered people, even in times of mortal danger, long burse on a Bill of Rights, is hard to subjugate or shut up, even after over a month spent locked up in their homes. Thank God, we have a Constitution quite different from those of European nations, which are themselves far superior to other alternatives. In these strange times, American individualism and the Bill of Rights that birthed it are still proving, for a while longer, too strong for the natural forces of fascism masquerading as 'we had to destroy freedom to save it'."

To being with, all development plans will not be realised. It will give room for the siphoning of resources and quality of life currently at the bottom level will seriously deteriorate. Most families that rely on remittances will be in great danger. It is estimated that remittances will drop drastically and the social and economic injury to various families will be devastating. Africa is in for a long haul of difficulties. The people are challenged to put their right-thinking cap to start salvaging the situation and as Ngwanyam (2020:11) points out: "we must put in place a new way of doing business in Africa by Africans for Africans (D I Y=Do it yourself. Africa must first wake up awareness and realise the need for change. The problem, just like the COVID, must be big enough to warrant us to think it is important to change."

According to McCormack (2020) writing in the National Review notes that: "Although there is still much we don't know about the coronavirus, we know enough to say that it is far dangerous and deadly than the flu. It took twelve months and 61 mill infections for the HiNi swine flu to kill 12,500 Americans in 2009-10. The Centre for Disease control estimated that the season's flu killed 34,200 Americans during 2018-19 flue seasons. In 2019, car crashes killed 38,800 Americans. As for the new coronavirus? On March 20, the death toll in the United States was 225. By April 20, the coronavirus had killed more than 42,000 Americans. The New Atlantis produced a chart that starkly portrays just how quickly COVID-19 has become one of the leading causes of death in the United States. No nation can afford to endure a lockdown until a vaccine is developed for the new coronavirus. But having a proper understanding of the virus's past and present danger matters. Knowing that it is extremely unlikely that the threat will be gone once the first wave passes will help guide the government, business, and individuals to take precautions that will limit the virus's death toll in the months to come."

These figures (which is not the end, and which will keep rising across the world) tell us something we have often forgotten about our governance structure and system. In short, if African democracy has so far failed to sustain itself under myriad pressures, then this period the period for serious rethinking and restructuring so that we have a truly functional democratic system that caters for the life and soul of the people and nation.

Many African countries failed to meet the Millennium Development Goals (MDGs), and very likely they will fail meeting Sustainable Development Goals (SDGs); and very likely AU Agenda 2063 will eventually face the same faith. Africa is getting back to the failure of the Lagos Plan of Action (LPA). COVID-19 will torpedo the AU Agenda 2063. With the inevitable arrival of COVID-19 in Africa is a challenge to the continent's democracy and development.

There is going to be a record collapse in the continents development even with the efforts being injected by the Africa Development Bank Group and the International Monetary Fund (IMF) for exempt some African countries from corona virus debt relief. The amounts will make the poor and most vulnerable members of the IMF to cover their debt obligations for an initial phase over the next six months as well as help them channel more of their scarce financial resources toward vital emergency medical and other relief efforts in the face of ramping coronavirus pandemic. The African Development Bank Group deploys its full weight of emergency response support to assist Africa at this critical juncture. According to Akinwani Adesina, President of the African Development Bank Group, "we must protect lives. This facility will help African countries to fast track their efforts to a contain the rapid spread of COVID-19.The facility entails 5.5 billion for sovereign operations in African Development Bank countries; and 3.1 billion dollars for sovereign regional operations for countries under the African Development Fund that caters to fragile countries. An additional 1.35 billion will be directed to private sector operations (Ntui, 2020:5).

With COVID-19 the truth is that there is no place for any African leader to hide anymore. Whether COVID-19 will put a stop for African leaders who spend the tax-payer money to go abroad of foreign medical trips at the slightest discomfort is one thing that will be reversed when the pandemic is over. In short, if African democracy is sustain itself under myriad pressure then this would be the moment. In the view of Hanson (2020); "Authoritarians and petty fascists, eager to issue endless edicts, moult their exoskeletons, as if under their chrysalis suits they were always caudillos, within to be reborn with sunglasses and epaulettes. But a free and empowered people, even in times of mortal danger, long nursed on a Bill of Rights, is to subjugate or shut up, even after over a month spent locked up in their homes. Thank God, we have a Constitution quite different from those of European nations, which are themselves far superior to other alternatives."

When rich nations are in panic mode stating thousands of ventilators are not enough, when the unwanted visitor – COVID-19 – come calling and taking permanent residence in Africa, is just to light how poor the 54 African nations in Africa are to fight against the encroaching COVID-19.

African countries have consistently neglected their country's health and education sectors despite several pledges to improve these vital sectors for the sustainable transformation of the society, and of which most countries have fallen through the cracks in fulfilling this fundamental commitment.

Africa is still in the early stages of the pandemic with fallouts we cannot predict at this stage, but what is sure it provides the structural anvil as a "wake-up call" for governments to prioritise quality health care for the people as well as improving on their status of human capital building.

The Awaited Great Recession

Africa should prepare itself in welcoming the awaited serious recession. The continent's economy could shrink by as much as 5.1%. Africa is seen as the world fast growing region in recent years; that growth is likely to drop drastically. Sub-Saharan Africa could need an economic stimulus of as much as USA$100bn (80bllion pounds) to help it recover. Africa alone will not be able to contain the disease and its impact on its own. It is predicted that Africa's economic recovery will be between 2.1% and 5.1% smaller by the end of the year from a growth of 2.4% of last year, Corona virus will cost Africa USA$37bn to USA$79bn in output losses this year because oil trade and value chain disruption among other factors.

The economies worst hit by the fallout from the COVID-19 pandemic will be those which are dependent on the export of oil and minerals such as Nigeria, Angola, South Africa. The spectre of a "serve food-security" as agricultural production and imports fall, notes the World Bank assessment. African economies are starving at an abyss. So bad would the situation be that "without help and action now, poor countries and vulnerable communities could suffer enormous devastation" (Tedros Adhanoums Ghebreyesus, WHO Director General).

From an academic and research perspective, it is hoped the pandemic can stimulate greater within and cross-border inter university cooperation and research related activities. Currently, there is little cooperation among African universities and research institutions. For example, what form of research cooperation that exists between universities within the same country? Here again we find another wrongly placed priority in the domain of human capital development which constitute the anvil for sustainable take-off to industrialisation, entrepreneurship, innovation and development. With more inter-university and research institutes co-operation and exchanged of ideas and knowledge within and between African institutions of higher learning, Africa can start cracking the code for industrialisation.

As already mentioned, the continent should start expecting serious drop in remittances. Those who remit financial support to their families back home are now in serious financial crisis abroad. The recovery period to normal financial support remitted back home may be longer than expected. The worst of the worst seems to be in the rear-view mirror. Ahead: The Future. For now, Africa is not at the centre of epic of COVID-19 and first wave is yet to strike the region and the consequences of the various waves will be horrific for the continent. Therefore cooperation, solidarity, understanding at this early stage and thereafter remains vital in addressing the pandemic. What to do about opening up is the challenge. How is Africa going to cope? Continuing hanging on the non-democratic governance system will be the doom. Whatever the case, Africa needs new pyjamas as the current generation is stuck in the old fashion way that does more harm than good. The response to the COVID-19 crisis is a case study in governmental ineptness.

Africa has been castrophysically stuck with centralised hegemonic governance construct and poor administrative structure which has been generally has been the misguided way of the continent for the past couple of decades. Africa is good only in constructing and reconstructing constitutions to favour the incumbent Head of State. It is time the private sector, civil society and the academia in African countries wake-up to facing the challenges that have befallen the country and people. A well-informed and enlightened public and a political educational structure now stand as the Godfather for making the vital decisions facing the continent. History comes back to provoke us in the new renaissance order – a strong and united African continent, and finally, rebellion as captured in the footage from the unholy Berlin Conference that partitioned Africa into more than thirty pieces of gold. Africa has to emerge out of the quarantine of colonialism and underdevelopment. The current image of Africa is so far away from the truth and reality that only makes the continent to sink deeper and deeper in the jungle of poverty and oppression and submission. Time for change is here; Africa must move fast now.

The Growing Terror-Crime Nexus and the New Danger Zone: Piracy and Armed Robbery

Deep in the Horn of Africa and along the Gulf of Guinea has a risen a new form of criminality terrorising the livelihood of citizens, making Africa an unsafe region. The Boko Haram's, piracy and terrorist activities make life unsafe for the silent majority. Our daily security is constantly threatened. State terrorism is fast growing in the name of keeping peace, a peace that does not hold an iota of justice. The entire continent is infested with arm robbery. Insecurity and injustices threatens the state of peace; the path to economic growth, sustainable development, thereby contributing to underscoring the state of quality livelihood of the people.

Entrenched bureaucratic machinery, authoritarian regime structures and lack of institutional capacity are existing obstacles to peace, stability, economic growth and development. When leaders become blind to justice, rule of law, job creation and inclusion, youths, as the bastion of society, start finding alternative means for quality livelihood. We do not need to go far to see why many young Africans force themselves into slavery as the escape route for their wellbeing. The continent's bourgeon human power is trained for export and use by the developed countries. Who is developing who, when, how and by what means? This chapter strongly advocates for a progressive Afro-centric, people-inclusive strategic approach for the continent's transformation. The departure from learning and the perusing of one's history has once again done the black race damage. There seems to be no mouth-piece to argue and push forward the kind development the continent greatly deserves.

Humanity under Threat

Insecurity in Africa and other parts of the world how vulnerable we are even in the wake of increasing technological developments. From the preceding pages, it is with the deep regret of all people that the arms arsenal race has become one of the signs of our times, primarily through actions of the developed countries. With the past couple of decades, the degree of insecurity and the arms arsenal race has acquired new characteristics. We live in a world of complexities which is changing faster than our capacity to learn its complexities. The new world forces us to cope with more and more complex situations, while leaving us with less and less chances to predict or even imagine our future. The rapid changing nexus requires leaders who stay ahead of the speed of change.

Humanity is under threat and Africa is at the receiving end, not only from these different kinds of weapons of mass destruction but also the effects of environmental destruction caused mostly by the developed polities and the fast-expanding forces of the 'globalisation' wave. World development is now at a turning point. This is true of all countries, regardless of their social systems, and is due to the scientific and technological revolution with its various consequences, to qualitative changes in the correlation of social and political forces in the world arena, and to the mounting struggle between the forces of war and peace, justice and injustice in which the cardinal question of our times is being decided: whether or not nuclear catastrophe; endemic poverty and a gross affluence will be allowed to break out and jeopardise the existence of humanity.

First, the perfection of weapons of mass destruction, factors propelling the state of insecurity have attained a high degree of sophistications and reached a point at which any further progress now constitute a serious threat to the existence of humanity on planet earth. Nobody is safe from accidents that could result in disaster whether from the outfalls of the weapons of mass destructions or from environmental factors.

Second, weapons that are innocuously called 'conventional' are now acquiring the qualities of weapons of mass destruction. Some of these weapons are constantly being tested across the world, and there are little differences between these 'conventional' weapons and those of mass destruction. With the passage of time conventional arms have acquired qualities that make them ever more dangerous. The various terrorist groups can now turn the simplest weapons into that of mass human destruction. And there seem to be no limits to their 'improvement'. No one is safe anywhere in the world today.

Third, new types of weapons are appearing on the scene. So far they are called weapons based on new physical properties, i.e. laser, radiological, particle-beam weapons etc. etc. The advent of these new types of weapons (along the 'third generation' nuclear arms) has spawned the 'Star Wars' concept. Who knows what technological developments would put in the market in no distant future?

Humanity is under threat in the nuclear age from many and varied perspectives. We are well aware of the great complexity of the-present-day world construct, and of the profound contradictions and inter-relationships that exist in it. In short, the global environment is multifarious, with each and every one state with its own interests and copes with its own problems. And yet, all the states are closely linked with one another. What is more, in many respects they depend on each other. This is the result of an objective and ongoing trend of internationalisation not only in the field of production but in the entire social life of contemporary humanity. In our day internationalisation is developing especially quickly on the basis of the scientific and technological revolution. Modern means of communication have made our vast planet fairly small. In these conditions it is vital that all of us learn to live together, irrespective of existing differences. And to leave together, means respecting each other's interests and to be especially considerate to the security interests of every nation (Zaggladin, 1986:41).

Our world is dominated by two opposing systems – capitalism and socialism; developed and developing countries; rich and poor. It is a question of the 'Global and National rich and the Global and National rich at the throat of each other. From the viewpoint of humanity's future, the most important contradictions in the present-day world affect relations between states belonging to the two opposing social systems. We are convinced that the contradictions between the two social systems and their historical dispute, in which humanity's further destinies are being decided, should be resolved by means of peaceful competition between these two systems. In other words, we need peaceful co-existence and cooperation among states, regardless of their social structures and irrespective of existing differences and contradictions between social systems, states or group of states.

Only through peaceful coexistence and peaceful competition, under the rule of law and justice can we address issues which currently place humanity in the realm of threat under the auspices of:

- **International Security: The Military Sphere** (i.e. (i)nuclear states to renounce war, both nuclear and conventional, against one another or against third states: (ii) to prevent the arms race from spreading to space, to discontinue all tests of nuclear arms and destroy all their stocks, and (iii) to ban and scrap chemical and other weapons of mass destruction: for African countries to silence the sound of war
- **International Security: The Political Sphere:** (i) to strictly respect in international practice for the sovereign right of every nation to choose its own way and forms of development: (ii)to settle existing international crises and regional conflicts effectively, by political means: (iii) to elaborate a complex of reliably verifiable measures aimed at improving trust between states and at providing them with effective guarantees that they will not come under attack from outside and that their borders will be inviolable; (iv) working out effective measures of preventing international terrorism, including those ensuring the safety of international land, air and sea communications.
- **International Security And Economic Problems;** (i) excluding all forms of discrimination from international relations and for rejecting the policy of economic blockades and sanctions, unless this is recommended by the international community; (ii)a joint search for ways to solve the debt problem in a mutually acceptable and fair manner; (iii) establishing a new world economic order which should guarantee the equal economic security of states.(iv) elaborate principles whereby part of the resources released as a result of military budget cuts should be used for the benefit of the international community,

especially the developing countries: (v) the need to pool efforts in exploring and peacefully using outer space and in coping with global problems crucial to the future of civilisation.

- **International Security; Humanitarian Aspec**ts: (i) cooperation in spreading the ideals of peace, disarmament and international security; in providing more objective information and enabling nations to learn more about one another's lives; and in promoting a spirit of mutual understanding and concord among them; (ii) eradicating genocide, apartheid, advocacy of fascism or any other racial, national or religious exclusiveness, and discrimination against people on this basis; (iii) expanding international cooperation in the implementation of people's political, social and personal rights on the basis of respect for the laws of each country; (iv) solving problems related to the reunification of families, marriage and promotion of contracts between people and organisation in a positive and human spirit; (v) strengthening, and searching for new forms of cooperation in the fields of culture, art, education, medicine, science and technology.
- **Specific African Situation Impacting On Its Security Nexus and the Global Community:** There are specific African scenarios like poverty, corruption, and poor governance seriously threatening the security nexus of the continent in particular. Even though corruption is a worldwide phenomenon that of Africa stings couple with poor governance places the people at the bottom of the ladder in greater vulnerability, jeopardy and serious threat of destruction. We are convinced that the persistent, undeviating and even more dynamic and creative implementation of policies designed towards averting insecurity, poverty and exclusion will help not only to preserve peace and reduce the threat of human destruction Africa needs to build a truly a national, regional and continental reliable system of security and create favourable conditions for the struggle of the nation-states for a better life. Africa needs sustainable democratic rule and economic growth to prevent and eliminate the threat of human insecurity and disaster without mobilising the broadest possible social force. It is imperative for the continent to continue to develop effective ties and cooperation with all democratic progressive and anti-war and insecurity forces.

Only by seeking the best possible, i.e. peaceful, internal and external conditions for the development of a people-focused society, we contribute to strengthening of sustainable peace and development throughout the world. In the spirit of these lofty ideals, African states should continue to regard it as their paramount duty to help strengthen the cooperation for unity and integration of the continent while respecting the right of every nation to live by its own laws and choose its own road of development for the overall security and wellbeing of the people.

The challenge of our time stems from the fact that human civilisation has created, unfortunately, highly effective means of self-destruction. We have placed ourselves in an unprecedented foolishness of a crime to have the worst things happen – poverty in the midst of plenty; insecurity without producing the weapons of human destruction but using these instruments to destroying ourselves. But human insecurity and destruction is produced through poor policy articulation, greed and governance. There is an enormous responsibility as it is our duty in helping to resolve this task in very best way possible. To achieve that goal, we should fall back on exploiting to the best of our ability existing concepts inherent in our cultural heritage and values which are part of our upbringing. I am talking of revitalising and beating together, the drum of *(Ubuntu, Harambee, and Batho Pele)* among others as strategic instruments piloting our drive for development and quality livelihood.

The recently signed continental Free Trade Area (CFTA) by 44 of Africa's 55 countries in Kigali (Rwanda) is an act rekindling Africa's Unity and integration and above all focused on improving on the quality wellbeing of the citizens - is the long-cherished dream of Kwame Nkrumah for a United continent – building the Africa We Want. The treaty should be seen as the first step towards a positive reconstruction of Africa as against the 1884 Berlin Conference which deconstructed Africa by various European powers and effectively led to the destruction of the region as a potential global force politically and economically. The Kigali accord constitutes the right step of putting together what 1884 Berlin Conference torn asunder. The CFTA is knitting back and should not be allowed to go the way of the Lagos Plan of Action.

As such the Kigali accord constitutes the beginning of a New African Political and Economic Development Strategy (NAPEDS) well-articulated by Cyril Ramaphosa (President of South Africa) in this these words: "We must rig ourselves of this colonial mentality that demands we rely on other people's currency. Perhaps the day, the hour and the moment could have arrived for us to create a single African currency. Our focus should not be on our individual countries but on the continent as a whole, to unlock greater opportunities and capabilities" (Versi (2018:13). Currently, intra-African trade is around 16% of the total African trade; its equivalent forms over 50% in Asia and 70% in the European Union. In both cases, greater trade integration has resulted not only in poverty alleviation but also, unprecedented rises in prosperity. As we trade more among ourselves, African firms will become bigger, more specialised, and more competitive internationally. There can be question that this is a historical moment in the unfolding history of the continent. It is a moment to cherish and celebrate, notes Versi Anver (2018:13). A common currency and passport will be the greasing icing of the cake of African unity and sustainable transformation with the people as the focus of development. African unity and integration is an issue the continent cannot afford to let such a golden opportunity pass by.

Currently, quality livelihood on the continent is the least in the world. Following the 2016 Human Development Index (HDI) 19 of the least-developed countries in the world are in Africa with Central Africa topping the list as demonstrated in Table 8:1: Top 10 Least-developed Countries in Africa.

Table 8:1: 1-0 Least Developed African Countries

Country	Ranking
Central African Republic	1
Niger	2
Chad	3
Burkina Faso	4
Burundi	5
Guinea	6
South Sudan	7
Mozambique	8
Sierra Leone	9
Eritrea	10

Source: Adopted from the 2016 Human Development Index, United Nations

Table 8:2: Africa's 10 developed Countries show the Seychelles ranked number 63 in the world with Norway leading the ranking. Seychelles is ranked the most the most developed country in Africa with the Central African Republic ranked the least developed in the world. The HDI emphasises that people and their capabilities should be the ultimate criteria for assessing the development of a country, not economic growth alone.

Table 8.2: Top Developed African Countries

Country	Ranking
Seychelles	1
Mauritius	2
Algeria	3
Tunisia	4
Libya	5
Botswana	6
Gabon	7
Egypt	8
South Africa	9
Cape Verde	10

Source: Adopted from the 2016 Human Development Index, United Nations

By and large, the security nexus of the continent builds and depends on a number of inter-related activities, concretely and comprehensively coordinated within the context of having strong democratic institutions, economic growth and equity in sharing the wealth of nation. Looking at the 2016 Democracy Index which according to the Economist Intelligence Unit, placing Mauritius as Africa's most democratic country. Mauritius is ranked number 18 in the world, with Norway leading the rankings. In contrast, the weakest democratic state in Africa is Chad, ranked number 165 in the world, with North Korea as the lowest-placed country. Tables 8::3 and 8.4 respectively depict these rankings of Top 10 democracies and 10 weakest democracies in Africa. Arguments in the democracy-development nexus show that one is not dependent on the other. For example, China is not considered as one of the least democratic states in the world, but is economic development has been impressive better than most democratic countries in the world. The link between democracy and development is weak in that there is a growing situation of authoritarian states which are showing signs of reaping the benefits of economic development while evading any pressure to relax their political control (Sikuka. 2017; Mesquita and Downs, 2005).

India and Singapore are countries that have managed to perform significantly better economically than democracies in the Western world.

African countries could do the same, provided they shone the orientation of the 'president for life' nexus which has eaten deep-into the marrow of African leaders.

Table 8:3 Top 10 African Democracies

Country	Ranking
Mauritius	1
Cape Verde	2
Botswana	3
South Africa	4
Ghana	5
Lesotho	6
Tunisia	7
Namibia	8
Zambia	9
Tanzania	10

Source: The Economist Intelligence Unit Limited (2017) UK

Table 8:4. 10 Weakest Democracies in Africa

Country	Ranking
Chad	1
Central African Republic	2
Equatorial Guinea	3
Democratic Republic of the Congo	4
Guinea-Bissau	5
Libya	6
Eritrea	7
Sudan	8
Burundi	9
Djibouti	10

Source: Adopted from The Economist Intelligence Unit Limited (2017) UK

The case of Seychelles and Libya is interesting in the development-democracy nexus. For example, Seychelles, a country not even among the top 10 democracies in Africa, is ranked as the most developed country on the continent. Libya which is ranked among the 10 worst democracies in Africa is regarded as one of the most developed. In contrast, countries like Namibia, Tanzania and Zambia considered among the most democratic states are not considered to be the most developed countries in Africa. On the whole, countries like Botswana, Cape Verde, Mauritius, South Africa and Tunisia are regarded as the most developed and the most advanced democracies in Africa (Said, 2000: Sikuka, op cit., Adejumobi, 2000; Svasand, 2011).

Apparently, African countries should key together a number of policy options, strategies and measures considered relevant and pivotal as major ingredients for the continent's development and democracy and as the linchpin towards ensuring a united, integrated, secured, peaceful and developmental continent and quality livelihood for all citizens. People all over the continent should be conscious of the fact that they can change a corrupt system and must work towards that goal.

As a result of poor governance, escalating inequalities and deepening poverty in society, the people are not able to benefit from the vast natural resources which, has unfortunately, become a curse rather than blessings. There is growing evidence of government failure and responsibility to protect citizens; rather there is mounting state use of force against its citizens as demonstrated throughout the continent, with the ongoing crisis in the two English-speaking regions of Cameroon. Growing military intervention in the domestic affairs of the state raises more questions about the role of the military and safety of citizens. Why has crime rates and insecurity soared throughout the continent? Something is wrong with the state of affairs in most African countries. We only need to look at the kind of governance system in place. Is it one that caters for the interests of the people or one that the people must cater for the interest of those elected to be at the helm of the state?

A vital function of government is providing welfare and security in all dimensions to citizens. Thus, the security in all dimensions, health, education, food, housing, water, safety to life and property must be a top priority of any meaningful government. One thing most needed is inclusiveness, participatory governance and great respect to the rule of law – creating or reinvigorating a legal system that keeps at bay any form of authoritarian systems of governance.

The Dynamics of Piracy – From Somalia to the Gulf of Guinea

Oil piracy in the Gulf of Guinea has to be understood within the dynamics of the huge hydrocarbon potential of the region. This area which stretches from West Africa to Southern Africa, covering a coastal arc of 6000 km include countries like Angola, Benin, Cameroon, Democratic Republic of Congo, Peoples Republic of the Congo, Cote d'Ivoire, Gabon, Ghana, Guinea, Guinea Bissau, Liberia, The Gambia, Sierra Leone, Nigeria, Sao Tome and Principe, Senegal, Togo. Chad could be included due to its oil resources being piped through Cameroon to the coast of the Gulf of Guinea. The region is endowed with large reserves of mineral and marine resources, such as oil, diamonds, gold, fish and so forth, which highlight the region's importance and value as an area of global geo-maritime importance.

Nearly 70% of Africa's oil production is concentrated in the area. It is estimated that since 1999, western oil companies have invested between US$40 to US$60 billion in the Gulf of Guinea alone. In addition, 2.5mn barrels of daily oil production capacity of Nigeria and pipelines have been shut down due to theft, lowering capacity by 400,000 barrels a day. Piracy tends to be conducted or supported by marginalised communities that have not been participating in economic development (Ben-Ari, 2013:12). But piracy is not the only security threat at sea. Piracy has drawn attention to wider problems of maritime insecurity such as trafficking and smuggling of humans, weapons and narcotics, and illegal and unregulated fishing activities.

The region's untapped oil reserves hold prospects of supplying significant quantities of oil to the global economy. The huge investment in oil extraction in the Gulf of Guinea means that seaborne oil trade increases with a high volume of maritime traffic, including oil-laden vessels. The region equally provides a shorter route to Europe. Therefore, keeping these shipping lanes open and safe is vital for world supply (Onuoha, 2012; Beazley 2012; Dretrich 2004; Obi 2011; Abubakar 2010; Engdahl 2006). It is a region which has become very attractive to piracy. Western countries have to inject their military might to ensure the free flow of movement within this vital coastal route. This explains the reasons of AFRICON.

Over the recent past, however, the dynamics of piracy in African waters has assumed a new direction. While the number of ships signalling attacks by Somali pirates has dropped, due to the intervention of foreign forces and use of vessel protection detachments, the incidence of piracy is rising in the Gulf of Guinea. Some of what is referred to as 'piracy' in the Gulf is, at best, armed robbery against ships, because it occurs mostly within 12 miles of the coast, which lies within the coastal state's responsibility. Piracy in the Gulf of Guinea has escalated from low-level armed robberies to more sophisticated violent hijackings and cargo thefts. As a result, piracy off the coast of the Gulf of Guinea is increasingly gaining the attention of stakeholders in the maritime domain – states, international and regional organisations, ship owners, crew members and insurance firms, among others (Onuoha op cit.). Each day, the Gulf of Guinea ships 1,5 million barrels of its oil to the United States, as well as 1 million barrels to Europe, 850 000 barrels to China and 330 000 barrels to India – altogether, 40% of Europe's and 29% of the United States' oil imports (Viroulon 2012).

The incidence and scope of piracy in the Gulf of Guinea has over the period varied from 64 attacks in 2003 to 56 n 2004 and 25 in 2005, but increased from 31 in 2006 to53 in 2007 and 59 in 2008. There was decline from 48 in 2009 to 39 in 2010, with a sudden increase to 53 cases in 2011 and further to62 in 2012. According to the International Maritime Bureau (IMB), 10 hijacks occurred in 2012, during which 207 crew members were taken hostage, 26 kidnapped and four killed (IMB, 2012; Onuoha, 2012). It is believed that modus operandi of oil piracy in the Gulf of Guinea is undertaken by a well-organised criminal gangs, mostly operating from Nigerian waters. Malaquais (2012) argues that: piracy in the Gulf of Guinea is organised, sometimes by highly sophisticated illicit taking of oil. They steal the oil, make a couple of black-market circles of the stuff, and then deposit it back into the global market. While Mukundan (2012) director of the IMB providing comparative insight, analysis points out that of the; 'attacks off west Africa follow some different modus operandi from pirate activity in other parts of the world. The majority of the attacks usually involve a high level of violence against the crew. After the hijacking the product is transferred on to a smaller vessel to be taken and sold illegally in the region.' All forms of criminality must be eradicated to create enabling and liveable conditions for all citizens. Why do these people take on themselves to terrorise the livelihood of people?

Fig. 1 Percentage of Distribution of Attacks in the Gulf of Guinea 2003-2012.

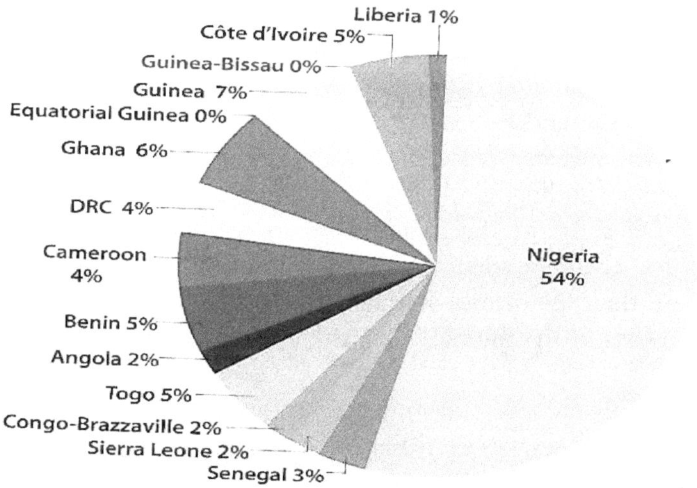

(Source: Credit: Conflict Trends, Issue 4, 2012, ACCORD, South Africa, p.30)

Apparently, the dynamics in the region is related to the growing upsurge in the activities of local militias in Nigeria's oil-rich Niger Delta region, who for a long period of time have been protesting their anger and revenge to the gross marginalisation they continue to suffer from the hands of successive Nigerian governments, the same situation the people of Southern Cameroons are suffering from the centralised regime of Republic of Cameroon, which has contributed to ongoing crisis in the country leading to nothing but *'the forgotten genocide'* of a country emerging in 2035.

Resources should be source of building the welfare of citizens. We have as a result of poor governance and greed made it curse to the people and nation. Interesting, we allow others exploit our resources for improving on their well-being and creating insecurity o ourselves in all forms. African governments continue to create unfulfilled expectations that subject the vast majority of their citizens to poor quality livelihood. Both external and internal forces take advantage to strengthen their grip and forces of exploitation on the people. The continent remains poor in the midst of plenty.

In short, Africans are facing hard times in the lands of plenty. We have failed in making or using our oil wealth and other resources in shaping and sustaining the welfare of citizens which only contributes to social dissent and instability. The continent is faced with resources wealth and regime failures. History will not blame our rich resources. It will blame the leaders and us for remaining passive and for only thinking about our individual stomachs. To the contrary, there are many reasons to pursue multiple methods, good governance, and the rule of law, justice and equality, beyond a simple, laudable commitment to inclusion, justice, peace, security and equality. There is need for creating an enabling environment to ensure, in a globalised world facilitated by tremendous growth in maritime transportation, the range of maritime threats requires collaboration among the various stakeholders, including national navies, which is very doubtful as these countries fall short of the required manpower necessary to combat piracy alone. The dependency of African countries on the West for the security of their maritime boarders is understood which, also has negative effects on the sovereignty and independence of these countries.

One can only recommend some preventive measures which include: (i) evolving sound resources management practices to leverage their oil affluence effectively to address the myriad economic afflictions; (ii) the Gulf of Guinea states should review, update, strategies, and harmonise their policies pertaining to piracy and other development related issues, plug legal loopholes leading to these culprits exploiting the resources of the region; (iii) the need to build capacity and other security forces in the region, as well as seek international alliances and cooperation with the developed countries.

Establishing peace and security in the Gulf of Guinea is important as it is defined as the region bringing together eight countries bordered by the Atlantic Ocean, namely: Ghana, Togo, Benin, Nigeria, Cameroon, Togo, Benin, Equatorial Guinea, Gabon as well as Sao Tome and Principe. However, it reality it reflects 25 countries located geographically in West and Central Africa. Being an important geostrategic area as major oil region of Africa, with one of the largest offshore deposits in the world, reserves comprising nearly 24 billion barrels – 4.5% of the world's oil reserves, it is imperative for the region to improve maritime security and safety in the Gulf of Guinea. There is need for concerted, regional and national strategy to deal with maritime piracy. This requires finances and capacity including infrastructures. Otherwise, it would be difficult to fight the criminal acts of piracy as well as armed robbery and other illegal activities committed at sea in this geographical area to ensure our shores are safe for navigations and as the centre of multiple geostrategic issues. The picture below depicts the Gulf of Guinea's coastal area of over 6.000 km, stretching from Senegal in West Africa to Cameroon in Central Africa and Angola in southern Africa.

OIL PIRACY IN THE GULF OF GUINEA
(Source: Credit – Conflict Trends, Issue 4, 2012, ACCORD, South Africa, p.28)

What Africa needs most is security, peace and justice (SPJ) to accelerate the process of transformation from an underdeveloped into a quality services delivery polity. The guns have to be silenced, rule of law and justice returned into the political activities of the people. Justice and peace-building remain paramount in curbing the degree of insecurity that clouds the continent without which African cannot transverse from its current status of a developing polity to that of services delivery society. Numerous failures and shortcomings can be registered the development path of African countries. It is imperative for the region to seek ways and means in ensuring that justice, security and peace reigns supreme to foster inclusive and sustainable development throughout the continent of Africa.

References

Abiola Segun & John Otte (2014). "Modern United Nations Peacekeeping: Towards A Holistic Approach to Addressing Conflict" Conflict Trends, Issue 2, 2014, pp3-10

Abubakar, Jibrin (2010). "Oil: Ghana Turns on the Tap, Egypt to Build Refinery in Ghana." Daily Trust, 16 December 2010, p.19

Adejumobi, Said (2000). "Between Democracy and Development in Africa: What are the Missing Links"? Paper presented to the World Bank Conference on "Development Thinking in the Next Millennium", Paris, 26-28 June 2000.

Ankomah Baffour (2013) "They Are at It Again: The Sponsors of African Wars", New African, 47th Year, No. 524, London, pp10-11

Annan Kofi (2001) Foreword: In McRae, Rob and Hubert Don (eds.) Human Security and the New Diplomacy. Montreal, McGill-Queens University Press.

Bay A. (2008) "Planet's Foremost Failed State". (http://www.strategy page.com/on point/2002010.asp).

Beazley (2012). "Specialist Piracy Cover Launched for Gulf of Guinea Risks', 5th December, Available at :(https://www.beazley.com/news/news_and_press/specialist_piracy_cover_launched_for_gulf_of_guinea_risks.html)

Ben-Ari Nirit (2013). "Piracy in West Africa: A bump Road to Maritime Security", African Renewal, Vol.27 No.3, December 2013, New York, USA. Pp12-13

Bruce, Bueno de Mesquita, Downs, George W. (2005) "Development and Democracy: Richer but Not Freer", Foreign Affairs, September/October 2005

Comoli Virginia (2015). Boko Haram. Nigeria's Islamist Insurgency. The Hurst Publishers, London

Dietrich, J. (2004). The Gulf of Guinea and Global Oil Market: Supply and Demand. In Traub-Merz, R. and Yates, D. (eds.) Oil Policy in the Gulf of Guinea: Security and Conflict, Economic Growth, Social Development. Bonn: Friedrich Ebert-Stiftung.

Dolek, C. (2008). "The Myth of Failed States' in Africa. A Question on Atomic Social Ontology? Journal of Turkish Weekly, April 29. (http://www.globalpolicy.org/nations/sovering/failed/2008/0429 .myth.hm)

Esterhuyse Abel (2009)." The Iraqization of Africa? Looking at AFRICOM from South African Perspective", in Africa and Francophonie (ASPJ), Winter 2009, Inaugural Issue, United States of America pp.21-34

Engdahl, William (2006). "USA Out-flanked in Eurasia Energy Politics?" Available at: http://www.321energy.com/editorials/engdahl/engdahl1060506.html>.

Fanon Frantz (1963). The Wretched of the Earth. Grove Press, New York.

Forje W. John (2002). The Disappointment of Independence", Futures Research Quarterly, Fall 2002, Vol.18. Number 3, pp41-60

Gill Peter (2016) Today We Drop Bombs. Tomorrow We build Bridges. Zed Books, London, United Kingdom

Groves, A. (2008). Explaining African State Failure. Does the State make the Nation, or Does the Nation make the State? (E-International Relations. June 23. http://www.e-rr.info/?-495).

Hanson Davis Victor (2020) "It's A Free Country, Brother". Politics and Policy, April 21, 2020. 6.30am See also National Review, April 21, 2020

Hirschmann, Gisela (2012) Peace Building in the UN Peacekeeping Exit Strategies: Organised Hypocrisy and Institutional Reform. International Peacekeeping, 19(2)

Howe Warren Russell (1981). Weapons: The Shattering Truth About the International Game of Power, Money and Arms. ABACUS Publishers, Sphere Books Ltd, London

Ikeda Daisaku (2012). "Human Security and Sustainability: Sharing Reverence for the Dignity of Life: ", in SGI Quarterly, No.68 April 2012, Japan, pp20-21

Joy Ibifuro Alasia (2015). "Demystifying Extremism in Nigeria: Understanding The Dynamics of Boko Haram", Current Trends,

Issue 3, 2015 African Centre for the Constructive Resolution of Disputes (ACCORD), South Africa, pp41-47

Keenan H, Jeremy (2017). "War Games in the Sahel", New African, No.568, January 2017, IC Publication, London, pp36-41

Malaquais, Assis (2012)." Ask the Expert: The Growing Threat of Oil Pirates in West Africa's Gulf of Guinea", ACSS News Spotlight, 29th March. Available at: http://africancenter.org/2012/03/ask-the-expert-the growing-threat-of-oil-pirates-in-west-africa%E2%80%99s-gulf-of-guinea/.

Mazrui A. Ali (1995) The Blood Experience," World Policy Journal, 12(1):28-35)

McCormack John (2020)'Coronavirus kills More Americans in One Month Than the Flu Kills in One Year" National Review April, 21, 2020, 12,25pm

Mercicca Charles (2012) "Role of Governments in Promoting Peace" Ala Barn A&M University. (Global community at telus.nt)

Mukundan, Pottengal (2012) as cited in IMB, p.32

Munson Robert (2009). "Do We Want to Kill People and Break Things in Africa"? In Africa and Francophonie (ASPJ), Winter 2009, USA, pp39-44, (www.airpower.au.af.mil)

Ngwanyam Nick (2020) "COVID-19 is a "Blessing" For Developing Nations", The Guardian Post No. 1855, Tuesday April 14, 2020. Yaoundé-Cameroon, p11

Ntui Obi N Cyprian (2020) AfDB Creates Coronavirus Response for Governments" The Guardian Post, No.1866, Tuesday, 14 April 2020, Yaoundé-Cameroon, p8

Novelli, M. & Robertson, S. (2007) The Politicisation of Development Aid to Education. (www.bris.ac.uk/edcation/academicStaff/edslr/publication/politics_of_disaster

Ntui Obi N. Cyprian (2020) AfDB Creates Coronavirus Response fir Governments." The Guardian Post No.1866, Tuesday, 14 April 2020, Yaoundé-Cameroon, 8

Obi, Cyril (2011). Democratising the Petro-state in West Africa: Understanding the Challenges. In Roll, M. and Sperling, S. (eds.) Fuelling the World – failing the Region? Oil Governance and Development in Africa's Gulf of Guinea. Abuja: Friedrich Ebert Stiftung, p.102

Ogoloma Fineface (2013) Niger Delta Militants and the Boko Haram: A Comparative Appraisal. International Journal of Arts and Humanities, 2 (1), pp114-131.

Ohamwe C. Augustine (2009). Post-Cold War Conflicts in Africa. Case Studies of Liberia and Somalia. Adonis & Abbey Publishers Ltd, UK

Onuoha C. Freedom (2012). "Oil Piracy in The Gulf of Guinea," in Conflict Trends, Issue 4, 2012, Accord, South Africa, pp28-35

Onuoha, C. Freedom (2010). Geo-strategy of Oil in the Gulf of Guinea: Implications for Regional Stability. Journal of Asian and African Studies, 45 (3), p.370

Pinar, W. E. (2008) The Subjective Violence of Decolonisation. In Decolonising Democratic Education: Trans-disciplinary Dialogues, edited by A.A. Abdi and G. Richardson, Sense Publishing, Rotterdam

Price-Smith T. Andrew (2009). Contagion and Chaos: Disease, Ecology and National Security in the Era of Globalisation, Cambridge, MA: MIT Press, 2009, 37

Price-Smith T. Andrew (2009). Contagion and Chaos: Disease, Ecology and National Security in the Era of Globalisation, Cambridge, MA: MIT Press, 2009, 37

Richards Paul (2016). How People's Science Helped End an Epidemic. National African Institute, London and African Argument.

Sani Shehu (2011). Boko Haram: History, Ideas and Revolt. Journal of the Centre for Constitutionalism and Demilitarisation, 11(4)

Shiva Vanadana (2016). Soil Not Oil. Zed Books, United Kingdom

Versi Anver (2018). "Celebrating the CFTA" in New African, No. 582, April 2018, London, p.13

Sikuka Kizito (2017). "Is There a Link Between Democracy and Development in Africa?" Conflict Trends, Issue 3, 2017, ACCORD, South Africa, pp3-10

Smith Benjamin (2007). Hard Times in the Land of Plenty – Oil Politics in Iran and Indonesia. Cornell University Press, Ithaca and London

Svasand Lars, (2011). Democratisation in Malawi: Moving Forward, Stuck in Transition or Backsliding? Forum for Development Studies, University of Bergen, Norway

Sörensen Jens Stilhoff & Soderbaum Fredrik (2012) "Introduction – The End of the Development – Security Nexus", in Development Dialogue, No.58, April 2012. The Dag Hammarskjöld Foundation, Uppsala – Sweden

United Nations (1992) Agenda for Peace, Report of the UN Secretary-General, 17 June 1992 (A/47/277-S/24111). New York, United Nations

United Nations Education, Scientific and Cultural Organisation (UNESCO) (2002) "Manual on the General Conference",

Available at :< http://unesdoc.unesco.org/Images/0012/00125/1255/125590s.pdf>

United Nations (2013) UN Security Council Resolutions 286 on United Nations Peacekeeping Operations, 21 January 2013 (S/Res/2086 (2013) New York, United Nation

United Nations Development Programme (UNDP) (2016) Human Development Index (HDI), New York, USA

Vircoulon, Thierry (2012)." Pirates of the Guinean". Foreign Policy, 20 December, (availableat:http://www.foreignpolicy.com/articles/2012/12/20/pirates_of_the_guinean?page=full)

Woldemariam Yohannes & Di Giacomo (2016) "Ebola Epidemic", in Africa and Francophone – ASPJ, Vol. 7, No. 1. 1st. Quarter 2016, Maxwell, AFB, USA, pp5472

Zagladin Vadim (1986). Our Aim: Universal International Security, Novosti Press Agency Publishing House, Moscow,

Chapter Nine

The Social Dimension

Africa is going through a very serious and trying period requiring policy strategies to stimulate economic growth, through job-creation, and increased productivity. The private sector has to be innovative, productive and competitive in the global market. The remnants of the economic and financial crisis and its impact on development activities present a poor picture with regards to the living standards of the citizens. Poverty is increasing not decreasing. Corruption is endemic. The health status of the people is the lowest in the world. Few on the continent have a social insurance policy. The continent fails in giving added value to its vast natural resources potentials. African countries continue depending on aid instead of generating income from its natural potentials. What kind of society is in the making and what does this generation intend to handover to coming generations?

There is no proper road-map in improving the living standards of the people. A dichotomy of social disharmony exists between poverty amid high economic growth rates which breeds dissatisfaction in society. The lack of political inclusion, limits to, the gross absence of the rule of law, the existence of a corrupt judicial system and law enforcing institutions and political repression are contributing factors to social disharmony in society. A number of African countries have registered 5 percent or 6 percent or even 8 percent growth for a long period. Unfortunately, this growth does not trickle down to the population; and the population who are below the poverty line are increasing more and more than ever before. There is need for good governance; have better employment, better health care among other services. Mobilising resources from within is fundamental and not to depend on foreign aid and the donor communities. African states should better manage their resources and do more in combating corruption. African countries expect more investment, more industrialisation and more employment, more social integration and more social and economic coherence. There are many rich Africans today than before independence. Create the enabling environment for these investors to invest at home.

Unfortunately, there is a lack of funds on this front and a decline in the percentage of aid for the international community to assist African countries, control over natural resources is very important. Most

African countries export natural resources as raw material, and then re-import them at five to six times the price. If only African countries can use natural resources for the benefit of the continent – that multiplying the price six times is for the benefit of the African people, then African countries will be doing better in African resources mobilisation and utilisation.

Poor economic growth impacts seriously on the social wellbeing of society. It equally fuels social tension and unrest especially when the benefits of economic growth do not trickle down to ordinary citizens. Rapid population growth, the quest for modern living style has equally increased social obligations and responsibilities. However, the social dimension should be contextualised within the premises of the 'social contract theory' which has roots in the idea that the state is created by a contract between the state and people; and in which the ultimate source of the power of the state is the people. Under the social contract theory all the people within the state create the state. The people are the state, and this notion is central to nationalism (Rodee & Christol, 1967:26-28). The failure of the state in meeting its social contract with the people fuels a social discontent atmosphere, with instability and conflicts threatening the democratic construct of the nation.

Inequality and socio-economic delusion in Africa can be attributed to a number of interrelated factors requiring interrelated holistic solutions. Attempts to minimise these differences insinuates an open and free society necessarily involving the use of coercive power for the ultimate good of society. People's incomes and their economic modus vivendi come largely under the control of politicians and civil servants. The extent of these consequences depends on the degree of economic equality the rulers wish to achieve; and also, on differences in the capacities, ambitions and differences of the groups and individuals among whom economic differences are to be curtailed or abolished. Importantly, the people have to be properly schooled on the intricacy that awaits the continent, particularly with penetrating role and impact of science and technology as a game-changer in the lives of the people's worldwide.

AU Agenda 2063 is equally explicit on the issues of social policy. Paying greater attention in this sector is laying the solid ground for coherent and meaningful social policies at the services of the people. Presently, social policies have failed to improve on the livelihood of citizens calling for a critical outlook and renewal of interest by governments and the academic community to strong focused on the social science policies currently in place. The reasons for these are clear; namely:

- looking critically in the rapid population of the continent and its positive and negative aspects to the transformation of each African country in particular and the continent in general;
- the presently unacceptable high levels of unemployment across the continent;
- the unacceptably increasing costs of social security or the non-existence of social security network in some countries; and how these impacts or not on the healthcare cost of African countries;
- the extent to which the continent deals with the issues of being a raw material producing and not moving towards becoming an industrial society, and the extent to which the basic fundamental rights of workers and citizens are addressed.

Rapid population growth is what the continent would need and how to maintain the quality of healthcare remains an outstanding challenge for the region in addition to ensuring the anvil on which its human capital development is anchored upon. A healthy and educated society is one anchored on the path of development and sustainable quality of livelihood for al. For now, the disparity in the quality of living is growing and not narrowing between the few rich and the great masses of poor. 'Widespread poverty, inequality and unemployment continue to characterise national socio-economic contexts, as skills, opportunities and capital remain concentrated within small centres of societies. Long-term strategies to reduce these social gaps include massive investments in education (especially primary education) and infrastructure. Successful investments in education and associated skills will enable citizens to meet the evolving demands of an increasing global economy. Stronger infrastructure will enable the development of complementary economies based in industrialisation and the information age – which are central for encouraging inclusive and broad-based economic development' (Gounden, 2016:2).

New policies are required in addressing issues of fundamental importance that improves the quality well-being of citizens; for example, curbing the high fertility rate by educating the people on proper birth spacing; education; employment, job security, equity in the distribution of social amenities in society; social security funds not only for workers but for all members in society; housing, healthcare, pipe-born water and electricity supply. As noted by Vasu Gounden (op cit,) advancing structural changed in education and infrastructural development can take, at a minimum, over 20-30 years to affect discernible change. This is precisely why the AUs Agenda 2063 charts

Africa's development trajectory over a 50-year time frame, instead of a 15-year frame. It is not surprising the Millennium Development Goals (MDGs) could not attain the envisaged goals; the time frame was short; and the governments ill-prepared in facing the challenges involved, even though these are things they should have been work on since the attainment of independence.

Of course, structural transformations are complicated by unprecedented convergence of global forces - namely threat multipliers - that amplify Africa's development challenges, some which include:

➢ Exponential population with: it is estimated that by 2050, the African continent will be home to over 2.4 billion people, representing 25 of the world's population. Over half of those 2.4 billion citizens will be under the age of 18 years. (UNICEF 2014)

➢ Rapid and unplanned urbanisation: Africa is the fastest urbanising continent and by 2050 approximately 56% of its inhabitants – over 1.3 billion people – will reside in urban areas (Mo Foundation 2015);

➢ Growing state of conflict, insecurity and political instability eroding the structural-functional bases of the society - come to think of the numerous crisis that have befallen the continent; beginning with war of independence, Algerian crisis, Congo ongoing crisis; Liberia, Mozambique, Angola, Central African Republic, Nigerian civil war, Rwanda, Somalia and Sudan, including the activities of the various insurgent's movements (Vera & Simon, 2010)

➢ The issue of 'collapsed state' and 'failed state' which signifies the consequences of a process of decay at the nation-state level, where the capacity of those nation-states to perform positively for their citizens has atrophied (Rotberg, 2004)

➢ The creation of post-independence African states were hampered by poor leadership, which lacked the capacity to define national priorities conducive to consolidating short-term, medium-term and long-term achievements related to the granting of political independent by colonial powers.

➢ Global economic challenges and decline in commodity prices: Africa has been affected adversely by the global economic decline – especially by China's shift from an investment – to consumption-oriented economy and the precipitous drop in commodity prices (AfDB 201; UNDP 2016)

➢ Climate change: the 2014 Intergovernmental Panel on Climate Change (IPCC) Report concluded that temperature increases across

Africa will exceed the 2C threshold by 2100 (IPCC 2014: Gounden 2016:2)

Africa needs a long-time frame to get things properly done. For the continent to achieve the aspirations of AU Agenda 2063, Africa must lay strong emphasis on preventing and mitigating conflicts efficiently and effectively. There is an urgent need to adequately address Africa's youth bulge and rapid urbanisation, ongoing wars, conflicts and instability, coupled with massive investments in education and infrastructure, present a unique opportunity for long-term transformation. Africa's ongoing wars, conflicts (from Algeria, Congo through Biafra to the various wars of independence in Angola, Mozambique, Liberia, Sierra Lone, Uganda, Sudan, Somalia, the ongoing Ebola epidemic and other killer diseases in the continent, present a unique opportunity for long term transformation: there is a need for comprehensive governance system designed to achieve the aspirations of Agenda 2063 or else Africa's chances at inclusive and sustainable development may be lost. The clock is ticking notes Vasu Gounden (2016:2). It means the real start to righting the wrongs of the colonial and immediate postcolonial era. "Africa's postcolonial disposition is the result of a people who have lost the habit of ruling themselves. We have also had difficulty running the new systems foisted upon us at the dawn of independence by our colonial masters. Because the West has had a long but uneven engagement with the continent, it is imperative that it understand what happened to Africa. It must also play a part in the solution. A meaningful solution will require the goodwill and concerted efforts on the part of all those who share the weight of Africa's historical burden|" (Achebe 2012:2). Africa today finds itself in a different world context, one governed by the forces of information and communication technologies (ICTs).

Elucidating the role of leadership in state failure, Reno (1998) opines that political leadership lacking capable administration finds market markets to be useful for controlling and disciplining rivals and their supporters, while intervening and disciplining rivals and their supporters, while intervening in markets enables rulers to accumulate wealth directly, which is then converted into political resources they can distribute at their discretion. Most African states bear the hallmark of a fragmented society divided along ethnic, clan and religious lines. Ethnicity is often used as a rallying point to mobilise society for war. Early post-independent states were caught in the trappings of poor leadership syndrome of distributing patronage along divisive clan affiliations that further weakened the state-creation process The phenomenon of state collapse is generally understood as the breakdown or disintegration of centralised political institutions and the system of authority that underlies them, and the unravelling of complex relationships between the state and society. With the consequences of a collapsed central administration, social services can hardly be adequately and fairly distributed in society.

Technology and Social Change

The world in general and Africa in particular has been subjected to dramatic changes due to advances in science and technology. These advances impact dramatically on our way of life. Technological advances will continue given human ingenuity especially since after World War Two. These changes conflict as well as impact on socio-cultural heritage and values of the African. Given that technology and technological changes affects our life; and looking at the social dimension of technological changes on our way of wellbeing, we cannot escape the fact that technology and social or cultural change necessitates several elements of change and interlink ages to meaningfully impact positively on the welfare of the people. To begin with, it requires an unambiguous definition of technology. Technology consists of individual, particular things, physical and observable. Bernard & Pelto (1987:360) defines technology as 'those machines, devices, and other physical apparatuses made and used by humans for instrumental purposes, and the physical products of those machines and devices. The use of machines and their products requires; 'knowledge', 'skills' and 'capital investments' among many other entities. The gruesome exploitation of the Third World, especially the down-trodden previously independent farmers and artisans are being driven from their land and displaced from their normal livelihood on a scale that makes the ravages of historical colonialism look pale in comparison. The neglect of the female gender as an important element and contributor to the development changes needed in society are some of the factors inhibiting the graduation of Africa from a 'backward' into a quality services delivery society.

We are in the world of *'techno-social system'* and technological change modifying the hierarchy of skills of workers. What do we mean by change in any system? What is social change as compared to 'cultural change'? Social change refers to changes in the pattern of recurrent behaviours in human social interaction. On the other hand, cultural change refers to modification – loss, addition, or transformation – of values, beliefs, attitudes, or other ideational elements relating to behaviours in given societies. In short, the concept, 'culture' means the internal states through which people give meaning and interpretation to observable behaviours and products of behaviour. The 'patterns of recurrent behaviours' of definition of 'social' refers to observable regulates large enough to 'make a difference' – patterns that can be aggregated into the stuff of general social evolution (Bernard & Pelto, op cit.pp360-1) For example, the reduction or decrease in the agricultural labour force in the agricultural labour force in industrial nations is a social change; getting more women in Africa into the public service and top administration positions is a social change; thus the concomitant changes in peoples' attitude and values toward rural life; the empowerment of women are cultural changes.

By the same logic, food, 'surplus' food and meat are being exported while children remain malnourished. Transnational corporations also contribute to infant mortality and disease by actively promoting 'modern; bottle-feeding in place of 'old-fashioned' breast-feeding. In addition, to feed the insatiable demands of the machines of the industrial nations and the equally insatiable desire for foreign exchange among Third World elites hungry for imported luxuries and armaments, large areas are being mined and undermined, forest destroyed, fields flooded, rivers silted, and farmers and tenants displaced from independent sources of income and livelihood (See World Order Model Project, 1978). In 2013, for example, Liberia, Guinea and Sierra Leone were at the bottom of the UN Development Programme (UNDP|) Human Development Index, appearing in the category of Low Human Development. At the same time, Liberia and Sierra Leone were ranked among the countries with the highest poverty headcount percentages, based on the UNDP Multidimensional Poverty Index, at 85% and 77% respectively (UNDP| 2013).

Technology has radically changed the cultural and social setting of many communities both in the developing and developed world context. African countries have and will continue to develop socially and economically in this epoch era of the scientific and technological revolution, and this exerts great influence on all aspects of society's life. No doubt the direction in which Africa, Latin America and Asian countries develop their science and technology base will contribute immensely to the solution of the most acute problems facing the former colonial periphery of the world capitalist economic system. The developing countries in Africa, Latin America and Asia – constituting more than 120 states or about four-fifth of the nations of the world. The export of technology to these countries on a preferential basis is supposed to promote the modernisation of the production structure on narrowly specialised foundations and the expansion of their export of natural resources.

African countries in particular taking advantage of *'the late-comer advantage'* in the latest achievements of contemporary science and technology, this would significantly promote their economic growth as well as the liquidation of abject poverty, hunger and disease. The all-round utilisation of new technologies makes it possible to solving the problems of industrialisation as well as this will sharply increase the efficiency of agricultural output. What is evidently clear is that the results of the scientific and technological revolution remain, for the most part, inaccessible for the rural poor in African countries. As earlier noted, the reality is that whatever scientific and technological development that trickles-down to the people is radically changing their pattern of lifestyle. Taking advantage of the low professional and technological level of the people and its working population and the shortage of skills personnel in places the utter absence of qualified human capacity, engineers, technicians, transnational corporations use their scientific and technological potential prowess very effectively and efficiently to control the most important branches of industry in African countries.

What prevents the spread of contemporary science and technology to African countries? The different sections of the publication make attempt in answering this and other related questions; the transfer of technology and expertise by the North to Africa; also, the issue of Africa neglecting the development and utilisation of indigenous knowledge as an inherent part of the transformation of the continent. Controlling the access to the latest scientific and technological achievements to Africa by the developed countries gives greater economic leverage to creating a system of technological neo-colonialism in the world capitalist economy, a system of exploitation and subjection of African countries, a system based on economic, scientific and technological supremacy by the industrially developed capitalist countries (UN Document 1981:48), which Peter Drucker sees as nothing that lays the foundation for a new and even more successful imperialism, the imperialism of technology? This new technological imperialism deepens the social divide between the rich and poor increasing serious tensions and conflicts within the society.

The Resurrection of the African Philanthropic Dynamism

The Africanness in us calls for the re-dynamism of the African socialist construct. African socialism has been with us and remains in our veins until the end of the world. Long before the arrival of slavery, imperialism and colonialism the ideological and humanitarian orientation of give and take, being your neighbours keeper was holy enshrined in the African social system; it is that spirit which has kept Africans alive; in spite of the great torture and challenges the people continue to endure. Revamping the age-old cultural heritage and values is extremely important. From Banjul to the Horn, from the cape to Cairo, you cannot enter an African home where you not offered water, kola nuts or something to drink or eat, whether a friend or stranger. That's the philanthropic dynamism in us the blacks which colonialism and imperialism destroyed. Unfortunately, the money economy has added disastrous behaviour in our cultural heritage and value belief systems.

Revamping and re-dynamising the cultural value of sharing; ubuntu, harambee, batho pelo' or any other of these cultural and chartable values should take paramount place in the continent's developmental nexus. These chartable features of the African society were coped by the West and the appellation of 'philanthropic' attached to it, subjecting the continent to believe strongly n 'ad-assistance' as the way towards development, thereby relegating the concept of 'self-reliance' to the background of the development nexus of the region. Apart from resurrecting n a proper way our lost heritage and die of 'sharing', being our neighbour's keeper, Africa must ensure to enhance, harness, consolidate and broaden the base of this wonderful gift of social capital that brings us together as Africans and human-beings. Importantly, 'African social movements, civil society activists, and progressive intellectuals must ensure that African governments do not sell their countries cheaply and mortgage their futures due to corruption, ignorance, incompetence, misjudgements, misguided euphoria, and short-term thinking' (Zeleza, 2014:166).

We have to give added value to the African social capital, as for ages past has provided a lifeline that has frequently rescued the continent from total collapse. Wambu (2017:90) post that the need towards formalising the African philanthropic spaces now as two African-wide institutions, the Africa Philanthropic Network (APN) and the African Philanthropy Forum (APF) seek to understand, improve, and broaden the base of philanthropic organisations across the continent. For now, the number of African most successful 'givers' – the Mo Ibrahim, the Aliko Dangote and Strive Mayisiwa have taken the lead in the 'politics of giving'. There are many yet to be discovered bodies that when properly harnessed should contribute to the sustainable transformation of Africa. For example, Dangote has established an endowment fund of USA$1.2bn, more than the Gross Domestic Product (GDP) of several African countries to address the education and health problems of African countries. The Mo Ibrahim African Leadership Award is USA$5m, far ahead the Noble Prize Award. The Dangote's and many other wealthy African men and women are resources to be harnessed, encouraged, mobilised and constructively put into use for the wellbeing of the African population. There are resources when properly harnessed and utilised can accelerate the economic transformation of the continent. To be blunt, stolen monies siphoned out of the country in European Banks should be used in developing the continent for the good of the people.

Bear in mind that when government works well, people thrive. Therefore, encouraging and promoting the activities of philanthropic groups aids the capacity development efforts of African government to enable them to provide better services such as schools, roads, hospitals and other services to the population. They foster a stable economic environment as well as help create jobs and improve sound economic growth. African governments should read into and exploit the positive, most feasible strategic aspects of the SDGs, AU Agenda 2063 and national development strategic plans in accomplishing some of the ideas advanced here. To be brief, the need to critically and objectively review both the backward and forward-looking components that facilitate the sustainable transformation of the continent in respect of:- (i) the backward-looking component that should consider the prioritisation, funding, monitoring and evaluation, and delivery of capacity development as set out in the SDGs, AU Agenda 2063, and National Development Plans (NDP);(ii) the forward-looking component that should provide the opportunity to outline reforms to increase the impact of capacity development will stronger emphasis on making capacity development more effective and efficient while building on its existing strength, and targeting the most important needs of each country as seen through the periscope of SDGs, AU Agenda 2063 and NDPs.

Another area for the continent to exploit is the ever-expanding forces of the continent's sixth region – the Diaspora, currently not adequately mobilised as a sounding partner in the development process (Aina & Bhehinkoh (Eds.). The philanthropy of the African Diaspora according to the World Bank through formal remittances sent to Africa stood at USA$40bn in 2015. It is believed that between 20-25% of the figure goes to various forms of investment leaving about USA$30bn for covering day-to-day living, education and healthcare expenses of families and relatives. These activities should help strengthen the self-reliance nexus much needed for the sustainable development of Africa. Here Wambu (op. cit. 2017) asserts that efficient government's investing in the people, infrastructure creating the right environment; a dynamic private sector providing affordable business solutions to market or social failures, a third sector working together with them and plugging the gaps – the tools are at hand for our internally driven development. With the rise of 'Trumpism', the anti-migration and the 'white nationalist populism' convulsing across Europe, Africa should not rely totally on 'remittances' from the Diaspora. Africa will have and must generate its sources of funding its developmental project. Domestic resources for invest must be mobilised, encouraged and judiciously utilised for the sustainable transformation of the continent. Here lies some of the reasons for the unity and integration of the continent; connecting the people, through good communications, road, railway, airways, seas transportation to facilitate the free movement of people and goods is crucial for the transformation of the society from a so-called back to a modern polity.

Given the importance of understanding and addressing the impact of Africa's state of underdevelopment, African leaders and peoples should regularly engage in seeking comprehensive, functional and amicable solutions to the barrage of problems affecting the region to better move forward in unionism for the progressive and development changes that are needed in the continent. Diversity, engagement, proper resources use, inclusion and management are key strategic concepts that must be adequately utilised in the transformation process of the continent. We have the tools – ubuntu, harambee, batho pele, nhimbe etc. Why do we shy away from putting into functional use these concepts which are inherent part of our cultural heritage and values?

Inferiority complexes constitute bad viruses that have eaten deep into the social fabric of the African mind seriously contributing to the failure of states on the continent. We disregard our values but fall prey to foreign cultural values we do not known and understand. The social dimension has much to do with the national or self-determination, emancipation and independence struggle as the input mechanism for socioeconomic transformation. The colonial powers saw the question of the colonies as a question of outlets which implicitly implied that colonies were one of the remedies for social conflict and underscores why science and technology have failed to take-off and inject the necessary momentum for the development of continent. Not only must Africa develop its indigenous knowledge but take opportunity to exploit to the fullest the advantages of the 'late-come advantage'.

Developing a well-informed citizen for Africa is a must for survival in the next century and beyond (Forje, 2001:72).

The region is faced and harassed by 'internal colonialism' defined as a failed state concept that conceives of the state along-a strong-weak state continuum, based on three core factors: the monopoly of legitimate use of force, effective institutions and consensus (Jackson, 2013). When a state is weak, a strong culture imposes its wishes on the weaker state. This is Africa. In that order, they relate to coercive power, administrative and infrastructural power, and cultural hegemony. Aberg John (2018) notes that: succeeding with these three core aspects of state making has historically been an internal colonial process, i.e. it involved (i) pacification and subduance of enemies of the state; (ii) dismantling of the existence of parallel institutions; and (iii) suppression of rival cultural frameworks. Ayoob (2002) points out that the fundamental contradiction between internal and external sovereignty in the Africa state system is evident with internal colonialism destroying the functional basis or fabric of the society. Much has to be done by African states to regain its sovereignty.

For now, the policy of internal colonialism adopted by African states is a structure of social relations based on domination and exploitation among culturally heterogeneous, distinct groups. It is the result of an encounter between two races, cultures, or civilisations, whose genesis and evolution occurred without any mutual contact up to one specific moment making possible intensive racial and cultural discriminations (Casanova 1965). The time for unchaining Africa's social dimension is now (Lema, 2019). It is in our power to change the continent by constructively and appropriately using what we have – indigenous knowledge system and concepts *–nhimbe, harambee, Ubuntu, batho pele*, and many others and to begin thinking like Africans in Africa and in the world construct. We are, unfortunately, governing on borrowed concepts.

Mashamaite Moss (2014:188) is equivocal on this issue, pointing out that 'when an African's thought is not originally his/her own because the owner of that thought becomes the owner of his/her mind becomes the owner of his/her destiny. Africans need to change the software in their brains. This will help us even when we come to solutions to our land and resources issues. We will be able to approach them Afrocentrically with our own heads not borrowed ones. We fail to understand and appreciate the reality that Eurocentricism cannot be on the side of Afrocentricism. There are two opposing forces on the development construct. The Nigerian activist, Chinweizu extends the discourse further; 'one of the weaknesses of black civilisation, particularly during medieval times, was the openness, the cosmopolitanism of these societies… And today, one of the basic weaknesses of African societies is that they still maintain this inherited cosmopolitan trait.' In all, Africa's development rests on the shoulders of Africans. There is no other way out. The African can only pursue and achieve his/her liberation by him/herself because he/she is the one who was a slave, he/she is the one that was discriminated against, he/she is the one that was dispossessed of his/her heritage. To invite other people into his/her struggle, his/her revolution, is Afrocidal and confused notes Mashamaite (op. cit. p220).

The social dimensions of the continent hinges on the utilisation of our cultural heritage knowledge and values – *nhimbe, ubuntu, harambee, batho pele* and others found in us not properly being used, or destroyed by the Eurocentric ideological agenda. We have to be on the alert as we prepare Africa for the future paying greater attention to the quality livelihood of the people. In fact, poverty and relatively high levels of material deprivation have become the rule, not the exception throughout the continent. Today, Africa is still ranked the poorest and most deprived part of Planet Earth, challenging everyone to regain its consciousness and vitality in confronting the plight of the continent. The developed polities are swallowing Africans because of the poor social dynamics and in- security characteristics of the state structure of the continent. Thus, the public choice and transformational process of the continent informs us that to enhance sustainable development in Africa in the future and beyond requires each African state be provided with efficient and self-enforcing rules to allow for the construction ad participatory, stable, transparent, accountable and viable governance systems. Let me once again, re-emphasis that most Africans today remain poor and severely deprived, exploited, oppressed, and marginalised group within our current world construct.

We have to accept the realities of the existing situation in order to move forward. We have had six or more decades of wasted opportunities. This the time to pick up the pieces by every state choosing efficient and self-enforcing social contracts or governance structures establishing economic systems maximising the participation of all citizens in national reconstruction; without the quality of the livelihood of Africans will continue to deteriorate. In short, Africa today presents a sad case, as it remains the only region of the world with very poor prospects for development, and relatively, bleak future even though blessed with vast abundant resources. These vast resources present an optimistic view of the future of the continent.

References

Aberg H. S. John (2018). 'Why States Fail – Internal Colonialism and The Challenges of State Making in the 21st Century", Conflict Trends, Issue 2, 2018, Accord – South Africa, pp51-56.

Achebe Chinua (2012). There Was a Country – A Personal History of Biafra. The Penguin Press, New York. United States of America;

African Development Bank (AfDB) (2016) African Economic Outlook 2016: Sustainable Cities and Structural Transformation Organisation for Economic Cooperation and Development

Aina Akin Tade & Bhekinkosi Moyo (eds.) (2015) Giving to Help - Helping to Give: The Context and Politics of African Philanthropy

Ayoob, Mohammed (2002). Inequality and Theorizing in International relations: The Case for Subaltern realism. International Studies Review, 4 (3), pp. 27-48

Bernard H. Russell & Pelto J. Pertti (1987) "Technology and Anthropological Theory", in Russell H. Bernard and Pertti Pelto (1987) (eds.) Technology and Social Change, Waveland Press Inc. Chapter 13, pp359-276

Casanova, Pablo Gonzalez (1965). "Internal Colonialism and National Development." Studies in Comparative International Development, 1 (4), p33

Ekwe-Ekwe Herbert (1991). The Biafra War: Nigeria and the Aftermath. Edwin Mellen Press, Lampeter, Ceredigion, United Kingdom.

Forje W. John (2001). "The State of Science and Technology in Africa. Deficiencies, Challenges, and Prospects for the 21st Century", in Stuart S. Nagel (ed.). Handbook of Global Technology Policy, Marcel Dekker, Inc., USA, pp65-108

Gounden Vasu (2016) Editorial – Conflict Trends Issue 2, The African Centre for Conflict Resolution of Disputes [ACCORD] 2016, South Africa, p2

International Panel on Climate Change (IPCC) (2014) 'Fifth Assessment Report – Impacts, Adaptation and Vulnerability', Chapter 22, Africa, p1202. <Available at : <http://ipcc.wg2.gov/AR5/images/uploads/WG11AR5Chap22_FINAL.pdf>

Lema Catherine Forje (201(9). Unchaining Africa's Economic Development Through Entrepreneurship Education. L'Harmattan Publishers, France/Cameroon

Mashamaite Moss (2014). The Moving Finger Writs. Vol. 2, Chatworld Publishers, Wapadrand, South Africa

Mo Ibrahim Foundation (2015). 'Africa's Urban\Dynamics – Facts and Figures', Available at (http://static.moibrahimfoundation.org/u/2015/11/19115202/2015-Facts-Figures-African-Urban-Dynamics.pdf 8 June 2016)

Reno William (1998) Warlord of Politics and African States. Lynne Reinner, Colorado, USA

Jackson, Richard (2013). Regime Security. In Collins, Alan (ed.). Contemporary Security Studies. Oxford University Press, Oxford, UK, pp. 11-75

Rodee, C. C. Anderson & Christol, C. Q. (1967). Introduction to Political Science, 2nd (ed.) McGraw-Hill, New York

Rotberg, Robert (2004). The Failure and Collapse of Nation States: Breakdown, Prevention, and Repair. In Rotberg Robert (ed.) When States Fail. Princeton University Press, Princeton, USA

United Nations Document, A/CN, 11/12, May1, 1981, p.48

United Nations Development Programme (UNDP) (2013). The Rise of the Global South: Human Development Report 2013, New York, UNDP

UNICEF (2014) "Generation 2030 Africa", Available at; (http: //www.unicef.org/publications/index_7475`, 8 June 2016)

Vera Achvarina & Simon Reich (eds.) "No Place to Hide: Refugees, Displaced Persons, and Child Soldier Recruits" in Gates, Scott and Reich Simon (eds.) Child Soldiers in the Age of Fractured States. University of Pittsburgh Press, Pittsburgh, USA

Wambu Onyekachi (2017). "The Politics of Giving – And Receiving". New African, No.568, January 2017, IC Publication, London, pp90.

World Order Models Project (1978). The Perversion of Science and Technology: An Indictment. Document signed by individuals at the Fourteenth meeting of the World Order Models Project in Poona, India, 2-10 July 1978. Poona – India

Zeleza Tiyambe Paul (2014) "The Africa-China Relationship: Challenges and Opportunities" Canadian Journal of African Studies, Vol. 48. No.1, 2014, pp145-169

Chapter Ten

The Pandemic of Corruption

"Politicians and public officials from the world's leading industrial countries are ignoring the rot in their backyards and the criminal bribe-paying activities of multinational firms headquartered in their countries."

(Peter Eigen, Chairman of Transparency International, May 2002]

"Corruption is not a charitable game; 'winners' have every intention of recovering their bribery costs"

[Donald Strombom, Former Chief of Procurement for the World Bank]

"Corruption is a powerful and insidious animal. You either fight or tame it, or it would fight you back"

(President Paul Kagame, Rwanda)

"Where power is derived from loyalty of others and wealth from the labour of others; where many citizens' failure is other people's success; and Where noble intentions and ignoble effects exist is equal abundance, the power of a man is his/her present means to obtain some future good."

(Parenti, M. 1987)

"Paying Government Officials to Preside Over Events Is Outright Corruption. I am very aware that administrators want special envelops. Unlike the practice when I was in the administration, the question of a Governor, an SDO or DO going to open an establishment or preside over a public event should not require special envelopes being given to them. This practice is outright corruption

[Hon. Enow Tanjong, Eden No.842. 28th April 2014.p1&2, Limbe Cameroon]

"Corruption has devastating effects on women's lives. Let's fight together. Corruption hinders progress towards gender equality and presents a barrier for women to gain full access to their civil, social and economic rights

(Transparency International, International Women's Day 2018 //WD2018))

"Do not accept a bribe, for a briber makes people blind to what is right and ruins the cause of those who are innocent."

(2. Ex.23, 8)

"Corruption is one of the large obstacles to development: it reduces the efficiency of development efforts, undermines justice, weakens democracy, makes the rich richer and supports dictators – less in the area of private aid, organisations, than within governmental, multilateral and private economy relations"

(Christoph Stuckelberger – Fighting Corruption)

Introduction: Building A Corrupt Free Continent

The corruption pandemic has gripped the continent distorting its governance and development parlance. The point is that governance remains a sensitive and misunderstood topic; it is being given a widely and highly priority in development circles. According to the Africa Commission report, *"good governance is the key … unless there are improvements in capacity, transparency, accountability, and reducing corruption, other reforms will have only limited impact."* But is good governance and controlling corruption really so fundamental for development and the future of Africa? According to (Warf, 2018) "corruption occurs at multiple scales and in different forms." Mauro et al. (2019) opines that corruption, or the abuse of public office for private gains, distorts the activities of the state and ultimately, takes a toll on economic growth and the quality of people's lives. Depending on its extent, corruption can have a profoundly detrimental effect on public finances as governments collect less in tax revenue and overpay for goods and services of investment projects. But the cost of corruption is greater than the sum of lost money: distortions in spending priorities undermine the ability of the state to promote sustainable and inclusive growth. The drain public resources away from education, health care, and effective infrastructure, the kinds of investments that can improve economic performance and raise living standards for all.

Combating corruption requires major political changes and other inter-related inclusive reform policies and serious proactive policy measures that include:

- The chances of success being greater when countries improve on mutually supporting institutions to tackle corruption;
- Governments need to keep pace with evolving technology and opportunities for wrongdoing;
- Promoting transparency and a free press helps increase accountability (Mauro, op cit.28) (see also Hatchard 2014)

Sobrinho and Thakoor (2019) notes that; "Sub-Saharan Africa stands to gain more from reducing corruption than any other region" in the world. The continent is faced with the uphill task of corruption versus transparency and accountability, for transparency and accountability as the apex of good governance constitutes the potent weapon in the battle against corruption, illicit financial flows and poor-quality living standards for the vast majority of citizens.

Therefore, the rule of law, transparency, accountability, good governance among others shines a light on the hidden corners of the continent's economic transformation from a backward to a quality services delivery society. The political will to fight corruption and poor governance plants the fruits of growth to be shared more equitably within society. The fast-changing global economy calls for good governance and respect of the rule of law and openness and a free, objective critical media sector as the voice of the voiceless. Countries mired in conflict and centralised authoritarian governance structures can never progress. Countless opportunities are abound for African countries as they open-up to the light of democratic governance with their citizens as active participants in the process.

Contextualising Africa within the rudimentary stages of development focusing mainly on infrastructure - building roads and bridges, constructing railroads stations, seaports and airports as well as upgrading grids and telecommunications while on the other hand, the developed countries power their economy through scientific and technological innovation (Yao 2019:15). With good governance, society can drastically curb vast sums of monies that could be used to improve lives that are currently stashed in tax havens or lost to corruption, Just consider how much of these lost vast sums of monies can do for health care, education, infrastructure development, investing in enterprises on a country. The engine of growth lies in the governance nexus of each African country; the powerful political will of building a united continent, free of poverty and corruption; and as the main focus of improved and sustainable quality well-being of all citizens as the winning formula.

Centralised authoritarian regimes will continue efforts to block access to the dark web and the threats to legitimacy that it poses by enabling dissidents to continue the practice of siphoning the resources of the country into private accounts. Every democratic or minimally accountable government should have great concerns about the state of corruption and underdevelopment of the society. Each African country needs more open constructive discussions, reporting, understanding, accountability and engaging the community as the pillars of development, and as Loungani (2019:55) points out; "when the three pillars of society are appropriately balanced, society has the best chance for providing for its people, particularly those who lose out from the effects of trade and technology" as becoming to a basket of deplorable.

Africa needs a sharper focus on the agenda sharpening the focus on democratic governance, open society and "creating a virtuous cycles, where honesty breads honesty; cautioning that reforms may be fragile and incomplete if policies do not shift expectations and behaviour sufficiently enough towards a new less-corrupt status-quo" (Mungiu-Pippidi and Johnston 2017). Essoungu (2013:11) is more categorical; "corruption frequently takes place in societies where there is considerable discretion for public officials, limited accountability and little transparency in governmental operations.

Civil society mobilisation against corruption in Africa has also been at the heart of recent waves of protest on the continent; the Arab Spring for example. On the other hand, centralised authoritarian regime structures constrains and depletes the arsenal of civil society organisation as powerful cabal that brings the government to order and holds it accountable. Despite courageous, sometimes heroic actions from civil society groups the fight against corruption and bad governance in Africa faces significant challenges.

In the case of Africa, it is rooting and stings; destroying every aspects of sustainable development. Apparently, governance has progressed in a number of African countries over the past decade. Some countries are still stifled with daunting corruption and other wrong doings. But beyond scandals, and the varying responses, the challenges of corruption are vast and destroying the continent. Good governance provides the best way forward. Good governance could be taken to imply the traditions and institutions that determine how authority is exercised and this includes:

- how governments are selected, held accountable, monitored, and replaced;
- government's ability to manage resources efficiently and formulate, implement, and enforce sound policies and regulations; and
- respect for institutions that govern economic and social transformation;

Curbing or eliminating corruption is a healthy move towards a capable developmental state. A capable developmental state is one in which the people's voices are heard, and accountability, political stability, and absence of violence, government effectiveness, regulatory quality, rule of law, and control of corruption ranks high on the priority action agenda of the government. The people's dissatisfaction with the current political system stems from at least two points – the total neglect of the welfare of the people and the aversion of public office holders to accountability. Neglect and dissatisfaction breed corruption. Take the case in Cameroon where you work for over a year before you are paid your first salary. How do you live? You are motivated to stretch your activities into other areas in order to fend for your livelihood. The joint impact results in frustrations with almost all governments throughout the continent to state the least. We can get out of jam through prudent management, accountability and responsibility. Prudent management and placing the interest of citizens first contributes significantly to curbing corrupt practices.

Following Kaufmann [2005:41] myths about governance and corruption centres on 10 myths; Fig. 10:1

Fig 10.1: 10 Myths about Governance and Corruption

---

1. Governance and anticorruption are one and the same: Governance is the traditions and institutions by which authority in a country is exercised for the common good of all. By contrast, corruption is defined more narrowly as the "abuse of public office for private gain."

2. **Governance and Corruption cannot be measured**: The World Bank has constructed aggregate governance indicators that cover more than 200 countries based on more than 350 variables obtained from dozens of institutions worldwide

3. The Importance of Governance and Anti-corruption is overrated: Research shows the impact of governance on development. That countries can derive a very large 'development dividend' from better governance is a reality not to dismiss. Corruption also matters for a country's competitiveness and for income distribution. Corruption undermines fledgling democracies. Governance is not the only thing matters for development.

4. Governance is not a luxury that only rich countries can afford. Higher income automatically translates into better governance. A number of emerging economies, e.g. Baltic's, Botswana, Chile and Slovenia have shown that it is possible to reach higher standards of governance without yet having joined the ranks of wealthy nations.

5. It takes generations for governance to improve: While it is true that institutions often change only gradually, in some countries there has been a sharp improvement in the short term. For instance, there has been a significant improvement since 1996 in the 'voice and accountability' indicator in countries ranging from Bosnia, Croatia and Ghana, to Indonesia, Serbia and Sierra Leone. And the improvements exhibited by some African countries in a short period of time challenging the "Afro-pessimists." A number of countries including the Ivory Coast, Nepal, and Zimbabwe there have been a sharp deterioration

6. Donors can "ring fence" projects in highly corrupt countries and sectors. With the possible exception of some humanitarian aid projects, the notion that the aid community can insulate projects from an overall corrupt environment in a country is not borne out by the evidence.

7. Fight corruption by fighting corruption. A fallacy promoted by some in the field of anti-corruption, and at times also by the international community, is that one 'fights corruption by fighting corruption'-through yet another anti-corruption campaign, the creation of; commissions' and ethics agencies, and the incessant drafting of new laws, decrees, and codes of conduct;

8. The culprit is the public sector in developing countries: A common fallacy is to focus solely on the failings of the public sector. The reality is much more complex, since powerful private interests often exert undue influence in shaping public policy, institutions, and state legislation. In extreme case, 'oligarchs' capture state institutions. And many multinational corporations still bribe abroad, undermining public governance in emerging economies. There are also weaknesses in the nongovernmental sector. Furthermore, traditional public sector management interventions have not worked because they have focused on technocratic 'fixes' often done through technical assistance importing hardware, organisation templates, and experts from rich countries.

9. There is little countries can do to improve governance: Given the long list of interventions that have not worked, as well as the role often ascribed to historical and cultural factors in explaining governance, it is easy to fall into the pessimist camp.(a)historical and cultural factors are far from deterministic-witness, for instance, the diverging paths in term of governance of neighbouring countries in Latin Americas, the Korean peninsula, the transition economies of Easter Europe and in Southern Africa; (b)strategies that offer particular promise. The coupling of progress on improving voice and participation-including through freedom of expression and women's rights-with transparency reforms can be particularly effective;

10. There is not much IFIs can do: Some development experts are sceptical about the ability of IFIs and donors to help countries improve their governance-either because of a conviction that 'the macro matters more,' a mistaken belief in historical 'determinism,' or a view that the interventions needed to improve governance are politically sensitive and thus difficult for outsiders to encourage. There are areas that fall outside the mandate of IFIs, such as promotion of fair multiparty elections. But initiatives to encourage transparency, freedom of information and an independent media, participatory anticorruption programmes led by the country, and gender equality-all of which have been underemphasised so far in the fight against corruption-may well be within the ability of IFIs and donors to do something about.

Source: Forje (2012) Complied from Daniel Kaufmann (2005) 10 Myths about Governance and Corruption, Finance and Development, Vol.42, No.3, September 2005, pp.41-4

Africa's tolerance for corruption and impunity is only plunging the continent into the deep blue sea. Attempts to fight corruption have never succeeded when they are narrowly focused on wrong initiatives such as yet another unenforced anticorruption law or one more anticorruption campaigned or agency. It requires determined political will and integrated governance approach that alters incentives and addresses corruption systematically, tackling capture and corrupt networks. It equally requires a strong and independent judiciary, meritocratic systems, transparency and accountability. All branches of government as well as civil society, the media and the private sector must be involved. Without the rule of law and good leadership backed a responsive proactive civil society the viruses of corruption cannot be arrested. Corruption virtually stings in most African countries, explaining why many of the countries have a low-ranking rate on the corruption index worldwide.

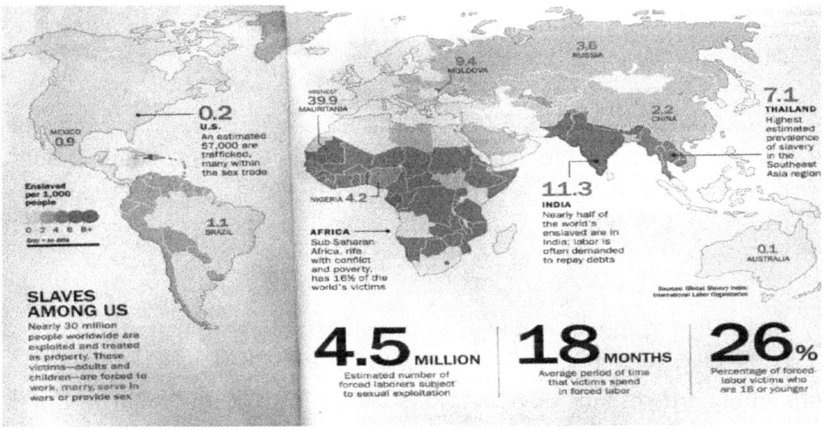

Source: Credit - New African, No544, November 2014, p32 AN IC Publication, London

Apparently the challenge of governance and anticorruption confronting the world today strongly argues against the "business-as-usual" modus operand. A bolder approach is needed, and collective responsibility at the global is called for. The rich world must not only deliver on its aid and trade liberation promises, it must also lead by example. On the other hand, Tajudeen (2010: 2) asserts:

> there is nothing particularly cultural or Africa about corruption. But we should not take cover under such blandishments. Corruption is destroying Africa more than any other region and it has greater impact on our lives than it does in most others. From drinking water to the dangerous 'licensed' aircrafts defying gravity that fly across our airspace, through hospitals and death traps on our roads, corruption is more omnipresent than God. Even in our temples, churches and mosques, corruption reigns. We reserve high tables at religious, cultural, social, political and other public events for thieves and rogues who continue to

rob us and wipe our noses in their acts. We elect them and complain afterwards

Apparently the challenge of governance and anticorruption confronting the world today strongly argues against the "business-as-usual" modus operand. A bolder approach is needed, and collective responsibility at the global is called for. The rich world must not only deliver on its aid and trade liberation promises, it must also lead by example. On the other hand:

> "There is nothing particularly cultural or Africa about corruption. But we should not take cover under such blandishments. Corruption is destroying Africa more than any other region and it has greater impact on our lives than it does in most others. From drinking water to the dangerous 'licensed' aircrafts defying gravity that fly across our airspace, through hospitals and death traps on our roads, corruption is more omnipresent than God. Even in our temples, churches and mosques, corruption reigns. We reserve high tables at religious, cultural, social, political and other public events for thieves and rogues who continue to rob us and wipe our noses in their acts. We elect them and complain afterwards" assert (Tajudeen 2010:2).

Corruption is as old as prostitution; and has become an inherent part of society because society has made it so; equally as society is embed with mechanisms to adequately address and eventually curb the pandemic. It can be brought to the lowest level possible minimum or given top priority of eradicating it if society so want. Every segment of society is affected. Within the public sector the temptation for public servants to bend official rules and regulations for different reasons are many; for example, (a) articulate self-interests to be rich overnight; and (b) the tendency to please friends and other benefactories; which helps in contributing to bureaucratic malpractices and eventually the destruction of society in the long run. Society becomes egregiously corrupt (see Roskin et al, 2000; Goldstein 2001:599; Parenti 1978:111; Weatherby et al 2000), inhibiting the rendering and ensuring equitable supply of quality services. The provision of goods and services requires skills to manage diversity as well as ensure transparency, efficiency, fairness and effective delivery systems (Chirawu 2012:51).

According to the World Bank estimates, $1-1.6 trillion are lost globally each year to corruption; however, "when countries tackle corruption they increase their national incomes by as much as four times in the long term. Business can grow as much as 3% faster, and child mortality can fall as much as 75%" (World Bank 2013).

Furthermore, the Africa Progress Report 2013 notes that "Africa loses twice as much to corruption as it receives in foreign aid" but that "good governance will help Africa out of poverty, joblessness and inequality" (Sepheka 2013). Since African states acquired their freedom in the 1960s, most of continent's states have been governed by either autocratic or semi-autocratic regimes. Nevertheless, Africa is far closer to realising its considerable potential in both economic development and social progress. The major impediment remains a lack of governance that would permit Africa to transform its economies and societies. Simply state, the concept of 'good governance' as the lawful control over the affairs of a political unity, such as a nation, describes certain forms of interaction between state and society.

Such intercourse is vital for the success of a nation. Good governance recognises the integrity, rights, and needs of everyone within the state. It offers a way of managing power and policy, while government serves as an instrument to do so. The absence of good governance contributes to the woes plaguing the continent as well as impeding the proper use of its vast resources potential for the wellbeing of the people. Good governance requires power-sharing democracy among the various stakeholders and institutions ensuring checks and balances as the sine qua non of a modern developmental state. The vitality of good governance as instrument for fighting corruption and underdevelopment and promoting quality livelihood of its citizen is characterised by the following;

Participatory, consensus-oriented, Good Governance accountable, transparent, responsive
Fight corruption and promoting effective and efficient and
Characteristics ===➔} equitable welfare to all citizens and the practice of the rule of law
// //
Corruption is minimised, views of minorities respected and taken into account as well as the voices of the most vulnerable in society is heard in decision-making & implementation process; and responsive to the present and future needs of society.

It is time corruption be shown the red card. How, when, where, by what means and by whom remains the task to overcome? The Panama and Paradise Papers tells a lot about the *'Global Rich and the National Poor'* in our world today. It is evidently clear that the war against corruption cannot be won in conference halls or the creation of anti-corruption organs and even laws. Corruption is as old as prostitution in our societies. It cannot be eradicated but reduced to the basic minimum. It requires a new mindset by the entire population to radically fight and reduce it. The best way of reducing corruption is a call to all to be true to oneself. How? This calls for every one of us willingly to be part of the mechanism for its eradication by doing something serious and radical about it. *First,* maintaining a stand of ethical and moral values.

Second, refusing to give or take bribes. *Third*, showing a high degree of 'zero-tolerance' of corruption no matter how small or big it may be. *Four*, institute a perfect control mechanism and justice system. Five, operate a functional democratic governance system with the rule of law give top priority. Corruption is a serious crime against humanity. As such it must receive a heavy punishment. Valuable lessons can be drawn from other parts of the world like China, Malaysia, Singapore and Thailand where acts of corruption are treated with the highest contempt and sternest sanction including capital punishment.

Without transparency, the perception of corruption is high. Since most African countries fail to exercise the basic tenets of democracy, that is do not operate on a system accompanied by development of a political system of checks and balances, corruption becomes the order of the day. It is even difficult to encourage foreign investment if there is no independent judicial system to properly address grievances. And it is hard to curtail corruption, which devours productivity, without an independent press or a strong parliamentary and judiciary system. Following Transparency International's Corruption Perceptions Index, Jordan fell from number 37 (of 178 countries) to number 58 (of 176 countries) 2003-2012; just before the revolution – Egypt's ranking fell from 70 to 98. The situation south of the Sahara is even worse where countries like Cameroon and Nigeria have hit Transparency International Perception Corruption Index on several occasions as the most corruption nations on planet earth.

Most governments afford any form of transparency and accountability, for the two are powerful disincentive for illicit activities. Progressive states sharing common ideals must quickly come together to strengthen a joint, multilateral regulatory framework flexible enough to adapt to rapidly changing technologies and financial movements that entrenches accountability, transparency curbing all forms of illicit transactions draining the financial capacity of the country. "Criminals and other devious groups operate in eco-political systems that permit rapid exploitation and anticipation of new communication technologies, financial instruments, and seams in the system" (Farah, 2017-21).

Corruption, money laundering and other criminal activities should be curtailed to the barest minimum and resources used in improving the quality livelihood of citizens. This is what Africa wants; not the elusiveness of political and ethnic corruption that has and continues to grip and govern the continent. The grey zone of political corruption propels the continent to destruction and underdevelopment. The political polyvalence of interests and party norms or adherences especially in monolithic political structures (and of course, in liberal political systems shows two forms of discrepancies or tensions, namely: (i) 'between institutional role-setting and norm-obeying action on the one hand, and their 'transition' into everyday conduct depending on the actors perceptions of the norms being 'rightly' applied to the other; and (ii) between the multiplicity of contesting organisation loyalties and norms on the one hand, and the unitary state norms on the other' (Maras 2007:21).

Defining Corruption

Given that corruption is known to permeate all levels of society affecting every aspect of society and even influencing foreign policy, can corruption be defined or what does it entails? One can define corruption as the deployment or use of public office for private or personal gain; government systems without competition; the privatisation of politics and thus concerns the distribution of benefits from economic transactions; and demanding additional payment for services that one is already officially paid for. Kaufmann (2015:20-23) points out that corruption is one among several measures of broader governance because it stems from weaknesses in other governance dimensions.

Traditionally corruption is defined in terms of individual public officials who abuse public office for private gain. But corruption has a wider reach. It is a costly symptom of institutional failure, often involving a network of politicians, organisations, companies, and private individuals colluding to benefit from access to power, public resources, and policy-making at the expense of the public good. Systematic political corruption particularly associated with campaign finance and related 'elite (or state) capture' – undue influence on laws, regulations, and policies by powerful corporate interests – plagues not only African countries but the developed polities as well. Corruption could be described as the act of 'giving or obtaining advantage through means which are illegitimate, immoral, and/or inconsistent with one's duty or the rights of others and often results from patronage (Roskin et al. 2000; Business Dictionary.com 2010; Chirawu 2012:52; Forje 2003).

Overall, Africa exhibits a major governance and leadership deficit. Unless it improves on these and other areas, sustained and shared growth is in jeopardy, the large middle class is under threat, and gross inequalities are unlikely to be addressed with the vast majority of the population sanctioned to perpetual poverty. Yet there is hope and opportunity for constructive and comprehensive change for the better.

Source: Credit - New African (2016) "Behind the Scenes" New African, No.566, November 2016, IC Publication. London, pp10,

Africa's previous high tolerance for corruption and impunity is declining in some countries. Civil society is demanding change, and some countries have embarked on reform. After all, the governance strength of a country can be inferred not from the unrealistic absence of any corruption but from the resolve and quality of its institutional response to addressing rightly this evil plaguing society. Poverty, inequality, dictatorial rule and ethnic divide being the no one challenging battle. The three parts to empowerment – consciousness, knowledge and action connote the transition from powerless to full citizenship. The logic of empowerment is to dichotomise power and powerless. State intrusion destroys the capacities of the people to govern them. State bureaucracies are responsible for blocking and defusing any restlessness or activities that might point towards citizen's cultural reawakening, self-help, or political empowerment that reduces what could be seen as hegemonic authoritarian rights of those in power to govern; and abrogate to themselves all the rights, powers and privileges. It is imperative to limit government hegemonic powers by getting the people to act as the true custodians of power in society.

Corruption has been described in certain quarters as initiation of transaction of goods and/or services to benefit the initiator, persons, or organisations of her/his choice which may include one's government. Or what Goldstein (2001:599) refers to as 'kind of politics which concerns the distribution of benefits' from economic transactions (exchange and capital accumulation) A serious draw back with the act of immoral and unethical behaviour is that it denies citizens important social and economic opportunities resulting in short, medium or long-term physical and psychological damage to those deprived of their rights, and yet improving the material gains for others thereby creating a situation where many citizens fail and a few succeed (Parenti, 1978:111).

It takes two to tango so goes the 'old-age' adage. The giver and taker are equally responsible in perpetuating the trade which is flourishing in leaps and bounds. Therefore, corruption exists within a structured environment where social, political and economic power relations instrumentally determine who gets what, when how much and for how long. In this regard, corruption is, therefore, inseparable from society's requirements for daily existence – professional opportunities, land ownership and delivery and receipt of a wide range of goods and services. The other characteristics of corruption are its victims' explicitly willingness to pay in order to get something done to survive. Bad governance promotes corruption and even institutionalised the process, in some societies it has become a creed an inherent component of the daily activities of the people. You look a fool if not involved in the process of greasing peoples' hands. Corruption occurs in an environment where there are either no measures to prevent the practice, or where anti-corruption laws exist but are reluctantly enforced, if at all. In addition, civil servants and senior politicians involved in the practice become oblivious to the phenomenon (Forje 2003; Chirawu 2012: op cit.). Corruption to a large extent is institutionalised. It is endemic requiring serious surgical operation to rid of the cancer destroying the region.

No country is corrupt free; from the least to most developed polity are involved at different levels of capacities and intensities. While avoiding the blame theory, it cannot be denied that the rich and powerful promote this act of immoral behaviour. To a large extent, the rich and powerful are leading proponents in influencing and perpetuating corruption in many parts of the world given the amounts of money they spend on bribing individuals and government officials in less developed parts of the world, Africa in particular. The multination enterprises are part of the racket. For example, "in the 1970s USA based Lockheed Company bribed top government officials in Japan to buy Lockheed jets for Japanese military, (and) in the early 1990s, the Bank of Commerce and Credit International (BCCI) was found to have operated a vast illegal worldwide network of money laundering, fraud, and corruption" (Goldstein 2001:429). The list is long and endless depicting the magnitude of the problem. Whether corruption is foreign or endogenous initiated and executed, the objectives remain the same. To reiterate the views of Acemah (2010) corruption is to: *"get what you want even if it means succeeding through the use of illegal or immoral methods. It could be argued that many Africans are sucked into corruption by the benefits they see accruing to fellow corrupt citizens, usually because of the absence of preventive measures – laws and policies"* or because of share weakness of leadership.

The famous statement by the Cameroon President *"show proof"* (Forje 2003) helped intensify corrupt practices in the country spreading like 'wildfire' which is now difficult to extinguish. The United States Ambassador to Cameroon, Janet E. Garvey sees the private sector in the country being hamstrung by a cumbersome bureaucracy, pervasive corruption and a dilapidated infrastructure. Many people are discouraged by the slow pace of reform in Cameroon. She decries the state of corruption in Cameroon whose position (154) in the 2007 World Bank Annual Doing Business Report; and Transparency International Corruption's Perception Index" (Pefok 200:3) In fact, one cannot dislodge the corruption mafia in Cameroon's Ministry of Finance and the Economy not to mention the educational sector from nursery through primary to the university. Corruption here remains a cankerworm that has eaten deep into all sectors of Cameroon society.

While Tanyi Mbi Joseph (2007:4) opines that: corruption, misappropriation and embezzlement, in general terms, are key elements that undermine economic development, performance and a major obstacle to poverty alleviation. Many high officials in Cameroon in particular and the third world countries in general, have plundered/mortgaged the national wealth, whereas citizens are in need of those resources to reconstruct and rehabilitate the societies. The lightening rates at which these shameless thieve misappropriate and embezzle public funds renders the State helpless in providing basic needs of its citizens. A country like Cameroon blessed with all sought of natural resources, yet unemployment, low salaries, no roads, all because a group of individuals and majority from a particular ethnic group have intentionally decided to plunder same and thus rendering millions frustrated. It is easy for a thief such as a Minister, Director or their accomplices when standing trial in court for charges of embezzlement, corruption and misappropriation to say, 'I am not guilty.' Where is the proof? The recent crime waves and insecurity, persistent strikes, poor output, are a clear indication that things are already falling apart. The next approach (terrorism) may be the physical attack on those tax officials, Ministers, Mayors, Directors etc., who, through their acts, are responsible for the misery and frustration of Cameroonians? The greatest and most dangerous criminals existing in Cameroon are embezzlers who through corrupt practices of the judiciary go free. They may decide with their huge high value foreign accounts to regroup themselves and topple the government or plunge the country into a civil war.

Apparently, those who misappropriate or embezzle private or public funds and corrupt officials are a new generation of international human right violators and a threat to world peace. According to Section 20 of the United Nations Convention against Corruption of 31 October 2003 states: *Subject to its constitution and the fundamental principle of its legal system, each State shall consider adopting such legislative and other measures as may be necessary to establish as a criminal offence, when committed intentionally, illicit enrichment, that is a significant increase in the assets of a public official that he or she cannot reasonably explain in relation to his/her income.* Article 31 of the cited convention provides the freezing, seizure and confiscation of assets procured in violation of this convention. Under this section, the thief is deprived permanently of the property by the order of the court or other competent authority. The existence and practice of the rule of law backed with good governance remain vital in ensuring that justice reigns supreme. The separation of powers to ensure proper checks and balance is primordial in ensuring that justice prevails. The Cameroon constitution gives executive powers to the Executive, The Cameroon Constitution Article 8 (12) states: The President of the Republic may, if necessary and after consultation with the Government, the Bureau of the National Assembly and the Senate, dissolve the National Assembly. Article 9(1) notes that: The President of the Republic may, where circumstances so warrant: declare by decree a state of emergency which shall confer upon him such special powers as may be provided for by law.

An individual holds the entire nation hostage Addams (2013:4) notes. "The political life of Cameroon has always been in Biya's armpit. There is no electoral calendar, or, rather, the political calendar is known only by him or decided by him alone. History is also being held hostage. Cameroon history belongs to President Biya and to him alone. Every aspect and every perspective of the preparations that are going on for the celebration of Reunification in the Cameroon are hinged on Biya. So, if Xmas were also dependent on the presidential visit, it would have been postponed." Such events can only occur in solid and stable centralised ethnic authoritarian regime or state structure. The developments offer at least two lessons, namely (i) governments that are either unable or unwilling to respond to their citizens' needs and to make transparent decisions will leader their countries to broader failures, corruption, violence, hunger, and poverty – and eventually to their demise; and (ii) in wave after wave of protests, the emerging, empowered youth in the developing world have shown that there is no return to autocracy, bad governance, and corruption (Mauduit 2013:3). Ghana has proved itself as the beacon of democracy in Africa; together with Botswana, Mauritius and South Africa, democratic government is beginning to emerge on the continent. Reynolds (2002:2-3) posit that democracy can be sustained even in countries that face daunting structural and cultural obstacles: poverty, inequality, and deep ethnic, national, or religious divisions. Structural and cultural factors help shape prospects for democracy, but a healthy dose of optimism regarding the potential for democracy under even adverse conditions has emerged.

Therefore, African countries must move in the direction of three important constitutional mechanisms for the inclusion of minority voices – autonomy, inclusive representation, and power sharing – in their asymmetry can be seen as compromising the form of classical liberal state. To avoid the state falling apart, African states should seek political solutions to political conflicts and not like in Cameroon where military force and might provide the answer to deep seated socio-political and cultural divide in society. For example, force cannot be used to impose on a people whose judicial system is based on the common law practice with a civil law judicial system. In addition, any society in which three institutions are corrupt – the education system; the security or law enforcing system and the judiciary – cannot make progress or graduate from the school of a capable developmental state. This is to state that corruption is institutionalised in Cameroon receiving the blessings of and protection by the legislative, executive and judiciary branches of government. What is fanning and legalising corruption in Cameroon is the *'bring proof syndrome'* backed by the lack of political will to fight the viruses of the disease.

Causes, Levels, Instruments & Categories of Corruption

Going back to the creation of humankind, we are told the story of Adam and Eva. Greed lies behind must of the corruption acts. Therefore, the causes of corruption are many and varied. They include the propensity of individual desires to get rich or to succeed in very endeavour of activities at whatever cost; the personal desire to socially, economically and politically ahead of others no matter the handicaps;

the competitive urge; desire for social; economic and political trappings, leadership pressure to be ahead or the desire to maintain personal or social status in society created by delusion of grandeur. According to Mawhood (1993:32), President Mobutu Sesse Seko of Zaire once told his people, "*if you want to steal, steal a little, cleverly, in a nice way.*" Whether this could be taken as invitation to enter the corruption trade or an appeal to citizens to moderate their corruption behaviour? That statement should be seen line with that of the Prime Minister of Cameroon: "*You scratch my back, I scratch your own*"; or the Cameroon proverb; "*you eat, I eat*" implying if you want to succeed, you should equally help me to succeed as well", which translate into bribing a government official or civil servant for the services rendered. There are those who are corrupt because it is fashionable to do no matter the consequences; they are those who do so for survival purposes; only when justice reigns that corruption can be brought to book. Until the rule of law and justice is pregnant in the African society, corruption will continue to expand its tentacles unprompted.

Corruption occurs at various levels, (a) political level; (b) organisation level; (c) personal or individual levels; (d) economic levels, (e) religious, and (e) within the public and private sectors. It is worse in the public sector since government machinery grinds slow and punitive measures are poorly and slowly to be implemented as compared with the private sector. Within the organisational level, especially in state institutions, bureaucracy and corruption are intertwined partly because bureaucrats become ingrained to the routine of corruption and find it difficult to do things as should be done properly. Deepings hands into one's pocket may accelerate the process of bureaucratic procedures fast than usual (Forje 2003, Roskin et al 2000; Weatherby et al 2000). Politically, the lure of power inevitably persuades leaders to cushion their positions as much as possible even reverting to the Machiavellian way; being rational and tough in exercising politics. The 21st century is witnessing such overindulgence, often proving that political processes are self-centred, which constitutes the driving force of the engine of government. Corruption in the public sector gives the government a bad check: a new check is necessary by cashing in the black cheque of corruption. In other worlds, now is the time to rise out of the black dust of corruption which is endemic shaking the very foundation of the nation/continent.

The instruments for corruption are often initiated by social, political and economic elites in most countries. More often than not, powerful government officials often with very strong ties with government are channels for multiplying the viruses of corruption and its vices. Which

Parenti argues, their *'interests never stand naked; there are enshrouded in the flag, fortified by law, protected by the policy, nurtured by the media, taught by the schools, and blessed by the church"* (1978:84). Different instruments such as the police, the law, the armed forces, school's institutions of higher learning, government-manipulated media and the flag among others like the churches which manipulated by the state are subtly used by government as instrument to enforce the state's control over its population. At the same time, government's action underlines the reality that power determines who gets what, when and how. And the state does so fully aware of this prevailing corruption (Weatherby et al. 2000:68; Chinawu 2012:57; Forje, 2003). The entire social fabric of society and its institutions are politicised curtailing the fundamental rights of the people. The establishment of monolithic party structure help to deepen the level of corruption, the divide and state of abject poverty. Consequently, party members in each institution knows who put him/her where and why to serve the interests of the party. More often than not, these political parties in Africa withhold development from areas or constituencies dominated by Opposition Parties.

It is indirectly or directly perceived as a form of 'punishment' meted out to convince the electorate in such regions to switch allegiance to the governing parties. Table 10:1 depicts some of the categories of corruption. There is no perfect human-being. Therefore, there is no perfect society. From the creation of the human-being, corruption was institute judging from the acts of Eva towards Adam. However, this should not be a cliché to act unethically and immorally. To expect perfect order in a social system only signifies the 'arrival of utopia' (Johnson 1966:9: Korda 1975:7; Chirawu 2012): corruption by design undermines the concept of 'moral community', or 'a collectivity of people who share certain 'definitions of the situation' (called values), which legitimise the inequalities of social organisation and cause people to accept them as morally justified'.

Table 10:1 Categories of Corruption

A	B
• Knowledge that others have benefited and continue to benefit from corruption	• The desire to fulfil political campaigns promises, particularly when the over prevailing conditions are not enabling;
• Desire to compete with socially and economically successful individuals	• Countering pressure to give in to national demand for a change of government;
• Absence of legal instrument to prevent/curb corruption;	• Fear for one's life after years of trampling on impoverished masses, which gives credence to the West African saying: "greet all the people that you meet going up, because you will meet the people when coming down;
• Compulsion to ensure one's success;	• Government's deliberate reluctance to enforce anti-corruption measures because enforcing them would wipe out the support the leader has among the current and prospective beneficiaries of corruption; and,
• Instinctive desire to move ahead economically in one's peer group;	• The necessity to secure one's future should political fortunes change (evident in the way Mubarak was deposed from power in 2011, for example).
• Government's failure to create jobs;	
• Outright greed;	
• Bad governance and leadership	

Source: (Complied from Chirawu 2012:51)

Korda insinuates further: 'to confess that one has power is to make oneself responsible for using it, and safety lies in and artfully contrived pose of impotence, behind which one can do exactly as one pleases.

The politicisation of power in Africa is too common and needs no further elaboration here but only highlight its impact in sanctifying the perpetuation of corruption and its dangerous effects impacting on the quality livelihood of the people. Why is corruption so entrenched in the African society? Some may argue that the African society is sucked into corruption simply by the benefits they see accruing to fellow corrupt citizens, usually because of the absence of preventive measures and mechanism to check such activities and render justice (Acemah 2010) and political leaders are effectively an inseparable part of the matrix. The poor and powerless are raped by the rich and powerful with the weak pushed to the edges of malpractices for survival purposes. The religious bodies are not free from this trade either. Others may argue that corruption is widespread due to the failure of the state to provide basic needs and services to the people – the rising level of unemployment, underdevelopment, marginalisation, exclusion, mistreatment and name the rest are contributing input factors fertilising the corruption saga throughout the continent. Absence of quality services delivery, poverty and destitution forces some of the people to migrate in search of greener pastures to fend for their families (Solimano & Avanzini (2010). It will take the continent a very long-time to free itself from this canker worm disease. While there are ongoing efforts to find a cure for devastating diseases like Ebola, malaria, HIV-AIDs, and the rest, government and society are promoting corruption and poverty. The choice before African leaders and the people is clear. On the one hand, social justice, radical, meaningful reform without delays not token measures. On the other, a continent of revolutions and fascist dictatorships and stagnant economies, perpetual wars and civil conflicts becoming proxy between different strata of society threatening national unity, cohesion under constant threat. An Africa, in other words, very much or even worse like the one we live

The Rottenness of the State: The Cancer of Corruption.

Corruption is clearly an absence both of accountability and of law and order. This is true whether it is basically bribe or extortion driven and even when it takes the form of camouflaged expenditure used for public purposes, but not disclosed to the public and representing the personal strategies and/or survival mechanisms of the head of state. Accountability requires not merely transparency but freedom to query, to criticise and to propose changes. Up to a point allowing this in respect to weak or erroneous implementation and individual malpractices can initially be popular even if there are distinct limits on allowable scope of querying or criticism. That is especially true after extended periods of war and capriciously oppressive dictatorships that exist in many African countries (Green, 1995:272).

Who guides the guards in a country riddle with corrupt? There are cases that you only need to hand over an 'envelop' to pass a driving test and obtain a driver's licence. The country is ridden with fake and false certificates as this is the passport to getting an employment where jobs are hard to come by. Customs officer sells stuff they have confiscated from people. In the Ministry of Finance, you have to pay upfront 30% of your due amount to be collected. The officer work on file does not know the pains you have gone through may be for over a year without a salary. He or she is only interested in the accumulated amount to siphon 30%. This goes on and on. This makes corruption to have its traditional antecedents in African countries. The sad side of all this is that corruption contributes significantly to mass poverty as well as it enriches the wealth of the ruling class.

Unfortunately, whenever power-holders and policy-makers become rich through corruption, the policies the articulate are less likely to threaten wealth or alleviate poverty. Bureaucrats who own large tracts of urban housing land will advise their ministers against urban land reform. Politicians who run factories or own estates will not vote in favour of more preferential treatment for small businesses (who may compete) or land reform. And, when politics comes to be considered as a path to wealth as well as power, it tends to attract few idealists and more opportunists, whose presence speeds up the degeneration process (Harrison, 1981:375).

Though this may solve the individual plight of the migrant, it also adds to the problems of his/her new environment. The will to livelihood and the desire to acquire and use power for whatever reasons underpins the desire to corrupt practices knowingly or unknowingly (governments, organisations, politicians, individuals etc.) express instinct through the cover of corruption, which manifest it in personal desires and political trappings. Indeed, corruption manifestation is intertwined by the acts of politicisation of state institutions, persuasion, inappropriate uses of force, economic deprivation, unfulfilled promises, exclusion and share greed. The inappropriate use of force leaves the powerless citizen vulnerable not only to corruption and deprivation of human rights, but equally exposed to numerous inhuman treatments by the state agents who fail to understand their functional roles in society. The worse thing a country can do is to politicise state institutions. Such act sow's seeds of exclusion and marginalisation fanning serious divide in society and paralysing the output functions of the government.

The output functions of government are for the entire society even those who voted against the ruling party in an election. Every society is expected to have unrestricted human networking that advances self-actualisation in the environmental milieu, ensuring mutually beneficial exchanges of goods and services offering material pleasure and benefits to the people. When these basic needs are denied the people, they often result to shortcuts to achieve certain goals and means of survival. Deprivation is factor that should be adequately addressed to better reduce the level of corruption in society. Unfulfilled promises are contributing factors in upholding the spread of malpractices in society. While corruption in the west could be seen as propelled by the forces of capitalist ethos at different levels, in Africa the principal causes are greed and poverty and exclusion making the continent most vulnerable to various forms of financial bribery.

In this respect, financial fraud and bribery are accepted and practiced as a means of survival and in an environment greased with inequality and vicious competition, prompting cunning strategies that disregard and/or absorb blame regardless of the inhuman consequence at different levels of governance These serve as attestation of the common and multifaceted nature of Africa's overwhelming corruption and other forms of malpractices (Chirawu 2012; Forje 2003;) that impedes the sustainable transformation of the continent. Imagine a country like Cameroon where 11 ministries have been blacklisted for refusing to collaborate with the National Anti-Corruption Commission (CONAC), with the State losing over FCFA 171 billion to various acts of corruption in 2015, and unscrupulous contractors abandoning 45 projects in 2015 (Nsomi, 2017:5). No legal actions are taken for such attitude. How do you expect society to comply to the laws of the state when the state fails in honouring laws its articulate? Society cannot develop with such prevailing attitude and behaviour. Fifty or more years after independence, we have only ourselves to blame for the continuous poor plight of the vast majority of the population. It is time to change course now, face the realities or for ever hold our mouth shut and stop propagating the blame theory.

What is clear is that corruption is a cancer at the heart of most countries, Cameroon in particular where it has eaten deep into the social fabric of the foundations of trust between people and their governors. In some countries, Cameroon for example, it is legalised by the activities and policies of the state; through and at least two key weaknesses of the state; (i) the unholy marriage of the ruling political party and economic power; whereby money buys influence, and power attracts money; and (ii) the 'softness' of the state, to deploy the words of Gunnar Myrdal – 'its inability to apply and enforce its own laws and regulations, so that reform – even if it is legislated – rarely gets put into effect' (Myrdal 1970; 1968, Harrison 1981). We can also add the fact civil society inherently contributes to the legalisation of corruption in society since it takes two to tango. Civil society can fight against corruption by building up a cadre of 'whistleblowers' with the mass media objectively acting as the voice of the voiceless. Presently, the mass media sector is not free from the hammer-sledge of the government. Advances in science and technology have contributed to wrongly enhancing the role of corruption in the transformation of transitional polities. Here, Karake et al (2019) highlights the quality and comprehensives of cyber security policies and strategies in developing and emerging economies. African countries need to put in place resources and infrastructure measures in addressing the wrong deployment of science and technology in the progress of a nation.

The constitution of the country following Law No.98/6 of 18 January 1996 Part V11 – The Constitutional Council, Article 46 called for the creation of the Constitutional Council. That aspect of the constitution went operation only in 2018. As for Article 66 which states that the President of the Republic, the Prime Minister, Members of Government and persons ranking as such, the President and Members of the Bureau of the National Assembly, the President and Members of the Bureau of the Senate, Members of Parliament, Senators, all holders of an elective office, Secretaries-General of Ministries and persons ranking as such, Directors of the Central Administration, General Managers of public and semi-public entries, Judicial and Legal Officers, administrative personnel in charge of the tax base, collection and handling of public funds, all managers of public votes and property, shall declare their assets and property at the beginning and at the end of their tenure of office (Cameroon Government 2008). This aspect of the constitution has not been implemented opening up the cankerworm for corruption. Seen from these perspectives, government has legalised and even institutionalised corruption.

Putting an end to the evil forces of corruption, call for joint efforts by the various stakeholders' state, civil sector, the private sector and international community working in synergy for the inclusive welfare of the country. Each side has an interests and a duty to act unconditionally to help wipe out the viruses of corruption and poverty. Presently, the kettle and pot are calling each other 'black' and this would go on for many years and generations to come for all eternity as the excuse for showing proof and not cleaning themselves

Beating the Cankerworm of Corruption, Poverty and Inequality

Without making the necessary changes, it is utopian to suggest that quality livelihood would come the way of the African people. But without constructive and meaningful changes reaching all parts of the continent, from Banjul to the Horn, Cape to Cairo, the play field is left wide open for changes through violence to take place. For long the powers that be have taken it as right that the poor or weak and will do nothing. As such, the status quo will continue for eternity. At the same time, we fail to understand and appreciate the fact that though the people may be poor and weak, they can be equally being dedicated to their plight and rising interest would one day succeed in taking power. Yet in some instances, possibly the majority or rich, increasingly strident demands for justice may be met by repression, which can be very long-lived if it is efficient enough. No condition is permanent. This is what the people of Southern Cameroons or other oppressed groups on the continent are witnessing. The quest for justice and change is striking hard with all forces on the corridors of power from East to West – South to North with all intensity.

The situation can be likened to the suppression of the female gender for centuries and their determination to brave the odds which is now yielding fruits. There is no need to detail the spectacular pains and violence, sexual and cultural inequities, dehumanisation that African women have and continue to encounter. All these acts of barbarism, dispossession, overlooked and overworked of the poor by the rich have contributed to the underdevelopment and exploitation of the continent. The siphoning of the nation's wealth by the ruling class, the oppression of the female gender by the male gender does not affect the poor and women alone. It affects society as a whole. The consequences on the continent remains clear, prolonged underdevelopment and exploitation.

No one could help but be appalled by the continued failure of the ruling class to escape a narrow, short term view of individual interests. They continue to place self-articulate interests above the collective interests of the people. The challenge is for the declassified group of the population to rally and pull-together their collective potentials, energies towards redeeming their fundamental human rights and freedoms. Now is the hour to work towards their sustenance, self-esteem and freedom. The only way forward is co-ordinated assault on poverty, inequality, injustice and discrimination of regaining their rights and prosperity.

References

Addams Bouddih (2013). Roughshod: Cameroon taken Hostage by Biya's Buea Visit." The Post No. 01490, Monday, 23 December 2013, Buea – Cameroon, p.4 (www.thepostwebedition.com)

Acemah, H. (2010)." Africa: Why is the Continent in Such a Mess"? 14 December 2010. Available at http://allafrica.com/stories/201210061:html, 9 March 2011)

Cameroon Government (2008) Constitution of the Republic of Cameroon. National Printing Press, Yaoundé - Cameroon

Commission For Africa Report [2005] our Common Interest: Report of the Commission for Africa, Penguin, London (http://www.commissionforafrica.org)

Charrawu O. Tapera (2012) "The Flip Sides of Corruption: A Challenge to Developing Countries", in Mammo Muche et al (eds.) (2012). The Africana World: From Fragmentation to Unity and Renaissance, Africa Institute of South Africa, Pretoria, South Africa.

Essoungou-Andre-Michel (2013). "The Rise of Civil Society Groups in Africa – These Major Groups have become Major Actors in the Fight Against Corruption", Africa Renewal, December, 2013,Vol. 27, No.3, United Nations, New York, pp10-11.

Farah Douglas, (2017).''The Terror-Crime Nexus: How International Groups of Criminals and Militants Team to Move Money Around the World", Finance and Development, Vol.54, No.3, September 2017, Washington, USA, pp19-21

Forje W. John (2003) Cameroon Without Corruption. The Search for a New Vision, Niba Publishers, Bamenda - Cameroon: (New enlarged edition (2018) Lambert Academic Publishing, Germany)

Goldstein, J. (2001). International Relations, 4th edition Longman, Paris

Green Herbold Reginald (1995) "Not Farewell but Fare Forward Voyagers: Africa into the 21st Century", in Bade Onimode and Richard Synge (eds.) (1995) Issues in African Development: Essays in Honour of Adebayo Adedeji at 65. Heinemann Educational Books (Nigeria) Plc and African Centre for Development and Strategic Studies, Ijebu-Ode, Nigeria, pp264-303

Hatchard John (2014). Combating Corruption: Legal Approaches to Supporting Good Governance and Integrity. Edward Elgar Publishing, Camberley, UK.

Harrison Paul (1981) Inside The Third World. Chapter 19, Something is Rotten in the State. The Politics of Poverty, pp366-406, Pelican Books Ltd, Harmondsworth, Middlesex, England, United Kingdom.

Johnson, C. (1966). Revolutionary Change Basic Studies in Politics. Little Brown Series, Brown and Company, Boston, USA

Karake Zeinab, Shalhoub A. Rana and Ayas Huda (2019). Enforcing Cyber security in Developing and Emerging Economies. Edward Elgar Publishing, United Kingdom

Kaufmann Daniel [2005] "10 Myths about Governance and Corruption," in Finance and Development, September 2005. Vol.42. No.3, International Monetary Fund, Washington, pp41-43

Kaufmann Daniel (2015). "Corruption Matters. Finance and Development, Vol. 52. No. 3, September 2015, Washington, USA, pp20-23.

Korda, M. (1975). Power! How to Get it. How to Use it. Ballantine Books, New York.

Loungani Prakash (2019) "Fixing Capitalism", Review of Raghuram Rajan (2019) The Third Pillar: How Markets and the State Leave the Community Behind, Penguin Books, New York, in Finance and Development, September 2019, Vol. 56 No.3, International Monetary Fund, Washington, DC. USA, p55

Maras Konstadinos (2007). Trace the Elusiveness of Political Corruption: A Discourse Analysis. Discuss Paper Series No.3. On Crime and Culture, University of Konstanz.

Mauro Paolo, Medas Paulo, and Fournier Jean-Marc (2019). "The Cost of Corruption – Graft Results in Lost-Tax Revenue, but it does takes a Social Toll", finance and Development, September 2019, Vol. 56, No. 3, International Monetary Fund, Washington, DC. USA. pp25-29

Mawhood, P. (ed:) (1993). Local Government in the Third World. 2nd Edition. Africa Institute of South Africa, Pretoria, South Africa.

Mauduit M. Remy (2013), "Editorial: Governance and Democratic Transaction" in Africa and Francophone (ASPJ), 3rd Quarter, Vol.4, No.3, pp2-3

Mungui-Alina and Johnston Michael (2017) Transitions to Good Governance. Creating Virtuous Circles of Anti-Corruption. Edward Elgar Publishing, UK

Myrdal Gunnar (1968) Asian Drama, Chapter 20, Vol. 11, Penguin Books

Myrdal Gunnar (1970) The Challenge of World Poverty, Allen Lane United Kingdom

Nsomi Kini Yerima (2017), "11 Ministries Blacklisted for Undermining CONAC", The Post, No. 01787, 9 January 2017, Buea, Cameroon, p5

Parenti, M. (1978) Power and Powerless, New York. St. Martin Press, New York,

Pefok Joe Dinga (2007). "US Ambassador Berates Cameroon for Slow Reforms: The Post No. 0899, Monday, 15 October 2007, Yaoundé – Cameroon

Reynolds Andrew (ed.) (2002) The Architecture of Democracy. Oxford University Press, United Kingdom

Roskin et al (2000) Political Science. An Introduction

Sepheka Mantsadi (2013). "Africa: Governance Gets New Emphasis at Economic Forum," All Africa, 16 May 2013. (http://allafrica.com/stories/201305161182.html)

Sobrinho Nelson and Thakoor Vimal (2019) "More Sand than Oil" Finance and Development, September 2019, Vol.56, No. 3. International Monetary Fund, Washington DC, USA, pp35-37.

Solimano, A. & Avanzini D. (2010). The International Circulation of Elites: Knowledge, Entrepreneurial and Political.

(WIP 113. (http://www.wider.unu.edu/publications/mewsletter)

Tanyi Mbi Joseph (2007). "The Most Dangerous Criminals in Cameroon Are Embezzlers." The Post. No.0899, Monday 15 October 2077, Yaoundé-Cameroon, p4

Tajudeen Abdul Raheem (2010) "Corrupt Leaders Are Mass Murderers" in Speaking Truth to Power – Selected Pan-African Postcards (Compiled by) Ama Biney and Adebayo Olukoshi, Pambazuka Press, London, pp20-22

United Nations (2013). "What is Good Governance?" United Nations and Social Commission for Asia and the Pacific2013 (http://www.unescap.org/pdd/prs/ProjectActivities/Ongoing/gg/governance.asp).

Warf Barney (ed.) (2018) Handbook on the Geographies of Corruption, Edward Elgar Publishing, United Kingdom

Weatherby, J.N. Cruikshanks, R. L Evans E. B. Jr., Gooden, R. Haff, E.D, Kranzdorf, R & Long D. (2000) World Issues and Politics of the Developing World, 4th ed. Longman

World Bank (2013). "Corruption: Lack of Integrity or Honesty – Especially Susceptibility to Bribery," World Bank 2013.

Yao Jiiaxiong (2019) "Illuminating Economic Growth – Satellite Images of the Earth at Night Reveals the Pace of Economic Growth and Much More", Finance and Development, September 2019, Vol. 56, No. 3, International Monetary Fund, Washington DC. USA, pp48-51

Chapter Eleven

Energy - The Engine of and Power for Development

"Industrialisation cannot be considered a luxury but a necessity for the continent's development. A rising middle class, an improved macroeconomic environment, a rising gross domestic product – all are low-hanging fruits that can nourish industrialisation."

(Nkosazana Dlamini-Zuma, AUC Chairperson)

Introduction: Energizing and Industrialising Africa

Energy is the life wire for the sustainable transformation of any African country. Therefore, emphasis should be focused on power development. The provision of reliable power, essentially through the generation and distribution of electricity to homes and industry, is recognised as a vital preliminary to fostering economic growth and development. Africa is blessed with all forms of energy supply facilities, hydro-electric power, solar energy bio-energy, and thermal energy for coastal nations; windmill energy given the hilly nature of the continent among others. Yet the continent suffers from erratic energy supply. Improving on all these energy possibilities will improve the continent's ability to provide power – thereby contributing to the general public's health and wellbeing and stimulating Africa's manufacturing activity.

The resources exist, from the Rift Valley to the North African deserts; from the Western coasts to South Africa's crops, the numerous mountains and hilltops provide vast areas for wind farms and the oceans to power the industrialisation of the continent. The oceans provide the geothermal energy needed to ensure that every household can be lit, and our industries powered to produce the goods needed for the welfare of the people. Some of the hydro-electric power dam projects funded by the Kuwait Fund include:

- Barge Dam Project in Burkina Faso which received USA$ 13.5 million
- Song Loulou in Cameroon with a loan of USA$15.3million in 1977 and $7.5 million in 1985;
- Kpong Hydro-Dam – Ghana a total of USA$ 44 million (1977 and 1981)

- Garafiri Hydro-electric project, guinea USA$30 million (1994 and 1997)
- Selingue Dam in Mali USA&16 million
- Kandadji Dam in Niger USA$19.38 million in 2009;
- Andekaleka hydro-dam in Madagascar USA$9.2 million in 1978 and S12.24 in 2006
- Mtera hydro-electric project in Tanzania with USA$11.11
- Aoulouz Dam in Morocco USA$24.23 million in 1990
- El Grass dam Morocco with USA$63.37 million in 199the Sidi Wahda Dam Morocco USA$48 million in 1995;
- The Raouz Dam in Morocco USA$42.5 million in 2012

Ethiopia's grand design to construct a USA$42.2 billion dam in the Benishangul-Gumuz region to provide 6,000 megawatts of electricity dubbed the Grand Ethiopia Renaissance Dam will be Africa's biggest dam; which will go a long way to boost power supply in the country and region. Although Africa is rich in oil, gas, coal and renewable energy resources, electricity is hard to come by, which traps people in endemic poverty. Presently only about 29 percent of the continent's population has access to power. Yet the continent is whitewashed with vast energy potentials. In respect of hydro-electric power, countries like Cameroon and the Democratic Republic of Congo have vast sources of hydro-power potentials still untapped. Plans by BHP Billiton (the world's largest mining company with the government Kinshasa over the construction of Inga 3 dam as one of the three dams of the USA$80 billion Grand Inga Dam project is yet to be realised. The Grand Inga Dam Project when completed will be the world's biggest hydropower scheme and could generate more than a third of the total electricity currently produced in Africa. Inga 1 and 2 are being rehabilitated with involvement from organisations including the World Bank and African Investment Bank (Whitby, 2011; 51) A country like Nigeria needs about 10.000 megawatts of electricity but generates only 4.500. With 12% of the world's oil reserve, 40% of its gold, about 90% of its chromium and platinum, 60% of its arable land and more, Africa should do better at ensuring proper energy supply and addressing poverty. Africa is blessed with vast alternatives of energy sources of power supply, ranging from hydro-power, solar, wind and its enormous gas resources to empowering manufacturing and improving the quality livelihood of citizens.

Nigeria for example, the world's sixth-largest producer of crude oil, should refine enough for local consumption rather than spending

USA$8 billion a year subsidizing fuel imports. Nigeria has been flaring gas for 40 years. It is estimated that the gas flared in Africa can supply half of the continent's electricity needs but it is burn with no value addition. Heavy dependence on oil revenues – which are volatile and unpredictable, and will, sooner or later, dry up – greatly complicates a country's fiscal policy. (see Akitoby, et al. 2012). Oil exporters in particular, are experiencing sharp declines in exports, putting pressure on foreign exchange reserves and exchange rates. (See Akitoby, et al. 2012: Chen, 2016:28-29) China's new growth strategy could hurt Africa's commodity-dependent economies. And slowdowns in large economies in sub-Saharan Africa, such as South Africa and Nigeria, affect smaller neighbours. It is time Africa's economy works for every African.

Africa is losing 2% to 3% of its GDP because of lack of reliable energy supply. With nearly 600 million people without electricity, Africa is the world's most energy-poor region. The continent cannot industrialise without regular supply of electricity. The current energy deficit is holding back the sustainable transformation of the continent. Erratic power supply makes the cost of running a business one of the highest in the world. Frequent power outages mean that most entrepreneurs have to rely on diesel-powered generator for back up, which are expensive to run, killing off many businesses in their first year of operations or forcing them to relocate to countries where the electricity supply is more stable. You cannot manufacture any product without a steady and reliable source of power supply. It is imperative for governments throughout the continent to introduce policies to develop alternative sources of energy for the country.

Serious structural transformation is imperative. This equally implies drastic shift from agriculture to industrial and service delivery sectors. Commodity-based industrialisation is the bridge from economic growth to jobs creation and social development. Growth trajectory is not sustainable because commodities are mostly exhaustible, and Africa has little control over disruptions in world demand and prices. Presently, average manufacturing in Africa's low-income countries is smaller as a percentage of GDP than it was some two – three decades ago. Not all African countries commodities to export, while others are landlocked and face high transport costs. In addition, most African markets are small and fragmented, which cancels out any competitive advantage smaller countries may have.

Source: Chen Wenjie & Roger Nord (2016). "A Fork in the Road – China's New Growth Strategy could hurt Africa's Commodity-dependent Economies" Finance & Development, No. 2, Vol. 53, June 2016,

The 'Black Gold - Oil as Cause Not a Blessing to the African Society

Source: BBC (2011) Focus on Africa: January-March 2011, Vol., 22, No.1 London, pp8 **(bbc.co.uk/focusonafricamagazine)**

Poor energy supply impedes their manufacturing capabilities. Africa cannot become an industrial region with erratic power supply. But even with all of these issues and concerns there is great hope and optimism for Africa in the near and long-term future. This is the biggest question facing the continent; how to make sure the current growth is continual and sustainable. If Africa is to be an 'Emerging Africa', we all wish, something drastic has to be done with energy to power the industrial phase of the continent. But with such erratic power and chaotic forms of energy supply, the continent's energy sector for now cannot empower the manufacturing sector's take-off in Africa and government alone cannot do it either. A synergy must emerge between the state and the private sector in enhancing the energy power sector of the continent.

Erratic and Chaotic Power Supply – A Common Feature in Africa.

Chaotic wiring in most African countries

Here men repair generators beneath a tangle of power lines on the rooftops of electronics stores in Oshodi Market in Lagos, Nigeria. Source: Ezerioha Damian (2015) "Empowering Manufacturing, News Africa, Vol.3. No.4, 31 January 2015, London, pp32

Erratic and Chaotic Power Supply cannot empower the manufacturing sector in Africa. The above picture shows men repairing generators beneath a tangle of power lines on the rooftops of electronics stores in Oshodi Market in Lagos – Nigeria. This is a common scene across the continent. Africa needs new sources of efficient energy supply to empowering its industrial take-off. Presently an energy revolution is rocking in the world: one triggered by an explosion of new energy technologies and supplies. It's a stark contrast to the energy shifts of the past half-century, which were sparked by acute supply shocks. New resource riches are popping up spottily across the globe and they are beginning to have profound and messy geopolitical and environmental repercussions. So far, their most straining effect is economic; today's new energy supplies are threatening powerful players at least as much as yesterday's energy crunches did. Why is everything in Africa up-side-down?

Yet energy is crucial and a significant input factor to power Africa into an industrial age. The creation of strong manufacturing and industrial base is vital to internal African growth. For example, Nigeria's manufacturing sector's contribution to Gross Domestic Product (GDP) – initially 6.8 per cent now revised to 9.2 per cent – is still relatively low when compared with those of her peers, such as Egypt (15 per cent), South Africa (16 per cent), Malaysia (17 per cent) and Singapore (24 per cent). In highly industrialised countries, contribution of manufacturing to GDP averages 20 per cent to 49 per cent. Progress in Africa entails a vibrant manufacturing sector is required for the sustained growth and development of the other key sectors especially agriculture and solid minerals. The increasing 'scope and scale of globalisation' has to be keyed into the development process of the continent. It is only with better infrastructure, lower costs of production and a friendlier manufacturing environment that African manufacturers will be able to produce cheaper and higher quality products competing effectively with imported ones. To fully diversify the economy, African countries should accelerate the process of looking towards non-traditional tradable goods and services beyond mineral and agriculture-based products.

Reliance on oil has exposed the economy of African countries to the volatility of the international oil market. Movement into manufacturing and exportable service activities would allow African countries to take advantage of the rising demand that derives from the growing income in the world economy. All these things cannot be achieved without sustainable power supply. The continent's development depends on empowering the energy sector and to implement policies that provide the necessary structures for rapid industrialisation, the acceleration of the development of manufacturing in Africa will depend on the creation of an appropriate enabling environment without which the desired growth will not be achieved; and the Africa We Want will never be realised.

In Sub-Saharan Africa, some 621 million people lack access to electricity, forcing people to rely on expensive and unhealthy sources of energy such as kerosene and charcoal, while the shortage of power also significantly inhibits economic growth. This is a region desperately in need of better access to energy and yet a region with vast energy resources potentials. The continent should take this as an opportunity to chart a new cleaner route for energy. Though Africa is only responsible for just 2.3% of global emissions despite accounting for over 15% of the world's population, current trajectories show that agricultural yields on the continent could fall by 20% in some areas due to unpredictable weather patterns, ground water levels in southern and west Africa could decrease by 50-70%. And huge areas of arable ground could dry out to become arid wastelands. These prospects would be damaging anywhere in the world, but would be particularly devastating on a continent in which around 70% of the population rely on agriculture for their livelihoods and most live on less than USA$2 a day" (Wan 2015:19). Africa only contributes a tiny fraction of greenhouse gas emissions, compared to what the US, China and the European Union contributing 42% of global emission with Russia, Brazil and India not far behind; but this does not mean that the continent cannot improve on its energy supply. Apparently, it takes a Tanzanian eight years to consume as much electricity as an American consumes in a single month. About 35 percent of South Africa's population still does not have access to the grid. Even the cheapest electricity will be out of reach for the majority. Today's challenge in Africa is not so much the privatisation of public services but the commercialisation of the public sector, where private sector operating sector operating principles are introduced, No. 421, July 2015, IC Publications, London, pp21.

Africa is challenged to take a judicious energy mix that will allow it to develop at the same time, which could include the use of fossil fuels and to ensure that the continent moves on a low carbon path. The bet on renewable would make sense not just from the perspectives of climate change but could be a double whammy in terms of being hugely attractive to investors as well. An alternative friendly energy source is what the continent needs. For example, it is well known, that covering just a fraction of the Sahara Desert with solar panels could power the entire world, while Ethiopia has estimated that it could generate 100GW through wind power alone. Sub-Saharan Africa's current grid capacity is just 90GW. The potentials are great across the continent. Ethiopia's Ashegoda wind farm, for example, has a 120MW capacity and is one of the central pillars of the country's bid to become carbon neutral by 2027 – it is also the largest wind project in Africa, though is set to be overtaken by the 300MW Lake Turkana Wind Power project when the Kenyan plant becomes fully operational. Elsewhere, Ghana's Nzema solar plant is set to be one of the biggest in the world and increase national capacity by 6%, while in South Africa, solar, biomass and wind systems have been cropping up across the country. Vast opportunities and possibilities exist across the continent in tapping and improving its energy power supplies without contributing to environmental and resources depletion. Many African countries are yet to initiate rigorous renewable energy policies that are necessary to attract foreign participation. There are a number of renewable energy funds available to support investors such as the USA$800m multilaterally funded Scaling Up Renewable Energy in Low Income Countries Programme and the USA$100m renewable energy fund established by the African Development Bank in 2014. Africa has to exert efforts in ensuring the proper use of renewable sources of energy. The picture show technicians installing panels for solar energy and the electric consumption for sub-Saharan Africa in comparison with electricity consumption in some developed countries, United States and the United Kingdom.

South Africa is in the process of construct the world's largest thermal energy store with a net generation capacity of 50 MW with nine hours of thermal energy storage. It enables the sun's energy to be stored during the day and released in the evening. South Africa has awarded its 120MW project to China's Goldwind. The Golden Valley project will be in the Eastern Cape, and the project will be Goldwind's first project in South Africa and it's second largest in Africa. South Africa has 294 wind turbines installed currently. The South African Wind Energy Association (Sawea) advises that it needs 2,500 by 2020 to alleviate electricity shortfalls. Egypt plans new solar and wind plants. An Egyptian company is developing a 50MW solar photovoltaic power plant 800km south of Cairo. Egypt intends that 20% of energy usage should come from renewable by 2020. Despite the risks, venture capitalists and angel investors are increasingly profiting from Africa's rapid growth and untapped opportunities. African governments should encourage investments in these untapped energy sources. Angels rush in where fools fear to tread. African business tycoons should hold this adage close to their heart.

Picture: Technicians Installing Panels in One of East Africa's Largest Solar Farms, Rwamagana District, Rwanda, and Electricity consumption for sub-Saharan Africa and selected countries/regions (kWh per capita, 2012)

Source: Wan James (2015) Can Africa Lead the Fight Against Climate Change? African Business No.421, July 2015, London, p21

The many hill-tops in a country like Cameroon, Lesotho, Kenya, Nigeria and others, provides vast opportunities for these countries to expand their energy wind-mill power potentials. These resources when added to the enormous hydropower potentials enable African countries to rich their energy capabilities in advancing their industrialisation programmes. All what requires is matching words with action and powering the continent to higher heights of industrialisation and quality services delivery in 21st century. People forget that Africa's power does not only lie in its tiny economies and large geography. The continent's power lies in controlling some of the most critical resources on the planet earth. If the continent shuts down all extractive resources and deny exports, Africa will bring the USA, Europe and China to their knees within months. Even though this may seem an extreme and highly unlikely possibility at present, but given how extreme the consequences of continuing on the current trajectory would be for Africa and many parts of the world, progressive radical solutions may soon be the only feasible ones. "There is no doubt that climate change is a threat to all humankind, Africa has the power; we are just being too nice, lacking the gouts to speak truth to the powers that be. May be it is time for the lion to bare its fangs" (Wan op cit. p21). Why does Africa shy-away from using the given natural resources of 'sun' in powering its economic growth? In Europe, 'snow' has been turned into a leisure form, but we cannot deploy the power of the sun in energising our development nexus.

A wind turbine farm in Tunisia. World Bank / Dana Smillie

(See also Dan Sheppard (2014)" Africa To Push Development Agenda at Upcoming Climate Summit" African Renewal, August 201. Vol.28, No.2, New York, Pp26-27

African countries need to be reimagining their internal relationships to respond to emerging forces and realities. The continent must plug into huge national and global opportunities in fostering creativity and innovation for economic growth, and practicing the very basic tenets of democratic governance and development in Africa. By our own efforts, Africa shall succeed. Africa can achieve only by what it does for itself and not by waiting for hand-outs, grants and services to be handed down. This is the hour to defend the values of our cultural heritage and for our children and their children protecting and securing the future of Africa. To build a better future for Africa, we must set the foundation for human capital development. This is extremely important as 'Education is the first and must crucial step in this direction, but true empowerment comes when you turn that education into economic progress, i.e. employment' (Lord Ahmad, 2017:40, in Versi Anver (2017:38-40).

Until and unless we can slay the demon of capacity deficiencies; it would be extremely difficult if not impossible to implement AU Agenda 2063, UN SDGs 2030 and national plans of 2020, 2025, 2030 and 2035. The reality is that with African countries working synergy with one-another, the continent is capable of achieving its own development, thus building a progressive future in partnership with the international community of nations. It is crucial at this stage for each country creating its own pool of talented youths and to stop blaming others for our failures. This is the hour for us to prime ourselves for a better tomorrow. Africa remains the land of opportunities and the continent of the future. Let us take advantage of that and continue building on it. The rest of the world is exploiting these possibilities and opportunities for its advantages – by exploiting the potential to leverage cutting-edge technologies to accelerate growth across Africa.

Africa, for example, is responsible for just 2.3% of global emissions despite accounting for over 15% of the world's population. Yet expert predicts that under current trajectories, agricultural yields on the continent could fall by 20% in some areas due to unpredictable weather patterns. Groundwater levels in southern and West Africa could decrease by 50-70%. And huge areas of arable ground could dry out to become arid wastelands. These prospect would be damaging anywhere in the world, but would be particularly devastating on a continent in which around 70% of the population rely on agriculture for their livelihoods and most live on less than USA $2 a day. Despite have played little part in driving human-made climate change, Africa is set to be disproportionately affected by the problem. But rather than being despondent, Africa could play a disproportionately large part in combating the global problem too.

In spite of everything, Africa is challenged to lighting up the path to change. One of the areas the continent could set an example to the rest of the world is in renewable energies, and the continent should just that. More than 620 million people lack access to electricity on the continent. Such adverse situation implies that many people rely on expensive and unhealthy sources of energy such as kerosene and charcoal, while the shortage of power also significantly inhibits economic growth. For example, it takes a Tanzanian eight years to consume as much electricity as an American consumes in one month. Therefore, the continent desperately needs better access to energy, but rather than following the typical path of cultivating a deeper reliance on fossil fuels, Africa could take the opportunity to chart a cleaner route. Advances in technology make this possible. The developed countries are polluting the world not Africa. China and Brazil have taken energy decisions that put them on a high carbon trajectory and are now contributing really high amounts of carbon, so it is in everybody's interest to help Africa leapfrog into a low-carbon trajectory. The USA, China and the European Union contribute 42% of global emissions, with Russia, Brazil and India not far behind, making the distribution of responsibilities to emission very obvious. The issue of cutting emission is of course, a global problem, beginning with the developed countries taken the bold move and doing something concrete about it. Of course, it does not exonerate Africa from not playing a useful part in the process.

We cannot deny Africa from industrialising. The rest of the world can help Africa industrialise from a totally different perspectives and using different strategies. The continent must take advantage of the 'late-comer advantage'. Africa should develop a judicious energy mix that allows it to develop at the same time, which could include fossil fuels, but everyone needs to ensure Africa moves on a low carbon path. Banking on renewable makes sense not just from the perspective of climate change, but could be a double whammy in terms of being attractive to investors too. Most African households live on less than USA$2per day but it is reportedly known to be spending USA$10bn collectively on energy-related products each year, pointing to a potentially lucrative market. There has been growing signs of investments in Africa's renewable energy sector in recent years.

Despite Africa's high-risk perception, this is perhaps not surprising given the continent's incredible potential for solar, wind and hydropower. It is well known, for example, that covering just a fraction of the Sahara- desert with solar panels could power the entire world, while Ethiopia estimates that it could generate 100GW through wind power alone. Sub-Saharan Africa's current grid capacity is just 90GW. Renewable energy should cover at least 24% of Africa's generation in 2030. There is also the Kalahari Desert in southern Africa to tape from. African governments are yet to take deliberate steps and measures of establishing renewable energy policies, which have solar, wind or thermal projects that attract foreign participation in the sector. It requires first of all redressing, unnecessary sluggish bureaucratic red tape and embarking on a more progressive, productive and efficient delivery bureaucratic sector.

Africa's energy vision should be premised on moving from the energy landscape based on underdeveloped and carbon intense pathways to a modern clean and decentralised energy system. This transition is a critical enabler of meaningful and endogenous socioeconomic development. While the continent may face a broad set of challenges in achieving this vision, it has at the same time the opportunity to avoid the fossil fuel lock-in that many industrialised countries face and to take advantage of vast supplies of untapped energy resources and / for any stranded asset problem. The African Energy transition Program (AFRETRAP) in the making under the auspices of the African Energy Commission forms a continent-wide and coordinated approach in facilitating the required transition for the realisation of Africa's development aspiration (Eralil and Sokona, 2020).

As an emergent continent, it has rethink very seriously on its energy policies and how to build the necessary infrastructure to power its drive towards industrialisation. Everything must change. The energy sector requires seriously attention by all the governments. Solutions must not only remain on paper. Concrete implementation actions must be effected to give the power necessary to drive the continent into a new industrial age.

References

Amhad. Lord of Wimbledon (2017). "Lord Ahmad, UK Minister for the Commonwealth and The UN' in conversion with Versi Anver, New Africa, No. 577, November 2017, London, pp38-30

Akitoby Bernardin and Sharmini Coorey (2012). Oil Wealth in Central Africa: Policies for Inclusive Growth. International Monetary Fund, Washington, DC.

Ball Jeffrey 2014. "New Powers", Finance and Development., Vol. 51, No. 3 September 2014, International Monetary Fund, Washington DC, pp32-34

Eralil Rajesh and Sokona Youba (2020). The African Energy Transition Program (AFRETRAP) – Climate Policy Brief 22, February 2020. See also African Energy Commission (AFREC), African Union (AU), Agenda 2063, Climate Change, Energy, Environment, Paris Agreement, Renewable Energy, Sustainable Development, Sustainable Development Goals (SDGs). See also South Centre Publications Newsletter – February 2020 (www.southcentre.int)

Sheppard Dan (2014) "Africa To Push Development Agenda At Upcoming Climate Summit" Africa Renewal, August 2014, Vol.28 No.2, New York, pp26-27

Versi Anver (2017) 'The Club' Is Uniquely Significant Today' (new Africa, No.577, November, London, pp38-40

Wan James (2015). "Can Africa Lead the Fight Against Climate Change" African Business, No.421, July 2015 IC Publications, London, pp18-21

Whitby Pamela (2011). "A Poor Effort" BBC – Focus On Africa, Vol. 22. No.1, January-March 2011, London (bbc.co.uk/focusonafricamagazine)

Chapter Twelve

Conclusion: A Wakeup Call for Africa

"All the indices of human welfare put us at the bottom of all humanity. All citizens of this nation must therefore full dedicate their energies and resources to the construction of a vibrant economy. We fought for freedom, justice and equality, yet once we got to power, we forgot what we fought for and began to enrich ourselves at the expense of the people."

(President Salva Kirr of South Sudan, 11 July 2011)

Is Africa sitting on a time-bomb or what? For now, the continent is wrapped up in numerous conflicts; chaos, poverty, corruption, exploitation instability spree. Of course, some progress has been made since the continent's Lost Decades of the 1980s. Outstanding is the issue of a continent with deficit leadership, poor governance and a very passive civil society in many African countries. Quality wellbeing cannot be said to have improved. Immigration has become one of the important questions for the continent. It has also been a source of income for a number of countries, more than the foreign aid received. Why are Africans evading their countries of plenty? What has gone wrong? What must be done, urgently to redress the pathetic situation-so that there can be a future for the continent?

The advent of democracy and self-government in African states were the main issues and justification for the struggle against colonial rule in which many lost their lives. Our inability to address the fundamental issues which the people fought for must be judiciously safeguarded. Our currently wrong policy actions constitute nothing but coups d'état against our brothers and sisters of blessed memory. We must not only end the exploitation of Africa by foreign powers, but of enabling each of us to realise his/her full human potential. Have the political regimes which we have installed met our aspirations for development and quality livelihood? Strengthening democratic governance is a sin qua non for Africa to take-off to sustainable development. To overcome the fragmentation of governance for sustainable development and ensure policy coherence, it is essential to re-arrange and re-configure the institutional arrangements that cover all aspects of the policy cycle: agenda-setting, policy analysis and formulation, decision-making, implementation and evaluation.

A desperation situation exists. How can hope and confidence be reinstated in the people that Africa holds the future of the world; and only Africans have the solution to their problems? Caught in this conundrum of Africa's underdevelopment syndrome as with any journey, it is crucial to know your starting point. Africa knows its starting point but refuses to understand the changing dynamics and its unfolding consequence of the situation. Therefore, implementing a successful transformation strategy and implantation action plans starts with knowing where you are coming and, where you are heading and why. The future of Africa requires a careful review of the continent's historical past, a critical and analytical surgical operation of the continent since independence, the objective and the why of where it's heading to. Where the focus of attention should be, things to be eliminated and streamlined and where and how the development focus should be structured and proceed; and importantly, the mobilisation of the masses to ensure that there is total participation of the masses in the development efforts and benefit-sharing as well as the sustainability of development efforts, without which Africa cannot carry greater weight in world affairs. The independence of African states injected new dynamics in global politics and will continue to do so in the foreseeable future. Africa's role at the United Nations and other international organisations remains significant in this respect.

At the dawn of the 21st century Africa finds itself at the most historic and challenging crossroads since the butchering and raping that occurred in Berlin in 1884-5. With the sad events following the slave trade, the invasion of the continent by the perpetrators of imperialism and colonialism, Africa has not been at peace with itself. Africa can never be peace with self with 'sit-tight presidents' or governments that do not have the interests of the citizens at heart. Recent events, in Gambia, Gabon and Cameroon testify governance system driven by greed or articulate self-interest with the sole goal of leaving the vast majority of citizens behind in the fast-moving development and quality services delivery bandwagon.

The struggle for independence saw the rise of great men and women with vision and determination. They did their best to bring us to where we are today. Mistakes were made on the way, but we finally got to the entrance of the Promised Land; but could not enter because of 'men without vision with nowhere to go.' Hope not despair has been the legacy bestowed on us by our leaders of vision. Africa moved from creating a weak organisation – the OAU (that served the purpose for which it was established) to a more structured entity – the African Union with its vision or Agenda 2063, So far, the continent's fragile political unity has only aggravated the difficulties of fostering effective cooperation particularly as African governments have not yet learnt how to insulate economic cooperation institutes and arrangements from the vicissitudes of political differences. What they have learnt is that of running and perfecting a rapacious oligarchy state across the continent. So far, Agenda 2063 is not enough. Nonetheless, it is better than having no vision. We need the Afro-centric vision that leaves no one behind, encouraging participation, mobilisation, reconciliation and equitable benefit-sharing.

Contextualised in this respect AU Agenda 2063 kindles hopes but raises the question, where are we likely to be going and where should we go if unity is not achieved before 2063? The forward-march towards African unity which started with 32 members in the early 1960s today with AU having 54 member states; but falls far short of the total integration of the continent. Regional Economic Communities (RECs) is not the answer for African Unity. But constitute a step in the right direction. There is still a long way to total unity which should create the world's most sophisticated and integrated trade area. The shift from OAU to AU is a notable achievement. Africa is integrating further; and we have to face a variety of inter-related issues of immediate significant importance. A heavy burden lies on our shoulders; for us to take our responsibilities seriously for nothing less than the diversity, unity and destiny of Africa. This is the time to chart a new curse of coherent action and concrete means of ensuring a continent that is integrated and united to bring happiness and quality livelihood to the peoples of Africa. Remember the flowers of tomorrow are the good seeds sown today. Sad enough, there is no African head of States spear-heading the 'unity drive' since the assassination of Libyan leader Ghaddafi. Africa today is like an orphan as far as the African Unity Government for the continent is concerned.

Since independence, the continent's development goals and objectives have not been properly guided by our values and perception of needs, resources and possibilities and it is here there is a dire need for rethinking, clarification and understanding of what we want, how and when? Therefore, we need elements of a genuinely African-oriented development strategy and their policy implications. For now, we have to address issues of self-reliance and self-sustain development, democratisation, and the creation of the right political and social environment, the recovery of self-confidence by the peoples of Africa in themselves and the determination and willingness to achieve effective and meaningful cooperation among African states. What is crucial now henceforth is that these main pillars of Africa's development strategy should be transformed from political slogans into a constructive framework for policy and implementation.

For now, Africa has bypassed the values of self-reliance and depended too long on external master's handouts. This dependency helps in snapping their own initiative and vitality – resulting in their exploitation by the master. Dependency injects loss of self-respect, with the dependent commanding no respect from others, constantly laughed at by the world and constantly despised and squeezed into a tight corner. Vision 2063 is spelled out; it requires the political will determination and implementation. It is better to depend on the Diaspora's handouts than that of the Eurocentric gesture with its hidden agenda.

The challenge, therefore, is proper stock-taking, understanding it and building a defence and development strategy important to the continent's effectiveness as a continental developmental force within the global force of the 21st century. Are you listening Africa? Or are we so ingrained in the loathing love and have forgotten the inherent ideal of being a pragmatic people, more comfortable with practice than theory within the parameters of "African Problems with African Solutions." Finding the right solutions means drawing a world of experiences of internal strengths and weaknesses as well as external opportunities and threats. We have to capitalise on strength and build strategies to counteract our weaknesses and threats. The long-term policy agenda should be construed within the paralysis of having a winning strategy to be able to compete effectively and efficiently to ensure the quality wellbeing of the people is not derailed. The sustainable quality livelihood of the people is the profit the states makes in this competitive world construct of our time. Analysing the way forward for Africa to compete is therefore an important part of the ideological orientation of *"African Problems with African Solutions"* (APWAS).

First, what are the continent's "strength, weakness, opportunities and threats?" What are the strategies, strength, weakness, opportunities and threats of your competitors? How real and sustainable are your opportunities? How organised or disorganised is Africa? How committed is the continent in pursuing these opportunities?

Second, what are the comparative advantages of the African continent and to what extend do they understand and appreciate their comparative advantage within the global context?

Third, apart from the established powers, who are the entrants or emerging competitors? Can these new entrants reshape Africa according to the aspirations of Africans? Or will these new competitors be attracted by your success or failure?

Fourth, for how long will the late-comer advantage prevail and continue to be an advantage for the continent?

Fifth, these developments processes and other related activities are equally conditioned by the input factors of Political, Economic, Sociological, Capacity and Technological Advancement (PECSTA). Therefore, Africa must build its human and natural capacities to take advantage of the latecomer advantage and of the PECSTA factors to protect and market itself within the rapidly changing global knowledge-based economy of this century. It means that Africa must identify growth opportunities as depicted in Diagram 1: Identifying Transformation Opportunities by African countries.

Table 1: Identify Transformation Opportunities by African Countries

Identifying Transformation Opportunities

New	*Transformation by developing*	*Rapid transformation by Diversification use of technology-with actions and roles*
Core	Develop new competences in developing new system capability and capacity to existing international **Competence** climate and environment	
Drive for Efficiency and Growth by Transformation and Effectiveness development	Building the requisite human capacity and infrastructural capability that puts on the path of competition with other nations. Africa has to transform by diversifying its activities; moving from a raw-material **exporting to finished product exporting continent, It has to give added value to its vast natural resources efficient in -its quality product so as to compete in the global market. Increased growth will bring**	
Development	**Development will increase quality services delivery and improved quality of life for the citizens.**	
Existing	Improve existing competence, and exploit **existing** core competence to add value to customer needs in the new international environment.	
	//	//
	International Environment	

Africa must develop the core competence drawing from her resources potentials and by building for productivity, efficiency and effectiveness to accelerate and sustain the quality livelihood of the people. In Table 1: Africa should radically improve existing advantages and competences as well as develop new ones to add significant value to existing environment. This makes it imperative for the continent to reinforce the process of integration and unity, curb its wave of conflict and reduce its dependency, build its human capital, instil a sense of patriotism and pride as well as develop a spirit of proactive and discard its current reactive development approach. The creation of the Diaspora as the sixth region of the continent is a new, constructive and sensible drive to converting the *'brain drain'* into the *'brain gain'* phenomena for the sustainable transformation of the continent.

Selected Case Studies

Take the case of the Democratic Republic of Congo (DRC) that has known no peace since independence. This is a country with protracted violence, with little or no shared experience of genuine peace to offset these negative interactions. Throughout its various incarnations as the Congo Free State (1885-1908) the Belgian Congo (1960-1971), Zaire (1971-1997) and then the Democratic Republic of Congo (since 1997-) an enduring feature and image that has held sway in all narratives and image that has been an entity immersed in an unrelenting sense of statelessness further embedded in perpetual state chaos. The Democratic Republic of Congo has become the epic-centre of conflict in Africa and the dearth of peaceful coexistence in the country has vividly revealed the numerous flaws that peace can possess if it is devoid of structural stability, integrity and most importantly the ability to address the underlying causes and factors that continue to torment and facilitates conflicts taking place in this war-torn nation (Sirrie Swart, 2012).

In Liberia and Somalia, Ohanwe (2009) writes: during the Cold War ideological and politico-military rivalries mostly dictated the actions of the competing blocs including their involvement in foreign conflict. In Africa for instance, the East-West rivalry of the time only fuelled conflicts but also appeared to undermine the use of diplomacy as a tool for peace-making and conflict resolution. With the fall of the Berlin Wall in 1989 and the demise of the Soviet Union however, there was a transformation of the conflict arena in the criteria which presented new opportunities and threats. This therefore raises a fundamental question of how the end of the Cold War affected the character of conflicts and their successful management in Africa (Othamwe 2009). Africa's youngest state South Sudan is in great turmoil tearing itself apart.

Though the Central African Republic has produced Africa's Third Woman Head of State, is not an easy with itself. South Africa emerged out from entrenched apartheid system only to embrace xenophobic attitude against other Africans who contributed to the liberation of the country from the ambit of white minority rule. Cameroon considered as the political laboratory of Africa is bracing up to prolonged conflict due to the injustices, greed and insensitiveness of the leaders engraved in the politics of majorities and neglect. The choice now is either a return to the federal system of governance or secessionist politics. The creation of more states in Africa is in the pipeline. A federal system is considered as the best options for the unity of the country (Forje, 1981). More than fifty years of the politics of exclusion and marginalisation, deceit and falsehood by the Francophone now threatens the unity, peace and stability of the country. The Soweto (South Africa) uprising in 1976, now sees its version in Cameroon through the teachers and lawyers strike in November- December 2016 which is ongoing in 2017.

Greed, the appointment syndrome, injustice and corruption is a cancer plaguing the future of the Cameroon nation.

The Horn of Africa remains the most dangerous spot on planet earth. While the Central African sub-region remains the most turbulent place. The Arab Spring changed the political dynamics not only of countries north of the Sahara but impacted in some countries south of the Sahara. Recent events in Mali demonstrate the need for a peoples' elected government and tolerance for different views and beliefs to co-exist peacefully in society. Religious intolerance is splitting countries apart. Nigeria has become the centre for religious insurgence, creating fear and distrust in the government's efforts to protect citizens. The legitimacy of the government is challenged as well as the capability to govern is questioned. The central African sub-region remains the most dangerous place on the continent. The Congo crisis has been ongoing since the 1960s; countries in the Great Lake Regions know no peace making the entire continent a shadow and illusion of itself. The Arab Spring instead of generating the democratisation and good governance the people hoped for is degenerating into religious radicalism and fundamentalism. Africa has become the endless wave of violence, destruction, underdevelopment misery to list but a few of the evils that plagued the continent. In addition, the continent is host the highest percentage of weak and failed states in the world. Can all these developments and weaknesses be attributed to the absence of democracy and hegemonic authoritarian rule or what? It looks the Middle East and North Africa (MENA) is one of the regions most resistant to democratic ideals yet to experience a wave of democratisation.

Given the scores of entrenched conflicts in Africa calls for a new constructive and comprehensive approach that involves a triumvirate of eminent men and women in conjunction with civil society from the continent, regional peace keeping forces, and the warring factions themselves working in concert to replace the power of firing rifle with the courage's tool of the 'talking will' till every one aggress should prevail. The United Nations Commission on Environment and Development in 1987 (the Bruntland Commission) defines sustainable development as 'development that meets the needs of the present without compromising the ability of future generations to meet their own needs." A concerted, consensual, conciliating and comprehensive approach by all stakeholders is imperative call in fortifying the continent's place and role in the fast-expanding global village of this century. Without building on common grounds, the continent exposes itself to enslavement. Military weapons must be silent on the continent.

At the same time, the arsenal of weapons for human development is put into full action.

Political Parties should be able to help the people to unlock their failure and state of poverty and corruption. In short the continent needs security in its totality – food, water, health, shelter, life and property, not only for this but coming generation as well. Apparently, violence, conflicts and wars occur when the democratic process based on dialogue, negotiation, reconciliation fail or are grossly inhibited by one or both parties and when justice, shared obligations and shared-prosperity is denied. When self-interests articulate overcomes collective interests and justice thrown into the ocean. Thus, the conditions leading to insecurity, conflict and wars include extreme inequality, injustice, repression, and abuse of power as well as extremism of various structures based on for example, ethnicity, class and religion. These man-made factors can be changed, with enlightened visionary servant leadership under enabling environment and backed by a proactive vibrant civil society.

On the other hand, natural factors such as drought and natural disasters can contribute to lack of peace, since these are random and cannot be controlled easily It goes without saying that articulate public policies promotes peace, security and development by establishing strong democratic institutions, fair legal and justice system to maintain and promote the process of change, development and progress, liberty, equality, freedom and human security based on checks and balances. Checks and balances calls for strong political parties and institutions; i.e. a governing party or parties and strong opposition party/parties ready to take over through legal and constitutional means when the opportunity for change exists. A credible coalition of opposition political parties should exist to challenge the political power monopoly of the ruling regime through competitive, fair, free, open and clean contested elections. Unfortunately, the liberation of Africa in the 1960s left the rural masses on the side-lines even though they did enthusiastically support the movements led by bourgeoisie of petty government officials. The rural masses, peasants and workers had no part as social classes in the fallouts of the economic goals and class struggles that eventually erupted.

Preparing for the Future and Curbing the Poisoned Chalice.

Preparing for the future of Africa is difficult based on issues outlined here. It is difficult not impossible. Importantly, one must select the time frame in order to build an innovative but realistic and reachable vision.

Prioritising the priorities is essential. Peter Drucker the economist argues that "the essence of planning is to make present decisions with knowledge of their futurity." (1974:121). Indeed, the next fifty to hundred years or more are already defined by the West – a programme of orders and deliveries. In Africa, we have *yet to reach the village* to capture the essence of Julius Nyerere's phrase. The West has gone past the moon. In the early 70s, the Swedes embark on creating (The Institute for Future Studies – Institute for Framtid Studio). Many thought it was a crazy idea.

The purpose of the institute, in nutshell was to start planning about the future. Many long-term studies and projections were made and are being crafted. Today, Sweden and other European countries know exactly what they want to come 2115. How to go about realising envisaged goals? For the developed economies the years between now and 2115 have already been defined by a programme of long-term political and economic strategies backed by military forces. The Military Industrial Complex (MIC) is at work coordinating the strategies and visions for the future of the West and of its hegemonic dominance over Africa. The establishment of AFRICOM is just one such strategies in the guise of helping Africa, while in reality is to secure and protect its sources of resources of raw materials and markets. It gives a breathing space for authoritarian sit-tight leaders to exploit in prolonging their stay in office.

How many African countries attained the 2015 Millennium Development Goals (MDGs)? Not many will attain the SDGs target even by 2025. Africa's flight towards the future is currently stuck on the runway laden with corruption and poor governance. The marginalisation of the private sector and civil society as veritable partners in Africa's transformation is a major drawback that should be adequately looked into. Africa's private sector did not evolve on its own. The private sector was set up by the colonial administration from other countries to stifle the sustainable transformation of the region. So, when the struggle for independence came in many African nations, it became almost synonymous with wanting to destroy the economy as well. The problem than arises when political independence is gained with no economic independence.

Psychologically we have internalised the economy as being owned by the enemy and the feeling is that it must be destroyed. For this reason, the relationship for the local people and the economy has become polarised between the colonised, and the coloniser. That is why the tensions in the public and private sectors have added complications and distrust. We need to get to a situation where the future of a nation is easy to identify: to a place where you can agree that your destiny is tied together, irrespective of what sector you are in. Given that colonisation is mutated from not wanting to do things with local traditions, you can see why it continues to be an issue (Moyo 2013) in post-colonial Africa. An issue which begs the question of what kind of development does Africa want now and in the future? What quantitative objectives is it reasonable to set for our development now and far beyond 2063? How well positioned is Africa to get the means required by its policy strategies? What kind of Africa should we begin to groom for the twenty-second century? Africa must begin look far beyond 2063.

Various approaches present themselves and numerous parameters require assessment for Africa to construct a strong and functional governance system. Creating a definite vision of the future that will not be misunderstood the concluding section offers some pathways for the construction of a new Africa. The continent is endowed with strong bargaining position enhanced by nature as certain natural resources found on the continent are vital to some or all of the world's powers. To benefit adequately from these natures gift to the African people requires serious strategic thinking, long-term planning, and visionary leadership. These are the most effective weapons in overcoming existing tenacious Western resistance and humiliation of the African people. The importance of education in our development and standing our grounds remains important. We are therefore forces to ask time and again: what kind of education should Africa articulate and achieve in order to ensure a higher contribution of its human resources to the sustainable transformation of the continent?

First: *"Overcoming Naive Thinking."* Africa must overcome current naive thinking which binds and undermines constructive future ideas for veritable development for the continent. The lessons of the past and present still represent a tremendous source of material and experiences that the people can revisit in anticipation of tomorrow's transformation. But the unfortunate side of the picture is that neither the visions of the future nor the lessons of the past, but the tyranny of today's governance system and commitments imposes constraints on our thinking and actions. Naive thinking has contributed to the derailment of constructing a strong and progressive continent. A new mindset is needed. A new generation of leaders is necessary. The founding fathers made mistakes but where committed nationalist with a common vision, the independence and unity of Africa though with varied approaches to its realisation. Nkrumah saw African unity even within the perspective of surrendering Ghana's sovereignty while

Nyerere had a different opinion though an ardent and passionate advocate of African unity. African unity for Nkrumah was through the lenses of *'continental unity'*, and for Nyerere it was through the perspectives of 'territorial nationalism'. The relevance of 'constructive strategic' thinking is needed to construct a better future for Africa. Naive thinking must be replaced by *'constructive and progressive scientific'* thinking that can define and construct Africa's future.

Second: *"Distinguishing among Effectors, Systems, and Platforms"*. Bear in mind that tomorrow's development will rely less on certain resources. It will rely more on knowledge, creativity, innovation and entrepreneurship. In short, more and more quality human capital development will be the pillar to build on. Resources are nothing in themselves. To what extent has the continent made proper use of its resources in transforming the quality livelihood of the people. Distinguishing among effectors, systems and platforms allows greater flexibility and certainly better adaptability. In short improving on the quality of human capital development creates more avenues for giving added value to the vast natural resources. Presently, added value is not given to these resources; hence Africa is poor in the midst of plenty. Mission effectiveness depends on the value given to human and natural resources.

Third: *"Constructing Capability Future Systems"*. Today's technology creates possibilities for creating capability future systems. Africa can draw valuable experiences from the developed economies. The continent does not need to develop the wheel. It is already there. It is a question of adding to and improving the wheel. Developing and utilising the human capital is essential. Capabilities must be constructed to increase mission effectiveness by integrating all the components – stakeholders, human and natural resources, evolving knowledge and providing them with updated information and situations. Cooperation among capabilities, the result of networking actors operating in all environments, will give the continent unlimited bounds to explore the future for the good of the people. Of course, limitations will become increasingly human, for instance the degree to which science and technology are handled and utilised will depend on the stability of the people, political will, determination and whether they want to own their development trajectories. The ability to integrate and fit into complex networks will likely become defining. It is a process of serious and drastic change and will not have an equally understanding of all people in society. Building a strong and efficient information and communication system for educating a broad-base population is imperative. Some people will have the capacity and training to devise networks and understand their place in uncertain environment in which they can determine their perimeter of responsibility; others will be destined to act only in a limited number of bounded networks.

Difference will exist among the various actors. These differences will prove fundamental in planning and articulating a forward-looking command, operations and control which may eventually create expansive disparities. Disparities should be kept at the minimum. These differences can and should be narrowed through the ***'ubuntu spirit'*** of reconciliation, consensus and caring for one another. What is important is adopting a policy of *'inclusion not exclusion'* as the way forward in thinking and constructing the present and future. Africa beyond 2013 requires the harmonious, constructive and comprehensive peaceful coexistence of different platforms and their communication capabilities to multiply their effectiveness manifold. At the same time, Africa must prepare for eventualities by analysing and building related skills and ensuring appropriate training. By understanding Africa's place in the new global complex world setting and complicated and interwoven networks involving many stakeholders the continent will have indirectly or directly prepared itself for future developmental environmental activities.

Fourth: *"Acknowledging Integration, Interdependence and Unity"*. Development is a joint effort and the environment requires inputs from all sectors to yield maximum results possible. All sectors of society and the economy are needed and dependent on each other. Understanding each sectors role in all aspects of activities facilitates true joint integration permitting more interconnect in common networks that are partitioned into the environmental segments, air, and land and sea segments. The form of governance as merging instruments permits and guarantees freedom of movement of people and goods. The intercourse between people will hasten and broaden the fertilisation of knowledge. No one, nation or continent has the total monopoly of knowledge. Knowledge should be created and shared. The networking coordinating capabilities of the system fosters better operations in their entirety with the continent developing and does not fall apart. The full integration of the capabilities of various actors will enhance joint cooperation in crafting a sustainable future. No single sector can achieve this alone. Integration or inclusion, interdependence and unity for the common good are vital as crucial in ensuring the construction of the future of Africa.

Fifth: *"Quality Human Capital development Driving Future Industrial Challenges"*. Building the human resources base now is essential to claim the future. Clearly, some countries are positioning themselves for these developments, having learned that investing in these fields is not as costly as commonly thought. Any country that wishes to become a major factor in the global environment of tomorrow must find a strategy which encourages evolution of the requisite know-how and technologies. The flight towards the future involves challenges, visions, choices, priority setting, new mindset, behaviour, attitude as well as risks. These challenges, changes and windows of opportunities depend on the existence, and proper exploitation of leadership, vibrant civil society and the responsive responsibility of the international community towards the aspiration of the continent. It requires regular investment in human resources development and financial resources necessary to guarantee the sustainable drive to the continent's future. The people of Africa must quote Martin Luther King Jr. ***"I have a dream"*** and should see to it that the dream is realised. The time of change is now. Africa has to change if it should be part of the emerging globalised world.

Sixth: *"Scientific and Technological Advancement"* will shape the future. This depends on the degree of and quality of human capital generated and gainfully utilised in the process of change, progress and development to attain sustainability. Financial input is imperative in the entire process. Here the continent's institutions of higher learning must play the significant role by staying out of any form of political interims. The academic must stay off political intrigues. Academic activity must not, in the first place, be interfered with or otherwise frustrated by the wider community or its agent, such as political party politics and government. It must remain true to its virtues of internal rationale of the pursuit of knowledge and allied processes such as training people for it, implying the need for detachment, open-mindedness, impartiality, and objectivity, that the liberal academic typically seeks to justify a certain range of claims that are closely connected tactically and, very probably, conceptually. The process of human capital development, scientific and technological development in Africa is constantly derailed due to the interferences of political party interferences. Such interference brings the name and role of the institution into disrepute. The university's independence and devotion to intellectual values and discourse should not be weakened by political interferences.

The flight towards the future will take place in a new scientific, technological and economic environment. It requires making a proper balancing act of the ***'The 'three T'*** approach – technology, technical assistance and training that should enable Africa governments to benefit from the late-comer advantage and address economic issues.

The future is laden with complexities as well as opportunities. All these dimensions will witness all manners of confrontations and challenges. These complexities will continue to encounter criticisms because that which is hard to understand tends to intimidate. Hence, a new dimension of mass awareness creation, communication, will become a priority in order to explain how the various actors will benefit from these developments, giving rise to challenges involving human capital development and integration of the various components in the future and as a consequence, the identity of those who direct the development process. The past should be the prologue for drawing immense experience in designing the future. Africa's flight to the future depends to a large extent to the products of its institutions of higher learning. The political party polarisation of educational system is what is destroying or delaying Africa's march into the future. That is why a new mindset and visionary leadership backed a proactive vibrant civil society is imperative in the construct of the future of the continent. To move forward and in constructive pattern, the education system of the continent needs objectivity, impartiality, open-mindedness, independence, excellence, transparency, quality output and an enabling environment.

More than ever before, we must shed light on the future in order to make the right decision today regarding our people and capabilities. Without such an open and holistic vision, the future of the continent will be subjected to greater exploitation and manipulation from those countries that did their homework. Only the decision made in the appropriate window of opportunity will prove correct. To be right too early is as useless as letting opportunities go by. Africa's future requires planning now. Planning for the future involves forecasting the consequences of today's decisions, taking into consideration lessons from the past. Has Africa learnt anything from centuries of colonialism? Is the continent prepared to imagine the future, more than any other thing it is subject to technological development? All aspects of development draw their inspiration from yesterday's activities and established principles of transformation, technological breakthroughs modify the evolution – the Gerschenkron (1962) concept of *"late-comer advantage"* should open new avenues for the continent to craft its future now by ensuring the existence of democratic governance, inclusion and equitable prosperity-sharing.

Modern means of communication have made our vast planet fairly small. In these ***Seventh,*** Africa needs a rebalancing act among the 54 member states, and with the rest of the world. The rapid growth witnessed by the new invaders of the continent and given the strong grip by the old colonial powers over their colonies necessitates a new balancing act, a new world economic order. For Africa it requires keeping a clean house, prudent economic management and practising democratic governance. African countries should turn-around lower government revenue in commodity-intensive countries (as well as corruption) which has forced them to cut public spending including so badly needed infrastructure and social services that continue to inflict hardship to those placed at the bottom of the ladder. The short-term pain is acute and bad for the continent. Of course, not all the news or events are bad; as the other sides of the new invaders' looking for more opportunities abroad provides a window of opportunity for progress. For example, Chinese enterprises and financial institutions are expanding their direct investment and lending in Africa, especially in non-resource-intensive countries, which continue to enjoy high growth. Over the medium term, this investment offers opportunities to African countries to become part of global value chains, boosting much-needed structural transformation on the continent. 'Every cloud has a silver lining' notes Roger Nord (2017); 'while falling commodity prices hurt Africa in the short term, China's shift to more consumption is an opportunity for Africa to accelerate its much-needed structural transformation'. The rebalancing act will be durable and pay-off when African countries exhibit prudence in good management and governance, ensure and boost domestic revenue collection mobilisation, foster diversification, and constructively address long-standing weaknesses in the business climate to attract foreign and domestic investment in new sectors.

Africa's future is challenged by a number of pending impediments, endemic corruption, abject poverty, poor governance, food insecurity, growing health crisis and imposed foreign hegemonic dominance among others. Policy decisions are imposed within the framework of 'master-servant' relationships. But if the past and present is any guide to the future, policy articulation should be framed within the realm of 'realism' (Morgenthau 1958). Given "that the strong do what they will, while the weak suffer what they must" (Thucydides trans Warner 1972) the essence of Africa's future must be framed within the context of 'survival'. The realist accord means putting all cards on the table which includes *'strength, weakness, opportunities and threats'* as the analytical strategic basis for the long-term construct of the continent. The continent must critically, scientifically and objectively define its strength, weakness, opportunity and threats to articulate forward looking policy measures as it constructs its future.

Jacobs (2018:78) asserts; "society evolves by a progressive organisation of human activities to an increasing extent in space and time, with increasing coordination between its myriad activities and increasing integration between the multiple layers of the social fabric....is an extraordinary product of human ingenuity, a social organisation capable of managing inconceivable and ever increasing levels of interconnectedness and complexity with ever greater velocity and precision." African countries should start thinking about the evolution of a human-centred economy and political governance system that brings the greatest happiness to the largest possible population. We need a democracy, economics sand other social technology, its value deepening the central purpose for which it is applied, the values by which it is guided and the principles on which it is founded to produce the right goods for the people. The failings of mainstream development approach recounted here are really minor in comparison with its fundamental flaw and effects on transition from backwardness to a service delivery society – deviation from the central purpose. All this is due to our constant marriage with the Eurocentric developmental approach totally alien from our values, needs and wants. Social institutions are created to serve society. We continue running away from the social institutions or concepts - *ubuntu, betho pele, harambee, etc.* - we better understand. It is time we strongly reverse the current model of thinking and development, we need to reposition human-beings at the centre of development activities and conceive a society as a system that maximises the freed, security, and welfare of all people. Recalling the views of Jacobs, there can be optimal private good for all individuals in this world without simultaneously optimising the benefit to society as a whole. Every achievement is founded on the cumulative achievement of all humanity over millennia (op cit. 79-80).

Here is the challenge for Africa's academia. Is Africa's scholarship rigid enough to exhibit the kind of structural changes required of it? Or is African scholarship subservient to the dictates of party politics. Naturally the universities should be important avenues of the continent's future leaders. The political independence of the university has a special importance in the future construct of the continent. Unfortunately, universities and the entire educational institutions has become the bedrock for deepening the corruption pandemic and propagating the ruling party's ideological; orientation not scholarship for the advancement of the country. Educational institutions should be the nursery for moral and ethical upbringing, transparency, accountability, objectivity and scholarship. They are not in many African countries. Until a serious attempt and vigorous pursuit of crafting a corrupt-free and free from political party orientation education institution to mould future generations of leaders, Africa will never rid itself of the pandemic of endemic corrupt practices as well as ensure genuine academic freedom and development.

Over the past couple of decades, Africa has witnessed an exponential growth of many forms of social power. Democracy, human rights, rule of law, open markets, entrepreneurship, scientific discovery, technological innovations, globalisation, higher education, and access to information have been major drivers of this growth. These gains have led to significant progress in enhancing human security, welfare and well-being, unfortunately, this progress has not been commensurate with the potential in many African countries because the distribution of power generated is skewed and biased to favour small economic and political elite. Whatever the case, let us continue building on these positive aspects of transformation to better consolidate our transition and future.

The problem is the urban petty-bourgeoisie regime that emerged after the independence struggle fuelled the idea of governance system construed on the manifestation of ethnic solidarity and regional patriotism which benefited the representatives of the urban petty bourgeoisie. The governance system was not built on the participation of the masses and in equity in sharing the fallouts of government activities. In order to consolidate its power and resist the promptly generated regional ethnic and social opposition, the new power-wielders had to call on the armed forces or relied on this group of citizens and not on the masses as the custodian of power and sovereignty of the nation. As might be expected, the armed forces appropriated power virtually everywhere and thereby initiated the second phase in the political history of independent Africa. On the strength of this, the educated class that had replaced the departed colonial masters became the instrument of selections for an emergent privileged class, yet a class which enjoys no autonomy and whose privileged are in no way connected with any productive activity.

Unfortunately, the academia instead of defending the interests of the down-threatened ganged with ruling political class in destroying the country. Africa became a battle-field or pyramid programmed for conflict, underdevelopment and destruction instead of progress and development. At the base of the pyramid lays a large mass of people lacking the basic needs of human existence. These are some of the issues Africa of the future should strongly guard against. To constructively correct the injustice of the past; and ensure we extend *'power to the people with equal opportunities for all'* to explore and benefit from their potentials. While the value of diversity in African society cannot be underplayed, it is equally important to underscore the value of a bridge-building cultural heritage of values and attitudes, which can contribute meaningfully to a national common purpose. It is in regard to these matters that we must speak truth to power to ensure that the welfare of the people is top on their priority agenda. The diversity of the continent is important so also the unity of Africa as the weapons for sustainable development and quality well-being of the citizens. It behoves us to reflect to the Brandt Report or Commission of 1980 which strongly appeals for a harmonious North-South relation (rich and poor) for remedying the economic and political situation. Africans must strive to make the continent a better place through its various actions such as their varied engagement in positive, constructive and progressive dialogues, and sensitisation amongst others in reinforcing the state peace, security, unity and sustainable development.

Transition and transformation in Africa should build on the trajectories of leaving no one behind, of linking the rural and urban centres, of narrowing the gap between the 'haves and have-nots. There is need for a new democratic dispensation and the management of confidence-building mechanisms to consolidate the process of fundamental social change ongoing in society. The continent has been face with discrimination, exploitation and marginalisation. A new era has emerged ushering a profound shifting political power relations and the inclusion of previously marginalised segment of society. Rephrased in another way, the future of Africa must seriously take into consideration two principal dimensions: a shift from minority rule to majority rule, and a shift from an exclusive to an inclusive political system. In short, it is power to the people or here the people rule (Forje 2009). The process of transition and transformation unleashes powerful centrifugal and centripetal forces. The reasons for this is not far to seek. Social transformation entails structural changes in power relations and the resultant shifts in the allocation of resources. No one captures is better than Claude Ake's (2000) dynamic description of the dilemma of democratisation: "The basic paradox of democratisation is that those who have the power tangentially [sic] have no interest or little inclination to democratise....for democratisation entails the redistribution of power against those who are in power and those who are privileged...The people who have an objective interest in democratisation are the ordinary people who stand to befit from a more equitable redistribution of power."

What are needed therefore are independent feed-backs of the effects of government policies, and independent assessments of the value of these policies, and there will very likely only arise in the presence of politically independent organisations and institutions. For now, the minority ruling elites are the winners or the *'emperors'* while the marginalised minority, the losers are branded as the *'bandits'*. What a joke and irony? Do you blame these wrongly accused citizens if they fell the states does not provide for theirs to take up arms or support political violence against the state? This hypothesis is grounded in the notion that individuals who have unjustly classified and discriminated upon will turn to political violence as a means of seeking redress and getting basic needs which have been denied them by the state. A state of anarchy prevails, and state failure is entrenched (Debiel 2002; Kreijen 2003). Strong states and institutions provide one basic, fundamental public good that weak states lack, namely security. Without security, it is difficult for states to offer other basic gods indicative of their stability. Clearly, personal insecurity has the potential leading support for and participation in political violence.

Conversely, the greater the State's presence in meeting its social contract with the people, the less likely will individuals participate in acts of political violence and the less likely will we observe state failure. What is behind this assumption or hypothesis is that leadership and the state sets the rules for development. Once people perceive state authority is transparent, accountable, legitimate, it is easy for the state to convince the people to shone violence and destructive activities that only roll back the progress of the country and wellbeing of citizens. Citizens within this context will adhere to the basic laws and institutional rules (Levi 1989:68-9). Law and order will prevail. But if the state and leadership style is such that is clothed in corruption, illegitimacy and other fraudulent activities it will be difficult to convenience the masses to keep away from acts that destroys society (Azam 2001). Absence of economic development and injustices in shared-prosperity, lack of job opportunities are all avenues breeding and sustaining conflicts and instability. These are hidden factors feeding the viruses of corruption. Lacking an inclusive economic system, and an open and participatory political structure, Africa has fostered grievances among able-bodied, educated, ideological youths who do not have gainful employment as wasting their lives. The restructuring process relates to the establishment of cohesive economic structures within the currently 54 states with strong emphasis on having order as regards the following areas:

- Population growth (which needs to be addressed, not based on the Chinese one-child agenda) but ensuring that our children are properly spaced to produce a healthy society;
- Ensure good public health and level of nutrition; for all citizens;
- Progressive and sustainable level of economic development and deepening the democratic and governance process; (open and inclusive government is strongly advocated).
- Equity in distribution of income (ensuring that there is equity in prosperity-sharing of the nation's wealth)
- Eradicating illiteracy and ensuring quality education and training for all
- Encourage the interplay between modern science and technology and indigenous knowledge.

These aspects are important, but the list is not exhaustive. That which has not been adequately perceived yet crucial and important is the linkage between technology as the instrument of development and the problems of the culture consideration. Therefore, the future of Africa lies within the parameters of winning hearts and minds through quality services delivery to the population, irrespective of political alignments, ethnic affiliations, religious creed or region of origin. Can African states use *"winning hearts and minds"* as the strategy to ensure, enhance and domesticate state legitimacy, trust and authority and ensure sustainable development? It is therefore time for African countries to seriously re-examine ways and means to survive in the fast moving 'globalisation train' The challenge is for both leaders and citizens to transform Africa from a battlefield of blood quagmire of failed states into a prosperous and more stable and secured area for the good of its people and humanity.

Currently Africa's growth is largely fuelled by demand for and exports of natural resources and by adopting prudent macroeconomic policies. The future will however draw on its youthful population, which accounts for sixty per cent of the 1 billion people living in the continent. This calls for massive investments in education, health, infrastructure, food security and requisite technology to add value to its natural resources that in tandem create jobs. The continent's resources should be converted into jobs and jobs to fuel economic growth; with economic growth ensuring the sustainable quality of welfare for all citizens. Here lie Africa's future challenges. Inequality, discrimination, and diktat are inherent in the imperialist system of international economic relations and manifest themselves fully in the field of technological exchange. The neo-colonial essence of western transnational corporations is especially clear, that of creating negative processes. Negative effects on Africa manifest themselves in the restraint of scientific technical growth through a monopolistic system of trade practices, the deformation of the technological structure of African economies, the destruction of many traditional kinds of production, and the formation of their industrial specialisation in accordance with the interests of the industrial north. The price of Eurocentric approach by African countries constitutes a significant burden for the economies of African countries; the flow of technology is usually not sufficient; and in many case technology does not meet local conditions and needs.

Africa must now reprioritise what it has to do and fast. Fifty years of independence should encourage policymaker to employ all available resources promiscuously in keeping the continent afloat of changes and ongoing development and out of needless troubles. Underdevelopment, poverty, corruption and poor services delivery must now henceforth be an issue of history. It should be thrown into the ghetto of the archives of slavery – the worse crime ever committed in human history. African states should eschew its present fascination with 'state sovereignty' and gun for a progressive *'Afrocentric'* agenda and action-plan as the counterinsurgency to Eurocentric attitude that has and continues derailing the progress of the continent. National will which should not be confused with 'state sovereignty' to meet the articulate self-interest of greedy leaders, should work hand in gloves with 'continental will' in shaping an Africa worth its salt. Victory is at sight as long as 'Afrocentric' people-focused approach is adopted and vigorously implemented to meet the needs and aspirations of the people. How can African countries overcome hardship, danger and surprise? But victory cannot be on the side of Africans as long as the leaders continuing perpetuating the Eurocentric agenda and operating a totalitarian regime structure. Victory is certain when the West is caught up in rhythm which confuses existing strategic plans. How to confuse existing strategic plans is what Africa should be working towards. In that process, 'putting people first' must be the guiding star.

This is the essence of the Afrocentric fighting spirit and which every African must research deeply so that in the end we can cross-fertilise our ideas and map out a common and encompassing strategic way forward. We need to develop Africa's 'drone' strategy. The continent has to escape and sealed once and for all the 'humiliation' agenda that has been ascribed to the people. Without a clear strategy with clear goals for victory, there is no good way to gauge progress, is victory even possible in a process that uses a population centric approach with a vague goal of winning the hearts and minds of the people. Drawing from the views of Nelson Mandela, *"war is won, or lost, in two phases – military out comes on the field of battle, and the battle to win peace through reconciliation and reconstruction afterwards; what is won on the battlefield can be lost entirely thereafter if the countries attacked are not turned into better and safer places."*

Africa must learn how to change and adapt to changing national and global situations. It is for this reason why a new mindset is imperative as counter-insurgency to the current Euro-centric approach. The Afrocentric agenda may be slow to take-off to maturity and requires visionary servant leadership that serves its people not a leadership to be served by the community. With visionary leadership, the masses are mobilised and ready to launch the assault – the total liberation of the continent and owning is development path. Now is the time to act in the proper way. And to build a solid foundation for a prosperous future is now. Attempts have been to paint as accurate a picture as possible. The challenge now is which way do we go from here as Africa stands at the crossroads of hope or despair; development or underdevelopment, wealth or poverty; chaos or stability; conflict or peace/security; justice or disorder/injustice; and name the rest. The past economic models are obsolete calling for a new approach to politics. As the political dilemma of the past and present are characterised by the present system's lack of legitimacy; widespread mistrust of the education system; judiciary, the law enforcement institutions; weakness of oversight institutions such as parliament; and widespread mistrust of the security forces looms large. Corruption has overtaken the machinery of governance and the justice system is trapped in upholding the phenomenon of illegality.

Apparently, there is retreat from formal institutions and an increased dependence on informal arrangements and institutions, non-delivery of services despite heavy taxation, which makes the state appear both distant and predatory, and increasing exploitation of ethnic and regional differences for political mileage. A system has been created that builds a nest with thorns around its structure and functioning mechanism. Each time we turn-around, the thorns prick us and shift our deliberate mistakes to external forces. The only answer is 'tear that nest of thorns' with an open democratic governance system that respects the rule of law and where justice reigns. For the better part of the six decades of the continent's independence, democratic rule was more or less on the retreat creating greater inequalities and social injustice in society. The situation has changed very little. Military dictatorship and centralised authoritarian ethnic hegemonic civil regimes became the order of the day leaving Africa where it is today. The shaping and future of Africa means embracing and practicing the rule of law and democratic governance system in its entire facet. The reinvigoration of democratic governance as the way forward for a New Africa will have to be structured on at least four interrelated pillars, namely:

- renewed commitment by democratic governments and international organisations to the defence of civil society against resurgent authoritarianism;
- the need for civil society to be better prepared to help protect fragile new democracies against the danger of backsliding to contribute to successful democratic transition for authoritarianism, and to guard against extremist movements and intolerant majorities;
- the need to protect cyberspace as a medium of free expression and the advancement of human rights and open societies;
- the need for the advanced democracies of the west to improve their economic and political performance, regain their confidence and sense of democratic purpose and recommit themselves to strengthening the liberal world order and to continuing the efforts by authoritarian's extremist to undermine it (WMD, 2016).

What is needed in Africa in order to move forward is nothing less than a new democratic resolve and political will for positive actions by the leaders and citizens of Africa to advance their transformation process towards attaining quality livelihood. The new generation of leaders must strive towards restoring the rule of law and to address difficult issues of transparency and accountability. They must avoid threading the path of democratic recession. This is the hour for Africa to break the chains of painful history from the colonial era, liberation, war and instability of the continent. So far Africa has failed to deliver basic goods and services which paves and enhances the emergence of authoritarian regime forms on the continent. That has to come to an end. This is not what we expect of the future of the continent.

Mother Africa beacons us to accomplish the task of unity and development, bearing in mind that the continent stands at a crossroads of decline or development, in this difficult and very trying times, when the future is uncertain and pessimism is rife, we should be spurred by the vision of our founding fathers to revive lost hopes and nurture progress to being the true Africans we are. It is the ardent mission of this generation to mobilise all resources possible to fight the down-thrusting impact of imperialism and colonialism on African values, more and the poor lifestyle inflicted on the peoples of the continent through the denigration of their culture and indigenous knowledge.

The continent faces a painful transition calling on the people to act in concert and remedy the political and economic problems though this will not come easily. But the people in unionism should stand-up to the devastating impact of poor leadership, poverty, corruption, inertia and indiscipline have on the development of the continent, issues that have contributed to state failure giving rise to destructive frustration, conflicts terrorism, underdevelopment, endemic poverty and poor living standards. With the will, there is way. Translating the will and local knowledge into positive action provides the opportunities and premises that Africa's future is up to Africans. For Africa to be what it should be requires a critical mass of well-educated and enlighten citizens. We are all challenged to break the chain of uncertainty, fear and hopelessness that clouds the future of the continent; and gun whole heartedly for an accommodating and progressive continent envied by all. Today there are better signs of hope and sense of a better future are more evident than fifty years back. One can realistically hope and have strong faith that the Afrocentric orientation provides the best way forward, as out of Africa there is always something new. From slavery, through imperialism and colonialism; through the dark days of structural adjustment, to the dark days of genocide and collapse of the apartheid governance system, Africa must be well equipped with the right agenda for action. Africa's past must now rest in perfect peace, as the structural adjustment halted the economic free fall to empower Africa on the new path of recovery and sustained development. There is greater willingness in many African countries to undertake economic and political reforms, this should be backed strong initiatives for creativity, innovation, entrepreneurship, productivity, accountability, justice and transparency in all undertakings; as earlier noted, the key and solution of the continent's perennial politico-socio-economic transformation rest solely in the hands of African governments and people.

Taking a Critical Look on the Highway of History

'Change will not come if we wait for some other person or some other time, we are the one's we've been waiting for. We are the change that we seek'

(Barack Obama, Former US President of America, New African No. 577, November 2017, pp13)

'I think that the trouble we now face in the world is caused mainly by the refusal to try and see another man's point of view, to try and persuade by example – and the refusal to meet a rather passionate desire to impose your own will upon others, either by force of means'

(Sir Seretse Khama, First President of Botswana, New African No.577, November 2017, p13

'Congo is the elephant of Africa. Now, it it's a dead elephant. Let's lift this elephant to go far'

(Moise Katumbi, DRC Presidential Hopeful and previous Governor of Katanga Province, New African, No. 577, November 2017, p13)

With this publication, we take what some could call a gamble on the highway to the future of the continent. Since the paper's synthesis is construed on speaking truth to power is not a gamble but a realistic perspective of what the past and present has been and to guide us towards a better future. The continent like other parts of the world has gone through the tsunami, tremors and humiliation of slavery, imperialism, colonialism and neo-colonialism with a difference. No continent in the world has suffered the terror of destruction, humiliation and oppression like Africa. Africa remains a special entity hence it holds the future of the world which gives us the basis of optimism for sustainable progress and development. We are now challenged to take a critical second look at the highway of history, stopping to impact a few of the more significant milestones of the Africa we want; and the role of that Africa within the context of global construction of our world of today. The physical and mental health of our leaders and the general population should be paramount in our policy strategy for transforming the continent.

Taking a critical look at the closing stretch – the road Africa has travelled challenges citizens of the continent to develop more resilience and determination to construct a continent that is not the play doll of the rest of the world. The energies contained in Africa's strengths must be potently released in targeted actions against isolation, deprivation; exploitation and exclusion; against malnutrition, affliction and poor-quality livelihood. Africans more than mere basic human needs. She wants new assets and new stature; new capabilities and new opportunities to constructively improve their quality living standards. The continent's corporate relations must not be iniquitous. Africa's access to technology, no less than technical learning, must not be impeded or inhibited. Importantly, Africa's voice must be heard clear and loud in the sustainable living of its people. Africa's action must be seen everywhere on planet earth. In short, no external advantages can supply the place of self-reliance and self-esteem. The force one's own being, if it has any force, comes from within. That force from within is what the continent must explicitly exploit to its growth and development. Africa must be well – armed to correct imbalances in the global economic structure. Therefore, UN Agenda 2063 should be the unifying military arsenal and assault against the forces that stifle development, growth and quality livelihood.

Africa is a sovereign continent like the rest of the continents that make up planet earth. This generation has to correct the wrongs of our forefathers/mothers. As these wrongs were committed in good faith without knowing what they were doing. They have to be forgiven or else this generation cannot make progress. This generation will equally commit its own mistakes in the process of development. Importantly, this generation and those who follow us will have to build the rest of the road, until Africa and the rest of the world is dissolved in flames or returns to the chill of everlasting night. We cannot deny the fact that the present is the past continuing, and generally continuing along lines already formed by the knowledge, habits, prejudices and fears of centuries gone by. Given a common platform for consultation, cooperation, coordination, consensus and conciliation in dealing with issues affect trade, finance, socio-economic and technological development the region would be well armed to forge a common and united effort in transforming itself from an underdeveloped into developed polity.

There are dramatic events, slavery, imperialism, colonialism and neo-colonialism which attempts have been made to record them in their different historical setting; there is seldom if ever, a clean break. It is that clean break that this paper attempts to navigate the reader so that we can jointly and constructively build the Africa we want without leaving any one behind. And so, the most important challenge facing the region is to lay the groundwork for the resumption of high and sustainable growth and equity in sharing the benefits of development. A clearly articulated agenda for structural reforms would support confidence – in a climate of stronger governance and rule of law – while political leaders clarify policy priorities and foster support for hard choices through social dialogue. Many African countries remain committed to their strong policies frameworks that build strongly on articulate self-interest of leaving the majority population behind. However, given the rapid change in economic performance and the surprising weakness in business and consumer confidence, it cannot hurt to reaffirm this commitment on an ongoing basis, especially with regard to macroeconomic policies. Anew dawn beacons the continent.

Democratic governance cannot force its interests but must enlist the willing participation of individuals in the pursuit of its object.

On the morning of 7th March 1957, the people of Ghana working in unionism with the rest of the states and peoples of African took the bold step towards sovereignty and independence. The wind of change was blowing across the continent and there was no turning back to the old order. Today, the chains of colonial rule to put it mildly have been broken as Africa is the only continent with 54 states. We are challenged to revise our assessment based on the realities that the Boer nation is no longer in existence since 1994; we have bid fare voyage to colonial since 1957 but we equally failed to unite, to construct a united continent one and indivisible. This tells us of a future with difficulties far bigger than before, challenges which must be overcome. The leaders of the continent must react more swiftly to great events with the unity the welfare of the people first as the focus. So far, this sense of perspective is lacking; because the next instalment is still to come we cannot assess the importance of what we have and what we want. The African commonwealth is not restricted to the continent but embraces the Diaspora and all black people with the African cultural heritage and value systems flowing in their blood.

Africa resurrected from colonialism, apartheid and domination. But to ensure that this gives priority to the welfare of the people we should be more proactive and working for the common good. We must work together to achieved something more important still, leaving no one behind as the society makes progress. History reminds us of the kind of people that we are; it shows our background, our limitations and our possibilities. Within these limitations, and with these possibilities, we may follow in what appears to be our predestined direction – and this is what most men and women and societies have done for most of the time; or we may turn this way or the other, this far but no further, and leave others to continue the journey we have started. However, we should bear in mind that in a society that is already bifurcated by inequality, the ever-growing youth unemployment statistics represent a poisoned chalice. Therefore, African governments should redouble their activities; use the rich natural resources potentials of the continent judiciously to ensure that the continent works better with quality livelihood for all. The continent's resources should not be 'curse' but a 'blessing' to the people.

History reminds us of the kind of people that we are; it shows us our background, our limitations and our possibilities. Within these limitations, and with these possibilities, we may follow in what appears to be our predestined direction – and this is t most people and societies have done for most of the time; or we may turn this way or the other, this far but no further, and leave others to continue the journey we have started (Kerr 1967:281). Kwame Nkrumah, Julius Nyerere, Nnamdi Azikiwe, Obafemi Awolowo, Kenneth Kaunda, Jomo Kenyatta, Tom Mboya, and many others started the journey in good faith and for the good of the continent. We should continue that journey under the prevailing context with a new twist as they started the travel under the prevailing political context of their era and with the interest of the people topmost in the agenda.

This generation is better placed and more enlightened than our founding fathers. Mistakes committed by them should not be repeated by this generation; of course, this generation will equally commit its own mistakes as no human being is perfect. Importantly, we must not put the interests of the experts against the interests and self-knowledge of the people. Rather, bio-power, through the administration and regulation of life and its needs, enacts the good of all society upon the antisocial bodies of the poor, deviant, and unhealthy. Therefore, good national policies must seek to unite the interests of the individual with the interest of society as a whole. Bear in mind that everything is dangerous, even democracy. The democratic discourses are embedded with hidden evils; they both enabling and constraining. The will to empower others and one-self is neither a bad nor a good thing. It is political; the will to empower contains the twin possibilities of domination and freedom. Even the most democratic modes of government entail power relationships that are both voluntary and coercive (Cruikshank 1999:2-3).

Africa of the future now needs an Afrocentric Revolution from within to construct the collective political front for building the Africa We Want and Without Leaving Anyone Behind. The continent needs a new liberation therapy of collective fulfilment as the social obligation in the discourse of building the future of the continent. Self-fulfilment is no longer a personal or private goal. It should be converted into collective fulfilment as something we owe to the present and next generation, something that will defray the costs of social problems, something that creates a 'true' and functional democracy. The solution to the continent's present underdevelopment or crisis of governability is discovered in the capacity of the people acting upon themselves, guided by the expertise of the social sciences and social service professionals.

The continent is where it is because it lacks self-esteem. A new social vaccine, 'self-esteem' must be injected in us to empower us to live responsibly inoculating in us the germ and power to fight all the

Eurocentric forces derailing the sustainable transformation of the continent. The power of education, and drawing from our cultural value heritage and systems acts as a guidepost against existing chronic foreign dependency. The lack of self-esteem is central to the continent's socio-economic and political ills plaguing our state and nation and continent as we approach the end of this century. We need just a simple vaccine shot in the arm, self-esteem is just the right kind of liberation therapy that should usher a complete reorientation to social problem-solving as well as mobilising every African to land on the quality services delivery Africa wants by 2063 or much earlier before.

Lacking esteem calls for strategic thinking, planning, and implementation and evaluating the rethinking spirit to pilot the continent through the dark seas of transition and transformation in a rapidly changing, unpredictable and turbulent global environment. A number of interrelated action plans must be grouped together to give a clear direction as to where Africa is heading. Therefore, the continent should be well-armed with the arsenals of:

Robustness ====➔ the potential for success under varying future circumstances or scenarios //

// //

Responsiveness=➔ ability to rapidly (a) sense change in environment; (b) conceptualise a response to that change; and (c) reconfigure resources to execute the response;

// // //

Performance===➔ overall output performance, or the combination of performance, business, and organisational effectiveness, and the ability to successfully invest in future capabilities;

Environment===➔ rapidly changing environment often referred to as turbulent or dynamic (see, Bettis and Hitt, 1995, Hart and Banbury 1994)

// // //

Critical issues impacting on the Future of Africa within the context of a rapidly changing complex and unpredictable and turbulent global environment.

// // //

Leadership **Reality** **Vision**

More often than not, we harp on the blame theory rather facing squarely the realities of our predicaments. We need to draw attention to this danger which have been maligned and derided. Africa should not continue to harp on the past, but with determination, zeal and esteem look forward to a better future. It has been demonstrated by Stiglitz (2002; Sachs, 2015) that there are choices of one kind or another during any transition and that in case after case governments can and have exercised choices that have benefited their countries and economic wellbeing, in spite of contrary directives from the International Monetary Fund (IMF). African leaders need to take that bold step in shaping the future of the continent but bearing in mind that when the 'wrong' decisions are made during transitions, the consequences for both the people and the economies concerned can be serious. We should also remember that when national economies fail to perform well, the legitimate moral claims of the poor for jobs, health, education and housing (all the basic needs and services) are undermined.

As Africa seeks to claim the 21st century, it must do more than at present. It should diversify its economies from commodity production to the industrial sector, and to small and medium scale industries that create jobs and add value to the production chain. The focus should be on unleashing creativity. This should include the agro-allied sector and beneficiation in the natural resources industry. Training and skills development should also be attuned to modern economy. The educational system inherited from colonialism cannot keep pace with the drive and technology of the 21st century; it requires a drastic overhaul. The state must take its rightful place not only in driving development of creating policies and regulatory regimes; it should be the force to mitigate poverty and inequality in society. In equality is not only an economic malaise; it is also a social and political liability to any society. If it is not tamed, it can consume whatever gains that the capitalist system might have accumulated. Thus, addressing inequality and the great divide in society constitutes a 'win-win' situation both for the powerful and powerless in society; It can equally create social harmony, mutual trust, hope, and confidence between the haves and have-nots, between state and society (Adejumobi 2014:47).

It can be argued that the future of Africa is that the age specific time horizons of any society at any given time are so strung together that the discounted future wellbeing of that society can act as a powerful motivator and is sufficient as a driving force to safeguard the well-being of future generations. The other important argument defining the responsibility for the future of Africa is the knowledge that is available about the present and future and the knowledge of the impact of our present actions on that future. Therefore, an understanding of the responsibility borne by present generations for the future generations has to begin with the acquisition of knowledge and value formation at the early stage of growth and development of the individual. The educational system has therefore a major role to play in this process. The school curricula in the present education system with its Eurocentric agenda seldom give attention to this respect. We need to begin now with an Afrocentric agenda to give new dimensions through innovative and imaginative programmes laying the foundations of knowledge and values relating to this major human responsibility towards the future of the continent. This requires major changes in the present learning system.

The concern with the future will always be subject to a number of fundamental objections which have their source in the way in which priorities are perceived or the potential for the future assessed. The objection on the basis of priorities is based on the argument that problems of poverty and deprivation of all types which afflict the present generation has to be the primary concern of the planners and policy makers at the national level as well as of the international community. The efforts to assume responsibility for unborn generations in a human predicament replete with pressing current problems would seem to be a luxury in which mankind cannot afford to indulge. The argument of those emphasising the long view of development is that future well-being is linked to present well-being and that the style of development which takes account of the well-being of future generations will intrinsically generate a high and sustainable quality of life for the present generation which it cannot otherwise secure through strategies which are neglectful of the long-term future. We must move away from individual to collective interests. Articulate policies that preserve the future by ensuring that the present is not wrongly exploited; we need a sense of moral responsibility and value system that protects the future as well as direct human beings on a gentler and more humane path of development.

There is a limit to growth. Over exploiting our resources now means leaving nothing to future generations. We should not fool ourselves that science and technology contain an unlimited potential to solve problems. Science and technology constitute but a means to achieving something. Overusing our resources today would lead to serious negative consequences for future generations. We must not put ourselves in a state of ignorance so as to jeopardise the future for oncoming generations. We need to articulate comprehensive policies that take the interests of future generations into account. If responsibility for the future is to be effectively fulfilled by this generation, this responsibility must incorporate all important aspects of society's system – the learning system which forms the growing mind, the choices of technology, the methodology for evaluating costs and benefits and the processes of national planning and decision-making must be tilted towards the interest of future generations.

The future of Africa should be contextualised within this premise and which has formed the basis of our discussion. An attempt has been made to identify the substantive issues and the problem areas which concern the future of Africa and the well-being of its citizens. We have examined how the present generation assumes its responsibility for a society's present concern with the future is related to the different time-horizons which are simultaneously held within it by its different age groups. Our responsibility towards the future of Africa must be grounded in knowledge building capacity of the people and from there providing African solutions to the continents problems. Africa today stands at a crucial crossroads in preparing and resolving enormous challenges and making the right choices for the continent's future. The book attempts to inculcate into the mindset of the people to start acknowledging that the future of Africa begins now and stimulating serious discourses on our responsibilities is imperative.

At this juncture it becomes imperative for the people of Africa to articulate and implement a strategic framework for critical thinking about the future of the continent. A number of processes have to be pierced together which (Lindgren and Bandhold 2009:39) sees as *'tracking, analysing, imaging, deciding and acting'.*

- *Tracking*: tracing changes and signs of threats and opportunities. This has to be seen within the context of the strength, weakness, opportunity and threat (SWOT) approach. Africa has to develop the ability to discover the unexpected; to search where the light is shining, taking into consideration the strength, weakness, opportunities and threats that exist. Africans should have their eyes and ears open.
- *Analysing:* analysing consequences and generating scenarios. What is really happening? Looking for possible alternatives; if tracking is about getting on the track of changes, discovering patterns, trends, threats and opportunities, analysing is about discovering future consequences of changes in the present, and the interplay between trends and tendencies. Analysing aims also at delving deeper into creative and intuitive models and visions and how necessary conditions for this to become reality.
- *Imaging:* identifying possibilities and generating visions of what is desired and how to achieve desired needs; imaging is realising the dreams of Africa. It is a question of the continent approaching changes and courses of events more intuitively, creating not only an intellectual understanding but also an emotional and ideological meaning as well as the determination to attain desired goals,
- *Deciding:* weighing up information, identify choices and strategies and making the right choice; Decision is the important critical link between vision and action. The ability to take decisions and make

the connection with concrete action separates the entrepreneur from the dreamer (Lindgren & Bandhold, op cit.)

- *Acting:* setting up short, medium and long-term goals; taking the first step followed by actions; Doing and acting are therefore central skills in this learning process with a strong focus directed on the future and the challenges that it provides.

Finally, both the predictability of the future of Africa and the impact of present actions on the future of the continent has been vastly increased by the advances in science and technology. Let us take advantage of science and technology to enhance the social responsibility for the future of the continent. Science and technology opens up unlimited potentials for solving the problems of today and the future, including those which are created by present technology. The future of Africa depends on how we build our human capital today without which we would only add to the cumulative and systemic damage of the future of the continent. We must now begin to plan for the future of Africa by learning from the mistakes of past generations or civilisations that have gone into long decline because they failed to plan for the future. Of course, every civilisation or generation has problems and choices. What this generation should ask itself is whether we are robbing our future heritage to pay for the present? We must therefore endeavour to work hard, honestly and genuinely to ensure that the generations of the future of Africa is bequeathed a continent worth living in. This generation taking its responsibility about the future of the continent means speaking up for those unable to speak for themselves, and that should represent the cornerstone of this publication as well as ensure the sound and sustainable development of continent.

There is a pressing concern for Africa to do better to regain its place within the community of nations. It requires defusing the continent's ticking time-bomb of poverty, corruption, injustice, disunity and ethnic divide. Blaming colonialism all the time for (an) embarrassingly slow pace in the socio-economic transformation of the area is both disingenuous and scapegoating. Constructively jumping that hurdle is what is required of us all now and making ourselves genuine development partners to bring forth deliverables for quality wellbeing.

May be colonialism implanted in us a perpetual form of weakness making us timid and entertaining foreign ideas. We allow ourselves to be bound by our colonial past. We must bear in mind that history cannot be rewritten, and neither can our dignity be restored without fighting for it. The struggle for self-determination must continue rigorously to better 'slay the demon of capacity deficits, or else it will be difficult to implement AU Agenda 2063 and the SDGs (2030), (Nnadozie, 2017:36-7) making it impossible to achieve AU Agenda 2063, the ideological orientation of building the Africa We Want and leaving no one behind. This entails not letting others turning us around, but Africa navigating its way through the dark clouds of the globalisation age.

We are challenged to plunge into the huge natural resources and vast development opportunities and possibilities offered by the global community of nations to make Africa working again (Mills et al, 2017). Yes, we can change; and positive and progressive changes are required to turn around the current predicament of the continent. Importantly, the people of the continent must beware of the 'second scramble' for Africa which leads to a massive depletion of the resources of the continent; and a gross displacement of the population (the brain-drain phenomenon); the growing '*dependency syndrome' and the 'endemic abject poverty factor.'* Africa is getting more and more dependent on the developed polities. For now, we pay less attention to cardinal issues that should drive the entrepreneurial and industrial wheels for a sustainable economic take-off. Africa's future for it to be sustainable calls for a comprehensive forward-looking policy strategy of 'reform or perish'. Like the academic world, it is either you publish or perish. "Publish or perish is the most significant of all pressures on young academics" (Moosa, 2018). African countries have no choice but to reform and develop or remain underdeveloped to be exploited by the developed countries. It underpins success with research, innovation, progress and development. This is what African countries must be gunning for to become part of the globalised world of our time. The people must develop a new ideological orientation to move progressively and comprehensively forward in the right direction.

The Future of Africa – Changing the Dynamics

The colonial era with the injection of Western Christian missionaries, traders and administrators preached the gospel of work, the dignity and sanctuary of labour to the African people to indolent in an effort to bring the black people in line with western values, (civilising the uncivilised), to which they succeed so to say. However, this form of western education but the indirect consequences of such colonial education consisted, or instilled, stimulate Africans to aspire to the possession of material goods (with raw materials from the continent produced in western factories) has been extremely successful. That inherited mentality should be changed. We need to ask the simple question, why have post-independence Africa in general failed to prosper while Asian countries with at least similar colonial history continue to prosper. This should be an eye opener to every Africa. Why change must urgently and drastically come the way of the people.

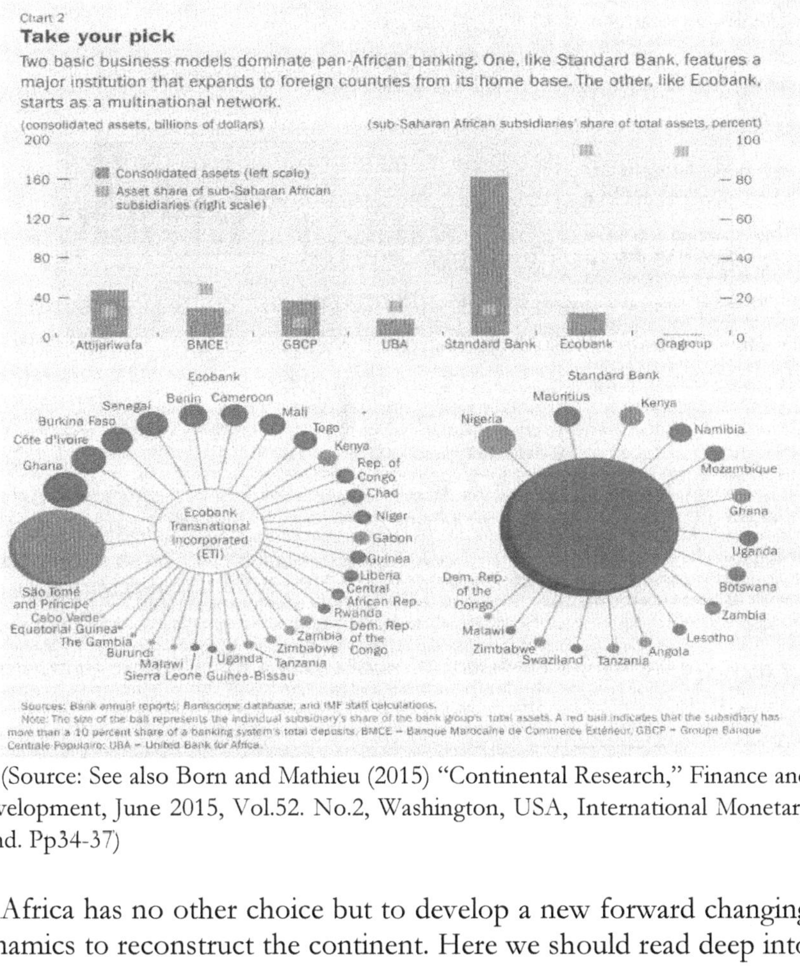

(Source: See also Born and Mathieu (2015) "Continental Research," Finance and Development, June 2015, Vol.52. No.2, Washington, USA, International Monetary Fund. Pp34-37)

Africa has no other choice but to develop a new forward changing dynamics to reconstruct the continent. Here we should read deep into and act constructively following the words of Rodney (1972:7) that 'African development is possible only on the basis of a radical break with the international capitalist system, which has been the principal agency of underdevelopment of Africa over the past five centuries. This same stand is taken up by Samir Amin and many other scholars in the theory of 'delinking and relinking' approach. There is a lot of truth in their positional thinking; however, a critical analysis of events during the past couple decades, one could aptly describe this as hasty, rash and drastic in light of current global economic and geo-[political trends; for example one never foresaw the collapse of the communist structure, the collapse of the Berlin Wall and the eventual rise of neo-liberalism, with its doctrine of deregularisation, liberalisation and privatisation, the spread of information and communication technologies in the context globalisation nor the emergence of new geo-political priorities after the horrendous events of 9/11 that worsen the plight and situation of African countries forcing them to seek feverishly – begging and pleading – outside assistance to constructing needed institutional and structural capacity; with the consequences of freeing and privatising their economies as a condition for their rapid integration into the world capitalist economy. Apparently, instead of African leaders 'delinking from the capitalist system (Rodney, Amin and others) our leaders see their salvation as lying in the countries effective integration in the new global economy (Owusu, 2004).

These developments intertwine to illustrate the pervasive influence of the colonial era on the structure and dynamics for socio-economic changes, heralding the dawn of a golden age of recovery and sustainable development throughout the continent. Why a new changing dynamics for the continent? By and large colonial policies and practices routinely cut off Africa from the new technology and capital investment from abroad with the exception of white settler states which alone could have released her full legacies of colonialism – political legal, educational, leaving black Africa, economically underdeveloped, exploited and dominated. The continent was left with the following interwoven fundamental problems, political, economic and psychological (PEP). The preponderant majority of Africa's 54 states are totally impoverished, divided, and weakened. Africa is became weakened because of the reverse flow of capital from the poor to the rich countries, producing severe debts of burden as well as prolonging its transition from a raw material producing exporting polity to one of a manufacturing and exporting continent.

Africa's development trajectory is stuck on the run-way unable to take-off to maturity. It is noteworthy and instructive that from a comparative basis, Asian success stories involves a combination of various dynamics of dictatorship, authoritarian and or at least regulated politics and a de facto one-party system, building consensus around the imperative of survival and the visible return of growth-shared growth benefiting the average citizen (Yergin & Stanislaw, 2002). But Africa's embracement of the single one-party structure, the practice of dictatorship, authoritarianism regulated politics failed to deliver the same kind of prosperity to the people like in the Asian countries. The impressive showing of Asian countries on economic performance and potential as contrasted with the poor economic record of African countries is rooted in psychological nexus, greed, and inferiority complex) and the failure to develop and use of the 'technology of the intellect'. It failed to develop its indigenous knowledge system (IKS). These with other factors could be seen in the words of President Nasser's book.: "I will continue to dream of the day when I will find in Cairo, a great African Institute dedicated to unveiling to our view the dark riches of' and that, 'it is our responsibility to support, with all our might, the spread of enlightenment and civilisation to the remotest depths of the jungle' (Theobald, 1960:129). Africa needs to undergo serious comprehensive and foresighted radical changes that place the human-being first in all activities, politically, economically and psychologically.

We are now faced with the realities; there is no African country, needless to say that can, so far, match the transformation in Asia, reporting similar stories of dramatic change in national economic prospects and improved standard of living, or of poverty alleviation and growing equality (Owusu, op cit.). The picture of a tired, malnourish African should ring a bell of consciousness in the heads, minds and hearts of African leaders to rethink seriously their roles as leaders of their people. We live in a different world context; and bearing in mind that the state of persistent poverty and inequality existing in Africa and these countries overwhelming dependence in the developed world; on neo-colonial partnership for economic survival and development cannot continue indefinitely, even if the neo-colonial partnership results in the cloning by compassionate western powers of the rise of a few African *Lions, Tigers and Elephants* to stimulate growth that accelerates Africa's take-off to developments that ensures a rise in living standards or sustainable quality livelihood out of abject poverty.

The alternative is for Africa to seek their solutions to the transformation of the region and drawing experiences from other countries. It should be African solutions or answers to African political and economic problems. As noted earlier, we can learn from best examples from other parts of the world. Gunnar Myrdal's (1970) publications together others by both African and non-African scholars provides great insights towards the transformation of the continent. What is fundamental is for Africa to invest in sound quality education system at all levels; empowerment of the female gender; and building the necessary infrastructures. The pursuit and use of knowledge remains crucial. With knowledge and other creative skills, we can build *an El Dorado* through adding knowledge to the existing abundant resources, which unfortunately is exported without added value. The views of Djanie Akua (2013) are significant in this context, and extensively reproduced here:

> "Africa is the new place to make money. And ultimately that is what everybody is chasing. The El Dorado: The land of Gold. The land of plenty: The land where any foreigner can be king. And this is my problem with all those singing about the new bright future for Africa. Certainly, it is a brilliant and bright new Africa if you are an Africa in the Diaspora. And it is a very prosperous Africa if you are an educated African in Africa, with contacts to society's movers and shakers. But the truth of the matter is that all the factors that are leading to a new African Renaissance are not provided by Africans on the continent. It is not Africans in Africa who will get the contract to build roads or work on a water project. It is not Africans who re investing in the booming energy and gas sector. It is not indigenous Africans in Africa who are consulting on oil and gas exploration and deals. No, the new African Renaissance is being led and enjoyed by an elite minority of people. There is no denying the potential for growth in all spheres of life in Africa. From music to fashion to banking to retail, Africa is fresh territory. And experts are moving fast and furiously to exploit this…."

For now, Africa stands at the cross-roads of progress or regression. No doubt we cohabit in an integrated world making political development the result of the need for rules to govern human interactions. In 1960 Dag Hammarskjold pointed out: "working at the edge of the development of human society is to work on the brink of one unknown. Much of what is done will one day prove to be of little avail. That is no excuse for the failure to act in accordance with our best understanding, in recognition of its limits, but will fail in the ultimate result of creative evolution in which it is our privilege to cooperate. There is always a challenge ahead, an historic opportunity to be grasped. There is also the certainty that our children will pay the price if we fail to grasp it. There is a disastrous human tendency to be killed by peaceful and prosperous times into doing nothing about great problems that still seem comfortably far off. It should be fatal mistake to evade or ignore the potential problems of globalisation just because they seem so vast and complex and we are still largely in the future (Urquhart 2000:18-19).

What future awaits Africa one is bound to question. Without any doubts the continent faces serious daunting challenges of development compared to other parts of the world. Africa is a region whose share of world trade continues to dwindle, and its resources plundered by external actors especially of war-torn countries like the Democratic

Republic of Congo, Sudan, Central Africa Republic, Cameroon to name but a few; and with the leaders breeding their countries to death and where war merchants are making a fortune out of the misery of the African people. The continent presently remains at the depth of economic and political despair and frustration. The situation undermines self-confidence and the ability of the African people, especially of its leadership, to ingeniously and creatively on the way forward for the continent. Yet, the responsibility for Africa's development lies primarily with African themselves (Adejumobi 2003:19-20).

Africa is walking down the lane of Paton's 'Cry their beloved Country'. Colonisation, with its intolerance of anything 'native' did its best to kill African indigenous knowledge and cultural traditions and to replace it with Europeans ones but it endured and after independence thrives. So far, the top-down approach – Eurocentric – has not and will not work or deliver the goods in Africa. Countries are in the end, people – the ideas they conceive about themselves and their approach and how hey organise to the realisation of their ideas is important; that is why a progressive Afrocentric or 'bottom-up' approach is crucial, and much needed by the continent. Africa must be on the move – the right way. In enunciating the goals of development, Africa has and for the nearest future vacillates from one extreme of quest for self-reliance, and self-sustaining development, to one of external dependence and externally-oriented policies and plans. Africa finds itself within the opportunity and insecurity of globalisation. Is this a blessing or curse for the continent? Since the wind of self-determination blew across the continent in the mid-fifties, Africa now finds itself in a most difficult situation.

Degeneration into the Abysses of no Return

Yes. The wind of change blew across the continent in the 1950s as it equally ushered a string of problems. For many, Africa was not freed but further subjected into more dilemmas. Today the continent has degenerated into abysses of greater destruction. It finds itself suffering from the viruses of:

□ The state of ingratitude	* The state of intimidation and gagging	
□ The state of intolerance	* The state of revenge	
□ The state of Apathy	* The state of apartheid	
□ The state of discontent)=====➔	* The state of fragmentation	
□ The state of denial	* The state of insanity) =====➔	*{Leads to state of*
□ The state of insecurity	* The state of injustice	*gross under-*
□ The state of lawlessness	* The state of endemic corruption	*development and*
□ The state of a new invasion	* The state of voluntary slavery	*destruction}*

The institutions of the state construct in Africa are massively politicised and feather bed of patronage, divide and rule phenomenon taking pride of place in the bureaucratic set-up of the structure-functioning of the country. This is one of the reasons why state collapse or state capture is more pronounced; and failure in quality services delivery extremely poor or non-existent. The bureaucratic machinery is bogged down with the appointment syndrome or motion of support syndrome; leading to wrong people placed in positions of responsibility on the basis of 'political party affiliation, ethnic connections, 'bribery and corruption' not on the basis of merit. No society can progress with such underlying deficiencies overriding its day-to-day functioning.

Only serious changes in mindset and attitude can usher meaningful restructuring of the society to transverse in the direction of progressive and inclusive development. It comes as no surprise that the continent is stuck on the runway – unable to take off to the next destination as signpost for quality welfare for all. Africa for centuries past has been bugged by the germ of colonialism. Colonialism is a common human malady, but proper analysis of it leads to deeper understanding of what ails us. Colonialism is a manifestation of wider phenomenon of greed and individual hubris. The impulse to exploit others explains how/why the rich get richer and the poor poorer; why African countries lost and continue to loose most of their valuable assets – human and natural resources potentials, even after the attainment of independence.

The struggle for self-determination must be intensified to get rid of the last grains of colonial rule inhibiting the sustainable transformation of the continent. And so, the need to decolonise the mind can no longer be exaggerated. To break the bonds of pains and sufferings requires progressive Afrocentric orientation and approach to rightly put an end to the current sufferings of the people. Africa needs an inclusive and holistic cleansing, a renaissance and purification that is not under the canopy of the Eurocentric ideology but profoundly embedded within an inclusive progressive Afrocentric ideological orientation and action plans that are embedded within the African cultural heritage knowledge. The continent needs to develop that knowledge and to deploy it appropriately for the sustainable transformation of the continent. Africa needs inclusive dialogue; this means building bridges rather than walls across the existing divide.

Stuck on the run-way tells us that certain forces are making a large fortune out of the misery of the African people. It also means that the continent remains at the depth of economic and political despair and frustration. Such a prevailing situation undermines self-confidence, trust, destroys the hopes, aspirations and ability of the people, especially its captured leadership to think strategically, constructively, ingenuously and creatively for a new forward for the continent. Yet, the continent runs from the fact that the responsibility for Africa's development is and lays primarily with us Africans. No one or any other country is going to develop Africa, but Africans developing the continent.

Globalisation now adds new dynamics in the process. Globalisation is a complex and dynamic process and has been analysed from various perspectives. These include the economic, political and socio-cultural dimensions. For the United Nations Development Programmes, (UNDP 2000:1) 'globalisation is a process integrating not just the economy, but culture, technology and governance'; while others like Goldhart et al, 1997; Mittleman 1993; Adejumobi 2002;Rosenau, 1997 and others) see globalisation as a shift in the spatial form and extent of human organisation and interaction to transnational or inter-regional level; globalisation widening and intensification of international linkages and interactions in trade, investment and economic policy orientation in the world. Globalisation is the internationalisation of production, capital, and marketing in which the world is integrated into a 'global factory', global money market', and 'global shopping centre'. Globalisation is seen as the whole trajectory of capitalist development. In short, it can be question whether globalisation is not a new euphemism for 'internationalism', 'universalism' and 'worldism' which depict the trajectory in the history of capitalist development. There are the losers and winners of the globalisation process. Without any hesitation, globalisation is recreating the world from the 'wealth of nations' to the 'wealth of the world'?

Globalisation provides many possibilities and obstructions towards striving for change and of keeping the region in perpetual underdeveloped status. Former World Bank, President James Wolfensohn, (April 2001) noted; "we cannot turn back globalisation. Our challenge is to make globalisation an instrument of opportunity and inclusion – not of fear and insecurity. Globalisation must work for all." The New Partnership for African Development (NEPAD) noted in October 2001: "in the absence of fair and just global rules, globalisation has increased the ability of the strong to advance their interests to the detriment of the weak, especially in the areas of trade, finance and technology. It has limited space for developing countries to control their own development, as the system makes no provision for compensating the weak. The conditions of those marginalised in this process have worsened in real terms. A fissure between inclusion and exclusion has emerged within and among nations."

There is a growing failure on the part of African governments investing in the people. Broadly stated, African leaders lack moral responsibility and patriotic sense of vision and direction of serving their people. They fail to realise the words written by Cywinski (2015) that;

> home is an intimate place. Known to us like no other place on Earth. We know exactly where we need to tidy, where to put dirty clothes, where the mementos and certificates of past successes are displayed and where evidence of past failures and shame remains hidden from the eyes of visitors. The walls are said to have ears, but they do not speak. What is said at home generally remains within the confines of its walls. The home is ours, and there we can be ourselves. Even in front of the bathroom mirrors; but sometimes at home. When we are alone we return to the past. We open old albums, pull out old photographs, ones of friends from the past, to whom we had once rashly albeit sincerely promised that we would write and stay in touch. Then we see ourselves without the embellishment.

When we think of Africa with the vast state of endemic poverty, chronic inequality, grossly poor and inadequate services delivery and entrenched corruption, we see also the growing state of affluence and optimism by a few we consider our leaders; we see the African holocaust, the barbed wire or nest of thorns our leaders have constructed around themselves to hide the stolen wealth of the people; we see the well-laid table with a cast-net under it to prevent even the crumps falling down from the tables for the have-nots to pick as means of survival for a second. Day after day we see Africa sinking deeper and deeper into abject poverty, obviation and the widening inequality gap, the violation of the fundamental human rights of citizens. Current deals that have the potential to create wealth are going to the Chinese, Americans and Europeans. The indigenous Africans are not forerunners in the New African renaissance. Why? These states of affairs builds castle of pessimism, making the next 50 years look bleak, not bright and full of optimism. We need to have optimism in building the Africa we want. The New Africa we want, or the New African Renaissance must not be constructed by foreigners but by Africans.

The past is never dead, so also the present, it is not even linked to its past; the future hangs on a balance. The gate of death, destruction and despair steers at us. The tragedy of Africa lies squarely in our leadership and in our inability to speak truth to power. It is needless to justify why we do not value dialogue; value other people like ourselves. So, we continue to have problems in Africa; and throw away the concept of a common good. We are unable to put a name to it and connect what we see in terms of cause-and-effect relationships. We continue to struggle with inadequate analogies. We become depressed in our inability into put order what we have stolen from the people. To find a common language with anyone else, we first must have to find our own words and actions, internal peace, thoughts that at least, we can understand. God Bless Africa. Has God been silent on Africa? Or has Africa turned its back against the most Supreme, the Just, Almighty and Benevolent One. The plight of the continent has been diagnosed rightly by Emmanuel Ifeanyi Ariwodo (Company Director at Quickwash in Dry Enterprise) in these captivating soul-searching words, lengthy reproduced here:

> frustration, aggression and violence is building up across the African continent, the result of poor leadership, governance, corruption and abject poverty, undernourished and nourished by high rate of unemployment and underemployment, faulty educational system, injustice and absolute disregard to the rule of law and court pronouncements, unimaginable looking of public treasury and week public institutions, unavailability of basic social needs, prebendalism and nepotism and ethno-religious intolerance may imminently lead to anomie, engineered crime and other social vices thereby threaten nation security and corporate existence of the continent. The time to act is now.

Indeed, the time to act constructively, holistically and in the overall interest of the people is now.

When COVID-19 pandemic penetrates into Africa, it is to show how negligent our leaders had been, and how the people have constantly failed speaking truth to power. If there was choice, it should penetrate Africa affecting those who have stolen from the poor and innocent.

Only through a progressive Afrocentric agenda can Africa recover and redevelop itself for a sustainable quality livelihood. Africa has to return to its roots with a difference. The difference is that of ensuring sustainable development, improved welfare and durable peace as well as security for everyone. It is important to emphasise that everything that leaders to accelerate the misfortune of underdevelopment, exploitation and oppression of people, to suffering and sorry, is deeply alien and unnatural to the African people will be resisted and resisted to their last drop of blood. The forces that are opposing the policy of aggression and interference in African countries are quite strong. Guided by common sense and the instinct for self-preservation, African countries most resolutely oppose by raising the voices as one people against the dangers of Eurocentrism. All of this gives us sufficient grounds to conclude our discourse about the ways and real possibilities to ensure a progressive march towards a better future for Africa on an optimistic note. Africa in the 21st century and beyond needs to building on Gandhi's legacy, not Hitler's might is right. Africa should avoid repeating the developmental saga, ecological and social mistakes of the North. Indeed, as reported by Shiva (2006), Gandhi observed: 'God forbid that India should ever take to industrialism after the manner of the West. The economic imperialism of a single tiny island kingdom (England) is today keeping the world in chains. If an entire nation of 300 million too to similar economic exploitation, it would strip the world like locusts."

We must envision an Africa beyond our current dependency on Western aid assistance; making the compelling case for a progressive Afrocentric ideological orientation as the way forward. It is argued that Africa's choice of return to the grass-roots conceptual heritage of harambee, batho pele, ubuntu, nhimbe etc., provides a people-oriented approach to returning to local and human realities, one which offers a decent and quality livelihood for all; remains a stark choice for the continent. Africa can either continue to pursue a Eurocentric market-centred approach or a people-centred approach. The North –Africa perspective has to be rigorously re-visited. This is a project that calls for all hands-on deck. It is time to dismantle the Eurocentric destructive agenda. We can only but agree and recommend the following wise views of; Annan, Fanon, Sadat. Maathai, Lumumba and Mandela:

> "African countries should now concentrate on transforming 'brain drain' into 'brain gain' by building and nurturing networks and developing strategies to harness the scientific and technical expertise of the Diaspora"
>
> **(Kofi Annan – Former UN Secretary General)**

> "Humanity is waiting for something from us other than an imitation of the West, which would be almost an obscene caricature"
>
> **(Frantz Fanon in The wretched of the Earth)**

"He who cannot change the very fabric of his/her thought will never be able to change the reality"

(Anwar Sadat, Former President of Egypt)

"In the course of history, there comes a time when humanity is called to shift to a new level of consciousness, to reach a higher moral ground. A time when we have t sheds our fear and to give hope to each is other. The time is now"

(Wangari Maathai. Noble Peace Laureate)

"Africa will tell the West that today it desires the rehabilitation of Africa, a return to the roots, a revalorisation of moral values"

(Patrice Lumumba – First Prime Minister of the DRC)

"Africa is beyond bemoaning the past for its problems. The task of undoing that past is on the shoulders of African leaders themselves, with the support of those willing to join in a continental renewal. We have a new generation of leaders who know that Africa must take responsibility for its own destiny, that Africa will uplift itself only by its own efforts in partnership with those who wish her well"

(Nelson Mandela, First Founding Black President of the New South Africa)

References

Adejumobi Said (2014). "The Pain of Inequality in Africa", New African No.541, July, 2014, IC Publication, London, pp46-47

Adejumobi Said (2003) Globalisation and Africa's Development Agenda. From the WTO to NEPAD. DPMF Occasional Paper, No.12, Development Policy Management Forum (DPMF), Addis Ababa, Ethiopia.

Ake Claude (2000). The Feasibility of Democracy in Africa. Codesria, Dakar, Sénégal

Azam, Jean-Paul (2001). "The Redistributive State and Conflicts in Africa." Journal of Peace Research 38, No.4 July 2001, pp429-44

Bettis, R. A. & M. A. Hitt (1995). " | The New Competitive Landscape," Strategic Management Journal, 16: 7-16

Busuttil Salvino et al (eds.) (1990). Our Responsibilities Towards Future Generations, Foundation for International Studies, University of Malta and in cooperating with UNESCO.

Cruikshank Barbara (1999). The Will to Empower: Democratic Citizens and Other Subjects. Cornell University Press, Ithaca and London

Cywinski M. A. Piotr (2015). Epitaph: Auschwitz-Birkenau State Museum, Austria

Debiel Tobias (ed.) (2002). Fragile Peace: State Failure, Violence, and Development in Crisis Regions. Zed Books, New York

Djanie Akua (2013). "A Future Made in Africa?" New African, Issue 531, August/September 2013, IC Publication, London, pp26-27

Drucker F. Peter (1974) Management Tasks, Responsibilities, Practice. Butterworth Heinemann, Oxford, UK

Forje W. John (2009) Here the People Rule: Political Transition and Challenges for Democratic Consolidation in Africa. Nova Science Publishers Inc. New York, USA

Forje W. John (1981). The One and Indivisible Cameroon. Political Integration and Socio-economic Development in a Fragmented Society. Department of Political Science, University of Lund, Lund Political Studies, No.35, University Printing Press, Lund, Sweden

Goldhalt, D. et al (1997). Economic Globalisation and The Nation State. Shifting Balances of Power. Alternatives, No. 22

Hart, S. and C. Banbury (1994). "How Strategy-making processes can make a difference,' Strategic Management Journal 15; 251-69

Held D. Et al (1999). Globalisation Transformations: Politics, Economics and Culture, Stanford University Press, Stanford, USA

Hoogvelt, A. (1997). Globalisation and Post-Colonial World: The New Political Economy of Development. John Hopkins University Press, Baltimore, MD, USA

Jacobs Garry (2018) "Foundations of Economic Theory: Money, Markets and Social Power|", ASPJ Africa and Francophonie, Vol. 9. No.1, 1st Quarter 2018, pp71-94

Keenan Jeremy (2009). The Dark Sahara. Pluto Press, UK.

Keenan Jeremy (2013). Global War on Terror in the Sahara. The Dying Sahara, Pluto Press, UK.

Keenan Jeremy (2013)." Mali Is Another African War. US and Algerian Convert Activities Sowed the Seeds of the Conflict", New African, 47th Year, January 2013, No.524, London, pp12-16

Kerr J. C. Anthony (1967) Time Past and Tim Present – The Modern World 1814 to the Present Day, Wheaton and CO Publishers, Exeter, United Kingdom.

Kreijen Hubert Peter Gerard (2003) State Failure, Sovereignty and Effectiveness. Leiden University Press, Leiden Netherlands.

Levi Margaret (1989). Of Rules and Revenue, University of California Press, Berkeley, CA,

Lindgren Mats and Bandhold Has (2009) Scenario Planning: The Link Between Future and Strategy, Palgrave Macmillan Publishers, UK and USA

Mills Greg, Jeffrey Herbst, Olusegun Obasanjo and Dick Davis (2017). Making Africa Work, Hurst Publishers, London, UK.

Mittleman, J. (1993). Globalisation restructuring of production and migration, African Journal of Political Economy

Morgenthau Hans (1958) Politics Among Nations: The Struggle for Power and Peace USA.

Moosa A. Imad (2018). Publish or Perish: Perceived Benefits versus United Consequences. Edward Elgar Publishing, United Kingdom

Moyo Nkosana (2013) "There is a Continued Imposition of Western Culture on Africans", New African, No.529, June 2013, London, pp74-77

Nnadozie Emmanuel (2017) 'Four Reasons Why African States Must Raise Their Game in Funding Capacity for Development', New African, No. 577, November 2017, IC Publications, London, United Kingdom

Nord Roger (2017)'A Balancing Act for China and Africa: The Effects of China's Rebalancing on Sub-Saharan Africa's Trade and Growth' see (http://www.imforg/en/publications/departmental-papers-policy-papers/issues 2017/04/07/a-rebalancingact-for-china-and-africa-the-effecta-of-chinas-rebalancing-on-sub-saharan-44711

North-South (1980) A Programme for Survival: Report of the North-South Commission. Pan Books, London [Otherwise known as the Brand Report or Commission]

Owusu Maxwell (2004), "Inside History: Why There Are No Africa 'Tigers', 'Dragons' or 'Elephants'. An Inquiry into the Nature and Causes of the Poverty and Wealth of African Nations in a Globalising World", (paper presented at the 14th Annual Conference of the Pan African Anthropological Association (PAAA) at The Institute of African Studies, University of Ghana, Legon, Ghana, 2-5 August 2004

Rodney Walter (1972). How Europe Underdeveloped Africa

Rosenau, J. (1997) The Complexities and Contradictions of Globalisation. Current History 96, No.613

Sachs D Jeffrey (2015). The Age of Sustainable Development Columbia University Press, New York, USA

Sieme Swart (2012) Department of Political Science, University of Stellenbosch, South Africa. (ed.) A Vanquished Peace; Prospects in

the Successful Reconstruction of the Democratic Republic of the Congo, Adonis & Abbey Publishers Ltd, London, UK.
Stiglitz (2002)
Theobald Robert (ed.) (1996). The New Nations of West Africa. The H. W. Wilson Co. New York, USA
Thucydides, (1972). History of the Peloponnesian War, (translated by Rex Warner), Penguin Books, 1972
Urquhart, Brian (2000), Between Sovereignty and Globalisation. Where does the United Nations fit in? The Second Dag Hammarskjold Lecture, Uppsala, Sweden. The Dag Hammarskjöld Foundation and Uppsala University, Motala Grafiska, AB, Sweden
World Movement for Democracies (WMD). The Eight General Assembly, Soule – Korea, November 1-4, 2015.
Yergin, Daniel & Joseph Stanislaw (2002). Commanding Heights: The Battle for The World Economy. Simon and Schuster, New York, USA.

Appendix 1

AGENDA 2063

The Africa We Want
Third Edition, January 2015

THE VOICES OF THE AFRICAN PEOPLE

1 **The people of Africa and her Diaspora** united in diversity, young and old, men and women, from all walks of life, deeply conscious of history, express their deep appreciation to all generations of Pan Africanists. In particular, to the founders of the Organisation of African Unity for having bequeathed an African free from slavery, colonialism and apartheid.

2 **We echo** the Pan African call that Africa must unit in order to realise its Renaissance. Present generations are confident that the destiny of Africa is in their hands, and that we must act now to shape the future we want. Fifty years after the first thirty-three (33) independent African states gathered in Addis Ababa to form the Organisation of African Unity, we are looking ahead towards the next fifty years.

3 We reviewed past plans and commitments, and pledge t takes into account the lessons as we implement Agenda 2063. These include putting mobilisation of the people and their ownership of continental programmes at the core; the principle of self-reliance and African financing its own development; the importance of capable, inclusive and accountable states and institutions at all levels and in all spheres, the critical role of Regional Economic Communities as building blocks for continental unity, and holding ourselves and our governments and institutions accountable for results;

4. We rededicated ourselves to the enduring Pan African vision of "an integrated prosperous and peaceful Africa, driven by its own citizens and representing a dynamic force in the global arena."

AFRICAN ASPIRATIONS FOR 2063D:

5. Our united voices paint a picture of what we desire for ourselves, for future generations and the continent.

6. The aspirations reflect our desire for shaped prosperity and well-being, for unity and integration, for a continent of free citizens and expanded horizons, where the full potential of women and youth are realised, and with freedom from fear, disease and want.

7. Africa is elf-confident I its identity, heritage and shared values, and as a strong, united and influential partner on the global stage making its contribution to peace, human progress and welfare. In short a different and better Africa.

8 We are confident that Africa has the capability to realise her full potential in development, culture and peace and to establish flourishing, inclusive and prosperous societies. We thus commit to act together towards achieving the following aspirations:

(1) A prosperous Africa based on inclusive growth and sustainable development:

(2) An integrated continent, politically united and based on the ideal Pan-Africanism

(3) An Africa of Good Governance, Democracy, Respect for human rights, Justice and the Rule of Law;

(4) A Peaceful and Secure Africa;

(5) An Africa with a strong cultural identity, common heritage, shared values and ethics

(6) An Africa where development is people-driven, unleashing the potential of women and youths

(7) Africa as a strong, united and influential global player and partner

ASPIRATION 1
A Prosperous Africa Based on Inclusive Growth and Sustainable Development

9 **We are determined** to eradicate poverty in one generation and build shared prosperity through social and economic transformation of the continent.

10 **We aspire that by 2063**, Africa shall be a prosperous continent, with the means and resources to drive its own development, and where:

- African people have a high standard of living, and quality of life, sound health and well-being;
- Well educated citizens and skills revolution underpinned by science, technology and innovation for a knowledge society is the norm and no child misses school due to poverty or any form of discrimination;
- Cities and other settlements are hubs of cultural and economic activities, with modernised infrastructure, and people have access to affordable and decent housing including finance together with all basic necessities of life as, water, sanitation, energy, public transport and ICT;
- Economies are structurally transformed to create shared growth, decent jobs and economic opportunities for all;
- Modern agriculture for increased production, productivity and value

addition contribute to farmer and national prosperity and Africa's collective food security;

- The environment and ecosystems are healthy and preserved, and climate resilient economies and communities.

11 By 2063, Africa countries will be amongst the best performers in global quality of life measures. This will be attained through strategies of inclusive growth, job creation, increasing agricultural production; investments in science, technology, research and innovation; gender equality, youth employment and the provision of basic services including health, nutrition, education, shelter, water and sanitation.

12 Africa's collective GDP will be proportionate to her share of the world's population and natural resources endowments

13 Africa's agriculture will be modern and productive, using science, technology, innovation and indigenous knowledge. The hand hoe will be banished by 2025 and the sector will be modern, profitable and attractive to the continent's youths and women.

14. Africa's Blue economy, which is three times the size of its landmass, shall be a major contributor to continental transformation and growth, advancing knowledge on marine and aquatic biotechnology, the growth of an Africa-wide shipping industry, the development of sea, river and lake transport and fishing; and exploitation and beneficiation of deep sea and mineral and other resources

15. Whilst Africa at present contributes less than (5%) of global carbon emissions, it bears the brunt of the impact of climate change. Africa shall address the global challenge of climate change by prioritising adaptation in our actions, drawing upon skills of diverse disciplines and with adequate support (affordable technology development and transfer, capacity building, financial and technical resources) to ensure implementation of actions for survival of the most vulnerable populations, including island states, and for sustainable development and shared prosperity

16. Africa will participate in global efforts for climate change mitigation that support and broaden the policy space for sustainable development on the continent. Africa shall continue to speak one voice and unity of purpose in advancing its position and interests on climate change.

Africa shall have equitable and sustainable use and management of water resources for socio-economic development, regional cooperation and the environment.

ASPIRATION 2

An Integrated Continent, Politically United Based On the ideals of Pan-Africanism and the Vision of Africa's Renaissance

17. Since 1963, the quest for African Unity has been inspired by the spirit of Pan-Africanism, focusing on liberation, and political and economic independence. It is motivated by development based on self-reliance and self-determination of African people, with democratic and people-centred governance.

18 **We aspire that by 2063,** Africa will:

> Be a United Africa;

> Have world class, integrative infrastructure that criss-crosses the continent

> Have dynamic and mutually beneficial links with her Diaspora;

> Be a continent of seamless borders, and management of cross border resources through dialogue

19. Africa shall be an integrated, united, sovereign, independent, confident and self-reliant continent

20. Africa will witness the rekindling of solidarity and unity of purpose that underpinned the struggle for emancipation from slavery, colonialism, apartheid and economic subjugation. By 2020 all remnants of colonialism would have ended and all African territories under occupation fully liberated. We shall take measures to expeditiously end the unlawful occupation of the Chagos Archipelago, the Comorian Island of Mayotte and affirming the right to self-determination of the people of Western Sahara. All kinds of oppression including gender, racial and other forms of discrimination would be ended.

21. The political unity of Africa will be the culmination of the integration process, including the free movement of people, the establishment of continental institutions, and full economic integration. By 2030, there shall be consensus on the form of the continental government and institutions.

22. Africa shall be a continent where the free movement of people, capital, goods and services will result in significant increases in trade and investments amongst African countries rising to unprecedented levels, and strengthen Africa's place in global trade.

23. By 2063 the necessary infrastructure will be in place to support Africa's accelerated integration and growth, technological transformation, trade and development. This will include high-speed railway networks, roads, shipping lines, sea and airport, as well as well-developed ICT and digital economy. A Pan African High-Speed Rail network will connect all the major

/ capitals of the continent, with adjacent highways and pipelines for gas, oil, water, as well as ICT Broadband cables and other infrastructure. This will be a catalyst for manufacturing, skills development, technology, research and development, integration and intra-African trade, investments and tourism.

24. The world-class infrastructure accompanied by trade facilitation will see intra-African trade growing from less than 12% in 2013 to approaching 50% by 2045. African share of global trade shall rise from 2% to 12%. This will in turn spur the growth of Pan African companies of global reach in all sectors.

ASPIRATION 3
An Africa of Good Governance, Democracy, Respect for Human Rights, Justice and the Rule of Law

25. Africa shall have a universal culture of good governance, democratic values, gender equality, and respect for human rights, justice and the rule of law.

26. **We aspire** that by 2063, Africa will:

* Bea a continent where democratic values, culture, practices, universal principles of human rights, gender equality, justice and the rule of law are entrenched; and

* Have capable institutions and transformative leadership in place at all levels;

27. The continent's population will enjoy affordable and timely access to independent courts and judiciary that deliver justice without fear or favour. Corruption and impunity will be a thing of the past.

28. Africa will be a continent where the institutions are at the service of its people. Citizens will actively participate in social, economic and political development and management. Competent, professional, rules and merit-based public institutions will serve the continent and deliver effective and efficient services. Institutions at all levels of government will be developmental, democratic, and accountable.

29. There will be transformation leadership in all fields (political, economic, religious, cultural, academic, youth and women) and at continental, regional, national and local levels.

ASPIRATION 4
A Peaceful and Secure Africa

30. By 2020 all guns will be silent.

31. Mechanisms for peaceful resolution of conflicts will be functional at levels. A culture of peace and tolerance shall be nurtured in Africa's children and youth through peace education

32. Africa will be a **Peaceful and Secure Continent,** with harmony among communities starting at grassroots level. The management of our diversity will be a source of wealth, harmony and social and economic transformation rather than a source of conflict.

33. **We aspire by 2063**, Africa shall have:
* An entrenched and flourishing culture of human rights, democracy, gender equality, inclusion and peace;
* Prosperity, security and safety for all citizens; and
* Mechanisms to promote and defend the continent's collective security and interests

34. We recognised that a prosperous, integrated and united Africa, based on good governance, democracy, social inclusion and respect for human rights, justice and the rule of law are the necessary pre-conditions for a peaceful and conflict-free continent.

35. The continent will witness improved human security with sharp reductions in violent crimes. There shall be safe and peaceful spaces for individuals, families and communities.

36. Africa shall be free from armed conflict, terrorism, extremism, intolerance and gendered-based violence as a major threat to human security, peace and development. The continent will be drugs-free, with no human trafficking, and where organised crime and other forms of criminal networks, such as the arms trade and piracy, are ended. Africa shall have ended the illicit trade in and proliferation of small arms and light weapons.

37. Africa shall promote human and moral values based on tolerance and rejection of all forms of terrorism irrespective of their motivations.

38. 2063, Africa will have the capacity to secure peace and protect its citizens and interests, through a common defence, foreign and security policy

ASPIRATION 5
An Africa with a Strong Cultural Identity, Common Heritage, Values and Ethics

39. Pan-Africanism and the common history, destiny, identity, heritage, respect for religious diversity and consciousness of African people's and her Diaspora's will be entrenched.

40. We aspire that by 2063:

* Pan-Africanism shall be fully entrenched; and

* The African Renaissance has reached its peak.

* Our diversity in culture, heritage, languages and religion shall because of strength

41. Pan-African ideals will be taught in all school circular and Pan- Africa cultural assets (heritage, folklore, languages, film, music, theatre, literature, festivals, religious and spirituality) will be enhanced. The African creative arts and industries will be celebrated throughout the continent and the Diaspora and contribute significantly to self-awareness, well-being and prosperity, and to world culture and heritage. African languages will be the basis for administration and integration. African values of family, community, hard work, merit, mutual respect and social cohesion will be firmly entrenched

42. Africa's stolen culture, heritage and artefacts will be fully repatriated and safeguarded.

43. Culture heritage and a common identity and destiny will be the centre of all our strategies so as to facilitate for a Pan-African approach and the African Renaissance

44. African women and youths shall play an important role as drivers of change. inter-generational dialogue to ensure that Africa is a continent that adapts to social and cultural change

ASPIRATION 6
An Africa where Development is People-Driven, Unleashing the Potential of its Women Youth

45. All Citizens of Africa will be actively involved in decision making in all aspects of development including social, economic, political and environmental.

46. Africa shall be an exclusive continent where no child, woman or man will be left behind or excluded, on the basis of gender, political affiliation, ethnic affiliation, locality, age or other factors.

47. We aspire that by 2963, Africa:

* Is People-centred and caring

* Puts children first

* Women are empowered and play their rightful role in all spheres of life.

* Has full gender equality in all spheres of life

* Has engaged and empowered youth

48. The African woman will be fully empowered in all spheres, with equal social, political and economic rights, including the rights to own and inherit prosperity, sign contract, register and manage a business. Rural women will have access to productive assets, including land, credit, inputs and financial services

49. All forms of violence and discrimination (social, economic, political) against women and girls will be eliminated and they will fully enjoy all their human rights. All harmful social practices (especially FGM) will be ended and barriers to quality health and education for women and girls eliminated

50. Africa of 2063 will have full gender parity, with women occupying at least 50% of elected public offices at all levels and half of managerial positions in the public and the private sector. The economic and political glass ceiling that restricted women's progress would have been shattered.

51. By 2063, African children shall be empowered with full implementation of the African Charter on the Rights of the child.

52. By 2063 the youth of Africa shall be socially, economically and politically empowered with full implementation of the African Youth Charter.

53. An Africa where the child and the youth's talent will be fully developed rewarded and protected for the benefit of society.

54. All forms of systemic inequalities, exploitation, marginalisation and discrimination of young people will be eliminated, and youth issue mainstreamed in all development agenda.

55. Youth unemployment will be eliminated, and Africa's youth guaranteed full access to education, training, skills and technology, to health services, jobs and economic opportunities, recreational and cultural activities as well as resources and financial means to allow them to realise their full potential

56. Young African men and women will be path breakers of the African knowledge society and will contribute significantly to innovation and entrepreneurship. The creativity, energy and innovation of African youth shall be a driving force behind the continent's political, social, cultural and economic transformation

ASPIRATION 7
Africa as a Strong, United and Influential Global Player and Partner

57. Africa shall be a strong, united, resilient, peaceful and influential global player and partner with a significant role in world affairs. We affirm the importance of African unity and solidarity in the face of continued external interference including, attempts to divide the continent and undue pressures and sanctions on some countries.

58. We aspire that by 2063, Africa shall be:

* A major social, political and economic force in the world, and with her rightful share of the global commons (land, ocean and space,).
* An active and equal participant in global affairs, multilateral institutions, a driver for peaceful co-existence, tolerance and a sustainable and just world
* Fully capable and have the means to finance her development

59. Africa will take its rightful place in the political, security, economic, and social systems of global governance towards the realisation of its Renaissance and establishing Africa as a leading continent. We undertake to continue the global struggle against all forms of racism and discrimination, xenophobia and related intolerances; advance international cooperation that promotes and defends Africa's interests, is mutually beneficial and aligned to our Pan-Africanist vision; continue to speak with one voice and act collectively to promote our common interests and positions in the international arena.

60. Africa shall continue to advocate for the reform of the United Nations and other global institutions; with particular reference to the UN Security Council, in order to correct the historical injustice with Africa as the only region not represented on the Council

61. Africa is on an upward trend and seeks mutually beneficial relations and partnerships with other regions and continents. It therefore looks at the nature of partnerships with a view to rationalise them and enhancing the benefits to its transformation and integration efforts. We shall do so by strengthening our common perspectives on partnerships and by speaking with one voice on priorities and views on global matters

THE ASSEMBLY OF THE AFRICAN UNION

62. We, Heads of State and Government of the African Union assembled in Addis Ababa, Ethiopia during the 24th Ordinary Session of the Assembly of the Union in January 2015;

63. Having taken note of the aspirations and determination of the African people expressed above, reiterate our full appreciation and commitment to these aspirations.

64. Re-affirm that Agenda 2063 builds on past achievements and challenges and takes into account the continental and global context and trends in which Africa is realising its transformation, including:

(A) The Pan-African vision and project, which guided struggles of African people and their descendants against slavery, colonialism, apartheid and racial discrimination; the commitment of the founders of the OAU to self-determination; integration, solidarity and unity; and which today forms the backdrop for Africa's renaissance, transformation and integration

(B) An African turning point, starting at the turn of the millennium with our renewed determination to end wars and conflicts, to build shared prosperity, the continent's marginalisation through the transformation of the OAU into the African Union and the adoption of the New Partnership for Africa's Development… Thus Africa, over the last decade has experienced sustained levels of growth, greater peace and stability and positive movements on a number of human development indicators. We recognised that sustaining this path and pace, though positive, is not sufficient for Africa to catch up and thus the need for radical transformation at all levels and in all spheres. Africa must therefore consolidate the positive turnaround, using the opportunities of demographics, natural resources, urbanisation, technology and trade as a springboard to ensure its transformation and renaissance to meet the people's aspirations

(C) Lessons from global developmental experiences, the significant advances by countries of the South to lift huge sections of their population out of poverty, improve incomes and catalyse economic and social transformation. We are part of the global drive through the United Nations and other multilateral organisations to find multi-lateral approaches to humanity's most pressing concerns including human security and peace; the eradication of poverty, hunger and disease; gender equality and climate change, including the Common African Position on the post-2015 Development agenda.

(D). Learning from past and present African development efforts and challenges and forging an African-centred approach to transformation. This includes lessons from post-independence state and nation-building, industrialisation and modernisation efforts, the fight against disease, ignorance and poverty; and the push for integration, as captured in the OAU Charter, the Monrovia Declaration, the Lagos Plan of Action, the Abuja Treaty, the AU Constitutive Act and, NEPAD

(E) People-centred development, gender equality and youth empowerment, which places the Africa people at the centre of all continental efforts, to ensure **their** participation in the transformation of the continent, and to build caring and inclusive societies. It recognises that no society can reach its full potential, unless it empowers women and youth and remove all obstacles to women's full participation in all areas of human endeavours. Africa must provide an enabling environment for its women, children and young people to flourish and reach their full potential

(F) The changing global context, and in our times the modern information revolution; globalisation; changes in technology, production, trade, knowledge and labour markets; the opportunities presented by global demographic trends, urbanisation and the growing global middle and working classes in the South; the move towards multi-polarity with strong elements of uni-polarism remaining, global security and the impact of climate change. Humanity today has the capacities, technology and know-how to ensure a decent standard of living and human security for all inhabitants of our earth. And yet children continue to die of preventable diseases; women continue to die whilst giving birth, hunger and malnutrition remain part of the human experience; and underdevelopment, fragility, marginalisation and inequality between regions and countries and within countries persist.

65. Stress that Agenda 2063 is:

- Our endogenous plan of transformation. It harnesses the continent's comparative advantages such as its people, history and cultures; its natural resources; its position and repositioning in the world to effect equitable and people-centred social, economic and technological transformation and eradication of poverty. It seeks to develop Africa's human capital; build social assets, infrastructure and public goods; empower women and youth; promote lasting peace and security; build effective developmental states and participatory and accountable institutions and governance;
- Africa's vision and roadmap for sequencing our sectoral and normative, national, regional and continental plans into a coherent whole.
- A call to action to all Africans and people of African descent, to take personal responsibility for **the** destiny of the continent and as the primary agents of change and transformation.
- A commitment from national regional and continental governments, leadership, institutions and citizens to act, coordinates, and cooperates for the realisation of this vision

66. Note that Agenda 2063 builds on the pledges made through the 50th Anniversary Solemn Declaration;

67. We are confident that our peoples' aspirations and the dream of an Africa that is integrated, peaceful and prosperous is achievable, provided that we construct this future based on actions taken now

A CALL TO ACTION

68. **We are deeply conscious** that Africa in 2015 stands at a crossroads and we are determined to transform the continent and ensure irreversible and universal change of the African condition

69. We recognise that island states confront problems similar to other developing countries, with their own peculiar characteristics, vulnerabilities and strengths and the need for mechanism to ensure that Agenda 2063 incorporates this.

70. We here adopt Agenda 2063 as a collective vision and roadmap for the next fifty years and therefore commit to speed-up actions in the following areas:

(i) Eradicate poverty in a generation by 2025, through concentrating all efforts, investing in the productive capacities (skills and assets) of our people, improving incomes, creating jobs and providing basic necessities of life.

(ii) **Provide opportunities for all Africans to have decent housing in clean, secure and well-planned environment by**

- Providing access to affordable and decent housing to all in sustainable human settlements;
- Ensuring balanced development of all human settlements while embracing a rural urban continuum;
- Improving the livelihoods of the great percentage of the people working and living in slums and informal settlements

(iii) Catalyse an Education and Skills revolution and actively promote science, technology, research and innovation, to build knowledge, human resources, capabilities and skills for the African century;

- Expand universal access to quality childhood, primary and secondary education;
- Expand and consolidate gender parity in education,
- Strengthen the technical and vocational education and training through scaled up investments, the establishment of a pool of high-quality TVET centres across Africa, greater links with industry and alignment to labour markets, with a view to improve the skills profile, employability and entrepreneurship of especially youth and women, and closing the skills gap across the continent;
- Build and expand an African knowledge society through transformation and investments in universities, science, technology, research and innovation; and through the harmonisation of education standards and mutual recognition of academic and professional qualifications. Establish an African Accreditation Agency to develop and monitor educational quality standards across the continent;
- Strengthen the Pan-African University, build the Pan-African Virtual University and elevate Africa's role in global research, technology development and transfer, innovation and knowledge production.

(iv) Transform, grow and industrialise our economies through beneficiation and value addition of natural resources;

- Implementation of the African Industrial Development Action Plan, The African Mining Vision at country and continental level, in particular fast-tracking the establishment of the Centre for African Mineral Development;
- Implementation of joint cross-border investments to exploit shared natural resources.
- Promote social dialogue, sectoral and productivity plans and regional and community value chains to support the implementation of industrial policies at all levels, with focus on SMMEs and Agribusinesses.
- The establishment of Commodity exchanges for strategic African products.
- Strategies to grow the African Blue and Green economies;
- The development of the African Private sector through engagement and an enabling environment, fostering Pan-African businesses through the growth of regional manufacturing hubs and scaled up intra-Africa trade.
- Productivity Agenda for Africa, as an essential engine for industrialisation, progressively enhancing the competitiveness of the continent in the global economy.
- Macro-economic policies that facilitate growth, employment creation, investments and industrialisation.

(v) Consolidate the modernisation of Africa agriculture and agro-businesses, through scaled up value addition and productivity, and by 2025:

- Eliminate hunger and food insecurity;
- Reduce the imports of food and raise intra-Africa trade in agriculture and food to 50% of total formal food and agricultural trade.
- Expand the introduction of modern agricultural systems, technology, practices and training, including the banishment of the hand-hoe.
- Develop and implement affirmative policies and advocacy to ensure women's increased access to land and inputs, and ensure that at least 30% of agricultural financing are accessed by women.
- Economically empower women and youths by enhancing access to financial resources for investments.

(vi) Climate change and Environment, implementation of the Programme on Climate Action in Africa, including:

- Identification of five regional technology centres, linking with national designated climate technology entities;
- Programmes on climate change targeting women and youths:
- A climate resilient agricultural development programme as CAADP;

- S sustainable forest management programme.
- National adaptation plans, systems and structures (National Designated Authorities and Implementation Entities)
- A sustainable exploitation and management of Africa's diversity for the benefit of its people

(vii) Connect Africa through world-class infrastructure, with a concerted push to finance and implement the major infrastructure projects in:

- **Transport**: connecting all African capitals and commercial centres through the African Integrated Speed Train initiative, the PIDA transport corridors; improved efficiency and connections of the African aviation sector and implement the Yamoussoukro Declaration, and strengthening the African port and shipping sector as regional and continental assets;
- **Energy** harnessing all African energy resources to ensure modern, efficient, reliable, cost effective, renewable and environmentally friendly energy to all African households, businesses, industries and institutions, through building the national and regional energy pools and grids, and PIDA energy projects.
- **ICT: a** continent on equal footing with the rest of the world as an information society, an integrated e-economy where every government, business and citizen has access to reliable and affordable ICT services by increasing broadband penetration by 10% by 2018, broadband and connectivity by 20 percentage points and providing access to ICT to children in schools and venture capital to young ICT entrepreneurs and innovators and migration to digital TV broadcasting by 2016

(vii) Fast-track the establishment of a Continental Free Trade Area by 2017, a programme to double intra-African trade by 2022, strengthen Africa's common voice and policy space in global trade negotiations and establish the financial institutions within agreed upon timeframes: African Investment Bank and Pan-African Stock Exchange (2016), the African Monetary Fund (2018), and the African Central Bank (2028/34).

(vii) Support Young people as drivers of Africa's Renaissance, through investment in their health, education and access to technology, opportunities and capital, and concerted strategies to combat youth unemployment and underemployment. Ensure faster movement on the harmonisation of continental admissions, curricula, standards, programmes and qualifications and raising the standards of higher education to enhance the mobility of African youths and talents across the continent by 2025

(viii) Silence the guns by 2020, to make peace a reality for all our people and by ending all wars, civil conflicts, human rights violations, humanitarian disasters, gender-based violence and violent conflicts, and to prevent genocide. We pledge not to bequeath the burden of conflicts to the next generation of Africans by ending all wars in Africa by 2020. We shall establish an African Human Security Index (AHSI) to monitor progress.

(ix) Achieve Gender Parity by 2020 in public and private institutions, and the removal of all forms of d=gender discrimination in the social, cultural, economic and political spheres. Mobilise a concerted drive towards immediately ending child marriages, female genital mutilation and other harmful cultural practises that discriminate against women;

(x) Introduce an African Passport, issued by Member States, capitalising on the global migration towards e-passports, and with the abolishment of visa requirements for all African citizens in all African countries by 2028

(xi) Consolidate a democratic and people-centred Africa, through the universal application of the normative framework of the Africa Governance Architecture, and all elections on the continent are free, fair and credible.

(xii) Enhance Africa's united voice in global negotiations, through pooled sovereignty, integration and the development of common African positions and integration of an African language as a UN working language Correct the historical injustice of Africa as the only region without a permanent eat in the UN Security Council within the next decade.

(xiii) Strengthening domestic resources mobilisation, builds continental capital markets and financial institutions, and reverses the illicit flows of capital from the continent, with view to by 2025:

- Reducing aid dependency by 50%;
- Eliminate all forms of illicit flows;
- Double the contribution of African capital markets in development financing;
- Render fully operational the African Remittances Institute, the African Investment Bank and the African Credit Guarantee Scheme;
- Elevation of Africa-multilateral lending institutions to global status (e.g. African Development Bank);
- Reduce unsustainable levels, heavy indebtedness and odious debt;
- Build effective, transparent and harmonised tax and revenue collection systems and public expenditure

(xiv) Set up an Implementation, monitoring, evaluation system to ensure the attainment of the African Aspiration by:

- Identifying leadership and stakeholders at the national, regional and continental levels and assigning roles and responsibilities to each of them;
- Providing broad policy guidelines that would be adopted/adapted by national, regional and continental stakeholders with respect to the implementation, monitoring and evaluation of Agenda 2063.
- Leveraging the strengths of the RECs as the focal point for coordinating the implementation, monitoring and evaluation of Agenda 2063 by member states;
- Leveraging the strengths of AU institutions as AUC/MEPAD, the PAP, and ECOSOCC amongst others to coordinate the implementation, monitoring and evaluation at the continental level.
- Leveraging the strengths of non-AU continental institutions as the African Development Bank, the UN Economic Commission, the African Capacity Building Foundation, and the African Public Services Commission Association amongst others to assist the AUC institutions in playing their roles effectively.
- Organising an annual continental level stakeholder platform to review the progress of implementation of Agenda 2063 at the national, regional and continental levels and submitting the outcome of its deliberation in the form of Annual Agenda 2063 State of the Union Report to the African Assembly

71. Towards continental unity: the political unity of Africa will be the culmination of the integration process, including the free movement of people, the establishment of the continental institutions, and full economic integration. By 2030, there shall be consensus on the form of the continental government and institutions

CRITICAL ENABLERS FOR AFRICA'S TRANSFORMATION

72. The determination, participation, self-reliance and solidarity of Africa's people's and leadership are preconditions for success and therefore recognise the following as critical enablers of continental transformation:

(a) The People's ownership and mobilisation: The continuous mobilisation of the African people and the Diaspora in various formations, effective communication and outreach, and sustained and inclusive social dialogue on Agenda 2063;

(b) African resources to finance its development: Looking inwards to mobilise African resources to finance and accelerate its transformation, integration, peace, security, infrastructure, industrialisation, democratic governance and strengthen continental institutions;

(c) Accountable leadership and responsive institutions: Build visionary and accountable leadership, democratic and developmental governance and institutions, through robust and transparent planning, implementation, monitoring and evaluation mechanisms at all levels;

(d) Capable and democratic developmental states and institutions: Revitalise African development planning capacities and rebuild career, professional and capable public services. Strengthen and transform regional and continental institutions and the manner in which we do business, so as to effectively lead and drive the agenda for transformation and integration;

(e) Changed attitudes and mind-set; To strengthen Pan-African values of self-reliance, solidarity, hard work and collective prosperity, and build on Africa successes, experiences and best practices to forge the African model of development and transformation;

(f) A Pan African Perspective, through solidarity, integration, implementation of our programmes and pooled sovereignty on critical issues of continental and global dimensions;

(g) Ownership of the African narrative and brand to ensure that it reflects continental realities, aspirations and priorities and Africa's position in the world,

(h) African approach to development and transformation, learning from the diverse, unique and shared experiences and best practices of various countries and regions as a basis of forging an African approach to transformation.

73. We reaffirm our pledge in the 50th Anniversary Solemn Declaration to immediately align and integrate Agenda 2063 in our national and regional development plans and ensure that we provide the AU Commission and other regional and continental institutions with the necessary capacities and resources to effectively drive the implementation of Agenda 2063;

74. We call upon the international community to respect Africa's vision and aspirations for herself and to align their partnerships appropriately

Our Journey towards the Africa of 2063 has started.......
As Africa is consulting on Agenda 2063
Let your Voice Be Heard

Contribute to, or follow the dialogue

Twitter: @_africaUnon. #Agenda2063. Face book: AfricanUnionCommission
African Union Website: www.au.int Email: agenda2063@africa-union.org
Address: African Union Commission, P O. Box 3243 Roosevelt Street Addis Ababa, Ethiopia

Appendix Two

United Nations Sustainable Development Goals [Sdgs]

AGENDA 2015-2030

The Outstanding mission of United Nations Sustainable Development Goals [SDGs] Agenda 2030 is structured on a seventeen-point nexus to attain the following objectives by 2030. This replaces United Nations Millennium Development Goals [2000-2015] which was built on Eight Objectives;

- Eradicate poverty in all its forms everywhere;
- End hunger, achieve food security and improved nutrition and promote sustainable agriculture
- Ensure healthy lives and promote well-being for all at all ages;
- Ensure inclusive and equitable quality education and promote lifelong opportunities for all
- Achieve gender equality and empower all women and girls;
- Ensure availability and sustainable management of water and sanitation for all;
- Ensure access to affordable, reliable, sustainable and modern energy for all;
- Promote sustained inclusive and sustainable economic growth, full and productive employment and decent work for all;
- Build resilient infrastructure, promote inclusive and sustainable industrialisation and foster innovation;
- Reduce inequality within and among countries;
- Make cities and human settlements inclusive, safe, resilient and sustainable;
- Ensure sustainable consumption and production patterns;
- Take urgent action to combat climate change and its impacts;
- Conserve and sustainable use oceans, seas and maritime resources for sustainable development;
- Protect, restore and promote sustainable use of terrestrial ecosystems, sustainable manage forests, combat desertification and halt and reverse land degradation and halt biodiversity loss;
- Promote peaceful and inclusive societies for sustainable development, provide access to justice for all and build effective, accountable and inclusive institutions at all levels;
- Strengthen the means of implementation and revitalise the global partnership for sustainable development

Can SDGs be achieved without the full participation of all working in unionism – state, civil society, private sector and other stake-holders? Reaping the rewards of SDGs and any other development plans requires building bridges across existing divides – between the 'haves' and 'have-nots', developing and developed polities. This puts the world at a crossroads, challenging all to seek new pathways to ensure that we all cohabit on planet earth in a peaceful and harmonious way. The SDGs provides a comprehensive pathway forward to addressing the world's issues – whilst creating laying the foundation for future generations to benefit from the resources of planet earth. The private sector plays a significant role in the achievement of the SDGs. Without job-creation, SDGs will only be another talk-shop agenda. The successful implementation of SDGs would therefore require a number of inter-related activities which would include: -

- Building comprehensive and coordinated support for SDGs as the right growth development strategy;
- Putting the SDGs at the core of all societal and business strategies;
- Working together to making transformative and developmental changes across the entire spectrum of society;
- The entire stakeholder's community pulling their resources and working together in unionism as the strategic framework for a better tomorrow;
- African countries should stop being raw material export-based economies as well as make sufficient efforts on its heavy reliance on foreign aid;
- A clarion call for all to make their voices heard, by seeing planet earth as a patrimony given to us and future generations for safe-keeping;
- Walking the walk and be the driver for constructive and sustainable development and change;
- Without collective action we cannot sustainable planet earth for present and future generations
- There is need for building an equal world and leaving no one behind.

The challenges are daunting for every passing day requiring urgent actions. We should learn from the outcomes of MDGs. The failures to attain the MDGs imply acting quickly, diligently, decisively and in unionism to ensure the full realisation of the SDGs for a fairer, prosperous, just and peaceful world. We must all redouble our efforts. In the words of President Nana Akufo-Addo of Ghana: "The achievement of the SDGs will require bolds ambition in thought and actions, creativity, innovation, hard work and most critically, connecting to the positive and abundant energies of the continent" (2018:35-36)

UNITED NATIONS MILLENNIUM DEVELOPMENT GOALS: [MDGs – 2000-2015]

The United Nations Millennium Development Goals (MDGs) 2000-2015 focused on eight points comprising the following;

- Eradicate extreme poverty and hunger;
- Achieve universal; primary education;
- Promote gender equality and empower women;
- Reduce child mortality;
- Improve maternal health;
- Combat HIV/AIDS, malaria and other diseases;
- Ensure environmental sustainability;
- Global partnership for development.

Comments:

Few African countries attained the envisaged goals due to a number of inter-related activities, including poor governance, corruption, poor economic growth; turbulences in global economic development. Many question if African countries could not meet the eight envisaged goals, is it possible for the enlarged 17 goals under the SDGs 2030 to be attained? The International Monetary Fund (IMF) Annual Report for 2015 - Tackling Challenges Together - highlights the continent's significant role in the global economy. It states: "By 2025, the number of sub-Saharan Africans joining the working-age population (ages 15-64) will exceed that from the rest of the world combined. This is a trend with significant ramifications for both sub-Saharan Africa and the global economy." Therefore, the continent must learn how to harness its demographic dividends, the magnitude of which will depend on how fast fertility rates decline and how strong the accompanying policies are.

The continent has been the second-fastest-growing in the world in recent years and has the potential to accrue economic benefits. The world economy also stands to benefit if sub-Saharan Africa's labour force is integrated into global supply chains in an era of declining working-age populations elsewhere. Holistic policy challenges of creating jobs and economic integration becomes an increasingly important and imperative driver of growth which African countries must take very seriously. Cooperation on cross-border trade as well as enhanced collaboration is critical. Investing in human capital development, institution building, prudent management, female gender empowerment, involvement of the youths and investments in infrastructure are areas to pay great attention. Presently, Africa's growing youth unemployment constitutes a serious time bomb ready to explode negatively. Rephrased differently, 'Africa's youths is the continent's single asset but also its greatest challenge ever' (Ankomah, 2018:4446).

There is an unnecessary expenditure on the purchase of weapons of mass destruction by African countries. The growing cost on military expenditure is the result of the establishment leaving many people behind; citizens not reaping the benefits of development and progress. Exclusion fans insecurity, fuelling those left behind to be destructive as their only hope of survival. The state of high and growing inequality, instability and underdevelopment in Africa is a result of its poor policies. False capitalism or capitalism without a human face is fast overtaking the development vision of African countries.

According to projections, shows Sub-Saharan Africa failing to reach most of the SDGs by 2030, which follows on from its relatively poor performance at the MDGs. Indeed, the MDGs emphasised the weak performance of Sub-Saharan Africa compared with other regions. This was notable in the Mid 2000s when it was found to be the only region not 'on track' to meet ant goals. Sub-Saharan Africa's failure to hit uniform global goals in 2030s is understandable in the context of its low standing position in 2015. Given absolute targets (getting to zero) in the SDGs, the target being set is the most challenging targets compared with other regions (Susan Nicolai, et al 2016). Nonetheless, negative scores do not predict failure but as a warning sign that sets out the scale of the challenges and what appropriate measures should be put in place to ensure success. The current negative scores should stretch African governments beyond current results trends as both the SDGs and the AU Agenda 2063 set out ambitious agenda to inspire action and good results (Rodriguez Takeuchi et al, 2015). The writing is appearing on the wall for African leaders to see as well as awaken measures before things get out of hand.

Africa is challenged to look deep into the crystal ball, unplug uncertainties and prepare for future economic and political challenges. Even though one can conclude that global power is gradually shifting from the West or developed countries to the emerging polities in Africa, Asia and Latin America, sharing the pie in these emerging economies is not following the pattern of equality. Income inequality is rising significantly to the greatest disadvantage of the currently vulnerable population especially in Africa even with its abundant resources. Globalisation and technological advances have lifted billions out of poverty (in polities with good governance and leadership style with a vision) but also contributed to the rise in income inequality and exclusion in Africa.

There are many reasons to believe that income inequality will persist, given its inertia and the interplay between inequality and political polarisation, which makes consensus on redistributive policies all the more difficult. Persistent inequality and bad governance threatens growth and macroeconomic stability with distribution of wealth becoming even more imbalanced (see Sun et al 2014:12-13; Cimadamore et al 2016).

African countries will have to redoubled efforts to ensure that National Development Goals (NDGs), the UN (SDGs 2030) and AU Agenda 2063 are attained. Measures would include articulating and implementing policy measures attracting foreign as well as domestic investments, improving the governance and management nexus; ensure the full participation of society in addressing longstanding challenges such as lack of capacity and infrastructure, job creation and improving inter-continental integration in facilitating the movements of people and goods. Diversifying the economy of African countries is pivotal in moving the continent forward. There has to be a big squeeze especially in terms of bringing order to its fast-increasing population without job creation and the basic needs facilities- education, infrastructure, healthcare among others.

However, one could see the MDGs as preparing the ground for a better onslaught towards building a capable developmental continent [CDC]. Building a capable developmental continent implies the democratic empowerment of citizens; (i) ensuring a holistic process of addressing the normative and empirical dimensions of citizens; (ii) learning from other times and places and the comparison between these and adapting to the specific circumstances of the continent, region, and nation; and (iii) a comprehensive utilisation of the human capital available on the continent and in the diasporas.

The MDGs has come and gone and its legacy lingers on but beaconing African countries to do better the next time round. We expect the SDGs to give new dynamism for comprehensive restructuralisation of the continent. The challenge is to ensure prudent management and good governance. Good and visionary leadership is and imperative in bulldozing Africa into the 21st century and far beyond. Africa is a continent on the move and needing servant leadership and a proactive civil society to lubricate and sustain the wheels of Africa's engines for development in constant rotation.

Leadership role is crucial in propelling the continent into higher heights. So far, and most unfortunately, the continent has had more than its fair share of poor and outright bad leaders who have and continue to set their countries back several decades as well as cause untold sufferings for the people, Of course, it has also produced some outstanding leaders. It should produce many more visionary leaders for the continent to take its rightful place within the global community.

In 1968, Ayi Kwei Armah in the *'Beautiful Ones are not yet Born*, was equivocal in stating; *'there is something so terrible in watching a black man trying at all points to be the dark ghost of a European'*. We are faced with the challenging question and diagnosis of '*How Africa Civilised Europe*'? And *'How Europe Underdeveloped Africa'*?

Africa now stands at the crossroads of *'How Africans Underdeveloped Africa;* and *'How Africans are voluntarily enslaving themselves*? Currently, non-Africans have freer access to Africa (i.e., visa-free travel and visa-on-arrival) than Africans themselves travelling in Africa. This beacons and begs the question: will Africa ever develop? We see the futility of making Africans suffer in their own continent when they want to travel or are restricted from articulating and implementing bottom-up development policy strategies.

A new dose of progressive political will, visionary leadership and conscience is needed. We need a mustard seed dose to re-open the continent for Africans to develop their region and improve on their quality wellbeing like other continents. Why must we continue groping in darkness? Where has the spirit of batho pele, ubuntu and harambee gone? The slogan of Pan-Africanism and African Renaissance needs a new coat of spiritual blessings from our ancestors, without which there is no future for the African continent. We need a new strategic vision for achieving justice, equality and combating chronic poverty and endemic corruption.

To achieve the visions of SDGs 2030 and AU Agenda 2063, all geared towards empowerment, poverty eradication, job creation, economic growth, and sustainable quality livelihood for citizens that they aspire to requires the following collective choices to be made namely: (i) how to achieve the growth and jobs needed to advance prosperity and ensure social harmony – i.e. a choice between acceleration and stagnation: (ii) how to integrate African economies – diversification, free movements of people and goods, which entails a choice between stability and fragility: and (iii) how to strengthen cooperation and multilateralism, instead of isolationism and insularity; i.e. making the choice between solidarity and seclusion; (iv) the policy strategy of delinking and re-linking into the global economy, and (v) most importantly, building, consolidating and utilising the human capacity of the people.

The SDGs explicitly highlight the need for progress to 'leave no one behind', identifying a series of groups that have typically been disadvantaged and excluded from progress. Reacting both the SDGs and AU Agenda 2063 requires universal achievement, and in particular African solidarity, unity and integration is critically dependent on the active efforts by African governments and other stakeholders. Going forward, a focus on equity and participation (involving all) is needed now than ever before, or else Agenda 2063 will never be attained, unless progress is made for all groups and sector of society. The views of Mammo Muchie (2017) is very appropriate in this context: *'it is time to un-think to rethink, un-learn to re-learn, un-design to re-design, un-engineer to re-engineer and un-science to re-science and un-political economies economics with human and nature wellbeing as the priority of priorities to bring about an African integrated sustainable development to make Africa forever free. Never again must Africa fail or fall. Let us unite to make free Africa for ever, colonised Africa never.*

This calls for serious intensification of political unity and economic integration among African countries; and a kind of isolationist short-term policy before reintegrating into the world economy. Whatever strategy adopted, Africa's future hangs on the choices made by the people – building the kind of Africa's future the people want today. We have the resources, an expanding market, a rapidly growing young population whose human capacity must be rightly moulded as the technology for future growth and development. On these and other factors should we building Africa's future with all the problems, progress, and prospects that entails.

The challenges of transforming Africa are enormous but surmountable as long as we face the reality of proliferating internal conflicts, injustice and unbalanced development strategies that alienates instead of uniting people. By putting the 'people-first' we can bring an end to contestation over state power and control of resources, together with issues of ethnic diversity; that drives an appealing humanitarian crisis, while engendering systemic corruption, looting, violence and economic disparities within society. Technology does not automatically translate into socially and ecologically sustainable environmental management and human development. There is thus a need to strengthen governance and justice codes to better eradicate endemic corruption and entrenched poverty as well as mapping a new African order for the continent of the future. Time is not on our side. Positive actions must be taken now. The challenge is urgent. Any passing day without proper action is another lost opportunity for action. Put the SDGs at the core of business strategies. The business world must be part of the transformation of society.

So far, Africa has turned political virtues of democracy and justice into vices. Sad enough and most unfortunately, the continent has converted its cultural heritage and traditional values by using these as a system of oppression, exploitation, destruction and class privilege; the principles of liberty and rules of law are thrown into the ocean or under attack from left and right. At a moment when authoritarianism, tribalism, identity politics, nationalism, and cults of personality worship are rotting our democracy and transition from within; adopting a progressive Afrocentric approach exposes the West and Africa's governing elite suicidal tendencies on both sides of the ideological aisle. For the developed countries to survive, be true partners in development with the continent, Africa must reinstate and renew its contribution to the world civilisation, rediscover the ideals of its cultural heritage and values that led us out of the wilderness and satanic acts of the West towards Africa for the continent to make progress. Changing the current landscape provides the best way to attaining the SDGs, AUs Agenda 2063 and national development plans. The right taxonomies must be applied.

Only serious changes in mind-set and attitude can usher meaningful restructuring of the society to transverse in the direction of progressive and inclusive development. Flight Africa is currently stuck on the runway unable to take off to the next direction. For centuries past the continent has been bugged by the germ of colonialism. Neo-colonialism and leaders in perpetuity have takeover. Colonialism is a common human malady, but proper analysis of it leads to deeper understanding of what owls us. Colonialisation is a manifestation of wider phenomenon of greed and individual hubris. The impulse to exploit others explains how/why the rich get richer and the poor, poorer; why African countries lost and continue to loose most of their human and natural resources potentials even after the attainment of independence.

The struggle for self-determination must be intensified to get rid of the last grains of colonial and neo-colonial rule inhibiting the sustainable transformation of the continent. And so, the need to decolonise the mind can no longer be exaggerated. To break the bonds of pains and sufferings of the people requires a comprehensive and holistic progressive Afrocentric orientation and action plan to approach to rightly put an end to the current dehuminsation of the people. Africa needs an inclusive cleansing, a renaissance and purification that are not under the canopy of Eurocentric ideological command, but under the command of The Peoples Power. Africa needs to be guided by an inclusive progressive Afrocentric ideological orientation action plan that is embedded within the African cultural heritage knowledge. We need to develop that knowledge and deploy it appropriately for the sustainable transformation of the continent.

The continent needs inclusive dialogue with itself for the good of itself; this means building bridges rather than walls across the existing divide. We must connect with one another; build trust and confidence for the good of society. Building walls rather than bridges has pushed the continent to degenerate into the abyss of:

- The state of ingratitude to ourselves and country;
- The state of intimidation and gagging;
- The state of intolerance and hatred
- The state of revenge and destruction;
- The state of apathy
- The state of apartheid and xenophobia;
- The state of discontent, corruption; Lacking power and involvement-
- The state of underdevelopment; ======➔ degree of effective political participation in society.
- The state of fragmentation;
- The state of denial;
- The state of insanity; //
- The state of insecurity; //
- The state of injustice; //
- The state of lawlessness and anarchy. //

Gross underdevelopment of the society/country contributing to poor quality services delivery, poor quality, livelihood, chaos, instability, serious inequality in society, division, conflicts, marginalisation, conflicts and all other malpractices that translate to the underdevelopment of the country. The country remains in a state of perpetual underdevelopment, while other countries are moving forward being party of the rapidly globalised knowledge-based economy of this century

---

The institutions of the state construct in African countries are massively politicised, ethicised, tribalistic, destructive and feather bed of patronage, divide and rule phenomenon taking the place of pride in the bureaucratic setup of these countries. This explains the reasons why state collapse or state capture is more pronounced and failure in quality services delivery extremely poor or non-existent. The bureaucratic machinery is bogged down with the 'appointment syndrome, wrong people placed in positions of responsibility on the basis of 'political party affiliation', 'bribery and corruption' or ethnic affinity. No society can progress with such underlying destructive deficiencies over-riding its day-to-day functioning.

Time for Africa to change is now. Africa struck on the runway tells us that certain forces are making a fortune out of the misery of the African people – (the ongoing crisis in South West and North West Cameroon) which is nothing short of the *'silent genocide'* committed against the people and which the world has forgotten) is a good example. It also means that the continent remains at the depth of economic and political despair and frustration. Such a situation undermines self-confidence; trust in government as it equally destroys the hopes and ability of the people, especially its captured leadership to thin strategically, constructively, ingeniously and creatively for a new way forward for the best interest of the people and continent. Yet, we cannot run from the fact that the responsibility for the continent's development is and lies primarily with us.

No one else or other country is going to develop Africa but Africans developing Africa. There is need for new and far-reaching proposals and action plans in enunciating the goals of economic, social and political development, since Africa has vacillated from one extreme of the quest for self-reliance and self-sustaining development, to one of external dependence and externally-oriented policies and development plans. As a result, the currents of global development is fast leaving Africa behind, and the ideology and interests of Eurocentrism are largely influencing and have taken control over the development thinking in Africa. Africa is shying away from sustainable quality livelihood. Apparently, only an inward-looking strategic approach of expanding domestic and regional markets, promoting intra-African trade, of developing factor inputs of encouraging local industrialisation, and of a structured interventionist role for the state in the economy and social sectors that development can take-off in Africa.

Therefore, it is time for us to get on board and take the right sit as well as be the commanders in chief in piloting the transformation nexus of the continent. We just have to be ready now, or never, fasten our seat belts for the take-off to the destination quality livelihood for all. The governance system of the continent is one construed on the basis of 'the failure to protect' the people. We need governments that focus on humanitarian interventions aimed at what Kivimaki (2019) sees as 'protecting citizens from terror, dictators and criminals in fragile states.' The African continent for now is made up of many fragile and dictatorial states.

We have to embark on the path of sustainable development as our common future for overcoming our current state of deficiencies in providing quality livelihood to all citizens. According to French (2018) and Meadowcroft et al (2019) questions what next for sustainable development – is sustainable development 'everything' or 'something'? Most unfortunately, sustainable development politics and policies is not taking the right perspective and analytical discourse that improves the well-being of all citizens, it has been seriously 'stymied' and 'diluted' at the international and national levels of implementation.

Africa is in turmoil needing fundamental changes. Of course, the entire world is turmoil, as too many people are tossed around in a global boom and bust; the world has been converted into a global casino, gambling with our lives, our security, our future and our planet. We live in a continent where the top 10 percent of the population enjoy more than 9o per cent of total income and those in the bottom quintile get only One per cent of the African income. Gains from economic growth and globalisation have been unevenly shared. In most African countries, the rich and powerful have become richer at the expense of lower income groups and the poor. Society can never progress with such a mindset, attitude and behaviour. There has to be a radical shift in the thinking faculty of the population.

Words That Remade Africa

We should bear in mind that democracy cannot survive inequality. If power and wealth are concentrated in the hands of a few, the fact that poor people can vote mean very little. There is no doubt that only the wealth and powers that be can mount expensive advertising campaigns, lobe effectively, bribes legislators, conduct protracted legal battles, and so on. It takes money to run for office. Poor people do not hobnob with judges, diplomats, and financial tycoons. Given these circumstance, the role is little more than a finger hold on democracy. What is happening in Africa since the attainment of independence is an increasing gap between the rich and poor – thus enhancing the power, wealth, immunity of the former and disenfranchising the latter.

Over the last fifty years or more, millions of Africans have slipped into the ranks of the destitute. The vast majority of the people have literally been dumped out of the African society as we have failed and continue failing to respect and implement the basic cultural values of *"harambee, nhimbe, ubuntu, batho pele".* The ongoing political crisis in Southern Cameroons presents a typical example, as people have lost their lives and properties and are living in bushes for fear of the genocide leashed on them though the acts of the armed forces that is expected to be their protectors. People have lost trust, confidence and hope in the government and their elected representatives. The infrastructure of these two English-speaking regions of Cameroon are destroyed and can no longer afford to provide any but the most rudimentary services; only the wealthy or heavily insured can afford medical care. It is not, too, surprising that the gap between the rich and poor invariably widens when such situation prevails.

The alarming increase in the gaps between the rich and poor is one of the most server threats to the advancement of African democracy. For the people of Southern Cameroons or any group of minorities across the continent, it is what Slater (1991) referred to as "A Dream Deferred". We cannot talk of a "democratising Africa" until the value of a true and genuine democracy is reflected in the reality of our daily lives. Unfettered economic growth characterised by accumulation and wealth concentration in a few hands has further increased social inequalities even though the resources it has generated could do the opposite and finance more equitable access to essential services. Persistent poverty, corruption, unemployment, social exclusion, and higher levels of inequality and insecurity are threatening care and health systems, social cohesion and political instability.

What has become of the famous or infamous 'trickle-down theory' which, in reality is 'a trickle-up effect' with the bottom feeding the upper stratum of society? How much, after all, is likely to slip through the fingers whose religion is greed and accumulation? The alarming increase in the gap between the *"haves"* and *"have-nots"* is one of the most serious threats to Africa's transformation today and will continue to be so if not adequately addressed here and now. The advocates of policies that have no other goal but to usher poverty, inequality and corruption are out to reinstate authoritarian administration of centuries past. It is for these reasons that corruption and bad governance flourishes throughout the continent of Africa.

If Africa is to progress, as pointed out in several sections of this publication, corruption, inequality, poverty and injustice must be shown the red card. To move forward, Africa needs a consolidate government. Of course, there is the outstanding question: will the rights of the people be secured by such a government. Suppose it should prove oppressive, how can it be altered? That is why the Bill of Rights provides in the declaration: "that a majority of the community hath an indubitable, unalienable, and indefeasible right to reform, alter, or abolish it, in such a manner as shall be judged most conducive to the public weal". We need progressive reforms for Africa to take-off from the runway.

Therefore, through participatory action, African citizens are better placed to join the battle for democracy. This would be a victory for the citizens when their representatives in government decide to fall into the ranks with their constituent, the people, and the moving force for any authentically democratic society. Political parties and pressure groups play a vital role in the process, see Key (1958). The book has discussed at great length, the past and present situation of the continent as it insinuates what to be done to avid the blame theory and move forward majestically, constructively for the good of the people.

This generation has itself to blame if our children, grandchildren and great-grandchildren point the failure debacle on this generation. We should take carefully to heart the lessons of the past mistakes. The inability of the African people to significantly improve their standard of living since the great wind of change started blowing across the continent in the mid-1950s constitutes the main aspect of this book. Prospects for the Future of Africa look relatively bright if only Africans are willing to design rules that holistically maximise the contributions of all citizens to national development for the common good of all. African can overcome entrenched difficulties and remake Africa for the overall good of Africa.

In other words, by seeking the best possible, i.e. peaceful, internal and external conditions for development of the true African society, we contribute to the strengthening of peace, eradication of poverty, corruption and the promotion of sustainable development throughout the world. In the name of these lofty ideals, all countries should strive to regard it as their paramount duty to help strengthen the cooperation of all countries, while respecting the right of every nation to live by its own laws and choose its own road of development. AU Agenda 2063 provides useful guidelines for transforming the continent; it should be constantly reviewed to keep it on track and for the good of all citizens. The monster of corruption, poverty and bad governance which continues to undermined the sustainable transformation of the continent is still with us, all waxing strong and destroying the social fabric and tranquillity of the society. It has to be eradicated, without which, it will surely be difficult to secure a peaceful future for the nations of Africa unless all forms of poverty, corruption, inequality, discrimination, racism and other kinds of exclusion are eliminated.

It is my utmost conviction that the persistent, undeviating and evermore dynamic and creative implementation of a progressive Afrocentric charter will help promote the sustainable transformation of the continent, will help not only to preserve peace and reduce the threat of another world war or catastrophe, but to build a truly universal and reliable system of national development, create favourable conditions for the struggle of the nations for a better livelihood. Africa now needs a breakthrough for a safe take-off and a soft-landing. Freedom and the struggle for equality and justice have been and will likely always remain a perpetual endeavour. The Future of Africa as a continent has been shaped by our past, and our present is shaped by too many forces, visible and invisible. The destiny of Africa remains as one of authentic equality, participation and sharing hence, we should rigorously explore and candidly implement our cultural heritage values of the concepts of *harambee, ubuntu, nhimbe, batho pele* and others in all our activities. This destiny of the continent will be shaped by fortune. Therefore, understanding our past provides us with some small ammunition and ability to shape the future Kwame Nkrumah, Julius Nyerere, Nasser, Nelson Mandela, Kenneth Kaunda, Kenyatta, Haile Selassie, Sekou Touré, Steve Biko, Oginga, Awolowo, Azikiwe, Tafawa and many others fought for.

We need structured, coherent, consensual and participatory pathways for dealing with our current predicaments to construct and forge our ways in the challenges that waits. We need to build common grounds that restore hope, confidence and trust and security to the people. We equally require proactive support from all citizens to engage in the new paradigm Africa seeks to continue to promote the economic well-being of all citizens. We need a new strategy to move forward. Bear in mind that Africa is a growing continent, it is the future of the world and must be preserved judiciously. We have behaved to ensure that it remains that way. Building on the African Free Trade Area should give the continent the leverage to lift millions out of poverty, endemic corruption and gross mismanagement. The continent should not miss the boat. Fundamental reforms, new mindset and behaviour are required to ensure more accountable, democratic and transparent governance that drives the continent towards a better and brighter future for all. Establishing a firm grasp on corruption and bad governance to ensure that public money and the vast resources of the continent no longer feeds corrupt systems is a vital first step.

The lesson African countries can take away from this publication is clear: the policy decision made now and in the near future will have a lasting effect on their long-term posture. Remember that even advanced countries face major challenges. We all have to adjust carefully to support our recovery and transformation to ensure a smooth soft-landing by deploying our cultural heritage values of ubuntu, harambee, batho pele, nhimbe and others. How African countries are judged prudent or profligate a few years from now all depend on policy decisions as well as on the extent to which long-lasting economic growth, resources and political stability ensures.

For now, the 'agony of Africa' lingers and jeopardises its future. Drawing from Morrow (1992:30-34), Africa has a genius for extremes, for the beginning and the end. It seems simultaneously connected to some memory of Eden and to some foretaste of apocalypse. Nowhere is day more vivid or night darker. Nowhere are forests more luxuriant. Nowhere is there a continent more miserable. Africa, at least, has begun to look like an immense illustration of chaos theory, although some hope is forming on the margin. Much of the continent has turned into a battle ground of contending dooms: social breakdown, poverty, starvation, corruption, illiteracy, social breakdown, vanishing resources, overcrowded cities, drought, war and homelessness of war's refugees. Africa has become the dumping basket continent in a free fall, a sort of neo-post-colonial breakdown.

Yet, with such a grim picture, we must monster the spirit for a better tomorrow; the desire to improve policies and people's lives: putting people at the centre of all activities. Since independence, there has been a growing public disillusionment that long-term has not led to happier, less stressful lives. Self-government has not produced the desire results; independence was meant to imply growth and quality livelihood; reflecting human creativity and a continuous quest to search for new ways of doing things better; but it has only turn out to a recipe for a society of lotus eaters. The Future of Africa depends on the game we play now; the strategies put in place and the kind of mind-set developed and strategic action plans envisaged. What type of strategic thinking and action plans are African countries developing?

In conclusion, one can only re-echo the views of Gounden (2018:2). This publication is a modest contribution toward building a new future for the continent, by Africans for Africans and humanity. But we must begin by facing the harsh realities of weak social responsibility and sustainability. What is our current population? How fast is that population growing? What proportion of the population is having an average income of below USA$1 per day? How many of the current population live up to 39 years or are at risk of dying before 40 years? How many have access to quality health services, clean pipe-born water, shelter, electricity, medical care, good roads and name the rest, not to talk of the rate of insecurity which grows by the day?

The views offered in the book are consistent with one stressing capabilities, governance, opportunity, security and employment. We need to dig deep into these depressing realities making Europe to be swallowing Africans in search of greener pastures. There are positive sides of our transformation on which to build strong social responsibilities. It challenges us to move from weak to strong social responsibility and sustainability. There is no single cause to weak governance, social responsibility and sustainability. Therefore, any single intervention is likely to fail. At the most basic level, governments in particular and industries in general, need to pay attention to both growth and distribution. African governments must develop a strong social and responsible contract with the people (Forje: 2003).

Democratic theory has to be rethought; new relevance, thought and action given to current development problems; along with the actual underlying principles and practices of democratic politics and respecting the basic fundamental human rights of citizens. Africa has to articulate the policy principles of self-reliant development strategies to reduce the constraints on growth stemming from the dependence of the periphery on the centres of economic power; ensuring policy actions strengthening and diversify the commodity economy. This is necessary if the continent is to make any meaningful progress in attaining quality welfare for the people. If people's immediate needs are unmet and they cannot fully participate in their political community, their potential for involvement in public and private life will remain unfulfilled. Their ability to make or not to make choices and to determine the course of their life projects will have been restricted, irrespective of the choices they would have made about the extent of their actual participation. It equally means that the democratic empowerment via institutional designs of extending rights to the African citizens to participate in policy-making stands at the centre of this book and as the inalienable rights of the people and for the people to be the key actors in shaping the future of the continent. Thus, the publication focuses on one particular claim of the peoples' right to self-determination and the respect of the fundamental human rights, freedoms and liberties of the people to determine and choice their form of state construct, which should not be imposed by another state over the other.

The book invites you to join the long bandwagon of optimists sharing similar hopes, visions and optimism for a true, brave and brighter Africa of tomorrow by using all possible means of media communication in driving home the message of a united, stronger, prosperous and progressive Africa of tomorrow. The right balance is yet to be found among the three levels of state formation, national, continental and global challenges. So far, some positive changes have occurred at the African continent level, for example, the shift from OAU to AU with the later taking on more constructive challenges and changes; while at the national level democratic governance has yet to take firm roots in the 54 countries. Some African countries have made progressive efforts in embracing democratic governance, improving on the welfare of their citizens; we expect all African countries to make progressive strides in the direction of improving on the well-being of their population, so that collectively, Africa becomes a great continent of tomorrow.

Ultimately, the objective must be to do far better in the twenty-first century and beyond with regards to democratic governance, to silencing the guns, eradication poverty, curbing the obnoxious issues of corruption and injustice in the calamitous years past. As long as wars and genocide within and among states remain rare, priority must be focused on building on the progress already made in enhancing the democratic process in all countries, ensuring the security of individuals and societies from the threats posed by centralised authoritarian hegemonic governance. People and governments must never do through something like it again in the kind of Africa we want for ourselves and our future generations.

We have to learn from history. The first great African thinker, Ptahhotep, advised nearly 4000 years ago that leaders should 'listen calmly to the speech of the man who pleads' and that *'not all one pleads for can be granted, but a good hearing soothes the soul'.* Wambu (2017:66) notes that the lack of 'good hearing which soothes the soul is quite often the first stone that is cast, leading to full-fledge civil war. When people feel slighted, or disregarded, or subjected to arbitrary violence, or denied justice, they are prepared to rise and fight'. The second lesson of history as noted by Winston Churchill is that; *'those who fail to learn from history are doomed to repeat it.'*

All in all, the various moments we have spent together in blousing through these random thoughts of mine and interest shown are hopeful signs and trends for the future of our great continent's cause in that they present alternatives and possible vehicles for organising ourselves for progressive changes that should constructively and systematically take place across the continent. We have to intensify balanced strategic discourses as well as action plans on putting the continent on the right path. Myths of existing reigning authoritarian hegemonic governance system to end, is imperative so that Africa can structurally and progressively move forward in the right direction.

The future of Africa is now. We have in various ways what needs to be done to address Africa's multiplicity of problems of underdevelopment and the virtues of sustainable development. Africa has to turn underdevelopment into progressive development; tears into happiness. We must have the objective desire to turn defeat into victory and deploy the experience of forceful separation into the era of slave trade and humiliation in the era of colonialism and beyond as a framework for total reconstruction and solidarity and rejuvenation in the new world. The details of African and global problems, challenges and changes, are outlined concisely, with an overview of the process that have led to the continent's current predicaments. Only by recognising the broader patterns can realistic alternatives be designed. Africans must work together for constructive and comprehensive beneficial changes to happen right now for the overall wellbeing of the people. We have to reassure ourselves that solutions are not too expensive, too difficult, or too complicated. In short, the catch word in this strategic point-in-time for change is to be *'optimistic and hopeful'* and be part of the progressive forward-march solution. The book is to heal a body, nation and continent that have been lacerated. We should be building and not destroying the future of the African continent. The truth is at stake. We must teach our children that they have a higher status as Africans. They have an identity in the current world construct as human-beings. We have to develop our own centres of power, the democratically minded government, established by the people's elected parliament for the people, and by the people. The continent is crowded with skewed priorities in all aspects of the development nexus of the region. The issue boils down to poor governance that seriously contributes to corruption. Poor governance impedes progress. African countries should aggressively crack down the issue of money laundering. Curbing corruption can be a daunting task, but it is necessary to restore public trust in government. The fight against corruption does promote significant economic and social gains over time.

Kind of Development and Future

We envisage a brave new Africa on the horizon, but what brave Africa do we need so that the problems of the continent might be solved. The African Union has advanced a new Africa by 2063. How many of us today do adults with all our qualities and failings, our genius and our mediocrity, will still have a considerable impact on the conduct of affair on which the continent's fate at that time will depend. What is most important for this generation is to plant the good seeds to that will blossom long after 2053. If we want to see serious radical and progressive changes on the continent in the future, now is the hour to sow the good seeds. It is also for this reason that it is not the right thing advancing clear-cut mathematical laws or prognosis and forecasts as this could be full of surprises.

Skewed priorities
Public spending on education and health is lower in countries where corruption is higher.

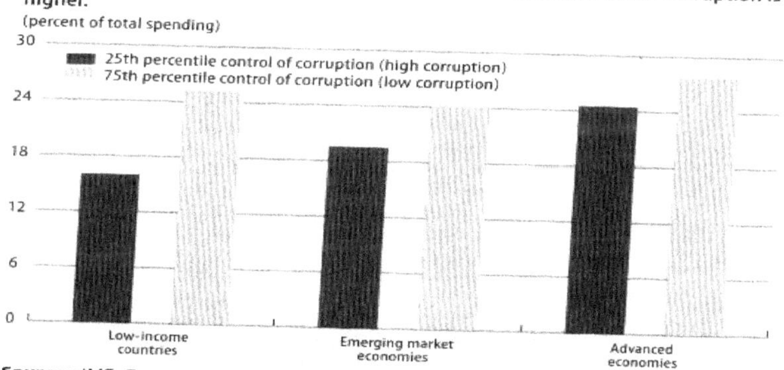

Sources: IMF, Government Finance Statistics; and IMF staff estimates.
Note: Data are for 2016.

Scientific and technological advancement are rapidly changing the dynamics of development. We are more connected today than before; that to the rapid changes in information and communication technologies (ICTs) that opens vast avenues and opportunities for extensive development, which equally leads to changes in the structure of the national economy; positive and progressive changes in the national economy should contribute to improve quality livelihood of the citizens. This is not the case because our political structure not undergoing a corresponding improvement to smoothen the path for progressive economic growth.

The slow pace of change in the democratic political structure of governance in African states slows down the pace of change in the structure of the national economy. The practice of centralised authoritarian hegemonic governance system slows down or derails the process of economic growth. Whether we focus on Aus 2063 or national development agendas of 2030, 2035, 2050 or any year as the emerging point for the continent, in the final analysis, the future is built on the activities of today. It is imperative and better we improve the elements from which the present is made. Gaining a better knowledge of our potential and organising ourselves better provides the anvil to overcoming possible obstacles now and in the years ahead.

As of now, the economic mechanism and governance construct is being reorganised in accordance with the demands made by the level of material, technical, social and intellectual development already attained by African countries. Very little structural and constructive progressive changes can be seen in the political and governance construct of many African countries. We need political and constitutional designs that creates the much needed enabling environment for inclusive growth and development that "provides the wherewithal for peaceful coexistence" (Mbaku, 2018); and the sustainable transformation of the continent. The acceleration of Africa's socio-economic development demands a constant improvement in the democratic governance and in the way the national economy is run, reliable and efficient functioning of the State. It is from these perspectives that we have to consider what kind of development and failure needed for the continent. To venture into the future, we must begin by confronting and critically situating what exists at the present. The past and present provides the structural root causes for us to visualise the future. We must start with a strong and proactive domestic political will, continuous strengthening of institutions ensuring their independency, promoting integrity and accountability, and of course working towards global cooperation.

Existing Realities: Searching for Solutions to Problems

The present realities require a comprehensive search for solutions to the problems, the content of the current predicaments can be summarised within the context of the following issues depicted below

---

Present Realities

- Economic growth is relatively low
- Food production is low
- Rapidly increasing population growth and poor human capital development
- High level of unemployment and underemployment including low incomes

- Poor state of industrialisation and infrastructure underdevelopment
- Poor situation of trade, and low share of intra-African trade is dropping not increasing
- Underdevelopment and poor inter-connectivity between African states;

The Future

Indicative qualitative objectives for the future would include

- Attaining a high degree of self-sufficiency, sovereignty and state of self-esteem, and owning its development trajectory
- Consolidating African solidarity – African Renaissance
- Structural democratisation of the continent
- Improving on its indigenous knowledge system and capability
- Building a strong human capital base
- Improved inter-African trade
- Diversification of the continent's economic standing
- Strengthening its presence within the evolving global community

It is time Africa gets beyond the polemics of the "blame game" and put together a framework for analysing and setting the framework of the vast growing challenging issues facing Africa. We need to re-examine the cost and benefits of what our actions or inactions means for the continent. Corruption causes leakages at multiple points as funds flow into, through, and out of the public sector which ought to be constructively used in improving the well-being of citizens.

Without doubts the benefit perspective provides a way for shaping on the future of the continent. We need to build on (i) the political and democratic governance of each state; (ii) financial sector development using the various opportunities provided by the Diaspora, mobilising domestic resources; encouraging domestic savings, encouraging foreign and domestic investments among other possible available means; (iii) institutional quality development and functioning; (iv) trade diversification and integration; and (v) sound relation with other bodies.

The dividend of these acts are best summarised in the words of Kwame Nkrumah and recalled by President Houphouet Boigny on the 10th anniversary of the OAU heads of States and Government Summit; "our chances of carrying our true weight in world affairs one day lies in gradually transforming inter-African economic relations by structuring them, expanding them and diversifying them".

All these adds to uncertainties of Africa's future development; and the chances of sustainable transformation of the region are affected or entangled with bad and good surprises or prospects.

Bad Surprises

- Ruining of development efforts
- Poor health leads to poor productivity and output;
- Individual wellbeing remain poor; and there is poor motivation to achieve their goals – and there is poor motivation to achieve their goals – strong indication of constrained economic opportunity pointing to persistent if not growing challenges;
- Poor job creation – growing unemployment, poor living standards that fuel discontent and which significantly undermine public sector reforms
- Diminution of African shine in global market
- Continuation or worsening of the crises in African states or the emergence of new crisis centres. The collective propensity of the continent's economy should be better managed, that transformation occurs under a nice and peaceful atmosphere.
- The need for a stable world economic situation, as any form of world crisis will unleash serious consequences and tremendous events that could be difficult to forecast'
- Poor institutional framework and entrenched corruption shaping an economic environment that stifles competition, discouraging job creation in the private sector.

Good Surprises

- Situation that are just the reverse of those already mentioned
- Important discoveries that add to the resources potentials of countries
- Availability of research break through and technological advances speeding up the transformation process of the continent and the world in general;
- New visions for growth and change
- A rapidly increasing population - middle class as potential consumer of resources and finished products for an emerging market nexus
- No magic wand for solving the numerous challenges associated with transformation, requires understanding for evolving situations, requiring political will, resolute efforts, coordination of policies;
- Emerging complementarities

What future for Africa begins with a number of interlocking activities; at the different levels, namely?

- The individual ➔ which requires radical restructure mindset. behaviour and attitude
- Community levels ➔ collective individual actions at the grassroots level
- National level ➔implementation of more vigorous policy of self-sufficiency, i.e. assuming fully the status

National level

- Implementation of more rigorous policy of self-sufficiency, i.e. assuming fully the status as sovereign nation-state;
- Better knowledge of existing potentials and possibilities with focus enhancing development and quality lifestyle
- Undertaking comprehensive reforms in the educational and management of development related activities;
- Comprehensive democratisation and of national development

Regional level

- Organisational reinforcement of greater economic solidarity through the establishment of regional economic communities – as first step toward the creation of an Africa Common Free Common Trade Area (AfCFTA,

World Level

- Taking advantage of opportunities offered by the forces of globalisation, advancement in science, technology and especially the rapid changing world of information and communication technologies.

What kind of future development does Africa need, and how can it achieve that kind of development? To tackle the challenges facing Africa of today and tomorrow requires that *"stand up, put our hands as one, and do look at others to do the stuff-do it yourself and not from a selfish perspective."* As the adage goes; *"do unto others what you expect others do to you."* Africa's motto for the future should read thus: "A continent of change and challenges." It is certainly a time of change as the continent seems to look as one big construction site to usher to usher a new dawn of modern conveniences that should compensate for decades of lost quality livelihood of the forgotten poor masses. The fear is that the construction site is poorly planned as many development related activities on the continent are, may eventually only led to disastrous consequences; with the usual plight of injustice prevailing and most of then placed once again in the scrap heap of destruction. Presently there exist a state of lack of trust and confidence in the governance system with no real relationship between the governments and governed. The governance landscape varies significantly around the world with African countries performing poorly as depicted in the diagram – Below average. Sobrinho and Thakor (2019:35-37) states: "there are some basic principles that apply across countries and can boost governance, such as strengthening laws, improving government effectiveness, and sharing up fiscal and anti-corruption institutions. Improving governance is difficult as the beneficiaries of corruption often fight back. It is a complex, drawn-out battle among the various players – government, institutions, civil society, media and the private sector and the international community."

Africa is at the turning point, reflecting a confluence of factors. A young fast-growing population with access to real-time information through digitalisation and open-access data is demanding transparency and accountability from elected officials. It requires a democratic structure-functional governance system. Democratic governance is a multifaceted issue which cuts across politics, economics, and institutions. Operating the various facets of democratic governance dimensions is a valuable indicator that challenges the dark side of issues impeding the sustainable transformation of the society. Even though corruption is a global problem, it should not be a passport for African countries to venture into the acts but to beat it with all the forces it can monster in fighting this pandemic. Africa should strive to adhere to good governance principles. Irrespective of the path African countries choose to improve governance, the dividends that eventually emerge will remain of significant and worth pursuing. For the Africa, good governance is more vital, important and most relevant than ever.

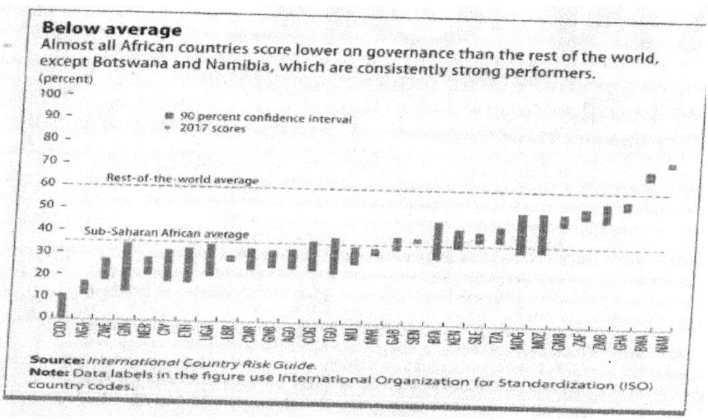

See also Sobrinho and Thakoor (2019) "More Sand Than Oil", Finance and Development, September 2019.p.36

Strong political commitment is thus an absolute requirement for success. These commitments require include political will, proactive stringent policy measures to reduce corruption opportunities, such as cutting red tape and lowering trade barriers, measures to constraint corruption behaviour and attitude (such as an independent judicial system, free and objective media landscape or a strong anti-money laundering framework, and improved fiscal institution with greater transparency and control mechanisms to oversee the progress in the change.

The Last Word – Change Must Come

"It is a bad habit to say another man's thoughts are and ours only are good and that those holding different views from ours are the enemies of the country"

(Gandhi in Hind Swaraji, or Indian Home Rule)

"It is always possible to bind together a considerable number of people in love, so long as there are other people left over to receive the manifestations of their aggressiveness"

(Freud Sigmund (1961 & 1930)

"Change will come, although not through commitment to simple lifestyle our human development projects alone. Poverty and excessive wealth, militarism and the arms industry, and the unjust distribution of capital, land and resources are issues of power and powerless. Without a shift of power through structural change these problems cannot be solved"

(Sainsbury Roger (1985)

So let Justice, Peace and Equality flow and reign, for inequality and poor governance is destroying Africa. Now is the hour for Africa to take centre stage in fighting the ills of the continent. Poverty, injustice and inequality are on the increase. The question of injustice, poverty and inequality and the need for the right response to it is a key test to the moral inadequacy of ourselves, our governments and society. All this creates a state of instability, insecurity and uncertainty. It creates what Sainsbury (1985:56) sees as ***'Fear''***. "Fear leads to anger and anger leads to destruction just as injustice contributes to both fear and destruction.

There is a real fear of the poor on the part of the rich. Powerlessness leads to frustration. There is a powerlessness of the rich as well as the poor. The question of poverty is therefore a problem for the rich as well as the poor" and it is vital for us to jointly face and rectify the situation. The Corona virus (COVID-19) shows that the poor and rich are in the same boat; this implies that "no amount of material wealth can justify a divided and unjust society, or a world divided into permanent haves and have not's" (Church of England Report, 1984). For now, it is difficult to say the kind of danger that awaits Africa following the COVID-19 Pandemic. Western medical doctors have started nursing the obnoxious idea of the vaccines for to be tested on Africans. Why Africans?

Is it because of the 54 African countries, of which 33 are classified among the least developed in the world? Besides, a 2016 report by the *think-tank* the RAND Corporation on the most vulnerable countries to infection outbreaks are on this continent. Therefore, almost all countries in Africa are unfavourable in many areas, from basic hygiene needs to health infrastructure. Other important and alarming factors are the presence of people living in unfavourable conditions in major cities, as well as communities of people displace in Sub-Saharan African countries, forced to migrate to other countries and living in non-sterile environments in camps. If the virus spreads to these areas where these people in the camps are struggling for life, what both the host countries and the international community can do may require serious restrictions and drastic measures as pointed out by Kaan Devecioglu, 2020:4). Devecioglu (2020) goes further to opine that the most negative impact of the outbreak - which has already begun to have devastating consequences on both international economics and politics – on African countries in these areas will result from the fact that oil prices in the last decades. There are oil exporter countries such as Algeria, Libya, Nigeria, Angola, Condo, Gabon, Cameroon, Mozambique and Equatorial Guinea, with their incomes dependent on oil, which will deeply feel this crisis in the short term

As such, Galbraith (1984) on the Affluent Society notes: "The miserable consumption of the poor is partly the results of the ostentatious demands of the rich" should be taken seriously as it depicts the evils of socio-eco-political injustices. Justice and equality for the powerless means changed attitudes on the part of the rich and powerful; it means the poor and powerless getting their rights; and putting people back into the right relationship leading to harmony in society. This could be seen as fundamental prescription for resolving the paradox of inequality and injustice in moving towards a poll of welfare functions.

Crowds celebrate the inauguration of the Chinese-funded Mombasa-Nairobi railway

Source (Credit David Thomas (2017) in African Business No.443, July 2017 London, pp54-55

We must take appropriate measures rectify existing industrialisation deficit, chronic unemployment on a massive scale decaying communities whose dreary housing depresses are signal of serious injustice in our society, exposing the state of poor governance in Africa today. Those in power often lack care, which the millions who feel these problems are powerless to bring about just solutions. These are fundamental issues that should not be side-lined. Sainsbury (1995:73) quoting Bishop David, Sheppard writes; "we live in a much-polarised society. In the same city people have widely different experiences and see the same events through widely different eyes. The church is one of the few bridges which reach across the different sides of that polarised society." We expect the religious bodies to bridge the gap and reconcile the divide society,

Africa needs a new game plan. The chain of poverty, inequality, corruption must be broken to free the continent from destruction. There has to be renewed dynamism and more regional integration as well as strengthening cooperation and improving on its structure-functional governance system. Greater regional integration will reinforce and compliment expanding and investment linkages. As Africa advances toward increased integration and strengthening cooperation; it is important to recognise the different regional strength and complimentary; together with those of the multilateral agencies, and the need to maximise synergies and avoid duplication of efforts (Aziz, 2007): 26-27).

Change has to occur or else the continent is doom to the abyss of gross under-development, exploitation and marginalisation. There is need for radical but positive changes that accelerates the industrialisation of the continent. Industrialisation should equally focus on internal markets, as there is rapidly growing middle class (i.e. increasing consumers on the continent, it is sad to note that a country like Nigeria imports about 80% of its tomato's paste from far away countries like China which makes no sense. Secondly, industrialisation means great improvement in renewable energy potentials. The continent has vast potentials for green energy; all it requires is leap-fogging capabilities, technologically speaking to have clean industrialisation; and finally, Africa's entry tickets are commodities. There exist across the continent 'pockets of efficiency' just to mention a few cases, textiles in Ethiopia, ICT in Kenya; Morocco which is identifying itself in aeronautic industry are segments that are known, others line up for investments and improvements to create new jobs.

The potentials are many to change the face and value of Africa for the better, by opening new era of innovation, entrepreneurship and development of Africa's infrastructure. Africa needs a commitment framework – AfCFTA for example that will support and accelerate the industrialisation and common market for the continent. The continent's economic transformation efforts must be embedded in constructive commitments of eradicating poverty, ending endemic corruption, harnessing all available resources to push the continent's development agenda. We need a new global politics of science that provides analytical insightful and impressively wide-ranging contemporary account of governance of "knowledge politics" (Benner 2018) across the world that contributes to the sustainable transformation of Africa. The continent needs to map its own new order with AU Agenda 2063 as the guideline contribution to understanding critical issues of our time and the convergence between Africa and the rest of the world. How can national, regional; continental and global institutions accommodate the irruption of Africa's as a new world economic power house?, The AU's Agenda 2063 and other well-articulated and progressive plans should constitute the Sustainable

Development Goals for Africa, holding ambitious political will needed to reverse existing trend of exclusion, exploitation and opening, for without equality the inclusive and transformative development envisaged by the AU 2063, Agenda cannot be achieved. Plans for the future of Africa evolve from the constructive basis building the African knowledge capacity. When leaders or countries invest in the creation of knowledge through proper education and skills development innovation and economic growth and enhanced quality livelihood of the people will follow. We can look at the examples of South Korea and other East Asian countries as testament to this truth.

Africa requires a kind of 'holy trinity', the interface of sustainable economic and political development (state, private sector and civil society) which must work together in harmony together a strong and well-structured institution as the interface and behaviour that contribute positively to the transformation of the people and society; without which we will only be heating differences and differently destroying political and economic incentives wrongly resulting in an array of economic problems including growth stagnation and constraint democratisation process changes.

The future of Africa must evolve within the context of a comprehensive and imprehensively well-articulated analysis of a trimly and socio-eco-political relevant issues and commonly explainable and predictable issues. It is our obligations to build the Africa we want and should do so without any qualms; and to realise such a future so that no one is left behind and within the context if the realities that given the world is unjust, a more just world is possible when we put our differences apart and exploit the positivity's of the good things that bind and divide us. Most unfortunately, historically, Africa has been a victim of one spoliator regime after another, and though these have assumed different forms across time, in essence, each nation can be distinguished from each other.

Africa of tomorrow is now challenged against meretriciously packaged devices that are systematically disempowering and asymmetrically disenfranchising. The Africa of tomorrow is in need of a Serious Africa Plan Strategy (SAPS) structurally and fundamentally specific to its post-SDGs revival. Africa cannot build unity or secure peace and stability and sustainable development without paying due attention to the suffering masses, without 'bread and butter' issues to be acknowledged and the challenges of globalisation, and without pointing out that African unity and xenophobia are incompatible. We need as the people of East Asia will in the Swahili language say ***'mijadala'*** (i.e. discourse), which underlines the purpose of this publication, generate serious discussion and action plans for the emergence of a Brave New Africa.

Throughout the various pages of the book we have embark on a journey of 'discourse' on ongoing conflicts, changes and challenges as well as prospects of prosperity in all forms and manifestation, and at different stages of the continent's transformation, to better provide policy-oriented actions plans and recommendations for a true Pan-African Programme or Renaissance. We are Africans and remain Africans but with a renewed African and world perspective. Change we must undergo at all cost is a call to all relevant partners to engage in structural fundamental changes that ushers Africa into a new level of transformation. We have to critically distinguish and face the problems caused by colonialism and neo-colonialism which is tearing African societies apart and the new problems of governance, instability, inequality, corruption, poverty, sit-tight-presidents being caused by African governments and people themselves, albeit sometimes with encouragement from outsiders. We cannot talk of a better future for Africa without tiding the wrongs truly and genuinely as well as facing the realities of our predicaments. Perhaps some 'marginal individuals, who are already disposed to such behaviour, will feel embolden upon hearing the appeal for constructive mind-set change.

Fighting for inclusion in the global knowledge based scientific and technological structure economy must begin in and with us – we need to keep our house in order for much needed socio-economic-political transition from the so-called backward society to a more open global one. We need enemies to help us reshape our strategy line of thinking and behaviour and to see things from a different significantly compelling perspectives and make people put aside not only rivalries even liberty. People can be persuaded to unite for a cause and from the same interest. It is for that common interest and good ***(Mijadala)*** that this publication is offered; ushering a new grasp and chance to shape the future though the guided principles of partnership, commitment and flexibility. We have to keep our differences away and unite for a common good.

Closing the rank and file or the "gap" does not entail being like the West, North or East. The concern is with bridging the huge gap in material well-being between the developed polities and Africa. Currently, Africa is at the tail end. Catching up necessitates comprehensive structural change including 'mind-set' and infrastructure building so that we can leapfrog over certain 'stages' of underdevelopment by taking advantage of the *'late-comer advantage'* and create a new brave continent in all its facet. It was Winston Churchill who said: "You must look at facts, because they look at you" and speak the truth and stand by it all the time.

At this moment in time, Africa finds itself facing numerous challenges, changes, dilemmas as well as opportunities and prospects for a better new continent. As already mentioned in the surprises and expectations, we cannot fail to pose the following soul-searching question.

- Why is the continent hunted by isolation and transformation?
- Economically speaking will Africa be competitive vis-a-vis the USA, Europe, China, Asia, Japan etc?
- Within the new framework – AU Agenda 2063 yet to realised will Africa through AfCFTA, NEPAD etc. really make full and judicious use of the opportunities and benefits from the emergence of a truly united continent?

- Why is it necessary for each country to develop its own vision path to reform?
- How will the benefits emanating from the above possible and constructive change be distributed to trickle-down to the vast majority leaving in slumps, chantey towns and refugee camps we have created because of greed and bad governance?
- Why is the continent haunted by slow economic, modernisation, limited transfer of technology and ultimately low competitiveness and productivity?
- How can we at present continue along the road towards implanting a full economic, political culture and financial union?
- What kind of transformation that the continent from the individual, community, national, regional and continent levels that best suits us?
- To what extent is the interest of the voiceless and exclude taken into consideration?
- How should an enlarged AfCFTA be sustained and made to function in the over inters of the 54 or more African states

Some of these soul-searching issues should instil in us a new pathway to develop new mental faculties and strength to and by judiciously reformed; to build a democratic system and operate a more open, transparent, accountable and credible system that all citizens can identify themselves with and be part of its operational mechanism. Let us in unity and consensual mode find the choice that unite not divide us in building the Africa we earnestly crave for so that the continent should take centre stage in our world of tomorrow. We should not be apologetic but aggressive towards the realisation of such a vision. We need leaders who can put this vision into real working practices. We equally need a civil society that is proactive and defends the rights of the people. Civil society should also educate the people to fight for their rights within the realms of the laws of the country. Laws should be enacted in defence of the interest of the people. Picture depicts civil society in Cape Town (South Africa) protested against the Protection of State Information Bill, dubbed the secrecy bill. Local and international critics saw the bill as a pretext for covering up state corruption (see Essoungou, 2013:10-11).

Source: Credit Essoungou, 2013, Africa Renewal, December 2013, Vol.27. No.3, New York

We are stuck and yet challenged by three fundamental natures of political justice and ensuring that wolves and sheep live together in peace and harmony. If means Africa getting extremely concern getting back to the position of harmony in society (what existed before the advent of colonialism) or before sin spoiled the relationship on the continent. In other words, Africa is search for the ideal political leader who operates within the contour of clean administration of just government; that is operate or runs a governance system characterised by a concept for political justice for the downtrodden and powerless; this entails, justice for the powerless meaning (a) changed attitude on the part of the powerful; (b) the poor and powerless getting their rights; and (c) justice means putting people hack onto right relationships leading to harmony in society; (ii) ensure harmony in society, i.e. operate and run a government where there is no violence and discrimination and where even the weakest and most vulnerable will have equally opportunities for all.

Africa is entangled within the parameters of politics and people bringing into sharp focus politicians/leaders working for the best interests of the society and people; politicians having a realistic understanding of the interests of their citizens, politicians/leaders aiming at the ends; politicians concern with justice and well-being for their citizens before their personal desire for power and wealth; and people responding positively to the good politics of leadership. The spread of the COVID-19 pandemic will eventually stop, and the international system will find a balance, but most of the damage will be permanent, particularly for the African countries. Ngwanyam Dick (2020:11) questions why are African youths running away from Africa to this Eldorado's? T hones answer to the question will show where the root problems are and what African countries should be doing.

The current crisis heavily hitting the economies on a local, regional and global scale, will also present opportunities at its final stage, but using these opportunities requires access to capital, knowledge and good health. Considering that the capital can only be provided by outsourcing for themselves while expecting help from the rest of the world, in most African countries, the situation does not seem pleasant at all. Developing countries and Least Developed countries (LDCs) in particular in Africa are especially vulnerable to the unfolding effects of the public health crisis. A priority area for global collaboration is advance research and development (R&D) for vaccines and medicines that are made available, affordable and accessible worldwide.

A good respond to politics and people can be dissected from the manifestos of three political parties in Britain in 1983, before George Orwell's famous 1984 world assessment. The three manifestos hammered on three fundamental interlinking concepts of wealth and power; working together and new hope for Britain. Can we not combine these acts to come out of the current predicaments? It means great improvement in the structure-functional governance system of African countries. It is not only the right to do; it is what must be done throughout the 54 member countries making up the continent. It requires joint action from all the implicit parties in shinning the light throughout all the dark corners of the continent.

Let us begin by considering how many rich Africans, civil servants and politicians stash secret assets in the developed polities and question ourselves, many rich people in the developed countries (not even Bill Gates and others) hide assets in Lagos, Cairo, Algiers, Abuja, Pretoria, Nairobi, Accra, Yaoundé, Harare. Lusaka, Maputo etc. They do not do so because of the state of our poor governance system. We deposit or stash huge amounts in the developed polities because of their high degree of good governance, transparency and accountability. It is incumbent on all of us to understand and carefully that our current acts of stashing fraudulent financial assets in the developed polities harms our future, the future of our children, and even distorts our present quality of livelihood.

The open and potent weapon for the continent to make progress into the future is through democratic good governance as the battle against illicit financial flows and fraudulent financial laundering. Good governance builds trust in institutions, increases accountability and diminishes perception of public corruption. We are urged to fixing our governance and development nexus. This equally poses a serious challenge to the African academia to put their heads together and get the continent out of its current underdevelopment quagmire so that the region is transformed into a quality services delivery polity. When the three pillars of society (State, private sector and civil society) are appropriately balanced society has the best chance for providing for its people, particularly those who are downtrodden.

So far, Africa has failed to prevent pre-colonial and post-colonial wars for the struggle of self-determination in order to build a strong and healthy society. We have instead established fragile and collapsed states and promoting wars and conflicts across the continent. These wars and conflicts continue to have devastating effects on the transformation of the continent.

Instead of building a structure of power-sharing and coexistence with the various partners, our leaders have gun for war and fraud which constitutes a serious threat to the sustainable development of the continent. The ongoing forgotten silent genocide osicatrated in Southern Cameroons, the situation of conflict in Northern Cameroons (Boko Haram), the existing conflict situation in Central African Republic, the situation in Mali and in the overall Sahel Regions, the situation on the Horn of Africa, among other tells the story of the great need of silencing the guns and promoting justice and peace throughout the continent.

What the continent need is a new mind-set for justice, peace and development sensitivity (JPDS) to bridge the gap between the rich and poor that continues dividing the society. Akinyoade (2019:85) notes; "....despite these encumbrances, there is a need to bridge the gap between theory and practice requiring concerted efforts, employing both qualitative and quantitative methodologies, to construct and build context – free and generalisable theories. To construct and build context-specific and generalisable theories, we can draw examples on the issues of theories and strategic approaches from three United Kingdom political parties – the conservatives, Social Democratic/Liberal and Labour - which present some of the issues in the discussion. These parties present their ideological arguments or orientation in an election manifesto as depicted in the table below.

Conservatives	S.D.P/ liberal	Labour
Only if we create wealth can we Continue to do justice to the old, and the disabled; It is economic success nothing that it will provides society. the surest guarantee of help for those who need it most. Conservatives believe in encouraging people to to have responsibility for their own decisions. We believe equally right! Strong in the duty of Governments to Help those best-able to help them- a	An attack on poverty is basic to the Alliance's strategy for creating Britain a more united and caring We seek a civilized community using the resources provided by a revived economy to guarantee to all the security and self-respect that are every citizens' These attach on poverty the Alliance sees as coming about by major overhaul of our welfare system	In this campaign documents we outline Labour's alternate to mass unem- sick ployment nothing truly enduring-can be done about anything else. Allow it to persist and it will corrode the rest of our society. it will make more deeply endemit then ever the injustice, the bitter hardship. which afflict so? many of our people.

Africa has no choice but to make progress by pulling together all the resources it has. The road to the continent's prosperity is by building its human capital and exploiting its natural resources for its transformation and by silencing all guns, ensuring justice as the means of promoting peace; and bearing in mind that the individual/people remain the hero either unleashed to transform the continent. Our current system of governance and development is biased against the weak, poor and vulnerable. Silencing the guns and putting an end to wars and conflicts is important in driving Africa forward in the right direction. Africa of today and tomorrow wants justice, peace, equality and development. The global economy will continue to grow in spite of COVID-19. Its growth will make everyone richer if only there is justice, peace, balanced development and growth as well as equity in the distribution of the wealth of each nation. At the first blush, Africa remains the locomotive of the world economy, posting impressive growth numbers. It is also the most vulnerable continent. For how long the coronavirus pandemic will persist remains a serious question which African leaders should pay attention too. The COVID-19 pandemic should stimulate positive actions on the part of Africa leaders especially in the domain of human capital development – Education remains the key in this aspect. Improve human capital development construed on science, technology, engineering and mathematics – (STEM) provides the way forward. Without proper human capital development Africa will remain a continent for exploitation and domination by those who master the domain of science, technology, engineering and mathematics.

Apparently from the current state of affairs continue appears poised to make history: even with is current status as a region plagued with fragile state construct. What is required is to move from an inefficient governance structure and inequitable economics construct to a new targeted well constructive development agenda that promotes education and supports both growth and income distribution objectives under the canopy of democratic governance and administrative platform. We need to re-balance our economic and political systems to create a balanced developmental process that benefits all in society. Without putting an end to centralised authoritarian governance, and ensuring a well-structured-functional political and administrative system, the continent cannot develop and face squarely the numerous challenges that come its way. First the guns must be silenced; second justice and the rule of law must prevail; third Africa must learn to take the bull by the horn. Her current status of remaining perpetually in slumber land and hanging on the 'blame theory' others would be marching forward.

Silencing the Gun

(Source: See Anke Hoeffler (2014) Centre for the Study of African Economies (CSAE) (2014) Research Summary (2014, p12, London

Once we start thinking about the gross existence of injustice, inequality, wanton poverty and endemic corruption throughout the continent, it is hard to think about anything else. It is only the though and concrete action on the distribution of the wealth of the product of growth – the wealth of the nation that will shape the economic and political nation of the African society and this is what demands our attention. If economics is the solution, politics is the problem. Africa has gotten is politics wrong. The ongoing situation in Cameroon proves that. There is an ongoing cleansing of Anglophones with the attempt of destroying the hope and aspiration of the self-determination of the people.

What message do the three manifestos send to Africa? Or what lessons can Africa draw from the ideological orientation of (i) creating wealth to logistics to the old, sick and disabled; (ii) working together for Britain *(Africa)* and (iii) bringing new hope for Britain *(Africa)*. Creating wealth plus working together plus a new hope for Africa putting Africa's development on the new Agenda strongly advocated here. How can AU Agenda 2063 **plus** NEPAD **plus** AfCFTA **plus** National Development Plans (NDPs) accelerate the sustainable transformation of the continent? This is the debt Africa leaders owe the people; and it is the responsibility of the people to elect and lent to leaders/political parties that can truly meet their aspirations. We are 'back to the future: The return to the ***Africa Must Unite*** syndrome as the only way forward for the continent.

References

Akinyoade Demola (2019)"A Case for Theory Building in Peace and Conflict Sensitivity" African Journal on Conflict Resolution, Vol.19, No.2, 2019, ACCORD South Africa, pp85-108

Armah Kwei Ayi (1968). The Beautiful Ones Are Not Yet Born, London

Aziz Akhtar Zeti (2007) "Asia's Decade of Transformation," Finance and Development, June 2007, Vol.44, No.2, International Monetary Fund, Washington DC, USA, pp 26-27.

Akufo-Addo, Nana (2018)" Sustainable Development Goals (SDGS) Can Propel

Africa Beyond Dependency on Aid", New African, No.583. May 2018. IC Publication, London UK

Ankomah Baffour (2018) "Youth Unemployment: A Bomb Ready to Explode", New African, No.583, May 2018, IC Publication, London UK

Benner Mats (2018) The New Global Politics of Science, Knowledge, Markets and the State. Edward Elgar Publishing, UK.

Cimadamore D. Alberto, Gabriele Koehler & Thomas Pogge (2016) Poverty and the Millennium Development Goals, A Critical Look Forward, Zed Books, UK

Church of England Report (1984) Perspectives on Economics, UK

Conservative Party (1983) British Conservative Party Manifesto 1983 – Conservative Headquarters, London

Devecioglu Kaan (2020)"COVID-19 Pandemic – Great Danger Awaits Africa", The Voice, Issue 216, April 07, 2020, Yaoundé-Cameroon

Gounden Vasu (2018). Editorial. Conflict Trend. Issue 4. 2018. An Accord Publication, Umhlanga Rocks, South Africa.

Forje W. John (2003)." Rethinking Social Responsibility and Governance Sustainability: Lesson from Developing Polities in Africa", Journal of Applied Social Sciences, Vol. 3, No. 1, 2003, pp 4-43

French Duncan and Kotze J. Louis (2018). Sustainable Development –Law, Theory and Implementation. Edward Elgar Publishing, United Kingdom

Freud Sigmund (1961, 1930). Civilisation and its Discontents. Trans. James Strachey, M.N. Norton, New York)

Gandhi. M.K. (1944) Hind Swaraj or Indian Home Rule. Ahmadabad, Navajin. India

Hoeffler Anke (2014). "Can International Interventions Secure the Peace?" in Research Summary 2014, Centre for the Study of African Economies, University of Oxfordpp10-12

Key Jr. V. O (1958). Politics, Parties, and Pressure Groups. 4th edition. Thomas Y. Cromwell Company, New York, USA, pp194-95.

Kivimaki Timo (2019). The Failure to Protect. The Path to and Consequences of Humanitarian Interventionism. Edward Elgar Publishing, UK

Labour Party (1983) Britain: Labour Party Manifestos 1983, Labour Party Headquarters, London

Meadowcroft James, Banister David, Langhelle Oluf, Linnerud Kristin and Gilpin Geoffrey (eds.) (2019). What Next for Sustainable Development? Our Common Future at Thirty. Edward Elgar Publishing, UK.

Morrow Lance (1992). "Africa: The Scramble for Existence,' Time Magazine, September 1992, No. 36, pp30-34

Muchie Mammo (2017). 'Still on the Journey to Regenerate Africans: The 7th AU Conference, 22-24 May 2017, Pretoria, South Africa.

Nicolai Susan, Chris Hoy, Tanyi Bhatkai and Thomas Aedy (2016). Projecting Progress. The SDGs in Sub-Saharan Africa. Overseas Development Institute (ODI) April 2016, London, United Kingdom.

Ngwanyam Nick (2020) "COVID-19 Is A 'Blessing" for Developing Nations", The Guardian Post No.1866, Tuesday April 14, 2020, Yaoundé-Cameroon. P11.

Sainsbury Roger (1988). Justice on the Agenda. Marshalls Paperback. Basingstoke Hants, UK, Zondervan Corporation.

Slater Phillip (1991). A Dream Deferred. Beacon Press, Boston. USA

Sobrinho Nelson and Thakor Vimal (2019) "More Sand Than Oil – Sub-Saharan Africa stands to gain more from reducing corruption than any other region", Finance and Development, September 2019. Vol.56. No.3, International Monetary Fund, Washington, DC. USA, pp35-39

Social Democratic Party (SDP) / Liberal Alliance (1983) Social Democratic Party/ Liberal Alliance (Britain) SDP/Liberal Part Alliance, Manifesto 1983

Sun Yan, Kalpana Kochhar, Evridiki Tsounta & Niklas Westelius (2014). "Crystal Ball: A Look at Trends and Uncertainties Can Help Prepare for Future Economic Challenges:" Finance and Development, Vol. 51. No.3; September 2014, Washington, DC. Pp12-1

Takeuchri L. Rodriquez and E. Samman (2015). Patterns of Progress Towards the MDGS and Implications for Post-2015. Target Setting. Overseas Development Institute (ODI) London, UK.

Wambu Onyekachi (2017)

Appendix Three

Carad Publications

- Unchaining Africa's Economic Development Through Entrepreneurship Education (2019) L'Harmattan Publication. France/Cameroon, **ISBN:978-2-343-16632-2**
- In the Heat of Africa's Development. Africa at the Crossroads – Time o Deliver (2019). Langaa International Publishers RPCIG, Bamenda – Cameroon. **(ISBN:978-9956-50951)**
- Shaping Africa's Future: Transforming African and Global Relations for A Just and Stable World **(2019)** Lambert Academic Publishing, Germany **(ISBN:978-413-9-4930-4)**
- Cameroon Without Corruption: The Search for A New Vision and Shared-Values. Challenges for Policy Choices, Articulation and Implementations. **(2018).** Lambert Academic Publishing, Germany **(ISBN:978-613-9-86151-4)**
- Withering or Constructing African Unity Fifty Years after Kwame Nkrumah. Implementing an Action Plan for the Realisation of 'Africa Must Unite' **(2017)** Lambert Academic Publishing, Germany **[ISBN:978-3-330-31786-4]**
- Gender Empowerment, Equality and Economic Development as Africa's Solutions to African Problems. **(2016)** Lambert Academic Publishing, Germany **[ISBN: 978-3-659-71046-9]**
- Perspectives on Democracy and Governance in Africa. Reorganising the State and Society for A Better Tomorrow **(2015)** Lambert Academic Publishing, Germany. **[ISBN: 978-3-659-56679-0]**

- Emerging Perspectives on Capacity Building and Quality Public Services Delivery in Africa **(2013)** Lambert Academic Publishing, Germany **[ISBN: 978-3-659-38368-7]**
- State Building and Democracy in Africa: A Comparative and Developmental Approach **(2013).** Nova Science Publishers Inc. New York, USA **[ISBN: 978-1-61209-025-2]**
- Century of Change – Symposium on African Unity, (ed.) **(2011)** Nova Science Publishers Inc., New York – United States of America [**ISBN: 978-1-61122-034—6]**
- Cameroon Without Poverty: Civil Society Empowerment: Growth and Poverty Eradication? Mapping New Strategies for the Future **(2010**). Lambert Academic Publishing, Germany **[ISBN: 978-3-8433-6951-0]**
- Here The People Rule: Political Transition and Challenges for Democratic Consolidation in Africa **(2009)** Nova Science Publishers Inc., New York, USA [**ISBN:978-1-60692-706-9]**
- The Challenges of Administrative Political and Developmental Renewal in Africa: Emerging Issues, **(2009)** Nova Science Publishers Inc. New York, USA**[ISBN:978-1-60741-265-6]**
- The Challenges of Administrative and Developmental Renewal in Africa: Essays on Rethinking Government and Reorganisation **(2009).** Nova Science Publishers Inc., New York USA **[ISBN: 978-1-60741-266-3]**
- Cameroon Without Corruption. The Search for a New Vision **(2004**). Niba Publishers, Bamenda, Cameroon
- Consolidating Democratic Governance and Quality Management in Africa**, (2003)** CARAD Readings in Policy, Governance and Management, Yaoundé - Cameroon
- Science and Technology in Africa **(1989)** Vol. 10. Longman World Series on Science and Technology, Longman, Essex, United Kingdom [**ISBN: 0-582-00086-6]**
- Science, Technology and Development Policy in Cameroon (Lund-Sweden, **1986**) **[ISSN: 0349-1684] [ISBN: 91-7810-970-1]**
- Third World Development and the Myth of International Cooperation (Lund-Sweden, **1984**)
- Science and Technology for Development in Africa South of the Sahara: A Bibliography **(1982)** Research Policy Institute, University of Lund, Sweden **[ISSN: 0349-1684]**
- The One and Indivisible Republic of Cameroon. Political and Economic Integration in a Fragmented Polity **(1981).** Department of Political Science, Lund Political Studies Series No.35, University of Lund Printing Press, Lund- Sweden **[ISBN:91-7222-450-9]**
- Cameroon's Five-Year Development Plans **(1977)** Publishers, Bokforlaget Doxa, Lund - Sweden

- The Rape of Africa in Vienna. African Participation in the 1979 United Nations Conference on Science and Technology for Development (ARGAD Publication, Lund-Sweden, **1970**)
- The Challenge of African Economic and Technological Development and the Influence of International Forums. **(1978)** ARGAD Publications, Lund, Sweden

CPSIA information can be obtained
at www.ICGtesting.com
Printed in the USA
LVHW080508151020
668815LV00021B/298

9 789956 551897